D1370568

Managing Projects

A Team-Based Approach

The McGraw-Hill/Irwin Series Operations and Decision Sciences

Managing Projects

A Team-Based Approach

Karen A. Brown
Thunderbird School of Global Management

Nancy Lea Hyer
Owen Graduate School of Management
Vanderbilt University

McGraw-Hill Irwin

MANAGING PROJECTS: A TEAM-BASED APPROACH

ISBN 978-0-07-295966-6
MHID 0-07-295966-5

Vice president and editor-in-chief: *Brent Gordon*
Editorial director: *Stewart Mattson*
Executive editor: *Richard T. Hercher, Jr.*
Director of development: *Ann Torbert*
Editorial coordinator: *Rebecca Mann*
Vice president and director of marketing: *Robin J. Zwettler*
Associate marketing manager: *Jaime Halteman*
Vice president of editing, design and production: *Sesha Bolisetty*
Lead project manager: *Pat Frederickson*
Lead production supervisor: *Carol A. Bielski*
Design coordinator: *Joanne Mennemeier*
Senior photo research coordinator: *Lori Kramer*
Media project manager: *Balaji Sundararaman, Hurix Systems Pvt. Ltd.*
Cover design: *Joanne Mennemeier*
Typeface: *10.5/12 Times New Roman*
Compositor: *Laserwords Private Limited*
Printer: *Quebecor World Versailles Inc.*

Library of Congress Cataloging-in-Publication Data

Brown, Karen A., 1949-
    Managing projects : a team-based approach / Karen A. Brown, Nancy Lea Hyer.
        p. cm.—(The McGraw-Hill/Irwin series operations and decision sciences)
    Includes index.
    ISBN-13: 978-0-07-295966-6 (alk. paper)
    ISBN-10: 0-07-295966-5 (alk. paper)
    1. Project management. I. Hyer, Nancy Lea, 1955- II. Title.
HD69.P75B7623 2010
658.4'04—dc22

                                                                                            2009021223

To our mothers, Betty Ann Preston Brown, 1925–2006, and Charlotte Feltner Hyer, 1934–2007, the best project managers we have ever known. We thank you and love you always.

About the Authors

Karen Brown is professor of Operations and Project Leadership at Thunderbird School of Global Management, where she delivers courses in MBA, EMBA, and corporate learning programs. She earned her BS, MBA, and Ph.D in business from the University of Washington, and was certified as a PMP in 2000. Since 1999, she has served regularly as a visiting professor at the China-Europe International Business School (CEIBS) in Shanghai, Beijing, and Shenzhen. She has also taught at IESE in Barcelona, Spain; Seattle University; and the University of Washington. Professor Brown has been recognized on several occasions for excellence and innovation in teaching. In 1999 she was the recipient of the Decision Sciences Institute's Instructional Innovation Award for her service-learning–based project management course.

Professor Brown's research is focused on socio-technical systems, the study of interactions between human and technical elements in the contexts of routine operations and unique projects. Her work has appeared in *Academy of Management Journal, Academy of Management Review, California Management Review, Journal of Operations Management, Interfaces, Project Management Journal, International Journal of Production Research, Human Relations, Journal of Applied Psychology, Business Horizons, Decision Sciences Journal of Innovative Education,* and other scholarly and practitioner outlets. Her chapters on project management and business-process benchmarking were published by McGraw-Hill as part of the Melnyk and Swink modular series *Value-Driven Operations Management.* She also has co-authored teaching cases for Harvard Business School, Thunderbird, and the European Case Clearinghouse. Professor Brown has been an associate editor of the *Journal of Operations Management* since 1994 and has served on the editorial review boards of *Academy of Management Journal* and *Decision Sciences Journal.*

In addition to her role as a faculty member, Professor Brown has consulted and led seminars for numerous private, non-profit, and public-sector organizations, including Boeing, Puget Sound Naval Shipyard, PACCAR, Maersk, ABB, Emerson Electric, Eli Lilly, Sony, Shanghai Media Group, Shanghai Stock Exchange, Sihuan Pharmaceuticals, Habitat for Humanity, and the Peace Corps.

Nancy Lea Hyer is associate professor at Vanderbilt University's Owen Graduate School of Management. She earned her MBA and Ph.D. in business from Indiana University and holds an undergraduate degree from the University of Richmond. At Owen, Professor Hyer teaches executive, MBA, and EMBA classes focused on project management, process development and improvement, and team leadership and facilitation. She has also taught at the University of North Carolina–Chapel Hill. She has won executive program, Executive MBA, and MBA teaching awards, and both school and university-wide awards for excellence in undergraduate education.

Before joining Vanderbilt, Professor Hyer was operations research manager at Hewlett-Packard's Network Measurements Division. In that capacity she was a project manager responsible for leading teams focused on operational and strategic improvement.

Professor Hyer's research focuses on lean processes and project management. Her publications have appeared in *Harvard Business Review, California Management*

Review, Decision Sciences Journal, IIE Solutions, Journal of Operations Management, Business Horizons, International Journal of Production Research, Manufacturing Engineering, and other scholarly and practitioner outlets. She is the co-author (with Urban Wemmerlöv) of *Reorganizing the Factory: Competing through Cellular Manufacturing,* which was awarded a 2003 Shingo Prize for "outstanding contribution to the body of knowledge in the field of manufacturing excellence." She serves on the editorial review boards of *Decision Sciences Journal of Innovative Education* and *Production & Inventory Management Journal.*

In addition to her corporate experience as a project manager at Hewlett-Packard, Professor Hyer has worked with a number of organizations to provide focused project management and process improvement training and to create and lead strategic planning sessions, retreats, and retrospectives. Recent clients include Community Health Systems, Commerce Bank, Provident Bank, Compaq, Hewlett-Packard, WebMD, Cheekwood Botanical Gardens and Museum, Cigna, and RR Donnelley.

Together, Professor Brown and Professor Hyer have co-authored several articles, jointly delivered presentations at academic and practitioner meetings, and team-taught highly successful Vanderbilt executive programs.

Preface

If projects touch your life in any way, this book is for you. We have written it for a wide range of stakeholders, including project managers, project team members, support personnel, functional managers who provide resources for projects, project customers, project sponsors, project subcontractors, and anyone who plays a role in the project delivery process. For each of these stakeholders, some parts of the book are likely to be more relevant than others, but the vocabulary we present and the big picture we paint should be useful to all who wish to see projects succeed.

We hope you have noticed how the title of our book differs from most others available in the market: "Managing Projects" versus "Project Management." The latter, which is the norm, implies a topic or category of knowledge. The former, ending in "ing," is intended to imply action and process; making it happen.

The need for knowledge and understanding about managing projects is on the rise as product life cycles compress, demand for IT systems increases, and business takes on an increasingly global character. These forces have led authors, educators, and organizations such as the Project Management Institute (www.pmi.org) to respond with a growing body of literature and training programs.

Managing Projects: A Team-Based Approach fills an unmet need by showing how teams can apply established tools and several tools that are relatively new to the field. We have combined the academic rigor found in many textbooks with the practical attributes often found only in trade publications. The book's defining characteristics include:

- **A team orientation:** We show how concepts and tools for managing projects can work in team settings. The book includes team-based tools not found, as a comprehensive set, in any other book on project management.

- **A process context:** We demonstrate how the various tools fit together as part of a cohesive process for managing projects, demonstrating the iterative nature of project planning and execution.

- **An integration of managerial and behavioral concepts:** We support our prescriptions about leader and team behavior with evidence from academic research.

- **A balanced tool set:** The most effective project managers are those who know when they need to be analytical and when a more creative and visionary approach is warranted—we offer ideas for making these distinctions and present tools for use in each type of situation.

- **A focus on pedagogy:** We have developed this book around teaching and learning. We present material in a way that will both enhance an instructor's ability to teach from the book, and support the solo learner.

- **Support for PMP exam preparation:** This book, first and foremost, is about managing projects. However, it will have great secondary value in preparing our readers to successfully pass the PMP (Project Management Professional) exam. Terminology used throughout this book fits with the vocabulary prescribed by the Project Management Institute. Our numerous former students who have achieved PMP certification endorse the test-preparation value of the material contained within this book. However, they express their deepest appreciation for how it has helped them to become better project leaders.

Knowledge is of little value if you are not able to act on it. And in the context of managing projects, acting on this knowledge means working in concert with others. You cannot implement these ideas alone, so you must become a teacher and coach for your colleagues. We believe this book equips you to do this.

SUPPLEMENTS

Microsoft Project 2007: The trial version of Microsoft Project software is included on its own CD-ROM free with the text.

Online Learning Center: www.mhhe.com/brown-hyer1e
The Student Edition of the *Managing Projects: A Team-Based Approach* OLC contains many tools designed to help students study, including PowerPoint presentations, text updates, and access to MindManager.

MindManager: A trial version of MindManager by MindJet software is available on the Online Learning Center. MindManager is a visual mind mapping software which enables users to tie together, visually map, and dynamically interact with all the information in a project. As described in the book, MindManager can be especially useful to teams who wish to document the results of work breakdown structure mind maps they have collaborated to create.

Project Flip: Project Flip is a multi-faceted exercise that combines technical project management skills, use of a project scheduling software, financial analysis, and a real-world case to immerse students in the management of a typical project. Developed by Janelle Heineke, Linda Boardman Liu and Jane Davies of Boston University and Larry Meile of Boston College, Project Flip won the 2008 Instructional Innovation Award from the Decision Sciences Institute, and is available for instructors on the Online Learning Center.

Online Learning Center: www.mhhe.com/brown-hyer1e
The Instructor Edition of the *Managing Projects: A Team-Based Approach* OLC is a password-protected and convenient place for instructors to access course supplements. Resources for professors include the Instructor Resource Guide, sample syllabi, text updates, solutions to the end-of-chapter questions, and access to MindManager and Project Flip.

Tegrity Campus: Lectures 24/7

 Tegrity Campus is a service that makes class time available 24/7 by automatically capturing lectures in a searchable format for students to review when they study and complete assignments. With a simple, one-click start-and-stop process, you capture all computer screens and corresponding audio. Students can replay any part of any class with easy-to-use browser-based viewing on a PC or Mac.

To learn more about Tegrity, watch a 2-minute Flash demo at
http://tegritycampus.mhhe.com.

ACKNOWLEDGMENTS

We thank both of our institutions for providing the superb professional environments in which we each work, and for their formal and informal support of the teaching and research on which this book is based. We are also indebted to the degree and executive students we have taught at Thunderbird, Vanderbilt, the University of Washington, Seattle University, the University of North Carolina, and the China-Europe International Business School (CEIBS). The bright, inquisitive minds with whom we have been privileged to work have inspired us to develop and refine team-based approaches for managing projects.

Many of the ideas contained within this book were germinated through interactions with our academic and business colleagues. Those who have contributed to our insights about managing projects include Ted Klastorin (University of Washington), Dwight Smith-Daniels (Wright State University), Bill Youngdahl (Thunderbird), Avi Shtub (Technion), and Jack Meredith (Wake Forest University). As Karen's mentor, co-author and doctoral advisor, Terry Mitchell (University of Washington) provided a foundation that supported our ability to integrate behavioral concepts throughout the book. Nancy offers special thanks to former co-workers and mentors at Hewlett-Packard, especially Sharon Zimmerman and Sam Scott; the experience she gained as a practicing project manager in a world-class organization was invaluable to us in shaping the unique team-based orientation of the book.

We are also grateful for the ideas offered by the following reviewers who saw the earlier versions of our manuscript. Their input and encouragement helped us immensely in reshaping the chapters, many of which were recrafted substantially in response to their good ideas and well-founded feedback.

Carl Adams
City University of Seattle

William Brauer
Bemidji State University

Larry Cornwell
Bradley University

Charles Daniels
Old Dominion University

Homer Johnstone
Golden Gate University

Timothy Kloppenborg
Xavier University

Frances Kubicek
Kalamazoo Valley Community College

William Lindsay
Northern Kentucky University

Daniel Mittleman
DePaul University

Cindy Nauer
Central Ohio Technical College

Hameed Nezhad
Metropolitan State University

Robert Ouellette
University of Maryland University College

Michael Petroski
Lynn University

William Teeple
Embry-Riddle Aeronautical University

Larry White
Eastern Illinois University

Stephen Whitehead
Hilbert College

We also appreciate the assistance we have received from Professor David Young of Boston University; Tamara Reid of Seattle University; Laura Clise, Jennifer Galek, and Meike Rapp, Gered Doherty, and Maria Gryskiewicz, recent Thunderbird MBA graduates; and Bryan Aaron, Melissa Shearer and Joanna Conley, recent Vanderbilt MBA graduates. Our administrative assistants, Cheri Hazen and Kathy Dewees at Thunderbird, and Linda Roberts and Cordy Cates at Vanderbilt, deserve a special thank you.

Their assistance in executing the many things we do as part of our academic jobs provided us the time we needed to complete this project. Members of the Media Services staff at Thunderbird, including Carlos de Jesus, Steve Rideau, Jason Hopkins, and Brett Byers have contributed time and genius to support our need for visual materials.

Our thanks also go to the staff of McGraw-Hill/Irwin, especially our editor, Dick Hercher and our editorial coordinator Rebecca Mann. We also greatly appreciate the support we received from Erika Jordan of Laserwords, our ever-patient developmental editor, Robin Reed at S4Carlisle Publishing Services, and our accuracy checker Charlie Daniels of Old Dominion University.

The authors welcome any comments or questions as well as corrections to the text. Please e-mail Professor Karen Brown at **karen.brown@thunderbird.edu** or Professor Nancy Lea Hyer at **nancy.lea.hyer@owen.vanderbilt.edu.**

Brief Contents

Contents

Chapter 10
Finishing Well: Project Closure and Learning   335

Appendix A
Quick Guide to Using Microsoft Project   363

Appendix B
Decision Analysis: Using Payoff Matrices, Decision Trees, and Implications Wheels in Project Management   391

Index   403

Chapter One

Managing Projects: What and Why

"If it weren't for all of these projects, I could get my work done."

Anonymous

Chapter Learning Objectives

When you have mastered the material in this chapter, you should be able to:

- Define and differentiate among projects, programs, and portfolios, and provide examples of each.
- Describe the reasons for the increasing importance of projects in organizations of all types, sizes, and global locations.
- Compare a set of projects based on drivers, sources, customers, degree of uncertainty, expected outcome, organizational reach, scope, degree of complexity, and strategic level. Describe how these differences will affect the way projects are managed.
- Evaluate a project based on its strengths and deficiencies related to key project success factors. Describe why each factor was important.
- For a given project, develop a list of performance metrics, including those that would be considered part of the triple constraint, as well as a larger set one might find in a balanced-scorecard approach.
- Discuss the benefits teams offer to projects and articulate examples of some challenges teams present to project managers.
- Describe the stages in the project management process and identify the options available to the project manager in synchronizing them.
- Offer arguments supporting the value of systematic approaches for managing projects and describe examples of implementation challenges.

"If we're going to stay alive as a company, we need to find a new market segment. I'd like you to head a task force to change our focus. This is big."

Chief marketing officer of a Fortune 500 company

"We've just been hit with a product recall from the FDA. I want you to fix the problem and get us back in production."

Vice president of supply chain management for a small, privately held medical devices company

"The board of directors' meeting is coming up in January. I'd like you to organize it."

President of a not-for-profit organization that provides mentoring services to at-risk youth

"We need to improve the way we manage the new client intake process. Will you look into this?"

Managing partner of a large law firm specializing in estate planning

Each one of these requests creates the seed for a project—a unique endeavor outside the realm of routine operations. This book is about what happens, or what should happen, in response to the kinds of inquiries highlighted in the quotes above. This chapter provides a general orientation to managing projects, emphasizing its importance, highlighting success factors, offering an overview of the process, addressing factors project managers should consider with respect to project teams, and stressing the value of systematic approaches.

PROJECTS IN PERSPECTIVE

A **project** is a temporary endeavor intended to solve a problem, seize an opportunity, or respond to a mandate. Some projects create or change processes, products or services, but others spawn events, produce information, or tackle crises.[1] Many projects require participation from a team whose members are drawn from diverse functional areas, but individuals, working alone, execute some projects in their entirety. Projects can be large (e.g., creation of the International Space Station) or small (e.g., planning the annual company picnic), and anything between. All types of organizations engage in project activities: families, governmental agencies, small businesses, and multinational corporations—any place people and teams are doing something to achieve a special purpose.

The term **program** sometimes is used to describe an effort that includes several subprojects. For example, a city government might charter a program with the goal of creating cleaner, safer streets. Within that program would be a set of interrelated

---

[1] This definition is somewhat broader than the one prescribed by the Project Management Institute (www.pmi.org), which defines a project as "a temporary endeavor undertaken to create a unique product, service, or result." As part of its mission, PMI works to set global standards for project management terminology. Throughout this book, we will draw from the PMI vocabulary, integrating it with terms from other sources as well, and embellishing where we believe it adds value.

EXHIBIT 1.1
Projects, Strategic Goals, and Organizational Mission

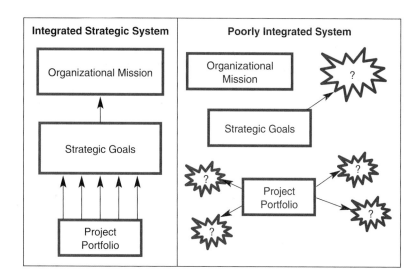

projects, including endeavors related to street repair, street lighting, public parking, services for homeless people, public restrooms, street cleaning, and policing plans. For the program to be a success, each project must meet its individual goals, and, as an integrated whole, they should all be executed in a way that supports program goals.

Beyond its program for clean, safe streets, the municipality would likely have numerous other projects under way (e.g., a new library, renovation of athletic fields, a new information system). The city's entire set of efforts would be known as a **project portfolio.** No project can stand alone; its leaders, contributors, and supporters must recognize how it fits with the larger set of efforts that compete for resources and attention within the organization. Successful organizations continuously review their project portfolios to ensure that, as a whole, they reflect strategic priorities.

If we look at an organization's entire project portfolio, we should see a set of endeavors that support its mission and strategic goals. Unfortunately, many organizations add projects to the mix without asking important questions about strategic fit. Also, some projects linger in the portfolio even though the organization's strategic priorities no longer justify their continuation. Exhibit 1.1[2] provides a conceptual illustration, with the figure on the left showing an ideal system in which the portfolio is closely aligned with higher-level purposes. In the figure on the right side of the exhibit, the organization has not properly aligned its project portfolio with its strategic goals. The result is a set of projects that consume organizational resources but do not move the enterprise forward. In Chapter 3, we introduce ideas for project selection and portfolio management that incorporate questions about strategic fit.

Project Attributes: Differentiating Project Types

As this chapter's opening quotes suggest, there are many types of projects. We can differentiate them along nine dimensions: drivers, source, customer, degree of certainty, expected outcome, organizational reach, scope, degree of complexity, and strategic level. These are shown in Exhibit 1.2, along with examples.

[2] Our thanks to M. Morgan, W. A. Malek, R. E. Levitt, *Executing Your Strategy: How to Break It Down and Get It Done* (Boston: Harvard Business School Press, 2008) for their inspiration with regard to Exhibit 1.1.

EXHIBIT 1.2   Project Attributes

Project Attribute	Examples
Driver	
Why are we doing this?	• Solve a problem. • Seize an opportunity. • Respond to a mandate or regulatory requirement.
Source	
Who decided we should do this?	• A request or command from an upper-level manager (i.e., a sponsor). • A grass-roots effort initiated by a lower-level individual or team.
Customer	
Who will be the ultimate beneficiary?	• A customer internal to the organization. • A customer external to the organization.
Degree of Certainty	
How much do we know at the front end of the project about how the end result will look?	• Customer or organizational expectations not clearly defined at the beginning. • Customer or organizational expectations defined at the beginning, but likely to change as the project evolves and more information is available. • Customer expectations clearly defined and unlikely to change.
Expected Outcome	
What deliverables will we see at the end? What will tell us we have achieved our objective?	• New/revised product or service. • New/revised process. • Improved information for decision making. • An event that enhances the company's public image. • Recovery from a crisis. • Increased market share. • Increased profit.
Organizational Reach	
Which functions or organizations will be involved?	• The project operates entirely within a functional unit or department. • The project spans several functional units or departments. • The project extends across several organizations (e.g., suppliers, partners, customers).
Scope	
How big is it?	• Small versus large budget. • Short versus long timeline or life cycle.
Degree of Complexity	
To what extent will it be necessary to integrate interrelated subsystems?	• Low complexity: very little need to integrate or coordinate across the project's elements. Deliverables and work packages may be completed independently. • High complexity: Project subcomponents, such as physical elements, information technology, social systems, cultural expectations, etc., must be carefully coordinated or integrated.
Strategic Level	
Is this strategic or tactical?	• Related to corporate-level strategy (e.g., launching a new product). • Related to work-unit–level tactical goals that ultimately support strategic goals. (e.g., changing the way an existing product is shipped to customers as a means of supporting strategic objectives associated with expanding market share through improved customer service).

WHY PROJECTS COMMAND OUR ATTENTION

A cursory glance at news headlines on any given day reveals many types of projects, from national election campaigns, to sporting events, to funerals for dignitaries, to animal rescue efforts. Many news stories highlight serious failures in high-profile projects. For example, in the aftermath of Hurricane Katrina in the United States in 2005, government officials at all levels apparently failed to understand that the crisis had created a project, and they fell into several typical traps: denial, failure to take responsibility, inaction, and shame-mongering.[3] Similarly, the ceiling collapse in one of the tunnels of Boston's Big Dig raises questions about how this structural failure could have happened in the most expensive public works project in U.S. history.[4]

In addition to notorious failures, the world also has witnessed remarkable project successes. Each year, the Project Management Institute (PMI) recognizes a Project of the Year. Past winners have included the Saudi Aramco's Hawiya gas plant project, the Olympic Winter Games in Salt Lake City, and the U.S. Department of Defense Fernald closure site project. One of these award-winning projects involved construction, another a major event, and the third involved ending the life of an existing facility and reclaiming the property for other future uses. All three are examples of highly complex projects that required coordination across multiple entities and the integration of many components. They received PMI recognition because they had, first and foremost, achieved their project outcome goals, but also because they had done so in a way that delivered results on time, within budget, and to the satisfaction of customers and other key stakeholders.

Projects, Projects, Everywhere

The need for project management has grown rapidly in recent years. As evidence, we offer statistics on the worldwide growth of the Project Management Institute (www .pmi.org). At the end of 2002, the organization had fewer than 100,000 members. Nearly 10 years later, the number had tripled to more than 300,000. Attention to the practice of managing projects undoubtedly is growing because organizations spend large sums of money on project endeavors. For example, according to the Standish Group, companies in the United States spend $250 billion on information technology (IT) projects annually. They forecast continued growth in these expenditures, and also note that nearly half of all IT projects end at nearly double their original budgets.

China offers another example of project growth. China's central plan for 2006 to 2010 called for construction of 2 billion square meters of new working, living, and governmental floor space per year.[5] The 2008 Olympic Games in Beijing created a project of proportion and complexity well beyond China's famous Great Wall, reminding the world of that country's long-standing capability for getting things done. India represents another region characterized by exponential growth in projects, ranking second only to China for economic expansion in recent years.[6] For example, India experienced the highest IT growth rate in the world (18.6 percent and $37 billion) in 2008.

In all regions of the world, the trend is toward greater and greater project complexity. The increased need to integrate information technologies, physical technologies, disparate subcontractor entities, cultures, languages, time zones, politics, and the interests of multiple and increasingly powerful stakeholders has pushed project complexity to new heights.

---

[3] J. Welch, "The Five Stages of Crisis Management," *The Wall Street Journal,* September 14, 2005, p. A20.

[4] J. Saltzman, "Big Dig Contractor Modern Continental Pleads Guilty," *The Boston Globe*, May 8, 2009, http://www.boston.com/news/local/breaking_news/2009/05/modern_continen_2.html (accessed July 6, 2009).

[5] www.buyusa.gov/china/en/ace.html (accessed July 6, 2009).

[6] www.newstrackindia.com/newsdetails/2869 (accessed July 6, 2009).

EXHIBIT 1.3
Factors Increasing
Project Activity

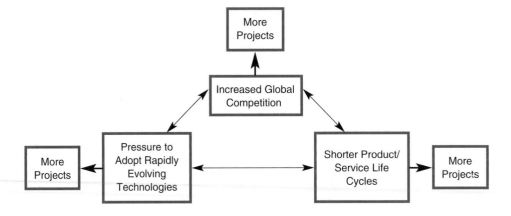

Projects are on the rise because businesses operate in what have been termed **hyper-competitive business environments,**[7] characterized by shortened product life cycles, the increasingly global reach of most businesses, and pressures to adopt rapidly evolving technologies. Each of these factors, by itself, has the capacity to increase the number of projects an organization undertakes to achieve strategic goals. When the three interact, they magnify the escalation, as shown in Exhibit 1.3. Note that the directional arrows are double-headed, signifying that each of the influence factors can affect the other two.

Consider an example that illustrates the concepts presented in Exhibit 1.3. An organization opens a manufacturing facility in Europe as part of a strategic plan to increase global market access. The addition of the new facility creates the need for better information systems to connect geographically dispersed operations and meet reporting requirements.[8] The new information systems give the company better access to customer information. This information, along with the company's new presence in Europe, prompts it to recognize the need for new products. Increased global competition makes it necessary to continue to add new products and shelve old ones. Each of these phenomena feeds on the others to escalate the need for new project initiatives. The cycle is unending.

PROJECT SUCCESS FACTORS

Most of us have been involved in both successful and unsuccessful projects. By reflecting on your own experiences, you probably can list factors that seem to have contributed to success and failure. Our work with project managers, along with evidence from research,[9] has led us to conclude that 10 factors are essential to project success. Exhibit 1.4 describes these factors and also shows where the reader can find more information about each one in this book.

[7] R.A. D'Aveni, *Hypercompetition: Managing the Dynamics of Strategic Maneuvering* (New York: Free Press, 1994).

[8] One example of a reporting requirement that is driving additional expenditures on IT is the Sarbanes-Oxley Act mandated by the U.S. Congress in 2002. Multinational corporations face these and other regulatory requirements and must find ways to manage all of them in a coordinated manner.

[9] D.P. Slevin and J.K. Pinto, "Balancing Strategy and Tactics in Project Implementation." *Sloan Management Review* 29, no. 1 (1987), pp. 33–34; J.K. Pinto and O.P. Kharbanda, "How to Fail in Project Management (Without Really Trying)." *Business Horizons* 39, no. 4 (1996), pp. 45–53; and C.L. Iacovou and A.S. Dexter, "Turning Around Runaway Information Technology Projects." *California Management Review* 46, no. 4 (Summer 2004), pp. 68–88.

EXHIBIT 1.4 **Project Success Factors**

Success Factor	Description and Chapter References
Factor 1	
Clear and shared purpose and goals	• All project participants must agree on the purpose or mission of the project (Why are we doing this?) and its measurable goals (What are we trying to achieve?). • Clear, shared, challenging but realistic goals have a powerful influence on individual and team performance.* • Chapters 2, 3, 4, 5, 7.
Factor 2	
Motivated project team and stakeholders	• Project team members must feel the project is important—that it is valued by the organization, the client, and other stakeholders. A project that seems worthless, marginal, or futile does not stimulate much excitement or involvement. • Although financial incentives can contribute to motivation in some situations, people in professional settings generally are more often motivated by being part of a successful endeavor than by contingent monetary rewards.[†] • Effective project managers tap into intrinsic motivation by recognizing and celebrating achievements and milestones throughout the project. • Chapters 2, 9, 10.
Factor 3	
Unfailing customer orientation	• In successful projects, team members know who the final customers are and what they need. Indeed, inadequate assessment of user needs is one of the primary causes of project failure.[‡] • Project managers must stay in continuous communication with customers, ensuring they are satisfied with progress at each milestone. • Chapters 2, 3, 4, 5, 8.
Factor 4	
Adequate support and resources	• Support from top-level managers is critical if a project is to be completed on time and meet its performance objectives. • Upper-level managers can ensure that the project has adequate resources in the form of money, people, physical space, equipment, logistics, support systems, and information. • If resources are not available when needed, even the most enthusiastic project manager will have difficulty achieving project goals. • Chapters 3, 4, 5, 8.
Factor 5	
Clear roles and responsibilities	• All members of the team, along with supporting stakeholders, must understand their roles in the project. • Roles must be choreographed such that they occur at the right time and complement each other. Chaos and conflict reign when people's roles are unclear, poorly coordinated, or both. • Chapters 2, 4, 5, 8.
Factor 6	
Attention to planning	• An effective project is carefully planned from the beginning and is planned again as new information becomes available. • Planning includes identifying the project's purpose, defining the scope, determining customer requirements, identifying tasks, estimating time and cost, assigning responsibility, and other activities. • The level of planning will vary with the size and complexity of the project. • Team members must be deeply involved in planning. • Chapters 4, 5, 6, 7, 8.

(continued)

EXHIBIT 1.4   *(Continued)*

Success Factor	Description and Chapter References
Factor 7	
Effective management of uncertainty	• Effective project teams consider possible uncertainties in advance. They determine ways to avoid or mitigate potential negative events and consider ways to leverage potential positive surprises, should they arise.
	• A well-planned project leaves a team with some reserves to effectively respond to unexpected crises.
	• Although it might seem that a successful project was simply blessed by good fortune, what appears to have been good luck was probably anything but random.
	• Chapters 3, 6, 7, 8, 9.
Factor 8	
Continuous, effective communication	• An effective project manager knows the importance of keeping key stakeholders informed of the project's purpose, goals, progress, and changes. A stakeholder is anyone who will be affected by the project, or who can influence the project's success or failure.
	• At the project's outset and as events unfold, key stakeholders must have the opportunity to comment and provide input. As a result, final project deliverables and outcomes should not come as a surprise to anyone.
	• Chapters 2, 4, 5, 9, 10.
Factor 9	
Effective scope management and change control	• Scope creep, the insidious tendency for a project to grow in scope as it unfolds, is among the most vexing issues for a project manager.
	• Although change is inevitable in project work, changes must arise from explicit discussions and formal decisions that consider resource, schedule, quality, and project goal-achievement implications.
	• Effective scope management entails having an appropriate change control process and carefully managing the expectations of customers and other key stakeholders.
	• Chapters 5, 8, 9.
Factor 10	
Leadership	• Different projects require different levels of leadership formality, but every project needs a leader.
	• The need for leadership formality depends on scope, complexity, strategic importance, and culture.[§]
	• Even in leaderless groups, someone should serve as facilitator, helping to steer the team at any given time.
	• Rotating leadership seldom works.
	• Chapters 2, 4.

[*]E.A. Locke and G.P. Latham, *Goal Setting: A Motivational Technique That Works!* (Englewood Cliffs, NJ: Prentice Hall, 1984).
[†]P. Smith and D.G. Reinertsen, *Developing Products in Half the Time: New Rules, New Tools* (New York: Van Nostrand Reinhold, 1998); and T. Amabile, "How to Kill Creativity," *Harvard Business Review* 76, no. 5 (1998), pp. 78–87.
[‡]S. McConnell, *Software Project Survival Guide* (Redmond, WA: Microsoft Press, 1998); and K. Beck and C. Andres, *Extreme Programming Explained: Embrace Change*, 2nd ed. (Boston: Addison-Wesley, 2004).
[§]A formal leader who holds authority is important, but more so in some cultures than others. For example, in countries where the culture is characterized by high "power distance" team members might not function well in the absence of a clearly designated authority figure. The Arabic-speaking nations, plus Latin America, Russia, and nearly all of Asia (especially India and China), are characterized by high levels of power distance. Most of Europe, Canada, Australia, and Israel are low in power distance. Japan, the United States, and Mediterranean Europe fall into the middle range (Hofstede, 1980).

MEASURING PROJECT SUCCESS

What is project success? How will we know it when we see it? A portion of the answers to these questions goes back to goal clarity and client needs, discussed above. **Key performance indicators (KPIs,** as they are often called) can help a team to

EXHIBIT 1.5
The Triple Constraint

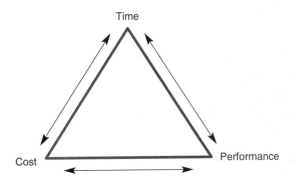

understand priorities among various goals and will guide team members' behaviors during the life of the project. Project **monitoring and control systems,** as well as **project closure and learning,** are built around the KPIs chosen for a project.

The Triple Constraint

The most commonly recognized project metrics are **time, cost,** and **performance.** In combination, they form a set of potentially competing project priorities known as the **triple constraint,** shown in Exhibit 1.5. As suggested in the exhibit, each constraint can affect the others. For example, if a project requires more time, the cost is likely to rise. However, if a project is time-compressed to a great extent, the inefficiencies that arise can lead to higher costs. Likewise, we generally assume that a requirement for higher performance will lead to greater cost. However, an excessive or out-of-control budget might lead team members to make work for themselves by adding unnecessary features to a product or extra tasks to a service-oriented endeavor, thereby degrading performance. The arrows in Exhibit 1.5 not only run in two directions but can represent nonlinear relationships.

Triple constraint definitions and examples from a successful program, China's first manned space shot,[10] are described in Exhibit 1.6.

An organization must clearly establish the relative priority of triple constraint criteria; the team cannot be expected to optimize all three. For example, a NASA motto, adopted in the 1990s, "better, faster, cheaper"[11] might have communicated an ambiguous message to team members, consequently contributing to some of the agency's widely publicized failures.[12]

Although some people joke about it, the old saying "Time, Cost, Performance, pick two" is actually quite valid.[13] Project sponsors and leaders must clearly communicate to the team and supporting stakeholders which two of these dimensions have priority over the third.

Balanced Scorecards

The triple constraint is deeply ingrained in project management culture and lore, and it offers a simple way for us to understand priorities and their interrelationships. However, it implies a somewhat limited perspective. For example, it typically does not place the project into a strategic context, considering bigger-picture corporate

[10] Numerous articles have been written about this space shot. One example is available at www.cbsnews .com/stories/2003/10/06/tech/main576804.shtml. Another is C. Hutzler, "Space Shot Is Tale of Precision Plan in Bolder China," *The Wall Street Journal,* October 16, 2003, p. A1.

[11] D. Leonard and D. Kiron, *Managing Knowledge and Learning at NASA and the Jet Propulsion Laboratory (JPL),* Harvard Business School Case (Boston: HBS Publishing, 2002).

[12] D. Vaughan, *The Challenger Launch Decision: Risky Technology, Culture, and Deviance at NASA* (Chicago: University of Chicago Press, 1996).

[13] D. Shirley, *Managing Martians* (New York: Broadway Books, 1998).

EXHIBIT 1.6   Triple Constraint Definitions Applied to China's First Manned Space Shot

The Shenzhou 5.
© AP Photo/Xinhua,
Li Gang

Photo source: www.space.com/
missionlaunches/shenzhou5_
launch_031014.html

Triple Constraint Dimension	Definition and Measures	Priority for the Chinese Space Shot
Performance	Performance is the most broadly defined of the triple constraint elements and may include scope, quality, extent to which specifications are met, ability of the product to perform required functions, and other factors.	The highest priority was technical performance; the spacecraft Shenzhou 5 had to reach a designated altitude and return the "taikonaut" safely to a landing site in Inner Mongolia. Chinese officials knew the entire world was watching, many with questions about the country's quick rise out of the ranks of developing nations.
Time	This dimension refers to measures of a project's ability to meet a specified deadline.	Time was the second priority for the space shot project. Sooner was better, but not at the expense of performance. Team members took the extra time to test the technology and support systems with unmanned flights to ensure performance effectiveness.
Cost	This dimension addresses measures of the cost of the project, which can be broken down to manageable components associated with individual work packages, labor, subcontracts, materials, equipment, etc., and also can include indirect and overhead costs.	Although neither the project team nor governmental agencies ignored cost, everyone no doubt was aware that the other two priorities were more important. The project is estimated to have cost about $2.2 billion,* although numerous indirect costs are probably not included in that figure.

*C. Hutzler, "Space Shot Is Tale of Precision Plan in Bolder China," *The Wall Street Journal,* October 16, 2003, p. A1.

financial objectives (e.g., return on investment) or the project's ability to meet its market goals or solve internal problems. Moreover, it does not explicitly include customer satisfaction or qualitative factors such as learning or team satisfaction.

Kaplan and his colleagues at Harvard Business School[14] have coined the term **balanced scorecard** to describe a comprehensive approach to companywide performance management. Their focus has been on the more routine aspects of organizational performance, but we argue that the balanced scorecard has value in project environments as well. They identify four measurement dimensions: **financial, internal business processes, customer,** and **learning and growth,** all of which are relevant to project environments. When emphasis on KPIs is not appropriately balanced, team members might focus on one aspect of performance to the detriment of others.[15] For example, imagine a new-product development project in which the leader and sponsor make

[14] R.S. Kaplan and D.P. Norton, *Execution Premium: Linking Strategy to Operations for Strategy Advantage* (Boston, MA: Harvard University Press, 2008).

[15] This sort of scenario has been documented in a variety of settings, as illustrated by S. Kerr in a classic article titled "On the Folly of Rewarding A while Hoping for B," *Academy of Management Executive,* February 1995 (This classic article was originally published in *Academy of Management Review* in 1975).

The Panama Canal, completed in 1914, was considered an engineering marvel in its day.* It changed the face of the global shipping industry by creating a 77-kilometer (48-mile) sea link between the Atlantic and Pacific Oceans through the isthmus of Panama. Enough time has passed that many people around the world have lost sight of the project's somewhat ugly history. A group of French investors initiated the first Panama Canal project in 1880, with a vision that involved a series of locks similar to those in the current design. Over several years, the project led to nearly 20,000 worker deaths, mostly from yellow fever and malaria. The French ultimately abandoned the project, and the site remained idle until 1905 when the U.S. government struck a deal with the sponsors to take over the effort and purchase the equipment on site.

The lessons learned in the initial effort led the new project leaders to begin with activities aimed at eradicating disease risks before restarting construction.[†] The canal project was completed two years ahead of schedule in 1914, and it certainly met its business objectives. However, worker deaths from construction activities added 5,000 more to the project's final toll. When reviewing the success of the Panama Canal project, we cannot overlook the loss of human life it caused. Clearly, this was a project that did not meet the expectation of 'do no harm,' and, thus, cannot be viewed as an unqualified success.

*For more information, we recommend the video titled *Widening the Panama Canal,* which is part of the Discovery Channel's *Extreme Engineering* Series. It is available for purchase through iTunes at www.itunes.com.

†The Americans might just as easily have made the mistakes the French did, but they had the advantage of learning from the French project.

daily announcements about project expenditures but mention nothing about product test results, customer satisfaction, or time to market. Under such a scenario, team members might ignore or give sparse attention to outcomes that may be even more important than adhering closely to the project's budget in ensuring the product's ultimate success in the marketplace.

Many organizations use **performance dashboards** to keep project team members focused on a balanced set of KPIs. Think of the dashboard in your car as a metaphor; it shows you your current speed, RPMs, engine temperature, fuel level, oil pressure, and other measures important to your understanding of the vehicle's performance. The same idea can be applied to a project, as we discuss in more depth in Chapter 9.

Do No Harm

In addition to meeting the criteria for effectiveness included in the triple constraint or, more broadly, in a balanced scorecard, a project should be accomplished in a socially responsible manner. We cannot call a project a success if it has harmed employees, the larger society, or the environment. The controversy over drilling for oil in the Arctic National Wildlife Refuge (ANWAR) in Alaska represents an example of this kind of issue. Those opposed to the project believed it would harm the fragile arctic environment and wildlife populations, even though it had the potential to help achieve other national goals such as reduced dependence on foreign oil. We present another example related to the warning about "do no harm" in Box 1.1.

THE PROJECT MANAGEMENT PROCESS

All productive work occurs in processes—the sequences of activities that transform inputs into outputs. Project work is no different. Projects take inputs (information, labor, materials, facilities, etc.) and, through a series of steps, transform them into deliverables (outputs).

Project Phases

Project work occurs in five widely acknowledged phases, described below. However, not all projects follow these phases in an entirely sequential fashion. They can overlap and often are iterative. Nonetheless, the five phases offer a useful guiding framework.

- **Selection:** Someone in the organization decides to embark on a project. Decision makers consider factors such as the importance of the underlying problem or opportunity, match with corporate mission, potential financial returns, fit or synergy with other projects in the company portfolio, available resources, and opportunities for learning.
- **Initiation:** The project sponsor issues a charter legitimizing the project within the organization and establishing ballpark guidelines for scope, time, and cost. The project manager and team are selected, the project's purpose and goals are clarified, and the KPIs are identified.
- **Planning:** Given a clear understanding of project purpose and measurable goals, the team selects a general approach and determines what needs to happen, when, by whom, and at what cost. Examples of outcomes for this phase include the **work breakdown structure (WBS),** the uncertainty assessment, the communication plan, and the schedule. These represent baseline elements and parameters that will be assessed against actual outcomes during and after the project.
- **Delivery and control:** The work of the project is executed and tracked against the plan, leading to real-time adjustments in project scope, schedule, cost, and specifications. KPIs are reviewed regularly. The team is in continuous communication with stakeholders, particularly customers. At the end of each phase or the completion of each major milestone, the team assesses lessons learned that indicate the need for changes in processes and practices as the project moves forward.
- **Closure and handoff to customer:** Project deliverables are handed off to customers, who must accept and approve the results. The team completes required documentation, assesses lessons learned, and celebrates.

In many cases, it also is appropriate to view the project from a **life cycle** perspective, considering its long-term effects on the organization, employees, the customer, the environment, the larger economy, the social system, and so forth. For example, think about a project to construct an offshore oil-drilling rig for a major oil company. The project might be considered complete when the rig is handed off to the oil company, but what about the long-term use and disposal of the equipment? A life cycle approach would consider projected costs of operating and maintaining the equipment, as well as the costs of decommissioning and disposing of materials at the end of the rig's useful life.

Graphical Perspectives on the Five Phases

Most projects involve considerable iteration as one stage of development leads to better understanding of parameters derived in previous stages. The left-hand side of Exhibit 1.7 depicts two ways these phases may be sequenced.

The figure in the upper left-hand corner of Exhibit 1.7 depicts what has been called a **waterfall** approach. One phase must be complete before the next one is started. Many

EXHIBIT 1.7

Project Phases: Sequential Relationships over Time

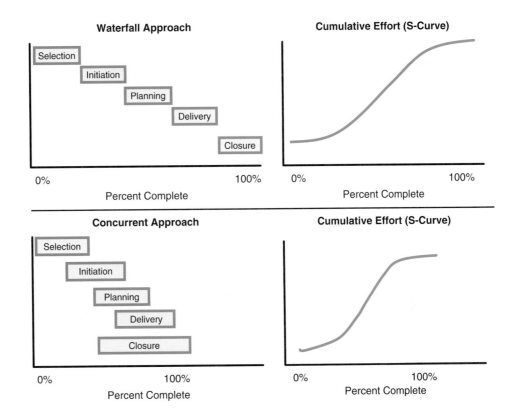

people view this approach as easier to manage because only one type of activity is happening at any given time, and there is a solid sense of closure at the end of each phase. However, it operates in what might be termed a **large batch size mode** in which there is a considerable investment in effort and a big commitment before the project moves to each new phase. The next phase could uncover flaws in the previous phase, potentially necessitating significant rework or even revealing that the project should be abandoned. Such discoveries can come at a high cost, as illustrated in the example in Box 1.2.

In contrast to the waterfall approach, the concurrent approach, depicted in the lower left-hand portion of Exhibit 1.7, follows a detailed plan for the early stages of the project (say, the first three months) and takes a less fine-grained approach for the remainder of the project (say, the next nine months). Some initiation work begins before the project is completely vetted, based on the understanding that early planning efforts can uncover something that renders the project infeasible. Team members can continue to add detail as they gain information. And, instead of viewing closeout and handoff as something to be done at the project's culmination, the team can identify key milestones where the customer is brought in for review (and celebration). Thus, closure is ongoing. The overlapped phases require greater communication and coordination, and they might, individually, take somewhat longer (as depicted in the bar lengths) than they would have in a waterfall approach. However, the concurrent approach has the potential to lead to higher quality in the finished product, and it can take less *total* time if it is effectively coordinated.[16]

[16] S. McConnell, *Software Project Survival Guide* (Redmond, WA: Microsoft Press, 1998); and Smith and Reinertsen, *Developing Products in Half the Time.*

When we view the cumulative effort associated with the phases of a waterfall-oriented project, we generally find **cumulative effort S-curves** similar to those shown on the right side of Exhibit 1.7. The S-shape characterizes most projects, but its steepness depends on the extent of overlap among the phases and where resource requirements are the greatest. Project managers and sponsors should be aware of the S-curve's implications and be prepared for a higher level of resource utilization and cash outflow during the middle portion of a project's timeline.

New Models for Concurrent Development Projects

The software industry has gone to new lengths in compressing project phases. These efforts began in the 1990s with what is known as Boehm's **spiral model,** an iterative approach that repeats project phases on a small scale as the project moves toward completion.[17] The general purpose of these models was to avoid the problems that arose when software engineers took an IT project too far before testing or checking back with customers. Boehm and his associates recommended the approach for software projects with uncertain requirements and staffed by experienced developers who had the capacity to respond to evolving information in a somewhat unstructured environment.[18]

Recently, practitioners of concurrent software development methods have embraced more sophisticated and structured approaches referred to collectively as **agile software development.** The idea behind agile development is to create software in a team environment where frequent testing and consultation with stakeholders allow team

[17] B. Boehm, "A Spiral Model of Software Development and Enhancement," *Computer IEEE* 21, no. 5 (1988), pp. 61–72.

[18] B. Boehm and R. Turner, *Balancing Agility and Discipline: A Guide for the Perplexed* (Boston: Addison-Wesley, 2004).

members to build a functioning system more effectively. Newer incarnations of agile development have added slightly more structure while retaining the underlying philosophy of adaptability, under the umbrella of what is known as **extreme programming.**[19] Proponents of this approach prescribe a series of daily, weekly, and monthly practices that involve frequent testing of incremental components, honest two-way exchange with customers, recognition that user requirements will become more clear with time, shared team knowledge as a substitute for excessive documentation, and simple solutions wherever possible. Agile development and extreme programming both result in a steepening of the S-curve, as depicted in the lower right-hand portion of Exhibit 1.7. Those who criticize extreme programming as a project management paradigm express concern that not all teams have the discipline to adhere to the process, leading the endeavor out of control and into a state of chaos.[20] Those who warn against extreme programming rightly point to its potential problems, but they appear to recognize its potential for positive results if it is done right.

We believe concepts from extreme programming and agile development have potential application beyond IT projects. The biggest potential appears to be for projects characterized by uncertainty at the front end; an example would be the development of a new product that is very different from anything the organization has created in the past. Continuous testing and communication with the customer can allow the project to grow in a way that identifies problems, solutions, and opportunities before the design is locked into place. But, as those who criticize agile development have observed, the team and supporting organizational functions must possess enough discipline to keep people's eyes focused on project outcome goals.

TEAMS IN PROJECT ENVIRONMENTS

"No man will make a great leader who wants to do it all himself, or get all the credit for doing it."

Andrew Carnegie

Although some projects involve an individual working alone, rarely does one person have all the skills and capabilities needed to effectively complete the work required by a project. Properly managed, a team of people with diverse skill sets, working in concert, creates synergies that lead to improved performance.[21] When the process is carefully coordinated, a team is likely to generate superior results more quickly than one individual acting alone.[22] But teams also present special challenges for project managers. This is particularly the case if the manager is overly focused on technical details and insufficiently attuned to the needs of team members. Exhibit 1.8 highlights the benefits and challenges linked with the potential contributions teams offer.

---

[19] K. Beck and C. Andres, *Extreme Programming Explained: Embrace Change,* 2nd ed. (Boston: Addison-Wesley, 2004).

[20] M. Stephens and D. Rosenberg, *Extreme Programming Refactored: The Case Against XP* (Berkeley, CA: Apress, 2003).

[21] J.R. Katzenbach and D.K. Smith, *The Wisdom of Teams: Creating the High-Performance Organization* (Boston: Harvard Business School Press, 1993).

[22] See J. Surowiecki, *The Wisdom of Crowds* (New York: Anchor Books, 2005) for numerous empirical studies to support this position.

EXHIBIT 1.8   Benefits and Challenges Associated with Project Teams

Potential Team Contribution	Benefits of a Project Team	Potential Challenges for a Project Team
Creativity	A team can generate more ideas than an individual working alone, resulting in a potentially better project. For example, a creative team might come up with a previously undiscovered strategy for achieving project goals.	The ideas the team generates might not be the best ones. The project manager may find it difficult to filter and prioritize the myriad ideas that emerge from a team brainstorming session. And the loudest voices can drown out quieter voices expressing superior ideas.
Synergy and cross-pollination of ideas	When people exchange thoughts and ideas with others who may come at the problem from a different perspective, the result can be better solutions than one individual might have thought of on his or her own.	Conflict may arise among team members who disagree and cannot reach consensus.
Motivational energy	Working in a positive work environment on a worthwhile project can energize team members to work harder than they might have if they were working alone.	The project manager must find a way to help team members see the project as worthwhile and involve them in a way that develops their sense of ownership. This can take extra time at the front end of the project.
Expanded workforce to complete project tasks	More people are available to get the job done.	In comparison to a project in which one person handles all of the work, more coordination is required when a team is involved. And, the project manager can experience frustration when team members are too busy working on other assignments to attend to project needs.
Technical expertise	The project manager can borrow technical expertise from various functional areas when it is needed for specific project tasks.	There can be conflicts when functional managers cannot or will not release the resources to a project when the schedule calls for their contributions.
Stakeholder communication	Team members can serve as emissaries for the project within and outside of the organization, helping to build necessary support. It would be more difficult for one person to do this alone.	Team members might communicate the wrong information or negative information about the project to key stakeholders. This becomes more of a problem as the size of the team expands.
Organizational development and personal learning	Working in teams provides opportunities for individuals to develop new competencies and promotes learning across the organization. This develops both the organization and the individual participants.	Providing appropriate professional development opportunities and being attuned to the learning needs of different team members represents one more thing to which the project manager must attend.

Visual Tools for Teams

"The soul never thinks without a picture."

Aristotle

Throughout this book, we will emphasize tools for team-based visual facilitation. Research and practice have illustrated the value of visual presentations in supporting effective team decision making, and what happens when needed information is not

Project Manager Discovers Visual Tools as an Aid to Teamwork   Box 1.3

Jack Zhang, a well-respected manager in a large pharmaceutical firm in China, had led many projects during his career. He had studied project management methods and was particularly adept at using Excel software for decision-analysis and MS Project software for scheduling. Before the team kickoff for any new project, Jack worked diligently to develop a list of tasks and enter them into a computerized project schedule. He proudly presented the project scope and schedule at the first team meeting, feeling that this would establish his credibility as a project manager. To his continuing disappointment, he was unable to obtain the level of team commitment he had anticipated.

After learning about visual tools for project teams, Jack changed his approach and began to engage his teams in visually oriented, mind-mapping processes to generate work breakdown structures. Instead of entering his view of the project into the scheduling software, he showed his team how to convert the work breakdown structure into a wall-mounted sticky note schedule. Later, when the team agreed on the schedule, he entered it into MS Project to record a baseline. He happily reported that this new approach had increased the level of motivation, commitment, and satisfaction for his project teams. *And* his projects have become much more successful in achieving their goals.

presented clearly. Tufte, well known for his work on visual displays, uses numerous examples to underscore this point.[23] One of his most often-cited case studies centers on NASA's doomed decision to launch the Challenger space shuttle in 1986.[24] The information presented to members of the decision-making team was displayed in ways that made it difficult for them to understand relationships among variables. In contrast, as Kepner and Tregoe observe, NASA's miraculous recovery of the Apollo 13 mission in 1970 may be attributed to good visual tools supported by a team well versed in sound decision-making methods.[25]

Examples of visual, team-based tools presented in this book include **decision trees** for project selection, **portfolio mapping, mind mapping** for WBS development, the **gut-feel method for uncertainty assessment,** and the **sticky-note method for project scheduling.** Box 1.3 tells the story of a real project manager who discovered the value of visual, team-based tools.

WHAT ORGANIZATIONS GAIN BY MANAGING PROJECTS SYSTEMATICALLY

What can organizations gain from following the ideas prescribed in this book? If an enterprise applies their best practices for managing projects, will it make a positive difference in short-term performance or long-term viability? The answer to both

[23] E.R. Tufte, *The Visual Display of Quantitative Information* (Cheshire, CN: Graphics Press, 1983); and *Visual Explanations* (Cheshire, CN: Graphics Press, 1997).

[24] D. Vaughan, *The Challenger Launch Decision: Risky Technology, Culture, and Deviance at NASA* (Chicago: University of Chicago Press, 1996).

[25] C.H. Kepner and B.B. Tregoe, *The New Rational Manager* (Princeton: Princeton Research Press, 1981).

questions appears to be a resounding "yes." Several authors, including Kerzner, Ibbs and Kwak, and Pennypacker and Grant,[26] observe that organizations with systematic project management processes are more effective and successful than those lower on the scale of what they call **project management maturity.** Quadrant Homes is an example of a company that ranks high in terms of project management maturity. Quadrant changed its approach to project management after poor financial results in the years preceding 1996 had threatened its continued viability as a subsidiary of Weyerhaeuser. It has achieved admirable financial and market success by finding ways to standardize across projects without making processes overly rigid. Box 1.4[27] presents information about Quadrant's systematic approach, along with performance results.

Although systematic approaches for managing projects are gaining popularity in organizations of all types, attempts at standardization in project environments can and will be met with resistance. For example, at a California-based subsidiary of an aerospace component supplier, the business unit president attempted to adapt standard processes and other lean manufacturing concepts for application within the engineering department. His intent was to streamline the product development process, which would have positive strategic implications for the company. As evidence of the potential benefits of standard processes, the president noted the degree of success the business unit had enjoyed as a result of implementing lean concepts in its manufacturing plant and in some of its back-office administrative functions. Engineers resisted the idea and sabotaged these initiatives, citing concerns that they would be forced into a box, and noting that creative work cannot be standardized. At the time of this writing, the project continues to be stalemated despite encouragement from the corporate CEO and business unit president.

Standardization can add value in project environments, as evidenced by the success at Quadrant Homes, but it can present at least three points of resistance. First, a one-size-fits-all approach can be overly restrictive for some types of projects.[28] Second, standardized processes generally introduce a higher degree of personal accountability, which can make people uncomfortable. And third, people nearly always resist change that takes them out of their comfort zones. The keys to success involve explaining why the change is necessary, convincing people that the change will benefit them, and involving stakeholders in the design of the new processes. Involvement not only enhances their sense of ownership; it also allow them to offer useful ideas that improve the potential success of the endeavor.[29]

---

[26] H. Kerzner, *Strategic Planning for Project Management: Using a Project Management Maturity Model* (New York: Wiley and Sons, 2002); C.W. Ibbs and Y.H. Kwak, "Assessing Project Management Maturity," *Project Management Journal* 31, no. 1 (2000), pp. 32–43; and J.S. Pennypacker and K.P. Grant, "Project Management Maturity: An Industry Benchmark," *Project Management Journal* 34, no. 1 (2003), pp. 4–11.

[27] K.A. Brown, T.G. Schmitt, R.J. Schonberger and S. Dennis, "Quadrant Homes Applies Lean Concepts in a Project Environment," *Interfaces* 34, no. 6 (2004), pp. 442–50.

[28] J.M. Hall and M.E. Johnson, "When Should a Process Be Art, Not Science?" *Harvard Business Review* 87, no. 3 (2009), pp. 59–65.

[29] J.D. Ford and L.W. Ford, "Decoding Resistance to Change," *Harvard Business Review* 87 no. 4 (2009), pp. 99–103.

Quadrant Homes Applies Process Standardization in a Project Environment

Box 1.4

© Quadrant logo reprinted with permission from Quadrant Homes.

Quadrant Homes, a subsidiary of Fortune 500 Weyerhaeuser Corp., began implementing standardized methods for custom home-building projects in 1996. A few examples of the outcomes of this change are as follows:

	1996	2006
Market share	1%	10%
Number of homes sold per year	175	2,000
Referral-based business	8%	36%
Cost per square foot	$60	$30
Net margin per home	2%	6%

QUADRANT'S STANDARDIZED PROJECT MANAGEMENT SYSTEM

Quadrant has developed a process for managing the opening of custom-home communities as part of a larger-scale, even-flow system. Before adopting its disciplined project management system, Quadrant treated each new community opening as a unique project. The most revered community-center managers were those who could heroically do battle with local jurisdictions and manage crises effectively.

Quadrant recognized that although each new community opening was a project, successive openings were very similar projects where standard processes could be used to great advantage. Under Quadrant's new system, teams follow a 40-task checklist, with columns for responsibility assignment, due dates, and progress. These standard procedures have allowed Quadrant to start and finish community openings more effectively, on-time, and within budget. As one community is built out and another is opened, intact teams move from one project to the next, carrying process knowledge and team relationships with them. These changes represent one aspect of an entire set of processes Quadrant uses to manage the flow of home-building projects in a standardized way.

Source: K.A. Brown, T.G. Schmitt, R.J. Schonberger and S. Dennis, "Quadrant Homes Applies Lean Concepts in a Project Environment," *Interfaces* 34, no. 6 (2004), pp. 442–50.

Chapter Summary and Onward

This chapter has set the stage for the remainder of the book by defining projects as unique endeavors. Projects originate because of problems, opportunities, or mandates, and may be large or small in scope. An organization's entire set of projects is known as a portfolio. Ideally, this portfolio is composed of a set of complementary initiatives that support the organization's mission and strategic goals.

Project-related work is on the rise. Underlying causes of this growth include global competition, shortened product life cycles, and pressures to adopt rapidly evolving technologies. These combined forces also have had the effect of making many projects more complex because of the need for coordination across systems, functions, continents, languages, and cultures.

The most successful projects are characterized by clear goals, motivated teams, strong customer orientation, adequate support, clear roles and responsibilities, appropriate planning, management of uncertainty, communication, scope management, and effective leadership. The triple constraint describes three potentially competing priorities and project success metrics: time, cost, and performance. It has great conceptual value, but can limit a project team's ability to appreciate a more complete and balanced set of metrics. The best measurement systems offer timely information about an array of key performance indicators that focus people's attention on a full range of relevant dimensions.

Project management occurs in five phases, which may be managed sequentially or in a more concurrent manner. Concurrent models offer advantages in information flow, improved quality, and time reduction, but are likely to require more coordination.

Most projects are executed in team environments, which present both opportunities and challenges for the project manager. Team-based, visual tools for project planning, which will be highlighted throughout this book, can play a major positive role in engaging and motivating team members. They offer another significant benefit, too: better project plans and better results throughout the five project phases.

Organizations that develop systematic approaches for managing projects can draw significant financial and market benefits from these efforts. However, individuals and teams working in creative environments might resist standardized project management approaches as being too rigid.

With this chapter as background, we hope you are eager to forge ahead and begin to master the details of selecting, initiating, planning, and executing projects. The majority of this book is dedicated to this process. However, before we move to that step, we establish an important foundation regarding the role of the project manager. This provides important contextual information that will be of continuing value to you as you work to put the ideas in this book into action. Chapter 2, titled "The Effective Project Manager," will help you to *(a)* understand the characteristics of the best project managers, *(b)* communicate with project stakeholders, *(c)* develop persuasion skills to attract resources to your project, *(d)* motivate project team members, *(e)* manage project conflict, and *(f)* lead project meetings. These skills will equip you to better manage the project management process.

Team Activities

1. Assemble a team of three or four classmates. On your own, or with the help of your instructor, make contact with an experienced project manager in an industry of your choice. Request a 45-minute interview with this person. Ask your interviewee to consider the best and worst project with which he or she has been affiliated. Assure your interviewee that his or her reflections will be used for assignment purposes only. For each of the two projects (best and worst), ask your interviewee to:

   a. Describe the project's purpose, the approach taken, and the extent to which it achieved or failed to achieve its goals.

   b. Name and describe at least four factors that helped make the project a success or contributed to its failure.

   Immediately after the interview, convene your team to prepare a two-page summary report, including at least one paragraph reflecting on how your interview results confirm, extend, or contradict the project success factors presented in Chapter 1.

2. Convene a team of four to six classmates to watch the Discovery Channel video about building the Panama Canal. (Although it is best if you watch the movie together, your instructor may offer you the option of watching the movie independently and convening later to discuss it.) This video is part of the series *Extreme Engineering* (you may download the video at www.itunes.com). As you watch the film, you will learn about the first canal project, which was completed in 1914. Following an historical overview of the first project, the second part of the film reviews the initial work and plans for the canal's widening and upgrade. After you watch it, work as a team to create a table with each of the two projects (original canal project and current expansion project) as the headers for the columns. Within the table, differentiate the projects based on the dimensions shown in the sample table below. (For more information on these attributes, see Exhibit 1.2 and the discussion related to that exhibit.) Offer a few sentences of narrative within the cells of the table. Feel free to consult the Internet for other sources of information about these Panama Canal projects.

Sample Table

Project Attribute	Original Panama Canal Project	Current Panama Canal Expansion Project
Project Drivers		
Project Source		
Customer		
Degree of Certainty		
Expected Outcomes		
Organizational Reach		
Scope		
Complexity		
Strategic Level		

After you complete the summary table, write a paragraph about sources of contrast between the two projects.

3. In a group of four to six classmates, watch the 2008 movie *Outsourced*. (Although it is best if you watch the movie together, your instructor may offer you the option of watching the movie independently and convening later to discuss it.) The movie tells the story of an American manager responsible for his company's call centers in the United States who is suddenly assigned the role of getting a new call center up-to-speed in India. As you watch the film, prepare to discuss the following questions:

   a. What underlying drivers motivated the company to undertake this project? Consider publicly stated reasons as well as those that may have been unstated. Do you think the company carefully thought through the reasons before initiating the project? Why or why not?

   b. What was the primary KPI (key performance indicator) for this project? What potential negative outcomes could arise if the project manager and sponsors focus only on this metric? What would you recommend as other possible metrics for assessing the performance of this project throughout its life cycle?

   c. As the story progresses, Todd involves the team more and more in the project. What advantages and disadvantages did he encounter when he expanded their participative roles?

   As a team, prepare a three- to five-page summary report that demonstrates your team's analysis and critical thinking with regard to questions a through c, above.

Discussion Questions and Exercises

1. List and briefly describe the reasons project work is on the rise. Select a well-known organization, or one where you have worked, and describe how these factors, individually and in combination, served to create more projects. Or, if they did not produce a proliferation of projects, explain why not.

2. Think back to the most and least successful projects in which you have been involved. Make a list of the project success factors presented in this chapter and create a table similar to the one below. Briefly describe how each of the 10 success factors played out in each of the two projects. What are your conclusions about which success factors tend to be most important? Name and describe at least one success factor you think is missing from this list.

Success Factor	Successful Project	Unsuccessful Project
	Brief description of project:	Brief description of project:
	How this factor contributed to success	How the absence of this factor or problems with this factor contributed to failure or detracted from potential success
1. Clear and shared purpose and goals		
2. Motivated project team and stakeholders		
3. Unfailing customer orientation		
4. Adequate support and resources		
5. Clear roles and responsibilities		
6. Attention to planning		
7. Effective management of uncertainty		
8. Continuous, effective communication		
9. Effective scope management		
10. Leadership		

3. Recall a project in which you have been involved. (This can be anything from moving to a new home, to hosting a Super Bowl or World Cup party, to launching a rocket.) Describe how each of the triple constraint priorities was defined for that project, and discuss their relative importance or emphasis. Comment about whether you believe the priorities were appropriately set and communicated.

4. Recall an instance from your own experience in which a work-related performance measure encouraged the wrong behavior from employees. Describe what happened and how things should have been handled.

5. Next week is your instructor's birthday. Class members have decided to surprise the instructor with a 10-minute, in-class birthday party. Each class member has donated $1 to fund the celebration. What KPIs (key performance indicators) could you use to measure the success of this project? Try to develop a balanced scorecard of measures.

6. Select a recent or vintage movie in which a project is central to the plot. Films for consideration include *Ocean's Eleven, Ocean's Twelve, Ocean's Thirteen, The Core, Mr. Blandings Builds His Dream House, Mountains of the Moon, The Italian Job, Return of the Jedi, Jaws.*

   a. Describe this project in terms of the project attributes highlighted in Exhibit 1.2 and offer a brief explanation for each one. So, for example, you will identify the project's key drivers, source, etc., and explain each one in the context of the project in the movie.

   b. List the five phases of project management presented in this chapter, and describe what happened during each of these phases in the project depicted in the movie.

7. Watch the movie *Apollo 13,* and find the scene where the astronauts discover they are about to suffocate from too much CO_2. A team of engineers on Earth is assigned the task of making "a square peg fit into a round hole" to make an air filter fit into a hole for which it was not designed. Note how the project turns out. List the project management steps or phases presented in Exhibit 1.7, and then describe what happened during each of these phases during this short crisis management project. Comment on whether you think this project followed a waterfall or concurrent approach and explain why you think so.

8. Visit the Web site of the Project Management Institute (www.pmi.org). Do the following:

   a. List and briefly describe the services offered by PMI.

   b. Name the countries where PMI has chapters and offers services.

   c. List the requirements one must meet to become a project management professional (PMP).

   d. For each PMP qualifying requirement, write a comment about whether or not you qualify, and why.

References

Amabile, T. "How to Kill Creativity." *Harvard Business Review* 76, no. 5 (1998), pp. 78–87.

Beck, K., and C. Andres. *Extreme Programming Explained: Embrace Change.* 2nd ed. Boston: Addison-Wesley, 2004.

Boehm, B., and R. Turner. *Balancing Agility and Discipline: A Guide for the Perplexed.* Boston: Addison-Wesley, 2004.

Boehm, B. "A Spiral Model of Software Development and Enhancement." *Computer IEEE* 21, no. 5 (1988), pp. 61–72.

Brown, K.A.; T.G. Schmitt; R.J. Schonberger; and S. Dennis. "Quadrant Homes Applies Lean Concepts in a Project Environment." *Interfaces* 34, no. 6 (2004), pp. 442–50.

Cooper, R.G. "Stage Gate New Product Development Processes: A Game Plan from Idea to Launch." In *The Portable MBA in Project Management,* ed. E. Verzuh. Hoboken, NJ: John Wiley and Sons, 2003.

D'Aveni, R.A. *Hypercompetition: Managing the Dynamics of Strategic Maneuvering.* New York: Free Press, 1994.

Ford, J.D., and L.W. Ford. "Decoding Resistance to Change." *Harvard Business Review* 87, no. 4 (2009), pp. 99–103.

Hall, J.M., and M.E. Johnson. "When Should a Process Be Art, Not Science?" *Harvard Business Review* 87, no. 3 (2009), pp. 59–65.

Hamilton, D.P. "Dose of Reality: Biotech's Bottom Line: More Than $40 Billion in Losses." *The Wall Street Journal,* May 20, 2004, p. A1.

Hartman, F. *Don't Park Your Brain Outside.* Newtown Square, PA: Project Management Institute, 2000.

Hofstede, G. *Culture's Consequences: International Differences in Work-Related Values.* Beverly Hills, CA: Sage Publications, 1980.

Iacovou, C.L., and A.S. Dexter. "Turning Around Runaway Information Technology Projects." *California Management Review* 46, no. 4 (Summer 2004), pp. 68–88.

Ibbs, C.W., and Y.H. Kwak. "Assessing Project Management Maturity." *Project Management Journal* 31, no. 1 (2000), pp. 32–43.

Kaplan, R.S. "What to Ask the Person in the Mirror." *Harvard Business Review* 85, no. 1 (2007), pp. 86–95.

Kaplan, R.S., and D.P. Norton. *Execution Premium: Linking Strategy to Operations for Strategic Advantage.* Boston, MA: Harvard University Press, 2008.

Katzenbach, J.R., and D.K. Smith. *The Wisdom of Teams: Creating the High-Performance Organization.* Boston: Harvard Business School Press, 1993.

Kerr, S. "On the Folly of Rewarding A While Hoping for B." *Academy of Management Executive* 9, no. 1 (1995), pp. 7–14. (This classic article was originally published in *Academy of Management Review* in 1975.)

Kerzner, H. *Strategic Planning for Project Management: Using a Project Management Maturity Model.* New York: Wiley and Sons, 2002.

Leonard, D., and D. Kiron. *Managing Knowledge and Learning at NASA and the Jet Propulsion Laboratory (JPL).* Harvard Business School Case. Boston: HBS Publishing, 2002.

Locke, E.A., and G.P. Latham. *Goal Setting: A Motivational Technique That Works!* Englewood Cliffs, NJ: Prentice Hall, 1984.

Locke, E.A., and G.P. Latham. *A Theory of Goal Setting and Task Performance.* Englewood Cliffs, NJ: Prentice Hall, 1990.

Mitchell, T.R., and D. Daniels. "Motivation." In *Comprehensive Handbook of Psychology, Volume Twelve: Industrial and Organizational Psychology,* ed. W.C. Borman, D.R. Ilgen, and R.J. Klimoski. New York: John Wiley & Sons, Inc., 2004.

McConnell, S. *Software Project Survival Guide.* Redmond, WA: Microsoft Press, 1998.

Morgan, M.; W.A. Malek; and R.E. Levitt. *Executing Your Strategy: How to Break It Down and Get It Done.* Boston: Harvard Business School Press, 2008.

Pennypacker, J.S., and K.P. Grant. "Project Management Maturity: An Industry Benchmark." *Project Management Journal* 34, no. 1 (March 2003), pp. 4–11.

Pinto, J.K., and O.P. Kharbanda. "How to Fail in Project Management (Without Really Trying)." *Business Horizons* 39, no. 4 (1996), pp. 45–53.

Project Management Institute. *A Guide to the Project Management Body of Knowledge,* 4th ed. Newton Square, PA: PMI, 2008.

Reinertsen, D.G. *Managing the Design Factory.* New York: Free Press, 1997.

Shirley, D. *Managing Martians.* New York: Broadway Books, 1998.

Slevin, D.P., and J.K. Pinto. "Balancing Strategy and Tactics in Project Implementation." *Sloan Management Review* 29, no. 1 (1987), pp. 33–34.

Smith, P., and D.G. Reinertsen. *Developing Products in Half the Time: New Rules, New Tools.* New York: Van Nostrand Reinhold, 1998.

Steers, R.M.; R.T. Mowday; and D.L. Shapiro. "The Future of Work Motivation." *Academy of Management Review* 29, no. 3 (2004), pp. 379–87.

Stephens, M., and D. Rosenberg. *Extreme Programming Refactored: The Case Against XP.* Berkeley, CA: Apress, 2003.

Tufte, E.R. *The Visual Display of Quantitative Information.* Cheshire, CN: Graphics Press, 1983.

Tufte, E.R. *Visual Explanations.* Cheshire, CN: Graphics Press, 1997.

Vaughan, D. *The Challenger Launch Decision: Risky Technology, Culture, and Deviance at NASA.* Chicago: University of Chicago Press, 1996.

Welch, J. "The Five Stages of Crisis Management." *The Wall Street Journal,* September 14, 2005, p. A20.

Chapter Two

The Effective Project Manager

"Leadership is the art of getting someone else to do something you want done because he wants to."

Dwight D. Eisenhower

Chapter Learning Objectives

When you have mastered the material in this chapter, you should be able to:

- Assess your core project leadership capabilities and identify areas where you need to enhance your skill or achieve greater balance.
- Apply strategies to encourage effective two-way communication in project environments.
- Apply influence strategies and appreciate why these skills are so essential to project managers.
- Recognize the keys to success in effective negotiation.
- Effectively lead project team meetings.
- Understand the sources of project team conflict and respond appropriately.
- Articulate the role of intrinsic factors, extrinsic factors, and goals in motivating team members and use this knowledge to best advantage in project environments.

This entire book is about managing projects. If you are reading this book, you probably want to become an effective project leader. We have placed this chapter here to provide important background for subsequent material.

The following scenario about a real project manager sets the tone for our discussion of attributes and skills that are the foundation for this chapter on project leadership:

> Over the course of several years, Barbara Briol[1] developed a reputation as a skillful project leader. One of her greatest successes was the Fever project, chartered to redesign the material delivery system for the large electronics plant where she worked as an engineer. When asked what made Barbara such a good project manager, stakeholders made the following comments:
>
> *From customers:*
>
> - Throughout the project, Barbara and her team solicited my area's views regarding system requirements and options and really listened to what we wanted. She made sure our input shaped the final recommendations.

---

[1] Pseudonym.

- Our area was kept informed of progress as the project moved forward; there were no surprises when the final solution was presented.

From general and functional managers:

- As a senior manager, I got just enough information about the project. I knew what was going on, but I wasn't overwhelmed by reams of data.
- Barbara made excellent use of the people in my area who worked on the project team. They were able to contribute their expertise to the project while still fulfilling their other job responsibilities.

From team members:

- Barbara really believed in what we were doing. Her sincere enthusiasm spilled over onto the entire team. I think all members of the team felt they, personally, were responsible for the project's success. Barbara's leadership was a big part of this.
- Even when we were struggling through the nitty-gritty detail, Barbara made sure we stayed focused on the project's ultimate goal.
- I knew why I was involved in the effort, what contributions I was expected to make, and when I needed to make them. Barbara made sure I got the information, resources, and support I needed to do my part.
- Our project team meetings were well run. I never felt my time was being wasted.

You might be tempted to conclude that Barbara was a one-in-a-million leader who possessed rare gifts, unattainable by mere mortals. How can anyone understand and satisfy the needs of such a broad spectrum of stakeholders? This is a true story, so we know it is possible, but it does require the project manager to balance a set of potentially conflicting capabilities. Effective project managers are visionary leaders *and* capable of managing details, technically savvy *and* interpersonally and politically astute, disciplined *and* flexible. This chapter describes the skills needed to effectively lead projects and suggests strategies for making them part of your personal tool kit.

WHO IS THE PROJECT MANAGER?

Project management has been referred to as "an accidental profession"[2] because many people prepare themselves to be engineers, accountants, programmers, administrators, marketing managers, or information technology specialists, but end up managing projects. As organizations initiate increasing numbers of projects to overcome problems or seize strategic opportunities, they will need more and more qualified people to lead and manage projects. You may be one of them.

No universal personality style characterizes the most effective leaders or managers, but a few traits increase a person's chances for success (see Box 2.1).

Individuals of many different personal styles can learn to be superb project managers. The project manager is responsible and accountable for planning and executing project tasks and often must operate with little formal authority. Consequently, he or she lacks the position power to obtain resources or make binding technical decisions. (See Exhibit 2.1 for Dilbert's view of these dilemmas). Despite these challenges, it is possible to become an effective project manager by balancing a core set of capabilities,

[2] J. Pinto and O. Kharbanda, "Lessons for an Accidental Profession," *Business Horizons* 38, no. 2 (1995), pp. 41–50.

Personality Traits of Effective Leaders

Box 2.1

Yukl summarizes the decades and volumes of research conducted to unlock the secrets of the most effective leaders.* One key conclusion he and others draw is that there is not just one universal personality style that makes for an effective leader. What is needed depends on the circumstances. However, the research appears to indicate that certain traits increase the likelihood of leadership effectiveness in most situations. Those most likely to benefit the project manager include:

- Energy level.
- Tolerance for stress.
- Self-confidence.
- Internal locus of control (belief one has control over what happens).
- Emotional stability and maturity.
- Personal integrity.
- Moderately high achievement orientation.

Notice that personal charisma does not show up on this list! Although some people think project managers must be extroverts, this is not a necessary characteristic.

* G. Yukl, *Leadership in Organizations,* 5th ed. (Upper Saddle River, NJ: Prentice Hall, 2002). Although some interesting ideas have emerged, limitations have been associated with the research methods used. Most results point to the importance of recognizing the role of situational factors. Yukl also suggests that, in addition to the importance of a contingency perspective, we also consider the interactions among the various traits and skills. That is, interpersonal skill may not explain much variance on its own, but in combination with personal integrity, we may see a significant result.

EXHIBIT 2.1   Dilbert on the Roles of Project Managers

DILBERT: © Scott Adams/Dist. by United Feature Syndicate, Inc

developing essential skills, and becoming proficient in a few key tools. This chapter is organized around these capabilities, skills, and tools.

THE PROJECT MANAGER'S CORE CAPABILITIES: A BALANCED SET

Effective project managers deftly balance a diverse set of contrasting core capabilities. In some respects, these capabilities are innate characteristics of individual personalities. If one recognizes his or her dominant orientation within each of the contrasting capabilities, this can be a first step toward achieving balance.

Visionary Leader *and* Detail-Oriented Manager

The effective project manager balances leadership and management roles, recognizing when each one is needed. The leader role involves a number of creative and visionary skills, which sometimes are viewed as right-brain capabilities.[3] These skills support the project manager in thinking about the big picture, brainstorming solutions, and motivating team members by creating a shared vision. However, to ensure that the work is actually accomplished effectively, the project manager also must apply a set of more analytical or left-brain skills for detailed scheduling, budgeting, resource allocation, and tracking progress.

Technically Savvy *and* Interpersonally and Politically Astute

It often happens that a person with sound technical knowledge is handed the reins of a project in his or her area of expertise. This person has been a great doer but might not have the interpersonal skills to accomplish work through others. Social and political skills are essential, and fortunately, they can be learned. Several ideas for communicating, enhancing persuasion skills, managing team meetings, and motivating team members are presented in this chapter.

Disciplined *and* Flexible

A final contrast is the need for project managers to be both disciplined and flexible.[4] "Formalization of process supports discipline, but it will reduce agility if it adheres excessively to processes."[5] We like to think about this as *just enough process*. Throughout this book we emphasize processes—tools, structures, and ways of working—that facilitate selecting, initiating, planning, executing, monitoring, and closing a project. However, these methods should be adapted, as needed, to fit each situation. As one of our MBA teams noted in a project retrospective, "We learned the value of tools, not rules" (or, as they quipped, "tulz not rulz.")

---

[3] Although research has demonstrated that the two sides of the brain do not operate as separately as some have imagined (T. Hines, "Left Brain/Right Brain Mythology and Implications for Management and Training," *Academy of Management Review* 12, no. 4 [1987], pp. 600–06), there are some distinctions along these lines (S. Springer and G. Deutsch, *Left Brain, Right Brain: Perspectives from Cognitive Science,* 5th ed. [New York: Freeman-Worth, 1998]), and the notion that creativity is a right-brain function and linearity and analysis are left-brain functions, has become a metaphorical distinction used frequently in management (D. Leonard and S. Strauss, "Putting Your Company's Whole Brain to Work," *Harvard Business Review* 75, no. 4 [1997], pp. 110–21; and K.A. Brown and N.L. Hyer, "Whole Brain Thinking for Project Management," *Business Horizons* 45, no. 3 [2002], pp. 47–57).

[4] R. Austin and L. Devin, *Artful Making: What Managers Need to Know about How Artists Work* (Upper Saddle River, NJ: Financial Times Prentice Hall, 2003).

[5] L. Applegate, R. Austin, and F. W. McFarlan, *Corporate Information Strategy and Management,* 6th ed. (New York: McGraw-Hill/Irwin, 2002), p. 278.

Mount Everest. © Pixtal / SuperStock.

In April 1990, an international team of 20 climbers from China, Russia, and the United States reached the summit of Mount Everest in what has been lauded by the *Guinness Book of World Records* as the most successful climbing expedition in history. Many factors (including good fortune) contributed to the project's success. The leadership structure was particularly noteworthy. Jim Whitaker, who in 1963 became the first U.S. citizen to reach the summit of Everest, served as the primary project leader. Whitaker was highly regarded by members of the international climbing community, and his visionary leadership provided the glue that held the diverse team together. Warren Thompson, a corporate tax attorney by trade, was deputy leader of the team; his role was to plan and monitor the schedule, manage resources, and handle the logistics of the expedition. In other words, Thompson focused on details. Whitaker's climbing knowledge clearly gave him the technical capability to lead the group, but he also was politically savvy and did a masterful job in bringing together disparate languages, cultures, power structures, and climbing styles. He knew how to persuade, negotiate, and find areas of compromise. He also knew when to be flexible and bend the plan and when to stick with the plan. For example, one of the teams was determined to reach the summit on International Earth Day, even though the weather and team preparation would have made it highly infeasible. Whitaker helped team members to understand that the Earth Day goal was a metaphor, and that a successful climb at a more appropriate time was a higher priority goal. Whitaker, with the support of Thompson's attention to detail, possessed an unusual capacity for balance.

Source: Personal interviews with Warren Thompson.

Concluding Remarks about Core Capabilities

We have presented several ways of thinking about the contrasting core capabilities of effective project managers. These can be difficult to balance, but, as the Mount Everest expedition story in Box 2.2 illustrates, it is possible.

THE PROJECT MANAGER'S ESSENTIAL SKILLS AND TOOLS

You can enhance your ability to successfully initiate, plan, execute, and close out a project by possessing a set of skills and tools that address several specific areas: communication, persuasion and influence, negotiation, meeting management, conflict management, and motivation.

Communication

Many stakeholders praised the communication skills of Barbara Briol, the effective project manager described earlier in this chapter. Projects run on communication—the exchange of information from one person to another. People, not plans and software,

EXHIBIT 2.2 Tips for Listening

Source: C. Lehman and D. DuFrene, *Business Communication* (Mason, Ohio: South-Western, 2005), pp. 61–62; D. Shilling, "Be an Effective Listener!" www.womensmedia .com/seminar-listening.html, accessed March 1, 2006; and PAR Group, "The Secrets to Listening Well," http://www.thepargroup.com/article_SecretsListenWell.html (accessed July, 2009).

- Focus on the speaker. Give him or her your full attention. Where possible, eliminate external distractions and try to clear your mind.
- Listen with empathy. Imagine yourself in the speaker's position so you can appreciate his or her point of view.
- React to the speaker, both after the speaker has concluded, and by responding nonverbally (nod, smile, as appropriate) while the speaker talks.
- Finish listening before you begin to speak. It is difficult to really listen if you are focused on formulating what you will say in response. Don't interrupt.
- Ask questions to clarify the intended meaning. Restate what you think the speaker has said in your own words. Respond in a way that lets the speaker know that you are taking him or her seriously.

complete projects. Team members and other stakeholders need information to know what and when to contribute or how the project will affect them. The project manager is at the hub of all these information exchanges and must be good at listening as well as sending information.

Listening

Listening is the foundation of two-way communication and essential for project managers and their teams. People must listen to one another to plan the work, report status, solve problems, and collaborate in accomplishing project objectives. The consequences of poor listening can be disastrous and, at minimum, can mean higher project costs because of mistakes and rework, missed project deadlines, and project deliverables that do not meet the client's goals. In addition, failure to listen effectively can damage working relationships.

Real listening is an active process in which we hear what is being said, understand the message in our own way, and test for understanding of the speaker's intent. As investigative journalist and TV personality Diane Sawyer so aptly puts it, "I think one lesson I have learned is that there is no substitute for paying attention." Exhibit 2.2 presents some tips for effective listening.

Sending Information

Although listening is essential, the project manager is often in the role of the sender of information—the person making the presentation or writing the memo that reports on status, requests resources, or asks for a decision. To do this effectively involves thinking through the objective of the communication, assessing the nature of the audience, selecting the appropriate communication channel or channels (written or spoken, individual or group, in person or via phone or other medium), and then actually developing the communication (e.g., presentation, memo, meeting plan). Exhibit 2.3 elaborates on each of these four steps and provides helpful guidelines in developing a communication strategy. Exhibit 2.4 provides targeted advice for making presentations.

When delivering your message orally, via a presentation or one on one, you must stay in tune with your audience and be prepared to adapt the tone, style, and content accordingly. The strategies noted in Exhibit 2.5 can help assure that you and your audience are "on the same page."

EXHIBIT 2.3
Developing a Communication Strategy

Source: Adapted from J. Dibble and B. Langford, *Communication Skills & Strategies: Guidelines for Managers at Work* (Cincinnati: South-Western Publishing Co., 1994).

1. Determine the communication objective.
   - What do you want this communication to accomplish?
   - What do you want your audience members to *do* after they receive this message?
   - How will you know if your objective has been accomplished?
2. Develop a clear and specific picture of the audience.
   - To whom are you directing this message? What do you know about them?
   - What do they already know about your subject and how are they likely to respond?
   - What questions will they likely have and how can you prepare to address them?
   - Consider the audience's most likely predisposition toward you, your team, and your message.
3. Choose the most suitable channel for your message.
   - It makes sense to use written communication (memo, e-mail, Web posting) when:
     - You need a permanent record of the communication.
     - The message needs to be very precise.
     - You need to send the message to a large number of people.
     - You don't need immediate feedback.
   - It makes sense to deliver the message through a presentation or conversation when:
     - You are dealing with a sensitive issue. It can be difficult to accurately convey tone and emotion in e-mail or other written format, which can lead to misunderstandings.
     - You need fast feedback.
     - You want to be absolutely sure the audience understands the message.
     - You want the message to have a big impact.
   - Choose a combination when no single channel will do everything you need.
4. Develop the communication (also, see the following sections on persuasion and influence, and negotiation).
   - Select the evidence to use in your message.
   - Arrange the material for best impact.
   - Develop a clear plan and follow it.
   - Carefully review your message once created. Does it say what you want it to say? Will it likely accomplish your intended objective? If not, then revise!

Persuasion and Influence

Influence is the use of personal energy to create an effect upon, redirect, or change the outcome of a particular situation. Influence is particularly important to project managers, who almost always lack the formal authority to obtain the resources they need. Drawing from a large body of research,[6] we highlight several principles of influence relevant to project management: reciprocity, consistency, social validation, liking, authority, potential loss versus potential gain, and request-magnitude sequence.

Reciprocity

Reciprocity is the fundamental social norm that obligates individuals to repay in kind what they have received.[7] In project management settings, you are far more likely to have individuals say yes to your requests if you have been cooperative or put favors

---

[6] For excellent reviews, see R. Cialdini, *Influence: The Psychology of Persuasion* (New York: Quill-William Morrow, 1993); R. Cialdini, *Influence: Science and Practice* (New York: Allyn & Bacon, 2000); and R. Cialdini, "The Science of Persuasion," *Scientific American* 14, no. 1 (2004), pp. 70–77.

[7] And, it pays. For example, in one study, charitable contributions increased from 18 percent to 35 percent when a small gift was included in the fund-raising solicitation; see R. Cialdini, "Harnessing the Science of Persuasion," *Harvard Business Review* 79, no. 9 (2001), p. 74.

EXHIBIT 2.4
Tips for Presentations

- Be certain that a presentation is the right communication vehicle for your message. In other words, work through the steps outlined in Exhibit 2.3.
- Practice the presentation!
  - This will assure a smooth delivery without hesitation or fumbling.
  - It will also give you a sense of the time needed for various segments.
- Be organized.
  - Provide audience members with a road map at the outset so they can follow the presentation.
  - Create a logical flow of ideas.
- Strive for good use of voice.
  - Be easy to listen to, energetic, and not monotone.
  - Demonstrate a sincere level of enthusiasm and passion for your ideas.
  - Avoid "uh," "um," and "you know."
- Maintain eye contact with the audience; avoid turning your back to the audience and reading from the screen.
- Use gesture and movement to keep audience attention.
  - Do not stand like a stone statue in one fixed position.
  - Maintain an energetic posture and good facial expression.
- Use effective visuals. Visuals should:
  - Look great from the back of the room (no tiny unreadable print).
  - Appropriately use color/pictures/graphics.
  - Be appropriate in number, neither too many nor too few.
- Pace the presentation. Be certain it does not drag or go too quickly.
- Anticipate likely audience questions and prepare responses.

in the bank ahead of time. Robert Cialdini, a well-respected expert on the power of persuasion, emphasizes that you can reinforce the likelihood of a reciprocal response to your own generosity by following a colleague's thank you with a statement such as "I know you would do the same for me if the tables were turned," rather than the more typical "Oh, sure, it was nothing."[8]

[8] R. Cialdini, "Harnessing the Science of Persuasion," *Harvard Business Review* 79, no. 9 (2001), pp. 72–79.

EXHIBIT 2.5
Are You Being Heard?

- Consider opening your presentation with a question for the audience that pulls members into the topic. For example, "How many of you have experienced delays in receiving reimbursement for travel?" might be a nice way to engage interest in a project to improve the travel reimbursement system.
- At appropriate points in the presentation, ask listeners if they are following you.
- Offer listeners opportunities to comment or ask questions. Some speakers encourage audience members to ask questions at any point during a presentation, and others express preference for end-of-presentation questions. Let your audience know what you prefer at the beginning of your talk.
- Look at the audience and be aware of body language that says, "I don't get it," such as rolled eyes, furrowed brows, and so on.
- Make sure the tone, style, content and the communication medium are appropriate to the audience. Adapt if necessary.

Consistency

Research in social psychology suggests that human beings like to *be* consistent, and *appear* consistent in their behavior. Project managers can use the principle of consistency to great advantage. For example, at the first check-off meeting for a final-assembly schedule project, a division's entire staff publicly signed a poster-size copy of the team's chartering document, indicating their support for the project and its objectives. Later in the project, when asked for specific time and resource contributions, managers were very reluctant to go back on their word. Commitments made actively—either spoken or in writing—are more likely to direct future conduct.[9] However, arm-twisting is not likely to garner long-term cooperation.

Social Validation

Social validation refers to the human tendency to look at what others are doing, especially similar or respected others, for cues about how to behave. For example, the manager of the order-fulfillment redesign team at a food service warehouse realized his project was likely to face strong resistance from warehouse associates, who were comfortable with established processes. The project manager selected two respected opinion leaders to serve as members of the design team. By being intimately involved in the analysis, these two became convinced of the need for change and became effective advocates for the process redesign. Their enthusiasm for the project provided social validation for other stakeholders. Horizontal influence may be more powerful than influence from above.[10] That is, people are more likely to identify with their peers than with their superiors.

Liking

"People prefer to say yes to those they like."[11] Short of getting a total makeover, how can you put the principle of liking to work for you as a project manager? The short answer is to win friends. This requires that you spend some time getting to know the people with whom you work. You cannot be a hermit if you want to build relationships. Learn about your co-workers, explore areas of common interest, and acknowledge their accomplishments. A sincere e-mail, handwritten note, or spoken "that was a great presentation" are not only gracious, but also can help you to build affiliations.

Credibility as a Source of Authority

Project managers rarely have control over rewards, promotions, and resources, but they can overcome this limitation by gaining respect for their capabilities and expertise. This was certainly true of Jim Whitaker in the Everest expedition example described in Box 2.2. He had no formal control over the other members of the international team, but people deferred to him because of his expertise.[12] This was his primary source of authority.

---

[9] D. Cioffi and R. Garner, "On Doing the Decision: Effects of Active versus Passive Choice on Commitment and Self-Perception," *Personality and Social Psychology Bulletin* 22, no. 2 (1996), p. 33.

[10] Cialdini, "Harnessing the Science of Persuasion," p. 76.

[11] Cialdini, "Harnessing the Science of Persuasion," p. 74.

[12] P. Hersey, K. Blanchard, and W. Natemeyer, "Situational Leadership and Power," *Group and Organizational Studies* 4, no. 4 (1979), pp. 418–28, reprinted in W. Natemeyer and T. McMahon, eds., *Classics of Organizational Behavior,* 3rd ed. (Prospect Heights, IL: Waveland Press, 2001), p. 322. Also, for a more general discussion see G. Salancik and J. Pfeffer, "Who Gets Power—and How They Hold on to It," *Organizational Dynamics* 5, no. 2 (1977), pp. 3–21.

It is not enough to be technically capable; others must know about your capabilities if you are to gain credibility. If you are a bit of an unknown, you may need to highlight your expertise, without sounding self-aggrandizing, for those who might not be familiar with your background. If you have a trusted associate within the organization, you might ask that person to let others know about your expertise and capabilities.

Potential Loss versus Potential Gain

Research by Shelley, Cialdini, and others demonstrates an important principle based on what is known as **prospect theory**—potential losses have a bigger influence on people's decision making than do potential gains.[13] This principle is used frequently in the field of marketing, but it also has great applicability for the project manager, especially when he or she is making requests for project resources (e.g., budgets, people, equipment, schedule extensions).

Imagine you have just learned about a new technology patent that, if purchased for $100,000, will enhance the performance of the new product your team is developing. One option for selling the idea to the sponsor would be to focus on the superior attributes of a product that has this technology. Another approach would be to warn that if your company does not purchase the patent rights, a specific competitor is likely to do so. This competitor could knock you out of the market, resulting in millions of dollars in lost sales. Research is clear on the choice; the loss-oriented communication will be more effective. (Warning: if you use this approach all of the time, people might become wise to your ploy!)

Request-Magnitude Sequence

The sequence in which we make requests of different magnitudes has a big impact on the responses we get. Think, for example, of how a teenager might sequence a request to her parents. "Could I travel around Europe this summer by myself? No? Well, how about letting me go to New York with my girlfriends for the weekend?" As a parent, you are more likely to say "yes" to the New York request if you receive the Europe proposal first. Cialdini has illustrated this principle in field experiments.[14] People who receive big requests first are more likely to say yes to a subsequent small request.

In the realm of project management, suppose you believe a major Web development project will have the greatest likelihood of meeting schedule commitments if you have four software engineers available full time for six months. However, you know that by extending the schedule, working some extra hours yourself, and possibly sacrificing another project, you might be able to complete the project in nine months with only two software engineers. Based on the request magnitude sequence principle, you should first make your largest request—for four software engineers. You may be surprised and get what you ask for. However, if the person granting the request tells you four are not available, your follow-up request for only two software engineers will seem small in comparison. This is another strategy the savvy project manager will take care not to over use.

Putting Persuasion and Influence to Work: Tips for Negotiating

To negotiate means to confer with another in order to come to terms. Beyond the influence strategies described above, additional tips can help you successfully negotiate. Let's look first at how *not* to handle a negotiation.

---

[13] M. K. Shelley, "Gain/Loss Asymmetry in Risky Intertemporal Choice," *Organizational Behavior & Human Decision Processes* 59, no. 1 (1994), pp. 124–60; and Cialdini, *Influence: The Psychology of Persuasion*.

[14] Cialdini, *Influence: The Psychology of Persuasion*.

Jacqueline: **(StarPanel project** **manager)**	Nathan, hi. Juan just stopped by and told me that you have asked him to work full time on documentation for the ISO audit. That means he is not available to complete the graphics for the StarPanel project.
Nathan: **(functional manager** **of communication and** **technical writing)**	Sorry, Jacqueline, I can't spare Juan for your project. I need my best designer to work on the ISO manual. Maxine is available, but you'll need to bring her up to speed on what you want.
Jacqueline:	Maxine? You're kidding, right? I need Juan for the project. Maxine has been on staff for only two months and she knows nothing about StarPanel! I should have expected that you would not stick to your commitment! You obviously don't know how important this project is!
Nathan:	Is that right? Come to think of it, Maxine is not available. You'll have to outsource the StarPanel work to one of the local design shops. It will cost you, but that's your problem, not mine.

The exchange between Jacqueline and Nathan illustrates a common but ineffective form of negotiation known as **positional bargaining.** This type of negotiation can produce unwise agreements—if StarPanel is more important to the company than ISO documentation, allocating Maxine to the task is certainly unwise. It is also inefficient—clearly this is *not* the last conversation that Jacqueline and Nathan will need to have regarding the graphics work for StarPanel. Positional bargaining also can endanger ongoing relationships; Jacqueline and Nathan's relationship is clearly degraded by this exchange.

In their highly regarded book, *Getting to Yes,* Fischer, Ury, and Patton of the Harvard Negotiation Project describe an alternative to positional bargaining, **principled negotiation,** which they define as "a method of negotiation explicitly designed to produce wise outcomes efficiently and amicably."[15] Principled negotiation, or negotiation on the merits, can be distilled down to four basic points.

Separate the People from the Problem

View yourself as working *with* the other person to solve a problem, not working *against* the other person to get your way. At the same time, recognize that you are dealing with a human being complete with ego and emotion. Pay attention to what and how you communicate. Jacqueline's angry remarks to Nathan inflame the situation and do nothing to move the negotiation forward. In fact, her comments actually work to her disadvantage: Nathan has become less compliant and less willing to give Jacqueline resources.

Focus on Interests, Not Positions

Interests are things a person really cares about. Position is where one stands on a particular issue. Jacqueline's *position* is that she wants Juan for her project. Her *interest* is having the graphics work for StarPanel done well and on time. Nathan's *position* is that

---

[15] R. Fisher, W. Ury, and Bruce Patton, *Getting to Yes: Negotiating Agreement Without Giving In* (New York: Penguin Books, 1993), p. 10.

Juan must do the work for the ISO documentation. His *interest* is in having the ISO work completed well and on time. Focusing on their interests (including a shared but unarticulated interest in overall company success) could help Jacqueline and Nathan reach an effective agreement.

One way to learn about a negotiation partner's interests is to simply ask. But in tense situations people are sometimes reluctant to expose themselves. Ask yourself, "If I were she, what would be important to me?" If you can find a way to spend more time with this individual, you can learn more about what makes her tick. You also may want to ask others who are close to her. With these perceptual underpinnings, you can seize the initiative by having a conversation in which you share information about your interests.[16]

Create a Variety of Possibilities before Deciding What to Do

Jacqueline and Nathan have tunnel vision. In their exchange, the world of possible solutions is limited to the resource assignments inherent in their positions. This will be unproductive, as the scenario suggests. At the start of a negotiation, take time to generate a large set of possible solutions that "advance shared interests and creatively reconcile differing interests."[17] A useful tool for generating a wide range of possibilities is the **mind map,** which we will introduce in Chapter 3 and expand upon in Chapters 4 and 5. Jointly creating a mind map of possible solution options encourages broad and expansive thinking about what might be considered, but also can enhance the sense that the negotiators are working as a team to attack a problem.

Insist the Result Be Based on Some Objective Standard

The outcome of a negotiation should reflect some fair standard (market value, expert opinion, legality, product performance, or meeting a target completion date) "independent of the naked will of either side."[18] If at the outset of a negotiation, the parties involved agree on what will make a fair solution, the negotiation quits being a contest of wills. Jacqueline and Nathan might agree that a fair solution supports the company's strategic plan, does not compromise customer satisfaction, and will meet the development and quality-of-work-life needs of staff. Exhibit 2.6 summarizes important points about negotiation.

[16] Adapted from Fisher, et al., *Getting to Yes: Negotiating Agreement Without Giving In;* and M. Federico and R. Beaty, *Rath and Strong's Six Sigma Team Pocket Guide* (New York: McGraw Hill, 2003).

[17] Fisher, et al., *Getting to Yes: Negotiating Agreement Without Giving In,* p. 11.

[18] Ibid, p. 12.

EXHIBIT 2.6
Negotiating Tips

Source: Adapted from R. Fisher, W. Ury, and B. Patton, *Getting to Yes: Negotiating Agreement Without Giving In* (New York: Penguin Books, 1993); and M. Federico and R. Beaty, *Rath and Strong's Six Sigma Team Pocket Guide* (New York: McGraw Hill, 2003).

- Identify the issue.
- Focus on interests rather than positions.
  - Think about what you have to offer the other person (how you might satisfy his/her interest), and how to make your offer attractive to this person.
  - Think about what he or she has that would satisfy your interests; don't be afraid to ask for what you want or to suggest trades.
- If the other person's style bothers you, don't let it get in the way of negotiating. The goal is a wise outcome, reached efficiently and amicably, not to become best friends.
- Explore objective criteria for a fair solution.
- Generate options, discuss them, evaluate, and then select.
- Keep in mind the essential elements of persuasion introduced in the previous section.

Leading Productive Team Meetings

Meetings are one of the most important venues for project communication, and the project manager has a major responsibility for making sure meetings offer value for all concerned and for the project. Someone who builds a reputation for effectively preparing and executing meetings becomes recognized as someone who can get things done and make things happen. On the contrary, anyone whose meetings are flaming disasters that accomplish little likely will attract few people to his or her projects.

When a project team assembles for a meeting, three things are actually happening: **content, process,** and **interactions.** *Content* is the "what" and refers to the agenda items themselves (e.g., the issues being considered or decisions to be made). *Process* refers to the methods, procedures, format, and tools used to address the topic at hand. *Interactions* encompass the interpersonal dimension—the communication patterns, group dynamics, and group climate. Unlike content, process and interactions are not as obvious and their importance is often underappreciated. This is unfortunate because process and interactions can have a *huge* impact on the effectiveness of any group.

The triple set of needs (content, process, interactions) demands a pair of complementary roles: that of leader and facilitator.[19] The leader typically wants to stay on task and address all of the content set forward in the agenda. The facilitator role centers on activities that can take considerable time and attention—guiding processes that ensure everyone has a voice, incorporating mechanisms for team decision making, and, more generally, creating a positive and productive group climate. Trying to do both the facilitator and leader job at the same time is a challenge. Some organizations provide resources for internal or external facilitators, but this is rare.

The project manager must prepare him or herself with some strategies for managing this role conflict. First, make it clear when you are switching roles. *"I've been asking for everyone's opinion. Now I would like to put on my leader hat and tell you what I think."* Making this role shift explicit can help you to avoid appearing manipulative. (Edward de Bono offers a clever approach for explicit role shifts.[20]) A second strategy is to acknowledge the conflict to the team. For example, *"I really appreciate hearing everyone's views and it seems we are developing some consensus around option A. However, I feel very unsettled by this because, personally, I feel that option A is the wrong choice because of the high risk it carries."* The project manager should use this approach with caution. If he or she takes a stand too often, it might stifle team members from offering ideas and dampen their enthusiasm as followers.

Documentation Is Essential

The worst meeting is the one that must be held again because the discussions, decisions, and action items were not recorded. If it is not documented, it never happened. Meeting minutes can be posted on a project Web site, distributed by e-mail, physically

---

[19] Decades of empirical research on organizational justice also demonstrate that leaders who pay attention to process and interactions will increase the likelihood of positive organizational outcomes; see T. Simons, "Why Managers Should Care about Fairness: The Effects of Aggregate Justice Perceptions on Organizational Outcomes," *Journal of Applied Psychology* 88, no. 3 (June 2003), pp. 432–43.

[20] Different colors of hats represent different thinking modes for a team. For example, team members would, at least metaphorically, wear black hats when they are trying to discover what is wrong with an idea, or green hats when they are in an idea-generation mode. See E. de Bono, *Six Thinking Hats* (London: Clays Limited, 1985).

EXHIBIT 2.7   Sample Issues Log

Source: Adapted from N. Hyer and U. Wemmerlöv, *Reorganizing the Factory: Competing Through Cellular Manufacturing* (Portland, OR: Productivity, 2002), p. 502.

Issue #	Date Logged	Originator	Description and Impact	Owner	Due Date	Status or Resolution
17	3/17	Danuta	Operators are not completing the tracking sheets we developed to log product flow and track lead time. We need this information for our analysis.	Danuta and team.	3/23	Resolved—Danuta and team have redesigned form; operators are now using it.
18	3/25	Sukran	Analysis of assembly activities in the 8517 area delayed by a week (due date: 4/10 in our original plan). The team needs training on analysis methods, and the key trainer is not available until 4/10. If the work is not complete by 4/25 it could delay our Design Week plans.	Sukran	4/25	Pending. We will analyze work during the next week and have an off-site scheduled for 4/17 to pull everything together.

distributed on paper, displayed in a project room, or all four of these. For example, one construction company places all written project records, including meeting minutes, on a Web site that the customer can access and search by keyword during and after the project. Open access to project documentation proves useful during and after the project, and it builds customer trust and loyalty.

In addition to, or as part of meeting minutes, the team should maintain an **issues log.** An **issue** is any problem or concern that arises in a project meeting that cannot be immediately resolved because there isn't enough time to discuss it thoroughly, the needed information is not available, or resolution will require actions outside the meeting. During the meeting, the team should identify the issue, who raised it, when it was raised, what steps will resolve the issue, who owns the resolution, and the expected resolution date. Exhibit 2.7 presents a sample format. The issues log should be reviewed and updated at each meeting. Afterward, it should be redistributed or posted on the project Web site or display board.

Meeting Tips

Exhibit 2.8 offers several ideas for designing and running productive team sessions. These highlight what to do (A) before the meeting begins, (B) during the meeting, and (C) after the meeting.

Technology-Enabled Meetings

Technology-enabled meetings rely on electronic means to facilitate collaboration among participants, in the same room or around the globe. Numerous technological options for collaboration are available. **Electronic meeting systems,** for example, consist of a network of personal computers equipped with special meeting software. Most versions of electronic meeting software have features that permit participants to contribute synchronously by typing in ideas that are displayed instantaneously and

EXHIBIT 2.8(A)
Meeting Tips for *before* **the Project Meeting**

Purpose

- Be sure you have a clear idea of the purpose of the meeting, and that you can articulate exactly what you hope to accomplish.
- Avoid "one way" meetings, where the only purpose is indoctrination. If you do not want group input, you probably do not need a meeting. There are more efficient ways to communicate one-way information.

Agenda

- Distribute the agenda in advance, ask for input, and highlight any work you expect people to do before the meeting.
- At the top of the agenda, state the meeting time, place, and date (some people will never read beyond this).
- For each part of the agenda (and the meeting as a whole) specify:
  - The subject.
  - The process you will use (brainstorm, discuss, multi-vote, etc.).
  - Who will lead or facilitate this part of the meeting.
  - The expected time you anticipate spending on this item.
  - The expected deliverable (what will be the output of this section).
- Send out a reminder on the meeting day, or the day before.

Venue

- For projects that require short, frequent meetings, consider holding these in a room without a table, or with a high stand-up table. Stand-up meetings tend to be faster than sit-down meetings.
- For major projects of long duration (say, nine months or more) see if you can use your persuasion skills to obtain a room dedicated to your project. Some organizations refer to these as **war rooms,** but we suggest the term **project room** because it has a more positive connotation. The walls of the room can display team member photos, diagrams depicting the end product, up-to-date project status charts, etc. Be sure to allow space for whiteboards and wall-mounted butcher paper the team can use to generate ideas and analyze emerging issues.
- Post your team's ground rules in the meeting room.*
- Assemble a facilitation kit with flip-chart markers, whiteboard markers, various sizes and colors of sticky notes, masking tape, extra pens and pencils, paper, adhesive-backed colored dots, and anything else that you might require in a meeting. Take this box with you to each meeting, or leave it in your meeting room.
- Especially if your meeting is planned for more than 90 minutes, arrange to serve refreshments; no one will need to leave the room for food or drink, and your meeting will have a more positive tone.

*This should be a list of behaviors and actions on which the group has reached consensus and may include items such as "Arrive and take a seat before the scheduled meeting time." Or "Listen carefully to the ideas and opinions of others before preparing your response." The content of these ground rules will vary based on the composition of the team and the general level of maturity of the organization. In some organizations, it might be necessary to include "Don't answer cell phones during meetings," whereas, in others, this would go without saying.

anonymously to the entire group,[21] and they can do so while in the same room or from distributed sites. Some meeting technologies offer the capacity for **instant polling** or **audience-response systems** that quickly produce anonymous polling results with graphical displays. According to some recent field studies, "Electronic meeting systems improved the productivity of projects, typically reducing labor costs by 50 to

[21] W. Tullar, P. Kaiser, and P. Balthazard, "Group Work and Electronic Meeting Systems: From Boardroom to Classroom," *Business Communication Quarterly* 61, no. 4 (1998), pp. 53–65.

EXHIBIT 2.8(B)
Meeting Tips for
during **the Project**
Meeting

Setting the Stage

- At the start of the meeting, review the agenda, objectives, expected deliverables, and previous meeting's accomplishments.
- Establish a context for each meeting by noting where the team is in the project plan.
- Prepare a flip chart of the agenda (with time estimates) that you can then post on the meeting room wall. This helps keep everyone focused and allows you to track progress.

Process

- When you use a particular process, make the steps in the process visible (list them on the flip chart or whiteboard, e.g., silent reflection, record on sticky notes, share in round robin).
- Make meeting *progress* visible by keeping notes on a flip chart or whiteboard (i.e., have a scribe). Consider having two scribes, one to keep notes on the flip chart and one to record notes on a laptop.
- If you are the scribe, your job is to record, not edit! If you want to paraphrase, ask for permission and if you are unsure, ask for clarification.
- Encourage balanced participation by paying attention to people's levels of involvement, and draw everyone in by using subgroups, round robins (each person in turn offers *one* idea or contribution), structured brainstorming, affinity diagrams, and colored dot votes, or simply asking questions such as: "Ling, you've been quiet, would you mind sharing your opinion on this matter?"
- If you use a process that will divide the team into groups, remember it takes time to disperse as well as reassemble. Build time into your agenda to reflect this. We offer a number of techniques for engaging team participation throughout this book.
- Use presentation software (e.g., PowerPoint) sparingly; it can discourage team involvement by creating a one-way communication climate, and it can seldom capture the richness of data or ideas needed for group decision making. Heed the warning of Thompson, who claims "PowerPoint Makes You Dumb."*
- Create a wait list or **parking lot** to capture important issues that do not fit with the current agenda but should be discussed later.
- Keep team members on track. If you think they are meandering away from the issue at hand, remind them of the goal of the discussion.
- Humor is your friend! One project team had two mascots, a stuffed rat and a stuffed horse. They were placed in a box of meeting supplies the project leader brought to every meeting. If anyone on the team felt someone else on the team was revisiting issues that had been decided or the team had tabled for later discussion, they were encouraged to retrieve the horse from the box and place it in the center of the meeting table. This signified that someone was "beating a dead horse." In a similar way, the rat was used to indicate that the discussion was heading "down a rat hole"—diverging from the intended topic. Small elements of humor can refresh a team and keep the atmosphere positive.
- Critique the meeting ("What worked well or not so well about today's meeting?" or "How did we do today with respect to our ground rules?") and ask for input on what to accomplish at the next meeting.

(continued)

EXHIBIT 2.8(B)
(*Continued*)

Timing
- Under most circumstances, stick to your schedule and end the meeting on time. If it appears the meeting may need more time, ask participants in advance if they would be able to stay for a specified number of additional minutes.
- Keep it short. Although all-day or half-day planning workshops can be very effective vehicles for project initiation and planning, they probably are not appropriate for most ongoing progress and problem-solving meetings. Try to keep meetings under 90 minutes or you may be viewed as a clone of Dilbert's boss.

DILBERT: © Scott Adams/Dist. by United Feature Syndicate, Inc

*C. Thompson, "The Third Annual Year in Ideas: PowerPoint Makes You Dumb," *New York Times Magazine,* December 2003, p. 88.

70 percent, and project cycle times by as much at 90 percent."[22] Box 2.3 lists several electronic meeting software systems. Keep in mind that technology is not a panacea. Like any meeting, an electronically facilitated meeting requires careful planning.[23]

The most common technology-enabled meeting is the conference call. These kinds of meetings have become increasingly necessary as the numbers of globally dispersed

[22] J. Nunamaker, R. Briggs, D. Mittleman, D. Vogel, and P. Balthazard, "Lessons from a Dozen Years of Group Support Systems Research: A Discussion of Lab and Field Findings," *Journal of Management Information Systems* 13, no. 3 (1997), pp. 163–207; R. Grohowski, C. McGodd, D. Vogel, W. Martz, and J. Nunamaker, "Implementation of Electronic Meeting Systems at IBM," *MIS Quarterly* 14, no. 4 (1990), pp. 369–83; and T. Connolly, L. Jessup, and J. Valacich, "Effects of Anonymity and Evaluative Tone on Idea Generation in Computer-Mediated Groups," *Management Science* 36, no. 6 (1990), pp. 689–703.

[23] F. Niederman, C. Beise, and P. Beranek, "Issues and Concerns about Computer-Supported Meetings: The Facilitator's Perspective," *MIS Quarterly* 20, no. 1 (1996), pp. 22–40.

EXHIBIT 2.8(C)
Meeting Tips for *after* **the Project Meeting**

- Spend three minutes thinking about what you could have done to make the meeting better. Record these improvement ideas in a small notebook and review it periodically. In a very short time you will discover that you are running better, more productive project team meetings.
- Write the minutes, or have someone else do it . . . soon! It is amazing what will be forgotten or redone without documentation.
- Update and publish your issues log.
- Follow-up on action items.

BRAINSTORMING AND POLLING OR VOTING*

Meetingworks (www.meetingworks.com)
GroupSystems (www.groupsystems.com)
FacilitatePro (www.facilitate.com)

INSTANT POLLING

www.turningpointtechnologies.com
www.elwayresearch.com

* These sites were operating at time of publication, but web addresses may have changed and new vendors become available.

---

teams escalate.[24] Managing a meeting in which people cannot see each other requires even more preparation and attention to process than a physical meeting. One cannot assess body language or levels of engagement when meeting participants are sitting half a country or half a world away. Similarly, a team member cannot point to an agenda item or refer to a graphic and expect the group to follow, unless these visuals are also available electronically. The potential for miscommunication is great; note that the NASA decision to launch the doomed space shuttle *Challenger* in 1986 was made during a conference call. Exhibit 2.9 provides conference-call guidelines.

[24] For insights about how meetings affect members of globally dispersed teams, see G.A. Fowler, "For the Asia-Based Staff, a Typical Workday Lasts 24 Hours," *The Wall Street Journal,* August 22, 2006, p. B1.

EXHIBIT 2.9
Getting the Most from Project Conference Calls

- If your team will be meeting virtually on a regular basis, develop ground rules for these virtual sessions. Examples include:
  - We agree not to multitask. We each will focus exclusively on the discussion topic and will not attempt to do other work as well.
  - We will each identify ourselves before speaking.
  - We will not interrupt the speaker.
  - Speakers will signal when they are finished speaking (think of 10-4 in radio communication).
  - When we are confused about something, we will ask for clarification.
  - Where possible, when there is something we want to present to the group (e.g., make a proposal, ask for input on a problem), we will send materials to the group (or to the team Web site) in advance.
  - We will have the agenda and any advance materials in front of us when the meeting begins.
- Have a clear objective/purpose and deliverables. This is even more important when players are dispersed geographically. Electronically distribute the agenda ahead of time so participants are sure of the rationale and expected outcomes of the call.
- Stop and test for understanding, agreement, disagreement more frequently than you would in a physical meeting.
  - Provide the chance to ask questions.
  - Ask "What is unclear about what we have covered so far?"
  - Do not assume silence means agreement; it doesn't!
- A round robin format can be helpful ("Let's hear from everyone on this").
- Document what happened in the conference call and distribute it to participants with a request for feedback.

Conflict Management

The effective project manager must set aside any preconceived notions suggesting that all conflict is bad. Conflict, a state of disharmony among incompatible persons, ideas, or interests, can play a powerful and positive role in the success of your project team. When misunderstood, ignored, or handled badly, conflict can destroy a team and compromise the success of the project. However, just as destructive is the absence of conflict and the emergence of what is known as **groupthink**—"the mode of thinking that persons engage in when concurrence-seeking becomes so dominant" that it "tends to override realistic appraisal of alternative courses of action."[25]

Two types of conflict may surface in project teams: **task-related conflict** and **interpersonal conflict.** The first of these is actually welcome: Divergent views regarding project tasks or decisions can actually lead to a more complete and thorough understanding of the issue at hand. For example, in a study of teams engaged in a simulated project, Brown et al. found that teams experiencing conflict in the project initiation stage ultimately performed better on objective outcomes (cost, schedule) than those who experienced harmony during the initiation period.[26]

Interpersonal conflict may be the result of personality differences or long-standing animosity. However, interpersonal conflict can also be a symptom of other issues with the team. Consider the **team iceberg,**[27] depicted in Exhibit 2.10. Apparent interpersonal conflict in a team actually may be the manifestation of underlying misunderstandings

[25] For a classic discussion of groupthink, see I.L. Janis, "Groupthink," *Psychology Today* 5, no. 6 (1971), pp. 43–46, 74–76. See also J. Harvey, "The Abilene Paradox: The Management of Agreement," *Organizational Dynamics* 3, no.1 (1974), pp. 63–80.

[26] K.A. Brown, T.D. Klastorin, and J.L. Valluzzi, "Project Performance and the Liability of Group Harmony," *IEEE Transactions on Engineering Management* 7, no. 2 (1989), pp. 117–25.

[27] CH2M Hill, *Project Delivery System* (Denver, CO: CH2M Hill, 2001), pp. 88–89.

EXHIBIT 2.10
The Team Iceberg

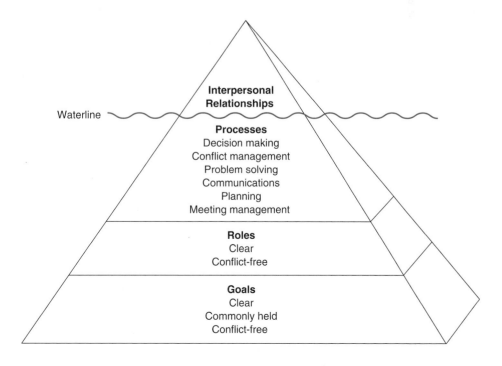

Attribution Theory: Something the Project Manager Must Understand Box 2.4

Attribution theory, a body of work within the field of social psychology, may be best described as the study of blame casting. Researchers have demonstrated, in numerous lab and field studies, a phenomenon known as the **fundamental attributional error.*** In the lexicon of the theory, it says an actor will attribute his or her own poor performance to **external factors** (outside of his or her control) and an observer will attribute the actor's poor performance to factors **internal to the actor** (e.g., motivation, attitude). In a project conflict situation, where two people experience strong disagreement, each party may attribute the conflict to something about the person with the opposing view ("She's such an idiot she just doesn't get it!" "He's just protecting his turf.") The project manager is likely to be subject to this bias as well. This will not only magnify conflict, but also potentially lead the project manager or team member to choose inappropriate corrective actions.[†] We all must keep in mind that the most likely causes of conflict are related to factors below the waterline in the "iceberg" shown in Exhibit 2.10—that is, factors external to the individual. By recognizing these underlying causes, we may guard ourselves against the fundamental attributional error. Conflict resolution strategies should focus first on these structural factors, which are more likely than personalities to be the true causes of a clash.

* Original classic works on this subject include F. Heider, *The Psychology of Interpersonal Relations* (New York: Wiley and Sons, 1958); and E.E. Jones and K.E. Davis, "From Acts to Dispositions: The Attribution Process in Person Perception," in *Advances in Experimental Social Psychology, Vol. 12,* ed. L. Berkowitz (New York: Academic Press, 1965). For an overview of how managers use information to formulate diagnoses in work environments, see K.A. Brown, "Explaining Group Poor Performance: An Attributional Analysis," *Academy of Management Review* 9, no. 1 (1984), pp. 54–63.

† S. Green and T. Mitchell, "Attributional Processes of Leaders in Leader-Member Exchanges," *Organizational Behavior and Human Performance* 23, no. 3 (1979), pp. 429–58; and T.R. Mitchell and R. E. Wood, "Supervisor's Responses to Subordinate Poor Performance: A Test of an Attributional Model," *Organizational Behavior and Human Performance* 25, no. 1 (1980), pp. 123–38.

about project purpose and goals, roles, or processes. When team members do not clearly understand or agree upon the project's purpose and goals, they may battle over what the project is actually about.

Finally, teams that have not clearly determined how they will work together—for example, how decisions will be made, who will make them, how meetings will be managed—often find themselves embroiled in contentious debate ("You have to accept this solution. We all voted for it!" or "Who put you in charge of making that choice for all of us?"). The project manager needs to be alert to conflict and sensitive to what underlying factors might be at work.

A vast body of research on **attribution theory** (see Box 2.4) may be extrapolated to project management; it suggests that project managers make the error of looking above the waterline at the tip of the iceberg shown in Exhibit 2.10, instead of below the waterline at organizational factors more likely to cause conflicts.

Conflict-Management Styles

Although the project manager may avert conflict by attending to the structures and processes below the waterline in Exhibit 2.10, some conflict will be inevitable, and the project manager must be ready for it. There are several possible approaches for

EXHIBIT 2.11
Conflict Resolution Styles

Conflict Resolution Style	When This Style Makes Sense in a Project Environment
Compromising	
Involves using a give-and-take approach to resolving conflicts. In this mode, the project manager might bargain and search for middle-of-the-road solutions that bring some degree of satisfaction to all parties in the dispute.	Use when the middle position between two conflicting parties is viable and would allow the project to proceed. The Biblical story of King Solomon offering to cut a baby in half is an example of a situation in which compromise would *not* be viable.
Smoothing	
Involves deemphasizing or avoiding areas of difference in divergent positions and emphasizing areas of agreement.	Use when tempers are running too high for the parties to be able to address the issue rationally. Smoothing might be the first step in a longer resolution process.
Forcing	
Is a command-and-control approach in which the project manager exerts his or her viewpoint, siding with one of the parties or insisting on a different solution.	Use when the issue is of paramount importance, you feel certain that you are right, and you believe the parties will follow your orders. It also works if their support is not necessary for the solution to be implemented. (If you are a parent, you may have used this one with your children!)
Withdrawing	
Is avoiding an actual or potential disagreement by ignoring the problem.	Use when the issue is not important, tempers are too high to allow for a reasonable discussion now, you believe the conflict may blow over if left alone, or you believe that talking about this issue now may actually harm instead of help the situation. It also works if you believe the two parties can work it out most effectively on their own.
Problem Solving	
Involves facing the conflict head-on using an approach that allows affected parties to work through their disagreements. Several of the tips we offered earlier in this chapter for negotiation (e.g., focus on issues rather than positions) will be useful for problem solving.	Use when the issue is a significant one for the project, it is important for the parties to commit to the resolution outcome, different perspectives are likely to lead to a higher-quality solution, the process of working through the conflict will enhance the team's understanding or performance, and the need to resolve the issue outweighs any potential difficulties the process of resolution might cause.

responding to a team conflict.[28] These include compromising, smoothing, forcing, withdrawing, and problem solving. Exhibit 2.11 describes the approaches and identifies the circumstances under which each one would be most appropriate.

[28] These approaches to resolving conflict were first proposed by R. Blake and J. Mouton, *The Managerial Grid* (Houston, TX: Gulf Publishing Co., 1964). See also R. Blake, H. Shepard, and J. Mouton, *Managing Intergroup Conflict in Industry* (Houston, TX: Gulf Publishing Co., 1964).

Sometimes It Really Is about the Person

What about situations in which interpersonal conflict has more to do with personalities and self-interests than with substantive issues of team process and task? Although we have warned against the fundamental attributional error and emphasized the importance of looking below the waterline on the team iceberg, sometimes the conflict really does have to do with individual personalities. At other times, the iceberg may hold the answer, but the project manager needs a way to defuse interpersonal issues until the underlying causal factors can be addressed. For example, what should the project manager do about the team member who dominates every team meeting, is unfailingly negative, can't stay on task, is always bringing up tangential points, and distracts his or her neighbor in animated side conversations?

First, remember that dealing with disruptive behavior is a group responsibility. So when Mary Jean whines that the surveys the team has agreed to conduct are a waste of time, ask the rest of the team to respond to Mary Jean. One member may wisely point out, "One of our ground rules was 'we look for ways for ideas to be right, not wrong.' Can you see any advantages with surveys, Mary Jean?" Second, the project manager might find it helpful to put himself or herself in the disrupter's shoes and consider what factors might be motivating the behavior. Does this individual have some unmet need (e.g., for attention or for respect) that lies behind his or her actions? To determine if this is the case, set up a private meeting with this individual to learn about his or her underlying concerns or needs. Finally, keep in mind, that if the project manager and team do not address disruptive behavior early in the project, it may become an unchangeable part of the group landscape.

Motivating the Team

One of the biggest challenges for the project manager is to psychologically engage team members in a project throughout its complete life. In this book, we offer numerous ideas for team-based planning methods that improve project plans while creating a sense of ownership that enhances motivation. Beyond these tools, the project manager should be familiar with several fundamental principles of team motivation. The best way to begin this discussion is to consider what motivates you, our readers, in project team environments.

We have asked more than 500 managers and team members about their most motivating project experiences. The following statements represent the recurring themes that have emerged from these discussions:

"I liked working on that project because it presented a new challenge for me."

"I felt energized when I worked with that team."

"The CEO had given the project a lot of attention and I felt honored to be part of it."

"I liked the amount of positive recognition I received for being part of this project."

"It was rewarding to be part of an effort that would result in a positive change for the company."

"The goal was clear and we felt confident in our ability to achieve it."

"I felt a sense of ownership in the project because the project leader listened to my ideas."

The theme of these statements centers on what are known as **intrinsic motivators:** factors having to do with the task itself that drive individuals and teams to participate and perform. Examples of intrinsic motivators include opportunities for learning, an appealing challenge, or opportunities to work with people we enjoy as colleagues. Of course, there generally will be someone who is motivated by the prospect of the bonus pay, but this is the exception rather than the rule. Motivators such as bonus pay, salary increases, or promotions are considered to be **extrinsic motivators** because they come from sources beyond the task or the individual.

Many project managers operate under the erroneous assumption that they need access to bonus money if they want to motivate team members. In most cases, intrinsic motivators will have more power than extrinsic motivators. The exception would be when base salary levels are so low that a bonus would allow an individual to rise out of an uncomfortable financial situation or to achieve a new and desired income status.[29]

Some of the work from the field of motivation theory can help us to understand why the relative importance of intrinsic and extrinsic motivators may vary from one person to the next. Herzberg identified what he called a **hygiene factor.**[30]

Hygiene was perhaps a poor word choice, as it had nothing to do with cleanliness, but it referred to fundamental attributes of the work environment and the individual's personal situation that must be present before intrinsic kinds of motivators could begin to be effective. In addition to a basic level of pay, other examples of hygiene factors include job security, fairness of company policies, and the physical work environment. We can see similar factors in Maslow's hierarchy, which depicts human needs as a pyramid where requirements for basic physiological well-being and safety represent the bottom of the hierarchy and must be satisfied before people will be motivated by higher-level factors such as social needs, self-esteem, and self-actualization.[31]

Although the theories of Herzberg and Maslow have come under fire in recent decades,[32] most organizational psychologists would agree that intrinsic motivators generally are effective only when living and working conditions are adequate to meet basic needs, and when there are few conditions present that block or disable people from performing to the best of their abilities. Thus, before considering what intrinsic motivators might be most important to employ in a particular situation, the project manager should ask the following questions:

1. Do individual team members have personal circumstances that provide for basic needs such as food, shelter, safety, or health?
2. Are there obstacles or situational constraints in the work environment that block individuals from working to the best of their ability?
3. Do individuals feel the workplace offers enough psychological safety such that they are not afraid to offer ideas, suggestions, or feedback?
4. Do team members feel they are treated fairly?
5. Do people possess the necessary skills and confidence for performing the assigned project work?

With respect to the last item in the above list, research in organizational behavior has shown that individuals with a type of task-specific confidence known as **self-efficacy** tend to apply more effort and persistence to a task.[33] Some of this confidence comes

[29] These circumstances do exist in some developing economies. However, China's example indicates this is changing rapidly. Financial incentives were at one time necessary for project work in China, but intrinsic motivators are becoming increasingly important.

[30] F. Herzberg, *The Motivation to Work* (New York: Wiley and Sons, 1959).

[31] A.H. Maslow, "A Theory of Human Motivation," *Psychological Review* 50 (1943), pp. 370–96.

[32] T.R. Mitchell, and D. Daniels, "Motivation," in *Comprehensive Handbook of Psychology Volume 12: Industrial and Organizational Psychology,* ed. W. Borman, D. Ilgen, and R.J. Klimoski (New York: Wiley and Sons, 2004).

[33] M.E. Gist, "Self-Efficacy: Implications for Organizational Behavior and Human Resource Management," *Academy of Management Review* 12, no. 3 (1987), pp. 472–85; and A. Bandura, *Self-Efficacy: The Exercise of Control* (New York: Freeman Publishing Co., 1997).

from experience with the task. Similarly, as members of a team work together, they can develop what is known as **team efficacy,** or a sense of confidence in their ability to perform the work collaboratively.[34] **High-efficacy teams** tend to be more satisfied with their work and more committed to the organization, and they typically set more difficult goals for themselves.[35] The project manager can enhance project-specific individual and team efficacy by making sure people have the training they need, finding ways to give them small bites of experience that build confidence, and offering encouragement by saying, "I know you can do it," "I have confidence in your ability," or "This is almost like the last project you did, and you did well on that." An important role of the project manager is to find ways to enhance and support team function and confidence.

Once the project manager has made the necessary corrections and feels confident that team members' basic needs are met, he or she may move to the next level, considering what motivates each individual and finding ways to tailor the environment and work assignments accordingly. As Nicholson observes, a team member who is underperforming is not a problem to be solved but a person to be understood.[36] In general, intrinsic motivators are more powerful than extrinsic motivators. Beyond that, some individuals may be motivated by recognition, others by the satisfaction of working toward and achieving a goal, and yet others by the enjoyment of working in a positive and fun team environment.

Although motivational forces may vary from individual to individual, there is one nearly universal truth: Clear, specific, challenging goals are the best of the intrinsic motivators available to managers. Moreover, we know that individuals are more likely to achieve their goals if situational constraints have been removed and if they feel confident in their ability to complete the work.

But what about money as a motivator? Based on academic research[37] and our own observations of management practice, we offer caveats about the use of monetary rewards in project settings. First, the amount of money available has to be sufficiently large so that individual payouts do not appear as an insult. For example, when Cisco Systems completed an ERP (enterprise resource planning) project in 1995,[38] the project manager was given $200,000 to distribute among 100 team members and possibly 100 other IT people who unexpectedly had to work full time on the project. This represented an average of $1,000 to $2,000 per person, depending on who was included. These were individuals who all probably had reasonably large salaries to begin with, and $1,000 for nearly a year's worth of hard work and very long hours may not have looked like much money. Also, a manager may distribute bonuses in a way that rewards top performers. Imagine what happens when people learn that others, whom they may perceive to be lesser performers, received more money than they did. This sense of unfairness could poison the organizational climate and put a stigma on the project manager that might create difficulties in new projects. So, the use of extrinsic motivators such as monetary rewards can lead to problems, particularly if the work is of a creative nature and difficult to measure.

[34] Mitchell and Daniels, "Motivation."

[35] Mitchell and Daniels, "Motivation."; G. Latham and E. Locke. "Work Motivation and Satisfaction: Light at the End of the Tunnel," *Psychological Science* 1, no. 4 (1990), pp. 240–246.

[36] N. Nicholson, "How to Motivate Your Problem People," *Harvard Business Review* 81, no. 11 (2006), pp. 56–65.

[37] T. Amabile, "How to Kill Creativity," *Harvard Business Review* 76, no. 8 (1998), pp. 78–87.

[38] See R.D. Austin, R.L. Nolan, and M. J. Cotteleer, *Cisco Systems, Inc: Implementing ERP,* Harvard Business School Case #9-699-022 (Boston: Harvard Business School Press, 2006).

To effectively motivate a team, the project manager needs to understand the following:

- Once people's basic needs are met, intrinsic motivators will be more effective than extrinsic motivators.
- Everyone has motivational potential, but the motivational forces will vary from one person to the next. The project manager should learn enough about individual team members to develop the best approach for each one. This involves getting to know the person, but also may include a direct approach: "What can I do to ensure that you get the most out of this project?"
- As noted above, of the intrinsic motivators available to the project manager, clear, specific, challenging goals are generally the most powerful.
- People will be more motivated if they feel a sense of ownership in the project.

The last point, addressing ownership in the project, is a central theme of this book.

Chapter Summary and Onward	One cannot effectively manage a project simply by learning a few terms or tools. The best project managers are visionary leaders *and* detail-oriented managers, technically savvy *and* interpersonally and politically astute, and disciplined *and* flexible. They are skilled communicators and are good at exercising influence and negotiating. They know how to plan and lead productive group sessions, and they manage conflict in ways that help raise and resolve important issues. They have a solid understanding of the factors that may motivate team members and are adept at creating project environments where team members want and are able to contribute their best. In subsequent chapters we will return to these skills and capabilities, illustrating how you put them to work throughout the life of the project.

Team Activities	1. With a group of three to four classmates, and using this chapter's content as a guide, create a job description for the position of project manager for an organization of your choosing. Your description should cover the minimum qualifications including education and experience, describe the attributes of a successful candidate, provide a job summary that identifies primary responsibilities and key functions of the project manager, and provide expected performance measures.
	2. Meet with a team of four to six classmates. Spend five minutes working individually to consider and respond to the following questions:
	a. What was the most motivating project experience you have ever had? (Note that this could be a personal, family, community, religious group, volunteer, or work-related project. Just think of the one that motivated and energized you the most.)
	b. What factors caused you to feel motivated? Make a list of at least six factors you can recall.
	After everyone has had a chance to work alone for at least five minutes, convene the team and share your experiences. Select a facilitator to take notes. As each person offers his or her list of motivating factors, keep a tally of how often

each one is mentioned. Discuss your shared observations about the themes that emerged. Summarize your findings by:

a. Compiling a complete list of motivating factors, along with the frequency with which each one was mentioned.

b. Writing a paragraph summarizing your observations about the themes that emerged and how you can use this information in your roles as project managers.

3. Gather a team of three to five classmates. Rent the 2008 movie *Outsourced* that tells the story of an American online retail executive who is sent to India, against his wishes, to set up a call center for receiving customer orders. Watch the film as a team, and prepare to discuss the following questions:

a. To what extent did Todd demonstrate or fail to demonstrate balance in the core capabilities of project managers identified in this chapter (vision/detail, technical/ interpersonal, disciplined/flexible)? What examples support your position?

b. Watch the first presentation Todd delivers to his new staff in India. Which of the tips for meeting management and presentations did he seem to ignore? What are your recommendations regarding how he could have improved this first presentation?

c. What factors motivated the staff members at the call center? How did Todd use his newfound knowledge of motivators to make a difference? How might the motivators have differed in another cultural or economic environment?

d. Which of the principles of persuasion and influence presented in this chapter were apparent in the behavior of characters in the film? Offer specific examples.

e. Beyond your observations about the questions listed above, what would you have done differently, or the same, if you had been the manager of the project to set up this call center in India?

At the end of your discussion, prepare a written summary with a one- or two-paragraph answer to each of the questions above. Include examples and demonstrate critical thinking.

4. Gather a team of three to five classmates. You will be attempting to sell an idea to your teammates, applying ideas from the section of this chapter on persuasion and influence. Your instructions are as follows:

a. Work silently for 5 to 10 minutes. Each person is to think of an idea he or she has for a project that would be of interest to other members of the group. The best choices might be projects that relate to issues on the campus where you are attending class. Examples might include a perceived need for better campus lighting during evening hours or a project idea to reduce campus energy consumption. During this silent period, make notes about what you will say to your team to influence members to adopt your idea. Consider how you will say it.

b. Gather your team and select a facilitator. The facilitator's role will be to keep time and ensure the process runs effectively.

c. Each person will be allowed five minutes, no more, to present his or her idea to the team. There will be no time allowed for questions and answers, so the presentation must be complete. The facilitator should keep track of time, but will also be a presenter.

d. At the end of the presentation phase, team members offer constructive feedback (begin with positives!) to each presenter, in the same sequence as the presentations were given.

e. After the feedback period, vote on the relative attractiveness of each proposal. A fun way to do this is with poker chips. Each participant begins with 10 chips, all of which he or she must distribute to other team members according to how much of an investment seems to be appropriate. You may give all of your chips to one team member if that is where you believe the money should go. You may not give the same number of chips to any two or more individuals unless that number is zero.

f. At the end of the voting or chip distribution process, count to see who received the most support for his or her project. Discuss what caused this project to be the most popular and write a report summarizing your observations. Within your report, identify the presentation guidelines and persuasion factors discussed in this chapter that you witnessed in the best presentations, as well as other factors. Consider the project itself as well as the way it was presented.

Discussion Questions and Exercises

1. Recall your experience in projects of all types. Who was the best project leader you have encountered so far in your career? To what extent did this individual effectively balance the roles we have described in this chapter? Did the individual have exemplary persuasion skills? Of the persuasion principles presented in this chapter, which ones did he or she apply most effectively? How did this project manager deal with conflict?

2. Recall accounts you have read about famous leaders in history. (You can seek information from the Internet or another reference.) Possibilities include Winston Churchill, George Washington, Joan of Arc, Martin Luther King, Catherine the Great, Peter the Great, or Chairman Mao. What projects did these people lead? (Yes, they all led projects!) What attributes and skills did they bring to their project management roles? For example, did they apply some principles of persuasion? What do you know about their communication styles?

3. Based on your experience in project teams (they might be work-related or teams in which you have participated as a student), recall a project manager you consider to have been highly ineffective.

   a. List the things this person did that seem to have contributed to his or her ineffectiveness.

   b. Compare notes with a classmate and write a paragraph summarizing your conclusions about common themes.

4. We have put forth the idea that effective project managers do not have to be charismatic. Do you believe this? Can you think of effective project managers with whom you have worked who are quiet, introverted types? What did they do to be effective?

5. Go to the Web site for the Keirsey Temperament sorter (www.advisorteam.com/temperament_sorter/register.asp?partid=1) and answer the questions in the short inventory provided. What is your type? Which parts of your personal orientation will be helpful to you in managing projects?

6. Go to www.queendom.com/tests/access_page/index.htm?idRegTest=703 and complete the listening self-test. What aspects of listening represent areas of opportunity for you personally? How might improving this aspect of your listening skills aid you as a project manager?

7. Revisit the dialogue between Jacqueline and Nathan in the chapter section on negotiation and influence. Rewrite the dialogue to improve Jacqueline's chances of obtaining the resources she needs for the StarPanel project. What could Jacqueline have done before the negotiation to help achieve a better outcome?

8. In Chapter 1, we introduced Jack Zhang, a high-ranking manager at a major pharmaceutical company who served as a project manager for new-product development efforts. He had studied books on project management and had learned to use Microsoft Project. Based on his knowledge, Jack created a complete project plan, including a computer-generated schedule, in preparation for his first team meeting. He began the meeting by presenting the plan, anticipating that team members would greatly appreciate his front-end efforts. Instead, he felt that team members were disengaged, and they did not seem interested in the tasks he had assigned them. Jack has come to you for advice on what to do differently. Please do the following:

   a. Develop a list of 5 recommendations for Jack, linking each to a concept or idea offered in this chapter.

   b. Describe for Jack the likely sources of conflict that may arise if he ignores your recommendations and, instead, continues with his current approach.

9. Dale, a materials/purchasing lead, and Michael, a manufacturing section manager, have worked together for a couple of years. You know from experience that they do not get along. The three of you are part of a six-member task force charged with analyzing and recommending improvements in your organization's vender selection process. In the middle of a two-hour meeting, Dale and Michael begin arguing over which aspects of the existing process need to be maintained. Their conversation quickly evolves into a heated exchange over the level of support that Dale's area provides to Michael's.

   Consider the five styles of conflict resolution described in this chapter. Select two of these and describe the potential advantages and disadvantages associated with applying each one in this situation. What additional information might be helpful to you?

10. One of your team members has just sent you the following e-mail message:

   "The next time I end up on a project team, I hope to have a leader able to successfully negotiate for needed resources. There is absolutely NO WAY John and I are going to be able to complete our section of the product manual without the graphics support from the CAD group. We both know that our heads will be on the chopping block for the delay, but it isn't our fault, it's yours! After all, you are the project manager!"

   Using the tips for developing a communication strategy described in Exhibit 2.3, plan a response to this e-mail. Be sure to specify the objective of your communication, the audience, the channel you would choose, and the content you would hope to convey. Explain each of your choices.

11. Read C. Thompson's article, "The Third Annual Year in Ideas: PowerPoint Makes You Dumb," from *New York Times Magazine,* December 2003, p. 88. Based on your experience, write a paragraph in which you either agree or disagree with the author's arguments.

12. Read G.A. Fowler's article, "For Asia-Based Staff, the Typical Workday Lasts about 24 Hours," *The Wall Street Journal,* August 22, 2006, p. B1. Imagine you are based in Dubai and that you have just been assigned responsibility to manage a project that will have team members in London, San Francisco, Shanghai, and Melbourne. Given observations presented in the article, advice on technology-enabled meetings

presented in this chapter, and your own personal insights, prepare a list of at least 10 guidelines you will keep in mind as you prepare to lead virtual team meetings. Briefly explain your rationale for each guideline you present.

13. Read K. Maher's article "The Jungle: The Inability to Run Effective Meetings Can Torpedo a Career," *The Wall Street Journal,* January 13, 2004, p. B6. Think about a meeting you recently attended and assess it using the criteria given in the article and the meeting tips presented in this chapter. In what ways did the meeting employ or violate the criteria and tips given in these two sources? What would you have done differently in planning and running the meeting?

References

Amabile, T. "How to Kill Creativity." *Harvard Business Review* 76, no. 8 (1998), pp. 78–87.

Applegate, L.; R. Austin; and F.W. McFarlan. *Corporate Information Strategy and Management.* 6th ed. New York: McGraw-Hill/Irwin, 2002.

Austin, R., and L. Devin. *Artful Making: What Managers Need to Know about How Artists Work.* Upper Saddle River, NJ: Financial Times Prentice Hall, 2003.

Austin, R., and R. Luecke. *Managing Projects Large and Small.* Boston: Harvard Business School Publishing Corp., 2004.

Bandura, A. *Self-Efficacy: The Exercise of Control.* New York: Freeman Publishing Co., 1997.

Blake, R., and J. Mouton. *The Managerial Grid.* Houston, TX: Gulf Publishing Co., 1964.

Blake, R.; H. Shepard; and J. Mouton. *Managing Intergroup Conflict in Industry.* Houston, TX: Gulf Publishing Co., 1964.

Brown, K.A. "Explaining Group Poor Performance: An Attributional Analysis." *Academy of Management Review* 9, no. 1 (1984), pp. 54–63.

Brown, K.A.; T.D. Klastorin; and J.L. Valluzzi. "Project Performance and the Liability of Group Harmony." *IEEE Transactions on Engineering Management* 7, no. 2 (1989), pp. 117–25.

Brown, K.A., and N.L. Hyer. "Whole Brain Thinking for Project Management." *Business Horizons* 45, no. 3 (2002), pp. 47–57.

CH2M Hill. *Project Delivery System.* Denver: CH2M Hill, 2001.

Cialdini, R. *Influence: The Psychology of Persuasion.* New York: Quill-William Morrow, 1993.

Cialdini, R. *Influence: Science and Practice.* New York: Allyn & Bacon, 2000.

Cialdini, R. "Harnessing the Science of Persuasion." *Harvard Business Review* 79, no. 9 (2001), pp. 72–79.

Cialdini, R. "The Science of Persuasion." *Scientific American* 14, no. 1 (2004), pp. 70–77.

Cioffi, D., and R. Garner. "On Doing the Decision: Effects of Active versus Passive Choice on Commitment and Self-Perception." *Personality and Social Psychology Bulletin* 22, no. 2 (1996), p. 33.

Connolly, T.; L. Jessup; and J. Valacich. "Effects of Anonymity and Evaluative Tone on Idea Generation in Computer-Mediated Groups." *Management Science* 36, no. 6 (1990), pp. 689–703.

De Bono, E. *Six Thinking Hats.* London: Clays Limited, 1985.

Dibble, J., and B. Langford. *Communication Skills & Strategies: Guidelines for Managers at Work.* Cincinnati: South-Western Publishing Co., 1994.

Federico, M., and R. Beaty. *Rath and Strong's Six Sigma Team Pocket Guide.* New York: McGraw-Hill, 2003.

Fisher, R.; W. Ury; and B. Patton. *Getting to Yes: Negotiating Agreement Without Giving In.* New York: Penguin Books, 1993.

Fowler, G.A. "For Asia-Based Staff, the Typical Workday Lasts about 24 Hours." *The Wall Street Journal,* August 22, 2006, p. B1.

Gist, M.E. "Self-Efficacy: Implications for Organizational Behavior and Human Resource Management." *Academy of Management Review* 12, no. 3 (1987), pp. 472–85.

Green, S., and T. Mitchell. "Attributional Processes of Leaders in Leader-Member Exchanges." *Organizational Behavior and Human Performance* 23, no. 3 (1979), pp. 429–58.

Grohowski, R.; C. McGodd; D. Vogel; W. Martz; and J. Nunamaker. "Implementation of Electronic Meeting Systems at IBM." *MIS Quarterly* 14, no. 4 (1990), pp. 369–83.

Harvey, J. "The Abilene Paradox: The Management of Agreement." *Organizational Dynamics* 3, no.1 (1974), pp. 63–80.

Heider, F. *The Psychology of Interpersonal Relations.* New York: Wiley and Sons, 1958.

Hersey, P.; K. Blanchard; and W. Natemeyer. "Situational Leadership and Power." *Group and Organizational Studies* 4, no. 4 (1979), pp. 418–28.

Herzberg, F. *The Motivation to Work.* New York: Wiley and Sons, 1959.

Hines, T. "Left Brain/Right Brain Mythology and Implications for Management and Training." *Academy of Management Review* 12, no. 4 (1987), pp. 600–06.

Hyer, N., and U. Wemmerlöv. *Reorganizing the Factory: Competing Through Cellular Manufacturing.* Portland, OR: Productivity, 2002.

Janis, I. "Groupthink." *Psychology Today* 5, no. 6 (1971), pp. 43–44 and 74–76.

Jones, E.E., and K.E. Davis. "From Acts to Dispositions: The Attribution Process in Person Perception." In *Advances in Experimental Social Psychology, Vol. 12,* ed. L. Berkowitz. New York: Academic Press, 1965.

Latham, G., and E. Locke. "Goal Setting—A Motivational Technique that Works." *Organization Dynamics* 8, no. 2 (1979), pp. 68–80.

Latham, G., and E. Locke. "Work Motivation and Satisfaction: Light at the End of the Tunnel." *Psychological Science* 1, no. 4 (1990), pp. 240–246.

Lehman, C., and D. DuFrene. *Business Communication.* Mason, OH: South-Western Publishing Co., 2005.

Leonard, D., and S. Strauss. "Putting Your Company's Whole Brain to Work." *Harvard Business Review* 75, no. 4 (1997), pp. 110–21.

Maher, K. "The Jungle: The Inability to Run Effective Meetings Can Torpedo a Career." *The Wall Street Journal,* January 13, 2004, p. B6.

Maslow, A.H. "A Theory of Human Motivation." *Psychological Review* 50 (1943), pp. 370–96.

Mitchell, T. R., and D. Daniels. "Motivation." In *Comprehensive Handbook of Psychology, Vol. 12: Industrial and Organizational Psychology,* eds. W. Borman, D. Ilgen, and R.J. Klimoski. New York: Wiley and Sons, 2004.

Mitchell, T. R., and R.E. Wood. "Supervisor's Responses to Subordinate Poor Performance: A Test of an Attributional Model." *Organizational Behavior and Human Performance* 25, no. 1 (1980), pp. 123–38.

Nicholson, N. "How to Motivate Your Problem People." *Harvard Business Review* 81, no. 11 (2006), pp. 56–65.

Niederman, F.; C. Beise; and P. Beranek. "Issues and Concerns about Computer-Supported Meetings: The Facilitator's Perspective." *MIS Quarterly* 20, no. 1 (1996), pp. 22–40.

Nunamaker, J.; R. Briggs; D. Mittleman; D. Vogel; and P. Balthazard. "Lessons from a Dozen Years of Group Support Systems Research: A Discussion of Lab and Field Findings." *Journal of Management Information Systems* 13, no. 3 (1997), pp. 163–207.

PAR Group. "The Secrets to Listening Well," 2005, **www.thepargroup.com/ article_SecretsListenWell.html** (accessed July, 2009).

Pinto, J., and O. Kharbanda. "Lessons for an Accidental Profession." *Business Horizons* 38, no. 2 (1995), pp. 41–50.

Salancik, G., and J. Pfeffer. "Who Gets Power—and How They Hold on to It," *Organizational Dynamics* 5, no. 3 (1977), pp. 3–21.

Shelley, M.K. "Gain/Loss Asymmetry in Risky Intertemporal Choice." *Organizational Behavior & Human Decision Processes* 59, no. 1 (1994), pp. 124–60.

Shilling, D. "Be an Effective Listener!" **www.womensmedia.com/ seminar-listening.html**, accessed March 1, 2006.

Simons, T. "Why Managers Should Care about Fairness: The Effects of Aggregate Justice Perceptions on Organizational Outcomes." *Journal of Applied Psychology* 88, no. 3 (2003), pp. 432–43.

Springer, S., and G. Deutsch. *Left Brain, Right Brain: Perspectives from Cognitive Science.* 5th ed. New York: Freeman-Worth, 1998.

Thompson, C. "The Third Annual Year in Ideas: PowerPoint Makes You Dumb." *New York Times Magazine,* December 2003, p. 88.

Tullar, W.; P. Kaiser; and P. Balthazard. "Group Work and Electronic Meeting Systems: From Boardroom to Classroom." *Business Communication Quarterly* 61, no. 4 (1998), pp. 53–65.

Yukl, G. *Leadership in Organizations.* 5th ed. Upper Saddle River, NJ: Prentice Hall, 2000.

Chapter Three

Project Selection: Doing the Right Thing

"NASA spent millions of dollars developing a pen that could write in zero-gravity conditions. In contrast, spending not a single ruble, the Soviets provided their cosmonauts with pencils that functioned very effectively in zero gravity."

Mykola Komarevskyy

Chapter Learning Objectives

When you have mastered the material in this chapter, you should be able to:

- Use the project selection funnel as a strategic tool.
- Establish project goals built on underlying problems, opportunities, and mandates.
- Generate and evaluate options for achieving project goals using financial analysis, as well as team-based methods such as advantages–disadvantages, factor rating, force-field analysis, SWOT analysis, and Pareto Priority Index.
- Create a formal or informal business case for a project.
- Build real-options concepts into a multistage project plan.
- Apply a team-based approach to assess a project portfolio.

Managing projects effectively involves *doing things right*. But, before people or organizations embark on projects, they must be sure they are *doing the right things*. This means doing not just any project, but the project that best serves the strategic needs of the organization. Consider the January 2007 fiasco created when Turner Broadcasting System's Cartoon Network used a guerrilla marketing scheme to clandestinely install electronic promotional devices on buildings, roadways, subway structures, and bridges around Boston's commercial, educational, government, and tourist centers. Project execution was flawless, but people seeing the wires protruding from the battery-powered devices feared a bomb plot. This led police and fire departments in the area to temporarily shut down several parts of Boston's transportation system as they worked to discover the nature and purpose of the devices.[1] Turner certainly had good intentions, but the fallout from the project cost the company millions of dollars in restitution and public relations damage control.[2]

The guerrilla marketing scheme might have been a project Turner Broadcasting should have left on the drawing board. Perhaps with more front-end analysis, using tools recommended in this chapter, company officials would have seen the folly of the idea and conceived a better option for grabbing consumer attention. The story is not unique; many organizations make errors in project selection. Although a good selection process cannot guarantee a successful project, it can increase the likelihood bad projects will be rejected before they begin.

This chapter introduces concepts and tools for **project selection** and **project portfolio management.** We begin with an overview of the process, introducing the concept of the **project funnel** and offering an example of how a project typically works its way through an organization's vetting system. We emphasize the importance of clearly specifying the underlying rationale for a project and introduce the process for building a business case in a team environment. In the later parts of the chapter, we examine the entire **portfolio of projects** within an organization, and present ideas for assessing them systematically in team environments.

THE PROJECT SELECTION PROCESS

An organization cannot adopt every proposed project. Doing so likely would overwhelm the resources of the enterprise. An effective project selection process may be viewed as a funnel (see Exhibit 3.1). The funnel's wide mouth represents the entry of all potential projects, which can be driven by problems, opportunities, or mandates from inside or outside the organization. These drivers can exist in real time, or they might represent future conditions for which the organization is preparing. For example, organizations initiate many IT projects to keep systems running with as few flaws as possible. These are intended to prevent *future* problems.

---

[1] One could also examine the law-enforcement response as a project with a questionable approach. Why didn't they first test one device, or contact Turner, before shutting down major parts of the city?

[2] For more information on this topic, see M. Levenson and R. Mishra, "Turner Broadcasting Accepts Blame, Promises Restitution." *The Boston Globe,* February 2, 2007. Or search www.boston.com for related stories.

EXHIBIT 3.1
The Project Selection Funnel

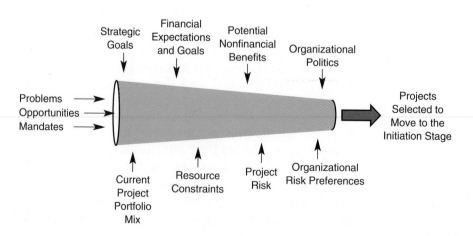

At Orem Corp., a manufacturer of heavy equipment, the vice president of operations has proposed outsourcing a set of key product components. She initially proposed the concept to her operations staff to get input on the idea's general appeal. The group's response was mixed, but members agreed the idea warranted further consideration. Two staff members volunteered to conduct a preliminary cost–benefit analysis. With these initial estimates in hand, the vice president of operations shared the project idea with the VPs of marketing, engineering, human resources, and finance. They asked her to clarify the need for the project. Was there a problem with current practice? An opportunity to open new markets? What was the goal? She offered rough initial estimates of cash outlays necessary, demonstrating she had considered several options for achieving desired outcomes. After conducting further research with the help of her team, she was able to return to the VPs with clearer and more compelling answers to their questions. They agreed to allow the idea to move into the funnel.

The VP of operations next took her idea to the company president. He challenged her to explain how the project would support the company's mission. Because outsourcing to low-wage countries was part of Orem's strategic plan, the fit was good. However, the president observed that Orem was currently engaged in several new-product launch efforts, a plant consolidation, a major acquisition, and a systemwide IT implementation. He questioned whether the organization could take on another substantial project.

After the discussion, the project moved past the initial screening and proceeded further into the selection funnel. Decision makers now wanted more information about costs and benefits, both financial (e.g., how much money will we save if we do this?) and nonfinancial (e.g., do we anticipate greater market share or better public goodwill from this project?). At that point, the VP of operations asked a team of four people to prepare a more detailed analysis in the form of a business case.

The business case team considered costs and benefits as well as the project's inherent risks. For example, certain parts planned for outsourcing were viewed as a core technical competency, and some key decision makers were concerned about potential loss of intellectual property.

As part of the business case development process, the VP group participated in a force-field analysis exercise (covered later in the chapter) that brought out driving and restraining forces. At the end of the process, the group made recommendations that slightly adjusted the project to fit the circumstances envisioned.

Ultimately, the project made it through the business case process. Observers noted that at least some of the reason it endured was because of the passion and persuasive capacity of the VP of operations. She strongly believed in the project and made it a topic of discussion in many of her formal and informal communications within the company.

The project moved into the initiation phase with a dedicated team working full time to develop a detailed project plan and execute it. However, project work came to a halt when union members in Orem's manufacturing plants went on strike to protest the impending job losses, resulting in production delays and negative media exposure for Orem. Following negotiation with the union, Orem scaled back the project such that about 50 percent of the designated parts were outsourced and the remainder stayed in Orem's U.S. plants.

The funnel narrows as projects are screened based on a number of criteria and influences, examples of which are shown above and below the funnel in Exhibit 3.1. Box 3.1 describes how a project might move through the funnel. It demonstrates that project selection involves a combination of idea generation from interested parties, data gathering, informal challenges from high-level stakeholders, formal analysis of costs, consideration of benefits and risks, portfolio and resource consid-erations, persuasion on the part of project champions, approval from sponsors, and, very often, unexpected derailment from stakeholders who were not involved in the decision process. This story does not necessarily prescribe how things *should* be done, but offers an example of how the project selection process often unfolds with a com-bination of formal and informal inputs. The best approaches offer opportunities for team members and other stakeholders to provide creative input and express concerns at critical points in the process.

THE BUSINESS CASE

Organizations with formal processes for project selection often require the develop-ment of a **business case.** This is a document that presents the justification for the project and recommends whether or not it should proceed to the initiation stage. The business case components presented in Exhibit 3.2 and described more fully below incorporate ideas from several sources[3] as well as our experience working with organi-zations in a variety of industries. Individuals and organizations can use these elements formally or informally.

The business case, when completed, goes before a decision-making body. For large projects, this could include senior-level leaders, company directors, or a strategic-planning council. Such a group conducts comparative evaluations of business cases for multiple projects. For smaller projects, decision authority rests within a department or work group. Those making the final decision should recognize the advocacy-related biases that underlie the recommendations in a business case and, consequently, should demonstrate diligence in their review. This is no place for rubber-stamp approval.[4]

---

[3] For examples, see C.H. Kepner and B.B. Tregoe, *The New Rational Manager* (Princeton, NJ: Princeton Research Press, 1984); and J.W. Brannock, *Business Case Analysis* (Plant City, FL: STS Publications, 2004).

[4] B. Frisch, "When Teams Can't Decide," *Harvard Business Review* 86, no. 11 (2008), pp. 121–26.

EXHIBIT 3.2   **Components of the Business Case (BC)**

Component	Description	Comments
Executive summary	This is a short summary of the main points of the BC. Although this segment appears at the beginning of the report, the BC team should write it after all of the other sections have been completed.	Most high-level decision makers will not want to read more than one or two pages, so it must be concise.
Project driver(s): underlying problems, opportunities, or mandates	This segment of the BC should answer the question, "What circumstances alerted us to the need for this project?" Or, if the proposed project is more future-oriented, it might answer the question, "What do we believe about future conditions that leads us to think we need to do something now?"	Imagine someone in an organization has proposed implementing an enterprise IT system in a retail company with 50 stores, at an estimated cost of $1 million. Spon-sors will want to know why the project champion thinks the expenditure is justi-fied. If the current system frequently breaks down and paralyzes company operations in ways that create annual costs in excess of $2 million, this offers validation that some-thing needs to change.

(*continued*)

EXHIBIT 3.2   (*Continued*)

Component	Description	Comments
Underlying causes	The BC should include as much information as possible about the reasons why the underlying problem or opportunity exists. The project initiation phase will allow time and resources for additional causal analysis, but decision makers should have some idea of the causes before adopting a project.	Without an understanding of problem causes, the organization might embark upon a course of action that does nothing to solve the core problem. For example, if the company's IT system is crashing because of power surges and interruptions, spending $1 million to implement a new system will not address the root cause.
Goal	The goal statement should answer the question, "What would we like to achieve?" It should be measurable and must go beyond work completion and budget targets to address desired outcomes.	The company with the IT downtime problem might set a goal of zero system downtime, 99.9% uptime, or some other metric directly linked to the underlying problem driving the project.
Options for achieving the goal	The options segment should present possible ways the organization could achieve the stated goal.	Many teams and organizations get stuck on one approach, without creatively thinking through other options. In the example where IT downtime has been caused by power outages and surges, solutions could include a power-stabilizing battery system, outsourcing IT functions, moving IT functions to a remote company site with stable power, or installing a generator.
Assessment of options for achieving the goal	Options are compared using one or more assessment methods. The team should recognize that in many situations, one valid option is to hold the status quo and do nothing.	Examples of methods for comparing options include: • Financial analysis of the options, including measures such as **payback period, net present value,** and **internal rate of return.** • A simple list of the **advantages and disadvantages** of each option. • A multiple-criteria, team-based approach such as **factor rating.** • Group decision tools such as **force-field analysis** and **SWOT.** • **Pareto Priority Index (PPI)** analysis. • A multiple-stage **decision tree** built on **real options** concepts.
Conclusion	This segment summarizes the findings from the assessment of options and includes a recommendation.	Conclusions should draw on all of the BC segments above and offer clear logic about how various factors were weighed in the final recommendation.

In the paragraphs below, we present information about tools and processes for formulating and evaluating a business case in a team setting. For large or important projects, a business case team and higher-level decision makers will use these formally and in detail. For less significant projects, an informal approach following similar logic will be appropriate. In Appendix 3A at the end of this chapter we offer an example of a business case for a volunteer-based community service project.

PROJECT DRIVERS: PROBLEMS AND OPPORTUNITIES

Every project charter, formal or informal, should begin with an answer to the question "Why?" The answer tells decision makers about current or potential problems and opportunities, as well as mandates driving the project. Box 3.2 describes examples of problem-, opportunity-, and mandate-driven projects at Schering-Plough, a multinational pharmaceutical company.

Problem Statements

A problem is a gap between actual conditions and desired conditions. The clearest and purest problem statements drill down to the point where the deviation can be described in terms of its critical effect on the organization or key stakeholders. A problem statement should include four dimensions: identity (What is it?), location (Where is it?), timing (When did it start; how often does it happen?), and magnitude (How big is the gap between actual and desired outcomes?). Exhibit 3.3 summarizes these questions and offers examples drawn from Emerald Sports, a London-based distributor of high-end sporting goods that is experiencing problems with late product deliveries to some customers.

The example in Exhibit 3.3 identifies specific attributes of the problem and can assist a team in homing in on a project proposal geared to the situation. The problem is focused on eastern Europe, where it began somewhat abruptly in January of this year. Furthermore, it is presenting serious consequences for Emerald's business.

Opportunity Statements

In contrast to a problem, an **opportunity** exists when there is a gap between current conditions and some desired future state. Everything could be fine just the way it is, but an organization might believe it could improve its performance or profitability if it seeks out a new opportunity. In this case, the four components of a problem statement can be recast, as shown in Exhibit 3.4. We use an example from Desert View

EXHIBIT 3.3
Problem Statement Components and Examples

Problem Statement Component	The Questions	Example for Emerald Sports
Identity	What is the problem?	Late deliveries to customers
Location	Where do we see it? (*Where* can refer to a product category, a market segment, a location, a machine, a person, etc.)	For all products sold in eastern Europe but not in western Europe
Timing	When does it occur or when did it begin?	Late deliveries began in January of this year and have occurred consistently since that time.
Magnitude	How big is this problem in measurable terms? What are the potential consequences for our organization?	On average, it takes two additional days to ship to customers in eastern Europe than to ship to customers in western Europe. Customers are complaining and some have dropped Emerald as a vendor because of the late deliveries.

Project Drivers at Schering-Plough Box 3.2

Fred Hassan, who took the reins of Schering-Plough Corp. in 2003, was hired for his reputation as a turnaround specialist. To quote *The Wall Street Journal:* "Schering-Plough was a mess when its board recruited Mr. Hassan from Pharmacia Corporation in April 2003." In the ensuing years, Hassan's methodical turnaround strategy involved a mix of projects with problem, opportunity, and mandated origins.

Problem-driven projects: In response to declining revenues associated with patent-expired drugs (a problem), Hassan chartered projects to uncover and cut unnecessary costs as a way of maintaining profitability in the short term. This was especially important during a period in which Schering-Plough was working hard to fill a somewhat limited development pipeline.

Opportunity-driven projects: Schering-Plough had several new products in development in 2006; these offered the company the potential to exploit new market opportunities. Examples of midstage drugs in development included compounds designed to treat Parkinson's disease, asthma, arterial thrombosis, and HIV. In addition to working on new products, Schering-Plough also was engaged in a major promotional project to increase public awareness of significant improvements in its already-popular nasal spray, Nasonex. The blitz resulted in substantially increased sales.

Mandate-driven projects: Because of some manufacturing problems identified by the FDA, Schering-Plough was forced to revamp its factories. Additionally, the company was required to change its processes for dealing with Medicare after it pled guilty to fraud charges. There was no choice in either of these matters, and both led to the initiation of projects.

Sources: J. Carryou, "Turning around a Drug Maker Takes Time," *The Wall Street Journal*, August 2, 2006, p. B1; and www.schering-plough.com.

EXHIBIT 3.4
Opportunity Statement Components and Examples

Opportunity Statement Component	The Questions	Example for Desert View Hospital
Identity	What is the opportunity?	Anticipated increase in the market for medical services for geriatric patients.
Location	Where do we envision it? (*Where* can refer to a product category, a market segment, a location, a machine, a person, etc.)	Located in Phoenix, Arizona, where there has been considerable growth in the over-65 population.
Timing	Are there any time constraints for this opportunity? Will it diminish in value if we do not act on it by a certain time?	There will be a first-mover advantage to having the facility operational within two years, when a large wave of baby boomers reaches the age of 65.
Magnitude	How big is the potential opportunity?	Census estimates indicate there will be over 8 million people living in Arizona in two years, which represents a projected 30% increase over a 10-year period. Analysts at the hospital estimate that the over-65 population in Arizona will grow to 30% of the total.

Hospital (a pseudonym), located in Phoenix, Arizona. The hospital's board members are weighing the possibility of finding ways to accommodate anticipated increases in demand for geriatric care.

CAUSES OF PROBLEMS AND OPPORTUNITIES

Once a business case team has a clear understanding of a potential project's driving problem, opportunity, or mandate, its members should consider the causes that underlie it. Even for mandated projects, such an exercise is useful because it can help team members understand the origins of the mandate.

Causal Configurations

Causes can take on many configurations. Some causes operate as a **constellation of interacting forces.** Financial recovery projects that grew out of the worldwide economic crisis that began in 2008 were based on the recognition of multiple causes, all interacting.[5] Causes included irresponsible lending, overextended credit, demand-supply imbalance in real estate, inflated oil prices, war expenditures, erratic investor behaviors, global monetary exchanges, and a variety of social factors. Each one affected others, magnifying the effects that any one had on its own. Governments and global alliance groups had to design projects aimed at recovering stability with all of these factors in mind. Correcting one while ignoring the others would be unlikely to solve the problems.

Some causes stand alone or predominate all others. For example, severe seismic events were the central and predominating cause of the 2008 earthquakes that hit China's Sichuan province, killing over 65,000 people.[6] Although observers implicated shoddy construction and poor evacuation practices in at least some of the deaths, the earthquake itself was the central factor.

Another causal pattern occurs when two or more causes feed on each other in a **reciprocal cause-effect** relationship. In the terminology of **system dynamics,** these are known as **positive feedback loops** because they represent situations where a system has no self-correcting mechanisms.[7] Consider the example shown in Exhibit 3.5. It depicts a potentially unending cycle of relationships that can emerge when demand for a company's products and that company's stock price interact based on perceptions of investors and customers.

A project team should consider the implications of the cause-effect loop shown in Exhibit 3.5 when devising a recovery plan. A good team approach would be to display the figure on a whiteboard and have team members discuss it before they move forward. In this case, a market initiative to increase demand by lowering prices might communicate that the company is in trouble, thus throwing gasoline on the fire rather than extinguishing it.

---

[5] Millions of pages have been written on this subject. One example of an article that summarizes some of the key causal factors as part of a discussion about the complexity of the solution is M. Mandel, "How to Get Growth Back on Track," *BusinessWeek,* October 27, 2008, pp. 34–38.

[6] Accounts of the number of people dead or missing vary from one source to another. For an article describing the quake, see C. McCleod, "Massive Quake Tests China on Reaction to Major Crisis," *USA Today,* May 13, 2008, p. 1A.

[7] J.D. Sterman, *Business Dynamics* (New York: McGraw-Hill, 2000).

EXHIBIT 3.5
**Reciprocal
Cause-Effect
Relationship
Example**

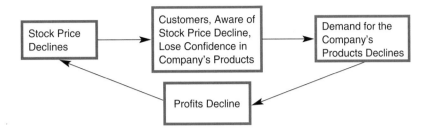

As a team investigates problem causes, it is important for members to avoid confusing correlation with cause—just because two events occur simultaneously does not mean they are related. For example, some in an organization might surmise that if business declines immediately following the installation of a new IT system, then the IT system is at fault. The timing could be coincidental. A more thorough analysis might demonstrate that the true cause was the surprise entry of a new competitor. A misdiagnosis surely would lead to an inappropriate project.

Team-Based Tools for Causal Analysis

Three useful tools for brainstorming possible problem causes[8] are **fishbone diagrams, affinity exercises,** and **influence diagrams.**

Fishbone Diagrams

A fishbone diagram is also known as an **Ishikawa diagram** or **cause-and-effect diagram.** To develop a fishbone diagram, a team mounts a large sheet of paper (about three feet or one meter square) on a conference room wall and places a problem statement in a box on the right side (left is OK, too, but the right side seems to be the convention). The team begins by identifying a few general categories of potential causes and writes these with a marker above or below the major ribs of the fish skeleton. Next, the team brainstorms specific examples of *possible* problem causes in each category. Of course, investigation will be required to verify which of these possible causes are the *actual* causes of the problem, but an inclusive orientation at this stage increases the likelihood the team will consider all possibilities.

The fishbone diagram in Exhibit 3.6 explores possible causes of Emerald Sports' late-delivery problem (see Exhibit 3.3 for the original description). The team developing the fishbone should include people who are close to the problem (e.g., truck drivers or customers in this example) as well as other stakeholders (e.g., IT staff members, salespeople).

The **fishbone diagram** in Exhibit 3.6 reveals several possibilities, but it is likely that one or a few are the primary culprits.[9] Imagine how different the project would be if the team determines *internal processes* versus the *transportation company* are the predominant problem source. For this reason, the team must gather more data and ask the right questions to assess which causes contribute most to the problem.

---

[8] See P.K. Scholtes, *The Team Handbook* (Madison, WI: Joiner Associates, Inc., 1993), which observes, "Cause-and-effect diagrams are most effective after the process has been described and the problem well defined."

[9] Ideas for this fishbone diagram were drawn from conversations with Professor Joseph Cavinato, Thunderbird School of Global Management, and I. Lewis, J. Semeijn, D.B. Vellenga, "Issues and Initiatives Surrounding Rail-Freight Transportation in Europe," *Transportation Journal* 41, no. 2/3 (2002), pp. 22–31.

EXHIBIT 3.6
Fishbone Diagram
for Emerald Sports
Late-Delivery
Problem

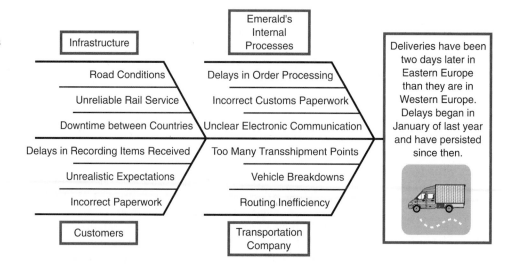

Infrastructure

Road Conditions
Unreliable Rail Service
Downtime between Countries
Delays in Recording Items Received
Unrealistic Expectations
Incorrect Paperwork

Customers

Emerald's Internal Processes

Delays in Order Processing
Incorrect Customs Paperwork
Unclear Electronic Communication
Too Many Transshipment Points
Vehicle Breakdowns
Routing Inefficiency

Transportation Company

Deliveries have been two days later in Eastern Europe than they are in Western Europe. Delays began in January of last year and have persisted since then.

Causes or reasons for *opportunities* could be assessed with a fishbone diagram as well. In the case of the Desert View Hospital geriatric facility introduced in Exhibit 3.4, the team might identify major skeletal elements in the diagram such as changing patient demographics, advances in available technologies, U.S. population migration, increased incidence of specific age-related maladies, and so on. The experience would offer them a conceptual framework for brainstorming, solidify their understanding of the reasons the opportunity has emerged, and guide decisions about how best to exploit it.

Affinity Exercises

In an **affinity exercise,** team members and other key stakeholders collaborate to brainstorm causes of a problem or drivers of an opportunity in a four-step process. First, the group discusses the problem or opportunity statement to ensure that everyone understands it. Second, individuals work silently for five minutes or so to imagine possible causes. They write each idea on a separate sticky note. Third, participants place the notes on a whiteboard in random order. Fourth, the team organizes the notes into categories by rearranging the sticky notes so similar or related items are physically clustered together. The end result will be similar to that created with a fishbone diagram, but the silent phase at the beginning of the process may generate more ideas.

Influence Diagrams

If the problem driving the project involves a constellation of interacting causes, the team can create an **influence diagram (ID).** By drawing an ID on a whiteboard or other vertical writing surface, a team can develop a sense of how causal factors interact. Exhibit 3.5, shown previously, offers an example of an ID that a team might create and discuss.

THE PROJECT GOAL

The next step in business case development is to create a specific and measurable project goal. The Emerald Sports business case team might envision a goal of reducing the delivery time in eastern Europe by two days. The team might also add "within a budget of 1 million euros, on or before June of next year." During the project initiation stage, described in Chapter 4, the team revisits and refines the goal statement.

OPTIONS FOR ACHIEVING THE GOAL

The team's choice of an option for achieving a project goal must be built on a solid understanding of project drivers. For example, what if Emerald Sports decided to find a new transportation carrier, even though the most important cause of the late deliveries in eastern Europe was its own failure to complete customs forms correctly? The team would find itself on a path to failure. Even when causes are well understood, there can be multiple ways to solve a problem or seize an opportunity.[10]

Continuing with the late delivery story, assume Emerald's business case team has determined that the predominant cause of the problem is related to the excessive number of transshipment points. Apparently, the transportation provider is moving materials from truck to truck as it seeks the lowest-cost carrier in each country or region. With this information, and verifying documentation, the team can move forward to brainstorm all the possible ways to solve the problem and achieve the goal of reduced delivery time. To do this, the team might use what is known as a **mind map.**[11] The process involves placing a large sheet of paper (about 3 feet by 6 feet, or 1 meter by 2 meters) on the wall horizontally. A facilitator writes the "Possible Options for . . ." in the center of the paper. The team brainstorms about various ways to solve the problem or seize the opportunity, and the facilitator writes these ideas and accompanying images around the central node. Exhibit 3.7 shows an example of a mind map of possible project options for Emerald Sports' delivery problem. Some of these options could stand alone, and others could be implemented in combination.

[10] Frisch, "When Teams Can't Decide."

[11] Mind-mapping concepts are covered in more detail in Chapter 5 within the segment on work breakdown structures, but they have many applications in project management. For an introduction, also see K.A. Brown and N.L. Hyer, "Whole-Brain Thinking for Project Managers," *Business Horizons* 45, no. 3 (2002), pp. 47–57.

EXHIBIT 3.7
Mind Map of Possible Approaches for Solving the Late-Delivery Problem at Emerald Sports

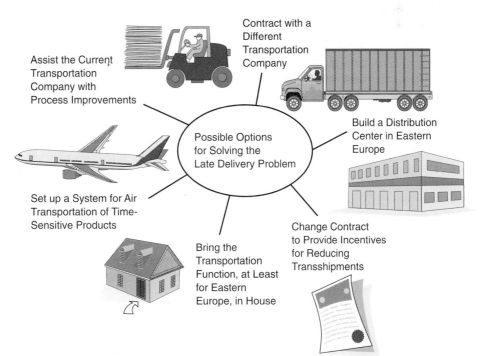

EVALUATING OPTIONS

Decision makers can use a variety of tools to compare options within a project or to compare the merits of projects with different goals as part of a broader examination of an entire portfolio of projects. Exhibit 3.8 summarizes the methods we discuss below, including recommendations about when or where each one would be appropriate.

EXHIBIT 3.8   Methods for Assessing Projects and Project Options

Project Assessment Method	Description	When This Approach Would Be Appropriate
Financial analysis	Projects or project options are compared based on metrics such as payback period, net present value, and internal rate of return. Potential financial returns should be weighed against preliminary risk assessments for each project.	• Appropriate when there is enough reliable information about project costs and financial benefits to justify the analysis. • Useful when the project involves a large budget and financial outcomes are important to the selection decision. • Should not stand alone as the only vetting mechanism, given that there are nearly always other, nonfinancial criteria to be considered.
List advantages and disadvantages	The team brainstorms advantages and disadvantages, listing them in two separate columns. At the end of the process, the team makes a subjective assessment of which projects or approaches offer the most significant advantages and fewest disadvantages.	• Appropriate as a stand-alone approach when the project is small and does not lend itself to financial or other complex analyses. • Useful as a precursor to more objective methods, as a way to get ideas out on the table and screen out infeasible options.
Factor rating	A team or an organizational policy predetermines a set of criteria for evaluating projects, which may incorporate expected financial performance. Each criterion is weighted according to its relative importance. Participants rate competing projects, or project options, and a total score for each one is calculated based on the weighted aggregate.	• Appropriate when selection criteria are necessarily broader than financial outcomes alone. • Helpful when team members do not initially have consensus on selection criteria. • Appropriate when team input and buy-in are important to the success of the project or option selected. • Adds a quantifiable element, which could appeal to some team members.
Force-field analysis	Solicits team members' ideas about forces that would drive the project or project option into reality, and opposing or restraining forces that might make implementation difficult. Forces are scored on a scale of 1–5.	• Recommended when social or cultural forces are pushing for or against a project. • Offers a vehicle to allow dissenting stakeholders to voice their views and feel as if someone is listening. • Provides a scoring aspect for those who want a quantifiable outcome.

(continued)

EXHIBIT 3.8   (*Continued*)

Project Assessment Method	Description	When This Approach Would Be Appropriate
Strengths, Weaknesses, Opportunities, Threats (SWOT) Analysis	Team members brainstorm strengths, weaknesses, opportunities, and threats associated with the project or project option.	• Especially useful when projects or project options are subject to negative and positive forces both inside the organization (strengths and weaknesses) and outside the organization (opportunities and threats). • Can work well when potential projects are being evaluated during a strategic planning session.
Pareto Priority Index (PPI)	An individual or team gathers information about a project or project option's cost and projected cost savings. A team of qualified people uses consensus or voting to assess the probability of the project's success. Using a formula prescribed in the tradition of Six Sigma, each project is rated for its PPI.	• Appropriate for projects where cost savings are anticipated project outcomes (IT and process improvement projects are examples). • Works well when input from key stakeholders plays a role in organizational commitment. • Quantitative aspect offers a sense of objectivity.
Real options and decision trees	Helps a team to see project selection as a multiple-phase process. Initial selection can involve a commitment to take the project only through a feasibility stage. A second decision about multiple options will be made once feasibility information is available. The process can continue through several subsequent phases.	• Useful when the project environment is dynamic. • Useful when the first phase of the project will determine the direction of later project phases. • Appropriate when seed money is available for the first phase of the project, but subsequent funding depends on the results of an initial phase.

Financial Analysis

Financial analysis is the centerpiece of many business case analyses and is an appropriate evaluation mechanism for projects that generate revenues or result in cost savings. In making financial assessments, a team must consider the timing and magnitude of net cash outflows directly attributable to the project as well as net cash inflows or cost savings specifically derived as project benefits. A project manager or team can assess these changes in a project's financial position with tools such as **payback period, net present value,** and **internal rate of return.**[12] These tools are generally covered in detail in finance courses; we describe them briefly here to ensure that we have addressed the full range of tools available. In keeping with the theme of this book, we focus on team-based tools for selection. But financial analysis often serves as an important input to team discussion.

---

[12] Other financial assessment tools are available. Refer to a finance or accounting source for a more in-depth treatment of financial analysis for project selection decisions. One source focused strictly on this topic is D.W. Young, "Note on Capital Budgeting," available from the Crimson Press Curriculum Center (www.thecrimsongroup.net). For broader coverage, see R.N. Anthony and D.W. Young, *Management Control in Nonprofit Organizations,* 7th ed. (New York: McGraw-Hill, 2003), chap. 9.

Payback Period

Payback period answers the question, "How long will it take us to get our money back?" It is typically applied in programs where benefits are projected to accrue incrementally over time after the project is complete. Mathematically, payback period is calculated as follows:

$$\frac{Estimated\ project\ cost}{Future\ annual\ benefits\ associated\ with\ project\ outcomes}$$

In this formula, the annual benefits term in the denominator must incorporate the cost savings or revenue the project is forecast to produce, minus the routine operating costs that will accrue in supporting the project outcome. Consider a proposed project to implement a new IT system to manage accounts payable. Analysts predict the $50,000 project will result in cost savings of $20,000 per year, but it will cost $5,000 per year to run the system. The payback period would be $50,000/($20,000 − $5,000) = 3.33 years. If the accounts payable IT system has a useful life greater than 3.33 years it might be worth the investment.

Payback period offers a quick way to assess a project's financial contribution, but it does not consider the time value of money. Below, we describe two methods based on discounted cash-flow concepts that address this limitation.

Net Present Value

Net present value (NPV) is based on the principle that an amount of money in hand today is worth more than the same amount available in the future. NPV is the difference between what we believe we will spend on a project and the present value associated with future cash inflows, or cost savings that will result exclusively from the project. NPV is built around a **required rate of return** (also known as a **discount rate**), which is a percent value reflecting a hurdle potential projects must surpass. The net present value for a proposed project is computed as follows:

$$NPV = \text{Present value of net cash inflows} - \text{Net investment amount}$$

Which is equivalent to:

$$NPV = (\text{Net cash inflows} \times \text{Present value factor}) - \text{Net investment amount}$$

If NPV is greater than zero, the investment is considered worthwhile from a financial standpoint. When an organization is considering several projects, those with higher NPVs receive priority.

Net cash inflows can occur at a single point in time, such as when a company contracted to perform work for another organization receives a single payment at the end of the project. Or, the net cash inflows can occur over several years. To account for multiple years of return, decision makers must agree on the **useful life** of a project outcome (e.g., number of years of market life for a new product), then estimate annual net inflows. Exhibit 3.1B in Appendix 3B shows the present value factor (PVF) associated with a project outcome having a single payout, and Exhibit 3.2B displays values for a several-year payback.

We again consider the accounts payable IT system mentioned in the payback period example above to illustrate how NPV works. The company has specified a required rate of return of 10 percent as the hurdle for all new IT projects. Elements of the assessment would be as follows:

1. Net project investment (I) = $50,000.
2. Economic life of the accounts payable system = 6 years.
3. Required rate of return = 10 percent.

4. Net annual cash flow from new system (CF) = $20,000 − $5,000 = $15,000.

5. Present value factor from Exhibit 3.2B = 4.354. To find this:

   a. Locate the row corresponding to 6 years in the future.

   b. Locate the column corresponding to the required rate of return of 10 percent.

   c. Find the cell of intersection and note that it contains the figure 4.354.

6. NPV = (CF × PVF) − I = ($15,000 × 4.354) − $50,000 = $15,310.

In this example, NPV is positive, indicating that the project should at least receive further consideration. However, competing projects or project options might offer better returns. A useful way to involve a team in assessing various NPV scenarios is to display an NPV table on the wall in a conference room during a selection discussion. The team considering the accounts payable system project could engage in some scenario analysis by asking what the result would be under different assumptions about useful life, project costs, net returns, or required rate of return.

Many organizations have specified a required rate of return on project investments as a way of accounting for the time value of money. Some organizations use a specified discount rate for all projects, but others apply different threshold rates based on the degree of project risk and other factors.[13]

One limitation to the NPV approach is that it does not overtly incorporate risk. More sophisticated financial tools, not addressed here, incorporate risk adjustments. Later in this section on evaluation, we present team-based assessment tools that incorporate a risk component.

Internal Rate of Return

Internal rate of return (IRR) is based on the same discounted cash-flow concepts as NPV, but IRR is the unknown variable (i. e., the discount rate) for which we must solve. Instead of producing a monetary value, it tells us the discount rate at which NPV would be zero. If the value of IRR is above the organization's required discount rate, the project will produce a positive NPV and it will be feasible to accept it. If the value of IRR is below the organization's required discount rate, the project should be rejected. For example, if the organization has a policy that all projects must achieve a return rate of 15 percent, and the IRR is 25 percent, decision makers would view the project favorably, assuming it satisfies other criteria.

Caveats about Financial Analysis

Financial analysis offers an objective approach to project evaluation. However, it can be corrupted by the biases or errors of those who decide on the parameter estimates. Also, a positive financial assessment offers no ironclad guarantee of success. Further, organizations select projects for reasons that extend beyond financial considerations. The team-based tools described below can build on financial analysis or stand alone in cases where financial analysis is not possible or necessary. Involving the team in the decision process can bring valuable insights to the surface, affirm team member contributions, and increase the likelihood key decision makers will support selected options or projects.

Listing Advantages and Disadvantages

A list of advantages and disadvantages offers the simplest approach to project evaluation. Imagine the business case team at Emerald Sports is considering the possibility of building a new distribution center in eastern Europe to reduce the number of transshipment transactions. Team members have decided they would like to begin the

---

[13] Anthony and Young, *Management Control in Nonprofit Organizations.*

EXHIBIT 3.9

Examples of Advantages and Disadvantages Associated with Building a New Distribution Center (DC) in Eastern Europe

Advantages	Disadvantages
• Capacity to stock regionally popular products close to the market.	• Added overhead cost to operate a second DC.
• Shortened delivery lead times.	• Large capital expenditure.
• Could potentially reduce customer complaints and defections.	• Items in the new eastern European DC could double Emerald's inventory investment.
• Offers Emerald a stronger presence in the region.	• Does not ensure Emerald will have the right items at the eastern European DC.
• Could serve as a transshipment point for growing business in Asia.	• Could necessitate investment in IT system upgrades or replacement.
• By moving products to the DC in large truckloads, Emerald can reduce shipping costs.	• Increases management complexity.
	• Does not necessarily ensure a reduction in the number of transshipment points.

assessment process by brainstorming advantages and disadvantages. A facilitator can gather information from the team in a **round robin** or **nominal group**[14] approach, in which participants first work silently, then each offers one idea at a time as the facilitator calls on each person in turn. Alternatively, people can brainstorm individually on sticky notes and arrange them by theme into two columns. The result of either approach might look something like the partial list in Exhibit 3.9.

The business case team would continue this process by brainstorming advantages and disadvantages for other project options. For many projects, this step can offer sufficient information for the team to make a selection decision or to reject certain options from the pool before moving to a deeper analysis.

Factor Rating

Factor rating offers a way for a team to compare projects (or options within a project) on multiple dimensions, which are weighted to reflect their relative importance.[15] Decision makers may use factor rating after they have reviewed financial figures. Or they may use factor rating in the absence of objective financial figures if none are available. The team-based process is as follows:

1. A team brainstorms possible selection criteria, either through discussion or through an affinity exercise with sticky notes. At this stage, no judgments are made about inclusion or exclusion. Team members discuss the meanings of any criteria that are unclear, and similar criteria are consolidated.

2. Based on consensus or voting, the team reduces the number of criteria to a manageable number. (We recommend four to six to keep the process manageable and to encourage the team to agree on some priorities rather than making a laundry list.)[16]

---

[14] For information on the nominal-group technique, see A.L. Delbecq and A.H. VandeVen, "A Group Process Model for Problem Identification and Program Planning," *Journal of Applied Behavioral Science* 7, no. 4 (1971), pp. 466–92; and A.L. Delbecq, A.H. VandeVen, and D.H. Gustafson, *Group Techniques for Program Planners* (Glenview, IL: Scott Foresman and Co., 1975).

[15] This concept is known in decision-theory circles as a weighted multiattribute utility model, which has been demonstrated to increase the quality and group acceptance of decisions. See R. Hogarth, *Judgement and Choice* (Chichester, England: John Wiley & Sons, 1980); and W. Edwards, "Use of Multiattribute Utility Measurement for Social Decision Making," in *Conflicting Objectives in Decisions,* ed. D.E. Bell, R.L. Keeney, and H. Raiffa (Chichester, England: John Wiley & Sons, 1977), pp. 247–75.

[16] We draw this conclusion from our own experience, as well as from the literature on survey design and psychometrics. Allocating points to a list of criteria is equivalent to rank-ordering them. People can find it cognitively difficult to rank the items in long lists, and the results can be meaningless. See, D.A. Dillman, *Mail and Internet Surveys: The Tailored Design Method,* 2nd ed. (New York: Wiley and Sons, 2000).

3. The team discusses and agrees on the relative importance of the chosen criteria, attaching weights as decimals that sum to 1 when all criteria are considered.

4. Team members, who are prepared with shared knowledge about all of the projects or project options, rate the projects for each selection criterion on a scale of 1–10, where a 10 means the project scores very high on a dimension, and a 1 means the project is weak on a dimension.

5. The team calculates an average score for each criterion, then multiplies it by the decimal value of the assigned weight. For each project, the weighted scores are summed and the projects are ranked according to these scores.[17]

6. As with all methods, the numerical scoring offers a foundation for discussion. Factor rating scores, alone, should not determine the decision.

A team at Emerald Sports applied factor rating to the decision about whether to initiate process improvements with the existing transportation provider or find a new provider. The five-person executive team followed the process described above, agreeing on four criteria and their weights. Information about the financial viability of each option was drawn from an NPV analysis with which all raters were familiar. Each member of the team rated each project option on the four criteria, as shown in Exhibit 3.10.

The factor rating results displayed in Exhibit 3.10 show that Option A meets the set of multiple criteria to a greater extent than Option B. Team members generally appear to agree that assisting an existing supplier supports Emerald's mission and values, that it fits slightly better with resource availability (which might mean special skills or sheer person hours), and that it will be quite a bit easier to implement than Option B. Consequently, this moves the team in the direction of recommending process-improvement activities with the existing supplier. No team is likely to view the results of the factor rating process as the definitive answer to a selection decision. Once it has a result, the team should continue the discussion both to ensure no critical variables have been omitted, and to check assumptions.

One limitation of factor rating is that it does not account for project attributes that could be deal killers because it is a **compensatory model.** That is, it is possible for a project that would be financially devastating to the company to receive high enough scores on other factors to come out ahead. Hammond, Keeney, and Raiffa offer a variation on factor rating that handles options sequentially, eliminating those that do not meet certain minimum criteria so the final set being considered includes the smaller set of more feasible choices.[18]

Force-Field Analysis

Force-field analysis is based on the concept that in any organization there will be forces that can help to move a project forward (e.g., "Everyone is aware of the customer complaints and lost revenue.") and other forces that can serve as obstacles to slow or stop the project from reaching its intended outcomes (e.g., "This represents a new way of doing things, and our employees might resist this project."). Force-field analysis can be especially useful for evaluating projects or project options when the proposed endeavor will involve social, cultural, power, or political change among stakeholders (Lewin, 1943).[19] A facilitator begins the process by reviewing the project goal, then draws a vertical line in the middle of a whiteboard and labels the left side as "driving

---

[17] Some meeting management software packages offer a means of quickly gathering and summarizing this type of analysis. One example is Meetingworks (www.meetingworks.com).

[18] J.S. Hammond, R.L. Keeney, and H. Raiffa, *Smart Choices* (New York: Broadway Books, 1999).

[19] K. Lewin, "Defining the Field at a Given Time," *Psychological Review* 50, no. 3 (1943), pp. 292–310.

EXHIBIT 3.10   **Factor Rating Example**

		Criteria and Weights				
		Supports Company Mission and Values	Anticipated Financial Outcome	Fit with Resource Availability	Ease of Implementation	Weighted Average
	Weights	0.2	0.3	0.25	0.25	
Option A: Assist Current Transportation Provider with Process Improvements	**Rater**					
	Depoorter	8	4	4	6	5.3
	Verkuil	6	3	2	7	4.35
	Da Pont	9	3	7	5	5.7
	Knudson	10	4	4	10	6.7
	Kalvenes	5	4	6	4	4.7
Average		7.6	3.6	4.6	6.4	5.35
Weighted Average		1.52	1.08	1.15	1.6	
			Factor-Rating Score for Option A			**5.35**
Option B: Find a New Transportation Provider	**Rater**					
	Depoorter	2	4	3	3	3.1
	Verkuil	3	5	7	2	4.35
	Da Pont	5	4	2	3	3.45
	Knudson	1	5	4	2	3.2
	Kalvenes	6	5	4	1	3.95
Average		3.4	4.6	4	2.2	
Weighted Average		0.68	1.38	1	0.55	
			Factor-Rating Score for Option B			**3.61**

forces," signifying factors that increase the likelihood the project or option will be successfully implemented. The right side is labeled "restraining forces" and is intended to prompt people to think about factors that could work against the plan.

Imagine Emerald Sports is considering assisting the current transportation provider with process improvement, one of the options shown in the mind map in Exhibit 3.7. This would definitely involve change management, so a force-field analysis would be an appropriate evaluation tool.

Results of the team's force-field brainstorming appear in Exhibit 3.11. The team has attempted to generate lists of about equal lengths, but this is not always possible. Following the brainstorming session, the team votes or reaches consensus about the strengths of these positive and negative forces, rating each one on a scale of +1 to +5 for driving forces and −1 to −5 for restraining forces. The results, in the example displayed in Exhibit 3.11, are scores of +11 and −16, suggesting the negative forces for this option might outweigh the positive forces. This could nix the project, depending

EXHIBIT 3.11
Force-Field Analysis for Assisting Emerald Sports' Current Transportation Provider with Process Improvement

Driving Forces	Restraining Forces
√ Current supplier will be motivated by desire to keep our business. (+3)	√ We might not have enough expertise to truly offer valuable consulting that makes a difference. (−2)
√ Fits with supplier's new lean process initiatives. (+3)	√ Our employees are too busy to take on the extra work. (−5)
√ We have a good relationship and communication flow with this supplier. (+2)	√ Employees working for current transportation provider may resist changes to their long-held practices. (−5)
√ Current practices of transportation provider in western Europe can be easily transferred to eastern European provider. (+3)	√ Might take so long to implement changes that we will lose a significant number of customers before the effects of changes materialize. (−4)

on whether the team views the restraining forces as immovable. But it opens the door for discussion and helps the team consider social forces at an early stage.

SWOT Analysis

SWOT (Strengths, Weaknesses, Opportunities, Threats) analysis has been a popular team-based tool for strategic planning because it stimulates thinking about factors inside and outside the organization that can affect a particular strategy. SWOT analysis has been criticized because it does not appear to increase the effectiveness of strategic plans.[20] However, those studying the issue have concluded that its weaknesses arise when teams attempt to use it in an open-ended manner in the absence of a clear objective.[21]

In a SWOT analysis, a team preparing a business case, or an executive body discussing the results of a completed business case, brainstorms forces that fall into the four quadrants shown in Exhibit 3.12. Like force-field analysis, SWOT involves a team in a structured discussion of positive and negative factors and can lead members to consider how they might redirect the project toward a higher likelihood of succeeding. However, SWOT typically does not incorporate numerical scoring.

[20] T. Hill and R. Westbrook, "SWOT Analysis: It's Time for a Product Recall," *Long Range Planning* 30, no. 1 (1997), pp. 46–52.

[21] J.S. Armstrong, "The Value of Formal Planning for Strategic Decisions," *Strategic Management Journal* 3, no. 3 (1982), pp. 197–211.

EXHIBIT 3.12
Dimensions for Discussion in a SWOT Analysis

	Positive	Negative
Internal Sources	Strengths	Weaknesses
External Sources	Opportunities	Threats

Consider an initiative to implement a new point-of-sale (POS) system in a retail electronics chain with 100 outlets. Team members generate multiple ideas for inclusion in each quadrant. An example of an internal opportunity might be the added capacity for data mining with regard to customers and product sales. An example of an internal threat might be the challenges associated with motivating retail employees to use the new system. An external opportunity might be that the POS system would open doors for better collaboration with suppliers, and an external threat might be that the data in the new system possibly could be accessed by external hackers. Based on a comprehensive SWOT analysis, the team can make a decision as to the relative strengths of the project and whether corrective actions are needed.

Pareto Priority Index (PPI)

Pareto Priority Index is a method for evaluating the merits of several projects that has grown out of the Six Sigma tradition for evaluating the relative merits of several projects competing for resources.[22] It is typically applied when the projects under consideration are aimed at cost reductions and is therefore especially useful for vetting process improvement or IT projects. It begins with a financial analysis that forecasts project costs and estimates cost savings the project will produce. These figures should include some consideration of the time value of money, applying concepts from financial analysis described earlier in this chapter. With these numbers in mind, along with a clear understanding of the project, a selection team works by voting or consensus to estimate the probability of success for each project or option. Input to the probability of success estimates can include force-field analysis or other methods that encourage team thinking about positive and negative factors that will influence the project. The team also should estimate how much time each project will require, which will necessitate some discussion of project tasks and timelines. With this information on hand, the team can use the following formula to calculate PPI for each project:

$$\text{PPI} = \frac{\text{Projected lifetime net cost savings} \times \text{Estimated probability of success}}{\text{Total cost of project} \times \text{Estimated project duration}}$$

An example of a real PPI analysis performed on a California avionics company's process-improvement initiatives is displayed in Exhibit 3.13. In this case, three projects rose to the surface, producing PPI values significantly greater than the others. Consequently, the company chose these three initiatives for immediate implementation and delayed the others. Decision makers also recognized that these three projects, if successfully completed, would have positive implications for the remaining projects deferred to the next year.

The downside to PPI analysis is that if team members have strong, predisposed biases toward some projects and against others they will game the system by over- or under-estimating parameters that go into the formulas.

Real Options

All of the project selection methods we have described so far are based on the assumption of a one-shot decision—the organization either selects the project or it does not. However, in reality, organizations continuously assess and reconsider projects as they progress, using multiple criteria. An organization that recognizes the iterative nature of the selection process might benefit from real-options thinking, applying the concepts either formally or informally. A real option is "the right to acquire some real-world

[22] P. Gupta, *The Six Sigma Performance Handbook* (New York: McGraw-Hill, 2004).

EXHIBIT 3.13   PPI Analysis for Process Improvement Projects at an Avionics Company

Project	Projected Lifetime Net Cost Savings	Estimated Probability of Success	Total Estimated Cost of Project	Estimated Project Duration (Years)	PPI	Status
1. Order-to-cash lead-time reduction	$1,900,000	0.8	$150,000	1.20	8.44	Begin now
2. Repairs project	$1,000,000	0.9	$160,000	0.90	6.25	Begin now
3. Standard switch project	$1,000,000	0.7	$150,000	0.90	5.19	Begin now
4. Inventory reduction project	$ 200,000	0.3	$ 90,000	0.40	1.67	Defer to next year
5. Company-wide barcoding system	$ 200,000	0.4	$100,000	0.50	1.60	Defer to next year
6. Document control enhancement project	$ 500,000	0.3	$190,000	0.50	1.58	Defer to next year
7. Export delay resolution	$ 100,000	0.4	$ 80,000	0.40	1.25	Defer to next year

asset without the obligation to exercise that right."[23] Real options concepts were first developed in the financial sector to assist investors in long-term investment strategies, but they have been applied more recently in IT and product development environments. Although the underlying mathematical concepts are complex,[24] the conceptual framework, handled more subjectively, can be useful to a selection team.

A selection team might break a project into several phases, with a decision point at the end of each phase. In a real options application, a decision-making team would consider multiple options at each designated milestone. This is different from a **Stage-Gate model,**[25] which typically considers only **go–no-go** alternatives at phase milestones. Consider Emerald Sports' decision options to improve the existing transportation provider or find a new one. One approach would be to engage in a **pilot project** to improve the existing supplier, then, at a specified milestone, evaluate how well things are going and consider what to do next. The pilot project could include lower-cost process improvements, but delay installation of technologies such as GPS or integration with Emerald's enterprise resource planning (ERP) system. If things are going well with process improvement, the organization would proceed with the technological aspects of the project. If initial efforts are failing, Emerald's project team might try different methods for process improvement, test technological solutions on a small scale, or abandon the project and reroute in quest of a new supplier. The key is for decision makers to lay out options ahead of time so any change of direction is part of a deliberate, carefully considered plan.

Decision trees, which have applications in many decision environments, lend themselves well to the graphical display of future-oriented, real-options scenario planning. Exhibit 3.14 shows an example of a portion of a stylized version of a decision tree for

---

[23] R.G. Fichman, M. Keil, A. Tiwana, "Beyond Valuation: 'Options Thinking' in IT Project Management," *California Management Review* 47, no. 2 (2005), pp. 74–94.

[24] Those interested in the application of Black-Scholes formulas and other mathematical models supporting real options in project selection decisions can find useful information in T.A. Leuhrman, "Investment Opportunities as Real Options: Getting Started on the Numbers," *Harvard Business Review* 76, no. 4 (1998), pp. 51–67.

[25] For more information on Stage-Gate models, see R.G. Cooper, *Winning at New Products: Accelerating the Process from Idea to Launch,* 3rd ed. (Reading, MA: Perseus Books, 2001).

EXHIBIT 3.14
Decision Tree Adapted for Depicting Real-Options Dynamic Scenario Planning

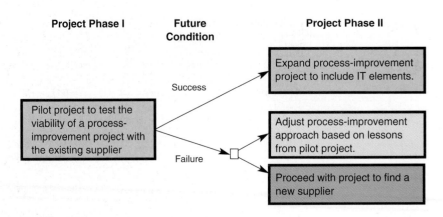

the Emerald Sports transportation project. As shown in the figure, the project team at Emerald will test the lower-cost option first to see if it meets specific performance criteria within a designated time period. Members want to be ready with another improvement approach if process-improvement efforts do not achieve performance goals. They can use the decision tree simply to uncover assumptions and brainstorm future scenarios, or they can apply more sophisticated probabilistic analysis as shown in Appendix B, "Decision Analysis: Using Payoff Matrices, Decision Trees, and Implications Wheels in Project Management," which appears at the end of this book.

Real options concepts are being applied increasingly in product development, even when the term is not explicitly used. For example, the U.S. Food and Drug Administration has begun allowing drug trials to shift midcourse as emerging information suggests that drugs may be effective for ailments other than those initially targeted.[26] Similarly, London-based GlaxoSmithKline is engaged in efforts to be more agile in product development and to shift resources among projects as more information becomes available.[27]

One downside to the real-options approach is that project leaders and teams can find it difficult to abandon or shift the direction of a project in which they have invested their time, energy, and egos. Even if a course of action is failing, it is human nature for those involved to want to continue.[28]

BUSINESS CASE CONCLUSION

At the end of the series of analyses included in the business case, the team should pull together all that it has learned to formulate a recommendation. This recommendation might include several sentences or paragraphs highlighting various aspects of the findings and explaining how the team reached its final conclusion.

[26] A.W. Mathews, "FDA Signals It's Open to Drug Trials that Shift Midcourse, *The Wall Street Journal*, July 10, 2006, p. B1.

[27] J. Whalen, "Bureaucracy Buster? Glaxo Lets Scientists Choose Its New Drugs," *The Wall Street Journal*, March 27, 2006, p. B1.

[28] This phenomenon, which is called "escalation of commitment" in the behavioral literature, has been shown to operate in all settings. As human beings, we cannot seem to let go of things. Escalation of commitment is at the root of many failed projects that are continued beyond the point where they should have been abandoned or rerouted. We will address this topic in more detail in Chapter 9 on project monitoring and control. A useful reference is I. Royer, "Why Bad Projects Are So Hard to Kill," *Harvard Business Review* 81, no. 2 (2003), pp. 48–56.

Eisner's Gong Shows at Disney   Box 3.3

Gong. © Photo Spin/Getty Images.

During his tenure as Disney CEO, Michael Eisner applied somewhat unconventional methods for project selection. For example, he introduced the "gong show," a practice he applied previously at ABC. "It started as a concept where, once a week, we'd invite everybody to come to a conference room, and anyone could offer up an idea or two and, right on the spot, people would react. We loved the idea of big, unruly, disruptive meetings; that's what the gong show was all about. *The Little Mermaid* came out of a gong show, and so did *Pocahontas*. Lots of ideas came out of those meetings, and people had a great time."

Although the gong-show concept might suggest that all decisions were made on a knee-jerk basis, this was not the case. Some associates complained that Eisner was too slow in deciding whether or not to adopt new project ideas. His response to these criticisms was: "Sometimes in our business, the best thing to do is nothing—because it buys you two things. First, it buys you time to incubate an idea, to let it simmer in your brain so you can edit it yourself or improve on it. And the second thing it buys is the ability to see the truth. Because a delay lets you know how deeply someone believes in the idea. If the person really believes, he'll fight for it. He'll create a stink—friction, that is. And if he doesn't believe, he'll back off. And then you can negotiate for what you want—like another version of the idea or another director for the movie."

Thus, with all we have said about the value of a systematic selection process, we must recognize that, in practice, there are other, less formal approaches that can work effectively.

Source: Michael Eisner quotes excerpted and reprinted by permission of *Harvard Business Review.* From S. Wetlaufer, "Common Sense and Conflict: An Interview with Disney's Michael Eisner," *Harvard Business Review* 78, no.1 (2000), pp. 114–24. Copyright © 2000 by Harvard Business Publishing; all rights reserved.

In the case of projects requiring large investments, or those with strategic implications, the recommendation of the team goes before a higher-level body of decision makers who approve and fund the project, reject it, revise it, or send the team back to conduct further analyses. It can be useful for these decision makers to engage in a structured team-based process such as factor rating, force-field analysis, and others mentioned in this chapter so they avoid hasty rejection of good but slightly flawed projects or outright rubber-stamping of bad ones.[29]

Every organization has its own processes for evaluating projects. These are most often built around company history and corporate culture. For example, Box 3.3 describes a unique process designed by Michael Eisner, the former CEO of Walt Disney Co.

PROJECT PORTFOLIOS

Organizations compare potential projects as they work their way through the project funnel, but they do not always consider project portfolio dynamics over time. Consequently, in some organizations, the number of projects seems to grow exponentially, and not all projects continue to be worthy of the resources initially allocated

[29] Frisch, "When Teams Can't Decide."

EXHIBIT 3.15
Project Portfolio Map

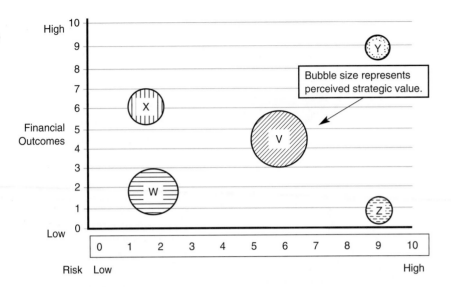

to them. Every one of these projects probably began with good intentions, and from someone's perspective, each one seemed like a really good idea. If the project load exceeds the resources available, what can the organization do? The answer is to drop, delay, combine, or reduce the scope of some projects.

Before making stand-alone decisions about which projects to select or drop, organizational decision makers can map their existing (and future) portfolios as a way of seeing the bigger picture. In developing **portfolio maps,** they should find a conceptual model that is appropriate to the kinds of projects under consideration. One approach recommended by Wheelwright and Clark plots new-product development projects based on degree of product change and degree of process change.[30] Another approach offered by Tjan examines IT projects based on strategic fit and viability.[31] We suggest a more generic, three-dimensional framework that may be applied to a variety of project types, based on anticipated risk, anticipated financial outcomes (e.g., NPV), and strategic value to the firm.[32] Exhibit 3.15 presents an example. Financial outcomes and risk are shown on the vertical and horizontal axes, respectively, and the size of the bubble represents the strategic value of each project. Of course, team members will need to discuss how each project rates on the three dimensions before they are ready to create this sort of schematic. Factor rating offers a useful approach for gathering this sort of information.

To achieve strategic balance, an organization should have a mix of projects in its portfolio. Too many high-risk projects and not enough moderate risk projects could lead to disaster. On the other hand, if the organization sticks with small, simple projects that present no risk and offer limited financial returns, it might miss out on significant market opportunities. Each organization has its own risk-preference profile, which is generally embedded in company strategy and culture.[33]

---

[30] S.C. Wheelwright and K.B. Clark, "Creating Project Plans to Focus Product Development," *Harvard Business Review* 70, no. 2 (1992), pp. 67–83.

[31] A.K. Tjan, "Finally, a Way to Put Your Internet Portfolio in Order," *Harvard Business Review* 76, no. 2 (2001), pp. 76–85.

[32] We thank Professor Bill Youngdahl, Thunderbird School of Global Management, for suggesting this framework.

[33] For examples, see the article about Motorola's CEO Zander titled "Cutting Edge," *The Economist*, October 7, 2006, p. 76; and R. Jana, "Deloitte Study: Emerging Market Innovation," *BusinessWeek Online*, March 15, 2007.

The map in Exhibit 3.15 shows at least two projects for which a team of decision makers might want to raise questions. Project Y offers potentially high returns and high risk, but apparently does not fit well with company strategy. Project Z is even less desirable than Y. Not only is it of low strategic value, it also promises very little financial return, even in the best of what appear to be risky circumstances. This is another one the organization could consider dropping, unless there is a compelling reason to keep it that is not captured in the map.

Creating a Portfolio Map

A decision-making team can create a portfolio map such as the one shown in Exhibit 3.15 by following these steps:

1. Assemble a team of managers who have responsibility for an entire set of projects. (This could be for the entire organization or within a particular group or division; for example, IT, manufacturing, or product development.)
2. List, on a whiteboard, all the projects currently under way or under consideration. (This, in itself, can be very enlightening.)
3. After discussing financial outcomes, risk, and strategic value for each project, use consensus or voting to create a table such as the one shown in Exhibit 3.16. This places all criteria on the same 1–10 rating scale where a 1 represents a low rating (low financial outcome, low risk, low strategic value) and a 10 represents a high rating.
4. On a sticky note, put the name of each project and a numerical rating for the strategic fit of each project. Or use different size notes for different degrees of strategic importance. There will be some arguments among project champions and project detractors or neutrals, but it can be productive to get these discussions out on the table.
5. On a large (about 1 meter by 2 meters) sheet of paper on the wall, draw the horizontal and vertical axes shown in Exhibit 3.15 (financial outcomes versus risk).
6. Work as a team to organize the notes on the map in the appropriate positions. Discussion and clarification of assumptions will emerge naturally.
7. Discuss, as a team, the mix of projects and the budget allocations. Questions to consider include:
   - Do we have appropriate coverage to achieve our strategic goals?
   - What is the relative importance of these projects? Have resources been allocated appropriately?
   - Where, in terms of progress, is each of these projects right now?
   - Do we have the resources to continue with all of these projects?

An executive team can follow the mapping process and discussion by making decisions to abandon some projects and reallocate resources among others. Members can do so by reaching consensus, voting on top priorities, using factor rating, or engaging in some other team-based process.

EXHIBIT 3.16
Sample Portfolio Matrix

	Project V	Project W	Project X	Project Y	Project Z
Expected Financial Outcomes	4.5	2	6	9	1
Risk	6	2	2	9	9
Strategic Value	8	6	4	1	1

One approach Frisch recommends for diverting an executive team from possible decision paralysis or as a way to prevent the leader from becoming dictator by default, is to use poker chips to represent funding allocations and have members distribute them.[34] This involves moving the portfolio map to a tabletop and asking participants to allocate their chips according to where they believe the company should invest. The process can be engaging, and the end result has high visual impact. To prevent biasing people from being influenced when they see the distributions of others, we recommend placing a paper bag next to each project on the map. The bags can be emptied once team members have distributed their chips.

Chapter Summary and Onward

In this chapter, we have emphasized the importance of selecting the right project. All of the project management tools in the world cannot salvage a project if it is not appropriate for the organization to undertake it. Individual project managers seldom have the opportunity to choose the projects the organization adopts. However, they need to understand the logic of the selection process in order to ask the right questions and make adjustments, as needed, in the project's general approach. We have introduced a framework for selecting projects using a business case approach, which first assesses project drivers (why are we doing this?) and their underlying sources. The business case next assesses various options for solving the underlying problem, seizing the opportunity, or responding to the mandate. Tools for assessment introduced here include financial methods, lists of advantages and disadvantages, factor rating, force-field analysis, SWOT analysis, and PPI. Project selection should not be a one-time decision; early phases often produce information the team can use to decide on courses of action for later phases. Real-options concepts offer useful frameworks for looking at projects along a dynamic timeline.

Individual projects are not islands unto themselves and should be viewed as part of a larger portfolio. Upper-level managers will benefit from having a mechanism whereby they periodically assess portfolio maps and make decisions about project continuation, modification, and resource allocation.

Once a project has made it through the selection process, it is ready to move to the initiation stage. Information the business case team has uncovered and recorded will provide important input to the initiation process, where preliminary concepts about the approach to take and project goals will be further developed. As we emphasize throughout this book, all project phases are iterative.

Team Activities

1. Gather a team of three to five classmates and watch the video, "Building Hong Kong's Airport," which is part of the Discovery Channel's *Extreme Engineering* series. You may acquire this by renting the DVD, purchasing it from a service such as iTunes, or downloading it from another Internet source. As you watch the video, consider the following questions and write a report summarizing your conclusions about each one:

   a. What were the project drivers in terms of problems and opportunities? Go beyond what is stated in the video to consider what the unstated drivers might have been. Include at least five drivers in your report and offer an explanation for each one.

[34] Frisch, "When Teams Can't Decide."

b. Given the goal of increasing capacity for passengers and cargo in the Hong Kong area, what options were available? Identify at least five mutually exclusive possibilities.

c. Conduct a SWOT analysis for the chosen course of action (i.e., the project as it was envisioned and executed). Include in your report a figure summarizing your SWOT analysis.

2. Request a 45-minute interview with an experienced project manager in a local organization. The organization should be large enough to have multiple projects, but can be in the public or private sector. Your team assignment is to learn about the organization's project selection process and write a two-page summary. In structuring your interview, consider asking some or all of the following questions, along with others you and your team have discussed as possibilities:

a. What process do you use for selecting projects in your organization? Is it formal or informal?

b. Are all projects required to go through your process? Is the selection process standardized across the entire organization, or do practices vary across departments and locations?

c. Do you have any project selection templates you would be willing to share?

d. What criteria do you use in comparing projects that are being considered for adoption?

e. When you apply financial analysis in project selection, what are the specific methods you use? If you specify a required rate of return, what is it?

f. What do you like most and least about your current selection process and what aspects would you change if you could?

3. Work with two or three classmates to discuss your personal project portfolios. Items on your list might include finishing your degree, finding a job, remodeling your house, finding a school for your child, getting married, or taking a vacation. Each person should prepare a portfolio matrix such as the one presented in Exhibit 3.16. Place your personal projects on the matrix and discuss them with your teammates. As a team, write a paragraph critiquing (remember to begin with the positives!) the personal project portfolio of each person. Then prepare an additional paragraph summarizing the group's general observations about project portfolio maps.

4. Work with a team of classmates to identify a project-worthy problem that affects all of you. If you are all enrolled in a project management course, consider a problem all of you are encountering in your educational process. This should be one for which you believe there is a need for a corrective project initiative. Examples might include arriving late to class, receiving poor grades on exams, getting indigestion immediately after lunch in the school cafeteria, weight gain you have experienced since you started school, etc. Once you have selected the problem, do the following:

a. Prepare a clear problem statement based on the problem statement elements described in this chapter (see Exhibit 3.3).

b. Use the affinity process described in this chapter to brainstorm possible causes of the problem you have described. Submit a photo of your team next to your wall-mounted affinity result that shows sticky notes representing causal categories and underlying causal factors.

c. Establish a goal for the end result of your improvement project (e.g., "Arrive to class five minutes before it begins 99 percent of the time" or "lose 19 pounds by December 1").

d. Describe at least three mutually exclusive approaches you could consider for achieving your goal.

Discussion Questions and Exercises

1. Discuss the concept of the project funnel, and use an example from your personal or work experience to explain how the process works (or doesn't).

2. Review current issues of *The Wall Street Journal, BusinessWeek, Fortune,* or *The Financial Times* for stories about project failures. Identify one example of a failed project that might have been the victim of a poor selection process. Use evidence from the article to support your position and highlight recommendations from this chapter that might have been overlooked.

3. Review the description of Michael Eisner's gong show approach in Box 3.3. In your own words, describe what you think might be the advantages and disadvantages of this approach. In what kinds of organizations would it be most appropriately used? Why do you think so?

4. Consider a problem you are currently facing. It could be large or small, personal or professional. Prepare a clear, crisp problem statement that incorporates the four elements described in this chapter: identity, location, timing, and magnitude.

5. Based on the problem you identified in question 4, prepare a fishbone diagram to show the possible underlying causes.

6. Again, based on the problem you identified and defined in question 4, list and briefly describe at least five options for solving it.

7. The Harvey Co. is considering the purchase of new Garland brand energy-efficient refrigerators for its chain of 60 restaurants. These new refrigerators will cost $10,000 each and will have useful lives of five years before they will need to be replaced. Installation of the *total* set of 60 refrigerators will cost $100,000. Fred Harvey, the owner of the company, has gathered information from other companies that have purchased these refrigerators and is confident they will produce a companywide, net cost saving of $200,000 per year. What is the payback period?

8. Fred Harvey would like to engage in further financial analysis of the purchase and installation project described in question 7. In addition to the option of purchasing the Garland brand refrigerators, he is also considering some less-expensive models from Bolger Appliances. The Bolger units will cost only $6,000 each, and it will cost the same ($100,000) to install all 60. These refrigerators will have a useful life of only four years and will produce net cost savings of only $100,000 per year because they are not as energy-efficient. Based on careful analysis of his company's financial position and goals, Mr. Harvey has set the discount rate at 12 percent. Calculate NPV for both projects and interpret the results. What other factors do you think Mr. Harvey should consider in his project selection decision?

9. You have been assigned to be the project leader for a plant closure at a company that produces medical devices for correcting circulatory ailments. Although the project is in preliminary planning stages, the company's top-level executives have asked you to make recommendations about whether to proceed with it or not, and to suggest changes or guidelines for the project that will help to ensure its success. The company is closing its U.S. plant on the West Coast and moving production to an existing company facility in Cork, Ireland. This will require you to lay off 300 employees in the United States, document all processes, transfer processes, train

operators, move equipment, gain U.S. Food and Drug Administration approval at the new site in Ireland, dispose of real estate, and other activities. Create a force-field analysis for this project, including at least five driving forces and five restraining forces. Make a rating for each one and calculate totals. Reflect on your analysis and recommend whether the project should proceed. What actions would increase the strength of driving forces and reduce the strength of restraining forces?

10. Dexter and Mitzi have both just completed their executive MBA degrees and plan to get married in June. They are trying to decide whether to elope to Costa Rica and travel in Central America for six months or have a big wedding in Vancouver, British Columbia. The elopement would combine a civil ceremony in San Jose, Costa Rica, with six months of eco-tourism in Central America. The large wedding at home would involve a two-week eco-tourism honeymoon in Costa Rica. Dexter and Mitzi prepared financial projections for each option. Revenues from the elopement, in the form of wedding gifts, will be delayed by one year because friends and family members will not know about the marriage for several months. Additionally, Mitzi's father, who is secretly opposed to the big wedding, has promised them $30,000 in Year 2 if they elope. He will pay their taxes on this amount, as well. The big wedding will involve lower travel costs, but will include the cost of the ceremony and reception. However, the big wedding will bring in large gifts in Year 0, and Dexter's Aunt Tootsie has promised to leave $100,000 to them in her will if they have a big wedding. Based on actuarial analysis, Dexter estimates Aunt Tootsie will die in 10 years, and that he will have to pay an income tax of 15 percent on the windfall.[35]

Dexter and Mitzi have decided on a discount rate of 10 percent. Calculate NPV for each option and make a recommendation about which one they should choose.

[35] Assumes 50 percent of the inheritance amount is taxed at the individual's personal income tax rate. If Dexter and Mitzi are in the 30 percent tax bracket in 10 years, the effective tax on the sum received would be half of that, or 15 percent.

Option 1: Elope to Costa Rica and Travel for Six Months in Central America

Expenses in Year 0		Revenues Expected in Year 1	
Air transportation	$ 3,000	Gifts from friends	$10,000
Ground transportation	$ 4,000		
Lodging	$ 2,000		
Meals	$ 2,000	**Revenues Expected in Year 2**	
Clothing	$ 1,000		
Miscellaneous adventure fees	$ 2,000	Bribe from Mitzi's father	$30,000
Total	**$14,000**		(Tax Free)

Option 2: Big Wedding Plus Two-Week Honeymoon in Costa Rica

Expenses in Year 0		Revenues Expected in Year 0	
Two weeks Costa Rica	$ 9,000	Wedding gifts	$20,000
Rental of wedding/reception venue	$10,000		
Reception food and beverages	$15,000	**Revenues Expected in Year 10**	
Wedding garments, bride and groom	$15,000		
Wedding party garments	$10,000	Bequeath from Tootsie	$100,000
Total	**$59,000**		(Taxable at 15%)

11. In question 10, Dexter and Mitzi were interested in determining the net present value for two options they were considering for their upcoming marriage. Extending beyond financial considerations, develop a list of advantages and disadvantages for the two options and discuss your conclusion.

12. Continuing with Dexter and Mitzi's wedding project, develop a force-field analysis figure and list at least five driving forces and five restraining forces for the elopement option. Use your imagination and feel free to go beyond any statements made in the project description presented in question 10. Rate each driving and restraining force on 1–5 scales as described in this chapter. Calculate total scores for the two categories and write a paragraph summarizing your conclusions. Describe at least two actions Dexter and Mitzi might take to increase the viability of the elopement option.

13. Mallard Saws produces table saws for the do-it-yourself (DIY) market and has been very successful financially. Lew Mallard, CEO, is working with his executive team, Hew, Dew, Don, and Daisy, on new-product development decisions. The group is considering the possibility of designing and launching four new products, which have been tentatively named Bubba, Butch, Brutus, and Buddy. A team of analysts has generated the following information about each product, based on market and technical studies:

Product	Market Life	Cost to Develop	Net Annual Income Expected
Bubba	5 years	$1,000,000	$300,000
Butch	4 years	$ 500,000	$200,000
Brutus	10 years	$2,000,000	$560,000
Buddy	3 years	$ 400,000	$150,000

Calculate net present value (NPV) for each potential project, assuming a discount rate of 18%. Use the present value table in Appendix 3B. Discuss the results and make a recommendation. What other factors should be considered in the selection decision?

14. Bisbee Aerospace has recently entered the market for commercial space flights. The executive team at Bisbee is considering proposals from its engineering group for five possible commercial space shuttle designs. The engineering group, in cooperation with the marketing division, has done a thorough job in preparing a business case for each design, and executive team members have carefully reviewed the documentation. Bisbee has a policy in place for weighting criteria used in new product development decisions. These are as follows:

Potential to increase market share	.40
Potential for financial gain	.20
Bisbee's technical capability for this project	.20
Fit with company mission and strategy	.20

Members of the Bisbee executive team have rated each shuttle project on the four criteria on scales of 1–10, where a 1 is a low score and a 10 is a high score. The results are as follows:

Rater	Project	Ratings			
		Market	Financial	Technical	Mission
Barry					
	A	10	5	9	9
	B	7	7	6	4
	C	4	5	4	3
	D	7	4	4	6
	E	2	3	9	5
Sandra					
	A	8	9	8	7
	B	7	6	6	3
	C	5	4	3	3
	D	7	5	7	4
	E	1	2	6	4
Mo					
	A	7	4	6	6
	B	5	5	5	3
	C	3	4	3	2
	D	6	3	2	5
	E	1	2	7	4
Janet					
	A	10	7	10	10
	B	9	8	7	5
	C	5	6	5	4
	D	6	5	6	7
	E	4	4	9	6

Prepare a factor-rating matrix using spreadsheet software, and interpret the results.

15. Dave is a successful home builder in Calgary, Alberta, who has $1 million Canadian available to invest in a project. He is considering two options. Option A is to purchase land and build five tract houses that would sell in the midrange of the local market. Option B is to invest in the land purchase and construction of a single high-end home. Option A would offer some economies of scale because the five tract houses, located right next to each other, would be similar in design and his crews could work very efficiently, moving from house to house. Houses in this price range often sell more quickly than higher-end homes. On the other hand, buyers in the lower-end category often have more difficulty qualifying for loans. In the case of the high-end home, Option B, Dave will not have the advantage of multi-house learning effects, and the high quality specifications will mean he has to monitor the work more closely. Additionally, buyers of high-end homes often insist on changes as a prerequisite to purchase, and Dave has found that these generally cost him an additional $30,000. But buyers in this category are more likely to qualify quickly for loans, and some of them (20 percent) pay cash. In addition to his construction and land purchase costs, Dave will incur a combination of sales tax and real estate broker commission fees of 10 percent of the selling price for each house. Based on past experience, Dave has created the table below to summarize financial and other comparative data for the two project options.

	Option A	Option B
	Build 5 Mid-Range Houses	**Build 1 High-End House**
Initial Investment	$1,000,000	$1,000,000
Time to Complete	12 months	18 months
Estimated Time to Sell After Completion	6 months (average over the 5 houses)	12 months
Sale-Contingent Upgrades	$0	$30,000
Selling Price (each)	$350,000	$2,000,000
Sales Tax and Real Estate Commissions	$175,000	$200,000

a. What is the NPV for each project, assuming Dave has set his discount rate at 15 percent? Assume the $1 million project expenditures are incurred when the project begins. All revenues, sales and real estate costs, and sale-contingent upgrade costs are incurred at the time of sale. Sales of the five houses in Option A will occur all at the same time because the six-month time frame shown in the table represents an average. If you use the NPV tables in Appendix 3B, you will need to interpolate to find values between years. Show your work.

b. Conduct a SWOT analysis for each of these projects. Demonstrate creativity in identifying factors, going beyond issues mentioned above. List at least three possible items in each of the SWOT quadrants shown in Exhibit 3.12.

c. Write a paragraph summarizing your recommendations to Dave, based on your financial analysis as well as your SWOT analysis.

16. Fred Farkle is the head of the IT Division at Rowen and Martin Bank. He and his team are evaluating six projects that represent potential cost savings to the bank, and they would like to apply PPI analysis to set priorities. They have thoroughly assessed project costs, estimating durations, and forecasting cost savings. Additionally, they have brainstormed implementation risks and used a voting process to estimate probability of success for each project. The projects and the results of this process are displayed in the table below.

Projects	Projected Savings	Probability of Success	Cost of Project	Time for Completion (in Years)
Online Banking Upgrade	$1,000,000	0.9	$ 75,000	0.8
Customer Relationship Management System	$2,000,000	0.5	$400,000	1.8
Payroll System Upgrade	$ 500,000	0.85	$100,000	0.5
Loan Processing System	$3,000,000	0.7	$500,000	1
Accounts Payable System	$ 90,000	0.9	$ 20,000	0.3
Vendor Management System Upgrade	$ 700,000	0.6	$100,000	1.2

Calculate PPI for this set of projects and discuss what the results mean to Rowen and Martin Bank. What are your recommendations?

References

Anthony, R.N., and D.W. Young. *Management Control in Nonprofit Organizations,* 7th ed. New York: McGraw-Hill, 2003.

Armstrong, J.S. "The Value of Formal Planning for Strategic Decisions." *Strategic Management Journal* 3, no. 3 (1982), pp. 197–211.

Bazerman, M.H. *Judgment in Decision Making,* 5th ed. New York: Wiley and Sons, 2002.

Brannock, J.W. *Business Case Analysis.* Plant City, FL: STS Publications, 2004.

Brown, K.A., and N.L. Hyer. "Whole-Brain Thinking for Project Managers." *Business Horizons* 45, no. 3 (2002), pp. 47–57.

Carryou, J. "Turning around a Drug Maker Takes Time." *The Wall Street Journal,* August 2, 2006, p. B1.

Cooper, R.G. *Winning at New Products: Accelerating the Process from Idea to Launch,* 3rd ed. Reading, MA: Perseus Books, 2001.

"The Cutting Edge." *The Economist,* October 7, 2006, p. 76.

Delbecq, A.L., and A.H. VandeVen, "A Group Process Model for Problem Identification and Program Planning." *Journal of Applied Behavioral Science* 7, no. 4 (1971), pp. 466–92.

Delbecq, A.L.; A.H. VandeVen; and D.H. Gustafson. *Group Techniques for Program Planners.* Glenview, IL: Scott Foresman and Co., 1975.

Dillman, D.A. *Mail and Internet Surveys: The Tailored Design Method,* 2nd ed. New York: Wiley and Sons, 2000.

Edwards, W. "Use of Multiattribute Utility Measurement for Social Decision Making." In *Conflicting Objectives in Decisions,* ed. D.E. Bell, R.L. Keeney, and H. Raiffa. Chichester, England: Wiley and Sons, 1977, pp. 247–75.

Fichman, R.G.; M. Keil; and A. Tiwana. "Beyond Valuation: 'Options Thinking' in IT Project Management." *California Management Review* 47, no. 2 (2005), pp. 74–94.

Frisch, B. "When Teams Can't Decide." *Harvard Business Review* 86, no. 11 (2008), pp. 121–26.

Gupta, P. *The Six Sigma Performance Handbook.* New York: McGraw-Hill, 2004.

Hammond, J.S.; R.L. Keeney; and H. Raiffa. *Smart Choices.* New York: Broadway Books, 1999.

Hill, T., and R. Westbrook. "SWOT Analysis: It's Time for a Product Recall." *Long Range Planning* 30, no. 1 (1997), pp. 46–52.

Hogarth, R. *Judgement and Choice.* Chichester, England: Wiley and Sons, 1980.

Jana, R. "Deloitte Study: Emerging Market Innovation." *BusinessWeek Online,* March 15, 2007.

Kepner, C.H., and B.B. Tregoe. *The New Rational Manager.* Princeton, NJ: Princeton Research Press, 1984.

Leuhrman, T.A. "Investment Opportunities as Real Options: Getting Started on the Numbers." *Harvard Business Review* 76, no. 4 (1998), pp. 51–67.

Levenson, M., and R. Mishra. "Turner Broadcasting Accepts Blame, Promises Restitution." *The Boston Globe,* February 2, 2007.

Lewin, K. "Defining the 'Field at a Given Time'." *Psychological Review* 50, no. 3 (1943), pp. 292–310.

Lewis, I.; J. Semeijn; and D.B. Vellenga, "Issues and Initiatives Surrounding Rail-Freight Transportation in Europe." *Transportation Journal* 41, no. 2/3 (2002), pp. 22–31.

Mandel, M. "How to Get Growth Back on Track." *BusinessWeek,* October 27, 2008, pp. 34–38.

Mathews, A.W. "FDA Signals It's Open to Drug Trials that Shift Midcourse." *The Wall Street Journal,* July 10, 2006, p. B1.

McCleod, C. "Massive Quake Tests China on Reaction to Major Crisis." *USA Today,* May 13, 2008, p. 1A.

Royer, I. "Why Bad Projects Are So Hard to Kill." *Harvard Business Review* 81, no. 2 (2003), pp. 48–56.

Scholtes, P.K. *The Team Handbook.* Madison, WI: Joiner Associates, Inc., 1993.

Sterman, J.D. *Business Dynamics.* New York: McGraw-Hill, 2000.

Whalen, J. "Bureaucracy Buster? Glaxo Lets Scientists Choose Its New Drugs." *The Wall Street Journal,* March 27, 2006, p. B1.

Wheelwright, S.C., and K.B. Clark, "Creating Project Plans to Focus Product Development." *Harvard Business Review* 70, no. 2 (1992), pp. 67–83.

Young, D.W. "Note on Capital Budgeting." The Crimson Press Curriculum Center, www.thecrimsongroup.net.

Appendix 3A

Sample Business Case for a Volunteer Community Service Project

BUSINESS CASE: PROJECT TO ASSIST HURRICANE EVACUEES*

Executive Summary

A massive Category 3 hurricane made a direct hit on New Orleans two days ago. Much of the population was evacuated to surrounding cities before the storm made landfall, and even more are expected to relocate themselves now that the city has been declared a natural disaster area. Government agencies estimate that approximately 50,000 displaced New Orleans residents will relocate to Dallas, Texas, within the next two weeks. Many of these evacuees will have lost their homes and most of their personal belongings. They are likely to be in need of food, especially during the early part of their resettlement here. Our neighborhood association has come together to assess the best way to help the victims of this tragedy who will soon arrive in our city. We would like these people to know we care about them and that we welcome them to our city.

Given the rarity of a storm of this magnitude, there is very little historical information available about how to respond to the resulting evacuation. We do know that the current aid organizations will need much more help than normal in their efforts to help such a large number of evacuees, and we would like to contribute in the best way we can. After careful analysis and discussion, we have decided to conduct a food and clothing drive. Our choice of this activity over other possibilities was based on three decision criteria:

1. Anticipated value to the evacuees.
2. Fit with the time and resources available in our neighborhood association.
3. Ease of implementation.

* Jennifer Galek, MBA, Thunderbird School of Global Management, 2008, created this business case based on her experience. Thanks, Jennifer!

We have set a goal of collecting enough clothing for 1,000 evacuees and enough food to feed 500 evacuees for two weeks.

Problem Statement

Within the next two weeks, the hurricane that hit New Orleans will force an estimated 50,000 evacuees to relocate to Dallas, Texas for safety while they await word about the damage to their city and their homes. For some, this might require a stay in Dallas of a few days or weeks. Others may not be able to return to New Orleans for several months. Regardless of the length of their stay in our city, the evacuees will be in desperate need of shelter, food, clothing, and social support. Governmental and nongovernmental aid agencies in Dallas are ill-prepared for an influx of so many people in need of assistance.

Given our interest in more completely understanding the problems faced by the evacuees, our community, and support agencies, we discussed the driving forces that have created the current situation and summarized them in a fishbone diagram, which is displayed below.

Fishbone Diagram for Project Drivers

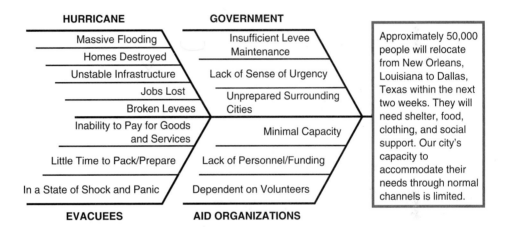

Summary Statement about Underlying Causes Creating the Problem

Primary causal categories underlying the problems associated with the evacuees include the hurricane, government agencies, aid organizations, and the evacuees. The full set of circumstances has made it very difficult for the evacuees to take care of themselves. The cost of immediate relocation for an undetermined amount of time is extremely high, and most of these people do not have the kind of savings it would take to cover the unexpected needs created by a catastrophic event such as a major hurricane. Because the hurricane came so quickly, people were unable to plan effectively and bring the things they needed for an extended trip away from home. Those who were in New Orleans at the time of the storm and are now traveling to Dallas have found that the majority of their possessions have been destroyed. And finally, the emotional state of the evacuees is one of shock because of the suddenness of their necessary departure and the uncertainty of their return.

Goal Statement

The essential needs of the evacuees will be shelter, food, clothing, and social support. Because of our size and resources, we have decided that we will be able to help most efficiently by focusing on meeting the food and clothing needs of a portion of these

Options for Achieving Our Goal

Options	Brief Description of Option	Arguments For	Arguments Against
Option 1			
Volunteer	Collaborate with an existing aid organization and serve as volunteers.	• Requires limited planning on our part. • We won't need to try to persuade others to contribute. • Involves less commitment and accountability. • Less stress for us.	• Small impact on the problem. • This disaster has caused more demand than existing organizations can handle. • Most organizations require volunteers to go through a training program that makes it impossible to meet urgent needs of the situation. • We might not feel as if we are making enough of a difference.
Option 2			
Hold a Food and Clothing Drive	Plan an event where people can help by donating goods and volunteering. We will then donate these goods to larger organizations (e.g., Red Cross) and involve ourselves in distribution of donated items.	• We believe we can collect the largest quantities of food and clothing this way. • Gives us an opportunity for more hands-on involvement. • Greater sense of satisfaction. • No training restrictions to limit our involvement. • Creates a way for others beyond our group to get involved. • Creates more capacity to help evacuees.	• Requires much more planning. • Will be time consuming. • We will have higher accountability. • We do not have the official credibility that an established aid organization has.
Option 3			
Fund Drive	We all make cash donations to a selected aid agency.	• All of the organizations are going to need money to help the large number of people. • Money is versatile and can meet specific needs that we might not be able to anticipate.	• It is difficult to get people to donate cash. They don't know where the money will go. • We do not have enough money to meet our goals. • We will not gain the personal satisfaction of helping people directly.
Option 4			
Do Nothing	Let others take care of the needs of the evacuees.	• It's not our personal problem. • We have other things to do.	• We should be willing to help others in time of need. • We would want help if we were in the same position.

evacuees. Based on our membership of 75 households and a two-week timeline we have set for ourselves, we have agreed upon the following goal statement:

The goal of our neighborhood association is to hold a food and clothing drive that will collect enough clothing for 1,000 evacuees and enough food to feed 500 evacuees for two weeks.

We considered four options for achieving our goal and brainstormed arguments for and against each one.

Factor Rating Analysis

We chose factor rating as opposed to a financial analysis because this is a volunteer situation where not much expense will be involved. Factor rating allowed us to discuss our decision criteria up-front and to involve key group members (i.e., the board of our neighborhood association) in a shared team decision.

		Anticipated Impact or Value	Fit with Resource Availability	Ease of Implementation	Weighted Average
	Weights	**0.5**	**0.4**	**0.1**	
Option 1: Volunteer					
	Jennifer	4	2	10	3.80
	Chris	3	3	9	3.60
	Rani	4	3	10	4.20
Average		3.67	2.67	9.67	
Weighted Average		**1.83**	**1.07**	**0.97**	
			Factor Rating Score		**3.87**
Option 2: Food and Clothing Drive					
	Jennifer	9	8	2	7.90
	Chris	8	7	3	7.10
	Rani	10	9	1	8.70
Average		9	8	2	
Weighted Average		**4.50**	**3.20**	**0.20**	
			Factor Rating Score		**7.90**
Option 3: Send Money					
	Jennifer	7	1	10	4.90
	Chris	9	3	10	6.70
	Rani	7	2	10	5.30
Average		7.67	2	10	
Weighted Average		**3.83**	**0.80**	**1.00**	
			Factor Rating Score		**5.63**
Option 4: Do Nothing					
	Jennifer	1	10	10	5.50
	Chris	1	10	10	5.50
	Rani	1	10	10	5.50
Average		1	10	10	
Weighted Average		**0.50**	**4.00**	**1.00**	
			Factor Rating Score		**5.50**

Concluding Statement about Chosen Course of Action

As leaders of our neighborhood organization, we have compared the four options based on three criteria: anticipated value, fit with available resources, and ease of implementation. We weighted anticipated value as most important because it is what truly compels us. The category of fit with resources was also highly weighted because this is a volunteer situation and we have to be able to achieve our goals without spending much money. The ease of implementation category was the least weighted because we do not mind working hard to help people.

Based on our brainstorming session to examine arguments for and against each option, as well as factor rating, we chose Option 2: Plan a Food and Clothing Drive. This was easily the best fit as far as meeting our goal of adding value. It also supports our fit with resources category because it can be as big or as small of an event as we want it to be, depending on what resources are donated. This option will be the most difficult to implement because we will have to create it from the bottom up, but we are sure, after comparing it to the other options, that it is by far the best choice.

Appendix 3B

Net Present Value Tables

Appendix Exhibit 3.1B: Present Value of $1

Years in the Future (N)	Required Rate of Return (Discount Rate)																	
	1%	2%	4%	6%	8%	10%	12%	14%	15%	16%	18%	20%	22%	24%	25%	26%	28%	30%
1	0.990	0.980	0.962	0.943	0.926	0.909	0.893	0.877	0.870	0.862	0.847	0.833	0.820	0.806	0.800	0.794	0.781	0.769
2	0.980	0.961	0.925	0.890	0.857	0.826	0.797	0.769	0.756	0.743	0.718	0.694	0.672	0.650	0.640	0.630	0.610	0.592
3	0.971	0.942	0.889	0.840	0.794	0.751	0.712	0.675	0.658	0.641	0.609	0.579	0.551	0.524	0.512	0.500	0.477	0.455
4	0.961	0.924	0.855	0.792	0.735	0.683	0.636	0.592	0.572	0.552	0.516	0.482	0.451	0.423	0.410	0.397	0.373	0.350
5	0.951	0.906	0.822	0.747	0.681	0.621	0.567	0.519	0.497	0.476	0.437	0.402	0.370	0.341	0.328	0.315	0.291	0.269
6	0.942	0.888	0.790	0.705	0.630	0.564	0.507	0.456	0.432	0.410	0.370	0.335	0.303	0.275	0.262	0.250	0.227	0.207
7	0.933	0.871	0.760	0.665	0.583	0.513	0.452	0.400	0.376	0.354	0.314	0.279	0.249	0.222	0.210	0.198	0.178	0.159
8	0.923	0.853	0.731	0.627	0.540	0.467	0.404	0.351	0.327	0.305	0.266	0.233	0.204	0.179	0.168	0.157	0.139	0.123
9	0.914	0.837	0.703	0.592	0.500	0.424	0.361	0.308	0.284	0.263	0.225	0.194	0.167	0.144	0.134	0.125	0.108	0.094
10	0.905	0.820	0.676	0.558	0.463	0.386	0.322	0.270	0.247	0.227	0.191	0.162	0.137	0.116	0.107	0.099	0.085	0.073
11	0.896	0.804	0.650	0.527	0.429	0.350	0.287	0.237	0.215	0.195	0.162	0.135	0.112	0.094	0.086	0.079	0.066	0.056
12	0.887	0.788	0.625	0.497	0.397	0.319	0.257	0.208	0.187	0.168	0.137	0.112	0.092	0.076	0.069	0.062	0.052	0.043
13	0.879	0.773	0.601	0.469	0.368	0.290	0.229	0.182	0.163	0.145	0.116	0.093	0.075	0.061	0.055	0.050	0.040	0.033
14	0.870	0.758	0.577	0.442	0.340	0.263	0.205	0.160	0.141	0.125	0.099	0.078	0.062	0.049	0.044	0.039	0.032	0.025
15	0.861	0.743	0.555	0.417	0.315	0.239	0.183	0.140	0.123	0.108	0.084	0.065	0.051	0.040	0.035	0.031	0.025	0.020

Appendix Exhibit 3.2B: Present Value of $1 Received Annually for *N* Years

Years in the Future (N)	Required Rate of Return (Discount Rate)																	
	1%	2%	4%	6%	8%	10%	12%	14%	15%	16%	18%	20%	22%	24%	25%	26%	28%	30%
1	0.990	0.980	0.962	0.943	0.926	0.909	0.893	0.877	0.870	0.862	0.847	0.833	0.820	0.806	0.800	0.794	0.781	0.769
2	1.970	1.941	1.887	1.833	1.783	1.735	1.690	1.646	1.626	1.605	1.565	1.527	1.492	1.456	1.440	1.424	1.391	1.361
3	2.941	2.883	2.776	2.673	2.577	2.486	2.402	2.321	2.284	2.246	2.174	2.106	2.043	1.980	1.952	1.924	1.868	1.816
4	3.902	3.807	3.631	3.465	3.312	3.169	3.038	2.913	2.856	2.798	2.690	2.588	2.494	2.403	2.362	2.321	2.241	2.166
5	4.853	4.713	4.453	4.212	3.993	3.790	3.605	3.432	3.353	3.274	3.127	2.990	2.864	2.744	2.690	2.636	2.532	2.435
6	5.795	5.601	5.243	4.917	4.623	4.354	4.112	3.888	3.785	3.684	3.497	3.325	3.167	3.019	2.952	2.886	2.759	2.642
7	6.728	6.472	6.003	5.582	5.206	4.867	4.564	4.288	4.161	4.038	3.811	3.604	3.416	3.241	3.162	3.084	2.937	2.801
8	7.651	7.325	6.734	6.209	5.746	5.334	4.968	4.639	4.488	4.343	4.077	3.837	3.620	3.420	3.330	3.241	3.076	2.924
9	8.565	8.162	7.437	6.801	6.246	5.758	5.329	4.947	4.772	4.606	4.302	4.031	3.787	3.564	3.464	3.366	3.184	3.018
10	9.470	8.982	8.113	7.359	6.709	6.144	5.651	5.217	5.019	4.833	4.493	4.193	3.924	3.680	3.571	3.465	3.269	3.091
11	10.366	9.786	8.763	7.886	7.138	6.494	5.938	5.454	5.234	5.028	4.655	4.328	4.036	3.774	3.657	3.544	3.335	3.147
12	11.253	10.574	9.388	8.383	7.535	6.813	6.195	5.662	5.421	5.196	4.792	4.440	4.128	3.850	3.726	3.606	3.387	3.190
13	12.132	11.347	9.989	8.852	7.903	7.103	6.424	5.844	5.584	5.341	4.908	4.533	4.203	3.911	3.781	3.656	3.427	3.223
14	13.002	12.105	10.566	9.294	8.243	7.366	6.629	6.004	5.725	5.466	5.007	4.611	4.265	3.960	3.825	3.695	3.459	3.248
15	13.863	12.848	11.121	9.711	8.558	7.605	6.812	6.144	5.848	5.574	5.091	4.676	4.316	4.000	3.860	3.726	3.484	3.268

Chapter **Four**

Project Initiation: Setting the Stage for Action

"The beginning is the most important part of the work."

Plato

Chapter Learning Objectives

When you have mastered the material in this chapter, you should be able to:

- Describe the importance of a sponsor-initiated project charter.
- Create a project charter where none exists by obtaining answers to key project initiation questions.
- Work with a team to establish a clear, shared understanding of a project's mission or purpose.
- Create a clear, specific objective statement with measurable goals.
- Assess stakeholder needs and develop a plan for gaining and maintaining their support.
- Define project deliverables and associated performance measures.
- Create an effective team in the context of organizational structure.
- Establish and maintain contractual relationships to support the project.

The beginning of any project sets the stage for what is to come. Some experts estimate that when a project has consumed 10 percent of its budgeted resources, the team has probably locked in 90 percent of the final project costs. So, if members of a project team sail lightly through the "fuzzy front end" of a project,[1] they may be squandering a significant opportunity to structure the project for best results. For a sense of the consequences of a poorly launched project, consider the following example:[2]

In 2000, Electronic Data Systems (EDS) executives were pleased to have secured an $8.8 billion contract with the U.S. Navy to design, install, manage, and support

---

[1] P. Smith and D. Reinertsen, "Faster to Market," *Mechanical Engineering* 120, no. 12 (1998), pp. 68–70.

[2] Drawn from a series of *Wall Street Journal* articles about the EDS project, beginning with G. McWilliams, "Sink or Swim: After Landing Huge Navy Pact, EDS Finds It's in over Its Head," *The Wall Street Journal*, April 6, 2004, p. A1.

"a single, hacker-proof network" connecting 345,000 computers at 4,000 Navy and Marine Corps locations. However, by 2004, the company had lost $1.6 billion on the project. Errors and omissions at the very start of the project were major contributors to the dismal financial performance and lost reputation EDS experienced. Examples included:

- *Poor project fit:* Adept at working with corporations, EDS was unfamiliar with the complex and highly regulated world of military contracts. Soon after the contract was signed, work was delayed for 18 months when Congress requested additional network performance tests. "The demands were very unlike requests from corporate clients," noted EDS Chairman Michael H. Jordan.[3]
- *Underestimation of project scope:* EDS anticipated transferring 5,000 software programs to the new network, but the actual number grew to 67,000. The nature of the contractual relationship required EDS to absorb the unexpected costs.
- *Failure to anticipate the realities of working with key stakeholders:* The Navy contract required that the computers be installed before EDS could bill for the work. However, many assembled computers sat waiting for installation for up to nine months because users were out at sea.
- *Unclear performance standards:* EDS promised to "bring the Navy up to corporate computer standards," a vague objective that opened the door for vast differences in interpretation that made it difficult for EDS to request contract revisions based on change orders.
- *Misunderstandings about organization structure:* The EDS and Navy aspects of this project operated from two separate functional structures. This made authority difficult to track, delayed the discovery of problems, and lengthened decision making lead times.

Beyond anecdotal evidence, such as the EDS example, research underscores the correlation between an effective project launch and a high-performing project team.[4]

Our goal for this chapter is to equip you with the knowledge and insight to successfully initiate a project and avoid the types of launch-related pitfalls EDS experienced. As depicted in Exhibit 4.1, the ideas we present here build on the business case discussion in Chapter 3. The business case directs those analyzing the project's fit and feasibility to consider several important questions before deciding whether a project is worthy of adoption. Once the project has been selected and a project manager has been assigned, many of the questions raised during the business case analysis are revisited during project initiation as flesh is added to the bones of the project plan. The culmination of this initiation work, again as depicted in Exhibit 4.1, is a project initiation

---

[3] Ibid., p. A1.

[4] J. Ericksen and L. Dyer, "Right from the Start: Exploring the Effects of Early Team Events on Subsequent Project Team Performance," *Administrative Science Quarterly* 49, no. 3 (2004), pp. 438–71.

EXHIBIT 4.1
From Business Case to Project Initiation Document

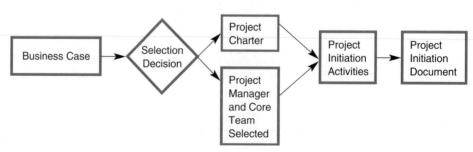

document. In this chapter we show how a team moves a project from "selected" to one that is fully defined in a completed project initiation document.

THE PROJECT CHARTER: SETTING OFF ON THE RIGHT FOOT

Once funding and corporate commitment have been established, the project is ready to move to the initiation stage. At this point, a project manager, along with a small planning team, should be assigned to take the project through its early stages. In large organizations, the sponsor, who typically authorizes and controls project resources, may issue a **project charter.** This document establishes the authority of the project manager and specifies several important project parameters. Although funding and deadlines sometimes can be modified as the detailed project plan unfolds, the baseline data provided in the project charter give the project team a general sense of the purpose and scope of its task.

Exhibit 4.2 presents an example of a charter for a project at Sapphire Medical Devices, which is in the early stages of creating a project management office (PMO). Many organizations concerned about improving the maturity of their project management process elect to establish a PMO as a center of excellence for project management. At Sapphire, company officials have decided that a PMO will offer opportunities for developing systematic methods for planning, managing, and supporting project endeavors across the organization. Further, the PMO will provide a "home base" for project managers and communicate their importance to the organization. This project was chosen based on a rigorous selection process, following the prescriptions presented in Chapter 3, and the business case outcome was strongly favorable. Senior-level executives view the project to be very important, and the president of the company, serving as the project sponsor, has issued the charter.

As illustrated in Exhibit 4.2, the *project charter* announces that a new project has begun and shows the project has been sanctioned by the organization. It also links this project to the organization's broader mission and strategic goals. In the absence of a charter, people in the organization might not know the project exists, and they might not recognize the project manager's authority. In the worst cases, an unannounced project can raise suspicions among the kinds of stakeholders who promulgate conspiracy theories.[5] The charter keeps the project out in the open.

Although the charter in Exhibit 4.2 was issued by the president, this need not be the case. For example, the director of manufacturing may be the sponsor for a process-improvement project that targets assembly activities, or the vice president for information systems may be the sponsor for an IT system upgrade. The more a project reaches into the lives of people across organizational lines, the more valuable top-level support will be. Nonetheless, the president or CEO cannot, and should not, issue every charter. If the organization's CEO and other high-level executives issue myriad project charters and testify that each project is of the utmost importance, individual project charters will have little influence on the organization and will not offer the intended benefits.

---

[5] We assume you know who we are talking about here and hope you are not one of these kinds of people.

EXHIBIT 4.2   Sapphire Medical Devices Project Charter

Project Management Office (PMO) Project Charter

Company Mission:* To maintain a premier position of leadership in the medical devices industry by designing, continuously improving, and producing high-end products for use in minimally invasive vascular surgeries.

Purpose of Project: The PMO project is being initiated to improve project selection, management, and learning on a corporatewide basis. Such improvements will support our mission by helping to ensure our ability to maintain a position of leadership in our industry. Although our company has been built on the results and lessons from many successful projects over the years, market and technological pressures have increased the volume and pace of project work. Recent project performance has not met expectations and has pushed us to realize we need a more systematic approach for handling unique, complex endeavors.

Expected Business Results: Ongoing improvement in our ability to select, plan, and execute projects will result in projects being completed on time, within budget, and with excellent technical results. This, in turn, will help grow the business, satisfy customers, increase market share, and improve overall company profitability.

Project Objective: To create a corporate-level PMO that will develop and sustain standard but adaptable processes for selecting, managing, and measuring projects; offer training; create avenues for best-practice sharing; maintain a repository of project lessons learned; facilitate problem solving; and encourage cooperation across projects.

Project Sponsor: Victor Eusebio, president

Project Manager: Barbara Tyndall, vice president of engineering

Project Stakeholders: All company employees involved in managing or supporting projects, including those related to product development, IT, testing, manufacturing, supply chain management, engineering, administrative services, marketing, and human resources. People across all functions at Sapphire will be customers of this project because all of them should, ultimately, be able to take advantage of the tools, support, and opportunities created by the PMO.

Preliminary Project Deliverables

- A standard project management process design.
- Reference manuals, including standard templates, documenting the standard project management process.
- Curriculum and materials for training programs to educate the organization on the standard project management process.
- A Web site to support and coordinate project activities across the company.
- Integrated project management software.
- A project measurement system.
- A system for capturing and disseminating lessons learned.
- Space design for six dedicated project conference rooms.

Preliminary Project Budget: $50,000 in outside costs, plus 2,000 hours of internal staff and management time. (These numbers may be revised after the project team has developed a more complete plan.)

Preliminary Completion Date: Based on initial estimates, the project is set to begin on June 1 and move to routine operational phase by December 15. (This, also, will be subject to adjustment based on the team's initial work.)

Notes from Victor Eusebio: I am pleased that Barbara Tyndall has agreed to spearhead this project. Her experiences as a successful project manager here at Sapphire, and the extensive benchmarking she has conducted this past year, make her the ideal person to lead this project. She and I have conferred about the project, and I have great confidence in her vision. She is especially aware of the importance of gaining input from stakeholders. So I believe you can count on her to listen to your ideas and concerns. I have asked the functional managers to assign their most qualified people to Barb's team. Staffed with the right people, and assured of our ongoing support, the team will be able to finish the project effectively and in a timely manner.

   I know we have several large-scale projects under way right now. Certainly our product development efforts must receive the highest priority. Time to market is critical in our highly competitive environment. However, if everyone can lend a hand to this background project, all of our product development projects will benefit.

Thanks, in advance, for your support of this project.

Victor Eusebio, President, Sapphire Medical Devices

---

*Although the company mission does not always appear in a project charter, we include it here to demonstrate the value of showing how a project relates to a company's overall strategy.

Not all project managers are fortunate enough to have comprehensive project charters issued for them by respected organizational sponsors. If you are asked to lead a project and are not provided a charter, you can create your own by asking, and documenting answers to, the following questions:

- What is the purpose of this project?
- What is the project objective—what is the project supposed to accomplish?
- What business result is expected from this project?
- Who is the customer and how will the customer judge the performance of this project?
- Who is the project sponsor?
- Who are the other project stakeholders?
- What specific deliverables are expected?
- What is the preliminary budget?
- When is the project expected to be complete?
- How will the project fit within the larger organization structure? (e.g., will it be contained within a single function, will it be cross functional?)
- Will the work be performed by existing employees, new employees, an outside contractor, or a combination?
- What is the relationship of this project to other current projects?
- How will my performance as a project manager be measured?

Based on the answers to these questions, a project manager can prepare a charter for discussion with the project sponsor. This will require tact but will offer a mechanism for the project manager to learn what is expected. The informally-generated charter can be distributed to key stakeholders once the sponsor has approved it.

PROJECT INITIATION ELEMENTS

Although the charter may include specified objectives, a list of deliverables, a preliminary budget, and other project parameters, these are just the beginning of the initiation process. It will be up to the project team to refine this information and develop a fuller statement of all the initiation elements.

Much of the process of initiating a project may appear to repeat content from the business case analysis, and it should. However, the business case is usually prepared with limited information, by people who are not necessarily going to be on the project team. (For example, they might be corporate staff members.) Now that the organization has sanctioned the project, funded it, and assigned a core team (that can grow in size), these people must revisit business case questions, gather information, add detail, and possibly reconceptualize the project, depending on what they learn during their investigation and analysis. The best way to start this process is with a project launch meeting. Exhibit 4.3 suggests an agenda.

The project manager can achieve multiple purposes during a well-designed project launch meeting that engages the team. First, it gets team members into the same room and begins to create a common sense of purpose. People who may not have worked together will have the opportunity to become acquainted. A participatory agenda demonstrates that team member contributions to this project will be valued. And it offers a framework for capturing their good ideas at this critical stage of the planning process.

EXHIBIT 4.3

Agenda for Project Launch Meeting

1. Project introduction (perhaps with a brief appearance by the sponsor).
2. Introduction of the core team. Highlights of the skills and interests they bring to the project.
3. Review and discussion of project drivers: What do we know about why this project has been chartered? Can we add anything? Are there any unstated or unofficial drivers we need to understand?
4. Discussion of intended business results. Are they achievable? Would we add, embellish, or delete anything?
5. Review and expansion of options for achieving intended business results.
6. Discussion of scope and major deliverables, including clarification, expansion, and identification of items that might be out of scope.
7. Identification of any contractual relationships that might be part of the project.
8. Agreement on a regular meeting schedule for the project.
9. Agreement on a reporting system for project activities, results, and lessons learned.

Confirming Project Drivers: Why Are We Doing This?

Before proceeding with any other initiation tasks, the team should revisit the various factors that have given rise to the project. These should have been identified during the project selection process, as discussed in Chapter 3, but time will have passed, and more information may be available. If the business case did not include information about project drivers, the team should discuss them before moving forward. The old saying "YB4WHAT" or "Why Before What" should be one of the project managers' mantras.

In the case of the Sapphire PMO project, the team reviewed the charter and the previously developed business case and confirmed five major factors driving the initial push for this project. They included:

- Product development times had increased dramatically during the previous five-year period.
- Sapphire had missed the market window on three recent product development efforts, resulting in estimated losses of nearly $200 million in sales.
- Recent IT projects had been over budget by 60 percent, on average.
- Some promising new-product initiatives had languished and died.
- Project stakeholders, especially project team members, complained that when they moved from one project to another they were confronted with a new set of procedures and terminology, making it very difficult to understand what was going on or develop transferable skills.

However, the PMO team, in the process of gathering more information, discovered other project drivers. For one, Sapphire's stock price had declined recently, and stock analysts were criticizing Sapphire for having a weak pipeline of potential new products. Additionally, team members noted that a potential FDA recall on a new product had raised questions about the rigor of Sapphire's product development processes. These newly discovered drivers would be added to the list the team keeps in mind throughout the project. Some implicit drivers might best be kept as "tribal knowledge" among team members and not added formally to the project charter document.

During the launch meeting, the team should confirm that the project supports the organization's mission and strategy. Projects that are not strategically driven are often candidates for cancellation. At Sapphire, the strategic importance of the project was clear. According to the project charter, a PMO would "support our mission by helping to ensure our ability to maintain a position of leadership in our industry."

Expected Outcomes

The core team's next step is to ask, "What does the organization hope to accomplish by successfully completing this project? What business or organizational result is expected?" If the team is starting from ground zero with no charter, or an incomplete one, articulating the project's expected effect on the business and then verifying it with the chartering authority should be one of the team's first steps. In the Sapphire PMO project, the initiative is expected to improve the company's market share, customer satisfaction, and bottom-line profitability by facilitating effective project delivery on time and within budget. These results are all measurable, and it is useful for the team to review and understand them. Teams can, in some instances, get so mired in project minutia they lose sight of high-level end results for the project. Exhibit 4.4 illustrates an example of a project in which participants have forgotten the purpose.

Deciding on the Course of Action

A course of action for the project is typically chosen during the selection process, as discussed in Chapter 3. But within a specified course of action, there can be more choices. In the case of the Sapphire Medical Devices PMO, the team could consider adopting a highly centralized approach, with project managers reporting directly to a powerful PMO director, or a decentralized approach in which the PMO operates with a lean staff and provides support without much authority. For the project Web site associated with the PMO, Sapphire could outsource the function through a vendor contract or develop and manage the site in house. If the team is not ready to make these decisions during the initiation stage, an early project activity will involve research and recommendations about the approach to take.

Project Objective Statement

A project objective statement is a simple statement of what the project will accomplish. The statement should be *shared,* reflecting the team's consensus regarding what the project will actually involve. It should also be relatively *short,* between 25 and

EXHIBIT 4.4

Keep Expected Outcomes in Mind: Don't Forget the Cattle

THE FAR SIDE®   BY GARY LARSON

"Say ... wait just a dang minute, here. ...
We forgot the cattle!"

EXHIBIT 4.5
Project Objective Statement Examples

Web Site Design Project: Create a Web site customers can use to search our product catalogue, order our products, and submit requests for specialized products and services. The site should load quickly (less than 15 seconds), have live links, work across platforms, and be browser independent. Customers should be able to find specific products and place orders by navigating through four or fewer pages. The Web site should integrate seamlessly with existing corporate accounts billing systems. It should be fully functional within three months.

Manufacturing Cell Design Project: By June of next year, develop a plan to reconfigure existing plant equipment to create a cell dedicated to the manufacture of SMA (Subminiature version A) connectors. The cell should manufacture SMA connectors in less than a day, with first pass quality of 99 percent. As part of the plan, recommend equipment layout, staffing assignments, production control procedures, and inventory levels.

New Curriculum Design Project: Design a distinctive 60-credit-hour health care MBA curriculum whose graduates will be attractive to and valued by employers in the health care industry. Gain faculty approval for the program by May of next year. Develop a draft program implementation plan, including recommendations regarding near-term (first year of operation) and long-term (two years out and beyond) program staffing, marketing, and student recruitment. Complete this work by mid-June of next year.

50 words.[6] Limiting the statement length forces clarity; if the team cannot explain the project goal in a brief paragraph, then the team itself may not understand the objective. The statement should also be simple, free of jargon and acronyms, specific, measurable, and time constrained. The objective statement for the PMO project appears in the charter displayed in Exhibit 4.2. Exhibit 4.5 provides other examples of effective project objective statements developed by project teams in three organizations.

During the project launch meeting, team members should review the objective to be sure they understand and are comfortable with it. If the previous discussion about courses of action has added detail or raised questions about the direction of the project, the objective statement from the charter should be revised.

Key stakeholders beyond the project manager and team should agree that the project objective statement accurately reflects the intent of the project work. If influential stakeholders have different views of the project objective, the project is doomed to fail before it starts. For this reason, each key stakeholder should be asked to review and approve the project objective statement. If there are disagreements, they should be ironed out (generally with the aid of the project sponsor) before the team proceeds further.

Once it has been confirmed (or modified with sponsor and stakeholder approval), the project objective statement should not change as the project unfolds. If circumstances evolve such that the original project objective statement no longer reflects the hoped-for outcome of the project, the project manager, team, and other stakeholders must acknowledge they are now pursing a *different* project. Suppose the Sapphire PMO team engages in discussion with key stakeholders, conducts industry research, and benchmarks other companies to gain insight about how to improve project performance. They conclude that what Sapphire *actually* should do, instead of creating a PMO, is to create a new organization structure that dismantles the company's vertical, functional orientation and redistributes all employees into a horizontal, project-focused structure. This, clearly, is a different project.

[6] IPS Associates, *Project Management Manual.* (Boston: Harvard Business School Press, 1996), pp. 10–11.

EXHIBIT 4.6
What Versus How

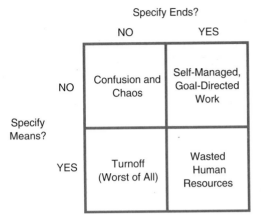

Specify Ends?

	NO	YES
NO	Confusion and Chaos	Self-Managed, Goal-Directed Work
YES	Turnoff (Worst of All)	Wasted Human Resources

Specify Means?

Specify What, Not How

Although we have called for a specific, unambiguous project objective, the project objective statement should not go too deeply into the "how" of the project. For example, the NASA *moon shot project objective* in the 1960s and early 1970s was, *by the end of the decade, put a man on the moon and bring him back safely.* Note the objective did not include *use solid fuel booster rockets and a liquid fuel propulsion system.* At the outset of the project, details such as this one might overly constrain the team in developing the best feasible solution.[7] Exhibit 4.6 displays an adaptation of Hackman's insightful perspective on the specification of "what" versus "how."[8]

As the matrix in Exhibit 4.6 shows, teams fare best when they are given clear goals but asked to apply their own talents and skills to determine the best means by which to achieve those goals (the upper-right-hand cell). The organization's resources are squandered and team members' contributions devalued when talented people are given a specific objective but also told *how* they should go about achieving it (the bottom-right-hand cell). Failing to specify the intended goal leads either to chaos—unspecified activities with no particular objective—or worker turnoff—people are told what to do but do not know where they are headed. Much research has been conducted on the effect of goals on human motivation and performance, and Exhibit 4.7 summarizes the aspects relevant to project management.

Project Metrics

After a team has reviewed, revised, and agreed on the project objective statement, the next step is to understand how the success or failure of the project will be assessed. In other words, the team needs to appreciate how key stakeholders will evaluate project performance. Some preliminary ideas may have been presented in the business case and charter, but the team must develop metrics in more detail.

One useful process for developing metrics is *success visioning.* This involves asking the team to imagine the project has concluded and has been wildly successful. How would the team know the project had been successful? What specific measures would indicate project success to each of the project's key stakeholders?

It is important to think not only about project success measures, but also business success measures. Typically, we can measure *project* success soon after the completion of the project by assessing whether tasks were completed, and the extent to which they

[7] M. LaBrosse, *Accelerated Project Management* (New York: HNB Publishing, 2002).

[8] J.R. Hackman, *Leading Teams* (Boston: Harvard Business School Press, 2002).

EXHIBIT 4.7

The Contribution of Goal-Setting Research to Project Management

Research on goal setting has concluded that most of human behavior is the result of a person's consciously chosen goals and intentions. This helps explain the importance of a clear, unambiguous project objective.[*] In short, the vast research in this area confirms that goals increase individual,[†] group,[‡] and organizational performance.[§] Moreover, the research is "uniform in its verdict that difficult and specific goals will result in higher levels of performance than easy or vague, 'do your best' goals."[**] The research also indicates that for a goal to have a motivational effect, individuals must be committed to achieving it[††] and have the ability and knowledge needed to achieve it.[‡‡] The project manager can benefit from understanding and applying these concepts: Guide the team in planning the project, but don't dictate, up front, how the project will look.

[*]T. Mitchell and D. Daniels, "Motivation," in *Comprehensive Handbook of Psychology, Volume Twelve: Industrial and Organizational Psychology,* ed. W.C. Borman, D.R. Ilgen, and R.J. Klimoski (New York: Wiley and Sons, 2006); and G.P. Latham, *Work Motivation: History, Theory, Research and Practice* (Thousand Oaks, CA: Sage, 2006).
[†]E.A. Locke and G.P. Latham, *A Theory of Goal Setting and Task Performance* (Englewood Cliffs, NJ: Prentice Hall, 1990).
[‡]A.M. O'Leary-Kelly, J.J. Martocchio, and D.D. Frink, "A Review of the Influence of Group Goals on Group Performance," *Academy of Management Journal* 37, no. 5 (1994), pp. 1285–1301.
[§]K.R. Thompson, W.A. Hochwarter, and N.J. Mathys, "Stretch Targets: What Makes Them Effective?" *Academy of Management Executive* 11, no. 3 (1997), pp. 48–60.
[**]Latham, *Work Motivation: History, Theory, Research and Practice.*
[††]M.E. Tubbs, "Commitment and the Role of Ability in Motivation: Comment on Wright, O'Leary-Kelly, Cortina, Klein & Hollenbeck," *Journal of Applied Psychology* 79, no. 6 (1994), pp. 804–11.
[‡‡]E.A. Locke, "Motivation through Conscious Goal Setting," *Applied & Preventive Psychology* 5, no. 2 (1996), pp. 117–24.

were on time and within budget. Business success measures, however, will require a more extended time horizon. Exhibit 4.8 shows some project and business success measures for the Sapphire Medical Devices PMO project. These grew out of some of the team's initial meetings. Note that they add detail and modify the performance metrics identified in the charter.

EXHIBIT 4.8

Success Metrics for Sapphire Medical Devices PMO Project

Project Success Measures

- Project completed on time.
- Project completed within budget.
- Team members satisfied with project involvement.
- Team members' personal learning enhanced by project involvement.
- Team members able to maintain responsibilities in their functional areas and on other assigned projects.
- Project stakeholders express satisfaction with interim milestones and deliverables.
- All project deliverables completed and specifications met.
- Test runs, pilots, and focus group activities demonstrate that the PMO concept can improve project outcomes and address stakeholder concerns.

Business Success Measures (Assessed Two Years after Project Completion)

- Project managers and team members successfully use processes designed under the leadership of the PMO.
- Project management stakeholders express satisfaction with PM processes, based on surveys administered annually.
- Sapphire projects are completed, on average, + or − 10% within original budgets.
- Sapphire projects completed, on average, + or − 10% within original due date targets.
- Sapphire new products meet target market windows at least 90% of the time.

Having measures that reveal—at the end of the project—whether the project has been successful is certainly important. However, project leaders and team members also need interim measures that indicate how tasks are progressing. We noted earlier the importance of specific and challenging project goals. Research also suggests that for goal setting to influence performance, those pursing the goal need feedback that enables them to gauge their progress.[9] This is why a system of ongoing project metrics is so important.

Chapter 9, "Monitoring and Controlling Project Performance," explores more fully the choice of metrics and specific tracking and measurement systems. For now, it is important to understand that as the project begins, the team should identify a set of measures that will provide a balanced assessment of how the project is proceeding toward completion and what should be different (better) when it is finished.

Determining Project Scope, Boundaries, and Deliverables

A scope statement expands on the project objective statement by articulating, in finer detail, what will be done, by when, at what cost, and with what resources. The starting point for these last two is the budget and resources information found in the project charter. However, the core team should conduct more research and discuss the scope to be sure it is appropriate in light of new information, the chosen courses of action, and the measures by which project success will be judged. Exhibit 4.9 shows the statement of scope for the PMO project. Note that the scope statement is more detailed than the charter, and also that it incorporates some changes, which have been underlined as a way of emphasizing that they are new additions or modifications. For example, the team's research and analysis about the volume of projects at Sapphire has led team members to recommend eight project rooms instead of the six prescribed in the charter. (Of course, they will have to obtain approval for this and other changes.)

Notice in Exhibit 4.9 that the statement of scope also describes what is *not* in scope. This makes clear what the team does and does not consider part of the project. This can help reduce the likelihood the project will later become subject to *scope creep*, the tendency for a project to grow in size beyond its initially envisioned boundaries. As with any of the outcomes of the initiation phase, the project manager should confer with the project sponsor and other key stakeholders about perceptions of what is in and what is out of scope. These conversations should occur before any work begins.

One key output of deliberations around scope, boundaries, and deliverables should be a set of acceptance criteria that define the finished product. In fact, as we will discuss more fully in Chapter 10, "Finishing Well: Project Closure and Learning," one of the smartest things a project team can do at the outset of the project is to secure consensus about the completion criteria. What, from the customer's (and other key stakeholders') perspective, will signal that the project or a major deliverable is finished?

Identifying and Understanding Stakeholders

Formally defined, a stakeholder is anyone who participates in the project or who will be affected by the results of the project, and may include the project manager, the project team, managers at various levels, the project sponsor, the customer, and

[9] M. Erez, "Feedback: A Necessary Condition for the Goal Setting-Performance Relationship," *Journal of Applied Psychology* 62, no. 5 (1977), pp. 624–27.

EXHIBIT 4.9
PMO Project Scope Statement

(Underlined items signify changes from the original charter.)

Project Objective Statement: By June 15 of next year, we will have a corporate-level PMO in place, ready to sustain standard but adaptable processes for selecting, managing, and measuring projects; offer training; create avenues for best-practice sharing; maintain a repository of lessons learned; facilitate problem solving; encourage cooperation across projects; coordinate benchmarking partnerships with other project-driven companies; and facilitate communication for globally dispersed virtual teams.

Resources: $100,000 in outside costs, plus 10,000 hours of internal staff and management time.

Deliverables in Project Scope: (Expanded from the charter)

- A standard project management process design, with structured options for different types of projects.
- Reference manuals, including standard templates, documenting the standard project management process.
- Curriculum and materials for training programs to educate the organization on standard terminology and on shared project management processes.
- Initial training for all project managers, project team members, functional leaders, and staff support personnel.
- A designed, programmed, and tested Web platform to support and coordinate project activities across the company.
- Integrated project management software.
- A designed, tested, and implemented project measurement system.
- A knowledge-management system for capturing and disseminating lessons learned.
- Eight dedicated project conference rooms, designed, constructed, and furnished.
- Two projects piloted using the new system, with opportunity for correction and feedback before going live across the company.
- Interim reports to Victor Eusebio, the project sponsor.

Deliverables NOT in Scope:

- A new performance evaluation system.
- A new enterprise resource planning (ERP) system.
- Ongoing training after the initial programs have been completed.
- Ongoing maintenance of the knowledge-management system.
- Ongoing maintenance of the project management software.
- Ongoing maintenance and updating of the project Web site.
- Revisions to PMO reference manuals and templates.

---

other people and groups within and outside the organization. Customers are those who will use the final deliverable and, depending on the project, can be external or internal to the organization undertaking the project. Beyond customers, external stakeholders might also include shareholders, the community in which the organization operates, the organization's supplier base, and so forth. Most projects have multiple stakeholders, and they can have different, even competing, perspectives. Early in the initiation stage, the team should identify the key stakeholders and examine their needs in detail. We describe a process for stakeholder analysis in Exhibit 4.10.[10]

[10] K.A. Brown and N.L. Hyer, "Whole Brain Thinking for Project Management," *Business Horizons* 45, no. 3 (2002), pp. 47–57.

EXHIBIT 4.10
Stakeholder Analysis Process

1. Draw a template on a whiteboard similar to the one shown below.
2. Gather the team around the whiteboard with one person (who is a good listener) serving as the facilitator.
3. Identify the key stakeholders or stakeholder groups and record them in the left-hand column.
4. How do you think each stakeholder or stakeholder group feels about the project? Mark on their row using the letter "C" to denote "current perception."
5. Identify the level of support the project needs from each individual or group to ensure that the project will run smoothly. Mark this position on the chart with a "D" to denote "desired perception."
6. As a team, discuss what issues or concerns you think the individual or group might express about the proposed project. Record in the "Issues" column.
7. Discuss the kinds of communications and actions the team could undertake to gain support from stakeholder groups with gaps between current and desired attitudes. Record in the "Ideas" column.
8. Keep these in mind as you develop the communication plan (discussed next) and work breakdown structure (discussed in Chapter 5) for the project.

Stakeholder Matrix

Stakeholder	Range of Support					Issues	Ideas
	Strongly Against	Mildly Against	Neutral	Mildly Supportive	Strongly Supportive		
Experienced project managers who are responsible for large, relatively autonomous projects	C				D	They have their own processes and don't want to reinvent something that is working well for them.	Seek their input and attempt to incorporate their best practices into standard procedures.
Managers of small projects		C	D			May find standard procedures too cumbersome and overkill for small projects.	Build in flexibility by creating decision rules for when scaled down procedures may be a better fit.
Project team members			C		D	May feel exposed when their performance is measured using standardized accountability methods.	Find ways to make sure the measurement system is used as a team problem-solving tool and not as a basis for evaluating individual performance.

C = current perception
D = desired perception

In facilitating a stakeholder analysis such as the one summarized in Exhibit 4.10, a team leader should ask team members to imagine themselves in the shoes of the stakeholders whose needs and concerns are being discussed. Doing so permits the team to take preemptive action by anticipating stakeholder concerns and addressing them before they arise. This proactive approach can result in stakeholders who are more satisfied with both the project outcome and project process, and it can turn potential foes into allies. A note of caution: The result of this analysis probably is best kept within the team. Making it public could raise concerns among stakeholders that they are being manipulated, even though this should not be the intent.

THE PROJECT COMMUNICATION PLAN

Continuous, effective communication is a defining characteristic of most successful projects. As part of the project initiation process, the core project team should develop a communication plan to get the right information to the right audience, at the right time, and via the most appropriate medium.

Two primary categories of project communication are (1) communication with key project stakeholders, and (2) communication within the project team. For key stakeholders, the team should seek answers to these questions: Who needs information about the project? What information do they need? How frequently do they need this information? What medium (or media) would convey the message most effectively to this particular audience? The stakeholder analysis conducted earlier is a key input to the communication plan. An effective way to organize ideas for communicating with key stakeholders is to create a communication matrix for each stakeholder group. Exhibit 4.11 shows an example. Notice that as part of the matrix, the team determines who will actually be responsible for creating and executing the communication.

Individuals have different styles and preferences when it comes to communication. If a key stakeholder for a lean-manufacturing initiative is a 30-year machine-shop

EXHIBIT 4.11

Sample Stakeholder Communication Matrix

Project Management Office Project at Sapphire Medical Instruments			
Stakeholder	**What Does This Person or Group Need?**	**Frequency of Communication**	**Medium**
Victor Eusebio, president and project sponsor	High-level information about the project progress, the budget, and schedule. Knowledge of any issues, problems and their proposed solutions that may require his authorization or intervention to resolve.	Every other week & monthly	E-mail for biweekly updates (the man lives on e-mail) with high-level bullet points; concise! Monthly, face-to-face meeting with project manager, Barbara. Provide written text to accompany the meeting.
Responsible for creating this communication: Project Manager Barbara Tyndall, with input from team.		Person responsible for sending this communication: Project Manager Barbara Tyndall	

EXHIBIT 4.12
The Distribution List
That Fills the Screen.
DELETE!

Delete

Have you ever received a project progress report or announcement that is sent to so many people the distribution list is one or two screens long and you have to scroll down to find the actual message? What is the chance you will read this report? It is highly likely you will hit the delete button before you even bother to scroll down. Why? Because you assume any message addressed to that many people must not be very important. Many project managers make the mistake of believing they have a communication plan if they send out mass e-mails to all possible stakeholders and beyond. When they learn people are uninformed about their projects, these project managers are shocked: "I sent out an e-mail!"

Remember this: Each stakeholder or stakeholder group has specialized needs for detail, frequency of reporting, and type of communication. And, most importantly, a stakeholder wants to be acknowledged.

veteran who shuns computers, sending him e-mail updates on project progress is probably *not* a good way of communicating. Tailor the format and content to the intended recipient. A one-size-fits-all stakeholder communication solution likely will be ineffective. (See Exhibit 4.12 for an example.) Although much of the stakeholder communication (e.g., sending status update e-mails) frequently is handled by the project manager, team members may be responsible for communicating project progress to their home departments. However, for communication with the customer and other key stakeholders, it is generally best to have one point of contact from the project team.[11]

The second dimension of communication planning focuses on interactions within the team. When team members are located within geographic proximity, the primary vehicle for most formal team communication is the project status meeting. The appropriate frequency for project status meetings is driven by the project itself. Too many meetings are a bad thing. (We know of one project manager at a Fortune 500 company who insisted on a daily, four-hour meeting for a project team. When did they get any work done?) However, meetings that occur with an appropriate degree of frequency will allow the team to uncover and fix small problems before they become big problems. For short-duration, high-intensity projects, it may be useful to have morning "traffic meetings" in which team members quickly report on the prior day's activities. Some organizations run these as stand-up meetings to encourage brevity and parsimonious presentation of key information.

Project meetings should not come as a surprise to team members unless there is a true emergency. Thus, during the initiation phase, the team should agree on how often, when, and where it will meet. This sets up a commitment and also allows team members to see how the project will fit with their other responsibilities. In addition to attending and participating in status meetings, team members also should be expected to submit progress reports on their assigned tasks. This is something else the team can establish during the initiation phase. If people know ahead of time when and what they are expected to report, they will be less likely to view requests for such information as micromanagement or believe the project manager is singling them out. Moreover, if they have input during the development of the status-reporting plan, they will feel a greater sense of ownership and commitment to using it. Exhibit 4.13 provides an example of a status report agreement.

[11] CH2M Hill, *Project Delivery System* (Denver, CO: CH2M Hill, 2001).

EXHIBIT 4.13   **Sample Status Report Agreement**

Type of Status Report	Contents of the Report	Frequency	Format
Weekly project progress reports prepared by each team member and submitted to the project manager.	• Major accomplishments, issues resolved, and decisions since last report. • Activities behind schedule, why, and plans for addressing behind-schedule activities. • Activities ahead of schedule and plans for moving subsequent activities forward. • Issues—problems that cannot be resolved immediately—identified since last report and plans for responding. • Potential problems on the horizon. • New risks or opportunities identified. • Help or assistance needed from others.	Weekly: submit to project manager by noon on Friday.	Word attachment to e-mail using the "Team Reporting Template"

As part of project initiation, the team should agree on a standard format for status reports that specifies both the structure and content of the update. Agreeing on a standard reporting format offers the advantage of establishing a reporting culture early in the project. It also ensures only value-added information is reported, makes the reports simple and easy to complete, keeps people focused on the essential information, prevents key points from being lost in mountains of extraneous communication, and makes the various status reports easy to consolidate. Exhibit 4.14 shows an example of a standard template.

EXHIBIT 4.14

Sample Team Reporting Template

Team Member Name:	Date:
Project Name:	
Project Manager:	
Major project accomplishments since last status report: • •	
Major decisions reached since the last status report: • •	

Activities behind or ahead of schedule and why: 1. 2.	Plan for getting activities back on track or adjusting schedules: 1. 2.
Issues encountered since last status report: 1. 2.	Plan for responding to these issues: 1. 2.

Potential problems on the horizon: • •
New risks or opportunities identified: • •
Input or assistance needed from others: • •

THE PROJECT TEAM

We considered calling this section "selecting your team." However, few project managers have the luxury of assigning whomever they wish to their projects. If you are fortunate, whoever has chartered the project and assigned you as project manager will seek your input and use his or her authority to secure your first-choice project team members. However, it is more common for the project manager to be in a position of negotiating (or begging) for team members. Although the persuasion and negotiating skills addressed in Chapter 2 are important, if the project manager has a charter legitimizing the project and encouraging stakeholders to support it, he or she will be in a stronger position to ask for resources. Regardless of how team members are selected, keep in mind the following points about team composition:

Knowledge and Technical Requirements

The project manager should begin by assessing the knowledge and technical requirements likely to be associated with the project work and advocate for (or select, if he or she is fortunate) individuals who, collectively, have the skills needed. A study by Ericksen and Dyer showed that high-performing teams selected team members based on competency, assuring that needed skills, experiences, and knowledge sets were present among the team members.[12] Low-performing teams selected team members perceived to have influence in "representing the interests of their units during the teams' deliberations and in promoting support and acceptance for the team's final products or solutions."[13] Although departmental representation is certainly important, a representative team that does not have the skills and knowledge needed to complete project tasks will accomplish little.

Exhibit 4.15 shows a portion of a matrix the PMO project manager used as a framework for considering the skills and team members needed for the project.

[12] Ericksen and Dyer, "Right from the Start: Exploring the Effects of Early Team Events on Subsequent Project Team Performance."
[13] Ibid., p. 450.

EXHIBIT 4.15

Assessing Team Skill Needs—Sapphire PMO Project Skill Requirements

Major Project Deliverable	Skills Required	Suggested Team Members
A standard project management process design		
Reference manuals, including standard templates, documenting the standard project management process		
Curriculum and materials for training programs to educate the organization on the standard project management process		
Web site to support and coordinate project activities across the company		
Integrated project management software		
A project measurement system		
A system for capturing and disseminating lessons learned		
Space design for eight project rooms		

Team Member Representation

Although the right skill mix is critical, the team should be representative of the areas that have a strong, vested interest in the project. Overlooking a key stakeholder group may lead to unpleasant surprises later. For example, the manager of the subassembly area of an electronics plant launched a project to redesign the way assembly occurred. No one from the inventory stores and material delivery group was included on the team. The project team came up with a "great" solution that optimized the flow of material within the area, but placed a huge burden on inventory stores and material delivery personnel. In fact, the overhead costs of the additional material personnel required to support the new design would more than offset any savings from the more efficient subassembly operation itself. Once the oversight was discovered, a material stores person was added to the team and the project was relaunched.

Working Together

A third criterion to consider is the ability of team members to work together. If Michael and Dale have a long work history of serious conflict, it may be best to avoid having both of them on the project team. However, if Michael and Dale possess unique skill sets needed for the project, they both belong on the project team. Plus, as we pointed out in Chapter 2, conflict, if appropriately managed, can make a positive contribution to team performance. The diversity of views, backgrounds, expertise, and perspectives helps explain why teams often are able to develop better solutions faster, than individuals working separately.

Team Size

Although there is no one optimal team size for all circumstances, laboratory research has found that when group size exceeds five, decision quality deteriorates.[14] Other investigations suggest that when team size exceeds 10 people, task groups become less effective.[15] As group size increases, communication, group cohesiveness, and job satisfaction may decline, and social loafing, absenteeism, and turnover are likely to increase.

For project teams, increased team size strongly affects communication. If there are four team members and every team member needs to speak with every other team member, there will be six two-way exchanges. If one team member is added, the number of two-way exchanges increases, not to seven, but to 10. And if a sixth team member is added, the number of two-way pairings jumps to 15! The mathematics here are that for every n members there are $(n \times (n - 1))/2$ two-way communication channels. So increasing the number of team members exponentially increases the communication effort required to keep team members informed.

Team size may not be constant throughout the life of the project. Individuals may rotate onto the team when their skills sets or contributions are needed, and then rotate off when their work is complete. Most teams, however, will have a core set of members who are with the project from start to finish. As suggested above, communication is less challenging and group dynamics are easier to manage if this core team is kept to a reasonable size.

---

[14] P. Yetton and P. Bottger, "The Relationship among Group Size, Member Abilities, Social Decisions Schemes and Performance," *Organization Behavior and Human Performance* 32, no. 2 (1983), pp. 145–59.

[15] R.L. Moreland and J.M. Levine, "The Composition of Small Groups," *Advances in Group Processes,* vol. 9 (Greenwich, CT: JAI Press, 1992), pp. 237–80.

Time Available

An additional consideration in team selection is the time people have available to devote to the project. A team can have the most talented, representative group of individuals, but if the project represents an overload for each team member, the project is unlikely to get the attention it deserves. For example, one study showed that low-performing teams had a higher average percentage of team members who were assigned to the project on an overtime basis (75 percent), than high-performing teams (42 percent). "The biggest problem is our inordinate workload and this was just another thing to do," observed one team member from a low-performing team.[16] When thinking through staffing decisions, be aware of the time team members will have available for the project.

The Team: Co-Located or Virtual?

In terms of physical proximity of team members, projects come in many configurations. At one extreme is the situation where project team members are physically co-located: Their actual work spaces are arranged so all team members work alongside one another on a daily basis. Such an arrangement generally happens only when team members are dedicated 100 percent to a given project and there is a high need for ongoing information exchange and collaboration that can best be accomplished face-to-face. As people, their work, and any project-related equipment move closer together, there is increased potential for continuous, natural communication among project team members. Information sharing will be an outgrowth of this phenomenon, and team members are more likely to be aware of activity status, problems, emerging risks, current issues, and other key performance factors if they are near each other. This position is supported by the classic work of Allen, who demonstrated in an R&D setting that people essentially stopped communicating with each other if their work spaces were farther than 10 meters apart.[17]

Despite the advantages of co-location, most project teams do not enjoy this luxury. This could be because of geographic dispersion of team members or because team members are working on other projects or routine work responsibilities that also require their physical presence. For example, it would be tough to be co-located with your teammates on the companywide ERP project, based at corporate headquarters in Denver, when you also run the company's European distribution center in Prague. Increasing numbers of organizations are using virtual teams for globally dispersed projects. Numerous communication and management challenges, many linked to cultural differences, have arisen as these types of teams become more prevalent.[18]

Several information technology tools can help project teams overcome the challenges inherent when people cannot meet face-to-face on a regular basis. Exhibit 4.16 provides URLs and a brief description of several Internet resources that can be helpful to teams that need to collaborate electronically.

---

[16] Ericksen and Dyer, "Right from the Start: Exploring the Effects of Early Team Events on Subsequent Project Team Performance," p. 453.

[17] T.J. Allen, *Managing the Flow of Technology* (Cambridge, MA: MIT Press, 1977).

[18] A. Malhotra, A. Majchrzak, and B. Rosen, "Leading Virtual Teams," *Academy of Management Perspectives* 21, no. 1 (2007), pp. 60–70; and G.A. Fowler, "For Asia-Based Staff the Typical Workday Lasts about 24 Hours," *The Wall Street Journal,* August 22, 2006, p. B1.

EXHIBIT 4.16
Internet Resources for Virtual Teams

- Discussion Web [http://dweb.waikato.ac.nz/dw/] a Windows/NT-based Web group discussion product.
- Global Chat [www.globalchat.com/help/mac/gcmac-netscape.1.0.html] provides information on configuring Netscape Navigator for chatting.
- Interaction/IP [http://interaction.in-progress.com/] is a Macintosh-based Web conferencing tool supporting threaded discussion forums and customizable chat rooms.
- Meetingworks [www.meetingworks.com] allows a virtual team to brainstorm and vote on priorities online.

When a project team is composed of team members who will work virtually, gathering the team physically together to engage in a formal project launch can pay huge benefits. A well-planned and executed project launch, with all team members physically present, can create a solid platform for the virtual project work that follows.[19] Team members, who may not know one another, will establish rapport that can be the basis for effective working relationships. However, this may not be possible in all cases.

WHERE AND HOW DOES THE TEAM FIT WITHIN THE ORGANIZATION STRUCTURE?[20]

As part of the chartering process, the team and project manager must establish how they fit within the larger structure of the organization. Additionally, they must consider how informal structures will interact with their efforts. These relationships will determine the authority of the project manager, the nature of the work assignments for team members (e.g., full or part time), how performance will be reviewed, how decisions will be made, and where there will be links with entities outside the boundaries of the organization (e.g., customers, contractors, governmental agencies). Many project managers have faltered because they failed to understand these contextual matters. For example, the leader of a software engineering project mistakenly assumed she had full authority to make major architecture decisions, only to learn several months into the project that she and her team had violated standards set within a functional area. The team had to re-start the project under the scrutiny of an untrusting functional manager. In another example, the leader of a project team involved in a new product launch was unaware of his role in managing the relationship with an advertising firm contracted to perform part of the work. Inattention to the outside firm's work resulted in an advertising strategy that did not match overall launch strategy. In the paragraphs below we describe several structural forms and how projects operate within them.

Functional Organization Structures

Many startup companies begin with a tightly knit team of co-located team members (think Hewlett and Packard tinkering in a garage or Gates and Allen developing hardware and software in a room in Gates' parents' home). As they grow in size, most ultimately split into functions such as engineering, operations, marketing, human

[19] Eriksen and Dyer, "Right from the Start: Exploring the Effects of Early Team Events on Subsequent Project Team Performance."

[20] Concepts from this section were drawn from *A Guide to the Project Management Body of Knowledge (PMBoK)*; N. Nohira, *Note on Organization Structure* (Harvard Business School Press, 1995); S.C. Wheelwright and K.B. Clark, "Organizing and Leading 'Heavyweight' Development Teams," *California Management Review* 34, no. 3 (1992), pp 9–28.

EXHIBIT 4.17
Functional Organization Structure

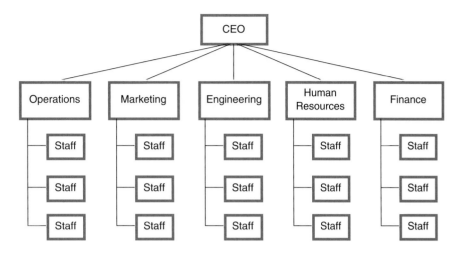

resources, and finance (clearly, every organization will have its unique set of functions). An example of a **functional structure** is displayed in Exhibit 4.17.

In a traditional functional organization, many local projects operate within the domain of a single department. For example, a process improvement project within the operations function could be conceived and completed without involvement of the other functions. (However, it is likely that important interfaces with other departments might be ignored under such a scenario.) Other types of projects requiring more cross-functional involvement are often run in phases as they move through the functions. For example, imagine a product development initiative in which the marketing department is responsible for identifying a customer need based on a market research subproject. When its work is completed, the marketing department sends its findings to the engineering department where the design phase takes place. The process continues as the project makes its way through operations, finance, and other departments. Each function brings its expertise to bear on the final project outcome. Although it might sound reasonable in theory, this approach can lead to suboptimal solutions because each function must either make do with what it is handed by working around problems, or send the project back to a previous function for revision, thereby increasing project cost and duration. Because there is little or no cross-functional input during the initiation and definition stages, people often refer to this approach as "throwing it over the wall." No one is really attending to the big picture.

In spite of its limitations in project environments, the functional form offers the advantages of maintaining technical expertise and economies of scale. It tends to work well in stable conditions where most work is routine and there are not large numbers of broad-reaching projects. Projects to upgrade existing departmental software or shorten manufacturing lead times are examples.

Projectized[21] Organization Structure

At the other extreme from the functional structure is a form in which an organization is built almost entirely around individual projects. A central core serves as the coordinating hub, but the rest of the organization is focused full time on various projects. A graphic representation of a **projectized structure** is displayed in Exhibit 4-18.

---

[21] Although this term causes us to grit our teeth from a grammatical point of view, it appears to have entered the lexicon of project management, as evidenced by its use in PMI's *A Guide to the Project Management Body of Knowledge.*

EXHIBIT 4.18
Projectized Organization Structure

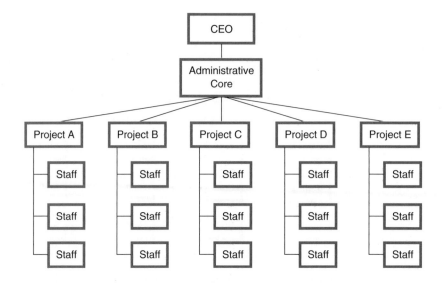

A project structure is characteristic of organizations involved in major engineering or consulting projects. Examples include NASA, Bechtel, and Bain and Company. People in these kinds of organizations are assigned for months or up to several years to work on major projects—constructing a dam, building a space station, installing a globally-networked ERP system, or constructing a shipping canal. A project form requires a high degree of fluidity because people must be moved to new projects (or leave the organization) when projects end. It also can require the organization to maintain excess human capacity in order to respond to changing needs. The upside is that people are generally assigned full time to a project, enabling them to focus. Teams are necessarily cross-functional, and decision authority is clear. The result can be a higher quality outcome than the project might have produced under a "throw it over the wall" scenario.

Although the project form offers advantages, it would be impractical for most organizations to operate completely this way. First, it can be challenging to continuously move people from one project to another. Second, if the organization has a high percentage of routine work, a functional form might be a more efficient way to deliver it.

Hybrid Structural Forms

The pure forms of functional and project structures represent two conceptual extremes that are rarely found in the real world. This is because most organizations have found it practical to blend them to meet the combined needs of projects and routine work. We highlight three possible hybrid forms—matrix, composite, and networked—below.

Matrix Organization

A **matrix organization** combines forms in a way that allows functions to exist on the vertical dimension of the organization chart, with projects running on the horizontal dimension. Team members can be assigned full or part time to projects, which generally span multiple departments. However, they still have their functional homes, allowing them to stay abreast of technical developments within their specialties and maintain relationships important to career development. Matrix forms have been described as **strong** or **heavyweight** when project managers enjoy a level of authority similar to that of functional managers. They are considered **weak** or **lightweight** when project managers carry more of a coordination role than a leadership role, and when they have

EXHIBIT 4.19   **Matrix Organization Form**

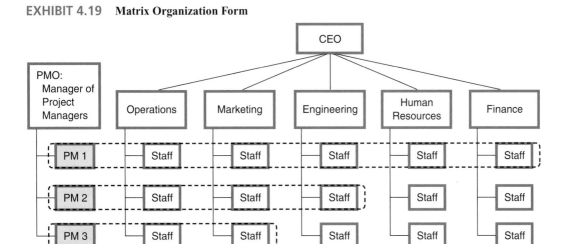

limited (or no) formal authority. A **balanced matrix** falls somewhere in the middle. An image of a matrix form is displayed in Exhibit 4.19.

The matrix example in Exhibit 4.19 shows project managers reporting to a manager of project managers who is the head of the PMO. This leadership position has authority equivalent to that of a functional head, giving him or her authority to request resources and discuss the relative priorities of various projects in the organization's portfolio. In other matrix forms, project managers might not report through a PMO but, instead, report within their functions or to an executive group under the CEO.

Matrix organizations offer the advantage of flexibility in resource allocation and have the potential to give project managers more clout than they would have in a traditional functional structure. However, they present some challenges. For example, unless clearly specified, there can be conflicts over who is responsible for evaluating the performance of team members who are permanently assigned to a function but have considerable responsibility to a project manager over an extended period of time.

Composite Organization Structure

Few organizations can be classified as purely functional, purely projectized, or purely matrix. Most organizations of any reasonable size represent a **composite.** Some projects operate within departments. Others, such as task forces, operate across functions and part time for limited durations. They are coordinated by a project manager who has limited authority. Projects representing major new business ventures might be run as entirely autonomous entities, or with limited affiliation with the organization's functions. An example of a composite form is shown in Exhibit 4.20.

Networked Organization Form

An emerging view of organization structures takes a more fluid and boundary-spanning perspective. It is built on the idea that project teams exist at the intersection of formal and informal structures, and that they often involve entities such as suppliers and contractors outside the organization. Project teams can take on many forms within a **networked** structure. Some projects are performed entirely by subcontractors who are coordinated by a single project manager or core team. Others operate within functions but rely on informal relationships with people in other functional areas.

EXHIBIT 4.20
Composite Form:
Functional,
Projectized, and
Matrix Combined

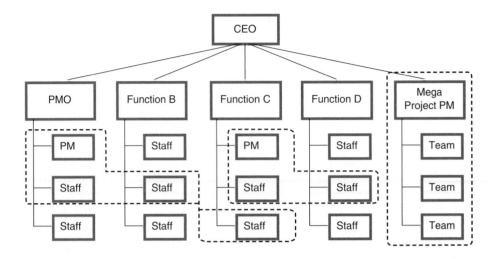

It is essential for the project manager and team to understand how they intersect with the larger organization. Although this is an important part of the chartering process at the beginning of the project, it is possible these relationships will change as the project moves forward. Each organization attaches its own terminology to what it views as its structure, so the terms are not as important as an understanding of who makes decisions, the nature of the team assignment, and how and by whom the team and project manager will be evaluated. The formal structure tells the project manager only part of the story. As you might have observed through your own experience, the most effective project managers are skillful in understanding and navigating the informal structures within the organization.

BEYOND THE CORE TEAM: UNDERSTANDING CONTRACTUAL RELATIONSHIPS

As was suggested in the section on organization structure, sometimes project teams extend beyond the boundaries of the organization to include outside individuals and entities. This creates the need to establish contractual agreements. At the beginning of this chapter, we described how EDS lost millions of dollars on a fixed-price contract project for the Navy. When costs to deliver the required work exceeded what EDS planned to spend, the company had little recourse. Had EDS negotiated what is called a "cost-reimbursement" contract, it may have fared better. Under such an arrangement, EDS would have billed the Navy for actual costs, plus a reasonable allowance for profit. A cost-reimbursement contract would have permitted EDS to bill the Navy for the hours required to migrate 67,000 computer programs to the new system. However, the fixed-price arrangement for the project, which was based on the cost of migrating 5,000 programs, meant EDS had to absorb the extra costs associated with migrating the 62,000 "extra" programs.

Fixed-price contracts are, in general, low risk for customers (they know in advance exactly what they will be charged for the work). These contracts tend to be higher risk for the supplier, who will bear the burden of any higher than anticipated costs. For the supplier, the key to an effective fixed-cost contract is accurate cost estimating. Or as the vice president of a global construction firm commented: "We live and die by our estimates." These types of contracts make sense when the work to be undertaken is very specific, well-defined, and involves little risk.

Cost-reimbursement contracts present just the opposite risk profile. Here, the customer bears most of the risk. If your home is being built on a cost-reimbursement contract and the foundation takes twice as many worker hours to pour than anticipated, you, not the contractor, will bear the additional labor cost. A cost-reimbursement contract is relatively low risk for the contractor because all costs are covered. However, a huge cost overrun is likely to damage the contractor's reputation (and discourage future business with this and other customers), so the cost-reimbursement contract is not a *carte blanche* to spend wildly. When cost-reimbursement contracts are used, customers will often require careful accounting throughout the project, including determining revised "cost at completion" estimates at various points. Customers may then make informed decisions about changing the requirements, adjusting timetables, or even abandoning the project if the cost becomes prohibitive.

As part of project initiation, the project team should review contractual relationships associated with the project. For example, if the project is being completed for an external customer, the team will want to know whether this is a cost-reimbursement or a fixed-price arrangement. This information helps inform decisions about resources and spending. Exhibit 4.21 lists specific elements you should consider if you are expected to form contractual relationships in support of your project. If this area is of interest to you and important for the types of projects you likely will manage, we suggest that you consult the references noted at the bottom of the exhibit.

EXHIBIT 4.21
Factors to Consider in a Project Contract

Factor	Options
Contract Structure	**Fixed price (also known as a lump-sum contract)** • Pay a given amount for a specific deliverable. **Cost reimbursement** • Pay for costs incurred in generating a specific deliverable, plus an allowance for profit.
Payment Schedule	**Progress payments** • Payment for work as it is completed (e.g., when a deliverable is 50% complete, 50% of the payment is made). **Time-based payments** • Payment is set to occur on specific dates.
Penalties and Incentives	**Delivery-based penalties and incentives** • Payment is reduced according to how late a particular deliverable is completed. • Cash incentives are paid for adherence to the schedule or for early completion. **Performance-based penalties and incentives** • Payment is reduced if a particular deliverable does not perform as expected. • Cash incentives are paid if deliverables meet or exceed a particular performance standard. • A portion of the revenue generated by the deliverable is shared with the contractor.

To learn more about contracting, see: Y. Chen and J. Davidson Frame, *Principles of Contracting for Project Management,* 2nd ed. (Arlington, VA: UMT Press, 2006); and H. Kerzner, *Project Management: A Systems Approach to Planning, Scheduling, and Controlling* (New York: Wiley and Sons, 2005), pp. 803–30.

FROM PROJECT CHARTER TO PROJECT INITIATION DOCUMENT

Earlier in this chapter, we introduced the project charter. Although some organizations routinely issue detailed charters for important projects, there will be many cases in which a project manager must create a charter, get it approved by the sponsor, and distribute it to those in the organization who need to know about the project. Once the project team has been selected and has worked through all the initiation elements described in this chapter, the team can expand the original charter to create a project initiation document (see Exhibit 4.22 for an example.) Copies of the document can be posted in the team's meeting area and distributed electronically or physically to team members. It will become part of the permanent project file. Some project managers find it helpful to condense the project initiation document to a single two-sided sheet, which they then laminate and distribute to team members to

EXHIBIT 4.22   Project Initiation Document

Project Name: Sapphire Project Management Office (PMO)

Project Manager: Barb Tyndal 3-3530 (btyndal@smd.com)

Project Sponsor: Victor Eusebio, president

Project Team Members (with phone and email):

Julianne Ross (0-9984) jross@smd.com   Ginny Coburn (2-7785) gcoburn@smd.com

Dave Onski (3-5579) donski@smd.com   Vic Melina (3-4783) vmelina@smd.com

Project Purpose: To improve project selection, management, and learning on a corporate-wide basis.

Expected Business Results: Ability to complete projects on time, within budget, and with excellent technical results. Doing so will grow the business, satisfy customers, and improve profitability.

Project Objective Statement: Within 12 months create a corporate-level PMO. This includes developing and documenting standard but adaptable processes for selecting, managing, and measuring projects, sharing best-practices, facilitating problem solving, and encouraging cooperation across projects. Creation of the PMO also includes designing a standard but adaptable curriculum to support project management education, consistent with the organization's project management process. Spend no more than $100,000 in outside costs, plus 10,000 hours of team, support staff, and management time (note: these were revised from the project charter, and approved).

Project Start: First team meeting   **Project End:** Sponsor and key stakeholder signoff on deliverables

Project Success Measures	Business Success Measures (To Be Assessed Two Years after Project Completion)
• Project completed on time. • Project completed within budget. • Team members satisfied with project involvement. • Team members' personal learning enhanced by project involvement. • Team members able to maintain responsibilities in their functional areas and on other assigned projects. • Project stakeholders express satisfaction with interim milestones and deliverables. • All project deliverables completed and specifications met. • Test runs, pilots, and focus group activities demonstrate that the PMO concept can improve project outcomes and address stakeholder concerns.	• Project managers and team members successfully use processes designed under the leadership of the PMO. • Project management stakeholders express satisfaction with PM processes, based on surveys administered annually. • Sapphire projects completed, on average, + or − 10% within original budgets. • Sapphire projects completed, on average, + or − 10% within original due date targets. • Sapphire new products meet target market windows at least 90% of the time.

Deliverables in Scope: (Expanded from the Charter)	Deliverables NOT in Scope:
• A standard project management process design, with structured options for different types of projects. • Reference manuals, including standard templates, documenting the standard project management process. • Curriculum and materials for training programs to educate the organization on standard terminology and on shared project management processes. • Initial training for all project managers, project team members, functional leaders, and staff support personnel. • A designed, programmed, and tested Web platform to support and coordinate project activities across the company. • Integrated project management software. • A designed, tested and implemented project measurement system. • A knowledge-management system for capturing and disseminating lessons learned. • Eight dedicated project conference rooms, designed, constructed, and furnished. • Two projects piloted using the new system, with opportunity for correction and feedback before going live across the company. • Interim reports to Victor Eusebio, the project sponsor.	• A new performance evaluation system. • A new Enterprise Resource Planning (ERP) system. • Ongoing training after the initial programs have been completed. • Ongoing maintenance of the knowledge-management system. • Ongoing maintenance of the project management software. Ongoing maintenance and updating of the project Web site. • Revisions to PMO reference manuals and templates. **Communication Plan (Team):** • E-mail status reports due to Barb every Friday by noon. • Team status meetings Mondays at 2:00, Room 4US **Contracting Plan:** Most work will be accomplished using company resources, but the Web platform design and implementation will be outsourced.

post in their individual work spaces. The document can offer a fast and easy way to explain the project to those unfamiliar with it, and it serves as a backdrop to the team's future work.

Chapter Summary and Onward

A project may begin with a formal charter or with less definition. When there is no charter, the project manager should ask a set of questions about the project's purpose and parameters, with a goal of creating a charter for approval by the sponsor. At this point, the project is ready for launch, and the project manager can initiate the project with a team kickoff meeting. During one or several meetings early in the initiation process, and with the support of background research efforts, the team expands and revises the charter to more fully develop project parameters and create a project initiation document. If this document differs in substance from the charter, the team will need approval from the sponsor before it proceeds. Project launch activities also include clarifying and gaining an understanding of who will be on the team, where team members will be located, how the project links with the organization's structure, and the nature of external contracting needs.

Initiation is a critical phase in the life of the project because everything that follows depends on it. Armed with a well-initiated project, the team is ready to move to the next phase of the project, project planning, covered in several upcoming chapters.

Team Activities

1. Assume you and three classmates work for the same small electronics organization. The four of you have just been asked by your division manager, Noah Tolk, to organize a two-day off-site year-in-review and "what's next" management retreat. The division manager has explained that he hopes the retreat will *(a)* provide an opportunity to celebrate recent accomplishments, *(b)* enhance community and interdepartmental cooperation within the organization, *(c)* provide time and space, without distraction, to focus on big-picture issues facing the organization, and *(d)* increase managers' ideas about, understanding of, and buy-in to a set of strategic initiatives for the coming year. Noah is concerned that a lack of interdepartmental cooperation and understanding is causing delays in customer service, compromising the organization's ability to get new products to market, and, in general, limiting the organization's performance. Approximately 25 managers will attend the retreat, which is to be held within driving distance of the company offices.

   Noah has asked that the program be organized so there are sessions/activities devoted to: (1) highlighting key accomplishments of each area, (2) gathering input to shape next year's divisional strategic initiatives, and (3) informal team building and energizing the team for the year ahead. The retreat should take place sometime in the next three months. Resources allocated to the retreat include: $15,000 to pay for facilities, materials and services, two hours per week per project team member and 20 total hours of an administrative assistant's time. Noah would like to see a draft plan for the retreat in four weeks and would like a written post-project report two weeks after the retreat. That report should briefly describe the retreat itself and the project that created it. Working with your team,

   a. Prepare a project charter for the two-day retreat project. Be sure the charter covers these elements: project name, project purpose, expected business impact, project objective, project sponsor, project manager (one of you should be named project manager), project stakeholders, preliminary list of deliverables, preliminary budget, preliminary completion date, and a note from Noah Tolk. Use the information presented above, but apply your own creativity as well.

   b. Based on what you know and what you infer from the information provided, develop a fishbone diagram which captures information about the factors motivating the project (i.e., the project drivers) (see Exhibit 3.3 for an example).

   c. Jointly develop an objective statement for the retreat project. Assess your statement against the criteria offered in the chapter. In other words is the statement shared, short, simple, specific, measurable, and time constrained? How could any deficiencies you identified be overcome?

   d. Imagine it is a week after the retreat, and the event has been judged a success. Your team is having a little celebration over bagels and coffee. Everyone on the team is pleased with how successful the retreat had been. How would you know the event had been successful? More specifically, with your team develop a set of project success measures that will assess the success of the retreat project from the perspective of key stakeholder groups.

   e. Determine a set of measures for assessing the degree to which the project is successful with respect to the intended impact on the business. Consider short-term and longer-term outcomes.

2. Find and read G. Kahn's "Crying Wolf about the 'Big One' Hasn't Worked, so Let's Party," *The Wall Street Journal,* November 11, 2008, p. A1. While you are reading

the article, consider the following assignment and be prepared to work with your team to discuss the scenario and prepare a report:

a. What do you believe are the reasons previous efforts to initiate earthquake awareness events have failed in the United States? In formulating your response, consider advice on project initiation presented in this chapter.

b. As a team, select an earthquake-prone part of the world that interests you. Possibilities include, but are not limited to, the west coast of the United States, eastern Brazil, Japan, central China, Tibet, India, South Africa, the Philippines, Russia, and Italy. Imagine that you have been assigned the task of creating an Earthquake Awareness Day in a major city within the region you have chosen. Use Internet sources to become somewhat familiar with earthquake history and risks in this city.

c. Prepare a project charter for your Earthquake Awareness Day. You will establish all of the parameters, including purpose, expected results, objective, sponsor, project manager, project stakeholders, deliverables, preliminary budget, preliminary completion date, and a letter of your own creation from the mayor of your chosen city, who will be the project sponsor. (You will need to do the appropriate research to determine the actual name of the mayor in the city you choose.) The assigned article should give you some ideas about content.

3. Work with a team of up to five people. Find an Internet-based virtual team collaboration tool such as Meetingworks (www.meetingworks.com) and download the free software available. Alternatively, you may select another collaboration tool that offers free trial software or that is available through your school. Using the sources, information, and assignment for activity 2 above, and working from remote locations, develop a project charter for an Earthquake Awareness Day in a city of your team's choice.

a. Create a sharable word-processing document and prepare a project charter based on the brainstorming and online discussion you conducted using the collaboration software.

b. Submit your project charter to the instructor electronically, along with a one-page discussion of the advantages and challenges you discovered when collaborating online. What lessons did you learn about virtual teamwork that you can apply in the future?

Discussion Questions and Exercises

1. Why is it necessary for the project team to revisit questions that were answered in the business case when developing the project initiation document? Use your own examples to illustrate your response.

2. Who is the project sponsor and why is this role important to the project manager? Create an example to explain your answer.

3. What does the term "YB4What" imply and why is it important in project management? Use an example of your own creation to illustrate your position.

4. What is the ideal team size for project planning? What is likely to happen if the team is much larger or much smaller than the ideal?

5. What role does goal setting play in project initiation? Why is it important? Offer an example from your own experience or observation to make your case.

6. What are the two major types of contracts and what are their advantages and disadvantages? Offer examples beyond those presented in the chapter to support your answer.

7. You have been assigned the role of project manager for a major company initiative to implement a new customer relationship management (CRM) IT module for your company, Wolford Technologies, which produces radio-frequency identification (RFID) hardware and software for consumer electronics manufacturers and

retailers. You have been given very little information about the project, and no charter has been issued. What questions should you ask the project sponsor, and what should you do with the information you receive? What challenges might you face in attempting to obtain this information in a tactful manner?

8. The Preston Co., located in Kansas City, Kansas, has a strong commitment to its community. Employees at all levels have agreed they would like to do something to support community needs, and they have chosen a local shelter for homeless people as a charity they would like to help. After an extensive brainstorming process, they identified several ways they could help the shelter, including a work party, serving meals, holding a raffle, and sponsoring a 10 kilometer run. They assessed advantages and disadvantages of each option, as described in Chapter 3, and decided they would like to sponsor a 10K run because it would generate funds for donation as well as draw attention to the homeless shelter and the problems of homelessness. Additionally, the event will offer positive public relations for Preston. The company president has assigned a team to plan and manage the project, and you have been selected as project manager. He has promised you and your team a seed money budget of $5,000 and, in consultation with you and your team, has agreed that raising $50,000 (after expenses) would be a reasonable goal. You have reached consensus with the project sponsor regarding the date of the event, and this allows you six months until the date of the race.

a. Create a project objective statement for this project.

b. What skills will you need on the team? What skills might you need beyond those available on the team?

c. The chapter identified several stakeholder roles typical of any project: project sponsor, project manager, project team, management, customer, and other peripheral groups. For the 10K project, what individuals or groups would be cast in various roles?

d. Develop a set of project success metrics. In other words, identify a balanced set of metrics that could be used to evaluate whether or not the 10K run was a success. Be sure to consider interim measures as well as those you would consider when the project is complete.

e. Develop a preliminary statement of scope for this project. As well as identifying deliverables within the scope of the project, be sure to identify those that others might reasonably assume to be "in scope" but that you and your team consider to be out-of-scope.

9. A recent project at a hospital had the following project objective statement: "Reduce the rate of ventilator-associated pneumonia (VAP) in the pediatric intensive care unit (PICU) to below the national average." Members of the project team that created the statement included five pediatric critical care nurses ranging in years of experience from 2 to 20, the PICU's nurse educator (a former PICU nurse with 20 years of experience at several different hospitals), the hospital's infection control specialist (a former PICU nurse who now tracks *nosocomial,* or hospital acquired, infections such as VAP and facilitates efforts to reduce them), a representative of the quality department (a trained facilitator skilled in data collection and quality analysis tools), and a respiratory therapist. One of the PICU nurses was selected as project manager.

a. How does the project objective statement given above fare with respect to the criteria for an effective project objective statement described in the chapter?

b. Critique the team composition for the PICU's VAP reduction project. Specifically, what do you think of the competency, representation, and size of the team?

10. Reflect on a project in which you recently participated, either school-related or in a past job or community organization. Describe the extent to which this project followed, or did not follow, the prescriptions for project initiation set forth in this chapter, and evaluate how this affected project outcomes.

Mini Case

Good Health Hospital Elective Admissions Project

PROJECT BACKGROUND

Congratulations! The Good Health Hospital process improvement steering committee has approved your request to study and improve the admitting process for elective hospital patients. (Elective patients are nonurgent, nonemergency patients for whom hospital admission reservations are made in advance.)

Your study has attracted the attention of Dave Wait, chief executive officer of the hospital. Recent customer survey data reveal that "long waits in elective admissions" are a major source of customer dissatisfaction. Dave regularly reviews the minutes of the steering committee and has long felt the elective admissions process was a key candidate for improvement. Apparently, Dave has been the recipient of numerous complaints from physicians and their elective patients about the long waits in admissions. He has sent your team a brief note of encouragement (see below).

Good Health Hospital, located in a rapidly growing semi-metropolitan area of northern California, is a 250-bed general hospital helping serve the medical needs of a district with an approximate population of 100,000 people. Opened in 1972, Good Health has as its mission to provide quality health care serving the inpatient disease and injury needs of the Santa Rosa community.

Your team consists of the admitting manager, two admissions clerks, a physician, two nurses, and an environmental services (i.e., housekeeping) supervisor. As individuals who work in or directly with admitting, you know the critical role the admitting process plays in smooth hospital operations. The admitting function, in fact, is a hub of activity that affects almost all other hospital operations and departments.

Your project began as the result of casual lunchtime conversation among the managers of nursing, environmental services, and admitting. In recent brainstorming meetings with their individual staffs, these three had discovered that problems in processing elective patients into the hospital were particularly frustrating to each area, although for different reasons.

Nursing complained that patient records that accompanied the patients from admitting were incomplete. Patients also arrived at nurse stations unexpectedly. In addition, according to nurses, elective patients seemed to arrive at the most inconvenient times. Environmental services complained that everything is always in a rush.

Admitting department personnel are frustrated because rooms seem never to be available. Patients and their loved ones get anxious and upset when they have to wait and, as the first point of contact in the hospital, admitting personnel must interface directly with dissatisfied customers. The admitting department, in fact, had recently gathered data on average elective patient wait time and had found it to be over an hour. They defined patient wait time as the elapsed time between a patient's arrival at the hospital reception desk and his or her arrival at either a room or one of the hospital departments for tests or procedures.

Admitting personnel also experienced frustration because parts of their jobs (for example, verifying insurance and tracking down missing test results) took lots of time. And, in some instances, these tasks had to be completed the day the patient arrived for a hospital stay. Occasionally, admitting personnel had to gather additional information from the physicians' offices and sometimes patients had to wait in admitting because no escorts were available to transport them to a room or test or procedure location.

In follow-up conversations, the admitting, nursing, and environmental services staffs agreed to collaborate on a joint improvement project; they were all involved in the process in one way or another, so a cross-departmental effort seemed to make sense. The three managers submitted a request, with a list of proposed team members, to the hospital process improvement steering committee. The committee approved the project, adding a physician to the proposed team. Everyone agreed the problem was an important one. Improving this process should increase external customer satisfaction and have a positive impact on internal hospital operations as well.

Letter from the CEO

GOOD HEALTH HOSPITAL
MEMORANDUM

TO: Elective admissions process improvement team
FROM: Dave Wait, CEO

I am pleased to learn your group will be tackling the important process of elective admissions. As you may know, Good Health's increasing occupancy rate (over 85%) coupled with our successful efforts to reduce average lengths of stay, has resulted in an increasing number of admissions. I am concerned by physician, patient, and nurse complaints about the excessive time required to admit an elective patient. I understand it has taken some patients as long as two hours to be admitted. I am especially disturbed that, in a recent customer satisfaction survey, the number one most frequent source of dissatisfaction among elective patients was "long wait time in admissions." Increasing patient satisfaction is one of several key initiatives at Good Health, and improving the elective admissions process will certainly contribute to achieving this important strategic objective.

Because we have some control over the schedule of elective admissions, I am confident your team will be able to significantly reduce wait times. At a recent Directions in Health Care CEO symposium, I learned that the best hospitals in our size and occupancy category are able to process incoming elective admissions in about 20 minutes. I am disturbed that we are nowhere near that figure. However, it is critical that, in reducing elective admission times, we do not compromise the quality of admission service. The information admitting provides to the rest of the hospital must remain timely, accurate, and complete.

Finally, you may be aware that we expect a visit from the Joint Commission on Accreditation of Healthcare Organizations sometime next calendar year. Because of their interest in efforts to improve operational performance, it would be ideal if you could complete your work and be able to demonstrate some real improvement in this area within six months. Doing so would provide us an opportunity to showcase a successful improvement effort.

I have encouraged your managers to provide you with the time you need—estimated at an average of two hours a week for the duration of the project—to address this important problem. In addition, a small budget of $2,000 is available to the team to cover expenses associated with meetings, data gathering, benchmarking, and the like.

I wish you the best of luck in your efforts. I hope you will keep me informed as the project unfolds, and I look forward to reading your final report and recommendations, and to hearing your team's final presentation.

Good Health Hospital Case Assignment Questions

1. Based on the information in the case, create a project charter for this project. In addition, answer these questions about the charter:

   a. From whom should the charter come?

   b. To whom should the charter be distributed?

2. What is the problem or opportunity motivating this project? In your answer be sure to describe the *what,* the *where,* the *timing,* and the *magnitude* of the problem or opportunity (see Exhibit 3.3).

3. Create a fishbone diagram that explores the possible causes of the problem (or opportunity) identified in question 2 (see Exhibit 3.6).

4. Imagine you are taking one of your parents to Good Health Hospital for an elective surgical procedure. Considering you and your parent as the customers, what would you want from the elective admissions process? Make a list of the "customer needs" for this process.

5. What possible courses of action could be pursued in improving the elective patient admission process? Name at least three mutually exclusive options.

6. Create a project objective statement for this project. Assess your statement against the criteria offered in the chapter. In other words, is the statement shared, short, simple, specific, measurable, and time constrained? How could any deficiencies you identified be overcome?

7. With whom would you want to share the project objective statement?

8. Who are the stakeholders for this project?

9. Create a set of project metrics for this project. What specific measures would indicate project success to each of the project's key stakeholders?

10. Identify the project boundaries; where does the project start and end?

11. Identify a preliminary set of project deliverables. For each deliverable you identify, determine what additional information the team may need to precisely specify the deliverable. In other words, what questions does your team need to have answered to clearly describe each deliverable?

12. Using Exhibit 4.11 as a model, develop a plan for communicating with Dave Wait, the CEO.

13. Critique the composition of the team as described in the project background information in terms of area representation, size, and time available. Why did the steering committee add a physician to the team? Do you agree with this decision? Should a patient be added to the team? Why or why not? What else might you want to know about each of these team members?

References

Allen, T.J. *Managing the Flow of Technology.* Cambridge, MA: MIT Press, 1977.

Brown, K.A., and N.L. Hyer. "Whole Brain Thinking for Project Management." *Business Horizons* 45, no. 3 (2002), pp. 47–57.

CH2M Hill. *Project Delivery System.* Denver, CO: CH2M Hill, 2001.

Erez, M. "Feedback: A Necessary Condition for the Goal Setting-Performance Relationship." *Journal of Applied Psychology* 62, no. 5 (1977), pp. 624–27.

Ericksen, J., and L. Dyer. "Right from the Start: Exploring the Effects of Early Team Events on Subsequent Project Team Performance." *Administrative Science Quarterly* 49, no. 3 (2004), pp. 438–71.

Fowler, G.A. "For Asia-Based Staff the Typical Workday Lasts about 24 Hours." *The Wall Street Journal,* August 22, 2006, p. B1.

Hackman, J.R. *Leading Teams.* Boston: Harvard Business School Press, 2002.

IPS Associates, *Project Management Manual.* Boston: Harvard Business School Press, 1996.

LaBrosse, M. *Accelerated Project Management.* New York: HNB Publishing, 2002.

Latham, G.P. *Work Motivation: History, Theory, Research and Practice.* Thousand Oaks, CA: Sage, 2006.

Locke, E.A. "Motivation through Conscious Goal Setting." *Applied & Preventive Psychology* 5, no. 2 (1996), pp. 117–24.

Locke, E.A., and G.P. Latham. *A Theory of Goal Setting and Task Performance.* Englewood Cliffs, NJ: Prentice Hall, 1990.

Malhotra, A.; A. Majchrzak; and B. Rosen. "Leading Virtual Teams." *Academy of Management Perspectives* 21, no. 1 (2007), pp. 60–70.

McWilliams, G. "After Landing Huge Navy Pact, EDS Finds It's In over Its Head." *The Wall Street Journal,* April 6, 2004, pp. A1.

Mitchell, T., and D. Daniels. "Motivation." In *Comprehensive Handbook of Psychology, Volume 12: Industrial and Organizational Psychology,* ed. W.C. Borman, D.R. Ilgen and R.J. Klimoski. New York: Wiley and Sons, 2006.

Moreland, R.L., and J.M. Levine. "The Composition of Small Groups." *Advances in Group Processes,* vol. 9. Greenwich, CT: JAI Press, 1992, pp. 237–80.

O'Leary-Kelly, A.M.; J.J. Martocchio; and D.D. Frink. "A Review of the Influence of Group Goals on Group Performance." *Academy of Management Journal* 37, no. 5 (1994), pp. 1285–1301.

Smith, P., and D. Reinertsen. "Faster to Market." *Mechanical Engineering* 120, no. 12 (1998), pp. 68–70.

Thompson, K.R.; W.A. Hochwarter; and N.J. Mathys. "Stretch Targets: What Makes Them Effective?" *Academy of Management Executive* 11, no. 3 (1997), pp. 48–60.

Tubbs, M.E. "Commitment and the Role of Ability in Motivation: Comment on Wright, O'Leary-Kelly, Cortina, Klein & Hollenbeck." *Journal of Applied Psychology* 79, no. 6 (1994), pp. 804–11.

Wheelwright, S.C., and K.B. Clark. "Organizing and Leading 'Heavyweight' Development Teams." *California Management Review* 34, no. 3 (1992), pp. 9–28.

Yetton, P., and P. Bottger. "The Relationship among Group Size, Member Abilities, Social Decisions Schemes and Performance." *Organization Behavior and Human Performance* 32, no. 2 (1983), pp. 145–59.

Chapter Five

Project Definition: Creating and Using the Work Breakdown Structure

"If you cry 'forward' you must make plain in what direction to go."
Anton Chekov

Chapter Learning Objectives

When you have mastered the material in this chapter, you should be able to:

- Transform a project charter into a plan for action.
- Work with a project team to develop a work breakdown structure using mind mapping, top-down outlining and bottom-up aggregation.
- Refine an initial work breakdown structure to meet structure and content guidelines.
- Identify task ownership and create a responsibility matrix for a project.
- Estimate working and calendar times for project tasks, applying concepts related to parametrics, learning curves, and PERT.
- Identify a comprehensive set of key performance indicators for project deliverables and tasks.
- Determine project resource requirements.
- Develop a project budget.

In this chapter, we illustrate how a team defines a project by decomposing it into its elements, assigning responsibility, identifying key performance indicators, and developing time and cost estimates. For small projects executed by a single person, a mental model of project tasks may be sufficient. But for large, complex projects involving multiple participants, a more formal definition will be necessary. At the center of project definition is a document known as the **work breakdown structure (WBS),** a tool that helps turn a large, seemingly overwhelming piece of work into a set of tasks that are doable, manageable, and measurable. We offer a mix of traditional and innovative approaches for generating the WBS and the planning steps it supports, focusing on tools and methods for use in team settings.

THE WORK BREAKDOWN STRUCTURE

According to the Project Management Institute, the WBS is:

> A deliverable-oriented hierarchical decomposition of the work to be executed by the project team, to accomplish the project objectives and create the required deliverables. The WBS organizes and defines the total scope of the project. . . . The planned work contained within the lowest-level WBS components, which are called work packages, can be scheduled, cost estimated, monitored, and controlled.[1]

The work breakdown structure is the project manager's best insurance against the risk of omitting important work from the project plan. It creates the core of any project, and almost every aspect of a project manager's job relates in one way or another to the WBS. Exhibit 5.1 illustrates the central role the WBS plays in any project.

Overlooked or forgotten work is one of the greatest sources of project delays and failures[2] and a significant source of stakeholder dissatisfaction. Matta and Ashkenas refer to these omissions as "white space risks."[3] The Far Side cartoon in Exhibit 5.2 offers an extreme example.

"The little things are infinitely the most important."

Sir Arthur Conan Doyle

WBS Hierarchy and Detail

The top level of the WBS is the project (or in some cases, the program), and the next level represents major deliverable work areas or phases in the project's life cycle.[4] A

---

[1] Project Management Institute, *A Guide to the Project Management Body of Knowledge* (Philadelphia: PMI Press, 2004), p. 112.

[2] IPS Associates, *Project Management Manual* (Boston: Harvard Business School Press, 1996), p. 18.

[3] N.F. Matta and R.N. Ashkenas, "Why Good Projects Fail Anyway," *Harvard Business Review* 81, no. 9 (2003), pp. 109–14.

[4] Project Management Institute, *A Guide to the Project Practice Standard for Work Breakdown Structures* (Philadelphia: PMI Press, 2002), p. 4.

EXHIBIT 5.1
WBS at the Center of the Project

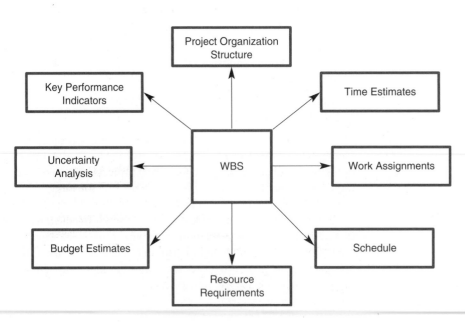

EXHIBIT 5.2
**An Extreme Example
of an Overlooked
WBS Element**

THE FAR SIDE® By GARY LARSON

"How many times did I say it, Harold?
How many times? 'Make sure that bomb
shelter's got a can opener—ain't much
good without a can opener,' I said."

team often develops a preliminary list of deliverables as part of the charter but refines it during project definition. At the lowest level of any branch in the WBS are work packages, collections of efforts intended to accomplish a particular result and that represent the real work of the project. The number of levels between the project level and the work package level depends on the size and complexity of the project. If you are creating a WBS for a personal computer software upgrade in your home office, you may need only one level. However, the WBS for an enterprisewide information systems upgrade might have four or five levels. A megaproject such as building a space station could have more than 60. WBS entities that fall between the deliverable level and the work package level can carry a variety of names, including activity, task, subtask, assignment, and so forth.

Imagine an accounting system upgrade as an example. Major deliverables might include system requirements, evaluation and selection of the software vendor, technical integration, and implementation. For the system requirements deliverable, work packages might include identifying user areas, obtaining input from users, and developing requirements. Exhibit 5.3 shows the hierarchy pictorially. Note that if the accounting system upgrade were part of a larger project involving upgrades of several systems within the organization, the hierarchy would shift, and the accounting upgrade would be one of several deliverables.

Some project teams organize the WBS around the functional areas that will be responsible for parts of the project, or according to the cost centers that will fund particular sets of project activities. Under this schema, the first level of the WBS for the accounting package upgrade might include accounting, IT, human resources, and so on. These approaches make it easy to see which functions own what pieces of the project, but they make it more difficult to see how individual activities roll up into the completed project. As a result, the team might overlook necessary activities, particularly those that integrate individual departmental contributions. Additionally, a functional division of work reinforces a silo mentality, where the area between functions is a no-man's-land and handoffs between departments are opportunities for mistakes and lost information.[5]

[5] Note that the *Project Management Institute Practice Standard for Work Breakdown Structures* argues against creating WBS elements by process or organization, noting that WBS structures that are not deliverable-focused may lead to project failure (p. 14).

EXHIBIT 5.3
Levels of Detail in a WBS for an Accounting Systems Upgrade Project

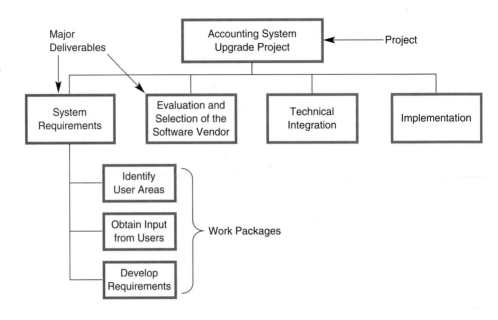

WBS Formats

Exhibit 5.4 shows three WBS formats for depicting a portion of a project to remove old underground fuel tanks. The three formats include the outline, mind map, and organizational chart. All convey the same content and structural hierarchy and are built around the same five major deliverables.

EXHIBIT 5.4
Three WBS Formats for a Fuel Tank Removal Project

Format A: Outline Approach		
Fuel Tank Removal Project		
Deliverable 1	Regulatory Compliance	
	Work Package 1.1	Process Environmental Review
	Work Package 1.2	Obtain Permits
Deliverable 2	Assessment	
	Work Package 2.1	Analyze Soil Sample
	Work Package 2.2	Assess Tank Condition
	Work Package 2.3	Identify Tank Substance
Deliverable 3	Tank Removal	
	Work Package 3.1	Remove Contents
	Work Package 3.2	Excavate Tank Site
	Work Package 3.3	Hoist Tank Out
Deliverable 4	Disposal	
	Work Package 4.1	Dispose of Tank
	Work Package 4.2	Dispose of Fuel
	Work Package 4.3	Dispose of Contaminated Soil
Deliverable 5	Site Reclamation	
	Work Package 5.1	Backfill Hole
	Work Package 5.2	Landscape Surface

EXHIBIT 5.4
(*Continued*)

Format B: Mind Mapping Approach

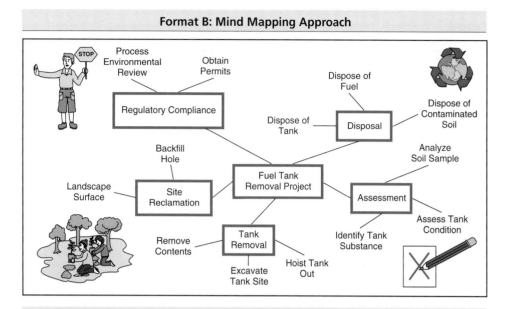

Format C: Organizational Chart Approach

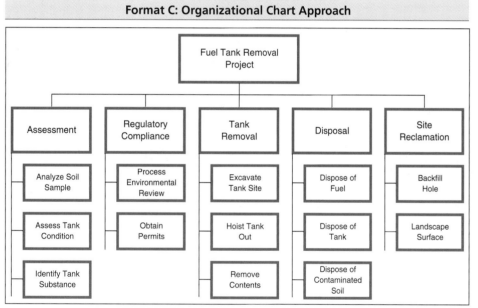

INVOLVING THE TEAM IN CREATING THE WBS

Once the project manager and the team have a clear picture of the project purpose or mission, customer specifications, measurable objectives, and a well-articulated statement of the project scope, they are ready to begin creating the WBS. Involving the team in WBS development offers many advantages. First, team members are the content experts. They are best equipped to know what is actually involved in generating each deliverable and how to break tasks down into doable work packages. Second, if team members are involved in WBS development, they will have a systems view of the total project and the interrelationships among project elements. Third, participation builds commitment

Disagreement over Project Mission: The Library Amnesty Week Project   Box 5.1

The CEO of a large public library system sponsored a project known as "Amnesty Week." As a result of this initiative, library patrons would be allowed to return overdue books to the library without paying fines, no matter how far overdue they were. (This had to be planned in great secrecy, or people would stop returning their books in anticipation of the fine-free week.) The CEO assigned all library directors to be on the project planning team, and they met for a facilitated, daylong project planning session. Once the major deliverables were identified, the group broke into subteams to develop WBS details. About 20 minutes into the process, conflict erupted in several subteams over WBS content. Comments such as, "We don't need to do that!" and "You are leaving out something really important!" and "You're crazy!" popped up around the room. The facilitator drilled down to the conflict's root causes and found participants had very different ideas about the purpose (mission) of the project. Some felt it was purely clerical—to clean up inventory files before a new information system was installed. Others thought it was to "catch all those scofflaws who haven't returned their books." And others felt it was primarily a public relations effort aimed at providing positive exposure and elevating the stature of the library within the community. After several rounds of discussion, the entire team finally agreed on public relations as the central purpose of the project. With this as a unifying mission, they were able to more quickly and effectively proceed with WBS development.*

*The project proved to be a smashing success, bringing in far more books than the library staff members had ever imagined. Some books that had been out for 50 years or more were returned in excellent condition.

to the project. People are far more likely to support what they have helped to create.[6] Fourth, collaboratively creating the WBS brings conflicting views and unresolved questions to the surface when it is not too late to address them. Box 5.1 offers an example.

THREE APPROACHES FOR TEAM-BASED WBS DEVELOPMENT

In this section, we offer three approaches for developing the WBS in a team setting: mind mapping, top-down outlining, and bottom-up aggregation. Each has strengths and limitations, as we shall discuss. Consistent with the team-based orientation of our book, we begin with a highly participative, though nontraditional, approach to WBS development: mind mapping.

Mind Mapping for WBS Development

Chapter 4 introduced mind mapping as a useful tool in project initiation and planning. One of the most powerful applications for mind mapping in project management is development of the WBS.[7]

To illustrate mind mapping for WBS development, we will use the example of the Preston Co., whose leaders have decided to sponsor a community service effort aimed at aiding homeless people in the company's metropolitan area. As part of this broader

---

[6] W. Kim and R. Mauborgne, "Fair Process: Managing in the Knowledge Economy," *Harvard Business Review* 75, no. 4 (1997), pp. 65–75; M. Wheatley, *Leadership and the New Science* (San Francisco, CA: Berrett-Koehler Publishers, 1996), p. 68.

[7] K A. Brown and N.L. Hyer, "Whole Brain Thinking for Project Management," *Business Horizons* 45, no. 3 (2002), pp. 47–57.

EXHIBIT 5.5
Getting a Start on the WBS Mind Map: Central Node with Project Name and Symbol

initiative, a fund-raising team has been chartered to stage a 10 kilometer (10K) run to raise funds to support a local shelter for homeless people. The stated objectives of the project are to raise $50,000 for the shelter and to enhance the company's public image. The team has thoroughly discussed and understands the mission, purpose, and objectives of the project and has a shared understanding of the scope of work. Equipped with this information, the team is now ready to create the WBS. This process should answer the question, "What are all of the things we need to do to complete the charity run?"

To begin the process, a facilitator places the project name and a representative symbol in the center of a large sheet (about 1 meter by 2 meters) of unlined paper that has been posted on the wall with the long edge running horizontally (see Exhibit 5.5). The symbol in the center of the map should capture an image representing the project, but does not have to meet any sort of artistic standards.

Next, the team brainstorms the high-level deliverables that represent major project components. For the charity run, high-level deliverables might include promotion, transportation, registration, route, safety, refreshments, prizes/recognition, and so forth. Each of these should be recorded as a branch emanating from the central node of the mind map using words and symbols (see Exhibit 5.6). Exhibit 5.7 shows a project team engaged in creating a WBS using a mind mapping approach.

EXHIBIT 5.6
Charity Run Mind Map with Major Branches for High-Level Deliverables

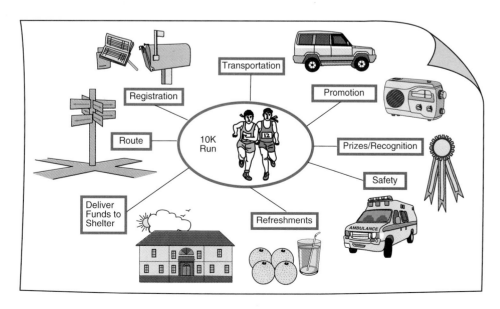

EXHIBIT 5.7
A Project Team
Developing a WBS
Mind Map

Branching Out

Once the team has agreed on high-level deliverables and recorded them on the mind map, the brainstorming focus shifts to identifying the lower-level activities required for each high-level deliverable. For example, activities or work packages for promotions might include research, TV and radio advertisements, and mailings. Each of these would be recorded as a twig off the promotions branch using words, colors, and symbols (see Exhibit 5.8). The team continues the process of subdividing deliverables until the WBS is sufficiently detailed. (We offer suggestions for deciding on the appropriate level of detail in a summary discussion below.)

Nonlinear Group Process

After the team has identified and agreed on the high-level deliverables, members can proceed in a nonlinear fashion, working in parallel on different parts of the map.

EXHIBIT 5.8
Charity Run:
Detailed WBS
Elements for
Promotions
Deliverable

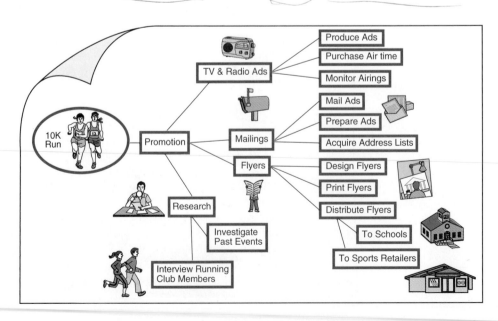

The flow of ideas can move across branches and levels; the team does not have to totally populate one deliverable or hierarchical level before moving to consider another part of the project. Because of these simultaneous mapping contributions, and the energy that seems to come from the mapping process, a team can develop a fairly complete preliminary WBS in 20 to 30 minutes. The first map is likely to be messy, but that is just part of the process.

Multiple-Stage Mapping Process for Complex Projects

If the project is complex, it may be appropriate to conduct the mind mapping in at least two stages. In the first stage, the team generates a map of all deliverables and identifies high-level tasks within each one. Once the team feels satisfied that the deliverable set is complete, members may work together or in small groups to develop separate subproject mind maps for each deliverable. If you use this approach, consider having teams rotate to offer ideas for the other maps as a way of increasing input. This helps to ensure coordination, identify overlaps, and increase the likelihood of completeness.

Advantages and Disadvantages of Mind Mapping

Mind mapping stimulates creative thinking about the project's activities, engages the team, helps generate enthusiasm and commitment to the project, gives the power of the pen (and thus the power of contribution) to all team members (including those who are less vocal), and is fast. The nonlinear nature of the process brings out many ideas, and because it does not involve sequencing or priorities, mind mapping steers people away from potential disagreements about what or who is most important.

Project managers occasionally run into resistance when they introduce mind mapping. Some people are uncomfortable with a nonlinear approach and may feel uneasy with the somewhat chaotic look of a first draft of a team mind map. However, most project teams find it extremely powerful once they try it. The following comment from one project team member is typical:

> To be honest, I was surprised by how useful the mind map turned out to be. We started our project plan by drawing a mind map on the whiteboard. This simple tool enabled us to take inventory of everything we needed to accomplish and helped us draw connections between closely related activities. Eventually, we distilled the results of this visual brainstorming session into our schedule. The mind map presents an easy and fun way to get a major project started; it's not intimidating and it allows participants to comprehend the project in its entirety.

Exhibit 5.9 offers a few tips for WBS mind mapping.

Mind Mapping Software

A team or individual can choose from several software packages to record the final results of a mind mapping session. Inspiration (www.inspiration.com), MindManager (www.mindjet.com), and iMindMap (www.imindmap.com) have been developed specifically for mind mapping. A number of mind mapping tools are also available for free (see www.mindmeister.com, http://freemind.sourceforge.net/wiki/index.php/Main_Page, and www.xmind.net). In addition, any graphics package (Visio, for example) can be adapted for use in recording mind maps, as well. However, a team can most effectively generate the initial version of the WBS mind map the old-fashioned way— with paper and colored pens and team members' brains and hands. Box 5.2 offers an example of how a virtual team uses the software when it is not possible for members to convene for a face-to-face session.

Virtual Mind Mapping for an IT Staff

The leader of an IT group for a large recreational equipment retailer wanted to use mind mapping for WBS development, but his teams were geographically dispersed and it was difficult to get them together in the same room. He posted a blank mind map on a shared Web site, with the project name in the center of the page, and invited team members and selected stakeholders to add deliverables, activities, and work packages asynchronously over several days. People added ideas, edited ideas, and restructured the map as they saw patterns emerge. In the end, team members enjoyed the satisfaction that comes from taking part in the design of their project, and the project was off to a good start. Although they agreed that a face-to-face meeting would have been helpful, the virtual approach was effective.

The Top-Down Outlining Approach for WBS Development

The top-down outlining approach begins the same way as mind mapping begins; the team reaffirms and clarifies key elements of the project charter and agrees on major deliverables. If there is enough wall space, the facilitator can write the names of the deliverables at the tops of separate pieces of flip-chart paper and display them across the front of the room. The facilitator then guides the team as members offer suggestions for subelements and work packages associated with each one. Another approach, useful if the team has more than six or seven people, is to break into subteams, with

---

EXHIBIT 5.9 **Tips for Mind Mapping the WBS**

1. In advance of the WBS session, ask participants to think about what they believe to be the project's major deliverables or components. They may wish to consult historical information about past projects of a similar nature, but they should be sufficiently open-minded to look beyond what has happened in the past.

2. Find a spacious work area with natural lighting and pleasant surroundings. Avoid locations where phones, competing tasks, and other distractions might interfere with the process.

3. Create the mind map on a large piece of butcher-type paper (at least 1 meter by 2 meters). Two or three flip-chart pages side by side will also work. Orient the paper horizontally and fasten it to a wall. (When the paper is oriented vertically, people seem to revert to linear thinking and list making.) Placing the paper on a table, rather than on the wall, discourages equal participation.

4. Stand up. Groups seem to generate the most ideas when everyone is standing. While standing, people can move freely to different positions in front of the mind map, making it easy to add ideas anywhere.

5. Use colored pens and draw images. Color and images stimulate creative thinking.*

6. Let people know it's OK to be messy. Some groups want to create a small-scale draft on a standard piece of paper before going to the butcher paper on the wall, but this defeats the creative purpose of the activity and does not encourage full-group involvement.

7. Use key words rather than sentences. This is sufficient for group understanding and can help uncover and quickly capture many ideas.

8. At the lowest or most detailed task level, include a noun and a verb (say, "build fence" as opposed to "fence"). This improves the clarity of the task definition.

9. Let everyone have a pen so people can work simultaneously on different parts of the map. This promotes involvement and also offers early clues as to team members' areas of interest.

---

*T. Buzan and B. Buzan, *The Mind Map Book* (New York: Plume Books, 1996); and R.N. Haber, "How We Remember What We See," *Scientific American* 222, no. 5 (1970), pp. 104–12.

EXHIBIT 5.10
**Outline for
the Promotion
Deliverable of the
Charity Run Project**

Project: 10K Charity Run
1.0 Promotion

1.1 TV and radio advertisements
   1.1.1 Produce ads
   1.1.2 Purchase airtime
   1.1.3 Monitor advertisement airings on radio and TV
1.2 Mailings
   1.2.1 Prepare ads
   1.2.2 Acquire address lists
   1.2.3 Mail ads
1.3 Flyers
   1.3.1 Design flyers
   1.3.2 Print flyers
   1.3.3 Distribute flyers
      1.3.3.1 Distribute to schools
      1.3.3.2 Distribute to sports retailers
1.4 Research
   1.4.1 Investigate past events
   1.4.2 Interview running club members

each one developing details for one or more deliverables. The full team will need to reconvene at some point to look for gaps and overlaps. Exhibit 5.10 displays an example of an outline for a portion of the 10K run. This conveys the same information as the mind map in Exhibit 5.8.

Top-Down Outlining: Advantages and Disadvantages

Most people have experience developing outlines, so the top-down approach has the appeal of familiarity. The disadvantages of this approach stem from its linearity. Typically, a team creating an outline develops detail for one deliverable at a time, and a facilitator records the results. This can make the process time consuming, and some weary participants might tune out if they are not interested in the deliverable under discussion. Further, it may be awkward to capture ideas that might emerge spontaneously about a deliverable that has already been discussed. Team members are sometimes reluctant to add ideas if the group is on a new topic, or if there isn't any room left on a flip-chart page. Further, in facilitating a team-based WBS outlining session, one must take great care to tap the ideas of less vocal team members: in an outlining session, they are likely to contribute less than their more effusive teammates will.

Comparing Mind Mapping with Top-Down Outlining

We believe mind mapping is a better team-based tool than outlining for top-down WBS development. The two approaches have the same structure, so the results of the mind map can be easily converted to an outline. If the team facilitator records the WBS in a mind mapping software program such as Inspiration or MindManager, he or she will be able to use the program's outline view to instantly make the conversion. MindManager offers the capacity to export a mind map into Microsoft Project where it is automatically converted to an outline.[8] An example of a WBS for a process-improvement project that was generated with MindManager is shown in Exhibit 5.11A, and MindManager's conversion from mind map to outline is displayed in Exhibit 5.11B.

---

[8] There are some problems with exporting the outline to Microsoft Project, however. Most importantly, it circumvents team involvement in developing the schedule.

EXHIBIT 5.11A WBS Mind Map Created with MindManager Software

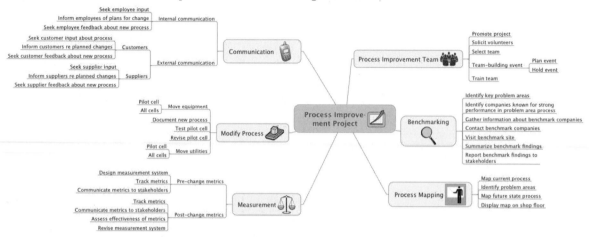

EXHIBIT 5.11B
MindManager WBS Outline Generated from Mind Map

Process Improvement Project

Process Improvement Team

- Promote project
- Solicit volunteers
- Select team
- Team-building event
  Plan event
  Hold event
- Train team

Benchmarking

- Identify key problem areas
- Identify companies known for strong performance in problem area process
- Gather information about benchmark companies
- Contact benchmark companies
- Visit benchmark site
- Summarize benchmark findings
- Report benchmark findings to stakeholders

Process Mapping

- Map current process
- Identify problem areas
- Map future state process
- Display map on shop floor

Measurement

- Pre-change metrics
  Design measurement system
  Track metrics
  Communicate metrics to stakeholders
- Post-change metrics
  Track metrics
  Communicate metrics to stakeholders
  Assess effectiveness of metrics
  Revise measurement system

Modify Process

- Move equipment
  Pilot cell
  All cells

EXHIBIT 5.11B
(Continued)

- Document new process
- Test pilot cell
- Revise pilot cell
- Move utilities
    Pilot cell
    All cells

Communication

- Internal communication
    Seek employee input
    Inform employees of plans for change
    Seek employee feedback about new process
- External communication
    Customers
        Seek customer input about process
        Inform customers re planned changes
        Seek customer feedback about new process
    Suppliers
        Seek supplier input
        Inform suppliers re planned changes
        Seek supplier feedback about new process

The Bottom-Up Aggregation Approach to WBS Development

Another way to create a work breakdown structure is to have the team start at the work-package level and build up the WBS. In this approach, begin by asking team members to individually brainstorm all the individual work packages required to make the project happen. Team members record each work package they identify on a separate sticky note and the notes are arranged randomly on a large whiteboard or piece of paper hung on a wall. The team then reviews the notes and uses an affinity diagram process (see Exhibit 5.12) to group related work packages into intermediate deliverables. These intermediate deliverables are then grouped into high-level deliverables, which, when taken together, should add up to the final project.

Advantages and Disadvantages of the Bottom-Up Approach

The bottom-up approach shares two advantages with mind mapping: it is participatory and it is fast. It has distinctive advantages, as well. Team members may find it easier to think at the detailed level about work packages because this is the work they do every day. People also appreciate having the time to work alone before conferring with the group.

However, the bottom-up method doesn't provide an *a priori* frame of reference or structure for the WBS and, as a consequence, the team might see the individual trees but miss the forest. Imagine writing a novel by beginning with a brainstorming process to describe all of the individual scenes and dialogues—you could group them by category, but you might not have much of a plot. Although we favor the mind mapping approach, for some teams and for some projects, the affinity method may be very appropriate.

THE WBS DOCUMENT

The work breakdown structure will become the centerpiece of the project plan, a document from which many other elements of the plan will be derived. Regardless of the approach the team uses, members ultimately will need a document in outline form. (An exception would be a small project in which a mind map on the wall may be sufficient.) To be useful, the WBS must represent an appropriate level of detail,

EXHIBIT 5.12   The Affinity Diagram Process for Bottom-Up WBS Development

The premise of the affinity diagram process* is that "birds of a feather flock together." It has numerous applications, but this is an adaptation for use in WBS development.

1. As with all WBS methods, begin the process by making sure everyone understands the project purpose, goals, scope, etc.

2. Allow 10 to 15 minutes for individuals to generate WBS elements, recording each on a separate note. Encourage participants to think of as many individual work packages as possible.

3. When the individual brainstorming is complete, team members place their notes on a wall-mounted whiteboard or paper.

4. The team gathers around the board and silently reviews the notes. When team members see two notes that appear to belong together (i.e., are related to the same deliverable or work package) they move them together. All team members work concurrently and there is no talking.

5. If a note is being moved back and forth between two groups, a duplicate of the same information may be created and placed in both groups.

6. It is OK for a note to stand on its own. This may represent a major deliverable or project component that needs further development, or it may suggest a topic the team has not fully considered.

7. Once the groupings are relatively stable (the notes are not getting moved around), the team reviews each grouping and creates a label. Each label will typically represent a high-level deliverable or major component of the project.

8. Once all groups have been labeled, the team reviews the deliverables to see if it may be appropriate to group two or more related components together. If so, then the team creates a high-level deliverable label for the related groups.

9. The process continues until the team is satisfied with the work package groupings and deliverable labels.

*M. Brassard, *The Memory Jogger Plus* (Methuen, MA: Goal QPC, 1996).

include actionable work packages, and pass the sum-of-the-parts test. Below, we embellish each of these recommendations and offer several additional prescriptions.

How Much Detail?

How far should a team go in breaking down the WBS? If it is useful for planning, accountability, or control purposes to break a task down into smaller component parts, then do so. If a finer resolution is not going to provide valuable insights, then stop. One simple guideline is the 8–80 rule (no work package with a duration less than a day—8 hours—or more than 10 working days or 80 hours). For fast-moving projects such as software development, the 4–20 rule may be appropriate (no work package duration smaller than 4 hours or greater 20). A more general recommendation is to continue to break the project into pieces until you get work packages that can be easily assigned to a single owner. In deciding how far to break tasks down, also consider the level of detail at which you plan to schedule the work.

The level of detail the project team uses in planning a project need not match the level of detail it uses for control. Suppose you have planned and scheduled the project in four-hour work packages. As project manager, however, you may not want to check the status of all tasks every four hours. Box 5.3 illustrates what can happen when tasks are monitored in too much detail.

Incorporate Project Management Tasks in the WBS

When brainstorming project activities, the team should not overlook the activities involved in actually managing the project. All activities essential to executing the project will take time and consume resources. These include: budgeting, milestone reviews, status report documentation, project closeout, and final celebration.

When a large shipyard reengineered its project management system, the first step involved implementing an improved monitoring and control system. The new system exposed underlying problems with the shipyard's estimating standards and practices. Nearly all tasks took longer than expected. Two predominating root causes accounted for these errors. First, the estimating standards had not been updated in decades. Consequently, they did not account for recent changes in technology (e.g., wire bundles now included several hundred wires instead of just 10 to 20), space available for people to work, and so on. Second, shipyard officials soon discovered that some of the inaccuracy stemmed from making estimates at an insufficient level of detail. In response, they revamped the entire estimating system. This appeared to be a good solution, until they discovered a dramatic increase in accidents on the shipyard's docks. When they investigated, they found that the time supervisors spent on the docks had decreased significantly; they were too busy filling out progress forms on detailed tasks to engage in management by wandering around or to pay attention to safety practices.

To address the problems associated with improper focus and micromanagement of progress reporting, shipyard managers reformatted the tracking system to focus on aggregated tasks. However, they continued to plan and estimate at the detailed level to reap the benefits of accuracy. Bottom line: plan in fine detail; manage at a more aggregate level.

Conduct a Sum-of-the-Parts Check

Regardless of the WBS approach used, team members should check their work at the end to be sure lower-level tasks sum up to their higher-level parent tasks. The project manager can conduct a sum-of-the-parts session in which the team reviews a cleaned-up version of the initial WBS. The project manager or a designated facilitator can ask "If we complete all of the work packages noted here, will we have completed the parent deliverable? Are there any extra tasks here that are not needed?"

Ask for Stakeholder Input

When sum-of-the-parts revisions are complete, the project manager can invite key stakeholders outside the project team to review a cleaned-up version of the WBS. (But, not too clean, or they will consider it to be final and will be less likely to contribute ideas.) As discussed in Chapter 4, stakeholders can make or break a project, so their involvement and commitment are essential.

Number the Final WBS Elements

For a large project, it can be very helpful to assign hierarchical numbers to WBS elements. Thus, for a four-level project, the top-level deliverables can be numbered 1, 2, 3, etc. The tasks that roll up to deliverable 1 would be numbered 1.1, 1.2, 1.3. The subtasks that together complete deliverable 1.2 would be numbered 1.2.1, 1.2.2, 1.2.3, and so forth. An example of this numbering scheme is shown in the outline for the 10K charity run displayed previously in Exhibit 5.10. Microsoft Project (and other project scheduling software) will assign these numbers when you input project information. Such a numbering system can facilitate project communication about specific tasks and work packages. This is especially important if, say, a task named "prepare documentation" appears several different places in the work breakdown structure. If each of these same-named tasks has a unique number, it will be easier for the team to know which is the focus of a specific discussion. In addition, the WBS codes can be used as account codes against which labor and other activity costs are charged.

ASSIGNING RESPONSIBILITY

Every task needs an owner—an individual, not a department—who will be responsible and accountable for its successful and timely completion. Making task assignments involves determining who on the team has the strongest interest and most appropriate skill set to tackle a given task. Depending on the size of the project, these responsibility assignments may be at the deliverable level, drill down to the work-package level, or fall somewhere in between. Box 5.4 offers insight about how the mind mapping process helps to uncover team members' interests.

Reviewing Task Assignments

Once task assignments have been completed, the team should do a global assignment review. If a particular task is unassigned, this may indicate that no one on the team has the necessary skill set, no one is interested, or that it has not been well defined. In these cases, the team should consider clarifying the task description, outsourcing the work, recruiting qualified team members, training existing team members, or finding ways to make the task more appealing. The project manager should also avoid overloading team members, because this can have serious effects on project schedules and quality. Research and practice demonstrate that the total work allocated to a single individual should not exceed 70 percent of the person's total hours, particularly if his or her time is distributed among multiple projects.[9] A person requires some setup time when shifting from one project to the next, and uncertainties are bound to arise.[10] Sometimes, and for some team members, even 70 percent is too much if uncertainties create a need for on-demand capacity. One law firm, for example, maintains several legal assistants who are purposefully underloaded with routine work so that they may be available to absorb additional project work.

As part of a comprehensive WBS check, the project manager should make sure a team member is responsible for each subcontracted or outsourced task. Someone needs to be in charge of managing the relationship with the subcontractor and ensuring a rich information flow about requirements, interfaces, progress, and problems. Outsourcing assigns the work to someone else but does not transfer accountability.

The Responsibility Matrix

In addition to assigning task ownership, the team should also think through other types of contributions to task performance. For example, some team members may provide

[9] For excellent discussions, see D. Reinertsen, *Managing the Design Factory* (New York: The Free Press, 1997), chap. 3; and E. Goldratt, *Critical Chain* (Great Barrington, MA: North River Press, 1997).

[10] Research on queuing theory demonstrates that the closer utilization gets to 100 percent, the more rapid the increase in waiting time for arriving customers or jobs. See N.L. Hyer and U. Wemmerlöv, *Reorganizing the Factory: Competing through Cellular Manufacturing* (Portland, OR: Productivity, 2002) for a review. The phenomenon also occurs in project environments, where the queue is represented by accumulations of project tasks waiting for team members to work on them. See Reinertsen, *Managing the Design Factory.*

One of the attractive features of mind mapping is that it can aid in task responsibility assignment. If each team member uses a different color marker when creating the mind map, you may easily be able to discern areas of interest. If a branch on the mind map is dominated by a particular color, the team member who worked with that pen color may be a good candidate to assume responsibility for tasks related to the deliverable in question. For example: "Harriet, you seem to have been very active in generating ideas for the intellectual property deliverable. Would you be willing to take responsibility?" Numerous managers have told us they are amazed at how well this works.

input to, participate in, or be responsible for reviewing or signing off on a task. A responsibility matrix (also called a responsibility assignment matrix, or RAM; a task assignment matrix; a linear responsibility chart; and other names) is a very helpful tool for keeping track of various roles. Project activities are listed as row headings and each team member as a column heading. Cell entries record the role a given individual plays in a particular project activity. Exhibit 5.13 shows a responsibility matrix for the promotions segment of the charity run. (The notation used is one of several ways to indicate various activity roles.) Although we have created our responsibility matrix indicating the role individual team members play in the lower-level work, one can create a responsibility matrix for any level of the WBS. For example, Julianne may have an entire research team working for her and maintain a separate, detailed responsibility matrix for that component of the project.

Project Organization Structure and the WBS

Responsibilities assigned at the deliverable level may form the basis for a project's organization structure. In fact, the WBS may be depicted as an organization structure, as shown in Exhibit 5.14 for the 10K charity run. The WBS also can be linked with the existing structure of the organization in what is termed an organizational breakdown structure or OBS.

The Project-Involvement Matrix

Functional managers in matrix organizations often find themselves needing to coordinate the work of those who report to them so that employees have adequate time to perform their routine work while simultaneously fulfilling the needs of institutional projects managed by people outside of their departments. A project-involvement matrix (PIM) can help a functional manager keep track of which individuals are involved in

EXHIBIT 5.13
Responsibility Matrix for Details within the Promotion Deliverable of the 10K Charity Run Project

Promotion Activities	Project Team Members						
	Natasha	Emily	Price	Nicole	Ricci	Allyson	Julianne
Research	I	I	I	I	I	I	A/S
Flyers		A			P		S
TV and Radio Ads		R	A			P	S
Mailings	P	P		A			S
P = participant		A = accountable			R = review required		
I = input required		S = sign-off required					

147

EXHIBIT 5.14   **Organization Chart for Charity Run**

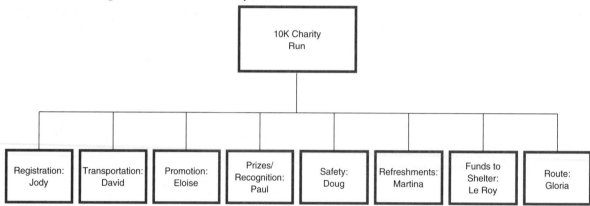

which projects. The rows on the PIM represent employees, and the column headings represent the projects in which these individuals are involved. A simple check mark can indicate an individual is committed to a particular project, or the manager can confer with team members to decide on percentage allocations. When new project opportunities arise, the manager has an easy and quick way of identifying available (and unavailable) resources and communicating this to others (e.g., project managers who request specific people). Exhibit 5.15 provides an example. Note that the savvy manager in Exhibit 5.15 has allocated no more than 70 percent of each resource's time to project work.

PROJECT ACCOUNTABILITY: TIME ESTIMATES, BUDGETS, AND PERFORMANCE INDICATORS

Time and cost estimation are natural outgrowths of the WBS process. Once team members have defined the work necessary to complete the project and they know who will do that work, they are ready to estimate how long it will take in actual work time and in calendar time. Work and calendar time estimates, along with estimates about material needs, service support, and assumptions about pay and benefits, serve as inputs to cost estimation and project budgeting.

Time Estimates for Scheduling and Accounting

Time estimates provide input for use in project scheduling, but they also support billing and accounting systems. These two needs are different, and, consequently, each task may require two separate types of estimates.

EXHIBIT 5.15
Project Involvement Matrix

Projects	Marketing Area Personnel*			
	Dorothy	**Peter**	**Harriet**	**Julianne**
Charity run				20%
Wifflers campaign		50%		
Gazebo launch		10%	60%	
Bellona Club promotion	45%			
Kaibab proposal	20%			40%

*Cell entries are percent of worker time devoted to this project. Project work not to exceed 70% of total time (30% devoted to routine tasks, administrative work and uncertainties).

Scheduling Estimates

A project manager uses calendar-time estimates as inputs to the schedule. This means elapsed time, from start to finish, not just the time invested in actually doing the task. If Sally is responsible for establishing supplier relationships for a product under development, it may require only 10 hours of her actual time to contact several vendors; discuss needs; review price, quality, and delivery information; and select a vendor. However, Sally is also the company's materials manager, so this work will need to be spread out over three weeks because she will work only part time on it. Additionally, the three-week estimate includes several anticipated delays in the process (e.g., waiting for information or responses from vendors).

Time Estimates for Billing and Accounting

Although elapsed time is the estimating focus for scheduling purposes, the project manager also may need to generate estimates based on actual working time for tasks. If the project involves hours billable to a client or an accounting system in which employees must allocate hours to specific projects, the project manager also will need to obtain estimates based on work hours. Think of an attorney who spends four hours working on a case for you. Although this work was spread out over five calendar days, you would want to be billed for 4 hours, not 40.

Improving Time Estimation Accuracy

The world is an uncertain place and project task times reflect this; they are estimates. The goal is to make estimates as accurate as possible. Here are some useful tips.

More Detail

The more detailed the WBS, the easier it is for those involved to develop accurate time estimates. (Box 5.3, "Details Derail Dockworkers," addressed this.) If we asked you how much time it would take you to read the entire online *Encyclopaedia Britannica*, you likely would be able to give nothing better than a wild guess. However, if we asked you to estimate how long it would take you to read an eight-line entry about the platypus, you could come a lot closer.

Ask Those Who Will Do the Work

Those who do the work (especially if they have done similar work before) may be in the best position to estimate the time required for a given task. Although some managers and team members might be concerned that individuals will over- or under-estimate task times, those who do the work generally have the most informed and realistic perspective on what the work will involve. It is best not to degrade trust by second-guessing or modifying their estimates. When individuals make time estimates for tasks they will perform, they are, in effect, setting goals for themselves. These serve as powerful motivators and will be more effective than time estimates the project manager imposes on team members.[11]

Get a Range of Times

One useful way to approach time estimates is to ask people to forecast a range rather than a single point. "An estimate is bound to be wrong, and a range, on the other hand, is more likely to be right, because it accounts for natural variations."[12] A good way to

---

[11] G.P. Latham, *Work Motivation: History, Theory, Research, and Practice* (Thousand Oaks, CA: Sage Publications, 2006).

[12] R. Austin and R. Luecke, *Managing Projects Large and Small* (Boston: Harvard Business School Publishing Corp., 2004), p. 74.

begin is to ask people for the longest, worst-case time first ("If things go badly and there are unexpected problems, or you are frequently interrupted to work on other assignments, how long is this task likely to take?"). This has a psychological advantage because it gives the person a chance to make the point that the worst case is possible. The project manager can then ask, "If everything goes smoothly, how long will it likely take to complete this task?" By asking for a range of times, the project manager may be able to extract more accurate estimates from those who will do the work. And the manager can more effectively manage stakeholders' schedule expectations by providing estimated ranges rather than single-point estimates.

Use Three-Point (PERT) Estimates

A more sophisticated approach to task time estimation that explicitly incorporates uncertainty is to use three-point, or PERT, estimates. PERT stands for Program Evaluation and Review Technique and is a methodology developed by the U.S. Department of Defense. In this approach, the estimated task time is determined by combining estimates for the optimistic time, pessimistic time, and mostly likely time. Specifically it involves calculating a weighted average as follows:

$$\text{Task time estimate} = \frac{(t_{\text{optimistic task time}} + 4t_{\text{most likely task time}} + t_{\text{pessimistic task time}})}{6}$$

As we will show in Chapter 7, time estimates generated in this way can be used to place probability bounds around the expected time to complete individual tasks and the project overall.

Ask about Assumptions

The project manager needs to understand the assumptions underlying the time estimates team members provide. For example, Julianne, who is working on the charity run promotions, estimates it will take her three weeks to complete the research. When asked, she explains she is assuming (1) she will be able to spend several hours each of the next three weeks working on this, (2) other people involved in promotions also will be available to work on this project for several hours each of the next three weeks, (3) she will be able to meet next week with key individuals outside the company, and (4) she will be able to get access this week to the promotion materials from two recent charity runs. Knowing the assumptions that underlie an estimate can help the project manager evaluate how realistic it is and the circumstances that might cause it to change.

Consult Historical Information

Where possible, it can be very helpful to consult historical information to find the time required for similar tasks in prior projects. Companies with mature project management practices maintain databases of project information from which employees can obtain figures on durations of similar past tasks.

Recognize that Outsourcing and Subcontracting Take Time and Resources

Some teams erroneously assume that outsourced or subcontracted tasks require no time because the work will be done outside of the organization. On the contrary, managing subcontractors well and assuring that all parties are informed about requirements, progress, and problems will require considerable time.[13] Additionally, the subcontractor's work will still appear in the schedule and will consume calendar time.

---

[13] N.W. Nix, R.F. Lusch, Z.G. Zacharia, and W. Bridges, "The Hand that Feeds You: What Makes Some Collaborations with Suppliers Succeed When So Many Fail?" *The Wall Street Journal,* October 27–28, 2007, p. R8.

Consider Parametric Estimating

Earlier we observed that while you would have a difficult time predicting the amount of time it would take you to read the entire online *Encyclopaedia Britannica,* you could probably give a fairly accurate estimate of how long it would take you to read the eight-line paragraph on the platypus. Suppose you estimated it would take you 45 seconds. Now, we tell you that the *Encyclopaedia Britannica* is composed of 250,000 paragraphs, which average eight lines each. You can now estimate the time required to read the entire encyclopedia. Your estimated time would be 250,000 × 45 seconds or 187,500 minutes or 3,125 hours or 390.6 eight-hour days or about 13 months. You have just made a parametric estimate. The "parameter" you used was "eight-line paragraphs," each of which you believe will take about 45 seconds to read.

Examples of commonly used parameters include square feet or meters in commercial construction, distance traveled for a space exploration project, or function points in software development. Based on historical data, the construction industry has developed reliable, detailed standards for use in estimating various types of construction (e.g., see www.corecon.com). Parametric approaches for some technical fields are quite complex, incorporating multiple variables and coefficients to create time-based forecasts. For example, some consulting organizations have developed methods for parametric time estimation in the IT industry. Construx (www.construx.com) is one well-known example.

Incorporate Anticipated Improvements in Efficiency with Learning Curves

If the work of the project involves tasks that will be repeated during the project (e.g., building several blocks of apartment buildings, developing multiple similar software modules, assembling multiple units of an aircraft component), the project team may need to account for improved performance over time. It probably will take more time (and hence, money) the first time a task is performed than the 10th time. If you have ever purchased two or more identical items from a furniture store such as IKEA and taken them home to assemble them, you probably noticed that the first unit took you considerably longer than the second or third. This is an example of what happens in project environments with repeated elements. Generally, the more labor-intensive a task is (i.e., the less it is machine paced), the greater the opportunity for learning to affect the time and effort required for successive iterations. An appreciation for learning curves is especially important in projects involving competitive bidding. If the bidding organization does not accurately account for the benefits it will gain through learning, it could over-bid for a project and lose the opportunity.

Years of industry practice have indicated that a learning curve (also known as an experience curve) exists when the time or effort to perform a task decreases by a fixed percentage of the previous value every time the volume doubles.[14] Imagine a framing task for a residential construction company. A team of framers can perform this work in 10 days on the first house, and historical records show that the learning rate for this kind of work is 95 percent. This means every time the output doubles, the task will require 95 percent of the prior time. So, if framing on the first house requires about 10 hours, the second house will require 10 × .95, or 9.5 hours, the fourth will require 9.5 × .95 or 9.025 hours, the eighth will require 8.574 hours, and the 16th will require 8.145 hours. Exhibit 5.16 displays this, showing the calculations for the first, second, fourth, and eighth houses. A project team can use learning curve tables such as those

---

[14] F.J. Andress, "The Learning Curve as a Production Tool," *Harvard Business Review* 32, no. 1 (1954), pp. 87–97; W.B. Hirschmann, "Profit from the Learning Curve," *Harvard Business Review* 42, no. 1 (1964), pp. 125–37; M. Lapré and L.N. Van Wassenhove, "Managing Learning Curves by Creating and Transferring Knowledge," *California Management Review* 46, no. 1 (2003), pp. 53–71.

EXHIBIT 5.16
Learning Curve
Illustration

Learning Curve Effects with a 95% Learning Rate

House #1 **10 hours**	**House #2:** **9.5 hours**	**House #4:** **9.025 hours**	**House #8:** **8.574 hours**

Framing for House #1:
10 hours

Framing for House #2:
.95 × 10 hours
= 9.5 hours

Framing for House #4:
.95 × 9.5 hours
= 9.025 hours

Framing for House #8:
.95 × 9.025 hours
= 8.574 hours

Learning Curve Graph for House-Framing: Units 1 through 30

Time Estimate for Unit X

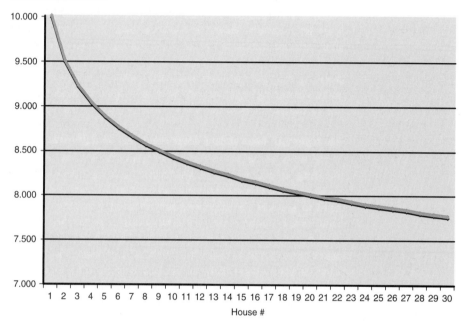

House #

developed by Crawford to determine the learning rates for units between the doubled figures.[15] The bottom of Exhibit 5.16 shows how the learning curve would look in graphical form as the framers advance to the 30th house. As the curve illustrates, learning increments fall off exponentially. Of course, there will be a lower bound, which will be reached when the time cannot be further compressed without completely redefining the task and methods.

Learning rates typically vary from a lower limit of 50 percent (extreme learning from repetition) to 100 percent (no learning from repetition).[16] A **steep learning curve** refers to a fast rate of learning.[17] According to Lapré and Van Wassenhove, learning may be of two types: conceptual and operational.[18] Conceptual learning involves improvements associated with gains in understanding of cause-and-effect relationships and typically involves systematic, scientific experimentation. Operational learning comes from trial and error on the job. A combination of "know why" conceptual learning and

[15] C.J. Teplitz, *The Learning Curve Deskbook* (New York: Quorum Books, 1991).

[16] Ibid.

[17] The term is sometimes misused in a way that suggests a steep learning curve is a circumstance in which it was very difficult to learn.

[18] Lapré and Van Wassenhove, "Managing Learning Curves by Creating and Transferring Knowledge."

EXHIBIT 5.17 **Learning Curve Tables with Unit and Cumulative Total Values for Rates of 60%, 75%, and 95%**

Source: Adapted from C.J. Teplitz, *The Learning Curve Deskbook* (New York: Quorum Books, 1991), Appendix D, Crawford Tables.

Unit Number	Unit Factor for 60% Learning Rate	Cumulative Total Factor for 60% Learning Rate	Unit Factor for 75% Learning Rate	Cumulative Total Factor for 75% Learning Rate	Unit Factor for 95% Learning Rate	Cumulative Total Factor for 95% Learning Rate
1	1.000	1.000	1.000	1.000	1.000	1.000
2	0.600	1.600	0.750	1.750	0.950	1.950
3	0.445	2.045	0.634	2.384	0.922	2.872
4	0.360	2.405	0.563	2.947	0.903	3.775
5	0.305	2.710	0.513	3.460	0.888	4.663
6	0.267	2.977	0.475	3.935	0.876	5.539
7	0.238	3.215	0.446	4.381	0.866	6.405
8	0.216	3.431	0.422	4.803	0.857	7.262
9	0.198	3.629	0.402	5.205	0.850	8.112
10	0.183	3.812	0.385	5.590	0.843	8.955
11	0.171	3.983	0.370	5.960	0.837	9.792
12	0.160	4.143	0.357	6.317	0.832	10.624
13	0.151	4.294	0.345	6.662	0.827	11.451
14	0.143	4.437	0.334	6.996	0.823	12.274
15	0.136	4.573	0.325	7.321	0.818	13.092
16	0.130	4.703	0.316	7.637	0.815	13.907
17	0.124	4.827	0.309	7.946	0.811	14.718
18	0.119	4.946	0.301	8.247	0.807	15.525
19	0.114	5.060	0.295	8.542	0.804	16.329
20	0.110	5.170	0.288	8.830	0.801	17.130
21	0.106	5.276	0.283	9.113	0.798	17.928
22	0.102	5.378	0.277	9.390	0.796	18.724
23	0.099	5.477	0.272	9.662	0.793	19.517
24	0.096	5.573	0.267	9.929	0.790	20.307
25	0.093	5.666	0.263	10.192	0.788	21.095
26	0.091	5.757	0.259	10.451	0.786	21.881
27	0.088	5.845	0.255	10.706	0.784	22.665
28	0.086	5.931	0.251	10.957	0.781	23.446
29	0.084	6.015	0.247	11.204	0.779	24.225
30	0.082	6.097	0.244	11.448	0.777	25.002

"know how" operational learning produces the most effective and sustainable learning. In the framing example shown in Exhibit 5.16, conceptual learning might come from experiments run in a company laboratory to test the relative effectiveness of different types of nail guns. Carpenters on the job might engage in operational learning when they experiment with different task sequences or teaming configurations.

Exhibit 5.17 displays tables for learning rates of 60, 75, and 95 percent based on the Crawford model.[19] These show the unit and cumulative total factor multipliers for

[19] Teplitz, *The Learning Curve Deskbook*. As Teplitz observes, although Wright's tables were the first to be developed, Crawford's approach, which produces slightly different results, is more widely used in industry today. Also, cumulative total figures shown here differ very slightly in some cases from the Crawford tables presented in the Teplitz reference, but this is because of differences in truncation and rounding.

units 1 through 30. More complete learning curve tables are available in references such as Teplitz' *The Learning Curve Deskbook.*

A team can use a learning curve table such as the one presented in Exhibit 5.17 to calculate unit and cumulative total estimates as follows. Imagine the team is working on an IT system upgrade in which several tasks such as programming and testing will be repeated across six IT modules: accounting, finance, human resource management, customer relationship management, logistics, and inventory. One of these repeated elements—user needs assessment—seems to offer potential for learning effects. It will involve gathering and compiling information based on interviews with users in departments related to each module, and members of the IT staff believe they will be able to work more effectively and quickly as they accumulate experience with this process. (They are accustomed to working on programming tasks and know that organizing an interview schedule, interviewing colleagues outside of their department, and summarizing results are not in their normal skill set.)

Based on data from previous, similar projects inside the company and at benchmark partner organizations, team members estimate that the learning rate will be 75 percent. Additionally, they estimate these data-gathering activities for the first module will require 15 calendar workdays or three workweeks. To determine the time required for the second module, they recognize it is simple to find 75 percent of 15 days, 11.25 days. For remaining modules, the table will be helpful. For the third module, as an example, they can find the cell corresponding to the unit factor for a 75 percent learning rate and unit number three. The multiplier to determine the third module's time would be .634, producing an estimate of 9.51 days (.634 $\times$ 15 days). Additionally, they can calculate the cumulative total time for modules one through six by using the multipliers in the cumulative total factor column for the 75 percent rate. Their full set of calculations, drawn from the Exhibit 5.17 unit and cumulative total columns for a 75 percent learning rate, would be as follows:

	Data Gathering Activity for Modules 1–6	
Module #	**Estimated Task Time**	**Cumulative Total Task Time**
1	= 15 days $\times$ 1 = 15 days	15 days $\times$ 1 = 15 days
2	= 15 days $\times$ .75 = 11.25 days	15 days $\times$ 1.750 = 26.25 days
3	= 15 days $\times$ .634 = 9.51 days	15 days $\times$ 2.384 = 35.76 days
4	= 15 days $\times$ .563 = 8.45 days	15 days $\times$ 2.947 = 44.21 days
5	= 15 days $\times$ .513 = 7.70 days	15 days $\times$ 3.460 = 51.90 days
6	= 15 days $\times$ .475 = 7.13 days	15 days $\times$ 3.935 = 59.03 days

Determining the learning rate has to be more than a best guess. For a new project, the team will need to find historical data, perhaps from similar past projects within the organization, from benchmark data provided by other companies, or through publicly available data for the industry. If historical information is available, the team may consider plotting data to discover patterns or applying least-squares linear regression of log-transformed data to determine the slope of the curve. However, not all learning effects are linear or log-linear. Some can follow an S-curve, others may have a plateau form, and others may have step functions. This is why an initial data plot is so important.

In the absence of historical, benchmark, or industry data, the team may wish to use learning curve tables in a scenario analysis as part of the estimating process. "What if the learning rate were 75 percent, how would our cumulative total time for that set of tasks look?" Or team members may wish to revise estimates to incorporate learning effects after the first few units have been completed and a pattern has emerged.

Determining Resource Requirements

Project resources include materials that will become part of a product (known as the bill of materials items), expendable materials, equipment, outsourced services, workspace, information, and people. Each element of the WBS will require resources from one or more of these categories. Exhibit 5.18 displays an example of a resource list for the 10K charity run.

EXHIBIT 5.18
Resource Requirements for Promotions Component of the 10K Charity Run

Research

Investigate Past Events
- Phone
- Computer
- Car
- Gas
- Maps

Interview Running Club Members
- Car
- Gas
- Phone
- Computer and paper
- Conference room
- Refreshments for focus group
- Tape recorder
- Flip chart
- Pens

Flyers

Design
- Photographic equipment
- Drawing desk
- Computer
- Illustration software
- Photo-editing software
- Flip chart
- Overhead
- Ruler
- Templates

Print
- Computer
- Printer
- Paper
- Photocopier

Distribute to Schools and Sports Retailers
- Car
- Gas
- Labels
- Stamps
- Envelopes

Estimating Projects Costs

Most projects begin with some preliminary expectations about what they will cost. If the organization has conducted a formal business case analysis, as described in Chapter 3, the core project team will have an initial idea of what the project should cost. This **ballpark** or **order of magnitude estimate**[20] served as the basis for the project selection decision, but once the project has been sanctioned, and especially for projects involving long duration, large scope or high complexity, the team may develop a second **budgetary estimate.** This number will reflect expectations regarding what financial resources, in aggregate, will be needed to support project work over its planned duration. Although more precise than the order of magnitude estimate, the budgetary estimate is developed before the WBS and, thus, is not based on a detailed understanding of the tasks and activities that will comprise the project.

Both the order of magnitude and the budgetary estimates sometimes turn out to be completely disconnected from the realities of the project. But they provide the team with a message from top-level managers about the relative importance of the project and the company resources available. Detailed planning will offer more realistic input, however, and may lead the project team to request more funding (or time), or to ask the sponsor for guidance about which WBS items may be eliminated.

With a description of the labor, time, and other resources required for each individual work package, the team is in a good position to estimate the cost for each project task or deliverable. Combining lower-level cost estimates will provide a total estimated cost for the project as a whole. An example from the 10K charity run promotion deliverable introduced earlier helps to illustrate how this occurs (see Exhibit 5.19.) Exhibit 5.20 shows a spreadsheet revealing the details underlying the estimates in Exhibit 5.19.

Many of the tips provided for time estimates apply to cost estimates, as well. Just as with time estimates, people may feel tempted to add extra budgetary cushions as a way of saving face or protecting themselves from reprimand. Conversely, they may

[20] K. Schwalbe, *Information Technology Project Management* (Cambridge, MA: Thomson Learning, 2000), pp. 150–51, for this cost estimating framework.

EXHIBIT 5.19
Charity Run Budget for the Promotion Deliverable

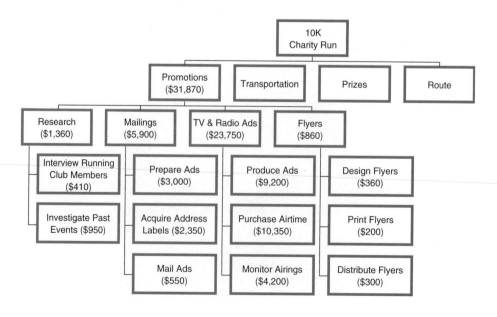

EXHIBIT 5.20   Underlying Accounting for Project Budget Displayed in Exhibit 5.19

Deliverable	Activity or Work Package	Estimated Working Time in Days	Estimated Calendar Time in Work Days	Human Resource Category	Burdened Cost Per Hour	Labor Cost	Cost of Purchased Materials	Cost of Purchased or Rented Equipment	Travel Expense	Outsource or Subcontract Costs	Subtotal Costs
Research	Interview Running Club Members	1	10	HR Specialist	$ 40	$ 320			$ 90		$ 410
	Investigate Past Events	2	5	Archivist	$ 50	$ 800	$ 150				$ 950
Mailings	Prepare Ads	8	15	Graphic Designer	$ 40	$2,560	$ 440				$ 3,000
	Acquire Address Labels	0.5	1	Purchasing Agent	$ 70	$ 280	$2,070				$ 2,350
	Mail Ads	0.5	4	Mail Clerk	$ 30	$ 120	$ 430				$ 550
TV & Radio Ads	Produce Ads	3	7	Media Specialist	$100	$2,400	$ 500	$1,300		$ 5,000	$ 9,200
	Purchase Airtime	0.5	4	Purchasing Agent	$ 70	$ 280				$10,070	$10,350
	Monitor Airings	0.5	20	HR Specialist	$ 50	$ 200				$ 4,000	$ 4,200
Flyers	Design Flyers	1	4	Graphic Designer	$ 45	$ 360					$ 360
	Print Flyers	0.1	1	N/A	$ 0	$ 0				$ 200	$ 200
	Distribute Flyers	2	5	Volunteer	$ 0	$ 0			$300		$ 300
										Total Cost	$ 31,870

EXHIBIT 5.21

Dilbert on Project Adjustment Factors

DILBERT: © Scott Adams/Dist. by United Feature Syndicate, Inc

underestimate expected costs to appear competent or to increase the likelihood they will be selected to do the work. According to Goldratt, overestimation is more common, but Reinertsen insists that engineers are especially prone to the underestimate the time required to complete work assignments.[21] Both padded and overly optimistic estimates can lead to poor resource utilization, resulting in excessive expenses, project delays, and starving of other projects in need of resources.

One may legitimately adjust time and cost estimates in anticipation of project risks. When you do so, you should be open about it. "Given the risk associated with using the new Cobra technology, we estimate the project could cost $400,000. However, if the technology is available earlier than expected, project costs should fall to about $375,000." As Dobson notes, "If your project has high risk, and that risk involves a cost adjustment, make it clear and obvious, not secret. You can legitimately argue for safety margins on projects, or contingency money for potential risks, and you'll be a lot stronger throughout if you are honest and up front about it."[22] However, avoid arbitrary approaches such as the one suggested by Dilbert in Exhibit 5.21.

Reality Checks

What happens when your detailed budget reveals total anticipated expenditures that exceed the initial budget for the project? In the 10K charity run, the budget estimate of nearly $32,000 is quite high for a project intended to raise $50,000 for a local homeless shelter. And this is for only one part of the project. If the project is really going to cost this much (and more), the project sponsor might decide to donate the estimated cost directly to the shelter and dispense with the hassle of the project. His or her input will be important here. Before abandoning the project, team members should recheck their assumptions about project scope. Perhaps they have included work that is unnecessary or too ambitious. For example, maybe the radio and TV ads are not necessary. The project manager might also investigate the possibility of using more volunteer labor for some of the tasks, by requesting the help of running club members when they are being interviewed. Another possibility is to set a bigger target for the donation amount.

[21] Goldratt, *Critical Chain;* and Reinertsen, *Managing the Design Factory.*

[22] M. Dobson, *Project Management: How to Manage People, Processes, and Time to Achieve the Results You Need* (Avon, MA: Adams Media Corp., 2003), p. 186.

During interviews with running club members, project team members could investigate how much people would be willing to pay to participate and explore ideas for increasing participation. Discovering that detailed estimates exceed the initial budget now, when the team can take proactive steps, is infinitely better than discovering this three months into the project when money has already been spent and precious time has been invested unwisely.

Defining Success Criteria and Determining Key Performance Indicators

In preceding chapters, we have emphasized the importance of determining how the project will be measured. As part of the chartering process, the project sponsor should inform the project manager about performance expectations. The project manager typically determines how to measure whether these expectations have been met. Once the WBS is complete, the project manager and team are ready to formulate more detailed performance goals and metrics for project deliverables and tasks. At this stage, the team asks, "What is our goal for this deliverable or task, and how will we know if we have succeeded?" This should certainly include on-time schedule performance and staying within budget, but should go beyond these traditional measures to include desired outcomes.

For example, imagine you are planning a major company event for your biggest clients. You have decided to send out invitations by e-mail. A naive approach to performance measurement would be to simply say, "We sent out the e-mail. It's done, so we've performed." If you take a more performance-oriented view, you would include key performance indicators (KPIs) such as number of e-mail bounce-backs for bad addresses, percent of people who respond, percent of people who commit to attend, and percent of those who commit who actually do attend. You could set targets for each of these and have a plan for follow-up or corrections if you do not meet your targets (e.g., "no more than 5 percent bounce-backs"). Exhibit 5.22 offers a set of performance goals and KPIs for the promotions deliverable associated with the 10K charity run. In defining performance metrics, the project manager and team members should consider what they will measure *during* the project as well as *after* the project is complete. This allows for a full life-cycle perspective on the project. Note that some goals and KPIs can be measured objectively, but others will be more subjective.

Deciding what to measure further clarifies project goals, encourages the team to discuss assumptions, and leads to the addition of items to the WBS. For example, the goal to have at least 50 percent of running club members sign up for the race might prompt the team to produce a preliminary application form to distribute during the interviews. Similarly, the recognition that pilot tests would help organizers to determine if the ads are likely to be effective would suggest that pilot testing should be added as a work package under "Produce Ads."

Iterative Examination and Revision of the WBS

As the planning process continues, the team may need to revise the WBS. In particular, members may decide to add activities that will alleviate or mitigate certain project risks. Or the team may need to change the WBS if the project budget and schedule on which they are based are unacceptable to one or more key stakeholders (especially the sponsor or customer). If the scope of the project changes as the team learns more about what will actually be required to meet customer or sponsor expectations, the WBS will change as well. The team should consider the WBS as a work in progress as it

EXHIBIT 5.22   Examples of Key Performance Indicators for 10K Run Promotions Deliverable

Task	Examples of Performance Goals and Metrics *during* the Project	Examples of Performance Goals and Metrics *after* the Project
Research	• Interviews with running club members are finished on time and within budget. • At least 100 running club members agree to participate in telephone or in-person interviews. • At least 50% of interviewees sign up for the race.	• Those who were interviewed form a positive impression of our company, according to a post-event online survey.
TV & Radio Ads	• Ads are finished on time and within budget. • Ads meet approval of sponsor. • Ads meet approval of managers at the homeless shelter that will receive the charitable funds. • Pilot tests show ads are effective. • Monitoring demonstrates ads are run at the volume and frequency for which the team contracted. • Ads prompt participants to sign up for the 10K run.	• Ads can be used as templates for future 10K runs with little or no modification. • Ads have a positive long-term effect on the company's public image, as measured by research conducted by an outside marketing firm. • Community donations to the homeless shelter increase as a result of the increased exposure these ads produce.
Mailings	• Mailing lists developed on time. • Mailings completed on time and within budget. • Fewer than 5% of promotional items mailed are returned because of incorrect addresses.	• Mailing list updated and retained for use in promoting future events. • Future event managers use the list and find it helpful.
Flyers	• Flyers printed on time and within budget. • Flyers distributed on time and within budget. • Schools and retailers display flyers in locations where people will notice them. • Schools and retailers do not run out of flyers.	• Flyers not found littering the streets. • Future event managers find the flyer format useful.

moves through the planning stages and on to execution. Beware, though, of significant changes to the WBS during execution. As we shall discuss in Chapter 9, the project team should have a change-management system in place for evaluating, rejecting or accepting, documenting, and implementing changes.

Chapter Summary And Onward

In this chapter we introduced the heart of the project plan—the work breakdown structure—and other project plan elements that build on the WBS foundation. The work breakdown structure is the project manager's best insurance against the risk of omitting important work from the project plan and it establishes the boundaries of project scope. This tool helps turn a large, seemingly overwhelming piece of work into a set of tasks that are doable, manageable, and measurable. It creates the core of any project, and almost every aspect of a project manager's job relates in one way or another to the WBS. Mind mapping is a powerful and visual team-based tool for WBS development, and the detailed task list the WBS produces is the starting point for assigning task responsibility, estimating task durations, determining required resources, and estimating detailed project costs. The WBS is also fundamental to uncertainty assessment, project scheduling, and establishment of a monitoring and control system. A team would be "putting the cart before the horse" if its members attempted to develop these remaining planning elements without a WBS. We address these extensions to the project plan in Chapters 6, 7, 8, and 9.

It is very important to involve the project team in creating the WBS and the follow-on activities of responsibility assignment and time and cost estimation. Their expertise and commitment are essential to a successful project.

Team Activities

1. Return to the management retreat project described in the Team Activities at the end of Chapter 4. As described there, assume you and three classmates work for the same small electronics organization. You have been asked by your division manager, Noah Tolk, to organize a two-day, off-site year-in-review and "what's next" management retreat. The division manager has explained that he hopes the retreat will (a) provide an opportunity to celebrate recent accomplishments, (b) enhance community and interdepartmental cooperation within the organization, (c) provide time and space, without distraction, to focus on big picture issues facing the organization, and (d) increase managers' ideas about, understanding of, and buy-in to a set of strategic initiatives for the coming year. Noah is concerned that a lack of interdepartmental cooperation and understanding is causing delays in customer service, compromising the organization's ability to get new products to market, and, in general, limiting the organization's performance. Approximately 25 managers will attend the retreat, which is to be held within driving distance of the company offices.

   Noah has asked that the program be organized so there are sessions and activities devoted to: (1) highlighting key accomplishments of each area, (2) gathering input to shape next year's divisional strategic initiatives, and (3) informal team building and energizing the team for the year ahead. The retreat should occur sometime in the next three months. Resources allocated to the retreat include: $15,000 to pay for facilities, materials and services, two hours per week per project team member, and 20 total hours of administration time. Noah would like to see a draft plan for the retreat in four weeks and would like a written post-project report two weeks after the retreat. That report should briefly describe the retreat itself and the project that created it.

   a. Working *on your own* and using the traditional top-down outlining approach, develop a rough work breakdown structure (WBS) for this project with at least three levels of detail and at least 30 work packages at the most detailed level. Be prepared to share your results with your team when you get to part b of this exercise.

   b. Working with a team of three other people, use the mind mapping format to create a work breakdown structure for this project. Again, your WBS should have at least three levels of detail and at least 30 work packages.

   c. As a team, discuss the differences and similarities between these two approaches. Prepare a one page summary of your discussion.

2. Gather a team of three to five classmates and locate the following article: T. Aeppel, "Attention, Shoppers: Global Scramble for Goods Gives Corporate Buyers a Lift," *The Wall Street Journal,* October 2, 2007, p. A1. Imagine you are staff members in the purchasing department of Manitowoc, one of the world's largest crane makers. As described in the article, Manitowoc is having trouble getting parts from a supplier in Poland. According to Robert Ward, the company's corporate purchasing

officer, the result of the parts shortage has been "a lot of angry customers." Imagine Mr. Ward has assigned you and your team to get these parts flowing to the company's plant in Lyon, France, within 30 days. Using a mind mapping approach on a large sheet of paper, develop a two-level WBS for this project. This means you will consider deliverables and their subordinate work packages. You may go to a third level if you wish, but two levels will meet the requirement of this assignment. Consider ideas presented in the article, but go beyond these to bring in your own ideas. Keep in mind all stakeholders involved, including suppliers and their extended supply chains, customers, the crane assembly plant in France, and others. (If you consider these stakeholders, you will be more likely to develop a comprehensive WBS.) When you have completed the WBS, convert it to an outline. Submit a photo of your group gathered around your completed mind map, a photo of the mind map, and a copy of the outline. Individually, prepare and submit a paragraph describing your experience and observations about the team process.

3. Gather a team of three to five classmates and locate the following article: C. Cummins, "Oil Tanker Waylaid by Pirates," *The Wall Street Journal,* November 18, 2008, p. A1, as well as one or two related articles detailing the outcome of this crisis for the owners and crew of this Saudi Arabian vessel. Imagine you are part of a crisis response team hired to return the crew, ship, and cargo safely. Work with your team to prepare the following:

   a. A list of desired project goals to use as a guideline in developing your project plan. Two of your goals will be: no loss of human life and no damage to the environment.

   b. A list of three mutually exclusive options for achieving the project objective.

   c. A paragraph describing the general approach you have chosen. Defend your choice. Recall your constraint: You cannot ultimately choose an option that intentionally results in the loss of human life or damage to the environment.

   d. A WBS of your project plan, in mind map and outline form, with at least four deliverables and at least 20 work packages at the most detailed level. Include a photo of your team gathered around your wall-mounted WBS.

   e. A responsibility matrix showing the work assignments of your project team members, as well as any subcontractors you may have chosen to involve in the project.

   f. Key performance indicators for each of the high-level deliverables you identified in part d.

   g. Calendar and work time estimates for each of the work packages you identified in part d. Explain the assumptions you have made in making your estimates. For at least four of the work packages, use the three-point estimation method and explain how you derived your optimistic, pessimistic, and most likely figures.

Discussion Questions and Exercises

1. What elements of the project plan depend on the WBS? Select four of these and explain the relationship with examples.

2. What are the advantages of organizing the WBS around deliverables rather than functions? What would be the advantages of organizing a WBS by function? Explain your answers with a specific example of your own creation and show how the WBS would look in each case.

3. How is a work package related to a deliverable in WBS terminology? Use an example to explain your answer.

4. Under what circumstances might it be appropriate to use a WBS from a previous project rather than developing a new one? What are the potential risks?

5. Name the three different approaches for developing a WBS presented in this chapter. What are the advantages and disadvantages of each? Go beyond statements from the text to explain your answer in your own words, and cite some advantages or disadvantages that are *not* mentioned.

6. What is a sum-of-the-parts check? Why is it necessary?

7. How does a responsibility matrix differ from a project involvement matrix? Which organizational members would find the most value in each one? Create an example to illustrate your arguments.

8. How do time estimates for scheduling differ from time estimates for budgeting? Create an example to support your explanation.

9. What is the value of using time estimate ranges rather than single point time estimates? Use an example to support your explanation.

10. Ratcliff Electronics has hired a company to create a movable exhibition to display and demonstrate its consumer products during a series of one-week shows in 32 cities around the world. This contractor, located in Bonn, Germany, has developed a system to transport and display the exhibit using cargo containers. Each container is a module that can be snapped into place with the others to create a self-contained, temporary facility at each location. At the end of the exhibit's run in each city, the modules will be dismantled and placed on trucks or trains, then transported over land or sea to the next location. The project manager has gathered data for setup times on similar traveling shows the company has managed previously for other customers. She has determined that the setup time for the first location will typically be about 30 working hours, assuming a staff of 20 people and all necessary equipment are available. She also has discovered setup teams tend to get faster over time as they move from city to city, and that their learning rate is 95 percent.

   a. Use the manual method shown in Exhibit 5.16 to determine estimated times for the first, second, fourth, eighth, 16th, and 32nd setups. Show your work.

   b. Use the learning curves table in Exhibit 5.17 to determine the estimated times for setup in cities one through 30. Show how your estimates would change if the learning rate were 75 percent instead of 95 percent. Draw a graph of the unit time estimates under these two learning-rate assumptions.

   c. Imagine you work for the contracting company and the president of Ratcliff Electronics has asked you to explain how learning curves affected your estimates. Write a few sentences offering an explanation in your own words, using hypothetical examples related to this traveling exhibition project.

11. Your family (you, your spouse, and five-year-old child) are planning a trip to Walt Disney World in Orlando, Florida. Representatives from upper management (your spouse and child) have specified that the trip will entail travel to Orlando, a four-night stay, and three days spent in Disney World itself. You and your spouse have allocated about $5,000 from your annual budget for this project.

   a. Develop a WBS for this project and submit your work in mind map and outline form. You should have at least 30 work packages as the lowest level.

   b. Select three of the deliverables included in your WBS and, for each, list three key performance indicators.

12. For two of the major deliverables or project elements you identified for the Disney World project, develop a detailed cost estimate in a spreadsheet format similar to the one shown in Exhibit 5.20. Your goal is to make the cost estimate as accurate as possible. Explain the approach you adopted in developing the estimate and the

strategies you used to increase the accuracy of the estimate. Also list any assumptions on which your estimates are based. How confident are you in the accuracy of these cost estimates? Why?

13. Imagine you and two classmates are about to collaborate in creating a 15-page research paper for one of your other classes. The paper is due six weeks from today. Your team's goals include earning an A on the paper, learning something about the topic, and maintaining or enhancing your interpersonal relationships. At the first meeting with your two colleagues you suggest creating a WBS for this undertaking. Your friends, who have not taken the project management course in which you are enrolled, respond with puzzled expressions.

   a. In 100 words or fewer, explain to your classmates what a WBS is, and how it can contribute to meeting the project objectives.

   b. Create a WBS for this project using one of the approaches described in the chapter (mind mapping, top-down outline, bottom-up affinity diagram). Explain why you selected this approach. (The WBS you develop should have at least three major deliverables and 15 to 20 work packages.)

   c. For two of the work packages you identified, estimate the time required to complete this work package. Using the information provided in the section on time and cost estimates, identify the approach you adopted in developing the time estimate and the strategies you used to increase the accuracy of the estimate. Also list any assumptions on which your estimates are based. How confident are you in the accuracy of these time estimates? Why?

14. You, your spouse, and your two children (ages seven and nine) have decided to hold a garage sale. The project objective is to reduce clutter in your home and raise spending money for an upcoming vacation. The sale is planned for three weeks from this Saturday. You have identified the following first-level WBS deliverables: select and price items for sale, promotions, setup for day of sale, selling and cashier activities, and cleanup. Develop a responsibility matrix for this project.

15. Develop a list of resource requirements based on the research paper project WBS you developed for question 13.

16. You and several of your musical colleagues have formed a rock band embarking on its first nationwide tour. You will be traveling by bus with a crew of roadies who will be responsible for setup in each location in advance of the performance. The roadies anticipate the setup time will be somewhat shorter in each venue as crew members gain experience working with one another and with the band's unique stage requirements. You have investigated learning rates for similar touring groups and estimate the learning rate will be 75 percent. If the time required at the first venue is 10 hours, or 600 minutes, what will be the time estimate for the set up at the 32nd venue? Show your work and explain your answer.

17. You are a member of the park and recreation services in the city of New Orleans and have been assigned to a team charged with creating a new one acre city park. In a letter announcing the project, the mayor has stated:

   Increasing the quality of life for the citizens of New Orleans is the number one objective of my office. After careful consideration with the city council, we have decided that a new neighborhood park within Orleans Parish will contribute significantly to achieving this goal. This park will provide more recreation for our citizens and also enhance the beauty of our city. I would like to thank you and your team for agreeing to work on this important project and know you will do an excellent job of selecting the location of the new park (please choose from the land the city has acquired through its abandoned house demolition program), creating the blueprint for the park (base this on citizen input, benchmarking, and council feedback on your draft plan – see below), complying with any legal or regulatory issues (e.g., permits, environmental impact, zoning, safety, etc.) and selecting, contracting with, and overseeing the work of a construction company to actually build the park.

The Mayor has designated a $225,000 grant from the federal government for the creation of the park. The park is to be completed within seven months. In addition, the Mayor has stated:

Three months from now, I would like to share the final location of the park and a draft of its blueprint with the city council. I would like to demonstrate to the council that the location and planned amenities have been based on citizen input, so please consider this as you plan your work. Four months from now, I would like to send finalized blueprints and your picks for possible construction companies to the city council office for final approval. Within seven months, a grand opening celebration, which highlights the new park's contribution to the city's available recreational options and beauty, and which attracts local media attention, should occur. Naturally, planning and executing the grand opening event is an important part of your work as the project team.

Based on the information provided (and on other issues you believe would be important in such an endeavor), develop a WBS for this project that includes at least 40 work packages. Use any of the three WBS formats discussed in the chapter.

18. You are leading a team to implement an integrated ERP (enterprise resource planning) system in your Madrid-based company, a contract manufacturer of electronic components for the consumer electronics industry. You currently have 3,800 employees in 19 plants in 10 different countries, and your sales revenue was 5 billion euros last year. Your company has expanded quickly and has outgrown its current enterprise systems, many of which were programmed in-house. The steering committee has decided to break the project into two phases, and to include the following modules in the first phase:
    - Finance
    - Accounting
    - Human Resource Management
    - Customer Relationship Management
    - Material Requirements Planning
    - Purchasing

    The steering committee has specified that the new system will be purchased from an outside vendor, and that a consulting company will be hired to provide guidance for requirements assessment and specification setting, training, testing, and implementation. Your task is as follows:

    a. Develop a list of goals for your project, focusing on systemwide issues such as system reliability as well as goals for the functioning of the modules.

    b. Make a list of the assumptions you will make as groundwork for developing your WBS (e.g., "An outside vendor will provide the training").

    c. Develop a WBS for this project in mind map, organization structure, and outline form (See Exhibit 5.4). Your WBS should have at least five deliverables or major components and you should define at least 30 work packages at the finest level of detail. Your deliverables need not focus on the six modules. Instead, you are better off structuring your WBS around action-oriented deliverables such as "Requirements Assessment" or "User Training." Keep in mind that even though an outside vendor will perform certain aspects of the work, that work needs to be included in the WBS. After all, the work still must be done!

d. List at least three key performance indicators (KPIs) for each of the deliverables in your WBS. Be sure to go beyond cost and schedule to consider more outcome-oriented metrics. Describe how you would measure these indicators.

References

Andress, F.J. "The Learning Curve as a Production Tool." *Harvard Business Review* 32, no. 1 (1954), pp. 87–97.

Austin, R., and R. Luecke. *Managing Projects Large and Small.* Boston: Harvard Business School Publishing Corp., 2004.

Brassard, M. *The Memory Jogger Plus.* Methuen, MA: Goal QPC, 1996.

Brown, K.A., and N.L. Hyer. "Whole Brain Thinking for Project Management." *Business Horizons* 45, no. 3 (2002), pp. 47–57.

Buzan, T., and B. Buzan. *The Mind Map Book.* New York: Plume Books, 1996.

Dobson, M. *Project Management: How to Manage People, Processes, and Time to Achieve the Results You Need.* Avon, MA: Adams Media Corp., 2003.

Goldratt, E. *Critical Chain.* Great Barrington, MA: North River Press, 1997.

Haber, R.N. "How We Remember What We See." *Scientific American* 222, no. 5 (1970), pp. 104-12.

Hirschmann, W.B. "Profit From the Learning Curve." *Harvard Business Review* 42, no. 1 (1964), pp. 125–39.

Hyer, N.L., and U. Wemmerlöv. *Reorganizing the Factory: Competing through Cellular Manufacturing.* Portland, OR: Productivity, 2002.

IPS Associates. *Project Management Manual.* Boston: Harvard Business School Press, 1996.

Kim, W., and R. Mauborgne. "Fair Process: Managing in the Knowledge Economy" *Harvard Business Review* 75, no. 4 (1997), pp. 65–75.

Lapré, M., and L.N. Van Wassenhove. "Managing Learning Curves by Creating and Transferring Knowledge." *California Management Review* 46, no. 1 (2003), pp. 53–71.

Latham, G.P. *Work Motivation: History, Theory, Research, and Practice.* Thousand Oaks, CA: Sage Publications, 2006.

Matta, N.F., and R.N. Ashkenas. "Why Good Projects Fail Anyway." *Harvard Business Review* 81, no. 9 (2003), pp. 109–14.

Nix, N.W.; R.F. Lusch; Z.G. Zacharia; and W. Bridges. "The Hand that Feeds You: What Makes Some Collaborations with Suppliers Succeed When So Many Fail?" *The Wall Street Journal,* October 27–28, 2007, p. R8.

Project Management Institute. *The Project Management Body of Knowledge.* Philadelphia: PMI Press, 2004.

Project Management Institute. *The Project Management Institute Practice Standard for Work Breakdown Structures.* Philadelphia: PMI Press, 2002.

Reinertsen, D. *Managing the Design Factory.* New York: The Free Press, 1997.

Schwalbe, K. *Information Technology Project Management.* Cambridge, MA: Thomson Learning, 2000.

Teplitz, C.J. *The Learning Curve Deskbook.* New York: Quorum Books, 1991.

Wheatley, M. *Leadership and the New Science.* San Francisco, CA: Berrett-Koehler Publishers, 1996.

Chapter **Six**

Assessing and Preparing for Project Uncertainties

"Anything that can go wrong will go wrong."
Murphy's Law

"Was I deceived, or did a sable cloud / Turn forth her silver lining on the night?"
John Milton

Chapter Learning Objectives

When you have mastered the material in this chapter, you should be able to:

- Describe the dimensions of project uncertainty as they apply to a specific project.
- Apply a systematic process for assessing potential uncertainties and preparing for them.
- In a team setting, apply uncertainty assessment tools such as risk mapping, failure modes and effects analysis (FMEA), gut-feel, Delphi, and fishbone diagrams.
- Design contingency plans to prepare for uncertainties.
- Revise a project plan to incorporate appropriate strategies for mitigating the potential outcomes associated with unfavorable uncertainties and enhancing the potential outcomes associated with favorable uncertainties.
- Develop a plan for monitoring uncertainties during a project's life cycle.

This chapter is about surprises or potential surprises, and how the effective project manager can anticipate, prepare for, monitor, and respond to them. In the context of surprises, we often think of risks with the potential to produce undesirable outcomes. However, uncertainties can lead to favorable outcomes, too, as noted in the Project Management Institute's *A Guide to the Project Management Body of Knowledge,* a project risk is "an uncertain event or condition that, if it occurs, has a positive or negative effect on a project's objectives."[1] In a slight departure from PMI, we use the word "risk" when referring to unfavorable uncertainties and we describe uncertainties with potential positive effects as "favorable uncertainties."

[1] Project Management Institute, *A Guide to the Project Management Body of Knowledge* (Newton Square, PA: PMI, 2008), p. 446.

EXAMPLES OF PROJECT UNCERTAINTIES

We begin with examples of **unfavorable project risks** and **favorable project uncertainties** that affected the outcomes of two projects. In each case, front-end brainstorming might have led the project team to envision the possibility of these uncertainties and appropriately adjust plans.

Example of an Unfavorable Project Risk: A Fence on the Neighbor's Property

In 2007, the U.S. government embarked on a controversial project to build a fence along its border with Mexico in several isolated areas where monitoring for illegal entrants was difficult. A few months into the project, Mexican officials determined that a 1.5-mile (2.4-kilometer) stretch of the fence had been built six feet (about two meters) south of the border on Mexican soil.[2] Crewmembers apparently had relied on the position of a rancher's fence line, rather than survey data, to determine the position of the border.[3] Existing Mexican opposition to the project was further inflamed as a consequence of the wrong positioning, and the U.S. government had to move the fence at an additional project cost of about $3 million. It seems possible that if project team members had brainstormed about the worst things that could happen, at least one person might have said, "We could put the fence in the wrong place!" This could have led the team to consider ways to avoid such a politically embarrassing and costly outcome through more diligence in fence positioning.

Example of a Favorable Project Uncertainty: Lilly Discovers Unexpected Drug Application

Eli Lilly and Co. has had many drugs fail in clinical trials, an accepted possibility in any scientific endeavor. One such drug, Evista, initially developed for birth control, was put into the category of bad ideas when it failed clinical trials. But this turned out to be an example of a missed opportunity—the drug later was found to be effective in addressing a completely different problem: osteoporosis.[4] Evidence of the alternative application emerged during the trials, but team members had been so focused on birth control they initially ignored it. This is a case where the organization could have been more aware of favorable uncertainties that had the potential to change the outcome of the project. Lilly has now implemented a formal process for uncovering other potentially missed opportunities in drug research.

THE ROLE OF PROJECT UNCERTAINTY ASSESSMENT

Uncertainty analysis occurs at every stage of the project management process, beginning with project selection and continuing to customer handoff and closure. In this chapter, we highlight tools that are especially useful during the planning stage,

---

[2] A.A. Caldwell, "Border Barrier Accidentally Crosses Border," *Seattle Times,* June 30, 2007, p. 1.

[3] Although one might attribute this to stupidity, it is helpful to consider that ranchers' fences and the border had lined up elsewhere, perhaps lulling team members into a false confidence about the accuracy of the fence lines. Risk analysis can help us to avoid doing stupid things.

[4] T.M. Burton, "Flop Factor: By Learning from Failures, Lilly Keeps Drug Pipeline Full," *The Wall Street Journal,* April 21, 2004, p. A1.

after the first-pass work breakdown structure (WBS) has been developed. Uncertainty assessment at this stage is likely to lead a team to alter or expand the WBS to prepare for newly recognized possibilities.

Any project, regardless of its size, needs uncertainty analysis. If you are planning a children's birthday party, you might run through what could go right or wrong in your head ("The children might really enjoy Bingo and want to play several more times than we have planned." "Billy is prone to temper tantrums when he loses at Bingo!") If you were responsible for implementing a new companywide IT system, you would conduct a much more formal analysis involving the team and key stakeholders.

Even with the best uncertainty analysis, some events will still come as surprises—the **unknown unknowns**.[5] However, if the team has planned carefully and anticipated as many eventualities **(known unknowns)** as it possibly can, members will be more likely to have the time and resources to deal effectively with those they were unable to anticipate. Anyone involved in project uncertainty assessment has good intentions, but several human biases can interfere with the ability of individuals and teams to see future possibilities as clearly as they should. Being aware of these biases, which we highlight in Appendix 6A at the end of this chapter, is a good starting point.

DIMENSIONS OF UNCERTAINTY

Project team members should consider several risk or uncertainty dimensions to ensure they have cast a wide enough net during the assessment phase. These include **source, outcome,** and **likelihood.** We highlight each of these below.

Uncertainty Sources

There are many perspectives on the sources of project uncertainty,[6] but most fit into the five categories, shown in Exhibit 6.1. Box 6.1 highlights examples of favorable and unfavorable uncertainties in these five categories as they could be applied to a project to develop a new airplane. Some aspects of the scenarios described in Box 6.1 are based on factual information and others are based on conjecture to illustrate future thinking.

Uncertainty Outcomes

An undesirable uncertainty in itself is not a problem to the project manager, and not every favorable uncertainty necessarily makes a project an unprecedented success. The *consequence* of the risk or favorable uncertainty creates headaches or opens

---

[5] R.M. Wideman, *Project and Program Risk Management: A Guide to Managing Risks and Opportunities* (Newtown Square, PA: Project Management Institute, 1992).

[6] For example, I. Mitroff, *Managing Crises before They Happen* (New York: American Management Association, 2001) includes economic, informational, physical, human resource, reputational, psychopathic (e.g., terrorism or product tampering), and natural disasters. T.D. Klastorin, *Project Management: Tools and Tradeoffs* (New York: Wiley and Sons, 2004) identifies technical, government, unexpected losses, market, legal, and natural hazards. Wideman, *Project and Program Risk Management,* includes scope, quality, information, contract, cost, time, quality, human resource, and integration. This last set, from our perspective, has more to do with the **outcomes** of risks, rather than sources.

EXHIBIT 6.1
Sources of
Uncertainty

Uncertainty Source	Unfavorable Uncertainty	Favorable Uncertainty
Financial	Financial conditions inside or outside the organization that could potentially threaten the success of the project.	Financial conditions inside or outside the organization that could enhance the viability or outcome of the project.
Technical	A possible technical challenge that could alter the course of the project in a negative way.	A possible technical breakthrough that could alter the course of the project in a positive way.
Business Environment	A possible market, political, or regulatory condition that could make the project outcomes less attractive than anticipated.	A possible market, political, or regulatory condition that could make project outcomes more attractive than anticipated.
Social	A project challenge associated with potential stakeholder interference in the project. Stakeholders can be inside or outside the organization.	Unexpected support for the project from a stakeholder group that might help the project advance. Stakeholders can be inside or outside the organization.
External or Natural Environment	Acts of nature such as disease epidemics, floods, earthquakes, tornadoes, weather patterns, or oceanic circumstances that could have a negative effect on the project.	Acts of nature such as the spontaneous end of a disease epidemic or changes in weather patterns that could make the project unexpectedly easier to execute.

doors.[7] Typical consequences of negative uncertainties include (but are not limited to) schedule delays, cost overruns, reductions in quality, project abandonment, physical or psychological harm to people, damage to facilities or the environment, and loss of reputation.

Likelihood of Occurrence

The project team must consider the likelihood of uncertainties to determine where it should focus attention. In most project environments, it is not possible to assess likelihoods with precision. In the absence of historical data, project teams typically take a subjective approach, based on opinion and judgment. But there are consensus-based or voting methods they can use to enhance their ability to forecast, as we discuss in this chapter.

"Prediction is very difficult, especially about the future."

Niels Bohr

[7] P.G. Smith and G. Merritt, *Proactive Risk Management* (Portland, OR: Productivity Press, 2002).

Dimensions of Uncertainty for the Boeing 787 Project

Box 6.1

© AP Photo/Elaine Thompson

In the mid-to-late 2000s, Boeing Commercial Airplanes was in the midst of a new development project for a mid-size (230–350) passenger jet to meet the needs of a variety of city-pair travel needs, including point-to-point, hub-to-hub, hub-to-point, etc. The airplane, initially called the 7E7 but later named the 787,* was promoted as fuel-efficient because it was to be made from lightweight composites supported by titanium structures.[†] The company had used this approach in military aircraft but had not tested it to any great extent in the commercial market. Not wanting to repeat the experience of high development costs associated with the 777 in the 1990s,[‡] Boeing transferred large portions of the development expense to subcontractors in several countries. At the same time, development speed was a major priority. For example, China represented a big market for the airplane, and Boeing officials promoted it for transport of spectators and tourists during the 2008 Olympic Games. Potentially big sales to China depended on Boeing's ability to meet the 2008 target. (Unfortunately, Boeing was unable to reach this goal.) Examples of possible uncertainty sources in each category shown in Exhibit 6.1 are highlighted below.

FINANCIAL UNCERTAINTIES

Unfavorable Uncertainty Example

A key supplier developing a critical component could go into financial default and be unable to deliver designs or build prototypes.[§]

Favorable Uncertainty Example

An airplane leasing company (often major customers for commercial jetliners) could become so optimistic about the 787 it would offer itself as a financial partner in the development process.

TECHNICAL UNCERTAINTIES

Unfavorable Uncertainty Example

Some informed observers warned that the 787's composite fuselage might not hold up in a crash because its structural properties made it more brittle than aluminum, the material used historically for airplane skins.**

---

* The "E" for "efficiency" in the 7E7 was later changed to an "8" at the encouragement of customers from China where the number "8" is considered lucky. Given the importance of China as a major customer, and the fact that this airplane was next in sequence after the 777, it made great sense to Boeing officials. Fact or urban legend, it makes a good story.

[†] S. Kotha and R. Nolan, *Boeing 787: The Dreamliner,* Harvard Business School case # 9-305-101 (Boston: Harvard Business School Publishing, 2005).

[‡] Although Boeing has not made any public statements, some financial analysts estimate the cost of the 777 development program at about $15 billion.

[§] As it turned out, when the first airplane was rolled out in July of 2007, it was actually missing several parts from suppliers and was not yet ready to fly (Gates, 2007a). See D. Gates, "First 787 Still Missing Parts," *Seattle Times,* August 21, 2007; www.seattletimes.com.

** D. Gates, "FAA Dismissed Criticism over 787 Safety Tests," *Seattle Times,* October 2, 2007; www.seattletimes.com.

Favorable Uncertainty Example

Boeing might be able to use technological advances from the 787 program to leverage developments in its defense and space programs to a greater extent than initially planned.

BUSINESS ENVIRONMENT UNCERTAINTIES

Unfavorable Uncertainty Example

Boeing was betting on the increasing demand for point-to-point and other short-haul air travel in medium-size airplanes. If Boeing's bet proved wrong, the company and its suppliers would not be able to recoup their huge investments (leading secondarily to a financial risk).[††]

Favorable Uncertainty Example

It was possible that increasing fuel costs (certainly a high possibility that did materialize) would increase demand for fuel-efficient commercial aircraft, raising demand for the 787 beyond that initially imagined.

SOCIAL UNCERTAINTIES

Unfavorable Uncertainty Example

Airplane components were to be built in large sections, in many cases outside the United States, and assembled in the company's Everett, Washington, facility. Union organizations objected to the new strategy because of the job losses it would produce.[‡‡] This could further evolve into bad public relations for the company.

Favorable Uncertainty Example

It is possible organized consumer-advocacy groups could become increasingly vocal about the inconveniences of hub-to-hub travel. If passengers see the 787 as part of a potential remedy to the problem, they might initiate public campaigns that would positively influence airline purchase decisions.

UNCERTAINTIES ASSOCIATED WITH THE EXTERNAL OR NATURAL ENVIRONMENT

Unfavorable Uncertainty Example

The Seattle area, home to the Boeing Commercial Airplanes group and the final assembly site for the 787, sits near a major geological fault.[§§] The fault is considered ripe for a devastating earthquake that could seriously damage Boeing's operations and facilities in the area, making it difficult or impossible to meet production schedules.

Favorable Uncertainty Example

In the process of preparing facilities for a big quake, Boeing might discover protective structural remedies it could patent and sell to other companies. Or, in creating a recovery plan for an earthquake, Boeing might develop strategies and processes that would be useful for responding to other types of disasters.

Source: As the references footnoted here suggest, some of the information in this example is drawn from newspaper articles about the 787 program. Other information is drawn from the authors' conversations with Boeing insiders and observers.

[††] As it turned out, Boeing received a record-high number of orders for the airplane (Lunsford, 2007). See J. L. Lunsford, "Boeing Vows On-Time Dreamliner," *The Wall Street Journal,* September 17, 2007, p. A8.

[‡‡] D. Gates, "Plan to Put 7E7 in Everett Tied to Boeing Transformation: Worker Support for New Production Strategy Is Key Factor as Board Weighs Site Proposal," *Seattle Times,* December 7, 2003, p. A1.

[§§] S. Doughton, "Pinpointing Devastation if Seattle Fault Ruptures," *Seattle Times,* February 20, 2005; http://seattletimes.nwsource.com/html/localnews/2002185299_earthquake20m.html; and T. Paulson, "New Shaky Ground in Seattle," *Seattle Post-Intelligencer,* October 12, 2007, p. A1.

LINKING LIKELIHOOD WITH DESIRABILITY OF OUTCOMES

Ultimately, a team looks for the relationship between likelihood and impact for each uncertainty. Utility theory describes how these two dimensions can be combined mathematically.[8] For example, imagine there is a 5 percent chance it will rain during a roofing project, causing a delay, requiring extra tenting equipment, and therefore costing an additional $2,000. Conversely, there is a 95 percent chance it will not rain, and there will be no additional cost. The expected value is $(.05 \times -\$2,000) + (.95 \times \$0) = -\$100$. We can use this general concept in terms of schedule, budget, and performance to weight the relevance of various uncertainties in cases where it is possible to estimate probabilities and where outcomes can be quantified. For more on utility theory, see Appendix B on decision analysis at the end of this book.

Exhibit 6.2 shows a traditional visual model combining likelihood with outcome desirability for unfavorable uncertainties (risks). The estimates of the two dimensions can be drawn from objective data or subjective assessments. This approach categorizes risks into three zones: red, yellow, and green. Risks in the red zone should receive the most attention, and a project team would seek ways to avoid these altogether. Those in the yellow zone might receive a wait-and-see status, and those in the green zone would be viewed in terms such as "Be aware, but don't worry too much about these." For the red zone, even those with low likelihoods are important because of the serious impact they can have on the project. Considering a space shuttle mission, we offer four examples (A through D) and locate them on the matrix in Exhibit 6.2.

- **Risk A, Food:** The astronauts might not like the food available on the shuttle. Given the nature of food delivery in zero-gravity conditions, this has a high likelihood.[9] However, it would be within the astronauts' expectations and probably would not have a negative effect on the project. Thus, it appears in the upper left-hand corner of the matrix.

---

[8] See J. Raftery, *Risk Analysis in Project Management* (London: E&FN Spon, 1994).

[9] One of our former students who worked for NASA insists that in-flight food on shuttles is delicious, but we don't believe him.

EXHIBIT 6.2
Traditional Risk Matrix Showing Relationships between Likelihood and Impact: Space Shuttle Example

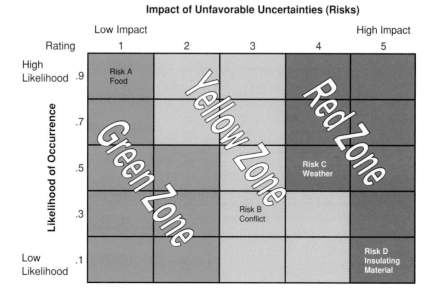

Impact of Unfavorable Uncertainties (Risks)

- **Risk B, Conflict:** The astronauts might experience interpersonal conflict during the mission. Given the close quarters and the potential for disconnects between individual and team goals, this carries a moderate likelihood. It could have some effect on the mission, but command structures would be likely to keep it from getting out of hand. Thus, it might best be placed in the yellow zone—something to watch.

- **Risk C, Weather:** Weather conditions might make it too dangerous to land the shuttle at the scheduled time and date. Although this is moderately likely, NASA has contingency plans in place (delay or reroute landing), so the impact would be serious but not devastating. This one might deserve to be on the inner edge of the red zone.

- **Risk D, Insulating Material:** If there is a breach in the shuttle's insulating material, the result could be catastrophic, as was the case with the space shuttle *Columbia* in 2003.[10] Although the probability of such an occurrence is low, it belongs in the red zone because of the disastrous outcome it would create.

A team could take the process a step further by adding numerical scores to the risks identified in Exhibit 6.2. The numbers adjacent to the vertical and horizontal axes can serve this purpose and may be used as somewhat subjective cutoff points for various types of actions. For example, a team or an organization might have a decision rule that any insurmountable risk with a 0.9 likelihood and a 5 on the impact scale (upper right-hand corner) would justify abandoning the project.

Expanded View of the Risk Matrix: Adding Favorable Uncertainties

The traditional risk matrix presented in Exhibit 6.2 does not include the possibility of potentially favorable uncertainties—things not currently within our expectations that have the potential to make the project even better or open doors for valuable opportunities currently outside the scope of the project. An historical example is Norway's international fishing boundaries negotiation in 1961.[11] At the time, Norwegian officials secured exclusive rights to the fisheries within 12 miles (about 19 kilometers) of the country's shores but did not anticipate that this maritime boundary offered an unseen opportunity for oil exploration. The story had a happy ending, but perhaps if Norwegian negotiators had anticipated the possibility of untapped oceanic oil reserves they might have been more aggressive than they were.

In keeping with the idea of anticipating potentially favorable uncertainties, Hillson has developed an expanded presentation, a version of which is shown in Exhibit 6.3.[12] The Project Management Institute also has embraced this perspective.

---

[10] On February 1, 2003, the space shuttle *Columbia* disintegrated in midair 15 minutes before its scheduled landing, apparently because a hole in one of the panels in the heat-protecting composite exposed the shuttle to the high temperatures (exceeding 3,000 degrees Fahrenheit or 1,649 Celsius) associated with reentry; see www.space.co/missionlaunches/caib_preview.

[11] H. Allen, *Norway and Europe in the 1970s* (Oslo: Universitetsforlaget, 1979).

[12] D. Hillson, "Extending the Risk Process to Manage Opportunities," *International Journal of Project Management* 20, no. 3 (2002), pp. 235–40.

EXHIBIT 6.3
Uncertainty Matrix Showing both Favorable and Unfavorable Uncertainties

Source: D. Hillson, "Extending the Risk Process to Manage Opportunities," *International Journal of Project Management* 20 (2002), pp. 235–40.

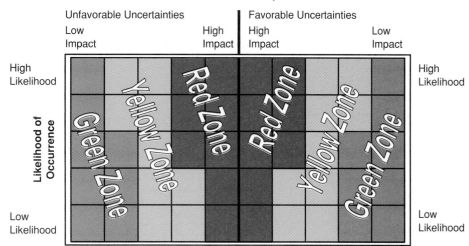

As in the case of the traditional risk matrix displayed in Exhibit 6.2, red zone uncertainties in Exhibit 6.3 should receive the most attention. The general rule is to look for high-likelihood, big-impact uncertainties on either side of the mirror-image matrix. High-likelihood, high-impact favorable events should be the target of most efforts because they offer relatively easy ways to enhance a project. However, drawing from work on implications wheels by Barker[13] and on Kepner and Tregoe's work on decision making,[14] we suggest a project team can sometimes find ways to increase the likelihood of *low probability* positive uncertainties. Consequently, the rules for selecting uncertainties for further consideration and action are more clearly cut for potential unfavorable risks than they are for potential favorable uncertainties. A caution is appropriate here: Going too far with favorable uncertainties can lead to scope creep, or the inappropriate expansion of a project beyond its mission.

THE UNCERTAINTY ASSESSMENT PLANNING AND ACTION PROCESS

Although uncertainty assessment should occur in every project phase, the team should engage in its most detailed analysis after it possesses a clear idea of project mission, goals, and scope, and after it has developed the WBS. Without knowledge of project content, it will be difficult for the team to imagine potential uncertainties. As shown in Exhibit 6.4, a team involved in uncertainty assessment typically gathers data and brainstorms possibilities, considers root causes, assesses likelihoods, envisions outcomes, considers risk preferences, selects relevant uncertainties, develops strategies, assigns responsibilities, and finds ways to monitor each relevant uncertainty. The extent of formality in this process, and the time spent, will depend on the size and complexity of the project.

[13] J. Barker, "Implications Wheels Training Video," 1994; http://strategicexploration.com/implications-wheel/ (accessed July 26, 2009).

[14] C.H. Kepner and B.B. Tregoe, *The New Rational Manager* (Princeton, NJ: Princeton University Press, 1981).

EXHIBIT 6.4   Project Uncertainty Assessment Process

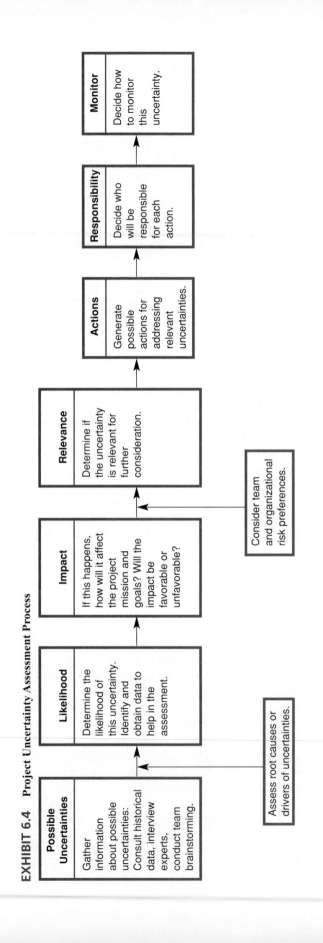

EXHIBIT 6.5
Uncertainty
Responses

Source: Adapted from
D. Hillson, "Extending the Risk
Process to Manage Opportuni-
ties," *International Journal of
Project Management* 20 (2002),
pp. 235–40, and *A Guide to the
Project Management Body of
Knowledge* (2008).

General Objective	Countermeasures for Risks or Unfavorable Uncertainties	Enhancements for Favorable Uncertainties
Modify exposure	Mitigate (Reduce the likelihood or negative effect of a risk event so it falls within acceptable threshold limits)	Enhance (Increase the likelihood or positive effect of an upside uncertainty or opportunity)
Shift ownership	Transfer risk to another party	Share opportunity with another party
Eliminate this uncertainty or ensure its occurrence	Avoid (Change the project plan to eliminate the threat entirely)	Exploit (Change the project plan to ensure the opportunity becomes a reality)
Accept and prepare	Accept potential for this risk to occur, and develop contingency plans	Accept potential for this uncertainty to occur, and prepare to take advantage if it emerges

A project team can devise several types of actions in preparing for negative and positive uncertainties. We highlight these in Exhibit 6.5.

Uncertainty Preparation and Response Strategies: Return to the Boeing Example

Returning to the Boeing 787 example highlighted earlier in this chapter, we examine an unfavorable financial risk and a potentially favorable technical uncertainty. Box 6.2 demonstrates how Boeing might respond using the strategies listed in Exhibit 6.5.

Some strategies for addressing uncertainties will create new WBS elements. As part of this process, the team must assign responsibility. If the newly identified actions blend well with the existing WBS, responsibility will reside with the individual or team associated with the related deliverable. If a significant new deliverable is added, the project organization structure will need to be expanded and new responsibilities assigned. In the 787 example, if Boeing decided to avoid the risk of a supplier's financial failure by in-sourcing fabrication and assembly of a key component, this would add a major deliverable, significantly expanding project scope. A project manager who can demonstrate that a request for change in scope and budget is based on a rigorous risk assessment process will be more likely (but not guaranteed!) to receive additional funding than one who simply asks for more money with only vague justification.

An uncertainty, by definition, is something that *might* happen,[15] but is currently not a goal or expected project outcome. Consequently, teams need monitoring systems that provide early warning signals, allowing them to respond appropriately.[16] In Exhibit 6.6

[15] As Martin and Tate so aptly observe, a risk with 100 percent probability is actually an assumption; see P.K. Martin and K. Tate, *A Step by Step Approach to Risk Assessment* (Cincinnati: MartinTate, LLC, 2001).
[16] M.D. Watkins and M.H. Bazerman, "Predictable Surprises: The Disasters You Should Have Seen Coming," *Harvard Business Review* 81, no. 3 (2003), pp. 72–80; and Mitroff, *Managing Crises Before They Happen.*

EXHIBIT 6.6
Monitoring Project
Uncertainties

Uncertainty Example	Monitoring Approaches
Unfavorable risk: Financial failure of a key supplier.	Require full financial disclosure from supplier, with a contract stipulation allowing quarterly audits. Run routine credit checks on the organization.
Favorable uncertainty: Composite nose cone technology proves appropriate for transfer to programs in other Boeing divisions.	Assign a team from defense and space division to meet at regularly scheduled times with key personnel from the 787 and receive technology briefings on progress and new findings.

Potential Financial Risk: Financial failure of a key supplier.
Outcome: Boeing would find itself without a supplier and have to delay the project while it seeks another partner.

Mitigate: To mitigate the potential risk, Boeing could ensure it has the most up-to-date digital designs stored in its databases and find a backup supplier who can be ready for quick ramp-up if needed.

Transfer: To transfer the risk, Boeing might place responsibility for this supplier under the control of an intermediary supplier with financial strength and the capacity to serve as a business advisor to the smaller supplier.

Avoid: To avoid the risk, Boeing could decide to in-source this particular part, building its own fabrication and assembly facility and ending the contract with the supplier.

Accept potential and develop contingency plans: Boeing might decide to accept the supplier-related risk, either because countermeasures are too expensive or because it views the likelihood to be low. In this case, the company still would monitor the situation closely and have a contingency plan for responding if the risk does materialize. For example, the company might identify one of its military facilities with composite capability as a backup.

The strategy choice (mitigate, transfer, avoid, accept) will depend on the overall risk tolerance associated with the project, the estimated likelihood of the risk and its outcomes, the impact the risk's outcomes will have on the project, perceived root causes, and the cost of each of the options. The company could decide to choose a combination of options.

Potential Favorable Technical Uncertainty: Potential to use nose-cone composite technologies for Boeing military applications.
Outcome: Boeing could use the technology transfer to its advantage in winning new military contracts.

Enhance: Initiate internal benchmarking activities that encourage people from other Boeing divisions to learn about composite developments on the 787.

Share opportunity: Bring in an outside consultant or supplier with expertise in composite applications to facilitate knowledge exchange. This might involve sharing patent benefits that result from the collaboration.

Exploit: Co-locate the composite team for the 787 with the composite team for a military program and create incentives for them to collaborate.

Accept potential and prepare to take advantage: Let the opportunity arise if it does, but do not necessarily take action to promote it. Keep good lab notes on development findings, and have informal plans in mind in case other applications materialize.

With respect to actions related to positive uncertainties, the strategy choice will depend on the relative desirability of the opportunity, root causes, estimated likelihood of its occurrence, and cost associated with leverage initiatives. Again, Boeing could choose a combination of these strategies.

* Recall that this case is based partly on information documented in the media and partly on hypothetical future events.

we consider two of the uncertainties associated with the Boeing 787 example and discuss how each might be monitored.

TOOLS FOR ASSESSING PROJECT UNCERTAINTIES

All project teams must understand the dimensions of uncertainty and possess a sense of the process required for assessing and preparing for unknown events. Many approaches are available for tackling project uncertainties, and several fit well with the team-based theme of this book. These include risk mapping, failure modes and effects analysis (FMEA), gut-feel, Delphi, fishbone diagramming, and various types of simulation.

Risk Mapping

For a small project, members of the project team can brainstorm a set of possible risks, writing them on sticky notes.[17] Using a matrix similar to the one shown in Exhibit 6.2, members can discuss assumptions about each risk's likelihood and impact, then reach consensus about where each risk should be placed on the matrix. At this meeting or at a later meeting, team members can decide how they will prepare for the most important risks (red and yellow zones) and what, if anything, they need to do about less important (green zone) risks. Although this is typically done in relation to unfavorable uncertainties in a traditional risk matrix such as the one in Exhibit 6.2, it can be expanded to include favorable uncertainties, as well.

Failure Modes and Effects Analysis (FMEA)

FMEA is a widely used tool with origins in the fields of safety and quality[18] and is a prescribed component of **Six Sigma.** It involves a systematic, team-based process for examining what could go wrong with products (e.g., a component that fails because it is not sufficiently durable to withstand the rigors of its intended use), or what can go wrong in the production process (e.g., failure of an adhesive curing process intended to fasten two components together). Although FMEA was created for use in product design and the analysis of routine manufacturing operations, it can be adapted to project management, as we demonstrate below. Note that FMEA is geared toward uncertainties with undesirable outcomes.

The FMEA process begins when a team brainstorms about possible failure modes—things that might go wrong during the project itself or technical failures with respect to what is actually delivered at the end of the project. Then, team members assign ratings for severity, occurrence (likelihood or frequency), and difficulty of detection for each possible failure mode. The product of the three ratings determines a risk priority score for each failure mode. Exhibit 6.7 highlights instructions

---

[17] Some readers may think we have a fascination with sticky notes. We believe they may represent one of the most useful tools available to a project team because of the opportunity they provide for quickly translating individual brainstorming into a flexible process of collaboration with a recordable result.

[18] R.E. McDermott, R.J. Mikulak, and M.R. Beauregard, *The Basics of FMEA* (New York: Productivity Press, 1996).

EXHIBIT 6.7 **Team-Based FMEA Process for Project Uncertainty Assessment Delivery**

1. **Foundation.** The team begins with FMEA only after it has developed a WBS and members have a shared understanding of project goals and expected outcomes.

2. **Individual Brainstorming.** Team members work alone, initially, to brainstorm possible failure modes for the project, keeping in mind things that could happen during the project that would cause execution to fail (e.g., a supplier is late to deliver a key project component), as well as possible flaws or risks associated with the project's final product (e.g., a design flaw in the product that does not become evident until the product is out in the market).

3. **List Failure Modes.** A facilitator uses a round robin approach to gather failure modes ideas from participants. The facilitator lists these on the left side of a whiteboard or large piece of paper mounted on the wall.

4. **Understand Meanings and Causes.** The group discusses the meaning, causes, and effects of each failure mode listed. The facilitator writes key information about each one in the column just to the right of the failure modes list. This activity helps the group develop a shared understanding of each risk.

5. **Rating.** The team rates each failure mode for severity, likelihood, and difficulty of detection* on scales of 1–10, where 1 is low and 10 is high. The facilitator can ask each person to complete his or her own ratings, then compute averages, or the group can use a consensus approach. To facilitate the rating process, it can be useful for the team to first agree on the meanings of the 1–10 scores. (Some organizations have formal definitions already in place. We offer an example in Exhibit 6.9.)

6. **Calculate Risk Priority Numbers (RPNs).** Team members multiply their three ratings for each failure mode to derive a score for each one. The facilitator calculates group averages.

7. **Prioritize and Discuss.** Some failure modes will emerge as higher priorities for action, based on their RPN scores. Before jumping to conclusions about what is important and what is not, the team should carefully review the ratings and underlying assumptions to ensure there are no serious flaws in logic. Given the multiplicative nature of the calculation, a small overestimate in one of the numbers can result in an exaggerated RPN. Thus, the team might wish to make adjustments before agreeing on final priorities. One way to summarize the discussion about priorities is to arrange the most significant failure modes on sticky notes on a whiteboard or wall-mounted paper from highest to lowest priority.

8. **Decide on Actions.** Once the team has agreed on which risks are most important based on RPN scores, the facilitator can guide members in a discussion of actions to limit negative outcomes, who will be responsible, how to monitor the failure mode, and what contingency plans to establish.

*For some projects, difficulty of detection might not be an important risk metric. In those cases, the team can decide to rate risks on severity and likelihood, but leave out the detection rating.

for the FMEA process, as adapted for project environments, and Exhibit 6.8 shows an example from a real project.

An example of an FMEA matrix based on a team effort is displayed in Exhibit 6.8. This example is drawn from a volunteer project executed by a team of MBA students who installed an irrigation system in the gardens surrounding a residential hospital for medically fragile children.

The criteria presented in Exhibit 6.9 are examples only. The team can create its own criteria to meet the needs of a particular project, or the organization can develop standards. We believe it is not necessary (or prudent) to develop descriptions for all 10 of the numerical scores. The 1–10 ratings should be treated as an interval scale, built on the assumption that gaps between all adjacent pairs of numbers are equidistant. Overspecifying the meanings of numbers within the scale could conflict with this assumption and create unnecessary complexity. Thus, it is sufficient just to specify high, medium, and low anchors.

EXHIBIT 6.8   Sample FMEA Results for a Project to Create an Irrigation System and Landscape the Grounds Surrounding a Residential Hospital for Medically Fragile Children

Type of Failure	Failure Mode	Potential Effect on Project	Possible Causes	Severity Rating	Likelihood Rating	Detection Difficulty Rating	RPN
Failure related to project *outcome*	Irrigation system fails to produce water	Grass and plants die	Leaks in irrigation pipes	8	5	10	$8 \times 5 \times 10 = 400$
Failure related to project *execution*	Crew accidentally cuts into underground electrical wires	Power outage affects crew's progress, medical care is dangerously disrupted, and neighbors become irate	Not having correct information about underground utility locations	8	2	4	$8 \times 2 \times 4 = 64$

EXHIBIT 6.9
Sample Rating Criteria for FMEA

Source: Adapted from R.E. McDermott, R.J. Mikulak, and M.R. Beauregard, *The Basics of FMEA* (New York: Productivity Press, 1996) to fit project environments.

Rating	Severity	Likelihood	Detection Difficulty
10	A rating of 10 indicates this failure mode would have a disastrous effect on the project.	A rating of 10 indicates it is almost inevitable (100%) this failure mode will happen.	A rating of 10 indicates this failure mode is not detectable with the current measurement approach.
5	A rating of 5 indicates this failure mode would have a moderately negative effect on the project.	A rating of 5 indicates there is about a 50% chance this failure will occur.	A rating of 5 indicates there is about a 50% chance of detecting this failure mode if it does occur.
1	A rating of 1 indicates this failure mode would have no effect on the project or its intended outcomes.	A rating of 1 indicates it is not at all likely this failure mode will occur.	A rating of 1 indicates this failure mode would be obvious.

The Gut-Feel Method

The **gut-feel method** is built on concepts from FMEA, but offers a more visual approach to uncertainty assessment.[19] The value of gut-feel comes from its use of group input to generate ideas and estimate likelihood and impact. Research has demonstrated that groups make more accurate judgments about uncertain events than individuals do.[20] Although the method was originally conceptualized to include only unfavorable risks, we have expanded it to include favorable uncertainties. The process, as we have adapted it from LaBrosse, is described in Exhibit 6.10. A board layout, examples of results, and a photo of a team in action are shown in Exhibits 6.11 through 6.13.

[19] M.A. LaBrosse, *Accelerated Project Management* (New York: HNB Publishing, 2001).

[20] J.A. Sniezek and R.A. Henry, "Accuracy and Confidences in Group Judgment," *Organizational Behavior and Human Decision Processes* 4, no. 3 (1989), pp. 1–28.

EXHIBIT 6.10
Gut-Feel Method for Uncertainty Assessment

1. **Identify Deliverables.** Using the team-generated WBS mind map or outline as a starting point, record the name of each major deliverable along the left-hand side of a large piece of wall-mounted paper or a whiteboard.

2. **Brainstorm Uncertainties.*** The facilitator instructs participants to spend 10 minutes working alone to brainstorm potential uncertainties associated with each deliverable. Participants write favorable uncertainties on one color of sticky note and unfavorable uncertainties on a different color. (One uncertainty per note.) The time working alone is critical to the process. To stimulate team members to cast a wide net around possibilities, the facilitator can remind participants to consider the five risk sources: financial, business environment, social, technical, and external or natural environment.

3. **Combine Uncertainties.** Team members place favorable uncertainty and unfavorable risk notes next to the corresponding deliverables, working collaboratively to discover and eliminate duplicates.[†] Participants may add new uncertainty statements as the exercise triggers ideas. At the end of the sorting process, the team steps back to see if it all makes sense and to ask if anything is missing.

4. **Discuss Uncertainty Meanings and Outcomes.[‡]** The team jointly reviews each uncertainty to ensure intended meanings are clear to all. Perhaps most importantly, the team discusses possible outcomes for each uncertainty. For example, if a subcontractor is late in delivering hardware, this would be a risk, but how would it affect the project? Would there be a schedule delay for the entire project? This will help the team focus on the most important uncertainties.

5. **Assess Likelihoods with Dot Voting.** Each team member affixes an adhesive-backed red dot along the periphery of any uncertainty note he or she considers high likelihood and affixes yellow dots on notes associated with uncertainties that seem to have moderate likelihoods. For those perceived to be of low likelihood, they affix no dot. Team members work silently and refrain from talking with or attempting to influence others.

6. **Assess Impacts with Dot Voting.** Use a dot-voting process similar to that used in assessing likelihoods. This time, each person places a blue dot next to any uncertainty that will, if it does occur, have a major impact on the project. A green dot is for moderate impact and no dot indicates low or no impact. (Remember, these effects may be either favorable or unfavorable depending on the nature of the uncertainty.) And, again, there should be no discussion or attempts to influence others during the dot-voting process.

7. **Assess for Significance or Relevance.** At the end of the voting, the team considers which uncertainties are most relevant. Relevant items are generally those with patterns of colored dots indicating high likelihood and significant impact, but a team can have other reasons for deciding an uncertainty is worthy of attention. Once the team has agreed on which uncertainties are most relevant, these are moved to the designated column, just to the right. The example in Exhibit 6.11 shows, in particular, one unfavorable risk and one favorable uncertainty that definitely should be moved to the right. Exhibit 6.12 provides a detailed example of two uncertainties that would be characterized as relevant based on dot-voting results. Exhibit 6.13 shows a team engaged in the gut-feel process.

8. **Discuss Root Causes and Drivers.** The team considers forces underlying uncertainties selected as relevant. For unfavorable risks, brainstorm potential root causes—factors that could potentially cause this risk and its associated outcomes. For favorable uncertainties, brainstorm key drivers—factors that would be likely to cause this to happen. Sometimes underlying causes are readily apparent and this discussion can be brief. In other cases, a more extensive discussion may be appropriate, and the team may wish to use a fishbone diagram, an example of which is shown in Exhibit 6.16.

9. **Consider Actions.** Drawing from the discussion of root causes and key drivers, the team brainstorms possible actions for (1) enhancing favorable opportunities, (2) mitigating high-likelihood, undesirable risks, and (3) creating contingency plans to prepare for uncertainties that cannot be controlled. (Recall the framework shown in Exhibit 6.5.) The facilitator plays an important role in guiding this process. If the list of relevant uncertainties is somewhat large, it can be useful to break the group into smaller subteams and have each one generate ideas for addressing the uncertainties associated with a particular deliverable.

10. **Assign Responsibility.** Determine who is responsible for each action, and add these actions to the WBS and responsibility matrix where appropriate.

11. **Develop a Plan to Monitor Uncertainties.** The facilitator asks the question, "How will we know if any of our relevant uncertainties materialize? Is there a way to watch for them?" The team brainstorms ideas for monitoring each uncertainty.

12. **Summarize the Results of the Analysis in a Risk-Response Matrix.** The risk-response matrix extracts key findings from the gut-feel process and summarizes them in an electronic document available to all team members for review, approval, and continued use during the project. Possible content for a risk-response matrix is shown in Exhibit 6.14.

*This is a departure from M.A. LaBrosse, *Accelerated Project Management* (New York: HNB Publishing, 2001), which emphasizes unfavorable risks but does not include positive uncertainties.
†This process follows the approach used in affinity diagramming; see M. Brassard and D. Ritter, *The Memory Jogger II* (Salem, NH: Goal/QPC, 1994).
‡This is another place where our adaptation differs from that originally prescribed by La Brosse. She does not explicitly include a step for uncertainty outcome discussion, although it may be implied in her process.

EXHIBIT 6.11   Gut-Feel Structure and Appearance after Dot Voting

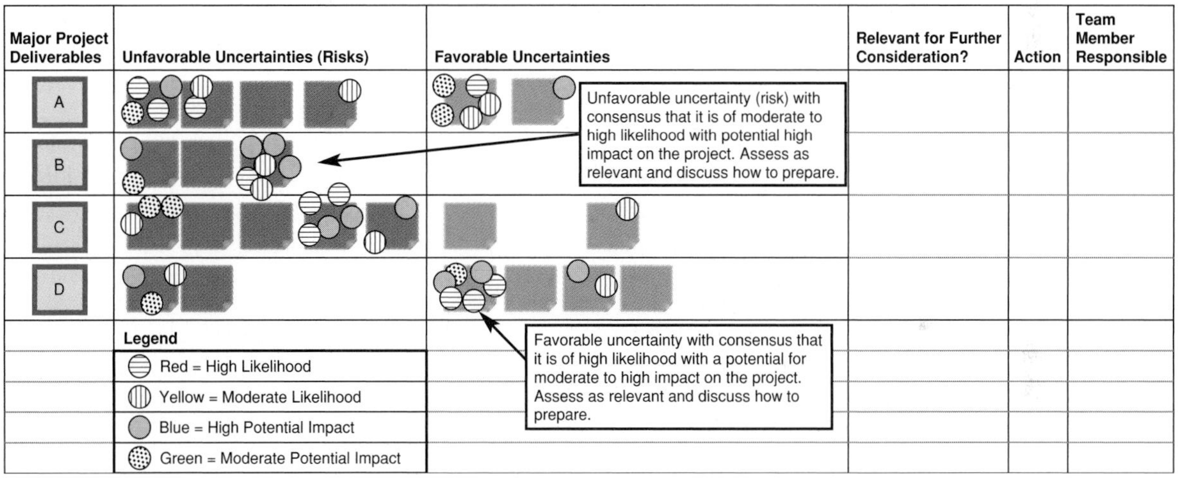

EXHIBIT 6.12
Examples of Relevant Uncertainties Identified through the Gut-Feel Method

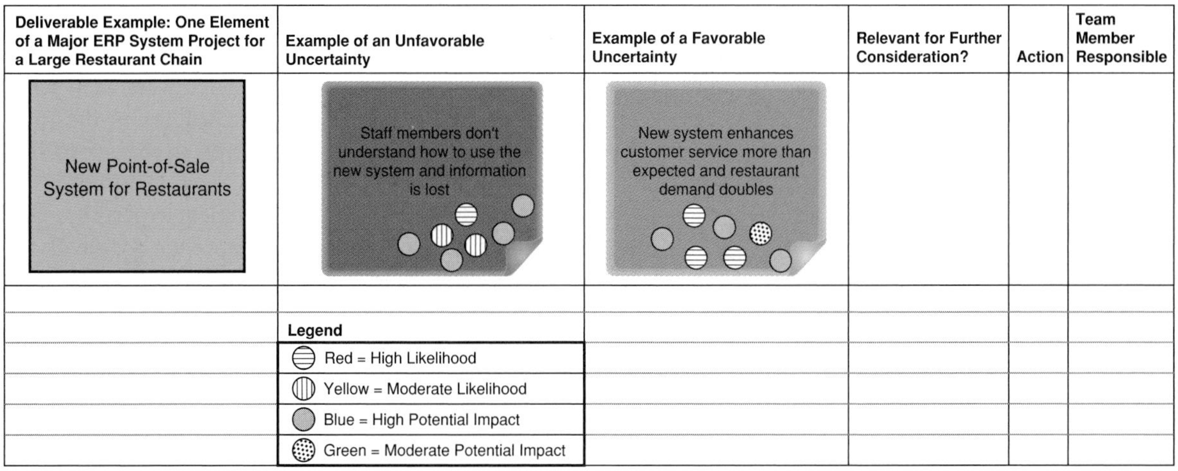

EXHIBIT 6.13
Gut-Feel Process:
Team in Action

EXHIBIT 6.14
Risk-Response
Matrix

Relevant Uncertainty	Preparation	Contingency	Trigger	Team Member Responsible
Short summary or full description of the favorable or unfavorable uncertainty	How will the team prepare for it? What must be added to the WBS? What will team members need to keep in mind?	What is the backup plan if the unfavorable uncertainty arises despite preparation? What is the backup plan if the favorable uncertainty does not appear, despite the team's best efforts?	What evidence will indicate this uncertainty has occurred, is occurring, or is imminent?	Who will take responsibility for preparing for this uncertainty? Who will develop and execute the contingency plan, should it become necessary?

The Delphi Method

The risk mapping, FMEA and gut-feel approaches discussed above work well when the project manager can gather the core team and critical stakeholders in the same room and take advantage of the synergies and commitment derived from face-to-face interaction. However, it is not always possible to hold an on-site brainstorming and analysis session, particularly when project team members or technical experts are geographically distributed. The Delphi method is an interactive approach for involving dispersed experts in forecasting that can be adapted for project uncertainty analysis.[21]

[21] G. Rowe and G. Wright, "The Delphi Technique as a Forecasting Tool: Issues and Analysis," *International Journal of Forecasting* 15, no. 4 (1999), pp. 353–75.

To do so, the project manager or process facilitator selects a group of 5 to 20 participants to form a virtual task force. All participants must have a clear understanding of the project's purpose, goals, and the content of the WBS. They then follow an interactive approach to risk brainstorming from their dispersed locations, as described in Exhibit 6.15.

A Web-based tool for a Delphi process is available at http://armstrong.wharton .upenn.edu/delphi2/. Additionally, some Web-based collaboration tools for virtual teams mentioned in Chapters 2 and 4 can be adapted for use with the Delphi method. For example, Meetingworks.com offers Web-based tools for anonymous brainstorming and for rating items to determine relative importance.

Delphi offers the advantage of bringing together a larger group than might be practical in an on-site session, and it opens the possibility of tapping into insights from external experts. Because it permits anonymous inputs, Delphi also can reduce the likelihood a high-status person can override others and bias results. However, it probably will not engage participants to the extent a synchronous, on-site meeting does. A team can partially compensate for this by using collaborative Web-based tools to conduct something like a Delphi process with dispersed individuals who are all participating at the same time from remote locations. Additionally, by scheduling participants to meet virtually at a specified time, the facilitator can increase the likelihood they will allocate time for the process. Moreover, they will be more likely to find appeal in the immediacy of the communication with other participants.

EXHIBIT 6.15
The Delphi Method for Uncertainty Assessment with Virtual Teams

1. **Brainstorming, Round 1.** In the first round, the facilitator asks team members to list the unfavorable uncertainties (risks) and favorable uncertainties (sometimes referred to as opportunities) that could potentially arise in relation to each project deliverable. The facilitator directs the team to consider potential uncertainties—events not currently expected or assumed as project outcomes or goals.

2. **Compilation of Round 1.** The facilitator compiles Round 1 results, consolidates similar items, and sends them back to participants without identifying who said what. In the next round, participants review the consolidated list and suggest items to add, delete, or clarify. The process can have two or three iterations, but, ultimately, an agreed-upon list emerges.

3. **Ratings.** To obtain likelihood and impact information, the facilitator can engage participants in a rating process similar to the one used in FMEA. (To keep things simple, it may be appropriate to include likelihood and impact ratings but omit the rating for difficulty of detection.) This will result in multiplicative scored ratings that enable participants to see which uncertainties are worthy of further consideration. Further online or telephone discussion will help to clarify assumptions.

4. **Selection of Uncertainties and Discussion of Strategies.** The next step, also handled interactively, is to engage team members in a numerical voting process to select the most important uncertainties. They may consider the numerical ratings from step 3 but also incorporate insights gained from online or telephone discussions.

5. **Ideas for Preparation.** Once the most important uncertainties have risen to the surface, virtual team members submit ideas for preparing or responding to them.

6. **Compilation of Results.** The facilitator compiles the results of the process and submits them to the team for final review. Once the team reaches agreement, the project manager makes the appropriate revisions to the project plan.

EXHIBIT 6.16
Fishbone Diagram for Risk Causes

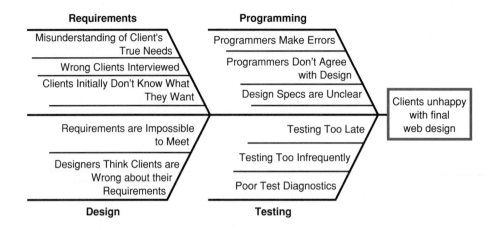

Fishbone Diagrams

A **fishbone diagram,** also known as a **cause-effect diagram** or an **Ishikawa diagram**[22] is a brainstorming tool that encourages a team to consider all possible causes of a problem. We introduced it in Chapter 3 as part of the assessment process for understanding project drivers. A fishbone diagram probably will not stand alone as an uncertainty assessment tool, but it can be used as an adjunct to risk mapping, FMEA, gut-feel, Delphi, or other team-based tools. Imagine that in a Web-design project, team members think there is some risk the client will be unhappy with the final product. If this happens, they would have to rework the design, extending the completion date and wiping out profits. If this were moderately or highly likely to happen, the team could dig more deeply into its possible causes. A team presented with the question, "What factors might contribute to unhappiness on the part of our client?" could generate a fishbone diagram such as the one shown in Exhibit 6.16. The fishbone diagramming exercise will alert the team to potential pitfalls and, in this example, should lead members to consider ways to increase diligence in requirements assessment, quality control, and testing.

Simulation

Technical simulation methods have broad applications, from queuing to virtual reality to analysis of manufacturing bottlenecks.[23] For project environments, simulation models are frequently associated with project risk analysis.[24] These tools can be useful when a full set of technical and financial risks is understood, when outcomes can be quantified (e.g., cost, time, or technical failure), and when probability distributions are known with relative certainty. Despite the interest in computer-based Monte Carlo simulation for project risk assessment, we believe these tools are too often used without input from team-based tools such as the ones we have described in this chapter. Consequently, a quantitatively based analysis, regardless of its rigor, may not include

---

[22] K. Ishikawa, *What is Total Quality Control? The Japanese Way* (Englewood Cliffs, NJ: Prentice Hall, 1985).

[23] J.J. Swain, "New Frontiers in Simulation," *ORMS Today* 34, no. 5 (2007), pp. 32–43.

[24] For examples, see Klastorin, *Project Management: Tools and Tradeoffs;* S.J. Mantel, J.R. Meredith, S.M. Shafer, and M.N. Sutton, *Project Management in Practice* (New York: Wiley and Sons, 2001); and A. Shtub, J.F. Bard, and S. Globerson, *Project Management: Processes, Methodologies, and Economics,* 2nd ed. (Englewood Cliffs, NJ: Prentice Hall, 2004).

EXHIBIT 6.17
Expanded Perspective on Simulation for Project Management

Timing of Use	Examples of Team-Based, Creative Simulation Tools	Examples of Analytically Based Simulation Tools
Before the project or early in the project	• Physical mock-ups • Rehearsals or dry runs • Tabletop exercises	• Three-dimensional design • Wind tunnel tests on preliminary designs • System dynamics modeling • Monte Carlo simulation
During the project, after some conceptual and design work have been completed	• Market tests • Clinical trials	• Test software on sample data • Wind tunnel test on a more fully developed prototype

all possible and relevant uncertainties.[25] Also, these tools cannot necessarily help a team envision the circumstances under which the project will ultimately operate. In response to these and other limitations, we offer a broader perspective on simulation, beginning with the following definition of **simulation** from *The American Heritage College Dictionary:* "Representation of the operation or features of one process or system through the use on another."

Based on this broad definition, Exhibit 6.17 highlights a few possibilities of simulation applications for project uncertainty assessment. We discuss each of these and offer examples in the paragraph below.

Physical Mock-ups

A **physical mock-up** is a three-dimensional representation of a product (the outcome of a project). A team can use it to assess the characteristics of a product in ways not possible with a computerized two- or three-dimensional drawing. Boeing used physical mockups of 777 lavatories to test options for designs that would offer access to people with disabilities. Hundreds of potential passengers, all with physical disabilities of various types, went through the mock-up and offered valuable insight. The result was a disability-friendly design that occupied a minimum amount of space.[26]

Dress Rehearsals

A **dress rehearsal** is a practice run for an event or activity. We generally associate these with theater, but they have applications beyond the stage.[27] For example, two teams preparing to beat the world's record for building a house each built a practice house two weeks before the final event so they could learn where the potential risks were. The result was a world record of two hours and 45 minutes to build a three-bedroom, two-bathroom house.[28]

---

[25] Smith and Merritt, *Proactive Risk Management.*

[26] K.A. Brown, K.V. Ramanathan, and T.G. Schmitt, "Boeing Commercial Airplane Group: Design Process Evolution," in *Technology Management: Text and International Cases,* ed. N. Harrison and D. Samson (New York: McGraw-Hill/Irwin, 2002).

[27] R. Austin and L. Devin, *Artful Making* (Englewood Cliffs, NJ: Prentice Hall, 2003).

[28] For more information, contact the Building Industry Association of San Diego. The organization has a great video that captures the event. An Internet search will produce the one-minute version of the project.

Tabletop Exercises

Tabletop exercises engage team members in imagining a scenario and placing themselves into the circumstances. A brainstorming process such as gut-feel might produce some critical uncertainties for which the team feels ill-prepared. The team can then gather around a table (or other surface), possibly using miniature props to get people into the right frame of reference to discuss possible favorable or unfavorable uncertainties and consider responses.

For example, a transportation team for a major international competitive sports event considered the following risk, based on past history of similar events:

> Boxers will be transported to the clinic where drug tests are administered. Tight timing requires us to get them out of the clinic and back to the bus so they can return to the athletes' village for a team photo. And we will need the buses for other purposes as soon as they arrive at the village. Based on past experience, we believe one or more of the boxers will not be able to urinate because he has dehydrated himself in order to stay under the weight limit for his class. If this happens, the entire team could potentially be delayed for two or three hours.

As part of the tabletop exercise built around this scenario, the team placed miniature buses, a clinic, roads, and so on, on a tabletop while they brainstormed the situation. This enabled the group to consider numerous options and to recognize which were within the group's purview and which were not. Ultimately, the team decided to add a small number of passenger vehicles to the fleet as a way of enhancing flexibility. Could they have done this without putting the props on the table? Perhaps, but team members contend the visual nature of the props allowed them to understand the situation better.

Market Tests and Clinical Trials

Market tests and clinical trials are team-oriented simulations intended to represent eventual realities for products. Both require extensive customer involvement, and the team's effective use of the results will determine their value. For example, software companies such as Apple often run tests of new or revised applications by releasing beta versions to enthusiastic expert users. These users subject the software to all sorts of tests the companies might not have ever imagined, thereby simulating many of the scenarios under which the software might be used. The results are invaluable in shaping the version ultimately released to the market.

Technical Simulation

New product efforts in technical environments often involve three-dimensional simulations of designs. For example, CATIA, a three-dimensional software package developed by Dassault in France, has come into widespread use around the world, with applications in automotive, aerospace, and computer design, just to name three examples. It allows a design team to see where interferences potentially exist among structural elements, reducing the chance assemblers will discover the problem when it is too late to fix in an economical manner.[29]

System Dynamics Modeling

System dynamics, a term coined by Jay Forrester,[30] describes a general set of simulation tools that allow users to examine the relationships among a constellation of interrelated social and technical variables. Such models can incorporate real data, or they can use subjective data generated by the user.[31] Although overuse of such models might

---

[29] Brown et al., "Boeing Commercial Airline Group."

[30] J. Forrester, *Urban Dynamics* (Cambridge, MA: MIT Press, 1969).

[31] P.M. Senge, *The Fifth Discipline* (New York: Doubleday Currency, 1990).

distract a team from getting down to project business, the models may be worthwhile to consider in the context of highly complex projects with multiple implications.[32]

Monte Carlo Simulation

Software tools such as @Risk or Crystal Ball use Monte Carlo simulation to assess risk profiles associated with time, cost, and other factors. (Swain offers a comprehensive listing of these software programs.[33]) One common application assesses probabilistic time estimates to gain insights into the range and distribution of project completion times. These programs can yield percentile probabilities of completing a project within various time frames. We discuss probabilistic time estimates in Chapter 7. For more information on Monte Carlo simulation in project environments, see Klastorin.[34]

ADDING TIME AND RESOURCES BASED ON PROJECT UNCERTAINTIES

Uncertainty analysis increases a team's awareness of unknowns that can affect project outcomes. To address these uncertainties, the team must adjust the project schedule, budget, resource distribution, specifications, and other project dimensions. For example, team members might discover the project will require more funding because of previously unforeseen items not included in the original plan. (Think about the need for additional lifeboats on the *Titanic*). In other cases, the project manager may request an increase in the project budget to provide contingency funds for use if an uncertainty does emerge. Another type of contingency can be linked to the schedule. Perhaps uncertain weather conditions or technical unknowns could extend the time required for the project. Major scope changes, budget increases, or necessary schedule extensions discovered as a result of uncertainty assessment will require approval from the project sponsor. The bottom line on uncertainty assessment is that it is not just an exercise in scenario planning, but an essential input to the WBS, schedule, and budget.

NEXT STEPS: MONITORING PROJECT UNCERTAINTIES

Uncertainty assessment is an ongoing activity in any project. The project team needs a way to keep tabs on uncertainties as they are uncovered throughout project planning and execution. An uncertainty or risk log can be the ideal tool for this purpose. Exhibit 6.18

[32] N. Repenning and J. Sterman, "Capability Traps and Self-Confirming Attribution Errors," *Administrative Science Quarterly* 47, no. 2 (2002), pp. 265–95.

[33] Swain, "New Frontiers in Simulation."

[34] Klastorin, *Project Management: Tools and Tradeoffs.*

EXHIBIT 6.18
**Sample Risk/
Uncertainty Log for a
Student Orientation
Session**

Current Date: 12 January						
Risk ID #	Date Logged	Priority	Person Responsible	Description	Response	Current Status or Resolution
15	12 January	High	Bobbette	Registrant no shows—prospective students who register for the weekend, but do not attend	Admissions staff will follow up with each registrant 2 weeks and again 5 days in advance of orientation	Action planned for 1 April and 15 April

presents a portion of a risk log for a student orientation program at a university. The team should review and update the log at each meeting.

<table>
<tr><td>

Chapter Summary and Onward

</td><td>

Projects are unique and nonroutine. Consequently, they present potential unknowns for which the team must prepare. We have emphasized the importance of recognizing both unfavorable risks *and* favorable uncertainties. Many tools are available for assessing potential project surprises, and all consider likelihood and impact of outcomes in some way. Ultimately, the project team must decide on actions to prepare for or respond to uncertainties, adjust the project plan accordingly, assign responsibility for managing them, and set up methods to monitor them.

Qualitative tools offer the advantage of engaging team members in interactive, visually based processes that can generate a wide range of possible uncertainties. Tools that involve team members in assessment of uncertainty include risk mapping, FMEA, gut-feel, Delphi, fishbone diagramming, tabletop exercises, dry runs, and dress rehearsals. Quantitative models for uncertainty assessment have their place, especially when there is sufficient historical information for making numerical parameters reasonably valid.

Once it has considered risks and modified the WBS accordingly, the team is ready to formulate a schedule. Uncertainty factors represent important inputs to the scheduling process. For example, if team members discover a material delay is highly likely, they might decide to schedule the order further in advance than they initially deemed necessary. Additionally, they could insert into the schedule a task called "confirm order" at some point during the order lead time. We move on to the project schedule with a full appreciation of the important steps that precede it.

</td></tr>
</table>

<table>
<tr><td>

Team Activities

</td><td>

1. Gather a team of three to five of your classmates. Imagine you are planning a celebration to commemorate the high school graduation of one of your children, a sibling, a niece or nephew, or the child of another relative or close friend. You have identified major project deliverables, including venue, guests, food and beverages, entertainment, and gifts. Do the following:

   a. Write the names of these deliverables on the left side of a large (about 1 meter by 2 meters) sheet of paper mounted horizontally on the wall.

   b. Follow the instructions in this chapter for executing the gut-feel method. Begin with individuals working alone to brainstorm unfavorable and favorable uncertainties for each deliverable, and take the process through dot voting, identification of relevant uncertainties, and development of actions associated with at least four of the most relevant uncertainties. At least one of the four should be a favorable uncertainty. Your result should be in a format similar to that shown in Exhibits 6.11–6.13.

   c. Summarize your results in a risk-response matrix either as a Word or Excel document. See Exhibit 6-14 for a framework.

   d. Submit your summary along with two photos of your team conducting the analysis on the wall-mounted paper.

2. Watch the movie *Ocean's Eleven* with your team. Make notes during the movie of all of the risks the *Ocean's Eleven* team identified in its planning process. How did the team prepare for each one? In other words, which actions did the team take to minimize negative uncertainties? Make a list of at least 10 risks and associated

</td></tr>
</table>

actions. Which of the methods described in this chapter were used, either explicitly or implicitly, in the project? Were there any risks the team failed to anticipate? If so, what were they? Submit the product of your analysis as a Word or Excel document.

3. Conduct an Internet search to find a video clip of "Exploding Whale." Watch this short clip with your team members. Write a three-page paper highlighting the following:

   a. A problem statement for the project (as described in Chapter 3, your statement should describe the nature of the problem, its location, timing, and magnitude).

   b. A project objective and key performance indicators. Include KPIs the team did not consider when the project actually occurred. How would *you* measure the performance of this project?

   c. Options for achieving project objectives. Be creative.

   d. Key deliverables of the WBS for this project as it was actually executed (at least four—be creative!).

   e. At least two potential unfavorable risks associated with each deliverable.

   f. For each of the unfavorable risks, conduct a failure modes and effects analysis (FMEA) that incorporates team member scoring. Calculate an RPN for each risk and identify the ones that are most significant.

   g. Describe how, in retrospect, you would have addressed the top three risks you identified in part f.

4. Form a team of classmates for a virtual teaming exercise on project uncertainty. Consider the graduation celebration project described in Team Activity 1, above. Do the following:

   a. Set up a time when you can all meet virtually. (It is also possible to do this asynchronously, so check with your instructor. We recommend the synchronous approach, however.) Each team member will need an Internet connection.

   b. With team members in separate locations, use the Delphi method to brainstorm possible project risks. For the sake of this exercise, consider *unfavorable* risks only. You may use one of the decision support Web tools recommended in Chapters 2 and 4 for virtual teams. Consider www.meetingworks.com, or the Web site specifically designed for Delphi processes: http://armstrong.wharton.upenn.edu/delphi2/.

   c. Use the features of the tool you have chosen to consolidate brainstorming results and move to the next stages, as prescribed in Exhibit 6.15.

   d. Summarize the results of your uncertainty assessment using a risk-response matrix. Include at least six risks in the table.

   e. Exchange e-mail messages relating your impressions of the virtual process—its advantages and disadvantages. Collaborate to write a two-page summary of reflections about your experience with the process.

Discussion Questions and Exercises

1. Why is it useful to consider both unfavorable risks and favorable uncertainties as part of the project planning process? Describe an example from your own work or personal life in which an unfavorable risk interfered with your ability to execute a project as you had initially envisioned it. Describe another example, also from your own work or personal life, in which an unexpected positive uncertainty caused a project to turn out better than you had envisioned it.

2. Why is it useful to have a complete WBS before engaging in formal uncertainty assessment? Use an example of your own creation to support your explanation.

3. Find the following article, H. Karp, "Why Protesters Are Playing Ping-Pong in Your Parking Space." *The Wall Street Journal,* September 21, 2007, p. W7. This article describes how activists are attempting to "raise awareness about the lack of open space in urban areas, and to draw attention to the gas wasted and pollution created by drivers circling the block for low-cost urban parking spaces." In short, they have set up lawn chairs, ping-pong tables, even a beauty parlor, in metered spaces in cities in the United States and Europe. Refer to Exhibit 6.1, which describes uncertainty sources. For each of these sources, describe a real or hypothetical unfavorable uncertainty and a real or hypothetical favorable uncertainty associated with the protestors' activities. Demonstrate connections with the content of the article, but use your imagination, as well.

4. Visit www.historylink.org and find links to Web pages describing the sinking of the Lake Washington Floating Bridge on November 25, 1990. Read several of these descriptions. A brief description from Historylink is as follows:

> On November 25, 1990, after a week of high winds and rain, the 50-year-old Lacey V. Murrow Bridge (Lake Washington Floating Bridge) breaks apart and plunges into the mud beneath Lake Washington. Since it took some time for the bridge to sag and finally crack apart, news cameras were poised and ready to show post-Thanksgiving TV viewers a once-in-a-lifetime telecast of the demise of the historic I-90 span. It is later discovered that hatchways into the concrete pontoon air pockets were left open, allowing water to enter, while the bridge was undergoing a $35.6 million renovation.

a. In hindsight (which we know is biased) where would you place the risk of water entering the pontoons in the uncertainty matrix presented in Exhibit 6.2? Discuss your rationale for the position you choose.

b. Of the five sources of uncertainty described in this chapter (see Exhibit 6.1) which one (or ones) best described the risk of water entering the pontoons on the bridge? Explain your answer.

c. Identify and discuss at least one positive outcome that could have emerged from this project crisis.

d. What tools could the team have used to uncover the possibility of water entering the pontoons? Name at least three and explain how they would be applied.

e. What biases (see Appendix 6A) may have prevented the team from seeing this risk as a possibility?

5. Read the article, E. Nelson and E. Ramstad, "Trick or Treat: Hershey's Biggest Dud Has Turned Out to Be Its New Technology," *The Wall Street Journal,* October 29, 1999, p. A1. This article describes a disastrous ERP (enterprise resource planning) system implementation at Hershey. Based on your reading of the article, as well as your own creative ideas, describe a negative outcome risk for each of the risk sources presented in Exhibit 6.1. For each of these risks, describe actions you could take to prevent it or prepare for it, and describe how you would monitor the situation so you were assured of being aware of the risk if it did occur.

6. A famous British expedition aimed at crossing Antarctica, led by Ernest Shackleton from 1914 to 1916, was derailed by unexpected ice floes.[35] Although this

---

[35] See www.shackleton-endurance.com (accessed July 26, 2009). Or C. Alexander, *The Endurance: Shackleton's Legendary Antarctic Expedition* (New York: Knopf, 1998).

act of nature presented an initial risk, Shackleton and his crew were able to later take advantage of ice floe movements to escape from a prolonged and cold entrapment that, remarkably, did not take any of their lives. Imagine yourself as Shackleton, and that you are developing an uncertainty assessment before you set sail. Prepare a gut-feel matrix similar to Exhibits 6.11 and 6.12. If you need more information about the Shackleton expedition, consult the sources cited in footnote 35 or conduct an Internet search. Identify three major project deliverables, and for each one identify one potential negative risk and one potential favorable uncertainty. Assess the likelihoods, outcomes, impacts on the project, and underlying causal factors. Discuss your analysis, use diagrams where appropriate, and demonstrate critical thinking.

7. A project team at Scanda Pharmaceutical is using FMEA to assess risks for a celebration to be held when a major project milestone, completion of clinical trials for a promising new drug, is completed. The celebration will be held on the luxurious gardens of Scanda headquarters in Bergen, Norway. Project team members, top company officials, and representatives from major customer groups will attend the event, which will include a gourmet meal, elaborate decorations, speeches, and live entertainment. The team responsible for planning the event decided to use FMEA, and members generated a long list of risks, five of which are shown in the matrix below. Each team member had the opportunity to give his or her ratings for these risks, which are shown in the matrix following the risk list.

Top Five Risks

Risk	Effect on the Project as It Is Currently Planned	Possible Causes
1. Invited VIP guests don't attend the event.	Major embarrassment to company. Loss of marketing opportunity.	Invitations sent to incorrect addresses. Invitations don't convey a sense of the importance of the event.
2. Guests get food poisoning.	Bad image for the company. Could hurt sales.	Food spoils in hot weather. Careless caterer.
3. Clinical trials prove to be unsuccessful but it is too late to cancel the event.	Bad publicity in the market. Delay in getting to market. Stock analysts produce negative reports.	Researchers giving falsely optimistic reports during the trials. Error in data analysis not caught soon enough. Event scheduled prematurely.
4. Another major event hosted by a competitor is scheduled for the same day.	Dilution of publicity. Some VIPs attend competitor's event.	Insufficient investigation of potential conflicts. Intentional move on part of competitor.
5. Major rainstorm.	Not possible to hold the event outdoors without everyone getting wet.	Atmospheric conditions outside the control of the team. Weather patterns characteristic of the time of year.

FMEA Ratings for Milestone Celebration

Risk #	Rater #	Severity	Likelihood	Detection Difficulty	Individual RPN	RPN Mean
1	Evelyn	9	3	4		
	Arve	8	5	6		
	Kyrre	6	6	2		
	Sindre	3	6	3		
2	Evelyn	10	2	7		
	Arve	9	4	5		
	Kyrre	6	4	3		
	Sindre	8	5	2		
3	Evelyn	10	4	6		
	Arve	9	4	9		
	Kyrre	7	2	4		
	Sindre	8	5	3		
4	Evelyn	8	5	1		
	Arve	7	6	1		
	Kyrre	9	3	4		
	Sindre	5	8	1		
5	Evelyn	10	5	2		
	Arve	9	6	1		
	Kyrre	5	3	3		
	Sindre	8	8	2		

a. Calculate individual and aggregated mean RPN scores for each of the five risks.

b. Based on RPN scores, identify the risks most relevant for further consideration. Would you completely trust the numbers, or would you seek further discussion or investigation? Why?

c. For the three most relevant risks, describe the actions you would take. For each action you recommend, identify which of the four unfavorable uncertainty action categories (see Exhibit 6.5) best describes what you are recommending.

d. Prepare a risk-response matrix. (See Exhibit 6.14.)

References

Alexander, C. *The Endurance: Shackleton's Legendary Antarctic Expedition.* New York: Knopf, 1998.

Allen, H. *Norway and Europe in the 1970s.* Oslo: Universitetsforlaget, 1979.

American Heritage College Dictionary, 4th ed. New York: Houghton Mifflin, 2002.

Associated Press. "Airlines: Fuel Costs to Compound Losses." *The San Diego Union-Tribune,* June 8, 2004, p. C4.

Austin, R., and L. Devin. *Artful Making.* Englewood Cliffs, NJ: Prentice Hall, 2003.

Barker, J. Implications Wheels Training Video, **www.joelbarker.com/downloads .php**, 1994.

Bazerman, M.H. *Judgment in Managerial Decision Making,* 5th ed. New York: Wiley and Sons, 2002.

Brassard, M., and D. Ritter. *The Memory Jogger II,* Salem, NH: Goal/QPC, 1994.

Brooks, F.P. *The Mythical Man Month.* New York: Addison-Wesley, 1995.

Brown, K.A.; K.V. Ramanathan; and T.G. Schmitt. "Boeing Commercial Airplane Group: Design Process Evolution." In *Technology Management: Text and International Cases,* ed. N. Harrison and D. Samson. New York: McGraw-Hill/Irwin, 2002.

Burton, T.M. "Flop Factor: By Learning From Failures, Lilly Keeps Drug Pipeline Full." *The Wall Street Journal,* April 21, 2004, p. A1.

Caldwell, A.A. "Border Barrier Accidentally Crosses Border." *Seattle Times,* June 30, 2007, p. A1.

Cohen, L. *Quality Function Deployment: How to Make QFD Work for You.* Reading, MA: Addison-Wesley, 1995.

Cougar, D.J. *Creative Problem Solving and Opportunity Finding.* Danvers, MA: Boyd and Fraser Publishing Co., 1995.

Dailey, K.W. *The FMEA Pocket Handbook.* DW Publishing Co., 2004.

Datta, S., and S.K. Mukherjee. "Developing a Risk Management Matrix for Effective Project Planning—An Empirical Study." *Project Management Journal* 32, no. 2 (2001), pp. 45–57.

Doughton, S. "Pinpointing Devastation If Seattle Fault Ruptures." *Seattle Times,* February 20, 2005, http://seattletimes.nwsource.com/html/localnews/2002185299_earthquake20m.html.

Ebert, R.J., and T.R. Mitchell. *Organizational Decision Processes: Concepts and Analysis.* New York: Crane, Russak & Co., 1975.

Forrester, J. *Urban Dynamics.* Cambridge, MA: MIT Press, 1969.

Gates, D. "7E7 a Shift to New Materials: Boeing Pioneers in Extent of Composite Use." *Seattle Times,* June 13, 2003, p. D1.

Gates, D. "FAA Dismissed Criticism over 787 Safety Tests." *Seattle Times,* October 2, 2007, www.seattletimes.com.

Gates, D. "First 787 Still Missing Parts." *Seattle Times,* August 21, 2007, www.seattletimes.com.

Gates, D. "Plan to Put 7E7 in Everett Tied to Boeing Transformation: Worker Support for New Production Strategy Is Key Factor As Board Weighs Site Proposal." *Seattle Times,* December 7, 2003, p. A1.

Hammond, J.S.; R.L. Keeney; and H. Raiffa. *Smart Choices: A Practical Guide to Making Better Life Decisions.* New York: Broadway Books, 1999.

Hillson, D. "Extending the Risk Process to Manage Opportunities." *International Journal of Project Management* 20, no. 3 (2002), pp. 235–40.

Hofstede, G. *Culture's Consequences,* New York: Sage, 1984.

Hogarth, R. *Judgement and Choice.* Chichester, England: Wiley and Sons, 1980.

Ishikawa, K. *What Is Total Quality Control? The Japanese Way.* Englewood Cliffs, NJ: Prentice Hall, 1985.

Janis, I.L. "Groupthink." *Psychology Today* 5, no. 6 (1971), pp. 43–46, 74–76.

Keaten, J. "New Scare at French Airport Terminal." *Seattle Post-Intelligencer,* May 25, 2004, p. A4.

Kepner, C.H., and B.B. Tregoe. *The New Rational Manager.* Princeton, NJ: Princeton University Press, 1981.

Klastorin, T.D. *Project Management: Tools and Tradeoffs.* New York: Wiley and Sons, 2004.

Kotha, S., and R. Nolan. *Boeing 787: The Dreamliner.* HBS case # 9-305-101. Boston: Harvard Business School Publishing, 2005.

LaBrosse, M.A. *Accelerated Project Management.* New York: HNB Publishing, 2001.

Lunsford, J.L. "Boeing Vows On-Time Dreamliner." *The Wall Street Journal,* September 17, 2007, p. A8.

Mantel, S.J.; J.R. Meredith; S.M. Shafer; and M.N. Sutton. *Project Management in Practice.* New York: Wiley and Sons, 2001.

Martin, P.K., and K. Tate. *A Step by Step Approach to Risk Assessment.* Cincinnati: MartinTate, LLC, 2001.

McCray, G.E.; R.L. Purvis; and C.G. McCray. "Project Management under Uncertainty: The Impact of Heuristics and Biases." *Project Management Journal* 33, no. 1 (2002), pp. 49–57.

McDermott, R.E.; R.J. Mikulak; and M.R. Beauregard. *The Basics of FMEA.* New York: Productivity Press, 1996.

Michaels, D. "Jumbo Bet: At Airbus, Picturing Huge Jet Was Easy; Building It Is Hard." *The Wall Street Journal,* May 27, 2004, p. A1.

Mitroff, I. *Managing Crises before They Happen.* New York: American Management Association, 2001.

Paulson, T. "New Shaky Ground in Seattle." *Seattle Post-Intelligencer,* October 12, 2007, p. A1.

Perrow, C. *Normal Accidents.* New York: Basic Books, 1984.

Project Management Institute. *A Guide to the Project Management Body of Knowledge,* 4th ed. Newtown Square, PA: PMI, 2008.

Raftery, J. *Risk Analysis in Project Management.* London: E&FN Spon, 1994.

Reiss, G. *Project Management Demystified.* London: Chapman and Hall, 1995.

Repenning, N., and J. Sterman. "Capability Traps and Self-Confirming Attribution Errors. *Administrative Science Quarterly* 47, no. 2 (2002), pp. 265–95.

Rowe, G., and G. Wright. "The Delphi Technique as a Forecasting Tool: Issues and Analysis." *International Journal of Forecasting* 15, no. 4 (1999), pp. 353–75.

Senge, P.M. *The Fifth Discipline.* New York: Doubleday Currency, 1990.

Shtub, A.; J.F. Bard; and S. Globerson. *Project Management: Processes, Methodologies, and Economics,* 2nd ed. Englewood Cliffs, NJ: Prentice Hall, 2004.

Smith, P.G, and G. Merritt. *Proactive Risk Management.* Portland, OR: Productivity Press, 2002.

Sniezek, J.A., and R.A. Henry. "Accuracy and Confidences in Group Judgment." *Organizational Behavior and Human Decision Processes* 4, no. 3 (1989), pp. 1–28.

Spencer, J., and C. Crossen. "Fear Factors: Why Do Americans Feel That Danger Lurks Everywhere?" *The Wall Street Journal,* April 24, 2007, p. A1.

Stein, A.J. "Lake Washington Floating Bridge Sinks on November 25, 1990." *Seattle Times,* November 26 and 27, 1990. Seattle/King Co. HistoryLink.org.

Swain, J.J. "New Frontiers in Simulation." *ORMS Today* 34, no. 5 (2007), pp. 32–43.

Tufte, E.R. *Visual Explanations.* Cheshire, CT: Graphics Press, 1997.

Tversky, A., and D. Kahneman. "Judgment under Uncertainty: Heuristics and Biases." *Science* 185, no. 4157 (1974), pp. 1124–31.

Vaughan, D. *The Challenger Launch Decision: Risky Technology, Culture, and Deviance at NASA.* Chicago: University of Chicago Press, 1996.

Watkins, M.D., and M.H. Bazerman. "Predictable Surprises: The Disasters You Should Have Seen Coming." *Harvard Business Review* 81, no. 3 (2003), pp. 72–80.

Weaver, R., and J. Farrell. *Managers as Facilitators.* San Francisco: Berrett-Koehler Publishers, 1999.

Wideman, R.M. *Project and Program Risk Management: A Guide to Managing Risks and Opportunities.* Newtown Square, PA: Project Management Institute, 1992.

APPENDIX 6A

Human Biases in Risk/Uncertainty Assessment

Human beings have a tendency to underestimate the likelihood of some types of risks[36] and overestimate the likelihood of others.[37] They can be unjustifiably over-confident or under-confident. These biases can affect uncertainty assessments in project environments.[38]

AVAILABILITY HEURISTICS

Availability heuristics describe human processes of recall based on vividness and recency. If a potential occurrence has happened to us (or someone we know) recently, or has been in the news, we are likely to overestimate its likelihood (think house fire, plane crash, hurricane, child abduction).

RETRIEVABILITY

Retrievability describes a pattern of human judgment biases based on familiarity. If a risk, opportunity, or issue is easy for us to retrieve because of our mental models, we will be more likely to recall it and associate it with the project. Imagine you are an expert programmer with strong technical skills and you are thinking about things that could go wrong in a software project. You might be more likely to consider technical problems because this is your area of expertise. Consequently, you might tend to over-look the possibility of social risks such as stakeholder resistance, which could carry a higher likelihood than the technical issues you are envisioning.

MISCONCEPTIONS OF CHANCE

People are not good mental statisticians and tend to make statistical inferences based on cognitive biases about how random event patterns should appear. For example, imagine you have experienced a sequence of independent, random coin tosses: H-H-H-H-H-T-T-T-T-T-T-T-T-T. You might be inclined to estimate a high likelihood the next toss would be heads (H). This is because you have a subconscious belief that the two possibilities should even out over the course of the toss series, even though each toss is an independent, random event. In fact, heads (H) or tails (T) are equally likely as the outcome of the next toss. In a project environment, this can lead people to believe a string of bad luck will even out—as a consequence, they underestimate the likelihood unfavorable conditions will continue. ("We're due for some good

---

[36] M.D. Watkins and M.H. Bazerman, "Predictable Surprises: The Disasters You Should Have Seen Coming," *Harvard Business Review,* March 2003, pp. 72–80.

[37] J. Spencer and C. Crossen, "Fear Factors: Why Do Americans Feel That Danger Lurks Everywhere?" *The Wall Street Journal,* April 24, 2007, p. A1.

[38] G.E. McCray, R.L. Purvis, C.G. McCray, "Project Management Under Uncertainty: The Impact of Heuristics and Biases," *Project Management Journal* 33, no. 1 (March 2002), pp. 49–57.

luck.") This bias, known as the **gambler's fallacy,** can play a role when a team is assessing project risks in relation to a series of past projects, or if members are making go–no-go decisions in the context of a series of failures within the project.

CONJUNCTIVE EVENTS

Individuals tend to *overestimate* the probability of conjunctive events occurring. Conjunction occurs when several things *all* must happen, or when several attributes *all* must be present. There is no compensation or tradeoff. In a project environment, an example of a conjunctive event would be an activity dependent on the merger of several predecessor activities. The project manager has a sense of the probability of each of the predecessor activities being completed on time, but might not intuitively apply joint probability statistical models to predict the likelihood of *all* of them being completed by a specified date. The following example illustrates: Imagine activities A, B, and C must be complete before D can start. Each of the three is estimated with a 90 percent probability to have a duration of 20 days. Based on conjunctive event biases, one might naively predict a 90 percent probability D can start at the end of day 20, but this would be incorrect. The actual joint probability would be the product of the individual probabilities, or $.90 \times .90 \times .90 = .729$

OVERCONFIDENCE IN ESTIMATES

Once they have made estimates, people tend to be far more confident than they should be about their accuracy. This has serious implications for the estimations project participants make about the impact and likelihood of potential uncertainties. Fortunately, group judgments tend to be more accurate than individual judgments, but unfortunately, groups are just as subject to the overconfidence bias as individuals are, particularly in instances where groupthink[39] rules. The result can be that a team wears blinders when it comes to seeing risks that might cause schedule slippages or cost overruns.

RISKY SHIFT

With respect to risk preferences, the project manager should be familiar with the potential for what is known as **risky shift.** Research and practice have consistently demonstrated that individuals are likely to take on more risks after a group discussion about the action under consideration than they would have without the discussion.[40] This can be a two-edged sword. On the one hand, it can lead reluctant team members to go along with a good idea they had initially feared. On the other hand, it could lead a team to make a foolish choice because of groupthink effects. A well-structured, balanced discussion will be important to the team in making the best decisions and avoiding risky shifts.

Source(s): Adapted from M.H. Bazerman, *Judgment in Managerial Decision Making,* 5th ed. (New York: Wiley and Sons, 2002); R. Hogarth, *Judgement and Choice* (Chichester, England: Wiley and Sons, 1980); J. Raftery, *Risk Analysis in Project Management* (London: E&FN Spon, 1994); A. Tversky and D. Kahneman, "Judgment under Uncertainty: Heuristics and Biases," *Science* 185, no. 4157 (1974), pp. 1124–31; and J.S. Hammond, R.L. Keeney, and H. Raiffa, *Smart Choices: A Practical Guide to Making Better Life Decisions* (New York: Broadway Books, 1999).

---

[39] I.L. Janis, "Groupthink," *Psychology Today* 5, no. 6 (1971), pp. 43–46, 74–76.

[40] Although some research has also documented the potential for **cautious shifts** in some circumstances, the risky shift is more common. R.J. Ebert and T.R. Mitchell, *Organizational Decision Processes: Concepts and Analysis* (New York: Crane, Russak & Co., 1975).

Chapter **Seven**

Project Scheduling: Adding the Time Dimension

"Time is a versatile performer. It flies, marches on, heals all wounds, runs out, and will tell."

Franklin P. Jones

Chapter Learning Objectives

When you have mastered the material in this chapter, you should be able to:

- Employ project scheduling concepts to engage team commitment and manage stakeholder expectations.
- Graphically illustrate the various project scheduling formats available and describe the key features of each.
- Given a network schedule, identify the critical path and float using visual and mathematical approaches.
- Facilitate a team session to create a project schedule.
- Discuss the application of project scheduling software and describe the advantages and challenges associated with its use.
- Apply the PERT approach to develop three-point time estimates and predict likelihoods for various project completion times.

In this chapter, we introduce concepts, principles, and tools for creating initial project schedules, including **network diagrams** (also known as **PERT** or **CPM** charts), **Gantt charts,** and **time-based networks,** emphasizing the importance of active team involvement in the scheduling process. We also demonstrate how these models can be extended to support **probabilistic analysis** based on **three-point time estimates.** The effective project manager is familiar with these tools, knows when each one is appropriate, understands the contingencies driving the level of scheduling formality to adopt, and recognizes how various scheduling tools support team decision making and scenario analysis.

WHY SCHEDULE?

There are many business news stories about projects with schedule overruns. One high-publicity example was associated with the serious schedule delays in the months and weeks leading up to the 2004 Olympic Games in Athens.[1] At one point, the International Olympic Committee warned that Athens was at risk of losing the games if it did not get the project back on schedule. Fortunately, the games began on time, but only because of a last-minute influx of international funding, a 24-hour-per-day work frenzy, and the elimination of some items from the WBS. Another example of a project plagued by scheduling problems was Boston's Big Dig, an ambitious effort to tunnel under the city and add aboveground enhancements that took five times longer than the original 16-month estimate.[2] More generally, it is not unusual for total durations of information technology projects to be nearly double their original estimates.[3]

A good schedule might not have completely prevented the overruns described above. However, if team members had paid more attention to the scheduling process they might have anticipated some of the delays and challenges that appear to have surprised them. Without good schedules, project team members can find themselves working in chaos because they have not purposefully considered sequential task relationships and priorities. The result might be the kind of trap depicted in the "Dilbert" cartoon presented in Exhibit 7.1.

A schedule can be formal and highly detailed, as in the case of minute-by-minute plans for an event such as an opening ceremony for the Olympic Games. Other projects warrant a less detailed approach. A minor office remodel or a company picnic might require only a simple checklist with target completion dates for tasks. Regardless of the approach a team uses, the act of creating the schedule brings members together in an environment that establishes and clarifies goals, exposes team member assumptions, highlights schedule risks, forms a foundation for further analysis and

---

[1] D. Franz, "Olympics; Athens Races to Prepare for Olympics," *The New York Times,* July 23, 2001; www.nytimes.com; and T. Weil, "Four Days Out, Athens Confident It'll Be Ready," *USA Today,* August 9, 2004, p. 1A.

[2] B. McGrory, "Another Dig, Another Day," *Boston Globe,* November 24, 2006; www.boston.com; and S. LeBlanc, "Boston's $14.8 Big Dig Finally Complete," *San Jose Mercury News,* December 26, 2007.

[3] C.L. Iacovou and A. Dexter, "Turning around Runaway Information Technology Projects," *California Management Review* 46, no. 4 (2004), pp. 68–88.

EXHIBIT 7.1   What Happens When There Is No Schedule

DILBERT: © Scott Adams/Dist. by United Feature Syndicate, Inc

EXHIBIT 7.2
Key Contributions Stemming from the Project Schedule

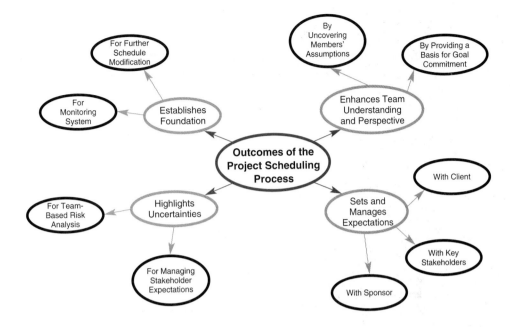

monitoring, and, ultimately, sets expectations for the team, client, and sponsor. Consequently, the schedule belongs to many stakeholders and is not just the domain of the core team or a single individual. Exhibit 7.2 highlights the key roles the schedule plays in a project environment.

Setting the Stage: Two Success Stories

Box 7.1 and Exhibits 7.3 and 7.4 describe two real-life scenarios to set the stage for further discussion about project scheduling. They involve vastly different project types, but offer a common set of lessons. First, both project managers used a visual approach to show when project activities were to occur. Second, the visual images facilitated team discussion, allowing members an opportunity for input and establishing ownership; this resulted in better schedules, and it enhanced team commitment to schedule goals. As we have discussed previously, clear, specific goals create one of the best forms of motivation available.[4]

The two stories in Box 7.1 also demonstrate that different display formats fit different circumstances. In the irrigation system schedule depicted in Exhibit 7.3, precedence relationships are implied but not specifically shown, and some activities are overlapped. For example, the diagram is based on an assumption that part of the crew can begin laying pipe before all of the trenching is complete. Crew members need to coordinate to a greater extent in an overlapping situation, and a bar chart can help them see where this is necessary. In the case of the tool-design project, the **time-based network** format allowed participants to see when activities would occur, but also gave them a clear understanding of **precedence relationships.** Additionally, the presentation format shown in Exhibit 7.4 revealed where some flexibility existed—as shown by the dashed line following Drawing 3, this activity could be delayed or stretched by one week without having a detrimental effect on the project deadline. Note, also, that Drawing 5 could start one week earlier if necessary. On the other hand,

---

[4] R.M. Steers, R.T. Mowday, and D.L. Shapiro, "The Future of Work Motivation," *Academy of Management Review* 29, no. 3 (2004), pp. 379–87.

SCENARIO 1: SCHEDULE GOALS MAKE A DIFFERENCE IN LANDSCAPING

Peter Roberts had operated a successful landscaping company in the southeastern United States for eight years. As his company grew, Peter noted an increasing tendency for major landscaping jobs to run beyond scheduled due dates. He knew from experience that it was possible to complete the work within the time frames he had promised his customers, but he was less and less able to spend time on every job site now that he had more employees and several projects running simultaneously.

After taking a course on project management, Peter decided to try posting, at each job site, a simple horizontal bar chart such as the one shown in Exhibit 7.3. In addition, Peter reviewed the schedule with each crew chief at the beginning and middle of each project. As time went by, he involved the crew chiefs and team members in decisions about the schedule.

These practices created some real magic; within just a few weeks, projects began to come in on time, consistently.

SCENARIO 2: SCHEDULE LEADS TO COOPERATION IN TOOL DESIGN

Brad Clemson, an industrial engineering manager at a Fortune 500 company, was experiencing schedule delays in the large machine-tool design process he managed. Designers produced tool drawings, which were then passed on to industrial engineers who created the shop drawings used in fabrication and assembly. Both sets of drawings were critical. Schedules were chaotic, and there was considerable finger-pointing between the two groups. Designers were unable to give time estimates for their work, and they often produced drawings out of sequence for the needs of the industrial engineering group.

Brad's solution was to get both groups to cooperate in developing a network-type schedule that incorporated (and made visible) the necessary precedence relationships among the various drawing tasks. He also assisted both groups in establishing standard methods for estimating realistic drawing development times; these factored in drawing complexity, tool type, and other relevant attributes. Team members created the schedules by hand on large sheets of paper and posted them on the wall in a common area. The most time-critical activities were highlighted in red. A simplified version of one of these schedules is shown in Exhibit 7.4.

EXHIBIT 7.3
Scenario 1: Gantt Chart for Installing a Garden Irrigation System

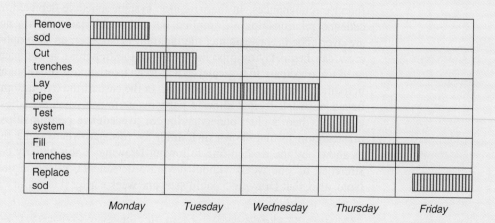

	Monday	Tuesday	Wednesday	Thursday	Friday
Remove sod	▓				
Cut trenches		▓			
Lay pipe			▓▓		
Test system				▓	
Fill trenches				▓	
Replace sod					▓

Project Scheduling: Two Real-Life Scenarios continued

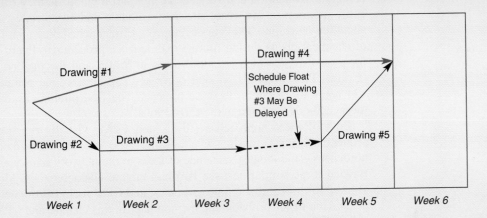

EXHIBIT 7.4
Scenario 2: Time-Based Network for Tool Design Project (Simplified Version)

Within four months of implementing this new system, schedule performance had improved dramatically, the quality of work had increased, cross-functional conflict was diminished, and people were generally more satisfied with their work.

the sequence of Drawing 1 and Drawing 4 offered no flexibility. Team members recognized this as the **critical path**—a sequence of activities that determines the expected duration of the project.[5]

In the remaining pages of this chapter, we demonstrate how these and other tools work, emphasizing their roles in team settings. Project managers and team members should recognize that a schedule developed in the early stages of the planning process will likely require modification before the plan is complete. Additionally, further revisions will become necessary as project realities unfold during the delivery phase.

History of Project Scheduling Methods

The pharaohs of ancient Egypt and the emperors of ancient China undoubtedly had schedules in mind when they built the great icons of their day, the Pyramids and the Great Wall, respectively. Perhaps these schedules were even recorded formally. However, they did not have the advantage of "modern" tools for project scheduling. These scheduling tools had their origins in **line-of-balance methods** developed in the early 1900s[6] and the work of Henry Gantt, who created the first horizontal **bar charts** for scheduling work activities.[7] These tools gained widespread use in job shop manufacturing environments in the early 1900s (e.g., Headen, 1936).[8]

---

[5] We discuss this terminology in more depth later, but introduce it here as a way of painting a big picture and indicating where we are headed.

[6] T. Uher, *Programming and Scheduling Techniques,* Construction Management Series (Sydney, Australia: UNSW Press, 2003), chap. 10.

[7] E.M. Knod and R.J. Schonberger, *Operations Management: Meeting Customers' Demands* (New York: McGraw-Hill/Irwin, 2001).

[8] E.B. Headen, "Pinpoint Planning: Stock and Production Control for the Small Plant—So Simple, a Girl Can Run It," *Factory and Industrial Management,* June 1936, pp. 233–34.

In the 1950s, the U.S. Department of Defense adapted line-of-balance and bar chart concepts for managing the Polaris program to create new weapons systems.[9] Previous military programs had been notoriously over budget and behind schedule. The **PERT** (**P**rogram **E**valuation and **R**eview **T**echnique) method, as they called it, brought the entire program in two years ahead of schedule and comfortably under budget.[10] At about the same time, Du Pont developed a similar scheduling approach for the closure of chemical plants during routine maintenance procedures. Every hour of downtime for a plant represented gigantic losses in profit, and the method they called **CPM** (**C**ritical **P**ath **M**ethod) brought order and substantial time compression (e.g., from 124 hours to 78 hours) to these projects. The first publicly available articles about these methods appeared in the early 1960s.[11]

Both of these approaches (PERT and CPM) visually represented parallel and sequential task relationships in a network form, and both allowed users to identify the bottleneck—the longest sequence of tasks in the network known as the *critical path*. Beyond these similarities, the two had unique characteristics. Most notably, PERT allowed for probabilistic time estimates, and CPM included time-cost trade-offs. (We discuss the PERT probabilistic method later in this chapter and CPM time-cost trade-offs in Chapter 8.) The strengths of both applications were their visual nature and the way in which they provided frameworks for examining assumptions and solving problems.

Despite their presence on the managerial scene for more than a half-century, project scheduling tools did not come into widespread use until the advent of powerful desktop computers and the subsequent development of scheduling software packages such as MS Project, Artemis, Primavera, and others.[12] Unfortunately, the use of project planning and scheduling software has proliferated more quickly than people's understanding of the underlying concepts that support it. Consequently, many people begin using the software before they understand how to properly enter data and how to interpret what the software tells them. Read on, and you will not be one of those poor souls!

CONCEPTS FOR PROJECT SCHEDULING

In this section we introduce several concepts project managers and team members must consider before they develop schedules. These include display formats, level of detail, types of logic, and precedence relationships. These concepts are applicable to projects of all types and can be employed in schedules that are developed manually or through the application of scheduling software. For those who are interested in the digital side of project scheduling, Appendix A at the end of this book, "Quick Guide to Using MS Project," offers a tutorial to guide first-time users (or experienced users with bad habits) through that software's features.

---

[9] F.K. Levy, G.L. Thompson, and J.D. Wiest, "The ABCs of the Critical Path Method," *Harvard Business Review* 41, no. 5 (1963), pp. 98–108.

[10] R.W. Miller, "How to Plan and Control with PERT," *Harvard Business Review* 40, no. 2 (1962), p. 93.

[11] For example, see Levy, et al., "The ABCs of the Critical Path Method"; A. Charnes and W.W. Cooper, "A Network Interpretation and Directed Sub-Dual Algorithm for Critical Path Scheduling," *Journal of Industrial Engineering*, July–August 1962, pp. 213–19; and J.E. Kelley, Jr., "Critical Path Planning and Scheduling: A Mathematical Basis," *Operations Research* 7, no. 2 (1961), pp. 296–320.

[12] Many software reviews are available on the Internet. One example is: http://project-management-software-review.toptenreviews.com/ (accessed August 14, 2009).

EXHIBIT 7.5
Activity-on-Node and Activity-on-Arrow Schedule Displays

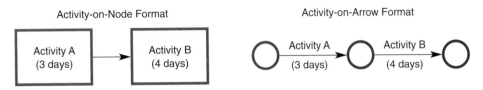

Activity-on-Node Format   Activity-on-Arrow Format

Schedule Display Formats

The examples presented previously in Box 7.1 illustrate two ways in which relationships among project activities can be depicted graphically. Both incorporate time estimates and both are based on the idea that some activities must occur sequentially and others can take place concurrently. Exhibit 7.3, related to the irrigation system project, represents relationships via a Gantt or bar chart. The bar chart makes it easy to see when work will occur, but it does not depict dependency relationships in a concrete way. Exhibit 7.4, related to machine-tool drawings, is a type of network schedule display known as a time-based network or schedule graph. It shows when activities will occur, but also makes clear their sequential relationships. Two other types of network schedule displays not depicted in these preceding exhibits are known as **activity-on-node (AON)** diagrams and **activity-on-arrow (AOA)** diagrams. Exhibit 7.5 shows the difference between these two types of network displays. Both indicate that Activity A must precede Activity B. In the case of AON, activity information is included inside the node, which may be a box, circle, or other two-dimensional shape. In the case of AOA, activity information appears on the connecting arrows or arcs, and the nodes (shown here as circles) represent the beginning and ending points of activities.

Level of Detail

An important early consideration in the development of a project schedule is the level of detail needed. A project manager for a multiple-year **megaproject** (sometimes known as a **program**) is not likely to want to see every work package in a network schedule; this could involve thousands of activities and require meters and meters of paper to display. Imagine a project to construct several dams on a series of rivers and tributaries. The program manager overseeing the entire set of dam construction efforts would probably want a high-level network showing summary deliverables or milestones, in parallel and sequential relationships. The managers of projects within this program are likely to require detailed schedules for their portions of the work. Exhibit 7.6 depicts these relationships for a hypothetical project to design two dams, construct them, and activate them. Note that **milestone** is a term used to describe a culminating event—the point at which a related set of activities has been completed—or to describe a point at which a set of activities may begin.

Exhibit 7.6 shows how a high-level milestone schedule could be used for big-picture thinking about project plans and progress, and how an underlying, more detailed schedule, depicts the tasks[13] that must occur to meet the goals of each milestone. In the dam construction example, Milestone A represents the completion of the design phase. Milestones B and C represent the completion of the construction of two separate dams. The activities leading to Milestone D, which involves rerouting the water flow through the two completed dams, cannot be started until both dams (Milestones B and C) have been completed.

---

[13] Reminder: throughout this book we interchange the words *task* and *activity.*

EXHIBIT 7.6
Dam Construction Megaproject (Program) with Subprojects

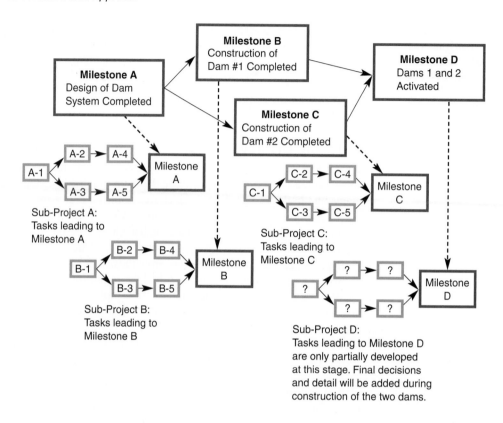

Levels of detail may also vary by phase. That is, task details and schedules within Milestones A, B, and C might be fairly well developed, whereas the team might decide not to develop details for Milestone D, activation, until the two dams are closer to completion and key questions have been answered. This approach is known as **rolling wave** planning because details about work to be done in the distant future are not developed until early work has been completed and the team has the necessary information to define work elements.

Types of Network Logic

Dependencies in network schedules can be based on what is known as *hard logic* or *soft logic*. **Hard logic** refers to sequences that are absolutely mandatory; there is simply no other way to arrange the relationship. For example, a construction crew would have to put the elevator shaft structure into a building before it could install the elevator. **Soft logic** refers to discretionary sequential relationships; the team does not really have to do it this way, but prefers it for some reason. For example, it is technically possible to program and install the two modules of an IT system concurrently, but because only one small team is available to do both, the project manager could set the schedule to program one first and then the other. We recommend that teams developing initial schedules try to adhere to hard logic at first. Otherwise, they could build in false dependencies based on initial assumptions about resource availability or other circumstances that later prove to be incorrect. With hard logic in place, the team can use schedule **float** for **noncritical activities** to adjust the schedule once members have a better idea of resource constraints and other project circumstances. We present tools and concepts for making these kinds of modifications in Chapter 8.

EXHIBIT 7.7
Finish-to-Start Relationships, without Lag and with Lag: Skydiving Example

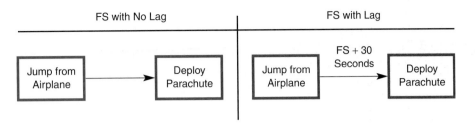

FS with No Lag | FS with Lag

Jump from Airplane → Deploy Parachute

Jump from Airplane → FS + 30 Seconds → Deploy Parachute

Types of Precedence Relationships

When tasks are sequentially related, we generally assume the first task must be finished before the next one may be completed. This type of relationship, the most common in project scheduling, is known as a **finish-to-start relationship.** For example, in skydiving: jump from airplane → deploy parachute would be an example of a finish-to-start relationship (and it certainly would be best not to reverse the sequence). The concept of finish-to-start can be expanded to include an intentional **lag** or **delay** between the end of the first task and the beginning of the successor task. In the skydiving example, some individuals might choose to delay the parachute deployment for 30 seconds[14] in order to experience the thrill of free-falling. Exhibit 7.7 depicts these two finish-to-start relationships.

In addition to the standard finish-to-start relationship, there are three other types of task linkages: **start-to-start, start-to-finish,** and **finish-to-finish.** In a start-to-start relationship, the second task in the sequence is scheduled to start at a specified time after the first task in the sequence has started. This can be useful in what are known as **fast-tracking** situations when tasks normally done in sequence are overlapped to some extent to compress a project schedule. There can be other reasons for using the start-to-start convention. Imagine you are planning a New Year's Eve party and you are putting together the guest list. You normally would complete the entire list before sending out the invitations, following finish-to-start precedence logic (Prepare Guest List → Send Invitations). However, you want to be sure your A-list friends receive invitations and commit to your party before they receive competing invitations from other people. The number of A-list friends who RSVP affirmatively also will determine how many people you can invite from your B-list. And, you might find some advantage in being able to mention in a note to B-list invitees, "Diddy will be there!" As a consequence of your careful scheming, you build in a five-day lag between the start of Prepare Guest List and the start of Send Invitations. Consequently, there will be a period of time when both of these tasks operate in parallel, as shown in Exhibit 7.8.

Although finish-to-start and start-to-start offer the most practical applications and cover most situations where lags or overlaps are appropriate, we acknowledge that some individuals might wish to use the other two types of precedence relationships. In a

[14] Using the authors as an example, Nancy would deploy immediately and Karen would wait.

EXHIBIT 7.8
Start-to-Start Relationship with Overlapping Tasks: Party Invitation Example

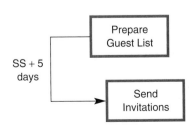

SS + 5 days

Prepare Guest List → Send Invitations

American Products (AP) sells memorabilia products through the Internet to customers primarily residing in the United States and currently has its primary call center in Seattle, Washington. Company officials have witnessed the cost savings their competitors have achieved by moving their call centers to India. India, with English as the official language, offers a large and capable workforce at wage rates significantly lower than those for equivalent jobs in Seattle. AP has enlisted its vice-president for sales, Todd Johnson, to work on-site to open a pilot call center with 50 employees in New Delhi. AP will continue to operate its Seattle call center until at least three Indian call centers are running effectively. The company has found a successful business agent in India, Srinivas Karuparti, who assures AP that he can cut the time for government approvals from the usual several months down to a few weeks. His other clients confirm that Karuparti is highly capable and ethical.

The call center project has gone through a complete business case analysis, and the sponsor has issued a project charter announcing the project to the entire company. The team has begun its initiation efforts and has developed a preliminary WBS with over 1,000 work packages, incorporating ideas from a thorough risk analysis. The team is experimenting with different types of schedule formats, each of which is presented in the next several exhibits. The schedules presented here are for one segment of the project and do not include all of the details in the comprehensive WBS. These schedules will be used for reporting to the sponsor, with time units in weeks. We discuss and graphically illustrate each of the scheduling formats the team is considering, highlight the advantages and disadvantages of each format, and describe how the team might use the information available to make inquiries and decisions.

start-to-finish relationship, one could specify that Task B cannot finish until so many time units (days, weeks, months) after Task A starts. A finish-to-finish relationship indicates that Task B cannot finish until so many time units after Task A finishes. Although these options are theoretically possible, we believe they add unnecessary complexity. Microsoft Project and other scheduling software packages offer a feature that allows the user to depict all four types of precedence relationships and show lags and concurrencies.

DISPLAYING AND INTERPRETING PROJECT SCHEDULES

We demonstrate how the scheduling concepts described above can be applied, based on a case about establishing a call center in India, presented in Box 7.2.

Activity-on-Node Network for the Indian Call Center Project

An AON diagram for the Indian call center project appears in Exhibit 7.9. Following AON convention, all activity information is depicted within the boxes (recall that circles are OK, too). In this example, we are assuming finish-to-start relationships, meaning no activity may begin until its predecessor has been completed. We have primarily applied hard logic here, designating activity precedence when it is necessary for one activity to be completed before its successor begins. One exception is the link between Activity J and Activity K: we have specified that Activity J,

EXHIBIT 7.9 **AON (Activity-on-Node) Schedule for the Indian Call Center Project**

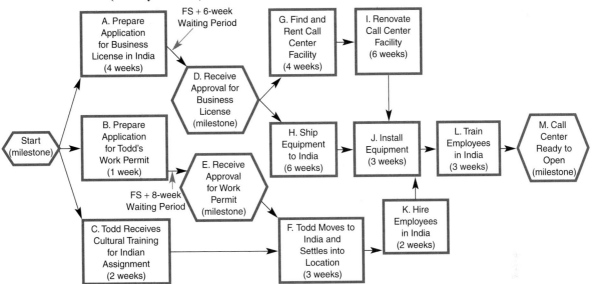

install equipment, cannot begin until Activity K, hire employees, has been completed because the new employees will assist with installation. This is an example of a soft-logic resource dependency. Note that we are not concerning ourselves with the lettering sequence in the network. Each activity is given a unique letter designator, but it is acceptable for Activity K to occur before Activity J. As we will discuss later in this chapter, when a team develops a schedule, activities are often moved around as insights and assumptions are uncovered. We believe it would be a waste of time and effort to become caught up in relettering activities as decisions about sequencing evolve.

In the AON diagram in Exhibit 7.9, four of the entities in the network are represented by hexagons[15] rather than boxes. These represent milestones, project events that theoretically require no time or resources. They can specify the beginning or ending of the project, or designate a project event where one or more important sets of work have been completed. There are instances when a milestone can be converted to an activity that does require time and resources. For example, the "Start" milestone might be converted to a one-day kickoff meeting, or the "Call Center Ready to Open" milestone could be converted to an opening ceremony for the call center.

Another feature of the AON schedule displayed in Exhibit 7.9 is that it shows two lags or delays associated with waiting time for approvals from the Indian government.[16] Thus, in each instance we have a finish-to-start relationship with a lag similar to the one introduced previously in Exhibit 7.7 for the skydiving example.

[15] The milestone does not necessarily have to be shown as a hexagon. It could be a parallelogram, a rhomboid, or any other shape that differentiates it from work packages, tasks, or activities.

[16] As with any international business venture, these delays can represent considerable duration uncertainty. However, in the American Products case, Mr. Karuparti, the trusty agent, has an impressive track record of keeping these approval processes on schedule.

EXHIBIT 7.10
Activity-on-Arrow
Diagram for the
Indian Call Center
Project

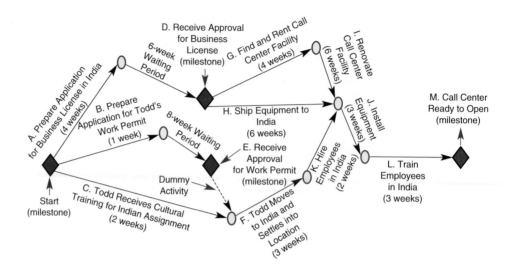

Activity-on-Arrow Diagram

Exhibit 7.10 shows the AOA network diagram for the Indian call center project. It conveys the same information as the AON network shown in Exhibit 7.9, but now the activity information is displayed along the arrows. Lags are depicted as arrows in this case, and the milestones and beginning and ending points of activities are nodes between arrows.

In Exhibit 7.10 there is a dashed line arrow connecting Activity (milestone) E to the node preceding Activity F. This is a **dummy activity.** These are sometimes necessary in AOA networks. In this case, it helps us to remain true to the hard logic dependencies in the AON network by avoiding the suggestion that C must precede E.

Although AOA has been popular in the past, AON has overtaken it in usage. We believe the AOA format has value because it allows for the use of a time-based network, a useful tool introduced previously in Exhibit 7.4 and described in more detail below. However, AOA does, in some circumstances, require the use of dummy activities, as shown above. These can create headaches for some people, but anyone who is truly comfortable with network logic will have no trouble with them. We have included another example of a project involving a dummy activity in Appendix 7A at the end of this chapter.

Visually Assessing the Critical Path and Float

A completed network schedule, inclusive of calendar time estimates,[17] serves as the team's information source for calculating several key project attributes and metrics, including the *critical path* and *float.* The **critical path** is the network path with the longest duration, and it determines the anticipated total amount of calendar time the project will consume. In Exhibits 7.9 and 7.10, we can see there are four paths in the Indian call center network. If we calculate the durations of these four paths, we can find the longest one, known as the critical path, which determines the expected duration of the project. The result of this path analysis, summarized with a spreadsheet in

---

[17] Some or all of the tasks in this network might require less working time than calendar time for the people who perform them. In project scheduling, we are focused on calendar time.

EXHIBIT 7.11   **Path Analysis for the Indian Call Center Project**

Path 1	A. Prepare Application for Business License in India	Lag: 6-week Waiting Period	D. Receive Approval for Business License (milestone)	G. Find and Rent Call Center Facility	I. Renovate Call Center Facility	J. Install Equipment	L. Train Employees in India	M. Call Center Ready to Open (milestone)	Path 1 Total Weeks
# Weeks	4	6	0	4	6	3	3	0	26
Path 2	A. Prepare Application for Business License in India	Lag: 6-week Waiting Period	D. Receive Approval for Business License (milestone)	H. Ship Equipment to India	J. Install Equipment	L. Train Employees in India	M. Call Center Ready to Open (milestone)		Path 2 Total Weeks
# Weeks	4	6	0	6	3	3	0		22
Path 3	B. Prepare Application for Todd's Work Permit	Lag: 8-week Waiting Period	E. Receive Approval for Work Permit (milestone)	F. Todd Moves to India and Settles into Location	K. Hire Employees in India	J. Install Equipment	L. Train Employees in India	M. Call Center Ready to Open (milestone)	Path 3 Total Weeks
# Weeks	1	8	0	3	2	3	3	0	20
Path 4	C. Todd Receives Cultural Training for Indian Assignment	F. Todd Moves to India and Settles into Location	K. Hire Employees in India	J. Install Equipment	L. Train Employees in India	M. Call Center Ready to Open (milestone)			Path 4 Total Weeks
# Weeks	2	3	2	3	3	0			13

Exhibit 7.11, reveals that path A-D-G-I-J-L-M, including a six-week waiting period (i.e., a lag) is the longest, at 26 weeks. The project manager and team must be very diligent in managing these seven activities, and attending to what is happening during the lag period, if they wish to contain the project's duration within 26 weeks. Also, if they would like to shorten the project's duration, they ought to concentrate their efforts on this set of activities. Activities not on the critical path possess what is known as **float** or **slack,** meaning they can be delayed somewhat without jeopardizing the schedule.

Gantt Chart for the Indian Call Center

We introduced the Gantt[18] chart in Exhibit 7.3 and now show in Exhibit 7.12 how the concept can be applied to the Indian call center case. The Gantt chart is very popular because of its simplicity and ease of use. A particular advantage of this format is that it makes it easy for a team to see where resource conflicts might exist. For example, if Todd is expected to take personal responsibility for completing his own work permit application (Activity B) while at the same time immersing himself in cultural training (Activity C) 10 hours per day, he and the project team would need to consider schedule adjustments. However, it will be difficult to make these adjustments based solely on a Gantt chart because Gantt charts do not reveal sequential relationships, the critical path, or float.[19] Thus, anyone using Gantt charts also must have a network diagram available for cross-checking.

[18] Gantt charts bear the name of Henry Gantt (1861–1919) who published his idea for the presentation format in 1910. It was later published as *Work, Wages, and Profits* (Easton, PA: Hive Publishing Co., 1974).

[19] Some project scheduling software packages such as MS Project offer modified versions of the Gantt chart that do show precedence arrows. This would be considered a hybrid between a network and Gantt format.

EXHIBIT 7.12   **Gantt Chart for the Indian Call Center Project**

Activity	Duration	Week 1	2	3	4	5	6	7	8	9	10	11	12	13	14	15	16	17	18	19	20	21	22	23	24	25	26
A. Prepare Application for Business License in India	4 weeks	A				Lag for Business License Approval					→																
B. Prepare Application for Todd's Work Permit	1 week	B	Lag for Work Permit Approval							→																	
C. Todd Receives Cultural Training for Indian Assignment	2 weeks	C																									
D. Receive Approval for Business License (milestone)	0 weeks										◆																
E. Receive Approval for Work Permit (milestone)	0 weeks									◆																	
F. Todd Moves to India and Settles into Location	3 weeks									F																	
G. Find and Rent Call Center Facility	4 weeks										G																
H. Ship Equipment to India	6 weeks										H																
I. Renovate Call Center Facility	6 weeks															I											
J. Install Equipment	3 weeks																				J						
K. Hire Employees in India	2 weeks											K															
L. Train Employees in India	3 weeks																							L			
M. Call Center Ready to Open (milestone)	0 weeks																							◆			
Week		1	2	3	4	5	6	7	8	9	10	11	12	13	14	15	16	17	18	19	20	21	22	23	24	25	26

Schedule Graph or Time-Based Network for the Indian Call Center Project

As we have established, AON and AOA network diagrams offer the advantage of making precedence relationships very clear, but they do not offer the time-scaled visual advantage of Gantt charts. A hybrid option, the schedule-graph or time-based network,[20] combines the advantages of networks and bar charts and provides a visual illustration of critical path and float. Exhibit 7.13 displays a spreadsheet-based schedule graph for the Indian call center project. In this presentation, every activity is depicted as starting at its earliest possible start time. This is known as the **early-start schedule.**

In the early-start schedule graph presented in Exhibit 7.13, the horizontal distance covered by the arrow for each activity is proportional to the duration of the activity. Dashed lines represent slack or float, areas where there is room for flexibility in the schedule. In recent years, the term *float* appears to have come into more common usage,[21] so we will use this term throughout the remainder of the book. There are two general types of float: **free float** and **total float.** Free float is the amount by which we can delay an activity from its **early start time** (earliest possible time an activity may begin, given its predecessors), without delaying the early start of any activity that immediately follows it. Total float is the amount by which we can delay an activity from its early start time without delaying the project beyond its anticipated end date. The critical path (or paths), by definition, does not have float and is shown as a sequence of solid lines at the top of the figure (A-lag-D-G-I-J-L-M).

In Exhibit 7.13 there is a seven-week dashed line representing float between Activity C, Todd's cultural training, and Activity F, Todd's move to India. This is because the

[20] We extend our appreciation to Wiest and Levy for introducing time-based networks in their classic book on project scheduling. See J.D. Wiest and F.K. Levy, *A Management Guide to PERT/CPM* (Englewood Cliffs, NJ: Prentice Hall, 1977).

[21] For example, see *A Guide to the Project Management Body of Knowledge* (*PMBOK Guide*), Fourth Edition (Newtown Square, PA: Project Management Institute, 2008).

EXHIBIT 7.13 **Early-Start Time-Based Network for the Indian Call Center Project**

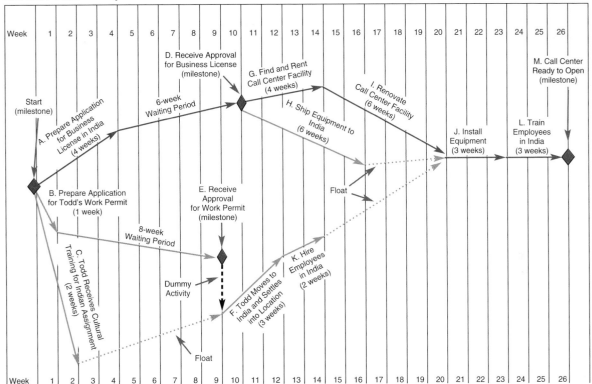

parallel Activity B and the eight-week lag that follows it require nine weeks and the training (Activity C) is only two weeks. We could, at least theoretically, delay Todd's training by seven weeks without interfering with the early start date for his scheduled move to India (Activity F). So, we can say Activity C has seven weeks of free float. Also, Activity K, hiring, could be delayed by six weeks without delaying installation. This is K's free float. Additionally, if Activity K is delayed by six weeks, it would now also be possible to delay Activity B and Activity F by six weeks without delaying Activity J or the project. This means each activity in this sequence has six weeks of total float. However, the total float is shared across this set of activities. One of the biggest misconceptions we have witnessed in project environments is that people responsible for different activities on a noncritical path assume they exclusively own the total float allocated to their activities. This is one reason we encourage teams to jointly develop time-based networks. In doing so, they develop a visual appreciation for shared float.

Imagine the call center planning team is considering the possibility of delaying all project activities to their latest possible start times. This would leave team members free to finish other projects before commencing with the Indian call center project. The result would be the **late-start schedule** graph presented in Exhibit 7.14.

The late-start schedule depicted in Exhibit 7.14 would be technically feasible if everything goes as planned. However, projects, by definition, carry uncertainty with them. What if it takes longer than six weeks to ship the equipment, perhaps because of a dockworkers' strike or snags with Indian customs? Or what if the lag for Todd's

EXHIBIT 7.14 Late-Start Schedule Graph for the Indian Call Center

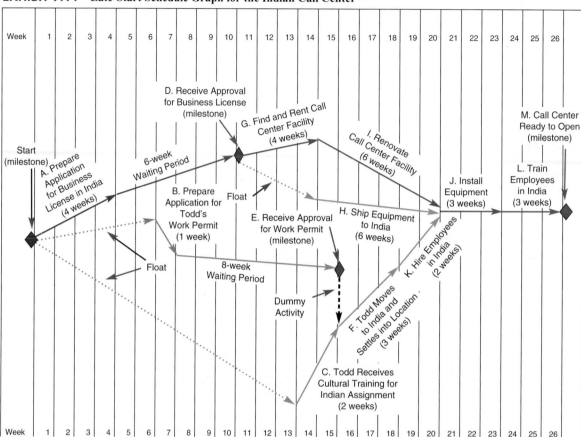

work permit is more than eight weeks? In either scenario, the project would be delayed because noncritical paths would have longer durations than the initially calculated critical path. A late-start schedule nearly always adds time and risk to a project schedule. Nonetheless, there are circumstances when it is worthwhile to delay noncritical activities (e.g., to accommodate resource conflicts or delay major capital expenditures). The project manager and team must clearly understand the uncertainties they introduce when they decide to delay activities.

A visual analysis of the sort just described can be effective for a small project, but for larger projects it becomes necessary to use a mathematical algorithm to calculate float and identify the critical path. Details of this algorithm are presented later in this chapter.

Project Scheduling Software

Several software programs are available for project scheduling. Examples of desktop packages currently available for use with Microsoft Windows platforms include Artemis, Planisware, Primavera's P6, and Microsoft Project, which currently holds the market lead. Two popular packages available for use with the Apple operating system are Merlin and Omniplan. Regardless of platform or product, the advantages of using these programs include ease of updating, availability of multiple report formats,

EXHIBIT 7.15   **MS Project Output for the Indian Call Center Project: Network View**

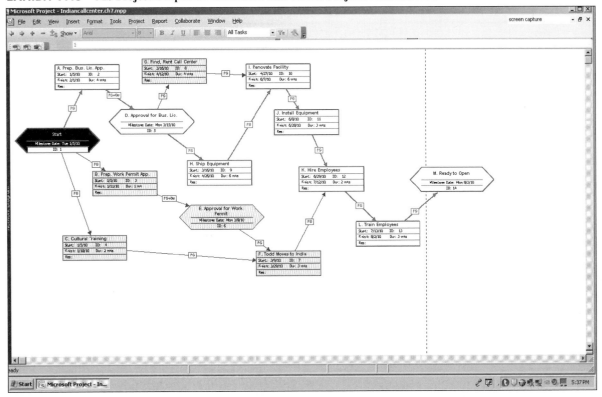

opportunity for file sharing among geographically dispersed team members, and standardization of schedule displays.

Despite the potential benefits of project scheduling software, project managers and team members should be aware of potential pitfalls. First, not all projects are big or complex enough to warrant the use of the software. In these cases, team members might spend more time fiddling with the software than they do actually delivering the project. Additionally, people can attach too much credibility to a computer-generated schedule, reducing the likelihood they will ask important questions about assumptions, time estimates, and the like. It also discourages big-picture thinking; for a project of any reasonable size, a team or individual can see only a portion of the schedule on a computer screen.

Many people who are starting out with software tend to believe it will manage a project for them. Consequently, they sometimes jump right into the software without completing all the important components that should precede the scheduling step (e.g., agreeing on goals, brainstorming the WBS, assessing uncertainties).

A screen shot of an MS Project network view for the Indian call center project is shown in Exhibit 7.15, and a Gantt view is shown in Exhibit 7.16. Task boxes in the network view shown here include Task Name, Start Date, End Date, and Resource. In this case we have not specified a resource. Other display options are available for the task boxes. Calendar dates reflect the passage of working and nonworking days such as weekends and holidays during the project's life. For more information about using MS Project, see Appendix A, "Quick Guide to Using MS Project," at the end of this book.

EXHIBIT 7.16   MS Project Output for the Indian Call Center Project: Gantt View

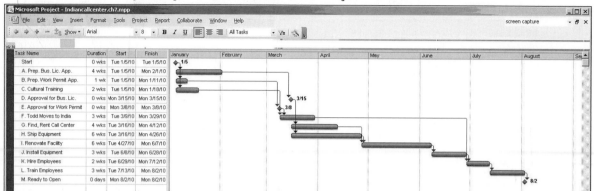

The Critical Path Algorithm

So far, we have explained the conceptual differences between free float and total float through our discussion of the graphical displays in Exhibits 7.13 and 7.14. These differences are important because an activity manager will be in error if he or she presumes ownership of total float that is shared with other activities on the same path. In a large network, it can be difficult to visually identify the critical path and float. Exhibit 7.17 presents a mathematical algorithm for assessing the location of the critical path, free float, and total float. This reveals the underlying procedural and mathematical logic used in project scheduling software packages. It involves making a forward pass through the network to determine the earliest possible start and finish times for each activity, then taking a backward pass to determine the latest possible start and finish times for each activity. With this information in hand, we can identify the critical path and calculate total and free float for noncritical activities. For the sake of simplicity in presenting the algorithm, we use points in time (0, 1, 2, etc.) rather than calendar dates.

We apply the **critical path algorithm** to the Indian call center project in Exhibit 7.18. Forward and backward pass calculations are displayed in the text lines above each activity box. The general procedure for the **forward pass** involves calculating the earliest possible start and finish time for each activity, beginning with all starting activities and working toward the end of the project. (The example uses sequential numbers rather than calendar dates, and adjustments for weekends and holidays are ignored.)

Assume the start date for the project is Time 0. This becomes the early start (ES) for the *Start* milestone, and given that it is a milestone that takes no time, its early finish (EF) will also be 0. The ES for Activity A will be 0 and the EF for A will be 4 (0 plus the activity time of four weeks). Activity D, another milestone, has an ES of 10 because it cannot occur until the six-week waiting period that follows A. However, because it is a milestone, its EF will be the same as its ES, week 10. Activity G can begin at the end of 10 weeks and its EF will be 10 plus its four-week duration, or 14. Shipping, Activity H, has an ES of 10, and its estimated time of six weeks means its EF will be 16. So, what is the ES of J, install equipment? It is preceded by H, with an EF of 16, and I, with an EF of 20. Following the logic prescribed in Exhibit 7.17, we correctly choose the latest EF, meaning that J cannot begin until *both* H and I are

EXHIBIT 7.17
Critical Path
Algorithm

Forward Pass: Calculating Early Start and Early Finish Times

1. Start time for starting node = 0
2. Early start (ES) for all starting activities (activities with no predecessors) = 0
3. ES for any other activity = Maximum or latest early finish (EF) for all activities that immediately precede the activity. Especially relevant at merge points where one activity has several predecessors.
4. Early finish (EF) for any activity = ES + Estimated activity duration.
5. Total estimated project time = Latest EF for any activity in the network (in other words, EF for the latest-running activity at the end of the network or the final milestone).

Backward Pass: Calculating Late Start and Late Finish Times

1. Late finish (LF) for last activity or milestone = Latest EF for any activity or milestone in the network.
2. Late start (LS) for latest EF activity or milestone = LF − Estimated activity duration.
3. LF for any activity = Earliest LS for all activities that follow it. Especially relevant at burst points where one activity has several successors.
4. LS for any activity = LF − Estimated activity duration.

Identifying the Critical Path and Float Using ES, EF, LS, LF Information

1. Critical path activities are those activities for which ES = LS and EF = LF.
2. Total float (TF) for any activity = LS − ES, which is equivalent to LF − EF. (If they are not the same, you have made an error.)
3. Free float (FF) for any activity = Difference between the EF of that activity and the earliest ES of all activities immediately following it. In other words, note the EF of each task in the network. Compare this figure with the ES of all activities following it. Wherever there is a difference between the EF of one activity and the earliest ES of a successor, there is free float. Free float always appears where a shorter path merges with a longer path.

finished, or week 20. The remaining steps for the forward pass follow the same logic, so now we move to the backward pass.

The **backward pass** involves calculating the late finish and late start for each activity, beginning with the ending project activity or milestone. For the call center project, the LF for Activity M, the final milestone, is 26, and, because it is a milestone, 26 is also the LS. The LS for M becomes the LF for Activity L, and subtracting L's time of three weeks we calculate an LS of 23 for Activity L. The LS of 23 for L becomes the LF for J, and subtracting J's time of three weeks, we determine J's LS of 20. As we continue to work backward on the upper path, ES = LS and EF = LF for all of the activities we previously identified as being on the critical path. In fact, in the upper two paths, the only activity where the early and late times differ is H, ship equipment. This is a noncritical activity that possesses some float. Moving to the lower set of paths on our backward pass, we see that Activity K, hire employees, can finish as late as week 20, its LF, and, thus, can begin as late as week 18 (20 − 2). Week 18 becomes the LF for Todd's move (Activity F), and the LS is 15 (18 − 3). This logic continues back to the start milestone or starting activity. Here, we have LS times for three initial activities to consider when deciding

EXHIBIT 7.18 Critical Path Algorithm Calculations for the Indian Call Center Project

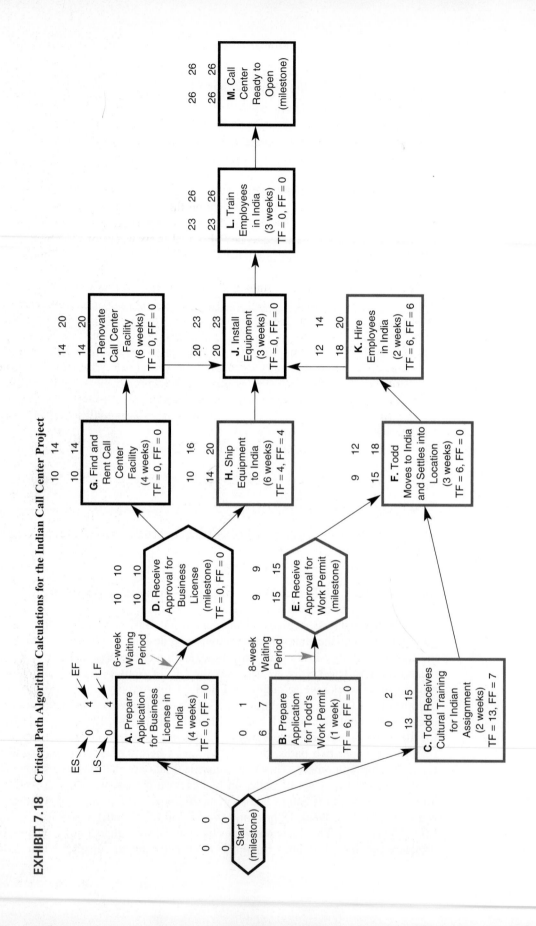

on the LF for the *Start* milestone. Following the logic described in Exhibit 7.17, we would correctly choose the earliest LS for all successors of *Start,* which in this case would be the 0 shown for Activity A.

The combination of information about ES, EF, LS, and LF provides the data needed for identifying the critical path and calculating total float and free float. Recall that total float (TF) is the amount by which we can delay an activity without delaying the project. TF can be shared by several activities on a noncritical path. As previously noted, the critical path of A–lag-D-G-I-J-L-M has no float because ES = LS and EF = LF for every activity on the path. For all noncritical activities, total float (TF) = LS – ES or LF – EF. So, for example, Activity H has four weeks of TF. And each activity in the sequence B-E-F-K has six weeks of TF, which we previously established in our visual analysis of Exhibit 7.13. Activity C, Todd's cultural training, has 13 weeks of TF.

The results of the CP algorithm also permit us to calculate free float (FF), which we previously identified visually as the dashed lines in Exhibit 7.13. Free float occurs when shorter paths merge with longer paths and is calculated as the difference between the EF of the predecessor and the earliest ES of any of its successors. So, for example, Activity K, hire employees, has an EF of 14 and its successor J has an ES of 20. Thus, K has six weeks of FF. Although it might appear that Activity B has eight weeks of free float, this would be an incorrect assumption, given the eight-week lag before Activity E. This is one of those areas where members of the project team must be very aware of how to interpret the network information or they will make serious judgment errors.

Negative Float

So far, we have proceeded under the assumption that all float is positive—that is, we have used it to signify the amount of wiggle room available for each task or series of linked tasks. In some situations, the initial schedule specifies a completion date later than the due date. Imagine that in the case of the Indian call center, the sponsor has demanded the project be completed in 24 weeks. In that case, critical activities would now all have a negative float of two weeks because LF for Activity M would be adjusted to 24 and this would affect all calculations in the backward pass. Negative float also may emerge after the project is underway. For example, if Activity H, shipping, takes 14 weeks instead of six and the LF for the project has been set at 26 weeks, all remaining critical activities would take on a negative float of four weeks. Unless the due date is negotiable, the team must consider methods for getting float back into a neutral or positive position by compressing activities, adding resources, reducing scope, or other actions. These topics are discussed in Chapter 8.

DEVELOPING THE SCHEDULE NETWORK

You are probably able to master scheduling concepts on your own, but to make them work in a project environment, you must involve the team. A team offers creative insight about task relationships, and the act of participating in the creation of the schedule increases members' commitment to meeting that schedule. A secondary benefit occurs in the realm of learning; by actively creating a network schedule, even those who are new at network scheduling will come away with a

EXHIBIT 7.19
A Team-Based Process for Creating Project Schedules

1. Place a large sheet of butcher paper (about two meters across by one meter high, or six feet by three feet) horizontally on the wall at standing-height eye level. Have colored pens, sticky notes, and pencils with erasers available.

2. Refer to the WBS, which should be posted on the wall next to the blank page prepared for scheduling. Revisit time estimates; for this purpose they should represent calendar-time durations based on underlying assumptions about the number of people available and their relative time allocations to the project. For example, if someone is available only half time to work on a 16 person-hour task, the effort will require four calendar days at four hours each.

3. Choose the appropriate level of detail. The team might decide to schedule at the lowest level of detail, or perhaps base the schedule on higher-level summary tasks.

4. Write the names of all work packages, activities, or tasks (depending on chosen level of detail) and their durations on sticky notes.

5. Initially, arrange the notes on the butcher paper into three groups: early, middle, and late, according to their approximate timing during the project. Attempt to reach group consensus on these clusters. This step is very important. Get a big picture first.

6. Determine detailed sequential and parallel relationships and rearrange the notes to reflect this. For example, which task absolutely must precede Task A? Could these two tasks progress in parallel without interfering with each other? Guard against making unnecessary assumptions about sequential relationships. In some of the most innovative and successful projects, planners have broken ingrained rules and traditions to find new ways to sequence activities. Once notes are arranged, draw lines in pencil to reflect these task relationships.
   Note: Be open to adding elements to the WBS. During the scheduling process, team members often discover WBS elements they previously overlooked. An iterative team process offers opportunities to discover white spaces in the plan.

7. The team leader or another member can clean up the schedule and present it for review at a later meeting. A second look often adds value after people have had time to reflect. The review version should be big enough to post on the wall, and we recommend *not* putting it into scheduling software at this stage. The sticky notes convey a certain flexibility and encourage more creative input. In contrast, a computer printout says, "This is a done deal" and discourages people from offering additional ideas.

8. Once the team has agreed on the initial schedule, a member can enter the information into a software package. However, a visible sticky note schedule can be sufficient for many projects. If the team uses a computer-generated schedule, print it with a plotter to make it large enough to view during project meetings. And remember it is OK to mark up a computer-generated schedule with changes.

better understanding of how to interpret the network and resolve scheduling problems once the project is underway. Exhibit 7.19 suggests a process for a team-based scheduling approach.

We recommend limiting the group size for the team-based scheduling activity to three or four people; however, we acknowledge that this sort of limit is not always possible. Creative tasks such as WBS development can involve more people, but analytical tasks are best done with smaller groups. To involve more team

EXHIBIT 7.20
A Project Team Collaborating to Develop a Schedule

members in scheduling, some organizations use a rotation system whereby one group creates an initial schedule and subsequent groups help to refine it. But, as we continue to emphasize, team involvement in scheduling increases the likelihood of schedule commitment. The process of developing the schedule may be the most important benefit of its use.[22] Exhibit 7.20 shows a team collaborating to develop a schedule.

Constructing a Network from a Precedence Table

Although a team-based approach may be the best way to develop a schedule in most project environments, there are times when an individual working alone wishes to put together the pieces of a schedule puzzle in a tabular format before creating a network (or, in the case of a small project, instead of creating a network). People who prefer a linear style of thinking may be more comfortable with such an approach. Consider an example. Kathryn is a lead programmer at Lewis-Nordfors Technologies. She will be responsible for coordinating a team of three people to upgrade the company's financial system, but she will work alone initially to plan the activities leading up to the project kickoff. Kathryn has listed the WBS elements in a table and is now considering sequential relationships. Her precedence table, which appears in Exhibit 7.21, lists each activity, identifies the activity or activities that immediately precede it, and includes time estimates. Kathryn can use the table to build a network schedule, as shown in the second half of Exhibit 7.21.

Exhibit 7.21 shows that a tabular approach leads to the same result as the visual approach we have prescribed for team environments. The critical path is Start-A-D-E-F-lag-G-I-J at 10.2 weeks. For some people, it is easier and more intuitively appealing to create a precedence table before creating a network.

[22] We paraphrase this from the project management classic by F.P. Brooks, *The Mythical Man-Month* (Boston: Addison-Wesley, 1995).

EXHIBIT 7.21
Precedence Table and Network Diagram for the Financial System Upgrade

Activity	Immediate Predecessor (s)	Estimated Activity Duration (Calendar Time)
A. Obtain charter from accounting department	Start milestone	1 week
B. Research past projects	Start milestone	2 weeks
C. Assess user requirements	A	2 weeks
D. Benchmark systems at other companies	A	3 weeks
E. Develop preliminary requirements and architecture	C, D	2 weeks
F. Prepare revised budget proposal and submit to sponsor	B, E	1 week
G. Approval	F (after a 1-week lag for the approval process)	0 weeks (milestone)
H. Form team	G	1 week
I. Review vendors available	G	2 weeks
J. Project kickoff meeting	H, I	.2 week (1 day)

Accounting System Network Schedule Built from above Precedence Table

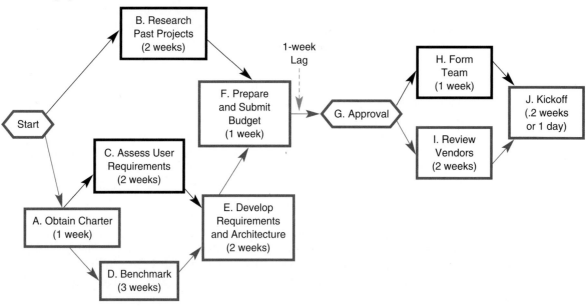

Technical Tips for Scheduling

When teams are learning to create network schedules in a collaborative mode, or when individuals work alone to create schedules, we have observed that they tend to make several common errors. This is part of the learning process. Exhibit 7.22 offers tips for recognizing them and correcting them.

EXHIBIT 7.22
Tips for Developing Network Schedules

- **Use Beginning and Ending Milestone Nodes If There is More Than One Activity at the Start or End of the Network.** Begin every project with a single starting node and end every project with a single finish node. In some networks, there is a single beginning and a single ending task. If there is not, the team should create start and finish milestones to tie things together in the beginning and end.

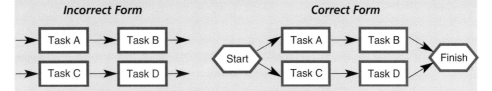

- **Place Task Information in One Place.** For AON networks, all task information should be inside the node (box, circle, hexagon, or other shape). The exception to this rule is when there is a designated lag between two tasks to show some sort of waiting time. For example, a project schedule might show that a team is waiting for concrete to dry or waiting for an order to be delivered. In that case, it is sometimes appropriate to show the waiting time on the arrows connecting two tasks. For AOA networks, all task information should be above or below the task arrow.

- **Avoid Cycles or Loops.** Eliminate instances where a set of connecting arrows would result in repeating a sequence of tasks that are meant to be performed only once.

Schedule Loop Example: $A \rightarrow B \rightarrow C \rightarrow D \rightarrow A$ ***This Project Will Never Be Finished!***

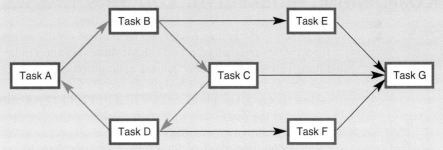

- **Be Sure All Tasks Lead to the End.** Every activity should connect with others leading to the end of the project. Nothing should be hanging without a place to go.

Task C Does Not Lead to Any Other Activity or to the End of the Project.

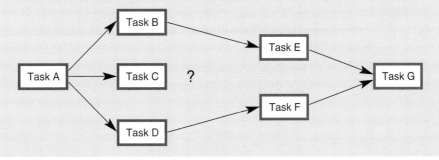

(continued)

EXHIBIT 7.22
(*Continued*)

- **Be Consistent with Line Styles.** Lines in an AON network should all be the same type, generally solid and not dashed. Dashed lines are reserved for use in specifying dummy activities in AOA networks and showing float in time-based networks.
- **Beware of Redundant Predecessor Relationships.** Consider the example shown below. In this case, the line connecting "Assess user requirements" with "Test Web site" would be redundant because the relationship is already shown with the sequence Assess user requirements → Develop Web site → Test Web site. Standard scheduling software programs currently available do not allow for decision options. If they did, something like the below figure, but with more information and a different set of tasks, might be legitimate. A method known as GERT, or Graphical Evaluation Review Technique,* does allow for decision options, but is not widely used because of its complexity.

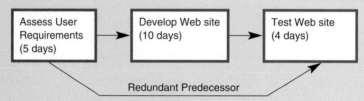

- **Recognize that Some Tasks are Ongoing.** A task that occurs during the entire life of a project and ends when the project is complete (e.g., monitoring performance or regular reporting to the sponsor) can be shown as a single task connected to the start node on one end and the finish node at the other end. These are known as **hammock tasks.**

*A.A.B. Pritzker, "GERT Networks," *The Production Engineer* 48, no. 10 (1968), pp. 499–506.

INCORPORATING PROBABILISTIC CONCEPTS INTO SCHEDULES

Up to this point in the chapter, we have relied on the assumption that time estimates for activities and paths represent single duration values rather than a ranges of possible times. This can be a rather gallant assumption in most project environments, where task times entered into a schedule are merely forecasts.

In Chapter 5, we introduced the idea of **PERT three-point time estimates.** Here, we extend the discussion to demonstrate how three-point estimates can be used to make probabilistic assessments of various project completion times. When people estimate the time required for a task, they often state a single point in time but have in the backs of their minds a range of possible times. For example, when you give someone an estimate of the time it will take you to drive, carpool, bicycle, or bus to work, you may say, "Oh, I'd guess about 25 minutes," knowing that if there is no traffic, and the weather is good, you can make it in 15 minutes. If the weather is bad or the traffic is heavy, you might estimate up to 65 minutes. If we translate this thinking into PERT terminology (see Chapter 5), we would break down your estimates as follows:

Optimistic commute time estimate ($t_{(o)}$) = 15 minutes

Most likely commute time estimate ($t_{(m)}$) = 25 minutes

Pessimistic commute time estimate ($t_{(p)}$) = 65 minutes

You may have your own mental model about the actual likelihoods of these times, but to apply the methods described here we assume the two extreme estimates are at

EXHIBIT 7.23
Beta Distribution
Example for
Commute Times

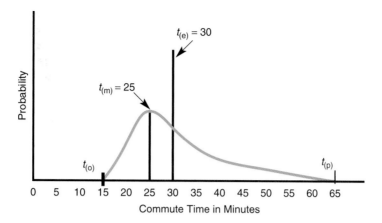

less than 1 percent tails of a distribution.[23] That is, there is some very small chance (less than 1 percent) the commute will take more than 65 minutes, and there is an equally small chance it will take less than 15 minutes. We will further assume the distribution of possible commute times may be described as a **beta distribution.** A **normal distribution** is bell-shaped and has tails of equal size extending from either side of the modal/mean value. A beta distribution allows us more flexibility in that it does not have to be symmetrical and, thus, can be skewed to the right or left. Additionally, and perhaps more importantly, a beta distribution and its **standard deviation** can be determined from only three time estimates. This is useful for project task estimation where an extensive historical data set is not likely to be available. A beta distribution for the commute time example is shown in Exhibit 7.23.

Applying PERT concepts, we can use the following weighted average formula to calculate the estimated completion time ($t_{(e)}$) for the commute:

$$t_{(e)} = \frac{t_{(o)} + 4\, t_{(m)} + t_{(p)}}{6} \rightarrow t_{(e)} = \frac{15 \text{ min.} + 4\,(25 \text{ min.}) + 65 \text{ min.}}{6}$$

$$= \frac{180 \text{ min}}{6} = 30 \text{ minutes}$$

The $t_{(e)}$ or expected time of 30 minutes is shown in Exhibit 7.23, just to the right of $t_{(m)}$. From a statistical standpoint, this weighted average $t_{(e)}$ is an estimate of the mean of a beta distribution for the commute task. Because PERT provides the foundation for probabilistic work, we must also calculate the standard deviation (σ) and **variance** (σ^2) of the distribution to make full use of the method. For the commute example, σ and σ^2 are calculated as follows:

Standard deviation for a beta distribution:

$$\sigma = \frac{(t_{(p)} - t_{(o)})}{6} \rightarrow \sigma = \frac{(65 \text{ minutes} - 15 \text{ minutes})}{6} = 8.33 \text{ minutes}$$

[23] Some experts recommend using 5 percent tails, suggesting this will reduce the potential for error. However, to remain true to the original assumptions of the PERT model, we will adhere to the rule of less than 1 percent estimation tails. See F.T. Hartman, *Don't Park Your Brain Outside* (Newtown Square, PA: Project Management Institute, 2000).

This division by 6 follows the assumption that by defining the distribution between two less-than-1 percent probability tails, we have captured approximately three standard deviations on either side of the mean (3 + 3 = 6). And, based on statistical principles, we calculate the variance (σ^2) as follows: $\sigma^2 = 8.33^2 = 69.39$.

Estimating Project Duration

To apply the PERT model more fully, imagine the commute time calculated previously is for the carpooling portion of a longer trip. The commuter must drive to a carpool pick-up point, ride with the carpool, and then take a short walk to get to her workplace. The schedule for the three commuting activities, along with time estimates and statistical calculations, is shown in Exhibit 7.24.

To comply with the requirements of PERT statistical analysis, we assume the time required for each of the commuting activities is an uncertain and random variable; thus, it may take on any value within the range specified by $t_{(o)}$ and $t_{(p)}$. We also assume the time required for each commute segment is independent of the time required for the other two. We are not saying one activity cannot delay another, just that the factors causing one to be delayed will not also cause the others to be delayed. This assumption is a bit hard to meet in reality, given that common factors such as weather and traffic could potentially influence all three segments of the commute. Common factors also exist in organizations, creating a challenge for this assumption in real-world projects, as well. We discuss this issue in more depth later in the chapter. For now, we will live with this limitation.

Information about expected times, standard deviations, and variances provides the foundation for PERT probabilistic calculations. In the commute example, there is only

EXHIBIT 7.24
Commuting Example with Three-Point Time Estimates

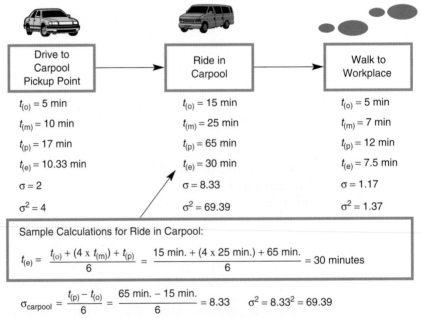

Here and in remaining examples all figures are rounded to two places to the right of the decimal point based on the rule that if the third integer to the right of the decimal is 5 or more we round up and if it is under 5 we round down.

one path (Drive → Carpool → Walk). Using the PERT approach, we can estimate total project time ($T_{(E)}$) as the sum of all three $t_{(e)}$ calculations:

$$T_{(E)} = t_{(e)\ \text{drive}} + t_{(e)\ \text{carpool}} + t_{(e)\ \text{walk}}$$
$$= 10.33 \text{ minutes} + 30 \text{ minutes} + 7.5 \text{ minutes} = 47.83 \text{ minutes}$$

Consider the type of distribution associated with the three-activity commuting project. As previously mentioned, we assume the individual $t_{(e)}$s for the commute are all independent random variables, and, thus, so is their sum, $T_{(E)}$. From a statistical standpoint, $T_{(E)}$ then has, at least theoretically, a normal distribution rather than the beta distribution that characterized its elements. (This is an outcome of the **Central Limit Theorem,** which you should recall if you have studied statistics.) Because we can treat $T_{(E)}$ as a normally distributed variable, its distribution can be described as a uniform, uni-modal, bell-shaped curve. A great deal is known about normal curves, and we can build on this knowledge to answer questions about a project's duration.

We have estimated values of σ and σ^2 for the individual activities in the project, but to get a clearer picture of the project as a whole, it is necessary to calculate σ and σ^2 for the entire set of activities. According to statistical principles, the variance of a sum is equal to the sum of the individual variances, assuming independence among elements (i.e., times, in this case).

Summing the variances for the three segments of the commute produces the following:

$$\sigma^2_{\text{commute}} = \sigma^2_{\text{drive}} + \sigma^2_{\text{carpool}} + \sigma^2_{\text{walk}} = 4 + 69.39 + 1.37 = 74.76$$

Taking the square root of σ^2, we determine the standard deviation (σ) for the total three-segment commute:

$$\sigma_{\text{commute}} = \sqrt{74.76} = 8.65$$

Remember this: to determine the standard deviation of a path, first sum the variances, *then* take the square root. Do not sum the standard deviations; this would produce a different, and incorrect, result.

Based on statistical theory, we know 68 percent of the area under a normal curve will fall within plus or minus one standard deviation of the mean. Additionally, we know 95 percent will fall within plus or minus two standard deviations of the mean, and we know more than 99 percent will fall within plus or minus three standard deviations of the mean. These attributes of the distribution are depicted for the commute project in Exhibit 7.25.

Estimating Duration Probabilities

In the case of the single path (three-leg) commute project, note that in Exhibit 7.23 the normal distribution of expected times has a mean ($T_{(E)}$) of 47.83 minutes (sum of all three $t_{(e)}$s), an upper end of 73.78 minutes ($T_{(E)} + 3\sigma = 47.83 + (3 \times 8.65)$), a lower end of 21.88 minutes ($T_{(E)} - 3\sigma = 47.83 - (3 \times 8.65)$).

Given the assumed normality of this distribution, there is a 50 percent probability the commute will take more than 47.83 minutes and an equally likely probability it will take fewer than 47.83 minutes. For the sake of simplicity, we round this up to 48 minutes. Imagine our commuter plans to leave her house at her usual time of 7:12 a.m. and she promises her boss she will arrive at work by 8 a.m. Given a $T_{(E)}$ of 48 minutes, she has only a 50 percent chance of meeting this commitment! Assume our commuter recognizes the folly of promising something that is as uncertain as a

EXHIBIT 7.25

Normal Distribution for Total Commute Time (Including Car, Carpool, Walk)

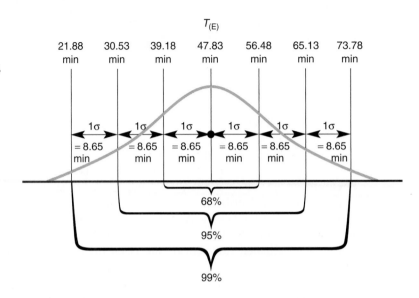

coin toss. Her boss is holding an important meeting at 8:05 a.m. Can she make it on time if she departs on her normal schedule at 7:12 a.m., thereby allowing 53 minutes?

Our commuter can use a **Z-table** to answer the question about the 53-minute commute time. *Z*-values provide a link to the area under a normal curve. As mentioned above, more than 99 percent of all values in a normal distribution will fall between plus and minus three standard deviations (σs) on either side of the mean. If we have information about the number of standard deviations a particular value falls above or below the mean, we can make some probabilistic estimates. In the case of the commute, we want to determine *how many standard deviations* beyond the mean of 48 minutes are represented by the target commuting time of 53 minutes. The calculation is as follows:

$$Z = \frac{D - T_{(E)}}{\sigma_{(total\ commute)}} = \frac{53\ min. - 48\ min.}{8.65} = .578\ (round\ to\ .58)$$

Where: D = Desired time or specified time
$T_{(E)}$ = Sum of $t_{(e)}$s on a path
Z = Number of standard deviations
$\sigma_{(total\ commute)}$ = Standard deviation of entire commute based on the square root of summed variances

This result tells us that the commuter's target time is .58 standard deviations beyond the approximate expected time ($T_{(E)}$) of 48 minutes. Exhibit 7.26 depicts the relationship between these two numbers. We can refer to a *Z*-table, as shown in Exhibit 7.27, to determine the likelihood of a 53-minute commute.

Referring to Exhibit 7.27, note that the *Z*-values representing standard deviations appear in the table column headings and corresponding probabilities appear in the columns beneath them. In the commute example, we wish to find the probability associated with a *Z*-value of .58. The area under the curve corresponding to .58 standard deviations (the cell value at the intersection of row .5 and column .08) is .7190. This is the basis of the answer to our commuter's question—moving the decimal point two spaces to the right, we can say there is a 71.9 percent chance she can complete her trip within 53 minutes because this represents .58 standard deviations beyond the approximate $T_{(E)}$ of 48 minutes. So, if our commuter is comfortable with an approximately 72 percent

EXHIBIT 7.26

**Probability of a
53-Minute Commute
Time**

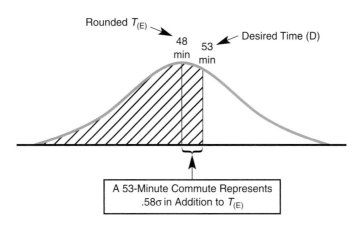

EXHIBIT 7.27

**Z-Table Cumulative
Single Tail
Probabilities (Area
under the Normal
Curve)**

Z	.00	.01	.02	.03	.04	.05	.06	.07	.08	.09
.0	.5000	.5040	.5080	.5120	.5160	.5199	.5239	.5279	.5319	.5359
.1	.5398	.5438	.5478	.5517	.5557	.5596	.5636	.5675	.5714	.5753
.2	.5793	.5832	.5871	.5910	.5948	.5987	.6026	.6064	.6103	.6141
.3	.6179	.6217	.6255	.6293	.6331	.6368	.6406	.6443	.6480	.6517
.4	.6554	.6591	.6628	.6664	.6700	.6736	.6772	.6808	.6844	.6879
.5	.6915	.6950	.6985	.7019	.7054	.7088	.7123	.7157	.7190	.7224
.6	.7257	.7291	.7324	.7357	.7389	.7422	.7454	.7486	.7517	.7549
.7	.7580	.7611	.7642	.7673	.7703	.7734	.7764	.7794	.7823	.7852
.8	.7881	.7910	.7939	.7967	.7995	.8023	.8051	.8078	.8106	.8133
.9	.8159	.8186	.8212	.8238	.8264	.8289	.8315	.8340	.8365	.8389
1.0	.8413	.8438	.8461	.8485	.8508	.8531	.8554	.8577	.8599	.8621
1.1	.8643	.8665	.8686	.8708	.8729	.8749	.8770	.8790	.8810	.8830
1.2	.8849	.8869	.8888	.8907	.8925	.8944	.8962	.8980	.8997	.9015
1.3	.9032	.9049	.9066	.9082	.9099	.9115	.9131	.9147	.9162	.9177
1.4	.9192	.9207	.9222	.9236	.9251	.9265	.9279	.9292	.9306	.9319
1.5	.9332	.9345	.9357	.9370	.9382	.9394	.9406	.9418	.9429	.9441
1.6	.9452	.9463	.9474	.9498	.9495	.9505	.9515	.9525	.9535	.9545
1.7	.9554	.9564	.9573	.9582	.9591	.9599	.9608	.9616	.9625	.9633
1.8	.9641	.9649	.9656	.9664	.9671	.9678	.9686	.9693	.9699	.9706
1.9	.9713	.9719	.9726	.9732	.9738	.9744	.9750	.9756	.9761	.9767
2.0	.9772	.9778	.9783	.9788	.9793	.9798	.9803	.9808	.9812	.9817
2.1	.9821	.9826	.9830	.9834	.9838	.9842	.9846	.9850	.9854	.9857
2.2	.9861	.9864	.9868	.9871	.9875	.9878	.9881	.9884	.9887	.9890
2.3	.9893	.9896	.9898	.9901	.9904	.9906	.9909	.9911	.9913	.9916
2.4	.9918	.9920	.9922	.9925	.9927	.9929	.9931	.9932	.9934	.9936
2.5	.9938	.9940	.9941	.9943	.9945	.9946	.9948	.9949	.9951	.9952
2.6	.9953	.9955	.9956	.9957	.9959	.9960	.9961	.9962	.9963	.9964
2.7	.9965	.9966	.9967	.9968	.9969	.9970	.9971	.9972	.9973	.9974
2.8	.9974	.9975	.9976	.9977	.9977	.9978	.9979	.9979	.9980	.9981
2.9	.9981	.9982	.9982	.9983	.9984	.9984	.9985	.9985	.9986	.9986
3.0	.9987	.9987	.9987	.9988	.9988	.9989	.9989	.9989	.9990	.9990
3.1	.9990	.9991	.9991	.9991	.9991	.9992	.9992	.9992	.9993	.9993
3.2	.9993	.9993	.9994	.9994	.9994	.9994	.9994	.9995	.9995	.9995
3.3	.9995	.9995	.9995	.9996	.9996	.9996	.9996	.9996	.9996	.9997
3.4	.9997	.9997	.9997	.9997	.9997	.9997	.9997	.9997	.9997	.9998

chance of meeting her boss's expectations, she can ride with her carpool group. If the meeting is career-critical, perhaps she would decide these odds are not good enough; in that case, she might choose to drive her own car or take a taxi directly to work.

This commute example has introduced PERT probabilistic concepts and offers enough information for a project manager to understand how to estimate likelihoods for various project completion times when considering the critical path in the analysis. For many situations, this will be sufficient. However, it is possible to extend the analysis by estimating joint probabilities for multiple project paths. We offer information and an example of how to use PERT analysis in multiple paths in Appendix 7B at the end of this chapter.

Managerial Implications for the PERT Statistical Model

The PERT model may be used in several ways in a project environment. The project manager could simply use the three-point time estimate approach ($t_{(o)}$, $t_{(m)}$, $t_{(p)}$) to determine an expected time ($t_{(e)}$) for each activity. This may make for better-informed estimates, add validity to expected time figures, or clarify communication with the client. Additionally, if a team goes through the exercise of developing three-point estimates, members will gain insights from each other about what will be involved in the tasks, sources of uncertainty, and assumptions. As one of our former MBA students reflected about a marine-industry product development team she led through a three-point estimation exercise: "It took much longer than I expected, but it was amazing how much we learned from the process. Each team member offered useful insights about assumptions and risks. In the end, our estimates were much more accurate than they had been in the past." Her experience about accuracy is supported by research: in a controlled experiment, teams trained in PERT three-point estimating methods and their underlying statistical principles proved to be more accurate in their time estimates than teams not trained in these methods.[24] Just having an appreciation for the 50 percent likelihood of expected times can help members of the project team recognize where time buffers might be useful. Microsoft Project 2007 includes a feature that calculates a weighted time estimate, $t_{(e)}$, from $t_{(o)}$, $t_{(m)}$, and $t_{(p)}$ estimates.

Extending PERT Concepts for Use in Simulation

A more advanced method for calculating task and path probabilities involves **Monte Carlo simulation.** The extended capabilities of software programs such as Excel, the market entry of products such as Crystal Ball, @Risk and Risk+, and the simulation features of high-end scheduling software such as Primavera, make simulation a practical possibility for a project manager. Using one of these packages, the project manager can generate random numbers for activity times based on specifications such as distribution type, mean, and range. After multiple simulation cycles, the program estimates the percentage likelihood a task will be on the critical path. Those with a high likelihood of becoming critical are said to have a high **criticality index.** This provides important insight. It highlights the fact that paths appearing to be noncritical in a deterministic or stable environment might become critical in the real, stochastic world.

A more extensive treatment of simulation methods for estimating project duration is presented in Mantel, Meredith, Shafer, and Sutton and also in Klastorin.[25] These authors warn the reader to take care in applying simulation tools. The user should begin with a mastery of the PERT methods presented here, then build an understanding of simulation and its underlying statistical assumptions before attempting to use or interpret the

[24] J.J. Moder and E.G. Rodgers, "Judgment Estimates of the Moments of PERT Type Distributions," *Management Science* 13, no. 2 (1968), pp. B76–B83.

[25] S.J. Mantel, J.R. Meredith, S.M. Shafer, and M.M. Sutton, *Core Concepts: Project Management in Practice* (New York: Wiley and Sons, 2004); and T.D. Klastorin, *Project Management: Tools and Tradeoffs* (New York: Wiley and Sons, 2003).

results of project duration simulations. Beware that a project team can become so engrossed in this sort of analysis that members lose sight of project goals. Also, many projects are neither large enough nor complex enough to warrant extensive simulation.

Chapter Summary and Onward

Project scheduling is a critical part of the project planning process that enhances team understanding and perspective, sets and manages expectations, highlights uncertainties, creates a foundation for the monitoring system, and generally helps everyone involved to visualize the action plan. Before a team develops a schedule, members must have established an understanding of the project's purpose, agreed on goals, selected the best course of action for achieving the goals, created a comprehensive WBS, assessed project uncertainties, and formulated activity time estimates. Schedules can be formal or informal, broad-brush or detailed, manually- or computer-generated. Several formats are available, including AON networks, AOA networks, Gantt or bar charts, and time-based networks. Project schedules are best created in a team environment. The result is better decision-making about sequencing, and a higher likelihood of commitment to time-based goals. Key concepts for project network schedules include critical path, total float, and free float. Anyone using project scheduling software should make certain he or she understands these concepts before "going digital."

PERT is an extension of basic network scheduling methods that incorporates three-point time estimates and allows for probability estimates of possible project completion times. Individuals who understand these concepts can apply them to varying degrees for improving time estimation accuracy, answering questions about possible scenarios, or managing client expectations. Those who wish to apply statistical concepts more extensively can use one of several simulation packages. However, we caution teams against allowing technical analysis to divert their attention from the project itself.

We have described how to develop an initial schedule during the project planning phase. A key message for this chapter and those remaining is that the first schedule is almost always wrong. This does not mean the team should avoid creating the first scheduling effort, but that members should recognize it as a starting point for further analysis, adjustment, and refinement. We address these concepts in Chapter 8.

Team Activities

1. Form a team of four to six classmates. Develop a work breakdown structure (WBS) for a simple project of your team's choosing. Select something for which all of your team members have a general understanding (they don't have to be experts, however). This will allow you to move quickly through the WBS stage. Examples of possibilities include a personal vacation or adventure, a wedding, a job search, a political campaign for local office, or something fun and humorous such as capturing your school's mascot and holding it for ransom.

   Once you have a detailed WBS with between 20 and 30 tasks at the lowest level of detail, follow the steps in the team-based scheduling method described in Exhibit 7.19. This will involve writing the names of tasks on sticky notes; making calendar-time estimates; separating them initially into early, middle, late groups; developing a network; and identifying the critical path. Be sure to develop your schedule on a large sheet of paper on the wall or on a whiteboard. When you have finished the process, prepare a report that includes the following:

   a. A cover page with your team members' names and the name of the project.

   b. A photo of your team gathered around your completed, wall-mounted schedule.

    c. A digital version of your schedule (created with any software you choose) showing the critical path and float.

    d. Two paragraphs describing the project, the process you followed as a team, and the lessons you learned from the experience.

2. Imagine you and your team have been selected as project management consultants for the 2012 Olympic Games in the United Kingdom. Your task is to develop time estimates and a network schedule for one component of the project: transportation of Olympic athletes to competitive venues in and around London. A high-level work breakdown structure for this project has been completed and appears in mind map form below:

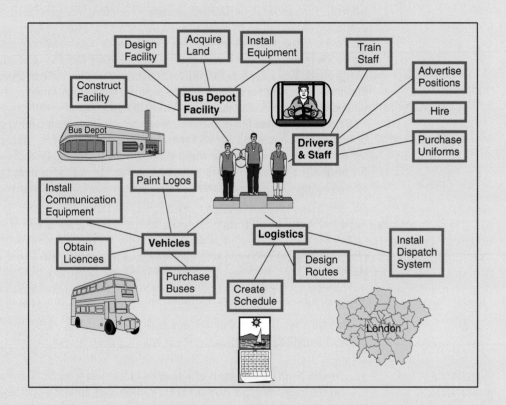

    a. Work with your team to add one more level of detail to the WBS. For example, you will need at least two work packages to describe what will be involved in installing the dispatch system or purchasing the buses. Be creative in identifying activities. (For this exercise, limit the total number of lowest-level WBS activities to 40 or fewer. This will keep the network schedule manageable.)

    b. Develop a calendar-day time estimate for each of the lowest-level work packages in the WBS. (Be creative.)

    c. Place names and time estimates for work packages on individual sticky notes. Place them on a piece of flip chart paper, mounted horizontally on the wall at standing height. First arrange the notes into early, middle, and late phases, then arrange them into parallel and sequential relationships. Pencil in lines to show dependencies and later darken them with a marker when you are sure of the precedence relationships. As part of your completed product, submit a photo of your team gathered around your wall-mounted team schedule.

d. Identify the critical path and estimate project duration.

e. Calculate total and free float for each activity.

f. Summarize your schedule digitally and include all of the information requested in parts d and e above.

g. Write a paragraph answering the following questions: Now that you see the project schedule, where do you think important actions might be missing? What are they? Where do you see potential for risk in the schedule?

h. Write a page describing your team experience and insights about the team-based process.

Discussion Questions and Exercises

1. Name, and in your own words briefly describe, the various formats available for depicting project schedules. For each one, offer an example of a circumstance or type of project for which this display format would be most useful to a project team. Explain the reasoning behind your conclusions about each format.

2. Based on ideas offered throughout this chapter, as well as your own insight and experience, discuss at least five benefits a project team is likely to gain if members collaborate in developing a project schedule. Cite examples not presented in this chapter.

3. In your own words, explain the difference between hard logic and soft logic for establishing dependency relationships in project schedules. Offer a creative example (not from the chapter) of each one.

4. Explain the relationships among project deliverables, work packages, and milestones as they would appear in a schedule. Use your own words and examples.

5. Imagine you work for an international telecommunications conglomerate that has just acquired a 300-person, family-owned telephone service provider. You have been asked to plan and manage a corporate off-site meeting in which 50 of the top-level people from the acquired company will meet for an entire day with 50 key people from your company. The purpose of the meeting will be to disseminate information, ease people's fears, obtain input, and gain buy-in. You have only one week to put this together. Should you use the scheduling tools presented in this chapter, or, given the short time horizon, should you just get right to work? Explain your answer. If you recommend using any of the scheduling tools from this chapter to plan this project, which ones would you use? Why?

6. You are planning a very complex two-year software system installation project and have observed that past IT projects have been completed significantly past their deadlines. You wonder if this had something to do with the time estimation methods employed, and you are considering using the PERT approach for this project. This would allow you to give probability estimates to your boss and other stakeholders. What would you consider as advantages and disadvantages of using the PERT approach?

7. You are managing the development of a new business-to-business sales Web site for a key customer. Your team includes five programmers as well as two representatives from the client company and a Web site interfaces expert. The project's mission and goals have been clearly defined and you have five months to complete it. Two months into the project, one of the programmers comes to you with an idea: "I think we could really add value for the customer if we extend the program to include a customized pricing feature. This part of the program is currently not on

the critical path, and I think it would take two people an extra week or two to make this addition." How would you respond? Explain your rationale.

8. Below is information about a project to implement a new manufacturing cell to assemble personal digital assistant devices.

Task	Duration Estimates	Immediate Predecessors
A. Determine process requirements	2 weeks	None
B. Benchmark competitor's processes	4 weeks	A
C. Prepare benchmark report	1 week	B
D. Design process and layout (preliminary)	2 weeks	A
E. Finalize design and set up manufacturing cell	2 weeks	C & D
F. Select and train operators	1 week	D
G. Pilot test new process	2 weeks	E & F
H. Finalize process design	1 week	G

   a. Draw an activity-on-node (AON) network.

   b. Identify the ES, EF, LS, LF, critical path, total float, and free float using the critical path algorithm.

   c. Which of these tasks should the project manager track most closely?

   d. Where do you see potential errors in network logic? Explain your reasoning.

   e. What would happen if a new estimate for Task D increases its expected duration from two weeks to six weeks? Would the project take longer? Would anything else change? Explain your answer.

9. You have decided to start a new business installing holiday lighting in wealthy neighborhoods. This will allow you to fill in some of the gaps in the schedule for a landscaping business you operate during the other parts of the year. You and your business partner have met to brainstorm about what will be involved, and, based on your shared understanding of the work to be done, you will develop a schedule. The following scenario is the result of your discussion.

Your first two steps will be to assess the market by conducting Web searches and talk to business owners in other cities who are likely to share information because you will not be a direct competitor. These two information gathering tasks should each take about two weeks. After you complete the information gathering, you will put together a business plan, which should take about a week. With your business plan in hand, you will contact your Uncle Dave to see if he is willing to lend you the seed money to start the new venture. Uncle Dave travels quite a bit, so you estimate it will take you about two weeks to get his approval. You believe he is highly likely to say yes and lend you the money because he is the one who suggested the business idea. Once you have Uncle Dave's funding, you will purchase a small inventory of materials and use them to install lights at the homes of several of your friends, and take photos. You have called this the "Sample Site" task, which you estimate will take about one week. Once you have the photos, you can develop your company Web site, which will take two weeks. Following completion of the sample site photos, and concurrent with Web site development, you can print flyers, which will take about a week. When the Web site is complete, you will be able to place ads in local papers. You think will take about a day, or .2 of a five-day workweek. Also, after you have printed the flyers, you will be able to distribute them in neighborhoods, which should take one week. Another task that can occur after the flyers are printed is "Mail Flyers to Friends and Relatives," which will require about a week's time. After the ads have been placed, the flyers have been distributed, and the flyers have been mailed, you and your team will have reached a milestone you have labeled, "Advertising Complete." Assuming you begin receiving calls from potential customers immediately after the advertising is complete you will visit their homes and give them bids on-site at the time of the visit. Given the timing of the holiday season, you estimate that the "Visits and Bids" activity will occur over a three-week period. The next step will be "Prepare and Sign Contracts," an activity that will occur over a four-week period, starting about one week after "Visits and Bids." The relationship between "Prepare and Sign Contracts" and "Visits and Bids" is start-to-start, with a one-week overlap. Once contracts are signed, you will be able to concurrently hire a crew (one week) and purchase materials (one week). Once the hiring and purchasing are complete, you will install the lighting over a two-week period. Given that you will require payment soon after the lights are installed, you will accumulate cash fairly quickly. Consequently, you will be able to pay your crew (a one-day or .2-week task) and repay your Uncle Dave (another one-day or .2-week task) immediately after you finish installing all of the lights. The project ends when all payments have been made.

Your assignment is the following:

a. Prepare a precedence table for the project scenario described above, following the approach shown in Exhibit 7.21. This will require you to give more definitive names to some tasks and to interpret the narrative. Within the table, also include task time estimates.

b. Comment on the logic of the schedule. Do you think the business partners have omitted any critical tasks or erred in their judgment about precedence relationships? If so, what would you change?

c. Using the table you created in part a, draw a network diagram for the project.

d. Using the critical path algorithm, identify ES, EF, LS, and LF for all tasks. Identify the critical path, free float, and total float.

10. What errors do you see in the AON diagram shown below?

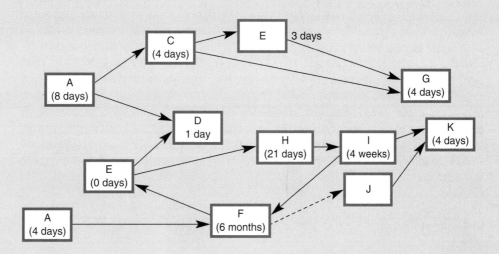

11. Below is a table of precedence relationships and task durations for a portion of a house-building project.

Task	Duration Estimates	Immediate Predecessor(s)
Prepare Site	4 days	None
Install Rough Plumbing	3 days	Prepare Site
Pour Concrete Foundation	2 days	Install Rough Plumbing
Cure Concrete	3 days	Pour Concrete Foundation
Preassemble Wall Frames	8 days	None
Erect Wall Frames	4 days	Preassemble WF, Cure Concrete
Install Roof	2 days	Erect Wall Frames
Install Wiring	3 days	Install Roof
Install Exterior Siding	4 days	Install Roof
Install Insulation	2 days	Install Exterior Siding
Hang Drywall	3 days	Install Insulation, Install Wiring
Install Windows	1 day	Hang DryWall
Paint Interior	6 days	Install Windows
Paint Exterior	5 days	Install Exterior Siding
Level Yard	2 days	Cure Concrete
Landscape Yard	4 days	Level Yard

a. Draw an activity-on-node diagram for this project and identify the critical path. (Tip: Write the task names and time estimates on sticky notes and arrange them to reflect precedence relationships.)

b. Draw a time-based network for this project.

c. What are some examples of assumptions that might have been made in the development of the time estimates and precedence relationships?

d. What will happen to the project if the materials needed for preassembling the wall frames are not available until the second day of the project? What if the materials were delayed until the 10th day?

e. Where are the potential conflicts in this schedule? Identify places where sequencing logic could lead to problems.

12. Based on the precedence table below, draw an AOA and an AON network diagram for this project. Identify the ES, EF, LS, LF, critical path, and total and free float using the critical path algorithm. (Tip: Write the task names and time estimates on sticky notes and arrange them to reflect precedence relationships.)

Activity	Duration (Days)	Immediate Predecessor
A	2	none
B	3	none
C	4	none
D	5	A
E	3	B
F	7	C
G	2	D,E
H	4	F
I	3	F
J	1	H
K	3	I

13. Below is the high-level project network for the development of a new performance evaluation system in a 10,000-employee company.

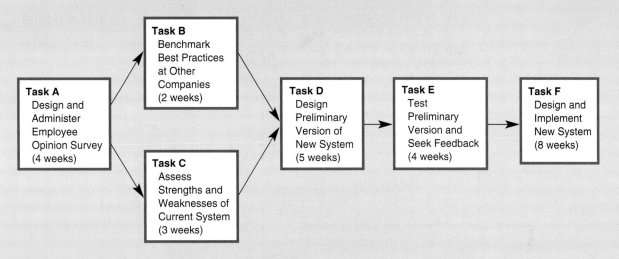

a. Use the critical path algorithm to determine ES, EF, LS, and LF times for all project tasks.

b. Calculate total float and free float for every project task.

c. Draw this network as a Gantt chart.

14. Given the network in problem 13, enter project data into a project management software program such as MS Project. Print a network and Gantt view. Interpret the results. Refer to Appendix A at the end of this book: "Quick Guide to Using MS Project."

15. The following precedence table provides PERT time estimates:

Activity	Immediate Predecessor(s)	Time Estimates (Days)		
		$t_{(o)}$	$t_{(m)}$	$t_{(p)}$
A	—	2	6	20
B	A	4	7	19
C	—	1	2	6
D	C	2	4	5
E	D	5	6	9
F	E	3	4	8

a. Draw an AON diagram of this project.

b. Calculate $t_{(e)}$, σ and σ^2 for each activity and $T_{(E)}$, σ and σ^2 for each path.

c. What is the probability path C-D-E-F will be completed within 20 days? Show your work and explain your answer.

d. What is the probability C-D-E-F will be completed within 18 days? What is the probability A-B will be completed within 18 days? As a project manager, what priorities would you set for monitoring these two paths? Why?

e. Instructor Option: What is the probability that *both* of these paths will be completed within 18 days? (To prepare your answer, review the material in Appendix 7B at the end of this chapter.)

16. A Canadian aerospace company has decided to design a new 100-passenger commercial jet. A key part of the design strategy is focused on manufacturability and ease of maintenance. Thus, a cross-functional team has been assigned to handle the project through its various phases. The research and development department has created a high-level preliminary schedule for the first part of the project, as shown below. For each major activity, members of the project team have developed optimistic, most likely, and pessimistic time estimates.

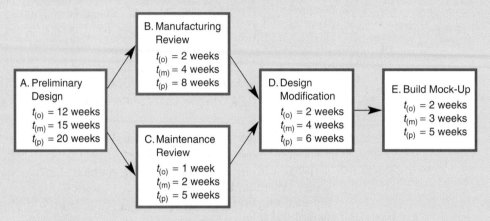

a. Calculate $T_{(E)}$, σ, σ^2 for each path. Show your work.
b. What is the probability path A-B-D-E can be completed within 27 weeks? Show your work.
c. What is the probability path A-C-D-E can be completed within 27 weeks? Show your work.
d. Instructor option: What is the joint probability both paths can be completed within 27 weeks? (To prepare your answer to this question, review the material in Appendix 7B at the end of this chapter.)

References

Brooks, F.P. *The Mythical Man-Month*. Boston: Addison-Wesley, 1995.

Charnes, A., and W.W. Cooper. "A Network Interpretation and Directed Sub-Dual Algorithm for Critical Path Scheduling." *Journal of Industrial Engineering,* July–August 1962, pp. 213–19.

Franz, D. "Olympics; Athens Races to Prepare for Olympics." *New York Times,* July 23, 2001; www.nytimes.com.

Gantt, H. *Work, Wages, and Profits*. Easton, PA: Hive Publishing Co., 1974.

Hartman, F.T. *Don't Park Your Brain Outside*. Newtown Square, PA: Project Management Institute, 2000.

Headen, E.B. "Pinpoint Planning: Stock and Production Control for the Small Plant—So Simple, a Girl Can Run It." *Factory and Industrial Management,* June 1936, pp. 233–34.

Hogarth, R. *Judgement and Choice*. New York: Wiley and Sons, 1980.

Iacovou, C.L., and A. Dexter. "Turning around Runaway Information Technology Projects." *California Management Review* 46, no. 4 (2004), pp. 68–88.

Kelley, J.E., Jr. "Critical Path Planning and Scheduling: A Mathematical Basis." *Operations Research* 7, no. 2 (1961), pp. 296–320.

Klastorin, T.D. *Project Management: Tools and Tradeoffs.* New York: Wiley and Sons, 2003.

Knod, E.M., and R.J. Schonberger. *Operations Management: Meeting Customers' Demands.* New York: McGraw-Hill/Irwin, 2001.

Levy, F.K.; G.L. Thompson; and J.D. Wiest. "The ABCs of the Critical Path Method." *Harvard Business Review* 41, no. 5 (1963), pp. 98–108.

Mantel, S.J.; J.R. Meredith; S.M. Shafer; and M.M. Sutton. *Core Concepts: Project Management in Practice.* New York: Wiley and Sons, 2004.

Miller, R.W. "How to Plan and Control with PERT." *Harvard Business Review* 40, no. 2 (1962), pp. 93–104.

Moder, J.J., and E.G. Rodgers. "Judgment Estimates of the Moments of PERT Type Distributions." *Management Science* 13, no. 2 (1968), pp. B76–B83.

Pritzker, A.A.B. "GERT Networks." *The Production Engineer* 48, no. 10 (1968), pp. 499–506.

Steers, R.M.; R.T. Mowday; and D.L. Shapiro. "The Future of Work Motivation." *Academy of Management Review* 29, no. 3 (2004), pp. 379–87.

Uher, T. *Programming and Scheduling Techniques,* Construction Management Series. Sydney, Australia: UNSW Press, 2003, chap. 10.

Weil, T. "Four Days Out, Athens Confident It'll Be Ready." *USA Today,* August 9, 2004, p. 1A.

Wiest, J.D., and F.K. Levy. *A Management Guide to PERT/CPM.* Englewood Cliffs, NJ: Prentice Hall, 1977.

Appendix 7A

Note on Using Dummy Activities in AOA Networks

Under some circumstances, AOA networks require a special feature known as a dummy activity. Dummy activities help to clarify precedence relationships and remove false dependencies but have no time or resources associated with them. Consider the following example.

The Fairchild Division of Cameron Mining Co. refines copper from copper cathodes and creates copper sheets and coils from the refined material. Its entire process is composed of a set of continuously linked subprocesses that operate 24 hours a day, year-round. One piece of processing equipment, a heat exchanger, has reached the end of its useful life and the company has decided to remove and replace it with a larger, heavier, state-of-the-art machine. After the old equipment is removed, members of the team will have to remove the existing concrete slab and replace it with a deeper one to support the new equipment, which weighs twice as much as the old equipment. When one piece of equipment is shut down, the entire plant must cease operation because of the interdependencies of the continuous flow. This will result in thousands of dollars per day in lost revenue. Consequently, team members responsible for the heat exchanger replacement project are paying close

EXHIBIT 7.1A   **Replacing Heat Exchange Equipment at the Cameron Co. AON Diagram**

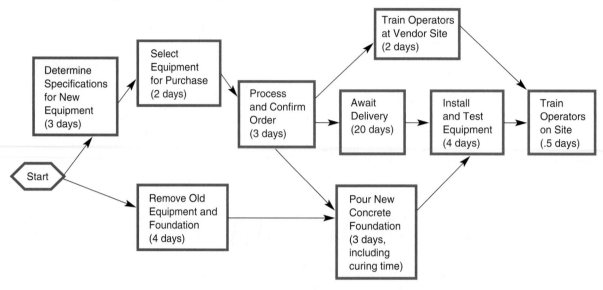

attention to the schedule. The schedule for this project is depicted as an AON diagram in Exhibit 7.1A. The same schedule, shown as an AOA diagram, appears in Exhibit 7.2A.

The dummy activity depicted as a dashed line in Exhibit 7.2A shows that it is necessary to process and confirm the order, *and* remove the old equipment and foundation, *before* pouring the new foundation. This is because the team must have information about the size and weight of the new equipment to know the dimensions of the concrete foundation they will form and pour. Without the dummy activity, this connection would not be apparent. If the dummy were removed and the nodes were merged, we could show "Remove old equipment and foundation"

EXHIBIT 7.2A   **Replacing Heat Exchange Equipment at the Cameron Co. AOA Diagram**

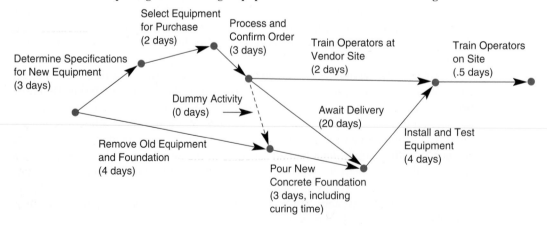

as linking directly into the node that follows "Process and confirm order." This would create a false dependency because training is not dependent on old equipment removal. Such a schedule would be illogical. The dummy activity simply clarifies the precedence relationship, but it is not a true activity because it requires no time and consumes no resources. Not all AOA diagrams require dummy activities.

The AON diagram for this project, shown in Exhibit 7.1A does not require a dummy activity to represent the schedule logic. Although this is a positive attribute of AON networks, we believe you will find some value in understanding AOA networks. Specifically, teams wishing to use the time-based networks introduced in this chapter must be aware of dummy activities in case the need arises for their use in that format.

Appendix **7B**

Multi-Path PERT Network Problem

The network displayed in Exhibit 7.1B shows the activities for a project to prepare a university stadium for the annual commencement ceremony. Members of the university's physical plant staff have kept data from previous years' commencement preparation projects. Although each year's project has been slightly different (based on class size, budgets, university politics, etc.) these records have offered the team useful information for developing three-point estimates. The team has identified three independent paths of activities leading up to the ceremony: (1). planting and associated activities, (2). painting, repairing, and cleaning the stadium, and (3). cleaning artificial turf, resurfacing the track, and setting up and decorating. Values of $t_{(o)}$, $t_{(m)}$, and $t_{(p)}$ are shown for all activities in the project. The time unit is days. At the bottom of the exhibit are path calculations for $T_{(E)}$, σ, and σ^2, as derived from the three values $t_{(o)}$, $t_{(m)}$, and $t_{(p)}$ for each activity on each path. The independence of the three paths allows the team to adhere, at least theoretically, to the assumptions of path and activity independence that underlie the PERT model.

Referring to Exhibit 7.1B, note that path D-E-F, at a $T_{(E)}$ of 23.83 days, is the critical path. Path G-H-I is nearly critical with a $T_{(E)}$ of 21.67 days, and path A-B-C, at only 11 days, has a significant amount of float. We know from our previous discussion that D-E-F, the critical path, has a 50 percent probability of being completed within its $T_{(E)}$ of 23.83 days. Given that the triple constraint for commencement clearly specifies time as the highest priority, there is not an option to delay the project. However, the crew does not necessarily need to begin work at a time that would ensure a 100 percent probability of hitting the deadline. In fact, there would be a disadvantage to doing so because activities such as cleaning must be done as close as possible to commencement day. Thus, the team has contingency plans in place. For example, crew members know that if they are running behind schedule in the days leading up to the ceremony they can eliminate some activities (e.g., seat repair), reduce the scope of some activities (e.g., paint only the areas most in need), or work overtime. They still would like to get a sense of the probability of various completion times because this will help them with their contingency plans.

EXHIBIT 7.1B **Network Diagram for Preparing the University Stadium for Graduation (Time Units in Days)**

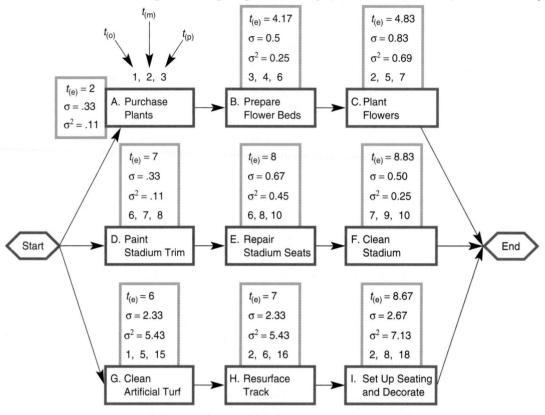

All time units are in days and figures are rounded to two places to the right of the decimal. Standard deviations are rounded before they are squared to calculate variance figures. Sample Calculation for Activity A, Purchase Plants:

$$t_{(e)} = \frac{t_{(o)} + 4\,(t_{(m)}) + t_{(p)}}{6} = \frac{1\,\text{day} + (4 \times 2\,\text{days}) + 3\,\text{days}}{6} = 2\,\text{days}$$

$$\sigma = \frac{(t_{(p)} - t_{(o)})}{6} = \frac{(3\,\text{days} - 1\,\text{day})}{6} = .33\,\text{days} \quad \text{and} \quad \sigma^2 = .33^2 = .11\,\text{days}$$

Given the $t_{(o)}$, $t_{(m)}$, $t_{(p)}$, $t_{(e)}$, σ, and σ^2 estimates for each activity, the team calculated the following path values:

	Activity Calculations				Path Calculations		
Activity	$t_{(e)}$	σ	σ^2		$T_{(E)}$	σ^2	σ
A	2.00	0.33	0.11 ⎫				
B	4.17	0.50	0.25 ⎬		11 days	1.05	1.03 days
C	4.83	0.83	0.69 ⎭				
D	7.00	0.33	0.11 ⎫				
E	8.00	0.67	0.45 ⎬		23.83 days	0.81	0.90 days
F	8.83	0.50	0.25 ⎭				
G	6.00	2.33	5.43 ⎫				
H	7.00	2.33	5.43 ⎬		21.67 days	17.99	4.24 days
I	8.67	2.67	7.13 ⎭				

Table Notes:
1. Times are in days.
2. $T_{(E)}$ for each path is the sum of the individual task $t_{(e)}$s. So, for example, $T_{(E)}$ for A-B-C = 2.0 + 4.17 + 4.83 = 11 days.
3. In this example, variance is calculated based on the unrounded result of the σ calculation.
4. We have summed individual activity variances (σ^2) to determine path variance (σ^2). Example for A-B-C: .11 + .25 + .69 = 1.05 days. Then, we calculated the square root to determine path standard deviation (σ). Sq. root of 1.05 = 1.03.

ANSWERING QUESTIONS ABOUT COMPLETION TIME PROBABILITIES

Imagine the university president, who is rather anxious because a major donor will attend the ceremony, has looked carefully at the project schedule and has some concerns. Team members have explained the concept of critical path to him and have shown him that activity sequence D-E-F represents the critical path for this work. He has asked the project manager to give him a probability estimate that this series of activities will be completed within 25 days. This number is slightly higher than the critical path $T_{(E)}$ of 23.83 days, so the project manager knows the probability will be greater than 50 percent. Using the formula we applied previously, and referring to the Z-table in Exhibit 7.27:

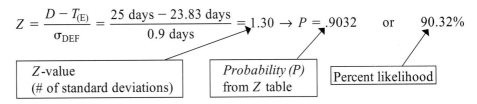

$$Z = \frac{D - T_{(E)}}{\sigma_{DEF}} = \frac{25 \text{ days} - 23.83 \text{ days}}{0.9 \text{ days}} = 1.30 \rightarrow P = .9032 \quad \text{or} \quad 90.32\%$$

Z-value
(# of standard deviations)

Probability (P)
from Z table

Percent likelihood

Thus, the project manager will be able to tell the university president there is a reasonable assurance (about 90 percent) the critical path can be completed within 25 days. This sort of information can be useful to any project manager who wishes to manage client expectations.

THE CASE OF LOW PROBABILITY OUTCOMES

The university president now wants to know if the crew can complete the critical path (D-E-F) within 22 days. The project manager knows the probability will be less than 50 percent because 22 is less than the $T_{(E)}$ of 23.83 days. The calculation is as follows:

$$Z = \frac{D - T_{(E)DEF}}{\sigma_{DEF}} = \frac{22 \text{ days} - 23.83 \text{ days}}{0.90 \text{ days}} = -2.03$$

This negative Z-value tells the project team the target completion date is 2.03 standard deviations below $T_{(E)}$ for the critical path D-E-F. A negative Z-value is produced when the desired duration (D) is less than $T_{(E)}$. It indicates a probability less than 50 percent. However, the Z-table included in this chapter does not include any negative Z-values. Given that a normal curve is symmetrical, the project manager can assume the probability of achieving a time with a Z-value of −2.03 is $1 - .9788 = .0212$, or about 2.12 percent.

PERT Tip: For a negative Z-value, the probability (P) of occurrence is 1 minus the probability (P) of Z.

Based on this analysis, the project manager can inform the university president there is less than a 3 percent chance of the critical path meeting an expected due date of 22 days. The portion of the normal curve represented by a Z-value of −2.03 is shown in Exhibit 7.2B.

If the president really wants the critical path to be completed within 22 days, the project manager is in a good position to propose ideas for increasing the likelihood beyond 2.12 percent. Possibilities include adding resources (e.g., people), hiring

EXHIBIT 7.2B
Percent of Normal Curve for a Low-Probability Outcome

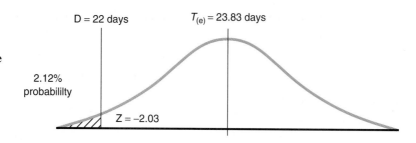

D = 22 days $T_{(e)}$ = 23.83 days

2.12% probabililty

Z = −2.03

subcontractors, authorizing the use of overtime, or eliminating some tasks from the WBS. The president's decision will be based on the relative value he places on time versus cost.

ESTIMATING JOINT PROBABILITIES

So far, we have considered the three paths as separate entities. This is a somewhat limited perspective; the project will not be complete until *all* of these paths are complete. To determine the likelihood of all three paths finishing at a specific time, the project manager must determine their joint probability. The likelihood of two or more events occurring is the product of their individual probabilities, based on the assumption that the events are independent. (As we discussed earlier in this chapter, the environment surrounding any project creates some degree of interdependence among activities, so we have to be cautious about this assumption.) With these limitations in mind, the project manager estimates the probabilities and calculates their product.

We have previously established that the probability of the critical path D-E-F finishing within 25 days is 90.32 percent. The project manager also must calculate the 25-day probabilities for A-B-C and G-H-I.

For path A-B-C, the calculation is as follows:

$$Z = \frac{D - T_{(E)\ ABC}}{\sigma_{ABC}} = \frac{25 \text{ days} - 11 \text{ days}}{1.03 \text{ days}} = 13.59 \text{ standard deviations}$$

According to the Z-table, the probability of A-B-C finishing within 25 days is completely off the chart with a Z-value of 13.5 standard deviations. This means that, for all practical purposes, there is a 100 percent chance path A-B-C will finish within 25 days.

A probability analysis for path G-H-I is as follows:

$$Z = \frac{D - T_{(E)\ GHI}}{\sigma_{GHI}} = \frac{25 \text{ days} - 21.67 \text{ days}}{4.24 \text{ days}} = .79 \rightarrow P = .7852 \text{ or about } 79\%$$

Even though path D-E-F is nominally the critical path, G-H-I has a larger standard deviation (4.24 versus .90). As a result, G-H-I has a lower probability of finishing within 25 days (about 79 percent) than the longer but more time-certain D-E-F does (about 90.32 percent). Had the project manager considered only the probability of completing the critical path within 25 days, she would have given an artificially optimistic likelihood estimate to the university president. Research has shown that human beings are subject to biases in these situations and that they tend to overestimate the likelihood of an outcome when it depends on several convergent events.[26]

[26] R. Hogarth, *Judgement and Choice* (New York: Wiley and Sons, 1980).

EXHIBIT 7.3B   Comparative Probabilities for Three Paths (Likelihood of Finishing within 25 Days)

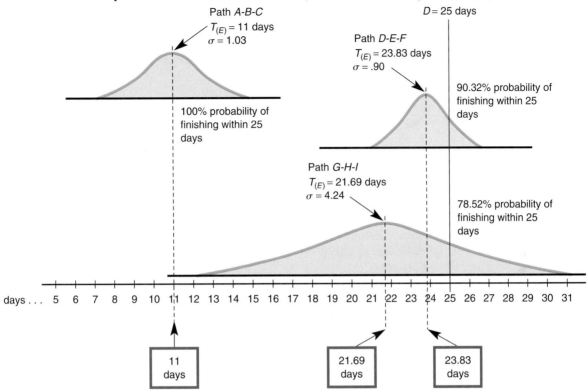

Thus, a PERT analysis might help to steer a team away from making unrealistic promises. Exhibit 7.3B shows the distributions associated with all three paths finishing within the 25-day time window.

Applying the concept of joint probability, the project manager calculates the product of the three probabilities (*P*s) as follows:

$$P_{(25\text{-day project})} = P_{\text{ABC(25)}} \times P_{\text{DEF(25)}} \times P_{\text{GHI(25)}} = (1.00)\times(.9032)\times(.7852)$$
$$= .7092 \text{ or about } 71\%$$

The preceding example illustrates how a team might develop probabilistic project time estimates in a multiple-path network. The network involved three separate paths. This allowed the project manager and team to adhere, at least nominally, to the independence assumptions underlying the PERT model.

In most projects there will be several instances where activities are shared by two or more paths. Even if network paths do not share activities, they are not likely to be entirely independent of each other; they probably share the same environment, culture, and organizational constraints. For example, if the project sponsor has cut back on project resources or struck fear into the hearts of project team members for some reason, these factors will influence every activity in the project—some to a greater extent than others. In the case of the commencement ceremony project, all outdoor activities and paths will be affected by the same weather. Thus, our assumptions about independence make it more difficult to justify using the PERT model in real projects. Anyone using it must recognize that mathematical outcomes will probably require some reality-based adjustments.

Chapter **Eight**

Modifying Project Schedules to Accommodate Time and Resource Constraints

"The first schedule is always wrong."

Frederick Brooks

Chapter Learning Objectives

When you have mastered the material in this chapter, you should be able to:

- Recognize project constraints and apply the appropriate combination of methods to modify existing schedules.
- Apply the logic of time-cost trade-offs to systematically shorten a project's expected duration by adding resources to key activities.
- Level-load project schedules to reduce variation in resource requirements or meet resource limitations.
- Estimate realistic project completion times by incorporating information about the availability of specialized resources.
- Differentiate between the critical path and the critical chain, and apply buffer concepts to reduce schedule risks.
- Explain project modification options to stakeholders and offer rational arguments for the most appropriate choices.

Scheduling is not a onetime effort. The first schedule becomes the starting point for adjustments based on the need to meet deadlines, reduce costs, or accommodate resource constraints. Additionally, project managers often must respond to unfolding project realities by adjusting schedules to get things back on track from a time, cost, resource, or performance standpoint. Possible reasons a project manager and team can find it necessary to modify a schedule include (but are not limited to) the factors highlighted in Exhibit 8.1.

EXHIBIT 8.1
Reasons for Schedule Modification

- To meet a customer-specified due date.
- To ensure the final product hits a market window.
- To delay cash outflows.
- To accommodate resource limitations.
- To respond to an emergency or crisis.
- To compensate for schedule delays during project delivery.
- To respond to cost overruns during project delivery.
- To respond to customer or technical requirements not initially considered.

The most effective project managers and their teams have a toolbox of methods for intelligently handling situations in which schedules require modification to meet internal and external constraints and demands. The contents of this toolbox include a sound understanding of project scheduling concepts, along with skills in negotiation and persuasion. Additionally, the project manager must be able to facilitate team discussions because schedule modification requires creative team problem solving. In this chapter we describe the technical side of schedule modification, but we embed comments about the softer side of modification within these discussions. We begin with an example involving various forms of schedule modification.

SCHEDULE MODIFICATION: PRODUCT DEVELOPMENT EXAMPLE

A project manager assigned to an effort to enhance an existing company product has presented a preliminary, high-level project schedule, shown in Exhibit 8.2, to the project sponsor and other key stakeholders. The project is currently scheduled to finish in 17 months. The critical path is highlighted. However, the project sponsor, based on her knowledge of a competitor's product development efforts, has requested that the team complete the project within 13 months.

EXHIBIT 8.2   Initial Network Schedule for Product Development Project with Early- and Late-Start Finish Times

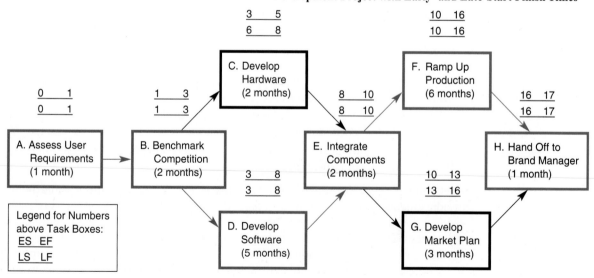

Legend for Numbers above Task Boxes:
ES EF
LS LF

→ Arrows connecting critical path tasks

The project team is considering several options to compress the project schedule:

1. **Crashing: Crashing** involves adding resources to reduce the time required for selected project tasks. For example, the manager could hire more programmers or use overtime to shorten the time required for Task D,[1] develop software, from five months to four months.

2. **Fast Tracking:** In **fast tracking,** the project manager and team can reschedule some sequentially related tasks to occur concurrently, applying start-to-start precedence logic introduced in Chapter 7. For example, the team could decide to benchmark the competition (Task B) and assess user requirements (Task A) simultaneously, shaving a month from the schedule.

3. **Delay Some Activities to Reallocate Resource Expenditures:** A project team can delay major cash outflows or resource loads by taking advantage of available float to shift a task to later in the project. It is best to do this after other modifications have been made and remaining float is visible. As described above, the project team could crash Task D by one month and perform Tasks A and B concurrently. Tasks C and G have available float. Task C, develop hardware, requires a major cash outflow, so the team could decide to start it one month later than its early-start time to delay a capital expenditure, leaving one month of float as a schedule buffer.

4. **Reduce Scope: Project scope reduction** involves eliminating tasks or deliverables from the work breakdown structure (WBS). For example, the project team might find a work package within Task F, ramp up production, that can be eliminated. Perhaps the production line could be redesigned to reduce the need for automation and rely on manual processes in the short term. These changes would reduce the estimated duration of Task F from six months to four months.

A rational approach to scope reduction can lead to schedule improvements that do not jeopardize project quality or performance. However, project managers often face pressure from higher-level managers to reduce scope by eliminating activities essential to the project's success in achieving its goals. An example is highlighted in the Dilbert cartoon shown in Exhibit 8.3. The most effective project managers do not

---

[1] Reminder: throughout this book we interchange the words *task* and *activity*.

EXHIBIT 8.3 **The Wrong Kind of Scope Reduction**

DILBERT: © Scott Adams/Dist. by United Feature Syndicate, Inc

EXHIBIT 8.4   Original and Compressed Schedules for Product Development Example Shown as a Comparative Gantt Chart

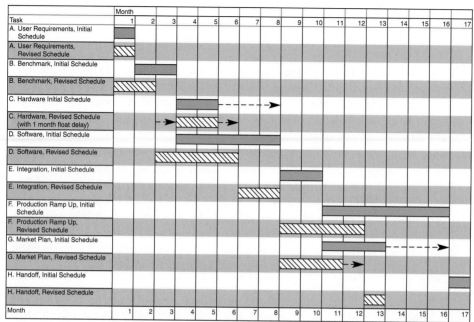
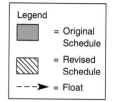

In this revised schedule, Task A, user requirements, and Task B, benchmark, are fast-tracked (performed concurrently), which shortens the planned duration by one month. This allows hardware, Task C, and software, Task D, to start a month earlier. However, it is not actually necessary to begin Task C, hardware, right after benchmarking is complete, so it has been delayed by one month, still leaving an additional month of float as a schedule buffer. Task D, software, can be crashed; more programmers can be hired to reduce duration from five months to four months. Integration, Task E, can start two months earlier than initially planned if software is completed at the end of month 6. Task F, production ramp up, can begin two months earlier than planned, and it can be reduced by two months because of a reduction in scope. The marketing plan, Task G, can also begin two months earlier than the initial plan, but could, if necessary, be delayed or extended by a month because it has float. And, Task H, handoff, can be completed at the end of month 13, meeting the expectations of the sponsor. Of course, whether or not this new schedule works will depend on everything happening smoothly. The project manager must clearly communicate the benefits, risks, and potential challenges, associated with this new schedule.

simply cave in to these kinds of pressures. They know what is essential and what can be scaled down or eliminated. Most importantly, they are capable of working with their teams to develop (and sell to the sponsor) creative options that will not detract from the project's success.

If the project team implements all four of the modifications described above, the resulting schedule would be as shown in Exhibit 8.4, which depicts original and revised Gantt chart bars differentiated by type of shading. It demonstrates that a combination of crashing, fast-tracking, scope reduction, and delays to accommodate resource constraints could be used to reduce the project's duration from 17 months to 13 months.

In the remaining pages of this chapter, we address in more detail how a project manager, cooperating with a project team, can effectively weigh the trade-offs associated with schedule modifications aimed at meeting triple constraint priorities. Although we present the concepts sequentially, in reality a team would be likely to consider and work with all of them simultaneously the way we have described in the preceding example.

CRASHING PROJECT SCHEDULES

Project crashing involves an analysis of trade-offs between prolonging a project or adding resources to shorten it. On one hand, the longer a project's duration, the greater the period over which administrative and overhead costs are incurred. On the other hand, if a team wants to shorten a project's duration to truncate the flow of overhead expenditures or avoid penalties, there likely is a price to be paid for compressing activities. Exhibit 8.5 depicts time-cost trade-offs.[2] Whether it is worthwhile to shorten a project's duration depends on the contrast between these two cost functions.

Knowing when and how to compress project schedules can involve some experimentation. Box 8.1 offers an example of a company that tried crashing programming projects by adding resources at multiple locations. Ultimately, the cost of coordination and rework exceeded the benefits of the crashing strategy.

Determining Crash Costs for Trade-off Analysis

Anyone making crashing decisions must have a sense of the cost of reducing task durations. Fortunately, a team does not need a tremendous amount of precision to get a rough idea of time-cost relationships.[3] Some activities can be shortened easily with an extra person or two, but others are more difficult to divide. If members of a planning team can estimate the cost of an activity when it is performed at its normal time, and if they have a fairly good estimate of the resources required, they can then ask the question, "What is the absolute shortest amount of time in which this activity could be accomplished?" This is the **fully crashed time.** If they then estimate the resources required for the tighter schedule, incorporating anticipated

[2] Adapted from J.D. Wiest and F.K. Levy, *A Management Guide to PERT/CPM* (Englewood Cliffs, NJ: Prentice Hall, 1977).

[3] P.G. Smith and D.G. Reinertsen, *Developing Products in Half the Time* (New York: Van Nostrand-Reinhold, 1998).

EXHIBIT 8.5
Trade-offs in Time and Cost

Cost of Prolonging a Project

Indirect project costs or end-of-project penalties accumulate over time, independent of direct costs associated with individual activities.

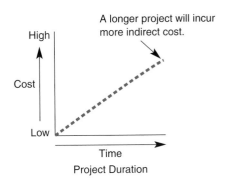

Project Duration

Cost of Shortening an Activity

Direct costs associated with individual activities can increase when an activity's duration is compressed. The normal time for a task is generally considered to be the lowest-cost option.

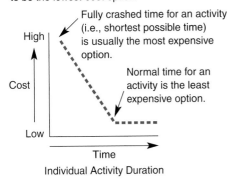

Individual Activity Duration

Round-the-Clock Programming   Box 8.1

A Canadian company specializing in data-mining software for enterprisewide IT systems attempted to speed up some of its projects with round-the-clock programming. Programmers in Canada finished their work at the end of each day and electronically handed it off to programmers in India as they began their workdays. This was intended to cut programming time in half. Unfortunately, the geographic distance and asynchronous timing made it impossible for real-time communication, and the receiving team had trouble understanding the details and rationale underlying the programming done by colleagues on the other side of the world. The series of handoffs, likened to a relay race, actually caused projects to take more, rather than less, time. Company officials realized that although this type of programming had become an industry trend, it was not effective for their work. Consequently, they divided the work so certain projects were performed entirely in Canada and others were performed entirely in India. Productivity improved and projects were completed in far less time, and with better outcomes, than they had been under the round-the-clock strategy.

training, coordination, and rework costs, they have the crash-cost estimate associated with the shortest possible time. Going back to the new product development project in Exhibits 8.2 and 8.4, consider the following information for Task D, develop software:

Normal Time	Resources Required	Resource Cost	
5 months	2 people for 5 months = 10 person months	2 × $3,000/month × 5 months	= $30,000

Crash Time	Resources Required	Resource Cost	
3 months	6 people for 3 months = 18 person months	6 × $3,000/month × 3 months	= $54,000

The number of **person-months** required (number of people × months of work) rises from 10 to 18 when we compare the normal time with the crash time. This reflects the anticipated loss in efficiency and the need for one of the people to serve, perhaps full time, in a coordinating and training role.[4] In this case, the **crash cost per month** is $12,000 (calculated as (($54,000 − $30,000)/2 months), assuming a linear relationship.[5] Thus, for each month the team shortens Task D, the project incurs an extra cost of $12,000. In the world of product development, where a month's delay in reaching the market can cost many times this amount in lost profit,[6] the project manager and sponsor would probably find this an attractive choice for crashing.

[4] As F.P. Brooks observes in his classic writing on project management in IT environments, *The Mythical Man-Month* (Boston: Addison-Wesley, 1995), p. 25, "Adding manpower to a late software project makes it later." In his more recent musings printed in the 1995 update of the book, Brooks concedes that the extra manpower might not make the project late, but it will increase the cost.

[5] It is reasonable to assume a linear relationship in order to keep things simple, but, as we demonstrate later in the chapter, it is also possible to handle crashing problems when there are step functions in the relationship between time and cost.

[6] S. Wheelwright and K. Clark, *Revolutionizing Product Development: Quantum Leaps in Speed, Efficiency, and Quality* (New York: Free Press, 1992).

EXHIBIT 8.6 **The Sponsor Who Does Not Understand the Increased Cost and Lost Efficiency Associated with Extreme Crashing**

DILBERT: © Scott Adams/Dist. by United Feature Syndicate, Inc

A general formula for calculating incremental crash costs is as follows:

$$\text{Incremental crash cost} = \frac{\text{Crash cost} - \text{Normal cost}}{\text{Normal time} - \text{Crash time}}$$

Where:

Normal time is the time required for a task under normal conditions, typically in the time specified in the initial project schedule.

Crash time is the least amount of time in which a task can be feasibly completed.

Normal cost is the cost of completing the task at its normal time.

Crash cost is the cost of completing the task at its fully crashed time.

Experienced project managers understand the trade-offs depicted in Exhibit 8.5, but they often are pressured by higher-level decision makers who do not appreciate the increased costs and lost efficiencies associated with crashing. The Dilbert cartoon in Exhibit 8.6 shows what can happen when an irrational sponsor thinks a horde of people can perform a task in the blink of an eye. Members of the team would serve themselves well if they were to read this chapter carefully and explain its contents to their pointy-haired boss.

Determining Ongoing Project Costs, Early-Completion Incentives, and Delay Penalties for Trade-off Analysis

During the life cycle of any project, a set of costs accumulates on a daily basis. These can include:

- Salaries and benefits of core team members, adjusted for the percent of their time allocated to the project.
- Apportioned percentages of salaries and benefits of personnel who provide support services to team members.
- Apportioned costs associated with the physical space where team members work (rent, utilities).
- Rental of equipment dedicated to the project.

Some might argue: "We're paying these people anyway and we own the building. Why should we charge these costs to the project?" The answer is that the time, space, and equipment dedicated to the project could be allocated to other projects or activities if this project were not underway. Any project competes for resources with other organizational activities. To understand the true costs of a project and make good decisions about compressing or extending (or even initially investing in) the project, these project-specific fixed costs should be considered.

In addition to costs that accumulate over the life of the project, other incentives for finishing a project sooner rather than later can include:

- Incentives offered by customers for early completion.
- Contractual penalties for late delivery.
- Lost profits associated with late market entry.

Beyond tangible costs and incentives, a project manager also should consider the potential for declining morale and associated losses in productivity and quality when a project is prolonged. Shorter projects hold people's attention better than longer projects.

For the product development case illustrated in Exhibits 8.2 and 8.4, here is a breakdown of the costs incurred by the project each month it is in operation:

Cost Category	Cost per Month
Salaries and benefits for four core team members dedicated at 50% to the project	$12,000
Apportioned salaries of clerical, maintenance, technical, and cleaning staff members who support the core project team	$ 5,000
Apportioned cost of office space and equipment for team members	$10,000
Estimated lost profits for every month of delay in product market entry	$30,000
Total Cost Per Month	**$57,000**

We previously determined that the cost of crashing one of the critical path tasks, develop software, was $12,000 per month. Even though the crashed time does not result in the lowest cost at the task level, it does produce a lower overall project cost because shortening this task eliminates a month of project time for a net gain of $57,000 − $12,000, or $45,000.

General Crashing Procedure

Once a team has estimates of crash times for project activities, as well as information about ongoing project costs, early completion incentives, and delay penalties, members are ready to evaluate a range of crashing options. Exhibit 8.7 describes this process, illustrated with an example below.

Crashing Example: The Garage Remodel and Car Repair Project

Paul has inherited four extremely valuable automobiles from a wealthy uncle. He plans to keep the vehicles, drive them regularly, enter them in collector auto shows, and maintain them himself. This represents the starting point for a new project to contract with outside specialists to perform initial repairs for the vehicles and remodel

EXHIBIT 8.7
Sequential Procedure for Crashing Project Activities

1. Identify the critical path.
2. Select the activity on the critical path with the lowest incremental crash cost. Crash it by one unit of time.
3. Reevaluate the critical path (additional critical paths will emerge at some point).
4. Make the next crashing decision, again looking for the lowest crash cost on the critical path. If there is more than one critical path, find the lowest-cost combination of activities to crash, or look for an activity that is common to the critical paths.
5. Repeat Steps 2 through 4 until the project cannot be crashed further. Crashing ends when crash costs exceed project compression benefits, or when critical activities have all been shortened to their limit, depending on the criteria that have been established.

his garage to accommodate them. Before he begins, he must develop a solid plan and decide whether to stretch the work or compress it into a tighter time period.

Paul recently purchased a house with a four-car garage that is equipped with a security system. However, the previous owner used the garage as a kennel for 200 dogs, so Paul plans to remove pen structures and make several upgrades.

The four vehicles are being stored temporarily in a high-security, insured storage facility at a cost of $400 per day.[7] An additional fixed cost associated with the project is Paul's work-related opportunity cost. He will take time away from his industrial equipment sales and leasing business to oversee the project, and estimates his company will lose $600 per day[8] in profits until the cars are safely in his garage. Thus, the combined incentive for completing the project as soon as possible is $1,000 per day.

Tasks involved in the car repair and garage renovation project include the following:

Task A: Repair Four Vehicles.

The mechanic has agreed to perform the work at the storage facility and fit the tasks around his other repair jobs over an eight-day period. He can give the work higher priority, reducing the time required to seven days or six days, at a higher fee.

Task B: Remove and Dispose of Existing Garage Structures.

Paul and a team of hired workers can complete this task in four days. However, Paul can outsource some or all of it and reduce the time required to three or two days at a higher cost.

Task C: Purchase Tools.

After he has finished the repairs, the mechanic will tell Paul what maintenance tools he needs to purchase. If he shops for tools online to get the best deals, the task will take three days, including delivery time. However, Paul can perform this task in two days if he goes to local hardware stores where he knows they have everything he needs. These stores charge higher prices.

---

[7] Perhaps he could have shopped around for a better price, but this is what the storage company is charging him.

[8] For the sake of simplicity, we assume all overhead and opportunity costs for this project are incurred over a seven-day week. We have calculated the daily, lost profit opportunity for Paul's company by dividing total profit by 365 days. He has employees who also produce revenue, but sales are higher when Paul is available full time.

Task D: Paint Vehicles.

A professional painting crew will touch up the paint on all four vehicles at the storage facility. Painting must follow mechanical repair because the mechanics might scratch the paint while they are working. Painting four vehicles one at a time is the cheapest option and requires 11 working days. However, if the painting company pays for overtime and brings in extra workers and extra equipment, the crew can perform some work concurrently, reducing the time required to as few as six days, but at a higher cost.

Task E: Apply Epoxy Coating on Garage Floor and Paint Walls.

After the kennel structures have been removed, Paul will coat the garage floor with epoxy material and paint the walls. The work can be done at a normal pace in five days if Paul does some of the work himself and hires a few laborers. The tasks can be done in four days, three days, two days or one day if he hires additional people, organizes longer workdays with premium pay for overtime, purchases more painting equipment, and rents fans to promote faster overnight drying.

Task F: Install Shelving and Other Fixtures.

After the epoxy and paint have dried, and after the tools are purchased, Paul can install the shelves and toolboxes and organize his tools. If he purchases shelving and toolboxes that are not preassembled and does all of the work himself, the task will take six days. If he hires expert help and rents a special lift, he can finish this task in five days at an extra cost of $200. If he purchases a few of the fixtures in prefabricated form for an extra $400 and hires a laborer for $100 (in addition to the expert helper he has already hired), he can finish this task in four days. Given that it costs more to crash this task a second day (a total of $400 + $100 = $500) than it does to crash it the first day (only $200), we would say that the crash costs for this task are nonlinear.

Task G: Move Cars to Paul's Garage.

The storage facility is a several-hour drive from Paul's home. It will take two days if he moves the vehicles with the help of an expert hired driver. Alternatively, Paul could move all four vehicles in one day if he rents a truck and trailer and gets special help from a crew experienced in loading and unloading.

Exhibit 8.8 presents a crash-cost matrix for Paul's project to restore his vehicles and remodel his garage. For each task, the matrix shows precedence relationships, normal time and crash time, and normal cost and crash cost. Paul has used this information to calculate the crash cost per day for each task. Total project cost at normal time, shown in the bottom row of the spreadsheet, is calculated as the sum of all normal task costs ($7,900) plus the overhead and opportunity cost of $1,000 per day for 21 days (duration of critical path at normal time).

Exhibit 8.9 shows the AON (activity-on-node) diagram for the garage remodel and car repair project. Task-time ranges, along with incremental crash costs from Exhibit 8.8, are displayed within each task box. Exhibit 8.10 shows a time-based network revealing the location of float with dashed-line arrows. Tasks A, D, and G comprise the critical path, and all others have float.

Exhibit 8.11 shows results of a **tabular approach** for displaying a series of crashing decisions. To use this type of matrix, identify all paths and list them, along with their durations, in the far left column. The next step is to calculate the path lengths when all tasks are performed at their normal times and record these in the second

EXHIBIT 8.8 **Crash-Cost Calculations for Garage Remodel and Car Repair Project**

Sample calculation:

$$\frac{\$3,000 - \$2,000}{8 \text{ days} - 6 \text{ days}} = \$500 \text{ / day}$$

Task	Immediate Predecessor (s)	Normal Duration (Days)	Normal Cost	Fully Crashed Duration	Fully Crashed Cost	Crash Cost Per Day
A. Repair vehicles	None	8	$ 2,000	6	$3,000	$500
B. Remove and dispose of existing kennel structures	None	4	$ 1,500	2	$4,000	$1,250
C. Purchase tools	A	3	$ 1,000	2	$1,400	$400
D. Paint vehicles	A	11	$ 1,000	6	$4,000	$600
E. Epoxy floor and paint walls	B	5	$ 1,000	1	$2,000	$250
F. Install shelving and fixtures	C,E	6	$ 800	4	$1,500	Crash from 6 to 5 days = $200 Crash from 5 to 4 days = $500
G. Move vehicles	D,F	2	$ 600	1	$1,500	$900
Total Task Cost at Normal Time			**$ 7,900**			
Total Cost of Project at 21-day Normal Time, Including Total Task Cost and Ongoing Project Cost of $1,000 Per Day			**$28,900**			

column. The details of each subsequent crashing decision are described below and recorded in tabular form in Exhibit 8.11.

Decision Analysis of the Garage Remodel and Car Repair Project

Step 1

Among the tasks on the 21-day critical path (A-D-G), Task A (repair) has the lowest crash cost per day ($500). This is a financially viable choice because A's crash cost is less than the project fixed cost of $1,000 that will be recovered when the project is shortened by one day. Therefore, Paul elects to crash Task A by one day. The duration of any path that includes Task A is reduced by one day, as well. Thus, after the first crashing decision, A-D-G is reduced from 21 days to 20 days and A-C-F-G is reduced from 19 days to 18 days. B-E-F-G does not change, as shown in Exhibit 8.11.

The net gain at the end of the first step is $1,000 − $500 = $500. Some might ask, "Why not just crash A by two days, given that it is the cheapest one on the critical path?" In this case, we could do that, but in some cases, crashing a critical

EXHIBIT 8.9   AON Diagram for Garage Remodel and Car Repair Project

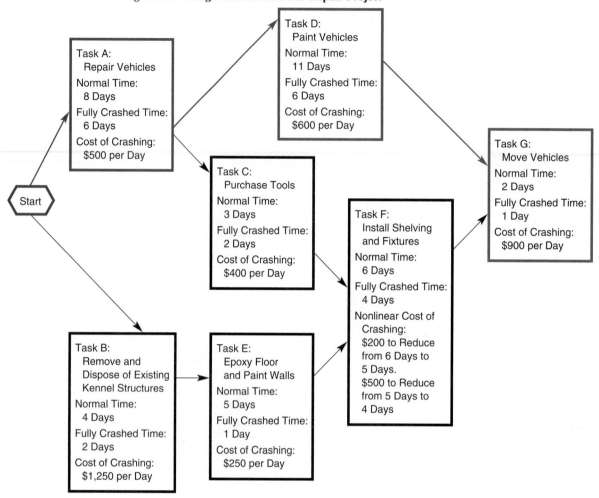

EXHIBIT 8.10   Time-Based Network for Garage Remodel and Car Repair Project before Crashing

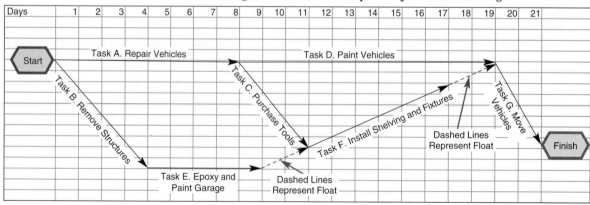

EXHIBIT 8.11   **Tabular Approach for Sequential Crashing**

Crashing Step		1	2	3	4	5	6	7	8
Number of Days Crashed	0 days	1 day	2 days	3 days	4 days	5 days	6 days	7 days	8 days
Path and Duration									
A-D-G	21	20	19	18	17	16	15	14	13
A-C-F-G	19	18	17	17	17	16	15	14	13
B-E-F-G	17	17	17	17	17	16	15	14	13
Activity Crashed	none	A	A	D	D	D, F	G	D, F	C, D, E
Crash Cost	$ 0	$ 500	$ 500	$ 600	$ 600	$ 800	$ 900	$ 1,100	$ 1,250
Fixed Cost Recovered		$ 1,000	$ 1,000	$ 1,000	$ 1,000	$ 1,000	$ 1,000	$ 1,000	$ 1,000
Net Gain or Loss	$ 0	$ 500	$ 500	$ 400	$ 400	$ 200	$ 100	–$ 100	–$ 250
Total Project Cost	**$28,900**	**$28,400**	**$27,900**	**$27,500**	**$27,100**	**$26,900**	**$26,800**	**$26,900**	**$27,150**

task by one time unit can reduce the critical path sufficiently to create a competing critical path. Consequently, we will crash one day at a time in this example to emphasize the importance of watching for the emergence of additional critical paths.

Step 2

No new critical paths result from Step 1. Paul can crash Task A (repair, $500) again because it is *still* the lowest crash-cost task on the critical path. Paths A-D-G and A-C-F-G are reduced by one more day (to 19 and 17 days, respectively). B-E-F-G is unchanged at 17. The net gain is again $1,000 − $500 = $500. Exhibit 8.12 shows a schedule graph depicting the first two crashing decisions involving Task A, which is now crashed to its limit.

Step 3

A-D-G is still the only critical path at the end of Step 2. Task A (repair) has been fully crashed from eight days to six days, so Task D (paint) is now the lowest-cost

EXHIBIT 8.12   **19-Day Schedule for Garage Remodel and Car Repair Project after Task A Is Crashed by Two Days**

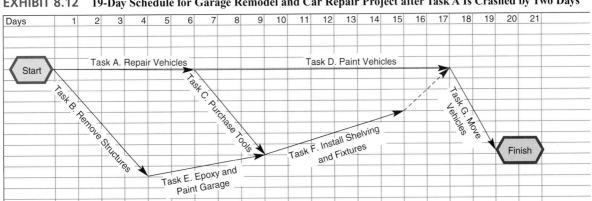

EXHIBIT 8.13 **17-Day Schedule for Garage Remodel and Car Repair Project after Task A Is Crashed by Two Days and Task D Is Crashed by Two Days**

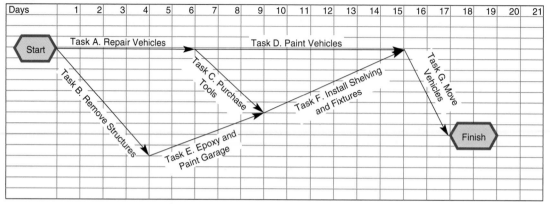

available critical activity to crash. Crashing D by one day at a cost of $600 is worthwhile because it will produce a $400 cost recovery ($1,000 − $600). This reduces path A-D-G from 19 days to 18 days, with other paths remaining the same.

Step 4

There is still only one critical path at the end of Step 3, and Task D (paint) can be crashed by another day for $600, reducing path A-D-G to 17 days and leaving the other two paths unchanged. The net gain for this step is $1000 − $600 = $400. Exhibit 8.13 presents a schedule graph depicting the results of the first four crashing decisions.

Step 5

At the end of Step 4, the project has three critical paths, as shown in Exhibit 8.13. One choice would be to crash Task G (move vehicles), which is common to all three paths, at a crash cost per day of $900. However, it is less expensive to crash both Task D (paint, $600) and Task F (shelving, $200) for a total of $800. The net gain for crashing D and F is $1,000 − $800 = $200. As shown in Exhibit 8.14, this produces a 16-day schedule.

EXHIBIT 8.14 **16-Day Schedule for Garage Remodel and Car Repair Project after Task A Is Crashed by Two Days, Task D Is Crashed by Two Days, and Tasks D and F Are Crashed Simultaneously by One Day**

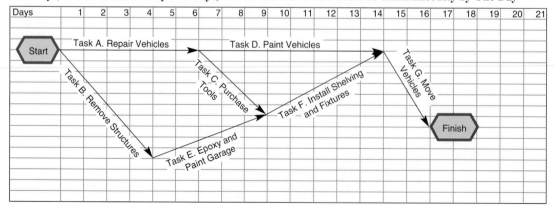

EXHIBIT 8.15   **15-Day Schedule for Garage Remodel and Car Repair Project after Task A Is Crashed by Two Days, Task D Is Crashed by Two Days, Tasks D and F Are Crashed Simultaneously by One Day, and Task G Is Crashed by One Day**

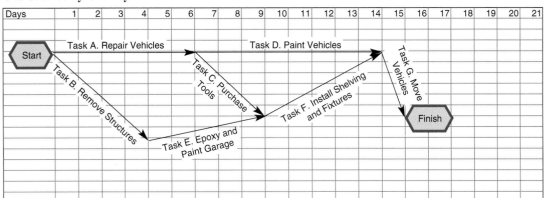

Step 6

The critical path durations are all identical at the end of Step 5, and it is technically possible to crash Tasks D (paint) and F (shelving) again. However, Task F has a nonlinear crash cost and the second day of crashing for this activity is $500, bringing the total for Tasks D and F to $1,100 and exceeding the $1,000 threshold. Paul's other choice is to crash Task G (move vehicles), which is common to all three paths, at a cost of $900. Task G is the better choice because it results in a net gain of $100. The new 15-day schedule, with Task G now crashed to its limit, is displayed in Exhibit 8.15. So far, total project cost has been reduced from $28,900 to $26,800 as shown in the bottom row of Exhibit 8.11.

Step 7

All three paths are critical at the end of Step 6. Task G (move) has been crashed to its limit, so this is no longer an option. The lowest-cost option is to crash Tasks D and F again. But, as mentioned in relation to Step 6, given the step function in the cost of Task F (shelving), the total for these two will be $1,100, producing a net change of $1,000 − $1,100 = −$100. From a pure cost standpoint, it is not worthwhile for Paul to crash the project down to 14 days. But he could have some other reason for doing so, and therefore has included this possibility in his scenario analysis.

Step 8

Although it might not be necessary to go further with the crashing scenarios, Paul wants to know all of his options. If he decides to reduce the project's duration any more, his only option is to crash Tasks C, D, and E at a cost of $1,250 ($400, $600, $250, respectively). As described in Steps 6 and 7, this exceeds the $1,000 cost recovery available and is probably not worth it to Paul. The net loss for this step would be $1,000 − $1,250 = −$250.

Assessing Crashing Options

The crashing analysis described above and summarized in Exhibit 8.11 allows the project manager, Paul, to assess his possibilities and also prepares him for midproject crashing should the need arise. Here are a few possibilities:

- Paul recognizes that if he is considering purely financial factors, and if he can assume his time and cost estimates are accurate, his rational choice is to execute the project in 15 days (i.e., stopping at crash Step 6 in Exhibit 8.11), where total project cost is lowest at $26,800.

- Paul could hesitate to compress the schedule to 15 days, however, because he recognizes that all paths will be critical, leaving no buffer in the schedule.

- Paul might recognize that if he compresses the schedule too tightly he will be too busy concentrating on the garage work to coordinate the repair and painting tasks. He will not have time to visit the work site where the mechanic and painters are working. Consequently, when he finally picks up the vehicles, he might discover the work is not completed to his satisfaction.

- Paul can use the matrix in Exhibit 8.11 to assess how to respond to new information. For example, if he learns he needs to finish the project within 13 days to qualify for participation in a garage competition, he might decide the increased overall cost is actually worth it for the value he places on the recognition. Or, if there is a prize associated with the competition, he could factor that into his analysis as a potential bonus payment for early completion. Imagine he learns there is a $20,000 prize for the best garage, and he estimates he will have a 5 percent chance of winning. In this case, the expected value of the early-completion bonus would be $.05 \times \$20,000 = \$1,000$. Assuming Paul is comfortable with the gamble, he would choose to compress the project to 13 days because the net gain would be $650 (the $1,000 expected prize value minus $350, which is the sum of the two net loss values shown in the bottom row of Exhibit 8.11) for crashing Steps 7 and 8.

- In another scenario, imagine Paul has decided to take a conservative approach and crash the schedule down to only 18 days (Step 3 in Exhibit 8.11). This leaves some float as a buffer. Partway into the project, he discovers mechanical repairs are running behind schedule. He can then look ahead to see where he might compress this or other tasks to get the project back on schedule. The more he understands the possibilities shown in Exhibits 8.11 through 8.15, the better prepared he will be to make these decisions logically.

- Finally, we must point out that Paul should not consider his fixed costs to be cast in stone. Perhaps he can enlist more help with his business while he is working on this project in order to reduce the profit reductions he anticipates. Or, maybe he can negotiate a better deal on the exorbitant garage rental. If he is able to change these parameters, he could reconsider decisions to crash various tasks in light of this new information.

Applying Crashing Concepts

Crashing is an important concept to understand, but real-world project managers seldom engage formally in the sort of process we have applied to solve the garage remodel and car repair project problem. Nonetheless, the example should help you to formulate your thinking when you make crashing decisions more subjectively. In selecting tasks to crash in the absence of objective crash-cost data, a project team should focus on the critical path. Beyond that, there are other factors to consider, including the following:[9]

- **Start-up activities.** It is generally better to compress early activities rather than late ones. This leaves room for unexpected contingencies that arise during project delivery.

[9] Adapted from T.B. Clark, W.E. Riggs, and R.H. Deane, "Guidelines to Compressing Project Schedules for Profit," *Business,* January–March 1985, pp. 18–21.

- **Activities in bottleneck positions.** Look for an activity at a major burst point; several dependent activities cannot start until this activity is completed. It makes sense to compress an activity that can affect so many others.
- **Long-duration activities.** In most cases, it is easier to find opportunities for compressing longer activities rather than shorter ones.
- **Labor-intensive or low-skill activities.** A simple activity that just requires lots of bodies is less expensive to compress than a technology-dependent activity that cannot be shortened without additional capital expenditures.
- **Activities subject to uncontrollable risks.** Some activities are more vulnerable to risks than others. For example, if a team is building a house during a rainy season, members will be wise to finish the roof as quickly as possible, particularly if a storm is anticipated.
- **Divisible activities.** Some activities are easier than others to divide and parcel out to several people. For example, some types of IT programming work cannot be easily divided beyond a certain point.[10] In contrast, other types of work related to the same project might be more easily broken into independent pieces; an example would be interviews with users during the requirements analysis phase.

In sum, a rational approach to crashing not only assists a team in choosing the best option, but it also provides a framework for offering solutions to key stakeholders in a logical manner that demonstrates thorough preparation.

FAST TRACKING

As described in the introduction to this chapter, fast tracking involves scheduling two or more tasks simultaneously. Fast tracking can be applied independently or in combination with crashing and scope reduction to shorten a project's duration. In the example summarized in Exhibit 8.4, Task A, user requirements, and Task B, benchmark, were overlapped to reduce project duration. Although this approach introduces risks and increases coordination challenges, it has become common in hypercompetitive, short product life cycle, new product development environments. For example, one Internet company reduced its time to market for a new product by starting feature design and coding before the specification process was complete.[11]

A project manager applying fast tracking can depict a concurrent activity relationship with a start-to-start precedence designator of the type introduced in Chapter 7. In the example of the Internet product design project mentioned above, the precedence diagram could appear as shown in Exhibit 8.16. Feature design is scheduled to start one month after specifications start, and coding is scheduled to start one month after feature design starts. If activities had been scheduled on a finish-to-start sequence, the project duration would be 13 months. With fast tracking and start-to-start logic, it can be reduced to seven months. This looks like a potentially easy solution, but as we have emphasized, fast tracking increases the need for coordination and communication.

[10] Brooks, *The Mythical Man-Month.*

[11] M. Iansiti and A. MacCormack, *Living on Internet Time* (Boston: Harvard Business School Publications, 1996).

EXHIBIT 8.16
Depicting Fast Tracking for an Internet Project Using a Start-to-Start Precedence Relationship

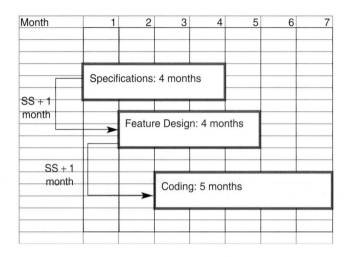

MODIFYING SCHEDULES TO ACCOMMODATE RESOURCE CONSTRAINTS

In describing crashing and fast tracking, we have operated under the assumption that the resources required are available. This is not always the case in project environments. Resources likely to create constraints include people, materials, services, information, equipment, money, and physical space. We will focus on human resource constraints because often these are the most significant determinants of a project manager's ability to deliver a project on time. However, the tools and concepts introduced here can be applied to all resource types.

Often, the first draft of a project schedule reveals that necessary resource loads exceed the availability of team members (this is known as **overallocation**). Or resource levels can be very uneven, producing situations in which people sometimes do not have enough to do (**underallocation**) and giving them impossibly heavy workloads at other times. Through the use of schedule float, it can be possible to smooth out the peaks and valleys in a resource load profile. Exhibit 8.17 shows a simple example. The early-start schedule calls for a peak requirement of 30 people in days three and four of the project. In the modified schedule, the peak has been dampened; Task E was moved to its late-start time, bringing the heaviest load down to 20 without extending the project schedule. In the paragraphs below, we expand on this concept, introducing tools and priorities for problem solving in more complex project schedules.

Resource Allocation Priorities

There are two competing priorities in resource allocation—resource availability and time. If a project schedule has an immovable deadline, it might be possible to reduce peaks and valleys to even out resource loads without delaying the project. However, if a project team is limited in size, or if a critical team member is needed for two tasks that have been scheduled simultaneously and have no available float, it might be necessary to increase the duration of the project to accommodate these constraints. Thus, it is important for the project manager to know which of these objectives (resource constraint versus time constraint) has the higher priority.

We begin with a **time-limited** scenario under the assumption of interchangeable or generic project team members who all possess the same skills. Such an analysis can be appropriate in large projects when the project manager wants a general idea of

EXHIBIT 8.17
Simple Resource Allocation Problem Demonstrating the Use of Schedule Float to Create Even Workforce Loading

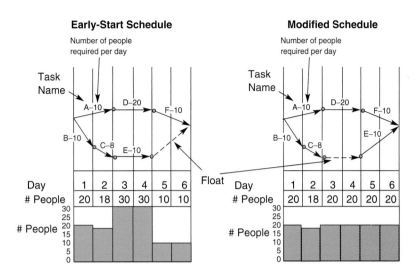

resource needs over the project's life. For example, project schedulers at a U.S. Navy shipyard use generic resource profiles to determine where a submarine overhaul project's peak loads will be. This helps decision makers anticipate when they will need to temporarily move workers across projects. Peak loads typically occur when ships are moved in and out of dry docks.

Resource Allocation Example with Interchangeable Resources

A movie director is planning the first phase of a wildlife documentary she and her crew will film in the northern and southern extremes of the world.[12] The second phase will include final editing, video retakes, and production of the finished film. She will develop plans for the second phase during the first phase as more information becomes available. As noted in Chapter 7, in PMI terminology this is known as **rolling-wave** planning because early activities in the project have been planned in greater detail than later activities. In planning the first phase, the director must determine staffing level needs. Crewmembers have considerable experience and, thus, can be moved around and interchanged depending on where they are needed. Exhibit 8.18 shows project activities, resource requirements, sequential relationships, and the rationale for sequencing.

In Exhibit 8.19, a time-based network identifies each activity and the number of team members it will require per week. In Exhibit 8.20, an Excel-based Gantt chart shows, numerically and in histogram form, what the loads are each week. This early-start schedule is considered **front-end loaded** because resource requirements are heavy in the beginning and taper off toward the end.

Why Level Resources?

If a preliminary project schedule shows front-end loading with the most heavy resource requirements at the beginning of the project (as in Exhibit 8.20), is this necessarily a concern for the project manager? Under some circumstances, the project manager favors a resource profile that tapers off. When team members are no longer needed they can be assigned to other projects. On the other hand, a front-end-loaded schedule can demand too many resources at the start of the project and might consequently be infeasible.

[12] The director is not concerned with the seasonal differences between the two hemispheres and, in fact, believes the summer-winter contrasts will add interest to the film.

EXHIBIT 8.18   Precedence Table for Wildlife Film Project

Activities	Immediate Predecessor (s)	Duration	Number of Crewmembers Needed per Week	Rationale for Sequencing
A. Filming of marine wildlife in Tierra del Fuego, Argentina	None	3 weeks	7	No predecessors
B. Filming during flights over wildlife sites in Siberia	None	2 weeks	9	No predecessors
C. Filming during flights over wildlife sites in Alaska	None	2 weeks	12	No predecessors
D. Marine filming by air and sea off the shores of Antarctica	None	2 weeks	6	No predecessors
E. On-the-ground filming of wildlife areas identified during flights over Siberia	B	2 weeks	11	The crew must first do the Siberian flight work to identify remote areas where game filming will be the best.
F. On-the-ground filming of wildlife areas identified during flights over Alaska	C	6 weeks	5	The crew must first do the Alaskan flight work to identify remote areas where game filming will be the best.
G. On-the-ground filming in the interior of Antarctica	D	3 weeks	5	The crew will gain insight about what to film on the ground while flying over Antarctica during Activity D.
H. Preliminary editing of northern wildlife scenes	E, F	3 weeks	2	Although final editing will occur in the next phase of the project, the director would like to pull together footage of northern wildlife and determine where the gaps and overlaps are. During the remainder of the project she will continue the editing based on what she and the crew have learned from the initial edits.

Uneven resource profiles can be problematic. For example, look ahead to the front-end-loaded scenario displayed in Exhibit 8.20. A team whose membership dwindles over time can lose its sense of morale or esprit de corps. Other types of lumpy resource profiles also can be undesirable. For example, if the resource load has a valley in the middle of the project, what should those who are idle do with their time? If the project manager temporarily releases them to another project, they might not return when they are needed. If she leaves enthusiastic team members with nothing to do, they might keep themselves busy by creatively taking on scope-creep tasks that disrupt other project work. A project manager who works with a team that remains intact throughout the project's life can avoid some of these challenges.

EXHIBIT 8.19   Early-Start Time-Based Network for First Phase of Wildlife Film Project

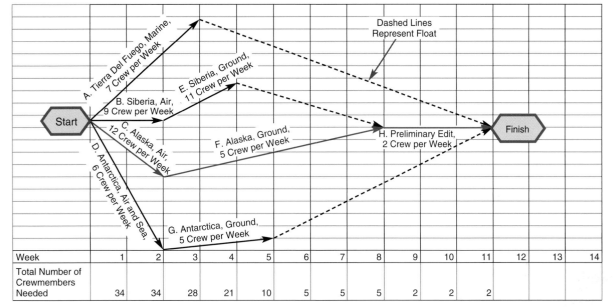

Week	1	2	3	4	5	6	7	8	9	10	11	12	13	14
Total Number of Crewmembers Needed	34	34	28	21	10	5	5	5	2	2	2			

⟶► = Critical Path

Time-Constrained Resource Smoothing

In some cases, project managers redistribute resources and float within the confines of a specified end date. This is known as **time-constrained resource smoothing.** The general approach for time-constrained resource smoothing is as follows:

1. *Schedule critical path activities.* Assuming the project cannot be delayed, the critical path is a given constraint.
2. *Schedule noncritical activities.* Use a combination of a few decision rules and common sense. For example, once the critical path has been set, compare activities that are eligible to be added to the schedule based on the float they have available. Activities with the least float should have higher priority. In cases where there is a tie between two activities based on float, research and practice suggest that giving priority to shorter activities near the beginning of the project is generally more effective than other decision rules.

Time-constrained resource smoothing problems are computationally complex and do not lend themselves to mathematical optimization. The only way to be certain we have the best solution is through complete enumeration of every possible combination. For projects of any realistic size, this is impossible. Although many project scheduling software packages offer features that perform resource leveling, they are generally not as clever as a team can be, as we discuss later in this section. Consequently, the best way to accomplish a workable solution is with a team whose members have a solid understanding of scheduling, a few rules of thumb, and a visual process that allows for experimentation. Visual approaches for teams include the following:

- Use a projector to display an Excel-based Gantt chart and histogram such as the one in Exhibit 8.20 on a conference room wall. Based on team input, experiment with different scenarios by adding cells to move activities to the right or deleting cells to move activities to the left. To be effective, the team must have access to a network diagram showing precedence relationships.

EXHIBIT 8.20 Excel-Based Gantt Chart and Histogram Showing Resource Loads for Early-Start Schedule of Wildlife Film Project

Activity	Crewmembers Needed per Week										
	Week 1	Week 2	Week 3	Week 4	Week 5	Week 6	Week 7	Week 8	Week 9	Week 10	Week 11
A. Film wildlife in Tierra del Fuego	7	7	7								
B. Film by air over Siberia	9	9									
C. Film by air over Alaska	12	12									
D. Film by sea and air off shores of Antarctica	6	6									
E. Film on ground in Siberia			11	11							
F. Film on ground in Alaska			5	5	5	5	5	5			
G. Film on ground in Antarctica			5	5	5						
H. Preliminary editing of northern wildlife scenes									2	2	2
Total Crew per Week	**34**	**34**	**28**	**21**	**10**	**5**	**5**	**5**	**2**	**2**	**2**
	Week 1	Week 2	Week 3	Week 4	Week 5	Week 6	Week 7	Week 8	Week 9	Week 10	Week 11

Crewmembers

Total Crew per Week	**34**	**34**	**28**	**21**	**10**	**5**	**5**	**5**	**2**	**2**	**2**
	Week 1	Week 2	Week 3	Week 4	Week 5	Week 6	Week 7	Week 8	Week 9	Week 10	Week 11

- Use a projector to display a Microsoft Project network and resource histogram, in split-screen view, on a conference room wall.[13] Set the software to "Show task links" and use this function to experiment with resource scenarios by specifying finish-to-start lags between activities.

- Prepare a wall-mounted paper with vertical lines corresponding to project time units. For each project activity, piece together a series of sticky notes sized in proportion to task duration. On each note, write the resource requirement per time unit. Move activities right and left to experiment with resource scenarios while keeping precedence relationships intact.

Regardless of the method used, a team developing a resource plan should be mindful of the schedule risks that emerge when float is consumed to accommodate resource conflicts and previously non critical activities become critical.

The Team's Solution

In the case of the wildlife film project, the director and her team projected a spreadsheet-based Gantt chart and histogram on the wall and worked through various scenarios before developing a time-limited resource plan. Exhibit 8.21 displays their solution. Following the procedure recommended above, they first scheduled critical path activities, then experimented by moving activities within the constraints of their precedence relationships. Note that Activities A, D, and G all have been delayed to their late start times. Activities B and E have each been delayed by two weeks. The resulting schedule has a much smoother, yet still imperfect, resource profile. There are other options with peak loads of no more than the 16 crewmember maximum shown in this solution. However, this team's solution offers the advantage of keeping activities at each location in sequence (e.g., Activity E, Siberia ground, is scheduled to occur immediately after Activity B, Siberia air). As this example illustrates, resource smoothing is part art, part science.

What about Activity Splitting?

Project management students often ask if it is acceptable to split an activity, perhaps working on it for a day when resources are available, then finishing a few days later when resources are available again. Although this is theoretically and practically possible, there is a downside to splitting. If you have ever started a complex activity, stopped because of an interruption, then resumed it later, the work probably took longer, in total, than it would have if you had done it all at once. And the quality of your work was probably compromised. This is true for individuals and teams; an activity interrupted will take longer because of the shutdown and startup time required. This applies to knowledge work such as computer programming, as well as to physical work such as painting a house. In acknowledgment of this phenomenon, and to keep examples consistent, we have not included activity-splitting as an option in the examples shown here.

Modifying the Schedule When There Is a Resource Limit

In the previous part of this wildlife filming example, we assumed the project end date was fixed. We had to smooth resource loads within that constraint. However, the director has now learned from the sponsor that the number of film crewmembers on the

---

[13] For information about split-screen displays, see Appendix A, "Quick Guide to Using Microsoft Project," at the end of this book.

EXHIBIT 8.21
Time-Constrained Resource Smoothing: Modified Schedule for Wildlife Film Project with Noncritical Activities Delayed

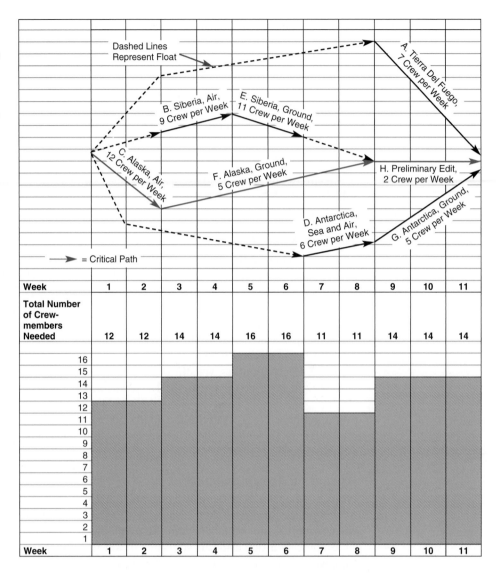

Week	1	2	3	4	5	6	7	8	9	10	11
Total Number of Crewmembers Needed	12	12	14	14	16	16	11	11	14	14	14

project is limited to 12. Refer to the smoothed resource profile in Exhibit 8.21. During seven of the 11 project weeks, loads exceed 12 people.

A procedure for solving a resource-constrained problem such as this one is to schedule the activities one week at a time, starting on the left. Identify all activities eligible to begin, and give priority to those with the least float. If there is a tie, it is reasonable to select those with resource loads that complement the loads of other eligible activities, or those that bring the resource load closest to reaching the limit. As with time-constrained leveling, the team engaged in scenario planning must consider other project-specific factors in addition to the resource profile when selecting options.

In **resource-constrained allocation problems** it is not appropriate to automatically schedule the critical path—it has priority, though, because it has no float. Here is how this process works in the context of the wildlife film project:

Activities eligible for the first week of the project include A, B, C, and D. Activity C has the least amount of float and also happens to require exactly 12 crewmembers, so the team decides to schedule it into the first two-week time slot. The second decision is what to start in week 3 after Activity C is complete. Eligible activities include A, B, D, and F, either individually or in some combination. Possibilities are summarized below:

Options for Activities to Initiate at the Start of Week 3	Resources Required	Remaining Activity Float	Evaluation of this Option	Conclusion
A and D	13	A, 6 D, 4	Not viable; exceeds limit of 12	Not a feasible option.
A and F	12	A, 6 F, 0	F has 0 float, making it a high priority, but A has 6 weeks of float.	A and F have less priority than D and F because D has less float than A.
D and F	11	D, 4 F, 0	D has 4 weeks of float. F has 0 float, making it a high priority.	More attractive than A and F because D has 4 weeks of float and F has 0. Also would allow the director to keep a crew in Alaska for two consecutive activities. The 11 crewmembers required for D and F put the director close to her goal of 12.
B	9	B, 2	Not as good as D and F because B has more float (2) than F (0).	Team decides against scheduling this one in favor of D and F because of float.

The planning team's choice, based on a combination of decision rules, forward thinking, and common sense, leads the director to schedule Activities D and F to fill the next three weeks of the project. An interim schedule graph for the first two decisions appears in Exhibit 8.22. The exhibit reveals that by scheduling Activity F to begin at the start of the third week the team has created an obligation to use five crewmembers in weeks 5 through 8. This means the next decision must include activities that, in combination with Activity F, do not exceed the limit of 12.

EXHIBIT 8.22
Modified Wildlife Film Project Schedule after First Two Resource Allocation Decisions under 12-Crewmember Constraint

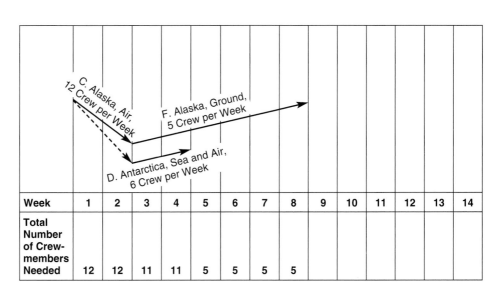

Week	1	2	3	4	5	6	7	8	9	10	11	12	13	14
Total Number of Crewmembers Needed	12	12	11	11	5	5	5	5						

For the third decision, Activity B is not a possibility to start in week 5 because it requires nine crewmembers, which, in combination with Activity F, would exceed the 12-crewmember limit. Eligible activities, given this restriction, include A and G. Either one will work because they both span the three of the four remaining weeks for Activity F. The team recommends Activity G because it makes sense to do the ground shooting in Antarctica immediately after the sea and air filming in Antartica. The next decision is between Activities A and B. Look ahead at what happens if the director schedules Activity A first. This delays Activity B by three weeks and there is nothing to combine with Activity H, with a two-crewmember requirement, at the end of the project. This leads the team to recommend starting Activity B next. Activity E follows B immediately, allowing the director to keep the team in Siberia for both activities. The final step is to schedule Activities A and H in parallel at the end of the project.

Exhibit 8.23 displays a schedule graph and histogram summarizing the results of the series of decisions described above. The filming project will now take four weeks longer than it did when a resource limit was not specified. There are other possible solutions, but this schedule keeps geographically linked activities together. Reflecting the realities of project life, the resource profile is not perfect and has a

EXHIBIT 8.23   Schedule Modification to Accommodate 12-Crewmember Constraint: Wildlife Film Project Is Extended by Four Weeks

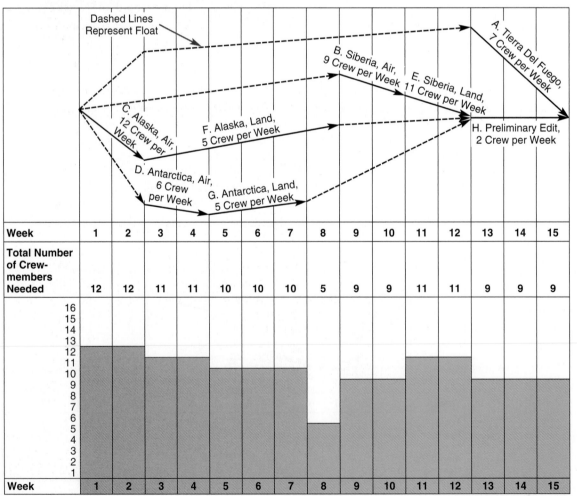

valley with only five crewmembers required in week 8. The director could accept this as a given, recognizing that extra crewmembers might be needed to respond to anticipated risks. Or she could consider concentrating resource usage for Activity F and crashing it from six weeks to five weeks. This would pull remaining activities forward and fill the gap. As in the time-limited scenario, the process requires the film director and her team to use a combination of decision rules, forward thinking about various scenarios, and a bit of common sense.

Resource Allocation Using Project Scheduling Software

A series of four screen shots from Microsoft Project appears in Exhibits 8.24, 8.25, 8.26, and 8.27. The first two exhibits show the early-start Gantt chart and resource histogram for

EXHIBIT 8.24   **Microsoft Project Gantt View of Wildlife Film Project Early-Start Schedule**

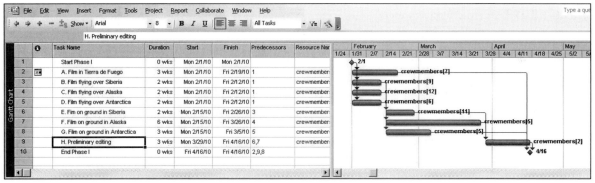

EXHIBIT 8.25   **Microsoft Project Resource Histogram for Wildlife Film Project Early-Start Schedule**

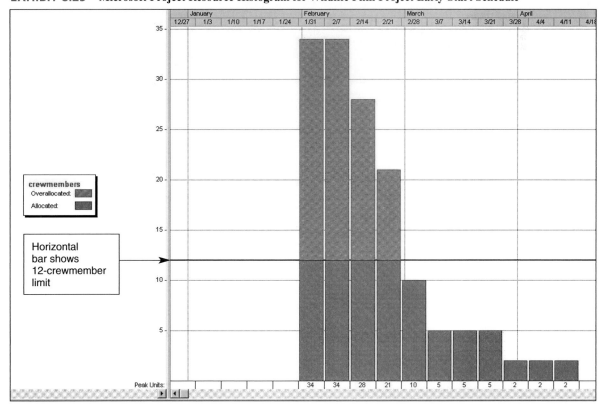

EXHIBIT 8.26 **Microsoft Project Gantt View of Film Project Schedule Following Software-Generated Resource Leveling**

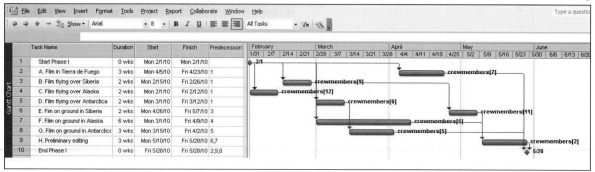

EXHIBIT 8.27 **Microsoft Project Resource Histogram for Wildlife Film Project Leveled Schedule**

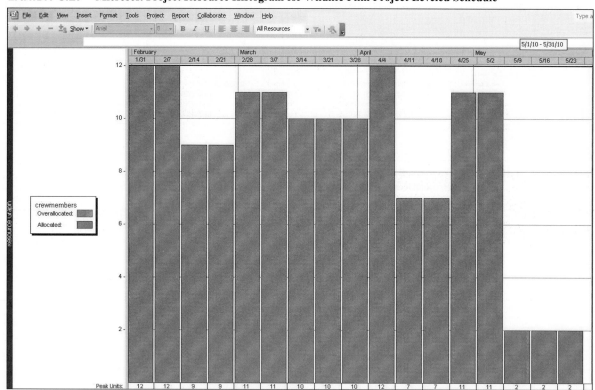

the wildlife film project. The second two exhibits show the results produced when Microsoft Project uses its own decision rules to modify the resource-constrained schedule.

Exhibit 8.26 shows that the Microsoft Project solution to the resource constraint extends the project to 17 weeks, exceeding by two weeks the human-generated solution. The software's decision to schedule Activity B at the start of week 3 led to a different set of subsequent decisions. Note the uneven use of resources in the Microsoft Project solution. Even if the software were able to look ahead at some of the scenarios from various decisions, it has no way of knowing any subjective preferences the film director might have for keeping some activities together (e.g., linking Activities D and G in Antarctica or C and F in Alaska.)

Some project managers find it necessary to use software for resource allocation in large, complex schedules,[14] but they should understand enough about the process to make educated adjustments to computer-generated leveling results. Most software packages allow the project manager to designate a set of priorities that can guide the decisions more than the default approach we used with Microsoft Project in Exhibits 8.26 and 8.27. However, priorities can vary from activity to activity, and some subjective preferences are simply outside the domain of the software. It could take more time to set up all of the priorities in the software than it would to simply lay it out on a large sheet of paper and work with a team to move tasks around, or shuffle tasks in a spreadsheet Gantt chart similar to the one shown in Exhibit 8.20.

Resource Allocation Example with Specialized Resources

In the wildlife-filming project described above, we operated under the assumption that film crewmembers were interchangeable. In many projects, especially those of a technical nature, each person or subteam possesses a specialized skill required for a particular type of activity. In this section, we build on the logic for interchangeable resource allocation to present an example involving team members with specialized skills.

Exhibit 8.28 depicts the schedule for an IT project to be completed by a team of four specialists whose names are shown in the table just below the network. The critical path for this project is A-C-F-H-I with a 16-day duration.

[14] But, as one experienced project manager remarked when asked for his advice on computer-generated scheduling, "Don't touch that button!"

EXHIBIT 8.28
Network Schedule for an IT Project with Constraints on Specialized Resources

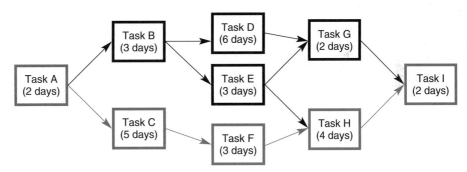

Task	Person who will perform each task
A Develop Web template and overall design with functionality goals	Bob
B Program customer order interface	Gail
C Program quote request interface	Gail
D Develop online purchasing security assurance for customer order interface	David
E Design graphics for order interface and review for consistency with other aspects of Web site	Bob
F Review quote request interface with design engineering team and revise as needed	Russ
G Review customer order interface with purchasing and revise as needed	Russ
H Review design engineering approved quote request interface for needed customer security enhancements	David
I Obtain final approval	Bob

EXHIBIT 8.29
**Early-Start Schedule
for IT Project with
Specialized Resources**

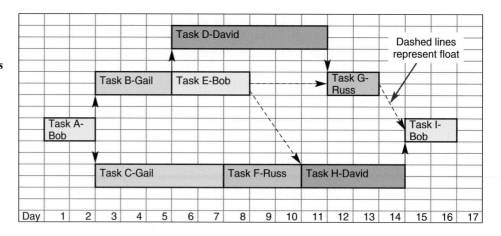

A Gantt chart with precedence relationships shown in Exhibit 8.29 reveals that the current schedule is not feasible because in some places individual team members are expected to perform more than one task at a given time. It is impossible to accommodate the resource constraints without extending the schedule. The challenge for the project manager is to determine how to delay the schedule by the least amount of time while avoiding conflicts for individual workloads. Another challenge is to logically demonstrate to the project sponsor why the delay is necessary. Visual illustrations such as the ones shown here will be much more effective than "I need more people."

Faced with an impossible schedule, as shown in Exhibit 8.29, members of the project team must collaborate to develop a feasible schedule that works for everyone. They know this will involve delaying some project tasks, and they are aware that software such as Microsoft Project might not produce an optimal solution. Moreover, they believe that by cooperating in the decision-making process they can discuss various scenarios based on multiple criteria. For example, perhaps one team member has planned her vacation during a certain period. Or perhaps there is a competing project with special needs. The team can test several scenarios with the help of visual displays (e.g., an Excel-based Gantt chart projected onto a wall, or sticky notes on a wall-mounted paper).

An example of a first-pass trial, shown in Exhibit 8.30, involves delaying Tasks B and D, as well as their successors, to eliminate resource conflicts for Gail and David. This schedule is feasible, but it extends the project completion date from 16 days to 27 days. The team believes there are probably better options, so members continue to brainstorm other possibilities, shown in Exhibits 8.31 and 8.32. The schedule shown in Exhibit 8.31 is similar to the one shown in 8.30, but it involves delaying Task H for David and having him perform Task D first. The 22-day result is an improvement over the 27-day schedule the team created in its first pass. However, team members explore further and discover that with some clever reshuffling they can keep the project within 19 days without violating resource constraints or prescribed network precedence relationships. This happens to be the shortest-duration, resource-feasible schedule for this project and is shown in Exhibit 8.32. Although

EXHIBIT 8.30 **27-Day Schedule for IT Project with Specialized Resources**

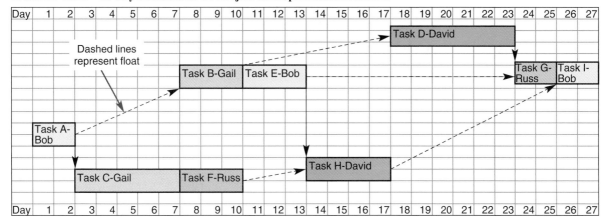

we do not show it here, Microsoft Project produced a longer-duration schedule when it leveled this project.

This is another example of a large, combinatorial problem that is difficult to optimize, but a few key principles can assist a team in making intelligent, systematic adjustments:

1. Consider delaying tasks with the most float.
2. For resource-conflicted tasks that appear *early* in the project, consider scheduling the shorter tasks *before* longer tasks for each resource.
3. For resource-conflicted tasks that appear *late* in the project, consider scheduling shorter tasks *later* than longer tasks for each resource.[15]

[15] The combination of principles 2 and 3 is drawn from a well-known job shop scheduling concept known as Johnson's Rule. We thank Ted Klastorin for this insight. We apply it here in a much less formal sense than the way it is prescribed in management science textbooks, but the general idea can be useful.

EXHIBIT 8.31 **22-Day Schedule for IT Project with Specialized Resources**

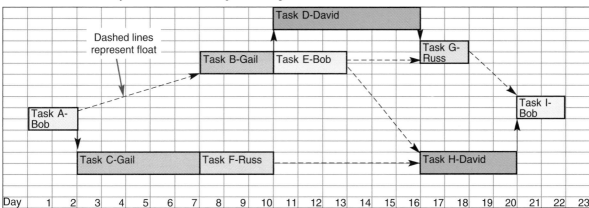

EXHIBIT 8.32   19-Day Schedule Is Shortest-Time Feasible Option

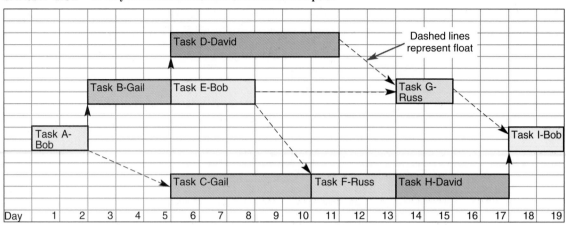

A slightly modified version of the adjusted schedule from Exhibit 8.32 is shown in Exhibit 8.33. It offers us the opportunity to introduce the distinction between the concepts of *critical path* and *critical chain*. Recall that the original critical path for this project was A-C-F-H-I. This was the sequence of tasks that, theoretically, could not be delayed without delaying the project. However, if we consider resource needs, a slightly different series of tasks is the sequence that *actually* determines the project's duration. This is known as the **critical chain** and is highlighted in Exhibit 8.33 with dashed lines around the boxes for the sequence A-B-C-F-H-I. The only difference from the critical path (shown in Exhibit 8.29) is that the critical chain for this project includes Task B. In other project schedules, it is possible for the critical chain to be an entirely different set of activities than the critical path.

The critical chain is the actual sequence of deliverables, activities, tasks, or work packages that cannot be delayed without delaying the project. It incorporates

EXHIBIT 8.33   19-Day Schedule with Critical Chain Highlighted

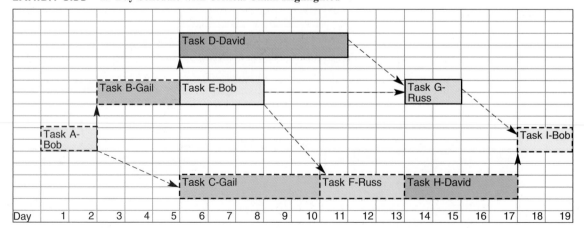

sequential logic as well as resource constraints. Note that none of the highlighted tasks can be delayed without extending the project beyond 19 days. However, the tasks without the dashed-line boxes (D, E, G) all have float, as shown in the dashed connecting lines.

Critical Chain Concepts

Critical chain concepts emerged as a significant addition to the project management body of knowledge in the late 1990s. Some readers may be familiar with the concept's originator, Eliyahu Goldratt, who wrote *The Goal,*[16] a popular operations management book that introduces a field of study and application known as **Theory of Constraints** or **TOC.** *Critical Chain,* a more recent book by Goldratt,[17] is based on a similar thesis: to manage any operation (service, manufacturing, project) effectively, we must focus our attention on system constraints. In a factory setting, the constraint is the bottleneck, or in the vernacular of *The Goal,* a "Herbie."[18] In a project, the constraint is the critical chain. The critical path, our focus so far, is represented only by activity sequences and does not account for resource availability. Goldratt's work offers several insights for managing the critical chain.[19]

Concept 1: Give Priority to the Critical Chain

In most situations, the project manager must negotiate with functional managers to ensure that the people required for critical chain tasks are available precisely when they are needed. If the project manager can communicate the significance of the critical chain, and perhaps show flexibility with respect to personnel needs for activities not on the critical chain, he or she stands a better chance of persuading functional managers to make critical team members available at the necessary times. If team members are assigned full time to the project, the project manager has more control. Additionally, the project manager should go out of his or her way to ensure that people on the critical chain have all of the materials, equipment, and support they need.

Concept 2: Use Schedule Buffers to Protect the Critical Chain

Critical chain advocates suggest three types of buffers: **feeding buffers, resource buffers,** and **project buffers.** *Feeding buffers* are segments of float intentionally scheduled at points where noncritical activities merge with the critical chain. According to critical chain principles, activities with float should be delayed as long as possible to postpone expenditures, thereby offering better cash flow management. However, if an activity is delayed too far, it will collide with the critical chain, adding to schedule risk. A feeding buffer specifies the limit on such delays. For example, in the schedule shown in Exhibit 8.33, Tasks E and G could each be delayed by two days without making the project late. However, this would put them right up next to the critical

---

[16] E.M. Goldratt and J. Fox, *The Goal* (Great Barrington, MA: The North River Press, 1996).

[17] E.M. Goldratt, *Critical Chain* (Great Barrington, MA: The North River Press, 1997).

[18] Herbie was a Boy Scout who slowed down his companions on a hike, thereby creating a constraint.

[19] For example, see, R.C. Newbold, *Project Management in the Fast Lane: Applying the Theory of Constraints* (Boca Raton, FL: St. Lucie Press, APICS, 1998).

chain. The team can delay each one of them by one day, thereby using only one day of float and specifying one day of feeding buffer.

A *resource buffer* provides information-based protection for critical chain activities. Referring to Exhibit 8.33, imagine Gail has the materials for Task C on her desk, but by the end of day 6 she has barely gotten started. She should be one-fifth of the way through this five-day task. Should she inform Russ, who is relying on her to be ready for handoff at the end of day 10? Yes. Will she? Probably not, if common human behavior is in operation here.[20] In fact, Gail's silence about her lack of progress will likely continue right up to the time when she is supposed to have everything ready for handoff to Russ. It will be better if Gail and Russ agree to meet at a certain point (the second day of the five-day time allowance for Task C, for example) to discuss her progress and work out solutions to potential problems. In this case, we would say they have agreed to a three-day resource buffer because the two plan to share information three days before the scheduled handoff of Gail's work. Russ could then volunteer to assist Gail if this is within his skill set, or he could get started on Task G while he is waiting for her to finish. The important thing is that the two of them recognize the significance of their positions on the critical chain and find ways to keep the project on schedule.

Project buffer generally refers to the time between a project's anticipated end date and the due date specified by the customer. A project buffer is not a new concept; traditionally it has been called *project float.* Goldratt adds value to the idea by suggesting that instead of padding time estimates for each individual activity to allow for uncertainties, the team agrees to accumulate some of this padding and place it at the end of the project where it can be shared. Many project managers argue that if they were to publicly expose all buffer at the end of a project, a powerful sponsor might decide to confiscate it, demanding an earlier completion date. Thus, they prefer to retain buffer within individual activities where it is less visible.

Concept 3: Beware the Effects of Multitasking

This critical chain concept focuses on how people's work time is scheduled. In many organizations, employees belong to functional organizations and their work time is loaned out to several projects. If people are assigned to too many projects at the same time, they can appear to be busy, but much of their time is unproductive. Switching from one project to another can be costly because of the setup time needed to change a train of thought, pull out the right materials, and recall where the project left off.[21] Exhibit 8.34 shows the results of a study Wheelwright and Clark conducted.[22] The chart shows that as the number of projects per engineer is increased, the amount of value-added time per project declines dramatically. (Box 8.2 offers an example.) Also, research has shown that a person's effective intelligence actually declines temporarily under multitasking conditions.[23] Although multitasking can be necessary in some

---

[20] J.B. Schmitt and R.J. Calatone, "Escalation of Commitment During New Product Development," *Journal of the Academy of Marketing Science,* 30, no. 2, (2002), pp. 103–18; and D.N. Ford and J.D. Sterman, "Overcoming the 90% Syndrome: Iteration Management in Concurrent Development Projects," *Concurrent Engineering: Research and Applications* 11, no. 3 (2003), pp. 177–86.

[21] T. DeMarco and T. Lister, *Peopleware: Productive Projects and Teams,* 2nd ed. (New York: Dorset House, 1999).

[22] Wheelwright and Clark, *Revolutionizing Product Development.*

[23] S. Shellenbarger, "Multitasking Makes You Stupid," *The Wall Street Journal,* February 27, 2003, p. D1.

The Advantage of Working on One Project at a Time

Box 8.2

The CEO of an international corporation that designs and manufactures industrial cutting equipment gave a speech at a professional meeting to explain some of his company's successes. Most notable was the company's 50 percent reduction in product development time. When asked what the company had done to make such a dramatic improvement, he replied: "We insisted that every engineer work on only one project at a time. I'm personally committed to this and regularly walk through the design department to ask people what they are working on. If an individual tells me that he or she is working on multiple projects, I make a visit to the supervisor to correct the problem." He went on to say, "Our goal as an organization is not to see how busy we can keep the engineers—it is to get the projects out the door in a timely manner."

circumstances (e.g., when an expensive or scarce resource has to be shared), a project manager should try to avoid or limit multitasking assignments on critical path or critical chain resources.

Conclusions about Critical Chain

Critical chain concepts complement our discussion of resource allocation, adding tools and ideas that are closely linked with the realities of project management. Although some authors argue that they replicate ideas already contained within the previously established body of knowledge on resource allocation,[24] most would agree that critical chain concepts provide new ways of looking at project constraints and draw managers' attention toward useful solutions. However, some critics have warned that too much attention to critical chain management can detract the team's attention away from customer-oriented KPIs that are not necessarily incorporated into critical chain procedures.[25]

[24] T.T. Wilkens, "Critical Path, or Chain, or Both?" *PM Network* 14, no. 7 (2000), pp. 68–74.

[25] T. Raz, R. Barnes, and D. Dvir, "A Critical Look at Critical Chain Project Management," *Project Management Journal* 34, no. 4 (2003), pp. 24–32.

EXHIBIT 8.34
Effects of Multitasking in Engineering Projects

Source: Adapted with permission of The Free Press, a Division of Simon & Schuster, Inc., from *Revolutionizing Product Development: Quantum Leaps in Speed, Efficiency, and Quality* by Steven C. Wheelwright and Kim B. Clark. Copyright © 1992 by Steven C. Wheelwright and Kim B. Clark. All rights reserved.

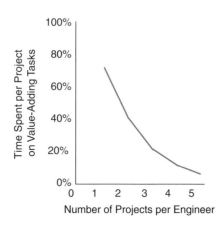

Warnings against multitasking direct our attention to the importance of not only managing resources *within* projects but also managing resources *among* projects. Leaders in many enterprises tend to ignore conflicts caused by multitasking across projects, hoping they will work themselves out. They rarely do.[26] The critical chain concepts introduced here can be effectively extended to an organization's project portfolio.

[26] Wheelwright and Clark, *Revolutionizing Product Development.*

Chapter Summary and Onward

This chapter presents several tools and concepts for modifying schedules to accommodate time and resource constraints. Creative solutions are available to those who have a solid understanding of network scheduling concepts and know how to use them as tools for problem solving and persuasion. So, before asking for more resources or time, the effective project manager investigates the potential to eliminate WBS activities (scope reduction), add resources to critical tasks to shorten their durations (i.e., crash), perform some sequentially related tasks concurrently (fast track), or delay tasks to reallocate resources. In the case of crashing, the project manager might have to ask for more money to compensate for potential lost efficiency, but the overall cost of a crashed schedule should be less than one without crashing when time-related fixed costs are considered. If the project manager and team have done a careful analysis of the options, they can present their case effectively, and with graphical displays, to key decision makers. In the next chapter, on project monitoring, we show how the adjusted schedule becomes the baseline against which the project is monitored, and through which the team engages in ongoing problem solving and further adjustment.

Team Activities

1. Gather a team of four or five classmates. Contact a project manager in an information systems environment (e.g., the IT manager for any medium- to large-sized organization) and arrange for a 45-minute interview. Inform your interviewee that you are in interested in learning more about how the company manages scarce resources in IT project environments. When you meet with this individual, ask the following questions and take good notes:

   a. In what ways do time pressures and human resource constraints affect your project schedules?

   b. What are one or two examples of project situations in which resource constraints presented special challenges? How did you handle these situations? As you listen to the answer to this question, assess whether any of the concepts covered in this chapter (crashing, fast tracking, reallocation of resources, scope reduction) would characterize the strategies the project manager describes.

   c. In addition to human resources, what other kinds of resource constraints affect your ability to complete projects on time, within budget, and at the desired level of performance?

   d. What advice would you give regarding resource management to people who wish to become effective project managers?

   Prepare a two- to three-page report summarizing the interview and your observations. Include information about the company and the name and relevant background of your interviewee. Link your report to concepts from this chapter, but also demonstrate insight that goes beyond the chapter. In your report, include a photo of your team with the interviewee.

2. Gather a group of three to five classmates. Review the following case study about Crash City and work as a team to answer the questions at the end of the case and prepare a report of your findings.

Crash City creates integrated Web solutions, including hardware, software, training, and implementation, for companies in the Shreveport, Louisiana, area. Company representatives have just delivered a proposal to a medium-sized, vinyl-framed window manufacturer to create an internal Web site that will serve sales employees and customers. Their proposal includes an initial schedule, as shown below:

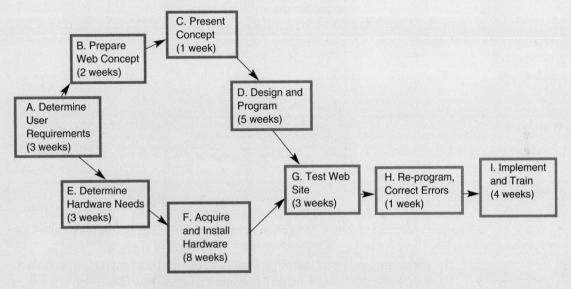

The following cost and resource information is included in the proposal:

Staff Category	Costs (Including Benefits)
User specialists	$50/hour
Web producers	$60/hour
Programmers	$40/hour
Hardware specialists	$70/hour

Begin with the assumption that all work is done in 40-hour workweeks and all staff members are dedicated full time to the project.

Activity	Duration in Calendar Weeks	Staff Requirements	Cost (Your Team will Calculate these Figures)
A. Determine user requirements	3 weeks	2 user specialists	
B. Prepare Web concept	2 weeks	2 Web producers	
C. Present Web concept	1 week	1 user specialist	
D. Design and program	5 weeks	3 programmers	$24,000
E. Determine hardware needs	3 weeks	1 hardware specialist	

Sample calculation:

5 weeks × 3 programmers × $40/hour × 40 hours = $24,000

(continued)

(continued)

Activity	Duration in Calendar Weeks	Staff Requirements	Cost (Your Team will Calculate these Figures)
F. Acquire and install hardware	8 weeks* (only 1 week of working time during this period)	1 hardware specialist	
G. Test Web site	3 weeks	1 user specialist, 1 Web producer, 1 programmer	
H. Re-program and correct errors	1 week	2 programmers	
I. Implement and train	4 weeks	1 user specialist, 2 Web producers, 1 hardware specialist	
Total project cost			

* Although the hardware acquisition and installation activity takes eight weeks, much of it involves waiting for the hardware to arrive. The actual work of the hardware specialist will take only one week of work time, spread out over eight weeks.

Your first task is to complete the calculations for activity costs and total project cost in the right-hand column of the above table. After doing so, consider the following:

The clients are very interested in Crash City's proposal, but find the current schedule undesirable in light of market pressures. They would like to have the Web site up and running in 20 weeks and they are willing to pay a $20,000 bonus to Crash City if it can deliver the project in this time frame. You and your team have been asked to analyze the situation and make a recommendation to the Crash City president. After a thorough cost assessment, you have uncovered the following information about ways to reduce the duration of the project:

- Crash City can hire an outside contractor to assist with Activity B, prepare Web concept. You have found someone who has special expertise in this area and who is available at an hourly rate of $100 per hour. With the addition of this outside contractor to work alongside the two in house Web producers, Crash City can complete the Web Concept task in one week.
- Crash City can add two more programmers to the Activity D, design and program, and complete it in four weeks (a one-week reduction). These two programmers are paid at the same rate as the others—$40 per hour.
- Crash City can spend less time talking with users at the front end, reducing Activity A, user requirements, by one week and eliminating one week's worth of cost.
- Crash City can perform Activity F, acquire and install hardware, in less time if the client company is willing to pay a premium price for factory expediting and transportation. The hardware can be delivered one week sooner if the client is willing to absorb an extra $8,000 in cost.
- Crash City can shorten the four weeks needed for Activity I, implement and train, to three weeks by treating training as a separate one-week activity and starting it right after testing. This change would add $4,000 to the total cost of the project. Implementation would become a three-week task and run concurrently with training.

Your team assignment:

a. Discuss and record all assumptions your team has made before proceeding further with your crashing evaluation. (You must make some assumptions!) Include these in your report.

b. Complete the activity cost table by calculating the cost of each activity and total cost for the entire schedule as it is initially planned.

c. Calculate a crash cost per week for each of the activities for which relevant information is presented above.

d. Assess the information presented here and make a recommendation to Crash City regarding schedule compression. Demonstrate that you have considered all of the options, highlighting the advantages and disadvantages of each. Consider costs as well as other variables such as quality or client satisfaction.

e. Prepare a Gantt chart or time-based network schedule reflecting your recommendations and contrasting them with the original schedule. See Exhibit 8.4 for an example.

f. Write a paragraph describing how your schedule would change if the hardware specialist were available only 50 percent of the time. What options would you have if this were the case? What could you do about it?

g. Prepare a report summarizing your results (include cost figures) and observations about the case and your solution.

Discussion Questions and Exercises

1. Imagine your boss has told you that you must compress a schedule for a product development project. Name and describe in your own words at least three strategies you could use. What would be the best way to present these to your boss?

2. A colleague who has not studied project management has asked you to give him your explanation of what crashing is. How would you explain it, in your own words, so that this colleague will understand it? Prepare an answer in only 75 words (or fewer), and include an example that has not been presented in this chapter.

3. Name at least two advantages and two challenges associated with fast tracking. Illustrate with examples other than those cited in the chapter. Bring in your own experience.

4. How does the critical chain differ from the critical path? Offer an explanation in your own words and illustrate graphically with a schedule example of your own creation.

5. Kingland Construction Co. has signed a contract to build a hotel on a mountaintop in Arizona. Leroy Kingland, who owns the company, is analyzing weekly costs he will incur during the life of the project. The initial project schedule sets the estimated duration at 24 weeks. Leroy has hired you as a consultant to assist him with decisions about crashing. He has secured a construction loan of $500,000 to cover his cash flow needs between progress payments from the customer, and it carries an interest rate of 0.2 percent per week. He will not repay the loan until the end of the project when he receives final payment from the customer. He also will pay $200 per week for construction insurance. Following some resource leveling, Leroy has determined that he will need 27 workers for the duration of the project. Their salaries, fully burdened for benefits, will result in a weekly cost of $45,000. Other costs to be incurred during the life of the project include rental fees for a construction trailer, portable toilets, and three trucks. Your assignment:

a. Calculate total cost per week for cost figures given above.

b. Conduct a Web search to determine weekly cost estimates for the construction trailer, portable toilets, and trucks. Describe how you conducted your search, cite your sources, and state the assumptions underlying your estimates. (For example, what type of portable toilet and how many will you rent?)

   c. Calculate a total cost per week for the project, combining the information provided with information you have gathered through your Web search.

   d. Prepare a consulting report for Mr. Kingland, advising him on how he can use
the information generated in Steps A, B, and C to make crashing decisions. Create an example to illustrate. Assume he has never heard of project crashing, and
use your own words.

6. An Australian movie director wishes to complete a surfing film and have it ready for
market before the beginning of the Southern Hemisphere's summer season. He determines that script writing is a three-month critical path activity with potential for crashing. His current plans involve using two young scriptwriters with minimal experience,
each of whom will be paid $4,000 per month. However, a more experienced script-
writer is available at $30,000 per month. The experienced scriptwriter works with two
savvy assistants whose salaries are $3,500 per month each. The director estimates that
he can reduce scriptwriting from three months to one month if he employs the senior
writer and the two assistants. What is the crash cost per month? Show your work. What
advice would you give to the director? What additional information would be useful?

7. It is the end of the second week of July. Kristin Anderson, the manager of a road
construction project, has noted in her contract with the city of Ketchum, Idaho, that
there will be a $15,000 per week penalty for every week the project extends past
its end-of-September due date. Additionally, the city has offered to pay a bonus of
$20,000 if her crew can finish the project by the end of the third week of September.
Ms. Anderson plans to start work at the beginning of the third week of July. The
mayor wishes to avoid problems with snow, which often arrives early because of
Ketchum's location at 5,853 feet (1,784 meters) above sea level. For the sake of simplicity, we assume exactly four weeks and 20 workdays for every month. The project
network, with normal times, is displayed below:

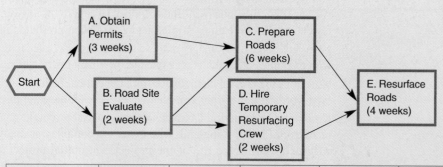

Activity	Normal Time	Crash Time	Normal Cost	Crash Cost	Crash Cost/Week
A. Obtain permits	3 weeks	2 weeks	$ 20,000	$ 32,000	
B. Evaluate	2 weeks	1 week	$ 10,000	$ 12,000	
C. Prepare	6 weeks	4 weeks	$100,000	$120,000	
D. Hire	2 weeks	1 week	$ 20,000	$ 25,000	
E. Resurface	4 weeks	2 weeks	$200,000	$250,000	

Remember: to
keep it simple,
assume 4 weeks
per month and
20 workdays per
month.

   a. Calculate the crash cost per week for each activity.

   b. Show the sequence of crashing decisions you would make to compress this project most cost effectively. (Recommendation: use the tabular approach, as shown

in this chapter.) Calculate total cost. Keep in mind that the penalty is incurred for every week past the end of September, and remember to consider the bonus.

c. Explain your rationale and describe how you would present the options to the Ketchum City Council.

8. You have been asked to manage a major IT project for which a preliminary schedule has been established. Based on historical data and your conversations with experienced company personnel, you estimated crash times and costs. It is fortunate you did this extra work because the project sponsor has now asked you to reduce the duration of the project. The current schedule and crashing data are shown below:

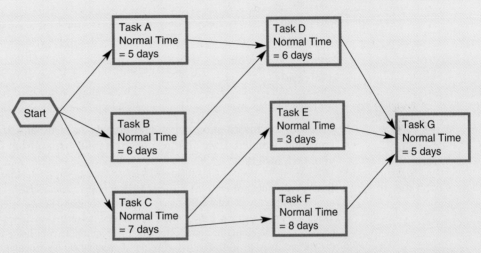

Task	Normal Time	Crash Time	Normal Cost (in Thousands)	Crash Cost (in Thousands)	Crash Cost per Day
A.	5 days	2 days	$100	$205	
B.	6 days	3 days	$140	$200	
C.	7 days	5 days	$140	$200	
D.	6 days	2 days	$100	$340	
E.	3 days	1 day	$120	$200	
F.	8 days	5 days	$580	$700	
G.	5 days	3 days	$400	$660	

a. Calculate crash cost per day for each task.

b. Draw a time-based network of the project with normal times.

c. The sponsor has asked you to reduce the project to 17 days, down from 20. Using a matrix similar to the one below, show the crashing decisions you would make by entering your answers into the first three empty columns. If the overhead cost for this project is $125,000 per day, would it be cost effective to take any of these crashing actions? Explain your answer.

d. Continue crashing the project until the cost of crashing exceeds the marginal gain associated with eliminating overhead cost ($125,000 per day).

e. Assume you have begun the project under the fully crashed schedule and you are now at the end of day 6. Tasks A and C are finished, but Task B will require two more days of work. What corrective crashing decisions might you make to increase the likelihood you can complete the schedule within the remaining 14 days? Are there any tasks you might consider uncrashing? What other actions could you consider?

Number of Days Crashed

Path	0	1	2	3	4	5	6	7
A-D-G								
B-D-G								
C-E-G								
C-F-G								
Activity(ies) crashed								
Crash cost								

9. Consider the information below and prepare to write an explanation for the phenomenon depicted. Base your response on information from this chapter as well as your own insight.

Eric Verzuh, author of *The Fast Forward MBA in Project Management,*[27] conducted a study of project complexity at Adobe Systems, a software company headquartered in San Jose, California. He found that when the number of software developers assigned to a project increased beyond a certain point, the complexity and time required to coordinate the project and handle rework increased as well. The graph below shows that for a particular type of project, using two developers instead of one can dramatically reduce project duration. However, the marginal effect of adding a third developer is not as great, and returns diminish after that.

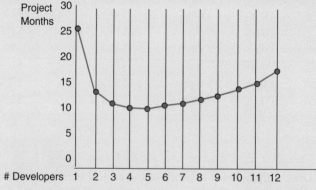

Source: E. Verzuh, *The Fast-Forward MBA in Project Management* (New York: Wiley and Sons, 1999). Reprinted with permission from John Wiley & Sons, Inc.

a. Write a paragraph explaining how and why such a phenomenon could occur, using concepts from this chapter and your own insight.

b. Write a paragraph explaining what you would say to a key decision maker about this phenomenon. Assume this person is attempting to persuade you to add resources to a programming activity.

[27] E. Verzuh, *The Fast-Forward MBA in Project Management* (New York: Wiley and Sons, 1999).

10. Based on the Crash City scenario in Team Activity 2, use Microsoft Project or another software package to display the initial (uncrashed) project in a network and Gantt format. Set the software to "Show Link Labels" (see Appendix A, "Quick Guide to Using Microsoft Project," at the end of this book). Then, revise the schedule using precedence diagramming features, as follows:

a. Separate Activity F, acquire and install hardware, into three components:
- F-1: Negotiate with vendors and place order: .5 week (2.5 days).
- F-2: Wait for hardware to arrive: 7 weeks (no human resources required).
- F-3: Install hardware: .5 week (2.5 days).

Schedule these three activities such that F-2 can start one week after F-1 starts and F-3 can start immediately after F-2 is finished.

b. Change the schedule to show that Activity E, determine hardware needs, can start two weeks after the start of Activity A, determine user requirements.

c. Change the schedule to show that Activity H, re-program and correct errors, can start two weeks after the start of Activity G, test Web site.

d. Print your initial and revised Microsoft Project (or other software) schedules in network and Gantt views. Include task link labels (e.g., SS +1) on connecting arrows. Write a few sentences highlighting your observations about the managerial implications of this new schedule.

11. You have developed an early-start schedule for a seven-month ERP programming and implementation project for Quigg Brothers Construction Co. You note that there will be a heavy human resource need at the beginning of the project, and requirements will taper off dramatically after the first three months. Would it be worth your effort to try to level the resource needs, or would you just leave the schedule the way it is? Explain your answer and discuss any additional information that would assist you in making a recommendation.

12. A project manager at Kippy Jo's Cosmetics wishes to determine total human resource needs for an upcoming marketing campaign involving three of the company's products. Each product will be marketed through a different medium. Precedence relationships for project tasks, along with resource information, are highlighted in the table below:

Task	Duration (Days)	Immediate Predecessor	Resource Requirement (# Staff Members Required per Day)
A. Research, Product 1	3	None	4
B. Research, Product 2	2	None	5
C. Research, Product 3	3	None	6
D. Create Web site, Product 1	2	A	6
E. Prepare TV ads, Product 1	9	A	5
F. Prepare print ads, Product 2	3	B	5
G. Purchase and place TV ads, Product 2	3	B	2
H. Purchase and place print ads, Product 3	2	C	4
I. Project completion milestone	0	D, E, F, G, H	0

a. Draw an AON and time-based network diagram and identify the critical path in each one.

b. Calculate the daily resource loads for the project. (You may wish to use Excel although this problem is small enough to lend itself to a manual approach.)

c. Scenario 1, Time Constrained: Revise the schedule to smooth resource requirements without changing the project's duration. No task splitting or task compression (crashing) will be allowed. Write a few sentences about the managerial implications of this revised schedule.

d. Scenario 2, Resource Constrained: Return to the original early-start schedule and assume the number of staff members has been limited to 10. Reschedule the project to accommodate this constraint. As in Part C, you may not split or compress tasks. You will have to change the project's end date, so your goal will be to meet resource constraints with the shortest possible project duration. Write a few sentences about the managerial implications of this schedule.

13. A new-venture electronics firm is setting up its production facilities in Mexicali, Baja California, Mexico, located just south of the border with the United States. Product design is complete. The plant manager has hired 30 people, who possess mostly interchangeable skills, to prepare the plant. He has asked you to help him with resource allocation. He is unsure if he can meet the 30-week deadline, given his resource constraint. Schedule and resource information are shown below.

Task	Immediate Predecessor(s)	Duration (Weeks)	People Required per Week
A. Select site	None	4	5
B. Design process	None	5	10
C. Assess materials needs	None	4	20
D. Arrange lease	A	4	10
E. Determine skill requirements	B	6	5
F. Purchase equipment	B	3	10
G. Establish supplier relationships	C	7	15
H. Order materials	G	8	10
I. Hire employees	D, E	5	5
J. Test equipment	F	5	25
K. Set up facility	I, J	6	20
L. Train employees	H, K	4	25
M. Ramp up production	L	4	30

a. Prepare an early-start schedule graph or Gantt chart and produce a histogram to show the resource loads.

b. Create a revised schedule graph or Gantt chart, with accompanying histogram, to address the resource constraint of 30 people.

c. Provide a short explanation for the plant manager about how you derived your revised schedule and what you recommend.

14. You are managing a new product development effort for the mixing division of a commercial kitchen equipment manufacturer. You have a team of five people, each of whom has special expertise. These people have been assigned specific tasks,

as shown. They will, of course, draw upon the resources of other people, but each one holds ultimate accountability for one or more activities. An individual must be available for the duration of an assigned activity and cannot do two things at once. No activity splitting will be allowed. Your initial schedule, along with team assignment information, is shown below.

Activity	Time (Weeks)	Immediate Predecessor	Team Member Responsible
A. Determine client needs	4	None	Preston
B. Conceptual design	5	A	Alesha
C. Manufacturing input	3	A	Davis
D. Marketing plan	5	B	Jack
E. Sales force input	4	D	Preston
F. Detailed design	4	B, C	Jack
G. Physical mock-up	3	F	Bett
H. Client review	3	G	Preston
I. Determine materials needs	3	F	Davis
J. Identify suppliers	4	I	Davis
K. Design manufacturing system	6	G	Davis
L. Ramp up production	4	J, K	Bett
M. Project completion milestone	0	E, H, L	____

a. Prepare two network diagrams, one in AON format, and one in early-start time-based AOA format. (If you need a dummy activity for the time-based AOA format, you might benefit from reviewing the appendix on dummy activities at the end of Chapter 7.)

b. Use the critical path algorithm to calculate ES, EF, LS, LF, free float and total float. Enter these figures next to the task boxes in your AON schedule. Highlight the critical path.

c. Reschedule the project to remove resource conflicts; find a minimum time schedule that does not require any of your team members to be in two different places at the same time.

d. Identify the critical chain.

e. Identify points where you think the schedule is vulnerable to uncertainties.

f. Show where you would place feeding buffers and resource buffers.

g. Write a paragraph explaining the results of your analysis. Consider your audience to be the project sponsor.

References

Brooks, F.P. *The Mythical Man-Month.* Boston: Addison-Wesley, 1995.

CH2MHILL. *Project Delivery.* Englewood, CO: CH2M Hill, 1996.

Clark, T.B.; W.E. Riggs; and R.H. Deane. "Guidelines to Compressing Project Schedules for Profit." *Business,* January–March (1985), pp. 18–21.

DeMarco, T., and T. Lister. *Peopleware: Productive Projects and Teams,* 2nd ed. New York: Dorset House, 1999.

Ford, D.N., and J.D. Sterman. "Overcoming the 90% Syndrome: Iteration Management in Concurrent Development Projects." *Concurrent Engineering: Research and Applications* 11, no. 3 (2003), pp. 177–86.

Goldratt, E., and J. Fox. *The Goal.* Great Barrington, MA: The North River Press, 1996.

Goldratt, E. *Critical Chain.* Great Barrington, MA: The North River Press, 1997.

Iansiti, M., and A. MacCormack. *Living on Internet Time.* Boston: Harvard Business School Publications, 1996.

Newbold, R.C. *Project Management in the Fast Lane: Applying the Theory of Constraints.* Boca Raton, FL: St. Lucie Press/APICS, 1998.

Project Management Institute. *Project Management Body of Knowledge.* Newtown Square, PA: Project Management Institute, 2004.

Raz, T.; R. Barnes; and D. Dvir. "A Critical Look at Critical Chain Project Management." *Project Management Journal* 34, no. 4 (2003), pp. 24–32.

Schmitt, B., and R.J. Calatone. "Escalation of Commitment During New Product Development." *Journal of the Academy of Marketing Science* 30, no. 2, (2002), pp. 103–18.

Shellenbarger, S. "Multitasking Makes You Stupid." *The Wall Street Journal,* February 27, 2003, p. D1.

Smith, P.G., and D.G. Reinertsen. *Developing Products in Half the Time.* New York: Van Nostrand-Reinhold, 1998.

Verzuh, E. *The Fast Forward MB in Project Management.* New York: Wiley and Sons, 1999.

Wiest, J.D., and F.K. Levy. *A Management Guide to PERT/CPM.* Englewood Cliffs, NJ: Prentice Hall, 1977.

Wilkens, T.T. "Critical Path, or Chain, or Both?" *PM Network* 14, no. 7 (2000), pp. 68–74.

Wheelwright, S., and K. Clark. *Revolutionizing Product Development: Quantum Leaps in Speed, Efficiency, and Quality.* New York: Free Press, 1992.

Chapter **Nine**

Monitoring and Controlling Project Performance

"Concentrate on finding your goal, then concentrate on reaching it."

Colonel Michael Friedsman

Chapter Learning Objectives

When you have mastered the material in this chapter, you should be able to:

- Prepare for the phenomena that can cause projects to detour from their plans.
- Design and manage a monitoring and control system based on effective project monitoring principles.
- Identify project-specific key performance indicators (KPIs) and develop systems for measuring and reporting them.
- Record earned value data, calculate variances and indices, and interpret the results in collaboration with project team members.
- Work with a team to modify project plans in response to variances.
- Design and manage a project change control system.

Project monitoring refers to any tracking system, from a simple checklist to sophisticated dashboard-style approaches, for identifying variances from the original plan. As part of the planning process, a project team should agree on the appropriate approach for monitoring key performance indicators (KPIs) during the life of the project. As we introduced in Chapter 1 and have emphasized throughout this book, these KPIs should represent a broad set of useful metrics with associated goals or targets. But monitoring is not enough. Even when the team has laid careful plans and endeavored to prepare for all possible contingencies, members still must be prepared to respond to gaps between KPI targets and actual performance. **Project control** refers to the set of processes, decisions, and actions involved in responding to project variances.

A project team also must develop and follow a **project change management** process for deciding when changes (e.g., addition of a new product feature) are appropriate and when to stay the course. Thus, in tandem with project control, project change management is an essential element of effective project delivery.

WHY PROJECT MONITORING AND CONTROL ARE NECESSARY

In an ideal world, project performance would be identical to the project plan. In reality, things seldom happen as anticipated. Several phenomena influence project execution and cause actual performance to depart from planned performance. Examples include **scope creep, Murphy's Law, Parkinson's Law, the student syndrome, Pareto's Law, escalation of commitment,** and **statistical variation among dependent events.** Effective project leaders and teams are aware of these and are prepared to collaborate in managing their effects.

Scope Creep

Scope creep describes the tendency for a project to grow beyond its initial size. It is caused by several factors, including team member enthusiasm, idle team members looking for ways to contribute during downtime, unanticipated issues discovered mid-project, and redefinition or clarification of customer needs. Closely related phenomena are **feature creep** (the tendency in technical environments for engineers to add features beyond what may be useful or marketable) and **quality creep** (the tendency for technical specialists to want to make a product incrementally better, often reaching beyond what is necessary in terms of specifications).[1] **Project change control systems,** introduced at the end of this chapter, offer a mechanism for controlling these types of project creep.

Murphy's Law

According to *Murphy's Law,* "Anything that can go wrong will go wrong."[2] (And some say Murphy was an optimist!) Although it is often used in humor, a great deal of truth is associated with Murphy's Law. Not all risks can be anticipated, but if project managers are vigilant about "looking for Murphy" they may be able to stem risks or dampen their effects by preparing for Murphy's inevitable delays and snags.

Parkinson's Law

C. Northcote Parkinson made the following observation: "Work expands so as to fill the time available for its completion."[3] In project environments, task duration estimates, especially if they are overly generous, can become self-fulfilling prophecies. Also, team member perceptions of activity float can lead them to dawdle over tasks longer than necessary. Consequently, noncritical tasks can become critical and jeopardize the project's target end date.

The Student Syndrome

Student syndrome[4] is the tendency for project team members to delay the start of their work until the last minute. If a team member sees float at the end of a task, he or she might not start working on it right away. Similar to Parkinson's Law, the student syndrome creates situations in which schedule buffers disappear and the critical path and critical chain are jeopardized.

---

[1] Feature creep and quality creep are sometimes called gold plating.

[2] A. Block, *Murphy's Law and Other Reasons Why Things Go Wrong* (New York: Price/Stern/Sloan, 1981).

[3] C.N. Parkinson, *The Law, Complete* (New York: Ballantine Books, 1979), p. 3.

[4] Goldratt identifies student syndrome as a major cause of project delays, but he was undoubtedly not the first to make the observation or coin the term. See E. Goldratt, *Critical Chain* (Great Barrington, MA: The North River Press, 1997).

Pareto's Law

Vilfredo Pareto, a 19th century Italian economist and sociologist, reflected on imbalanced distributions in general, and more specifically as they applied to societal wealth: He estimated that 80 percent of the people had 20 percent of the wealth and 20 percent of the people had 80 percent of the wealth.[5] The concept, also widely known as the 80-20 rule, has since been shown to apply to a number of phenomena in life. A commonly cited example is that a business often obtains 80 percent of its revenue from 20 percent of its customers. The project management application is as follows: 80 percent of project problems and delays are likely to be caused by 20 percent of project activities. An effective project monitoring system should focus on activities that carry the highest risks for delays, cost overruns, or performance challenges.

Escalation of Commitment

Human beings tend to continue pursuing failing courses of action, even when all signals point to the fallacy of the strategy. This phenomenon, known as escalation of commitment,[6] appears in projects of all types, with software projects receiving a good deal of notoriety.[7] When things keep going badly, project teams often increase their commitment to the current approach rather than seek a new approach. This can result in failure to correct good projects that need redirection, or failure to kill bad projects.[8] The monitoring system can have a significant influence on people's decisions to escalate or de-escalate commitment.[9]

Statistical Variation among Dependent Events

When a team executes dependent activities in a project schedule, it is possible some will be completed ahead of schedule and some will be completed behind schedule. On average, one might expect things to even out. But, unfortunately, late activities always delay subsequent activities, and early completions rarely benefit successor activities because team members hesitate to communicate with their handoff colleagues when they anticipate early completion.[10] Consequently, those performing successor activities are unable to capitalize on the opportunity to begin their work sooner.

PROJECT MONITORING PRINCIPLES

Different projects require different levels of monitoring detail. If you were planning a party you would probably not use the same monitoring tools you would for implementing a multimillion-dollar ERP system. Although the methods available

---

[5] He initially made the discovery when he observed that 20 percent of the pea pods in his garden produced 80 percent of the peas. V. Pareto, *The Rise and Fall of Elites: An Application of Theoretical Sociology* (New Brunswick, NJ: Transaction Publishers, 1991).

[6] B. Staw and J. Ross, "Knowing When to Pull the Plug," *Harvard Business Review* 65, no. 2 (1987), pp. 68–74.

[7] M. Keil, B.C.Y. Tan, K.K.Wei, T. Saarinen, F. Tuunainen, and A. Wassenaar, "A Cross-Cultural Study on Escalation of Commitment Behavior in Software Projects," *MIS Quarterly* 24, no. 2 (2000), pp. 299–325.

[8] I. Royer, "Why Bad Projects Are so Hard to Kill," *Harvard Business Review* 81, no. 2 (2003), pp. 48–56.

[9] G. McNamara, H. Moon, and P. Bromiley, "Banking on Commitment: Intended and Unintended Consequences of an Organization's Attempt to Attenuate Escalation of Commitment," *Academy of Management Journal* 43, no. 2 (2002), pp. 443–52.

[10] For more on this topic, see Goldratt, *Critical Chain*.

vary in their levels of sophistication, several attributes describe an effective monitoring system:

- *Identifies metrics relevant to the project.* A project manager and team must measure a balanced set of performance indicators. Of greatest priority will be metrics tied to project goals.[11]

- *Is built into the project plan.* A monitoring system cannot be an afterthought inserted into the management process after the project is underway. As part of the planning process, the team must establish performance metrics and baseline data as well as determine who will be responsible for keeping records, the frequency of reporting, and the level of detail or granularity of reporting.

- *Provides accurate information.* To effectively manage a project and make ongoing adjustments, the project manager and team must be able to trust that the performance information they receive is accurate. Otherwise, performance reports will go into a drawer and the reporting effort will be wasted.

- *Provides timely information.* Project data must be available to the project manager and team as soon as possible. Finding out in March that a task was two weeks behind schedule last December does not give the team the information it needs to take corrective action.

- *Facilitates management by exception.* Management by exception is a general approach for weeding important information from vast quantities of data and using threshold signals to determine when there is a problem. Statistical process control (SPC) is a good example of a management-by-exception tool—an operator or supervisor knows to become concerned only when data points fall outside control limits or exhibit certain patterns. Project managers can use similar concepts to manage by exception, making special note of performance when metrics fall outside preestablished parameters or reveal undesirable trends.

- *Is visible to team members.* The old saying "You get what you measure" applies here; if people know what is being measured and have ready access to the information, they are likely to behave in ways that keep performance on course.

- *Provides a basis for problem discovery and solution.* The monitoring system must be a problem-solving tool and not a "big brother is watching" mechanism that strikes fear into the hearts of participants. Also, if the team uses a monitoring system simply to comply with customer or sponsor requirements and does not use it to benefit the project, the effort is wasted. In either case, the data in the system are likely to be based on efforts aimed at self-protection and game playing, and no one is likely to believe or trust the results. Consequently, opportunities for using variance data to trigger root-cause analysis are lost, and monitoring becomes a pointless exercise.

PROJECT MONITORING TOOLS

Given a balanced set of metrics, the project team needs a process for gathering and consolidating data so key stakeholders can easily see how things are progressing and where problems or potential problems call for action. Many organizations have adopted a **dashboard** approach for this purpose. An example of a dashboard is the display panel in the cockpit of an airplane. It shows the pilot, in real time, metrics such

---

[11] N.F. Matta and R.N. Ashkenas, "Why Good Projects Fail Anyway," *Harvard Business Review* 81, no. 9 (2003), pp. 109–14.

EXHIBIT 9.1 **Example of a Project Dashboard**

Source: American Systems Project Control Panel, http://www.americansystems.com/Services/ProfessionalTechnicalITServices/RiskManagement/DownloadProjectControl
PanelDemo.htm. Reprinted with permission from American Systems.

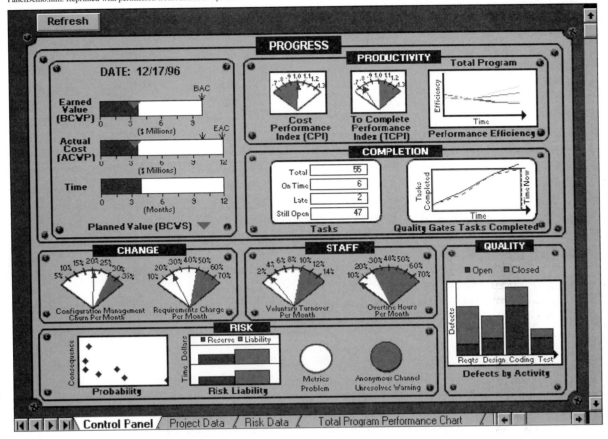

as altitude, coordinates, airspeed, wind velocity, temperature, and fuel levels. These are displayed in a way that allows the pilot to see, at a glance, how all systems are functioning and what is happening in the external environment. The idea of a dashboard is becoming increasingly popular in project environments, and several vendors have developed tools for aggregating data important to a project. Exhibit 9.1 shows an example of a project dashboard.

Although it is important to measure a broad set of project-specific metrics, time- and cost-related metrics are universal to all projects. Methods for measuring these universal indicators include **checklists, spreadsheets with variance data, Gantt chart tracking, percent-complete method,** and **earned value.** Each of these is discussed below, but earned value receives the greatest attention in this chapter.

Checklists

As the name implies, a checklist includes a list of activities, tasks, or work packages from the WBS and space for marking off each one as it is completed. Although its simplicity makes it attractive, a checklist is not sophisticated enough for large or complex projects. Also, it lacks a graphical dimension and consequently does not show relationships among activities. Still, it has its place. Exhibit 9.2 offers an example of a simple checklist that is probably sufficient for a small project.

EXHIBIT 9.2
Simple Checklist for Project Tracking
Example: Planning a Surprise Birthday Party for Your Sister

Task	Status
Prepare Guest List	✓
Send Invitations	✓
Prepare Menu	✓
Purchase Food	
Purchase Beverages	
Clean House	
Purchase Decorations	
Decorate House	
Invite Sister to Dinner	✓
Purchase Gifts	
Wrap Gifts	
Host Party	
Clean Up	

Spreadsheets with Variance Data

Many project teams find it useful to track performance metrics and variances with a spreadsheet such as that shown in Exhibit 9.3. One way to raise the level of sophistication is by adding colors to show the status of a deliverable or other WBS entity:

- Green shading means things are going as expected.
- Yellow shading indicates a caution that small variances could widen.
- Red shading indicates the deliverable or work package has run over budget, is behind schedule, or is challenged in other ways.
- Blue shading indicates the deliverable or work package is complete.

To make full use of a monitoring spreadsheet, the team should have access to a schedule with information about precedence relationships so members can use the two together during project status meetings.

Gantt Charts

Gantt charts, described in Chapters 7 and 8, can include tracking information. Exhibit 9.4 displays a Microsoft Project Gantt chart with progress indicators for an office remodel project. The darker horizontal line within each task bar represents the percent complete. For example, Task A is 100 percent complete because the dark bar runs the full length of the task bar.

A team can operate very effectively with a Gantt chart printed on large wall-mounted paper that allows members to collaboratively record updates manually. This approach seems to encourage problem solving more than IT-based information sharing. If the team combines this approach with periodic progress updates in spreadsheet and project scheduling software, it gains the benefit of a historical record as well. Exhibit 9.5 shows a project team involved in a community service project monitoring performance using a wall-mounted Gantt chart to record task completion updates and solve problems in real time.

EXHIBIT 9.3   Project Monitoring Spreadsheet with Variance Data

Office Renovation Project							
Task	**Estimated Duration**	**Start Date**	**Status**	**Schedule Variance**	**Budgeted Expense**	**Actual Expense to Date**	**Budget Variance**
							Negative = over budget. Positive = under budget
A. Design	3 weeks	12-Jan	Complete	On time	$ 10,000	$ 8,000	$ 2,000
B. Prepare temporary office	5 weeks	12-Jan	60% Complete	Behind schedule	$ 20,000	$ 18,000	To discuss at status meeting.
C. Order/ Purchase furniture	3 weeks	2-Feb	100% Complete	On time	$150,000	$190,000	–$40,000
D. Order/ Purchase artwork	4 weeks	2-Feb	100% Complete	On time	$ 20,000	$ 22,000	–$ 2,000
E. Relocate staff	1 week	16-Feb	Not started	Behind schedule. Wating for B.	$ 5,000		
F. Advertise construction contract	5 weeks	2-Feb	100% Complete	On time	$ 5,000	$ 4,000	$ 1,000
G. Review bids and select contractor	2 weeks	9-Mar	100% Complete	On time	$ 10,000	$ 3,000	$ 7,000
H. Move old furniture	.4 weeks	23-Feb	Not started	Behind schedule. Waiting for B, E.	$ 6,000		
I. Renovate	6 weeks	23-Mar	Not started	Behind schedule. Waiting for H.	$200,000		
J. Paint	1 week	4-May	Not started	Behind schedule.	$ 5,000		
K. Install carpet	1 week	11-May	Not started	Behind schedule.	$ 20,000		
L. Install new furniture	1.5 weeks	18-May	Not started	Behind schedule.	$ 10,000		
M. Hang art	.2 weeks	18-May	Not started	Behind schedule.	$ 4,000		
N. Move in	1.4 weeks	27-May	Not started	Behind schedule.	$ 6,000		
O. Office celebration	.2 weeks	7-Jun	Not Started	Behind schedule.	$ 4,000		

Today's Date: 10-April

EXHIBIT 9.4
Microsoft Project
Gantt Chart with
Progress Bars for
an Office Remodel
Project

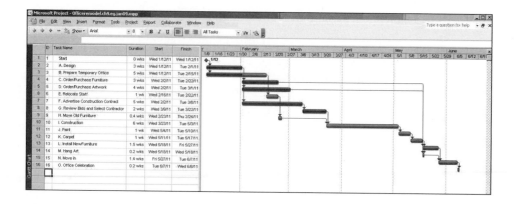

Percent-Complete Method

Applying the percent-complete method, a project team reports the number of time units (days, weeks, months) the project has been under way and compares it with the total time allotment for the project. For example, if a team has worked for 4 weeks on a 20-week project, members could say they were 25 percent complete. However, just because a team is 25 percent into a project's expected duration does not mean 25 percent of the work has been finished. The same would be true for a method that tracks only expenditures; do not assume a 50 percent budget expenditure implies 50 percent progress on project tasks. Although it has its weaknesses, the percent-complete method can work as a tracking tool for short-duration, low-priority projects. And it might be appropriate for work within a project that is difficult to monitor at a granular level (e.g., ongoing HR or accounting support for the project). Ongoing activity that is difficult to break into measurable subcomponents is known as **level of effort** work.

Earned Value Systems

Earned value systems address some of the limitations of other monitoring approaches and provide filtering capabilities that support a project team's need to identify the most important problem areas (i.e., exceptions). The comprehensive nature of earned

EXHIBIT 9.5
Project Team Using a
Wall-Mounted Gantt
Chart to Monitor
and Manually Update
Project Performance

value systems has contributed to their increasing popularity in industry.[12] The three fundamental metrics gathered during the life of a project include **planned value** (PV), **actual cost** (AC), and **earned value** (EV). **Earned value reports** combine these metrics into tables and graphical displays, and they are the basis for several variance and index calculations.

The U.S. Department of Defense introduced earned value concepts in 1967 when it began requiring its contractors to follow new project tracking rules.[13] As a formal tool, earned value is probably best applied to large or complex projects. As the basis for a conceptual framework for understanding project performance, its potential application is much broader.

Exhibit 9.6 shows two forms for the three fundamental metrics used in earned value systems, offering terminology most widely used today, as well as older, military-based acronyms.[14] In the remainder of this chapter, we use the terms and acronyms shown in the left hand column of Exhibit 9.6. Variance and index calculations derived from these metrics are described in Exhibit 9.7.

Exhibit 9.8 shows two generic examples of possible earned value scenarios. These offer perspective on how different combinations and patterns of PV, AC, and EV produce different variances. In Example A, the project is *over budget* because EV is less than AC. This reveals that the team has spent more than the planned value (PV) on work

---

[12] F. T. Anbari, "Earned Value Project Management Method and Extensions," *Project Management Journal* 34, no. 4 (2003), pp. 12–23; and E.H. Kim, W.G. Wells, and M.R. Duffey, "A Model for Effective Implementation of Earned Value Management Methodology," *International Journal of Project Management* 21, no. 5 (2003), pp. 375–82.

[13] It was initially called Cost/Schedule Control Systems Criteria (C/S CSC) and included more than just earned value concepts. Earned value has emerged as the most universally applicable idea within C/S CSC.

[14] Project Management Institute, *A Guide to the Project Management Body of Knowledge* (Newtown Square, PA: Project Management Institute, 2008); and Project Management Institute, *Practice Standard for Earned Value Management* (Newtown Square, PA: Project Management Institute, 2005).

EXHIBIT 9.6
Earned Value Terms

Currently Used Term	Military Term	Definition
Planned value (PV)	Budgeted cost of work scheduled (BCWS)	A future-oriented forecast. The amount the project team plans to have spent at any given project date, given all of the activities it expects to complete by that point in time. The ending PV represents the total project budget, which is known as Budget at Completion or BAC.
Actual cost (AC)	Actual cost of work performed (ACWP)	The actual, cumulative expenditures up to a specified date in the project. The ending value of AC is the total actual cost of the project.
Earned value (EV)	Budgeted cost of work performed (BCWP)	The value of the work completed up to a specified date in the project, based on the *initial value* specified for each deliverable or work package during the budgeting phase. (Disregards actual cost.)

EXHIBIT 9.7   **Earned Value Variance and Index Definitions and Formulas**

Earned Value Metric	Formula	What This Metric Tells Us
Cost variance (CV)	Earned value − Actual cost or EV − AC	What is the gap between the value of the work we have performed and what we have actually spent to achieve it? Negative values indicate poor performance; the project is over budget. Positive values indicate good performance. However, a large positive cost variance suggests potentially serious errors in estimating and a misallocation of resources. Small variances within prespecified tolerance limits generally should not raise serious inquiry but indicate a need to wait and see.
Cost variance % (CV%)	Cost variance/Earned value or CV/EV	What is the percentage relationship between the cost variance and the value of the work completed to date? Positive values are good; negative values indicate poor performance.
Schedule variance (SV)	Earned value − Planned value or EV − PV	What is the gap between the progress we have actually made and the progress we planned to have made by this point in the project? Negative values indicate poor performance; the project is behind schedule. Although positive values indicate good performance, they should not be ignored if they are significant. Perhaps there have been errors of omission or perhaps resources are being wasted. Small variances within prespecified tolerance limits generally should not raise serious inquiry but indicate a need to wait and see.
Schedule variance % (SV %)	Schedule variance/Planned value or SV/PV	What is the percentage relationship between schedule variance and the value of the work we intended to have completed to date? Positive values are good; negative values indicate poor performance.
Cost performance index (CPI)	Earned value/Actual cost or EV/AC	A ratio indicator of cost performance in relation to earned value where a value of 1 indicates performance to plan. A CPI greater than 1 indicates good performance and a CPI less than 1 indicates poor performance.
Schedule performance index (SPI)	Earned value/Planned value or EV/PV	A ratio indicator of schedule performance in relation to earned value where a value of 1 indicates performance to plan. An SPI greater than 1 indicates good performance and an SPI less than 1 indicates poor performance.
Budget at completion (BAC)	Final or end-of-project value of PV	Specifies the initial budget for the entire project based on planned expenditures.
Estimate at completion$_{(cost)}$ (EAC$_{cost}$)	Budget at completion/Cost performance index or BAC/CPI	What is the final cost of the project likely to be if cost performance continues in the current pattern? There are other formulas for EAC cost, which we do not present here (see PMI's *Practice Standard for Earned Value Management*).
Revised duration or Estimate at completion$_{(time)}$ (EAC$_{time}$)	Planned project duration/SPI*	If schedule performance continues as it has, how long will it take to complete this project?
To-complete performance index (TCPI)	Work remaining/Budget remaining or (BAC − EV)/(BAC−AC)	From the data date forward, what level of performance is needed to complete the project within the baseline budget?

*In *Practice Standard for Earned Value Management* (Newtown Square, PA: Project Management Institute, 2005), PMI uses the following, more cumbersome formula: EAC$_{time}$ = (BAC/SPI)/(BAC/time units forecast for project duration). This is algebraically equivalent to (time units forecast for project duration/SPI), which is much simpler.

EXHIBIT 9.8
Interpreting Earned Value Carts (Generic Examples)

Example A: Over Budget and Behind Schedule

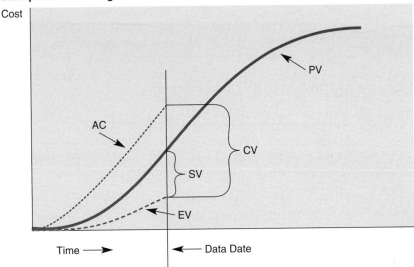

Example B: Ahead of Schedule and Under Budget

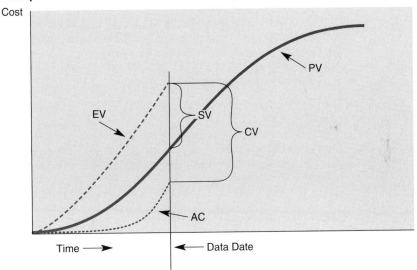

completed so far. Additionally, the project in Example A is behind schedule because EV at the data date is less than planned value (PV). **Data date** refers to the point in time at which the measurements were taken. In Example B, the project is under budget because EV is greater than AC. And it is ahead of schedule because EV is greater than PV. There are two other possible combinations, which we have not shown here. It is possible for a project to be ahead of schedule and over budget or to be behind schedule and under budget.

Studies of hundreds of military projects employing earned value methods have shown that project performance at the 10 to 20 percent complete stage is highly predictive of actual total project costs and complete dates.[15] These results show the power of the early warnings earned value systems can provide. Unfortunately, the fact that project performance did not change from what it was in the early stages of these projects suggests that people in these studies were using earned value as a reporting system and not as a problem-solving tool.[16]

APPLYING EARNED VALUE CONCEPTS

To demonstrate how earned value works in project settings, we present two examples. Both emphasize not only the EV calculations but how the data are combined with team observations to create a comprehensive picture of project status. Following these examples, we discuss some of the realities of earned value implementation and offer suggestions based on best practice.

Saskatoon Floors: Earned Value Example with a Linear Schedule

Jake Cheha, an entrepreneur in Saskatchewan, has recently purchased Saskatoon Floors, Ltd., from his former employer. He has worked in all aspects of the business but has never been responsible for managing an entire flooring project from start to finish. He has decided to apply earned value methods to his first job involving a $15,000 (Canadian) fixed-price contract to remove and replace the flooring in the public spaces of a downtown hotel that was built in the 1930s. The owner of the hotel has purchased all the tile and carpet materials and has them on site. Jake's only costs will be for labor. He wants to manage time and money to maximize his profits (currently estimated at $6,000) and establish the credibility of his time estimates to ensure future business.

Exhibit 9.9 displays a Gantt chart for the project schedule. Because the floors cannot be occupied by any more than one activity at a time, there can be no parallel paths

[15] Q.W. Fleming and J.M. Koppelman, *Earned Value Project Management* (Newtown Square, PA: Project Management Institute, 2005).

[16] D. Christensen and C. Templine, "EAC Evaluation Methods: Do They Still Work?" *Acquisition Review Quarterly* 9 (2002), pp. 105–16.

EXHIBIT 9.9 **Excel-Based Gantt Chart for Saskatoon Hotel Flooring Project Plan**

Activity	Day 1	2	3	4	5	6	7	8	9
A. Remove existing flooring and haul away	$1,000								
B. Prepare and level floors		$1,000							
C. Lay out tile design			$1,000						
D. Lay tile, grout, clean up				$1,000	$1,000	$1,000	$1,000	$1,000	
E. Lay carpet									$1,000
Planned Value (PV) (Cumulative)	$1,000	$2,000	$3,000	$4,000	$5,000	$6,000	$7,000	$8,000	$9,000

in this schedule. Also, there is a necessary overnight drying time between Activity B (prepare) and Activity C (lay out tile design). Jake has other jobs running concurrently, but he is giving the hotel project highest priority. This means that if workers from other jobs are available, he will assign them to the hotel project wherever activity crashing (see Chapter 8) seems appropriate.

During the first six days of the project, Jake has tracked three earned value metrics and kept a performance log, as shown in Exhibit 9.10. Building on this information, he has calculated earned value for each day of the project, as shown below. (Recall that EV represents the value of work accomplished based on its original budget (PV),

EXHIBIT 9.10 **Performance Log for Saskatoon Hotel Flooring Project**

Day	Planned Cost by Day	Planned Cost, Cumulative	Actual Cost by Day	Actual Cost, Cumulative	Progress	Comments and Observations
1	$1,000	$1,000	$1,500	$1,500	A. 100% complete B. 20% complete	Activity A was finished in half a day because extra workers were available from other projects. This made it possible to begin Task B earlier than planned. Added cost of $500 reflects compensation for a larger crew for Activity A, and also because B was started earlier than expected. But only minimal progress was made on Activity B.
2	$1,000	$2,000	$1,500	$3,000	A. 100% complete B. 40% complete	Activity B progressed more slowly than expected because some of the subfloor had rotted and required replacement. This added unexpected cost of $500.
3	$1,000	$3,000	$ 500	$3,500	A. 100% complete B. 100% complete	Activity B was finished by mid-day, but Activity C could not start because the leveling material had to dry overnight. Idle workers were sent to other jobs.
4	$1,000	$4,000	$1,000	$4,500	A. 100% complete B. 100% complete C. 50% complete	Activity C was started and nearly completed when the customer representative changed her mind, requiring considerable rework.
5	$1,000	$5,000	$2,000	$6,500	A. 100% complete B. 100% complete C. 100% complete D. 20% complete	Activity C was complete by mid-day with the help of some crashing at extra cost. Crewmembers worked overtime to catch up with Activity D. They made good progress but the overtime pay added to expense.
6	$1,000	$6,000	$1,500	$8,000	A. 100% complete B. 100% complete C. 100% complete D. 30% complete	To get Activity D back on track, the crew worked overtime at an added cost, but some problems with tile matching created unexpected delays and rework.

regardless of how much it actually costs or when it actually occurs.) Here are the EV calculations for the first six days of the Saskatoon flooring project:

Day 1 EV Calculations

Activity	Planned Value	Percent Complete	Earned Value
A	$1,000	100%	= $1,000
B	$1,000	20%	= .2 × $1,000 = $200

Total EV Day 1 = $1,000 + $200 = $1,200

Day 2 EV Calculations
(EV of previously completed activities carries forward.)

Activity	Planned Value	Percent Complete	Earned Value
A	$1,000	100%	= $1,000
B	$1,000	40%	= .4 × $1,000 = $400

Total EV Day 2 = $1,000 + $400 = $1,400

Day 3 EV Calculations
(EV of previously completed activities carries forward.)

Activity	Planned Value	Percent Complete	Earned Value
A	$1,000	100%	= $1,000
B	$1,000	100%	= $1,000

Total EV Day 3 = $1,000 + $1,000 = $2,000

Day 4 EV Calculations
(EV of previously completed activities carries forward.)

Activity	Planned Value	Percent Complete	Earned Value
A	$1,000	100%	= $1,000
B	$1,000	100%	= $1,000
C	$1,000	50%	= .5 × $1,000 = $500

Total EV Day 4 = $1,000 + $1,000 + $500 = $2,500

Day 5 EV Calculations
(EV of previously completed activities carries forward.)

Activity	Planned Value	Percent Complete	Earned Value
A	$1,000	100%	= $1,000
B	$1,000	100%	= $1,000
C	$1,000	100%	= $1,000
D	$5,000	20%	= .2 × $5,000 = $1,000

Total EV Day 5 = $1,000 + $1,000 + $1,000 + $1,000 = $4,000

Day 6 EV Calculations
(EV of previously completed activities carries forward.)

Activity	Planned Value	Percent Complete	Earned Value
A	$1,000	100%	= $1,000
B	$1,000	100%	= $1,000
C	$1,000	100%	= $1,000
D	$5,000	30%	= .3 × $5,000 = $1,500

Total EV Day 6 = $1,000 + $1,000 + $1,000 + $1,500 = $4,500

EXHIBIT 9.11

Planned Value versus Earned Value: Excel-Based Gantt Chart for Saskatoon Hotel Flooring Project after Six Days of Work

	Activity	Day 1	2	3	4	5	6	7	8	9
Planned Value	A. Remove existing flooring and haul away (PV)	$1,000								
Earned Value	A. Remove existing flooring and haul away (EV)	$1,000	$1,000	$1,000	$1,000	$1,000	$1,000			
Planned Value	B. Prepare and level floors (PV)		$1,000							
Earned Value	B. Prepare and level floors (EV)	$200	$400	$1,000	$1,000	$1,000	$1,000			
Planned Value	C. Lay out tile design (PV)			$1,000						
Earned Value	C. Lay out tile design (EV)				$500	$1,000	$1,000			
Planned Value	D. Lay tile, grout, clean up (PV)				$1,000	$1,000	$1,000	$1,000	$1,000	
Earned Value	D. Lay tile, grout, clean up (EV)					$1,000	$1,500			
Planned Value	E. Lay carpet (PV)									$1,000
Earned Value	E. Lay carpet (EV)									
	Incremental Planned Value	$1,000	$1,000	$1,000	$1,000	$1,000	$1,000	$1,000	$1,000	$1,000
	Cumulative Planned Value (PV)	$1,000	$2,000	$3,000	$4,000	$5,000	$6,000	$7,000	$8,000	$9,000
	Incremental Actual Cost	$1,500	$1,500	$500	$1,000	$2,000	$1,500			
	Cumulative Actual Cost (AC)	$1,500	$3,000	$3,500	$4,500	$6,500	$8,000			
	Cumulative Earned Value (EV)	$1,200	$1,400	$2,000	$2,500	$4,000	$4,500			

The shading intensity differentiates planned work period versus actual work period for each activity. Also, the EV figures shown to the right of planned or actual activity bars represent amounts carried forward after work on an activity has been completed.

A summary of EV calculations for the flooring project is displayed at the bottom of the Gantt chart in Exhibit 9.11. Shaded areas in EV rows in Exhibit 9.11 indicate the period during which work *actually* was performed on an activity, allowing for a comparison with the time period during which it was *initially scheduled*, shaded in a different color. Exhibit 9.12 depicts all three metrics, PV, AC, and EV, graphically.

Evaluating the Flooring Project

As shown in Exhibit 9.12, the flooring project appears to have gotten out of control. The three earned value metrics, PV, AC, and EV, have continued to diverge from each other during the first six days of the project, despite Jake's efforts to keep things on track. The amount of work accomplished is less than what Jake had planned to complete by the end of the sixth day. Making matters worse, the work he has completed has cost him more than he had estimated. He can put these contrasts

EXHIBIT 9.12
Earned Value Graph for Saskatoon Hotel Flooring Project

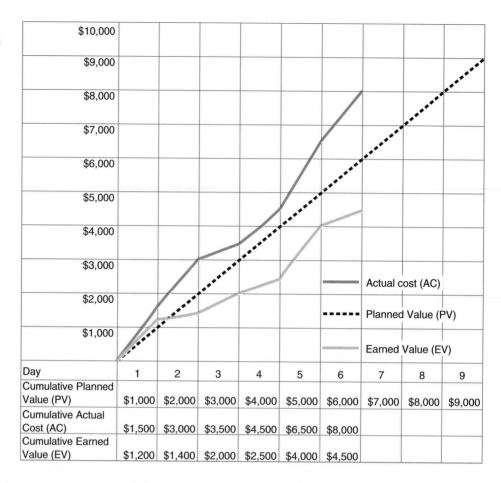

Day	1	2	3	4	5	6	7	8	9
Cumulative Planned Value (PV)	$1,000	$2,000	$3,000	$4,000	$5,000	$6,000	$7,000	$8,000	$9,000
Cumulative Actual Cost (AC)	$1,500	$3,000	$3,500	$4,500	$6,500	$8,000			
Cumulative Earned Value (EV)	$1,200	$1,400	$2,000	$2,500	$4,000	$4,500			

into earned value terminology by calculating key variances and indices for day 6. These are:[17]

Cost variance (CV) = EV − AC = $4,500 − $8,000 = −$3,500

Cost variance % = CV/ EV = −$3,500 / $4,500 = −.7778 (about 78%)

Schedule variance (SV) = EV − PV = $4,500 − $6,000 = −$1,500

Schedule variance % = SV / PV = −$1,500 / $6,000 = −.25 (25%)

Cost performance index (CPI) = EV / AC = $4,500 / $8,000 = .5625 (about 56%)

Scheduled performance index (SPI) = EV / PV = $4,500 / $6,000 = .75

Budget at completion (BAC) = Final PV = $9,000

Estimate at completion (EAC_{cost}) = BAC / CPI = $9,000 / .5625 = $16,000

Revised duration (EAC_{time}) = Planned duration/SPI = 9 days / .75 = 12 days

To-complete performance index (TCPI) = (BAC−EV) / (BAC − AC)
= ($9,000 − $4,500) / ($9,000 − $8,000) = 4.5

The calculations shown above reinforce our visual assessments from the graph displayed in Exhibit 9.12. The project is over budget and behind schedule. If things

[17] Rounded to four places to the right of the decimal.

continue as they have been, the project's final cost (EAC) will be $16,000, leaving Jake with a loss on his fixed-price $15,000 contract with the hotel. Also, the project is likely to require 12 days, exceeding Jake's nine-day promised delivery date and potentially delaying the hotel's reopening. If Jake wants to put the project back on track, his crew will need to work at over four times their previous efficiency, based on the TCPI figure, which is probably impossible.

But earned value figures do not tell the complete story, and the performance log presented in Exhibit 9.10 offers important information for Jake. In retrospect, he should have inspected the subflooring for rot before making his estimates or signing the contract. And he should have renegotiated the contract when the customer had a change of mind about the tile layout. Also, Jake should have inspected the tiles to be sure they all matched before he finalized the contract. Jake must take some responsibility for possible errors in estimation, crew selection, and project management. Given that he instituted EV methods on this project as a learning opportunity, we can say that Jake has probably captured quite a few lessons for application in future projects. EV methods allowed him to see his errors more clearly and to appreciate that careful vetting of contract details and quicker reactions to early variances would have produced a better result.

The flooring example shows an application of earned value terminology and calculations. However, it does not represent the complexity of a typical project with a network schedule involving multiple paths. The following example has these features.

Advanced Example: Earned Value with a Multiple-Path Schedule

This project involves the physical assets portion of a larger project to close a manufacturing plant in China and transfer production of a family of electrical devices to a new plant that has not yet been constructed in Malaysia (an actual project executed by a French multinational company). The company initiated this project to take advantage of major tax incentives and subsidies from the Malaysian government, as well as attractive wage rates. Some equipment from the China site will be moved, but the Malaysian plant also needs some new equipment. The full project involves many other deliverables (such as knowledge transfer, supply chain reconfiguration, information systems, human resource activities, and so on), but we limit our focus to the physical assets component of the project. The deliverables for this portion of the project, each of which has its own set of work packages not shown here, are listed below in Exhibit 9.13 and displayed as a network schedule in AON (activity-on-node) form in Exhibit 9.14. Calendar time estimates for deliverables are based on the project team's initial assumptions about the number of people assigned to each one, the complexity of work packages, and waiting time incorporated into the calendar. The team has given careful consideration to sequential relationships.

The project team converted the AON diagram in Exhibit 9.14 to a time-based network, as shown in Exhibit 9.15. This network is very similar to the ones we presented for resource allocation decisions in Chapter 8. In this case, however, the resources are planned expense dollars. Dashed lines represent float.

At the bottom of Exhibit 9.15 are two rows showing monthly and cumulative planned expenditures (PV). For the sake of this example, assume the expenditure rate for each deliverable is linear. Even if it is not exactly linear in reality, the assumption provides a reasonable approximation in many cases. (However, if a long-duration activity has an extremely lumpy PV profile, we recommend splitting it into two or more subactivities, each with a different spending rate.) We can also

EXHIBIT 9.13   Major Deliverables for Physical Assets Portion of Plant Relocation Project

Deliverable	Calendar Time Estimate	Immediate Predecessor (s)	Cost Estimate	Monthly Spending Rate
A. Purchase land and obtain permits	4 months	None	$ 80,000 (subsidized by Malaysian government)	$ 20,000/month
B. Remove usable manufacturing equipment from closure site	2 months	None	$ 50,000	$ 25,000/month
C. Design new plant	2 months	A	$ 60,000	$ 30,000/month
D. Construct new plant in Malaysia	12 months	C	$2,400,000	$200,000/month
E. Move old manufacturing equipment from China site to receiving site, and perform repairs and upgrades	4 months	B	$ 120,000	$ 30,000/month
F. Remove nonmanufacturing equipment and other materials from China site	4 months	B	$ 40,000	$ 10,000/month
G. Upgrade product designs for Malaysian site	6 months	A	$ 90,000	$ 15,000/month
H. Purchase new manufacturing equipment and await delivery	9 months	G	$ 360,000	$ 40,000/month
I. Redistribute, sell, recycle, or dispose of nonmanufacturing assets	3 months	F	$ 300,000 (net cost after equipment re-sale)	$100,000/month
J. Install and integrate new and old equipment at Malaysian site	3 months	D, E, H	$ 120,000	$ 40,000/month

present information about this project in a spreadsheet-based Gantt chart, as shown in Exhibit 9.16.

The plant relocation project has progressed through month 7. Actual expenditures for months 1 through 7, by deliverable, are shown in the comparative Gantt chart in Exhibit 9.17.[18]

By comparing PV and AC for the end of month 7 in Exhibits 9.16 and 9.17, members of the project team realize they have spent more than they had planned to spend ($835,000 [AC] versus $695,000 [PV]). In addition to these planned values (PV) and actual costs (AC), they also have information about progress on Deliverables A through G during months 1 through 7, as shown in Exhibit 9.18. These are the only deliverables that have been started, and not all are complete.

A spreadsheet summarizing earned value performance appears in Exhibit 9.19. This combines data from previous exhibits and shows the relationships among PV, EV, and AC over the first seven months of the project. A graphical view of PV, EV, and AC appears in Exhibit 9.20.

[18] Note that this comparative Gantt chart in Exhibit 9.17 is different from the one displayed for progress information related to the flooring project example, which offered comparisons between planned value and earned value. By using two different types of comparative Gantt charts, we demonstrate that there is no single, best way to present project information in earned value systems.

EXHIBIT 9.14 **Activity-on-Node Network Schedule for Physical Assets Portion of a Plant Relocation Project**

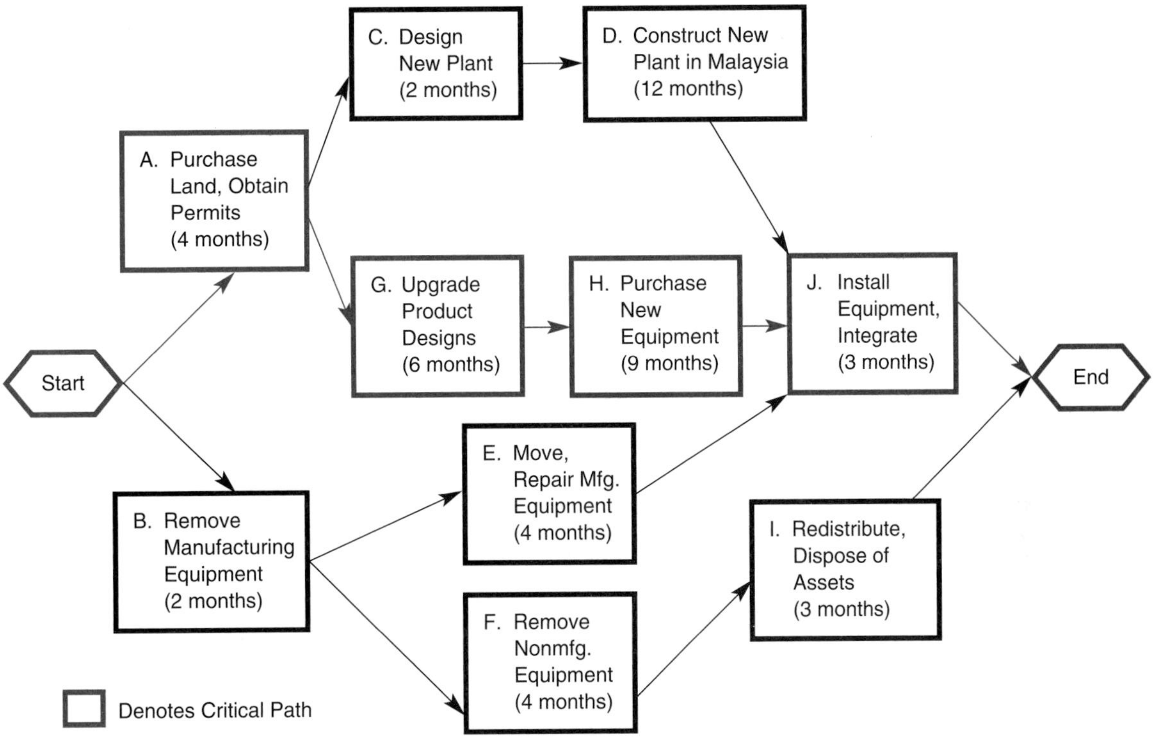

EXHIBIT 9.15 **Time-Based Network Showing Planned Expenditures for Plant Relocation Project**

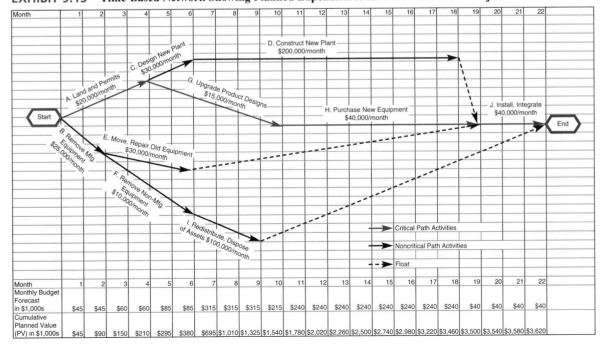

EXHIBIT 9.16 Spreadsheet-Based Gantt Chart for Plant Relocation Project—Planned Value (PV) Data

Planned Expenditures per Month in $1,000s

Deliverable	1	2	3	4	5	6	7	8	9	10	11	12	13	14	15	16	17	18	19	20	21	22
A. Land and permits	$20	$20	$20	$20																		
B. Remove manufacturing equipment	$25	$25																				
C. Design new plant					$30	$30																
D. Construct new plant							$200	$200	$200	$200	$200	$200	$200	$200	$200	$200	$200	$200				
E. Move, repair old equipment			$30	$30	$30	$30																
F. Remove nonmanufacturing equipment			$10	$10	$10	$10																
G. Upgrade product designs					$15	$15	$15	$15	$15	$15												
H. Purchase new equipment											$40	$40	$40	$40	$40	$40	$40	$40	$40			
I. Redistribute, dispose of assets							$100	$100	$100													
J. Install equipment, integrate																				$40	$40	$40
Cost/month	$45	$45	$60	$60	$85	$85	$315	$315	$315	$215	$240	$240	$240	$240	$240	$240	$240	$240	$40	$40	$40	$40
Planned Value (PV) in $1,000s	$45	$90	$150	$210	$295	$380	$695	$1,010	$1,325	$1,540	$1,780	$2,020	$2,260	$2,500	$2,740	$2,980	$3,220	$3,460	$3,500	$3,540	$3,580	$3,620

EXHIBIT 9.17   Comparative Gantt Chart for Plant Relocation Project Showing Planned versus Actual Expenditures by Month

	Deliverable	1	2	3	4	5	6	7	8	9	10	11	12	13	14	15	16	17	18	19	20	21	22
	Planned Versus Actual Expenditures per Month in $1,000s																						
	Month																						
Planned Value (not cumulative)	A. Land and permits	$20	$20	$20	$20																		
Actual Expenditures (not cumulative)	A. Land and permits	$30	$40	$25	$30	$10																	
Planned Value (not cumulative)	B. Remove manufacturing equipment	$25	$25																				
Actual Expenditures (not cumulative)	B. Remove manufacturing equipment	$30	$30																				
Planned Value (not cumulative)	C. Design new plant					$30	$30																
Actual Expenditures (not cumulative)	C. Design new plant						$90																
Planned Value (not cumulative)	D. Construct new plant							$200	$200	$200	$200	$200	$200	$200	$200	$200	$200	$200	$200				
Actual Expenditures (not cumulative)	D. Construct new plant							$300															
Planned Value (not cumulative)	E. Move, repair old equipment			$30	$30	$30	$30																
Actual Expenditures (not cumulative)	E. Move, repair old equipment				$20	$30	$30	$30															
Planned Value (not cumulative)	F. Remove non-manufacturing equipment			$10	$10	$10	$10																
Actual Expenditures (not cumulative)	F. Remove non-manufacturing equipment			$15	$15	$10	$10	$30															
Planned Value (not cumulative)	G. Upgrade product designs					$15	$15	$15	$15	$15	$15												
Actual Expenditures (not cumulative)	G. Upgrade product designs						$20	$40															
Planned Value (not cumulative)	H. Purchase new equipment											$40	$40	$40	$40	$40	$40	$40	$40	$40			
Actual Expenditures (not cumulative)	H. Purchase new equipment																						
Planned Value (not cumulative)	I. Redistribute, dispose of assets							$100	$100	$100													
Actual Expenditures (not cumulative)	I. Redistribute, dispose of assets																						
Planned Value (not cumulative)	J. Install equipment, integrate																				$40	$40	$40
Actual Expenditures (not cumulative)	J. Install equipment, integrate																						
	Planned Value (monthly) estimates in $1,000s	$45	$45	$60	$60	$85	$85	$315	$315	$315	$215	$240	$240	$240	$240	$240	$240	$240	$240	$40	$40	$40	$40
	Planned Value (PV) (cumulative)	$45	$90	$150	$210	$295	$380	$695	$1,010	$1,325	$1,540	$1,780	$2,020	$2,260	$2,500	$2,740	$2,980	$3,220	$3,460	$3,500	$3,540	$3,580	$3,620
	Actual Expenditures (monthly)	$60	$70	$40	$65	$50	$150	$400															
	Actual Cost (AC) (cumulative)	$60	$130	$170	$235	$285	$435	$835															

Although the project team assumed linear expenditures when it calculated planned value (PV) by deliverable and time period, actual cost (AC) proved to be lumpy.

EXHIBIT 9.18   **Worksheet for Plant Relocation Progress Data (Earned Value or EV) through Month 7**

Progress Data in $1,000s							
Month	1	2	3	4	5	6	7
% Complete A	20%	30%	45%	95%	100%	100%	100%
EV A	$16	$24	$36	$76	$80	$80	$80
% Complete B	40%	100%	100%	100%	100%	100%	100%
EV B	$20	$50	$50	$50	$50	$50	$50
% Complete C						100%	100%
EV C						$60	$60
% Complete D							10%
EV D							$240
% Complete E				25%	30%	60%	90%
EV E				$30	$36	$72	$108
% Complete F			15%	20%	60%	70%	90%
EV F			$6	$8	$24	$28	$36
% Complete G						10%	20%
EV G						$9	$18
EV	$36	$74	$92	$164	$190	$299	$592
AC (From Exhibit 9.17)	$60	$130	$170	$235	$285	$435	$835
PV (From Exhibit 9.17)	$45	$90	$150	$210	$295	$380	$695

Regardless of what the deliverable has cost, earned value cannot be more than its originally budgeted amount (PV). Also, recall that earned value is a cumulative figure that carries forward to subsequent periods after work is complete.

Sample Calculations from Exhibit 9.18

1. Deliverable F is 90% complete by month 7. Earned value is calculated as .9 multiplied by its final planned value of $40,000 = $36,000.
2. Project EV for month 2 = Sum of earned values for all deliverables in process or completed (at this point, A and B only) = $24,000 + $50,000 = $74,000.

EXHIBIT 9.19   **Summary of Data, Variances, and Indices for Plant Relocation Project through Month 7**[19]

	Calculations of Key Project Metrics (Dollar figures in 1,000s)						
Month	1	2	3	4	5	6	7
EV	$ 36	$ 74	$ 92	$ 164	$ 190	$ 299	$ 592
AC	$ 60	$ 130	$ 170	$ 235	$ 285	$ 435	$ 835
PV	$ 45	$ 90	$ 150	$ 210	$ 295	$ 380	$ 695
CV	–$ 24	–$ 56	–$ 78	–$ 71	–$ 95	–$ 136	–$ 243
CV%	–67%	–76%	–85%	–43%	–50%	–45%	–41%
SV	–$ 9	–$ 16	–$ 58	–$ 46	–$ 105	–$ 81	–$ 103
SV%	–20%	–18%	–39%	–22%	–36%	–21%	–15%
CPI	0.60	0.57	0.54	0.70	0.67	0.69	0.71
SPI	0.80	0.82	0.61	0.78	0.64	0.79	0.85
BAC	$3,620	$3,620	$3,620	$3,620	$3,620	$3,620	$3,620
EAC$_{cost}$	$6,033	$6,351	$6,704	$5,171	$5,403	$5,246	$5,099
EAC$_{time}$ (months)	27.50	26.83	36.07	28.21	34.38	27.85	25.88
TCPI	1.01	1.02	1.02	1.02	1.03	1.04	1.09

[19] All figures are rounded to two places to the right of the decimal in Exhibit 9.19.

Details of the calculations from Exhibit 9.19 are shown below in $1,000s for month 7:[20]

Cost variance (CV)	=	EV − AC	=	$592 − $835 = −$243	
CV %	=	CV/EV	=	−$243 / $592 = −.41(−41%)	
Schedule variance (SV)	=	EV − PV	=	$592 − $695 = −$103	
SV%	=	SV/PV	=	−$103 / $695 = −.15 (−15%)	
CPI	=	EV/AC	=	$592 / $835 = .71	
SPI	=	EV/PV	=	$592 / $695 = .85	
EAC_{Cost}	=	BAC/CPI	=	$3,620 / .71 = $5,099	
Revised duration, or EAC_{Time}	=	Planned Dur./SPI	=	22 months / .85 = 25.88 months	
TCPI	=	(BAC − EV)/ (BAC − AC)	=	($3,620 − $592) / ($3,620 − $835) = 1.09	

CPI and SPI are plotted in Exhibit 9.21. As shown in the exhibit, both measures fall below the target of 1 for each of the seven months of the project. After month 3, there appears to be a slightly upward trend for both indices.

From all of the information presented here, the team sees clearly that the plant relocation project is not tracking well with plans. Nearly one-third of the project's allotted time has been consumed, and the project is over budget and behind schedule, as evidenced by the CPI of .71 and the SPI of .85. If things continue in this manner, the project could cost considerably more than its original budget (EAC_{cost} is $5,099,000) and require more time than initially allotted (revised duration or EAC_{time} is 25.88 months). With two-thirds of the time remaining, there is still time to recover, but what options are available to the project manager and team? They need to answer two important questions before they proceed:

- What has caused the project to get out of control?
- What are the triple constraint priorities? What is more important—cost, time, or performance? Some organizations set control limits for CV% and SV% indicating relative priorities for two of the three triple constraint factors.[21]

In diagnosing causal factors, the team has dug into the data about individual deliverables, reviewed performance logs, assessed needs of remaining deliverables, and interviewed those involved. This exploration has revealed several key points:

- Deliverable A, land and permits, which is on the critical path, took a month longer than expected because an important document sat on an executive's desk for three weeks. As a result of this problem, the project manager has modified the communication plan and resolved to engage in more informal interactions with key stakeholders. The budget overrun for Deliverable A was the result of fees paid to an agent in Malaysia on a cost-plus contract. The project manager is wondering if

[20] All are rounded to two places to the right of the decimal.

[21] For example, one US shipyard with which we are familiar sets control thresholds at +/− 10% for time and +/− 5% for cost, indicating that cost is a more important priority than time.

EXHIBIT 9.20   Graphical View of PV, EV, and AC for Plant Relocation Project with Performance Data through Month 7

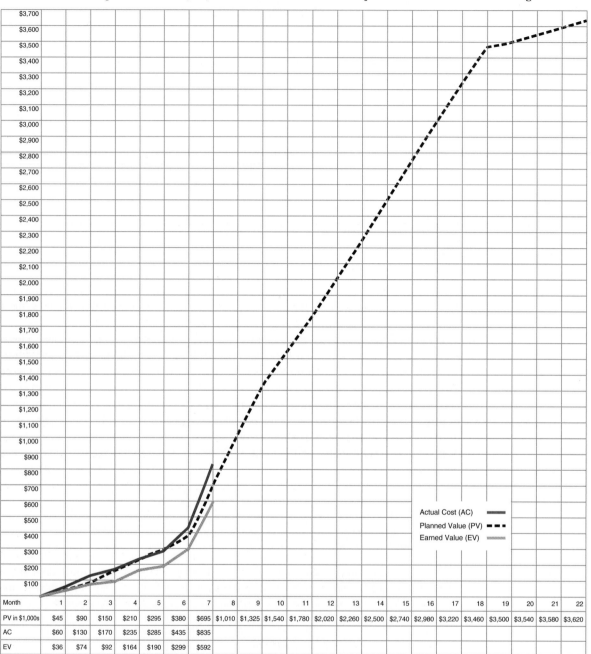

Month	1	2	3	4	5	6	7	8	9	10	11	12	13	14	15	16	17	18	19	20	21	22
PV in $1,000s	$45	$90	$150	$210	$295	$380	$695	$1,010	$1,325	$1,540	$1,780	$2,020	$2,260	$2,500	$2,740	$2,980	$3,220	$3,460	$3,500	$3,540	$3,580	$3,620
AC	$60	$130	$170	$235	$285	$435	$835															
EV	$36	$74	$92	$164	$190	$299	$592															

a fixed-fee contract would have been better and has initiated new negotiations with the agent.

- Deliverable B, remove manufacturing equipment, was completed on time but exceeded its budget. An investigation reveals that the team did not have clear

EXHIBIT 9.21
Tracking CPI and SPI for Plant Relocation Project through Month 7

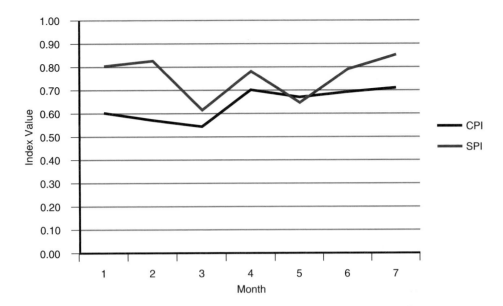

guidelines for what was manufacturing equipment and what was nonmanufacturing equipment. The confusion created coordination problems with the team assigned to Deliverable F, remove nonmanufacturing equipment, resulting in a delay and significant extra expense. Given that neither deliverable was on the critical path, it might have been better to stretch them out and perform them concurrently, allowing for better coordination and communication between the two teams.

- In an effort to keep the critical path on schedule, Deliverable C, design new plant, was crashed from two months to one month, allowing Deliverable D, construction, to start on time. Although Deliverable D is not on the critical path, it has only one month of float preceding its merger with the critical path. Consequently, the extra push was probably worthwhile. In light of the limited progress reported, AC for the first month of construction has raised concerns among team members and they are investigating root causes.

- Deliverable E, move and repair old equipment, started a week late because resources were being used elsewhere, but it still has float.

- Deliverable G, upgrade product designs, is on the critical path. It started a month late, but the team crashed it by adding more designers. Unfortunately, the crashing effort might have had an effect opposite of the one intended, given that progress is slower than planned. (Two months of work on a six-month task should have produced 33 percent progress instead of only 20 percent.)

Although overall performance is shy of PV targets, if we focus on the critical path we can see recovery is a real possibility. It is possible resources from non-critical deliverables could be diverted to critical path deliverables. However, more resources are not always the answer, as the team discovered when it added more designers to Deliverable G. With a clarification regarding triple constraint priorities, the team can make intelligent decisions about what to do next. We suggest several general possibilities following.

Responding to Project Variances Identified by the Earned Value System

The way the project team uses an earned value system is probably more important than details such as software, reporting methods, terminology, calculations, and forms. Faced with variances that exceed control thresholds, and armed with information about the causes of these variances as well as triple constraint priorities, the team has several options for getting a project back on track. These include:

- Crash or compress remaining critical activities to bring the project on track with initial plans and commitments.
- Negotiate a new due date with the customer to manage expectations about project delays.
- Provide appropriate assistance to teams whose activities have undesirable variances.
- Work with suppliers (internal and external) to ensure on-time or expedited delivery of critical materials.
- Re-evaluate the WBS to determine if project scope can be reduced.
- Check for scope creep and engage the change control process.
- Revise the project schedule, budget, or both, if scope or specifications have legitimately changed.

Exhibit 9.22 depicts Dilbert's view of how some project sponsors react to projects with schedule variances. Although it is not unusual for project sponsors to request more frequent status reporting in response to delays or cost overruns, an overzealous approach can distract team members and further degrade project performance.

Aggregating Earned Value Data across Projects

A firm that has achieved a relatively high level of project management maturity[22] is likely to have a system in place for tracking multiple projects simultaneously. Exhibit 9.23 illustrates one tool for broad-spectrum monitoring. The chart shows cost performance index (CPI) and schedule performance index (SPI) values for four projects on a two-dimensional grid.

---

[22] For more information on project management maturity, see H. Kerzner, *Strategic Planning for Project Management Using a Project Management Maturity Model* (New York: Wiley and Sons, 2001).

EXHIBIT 9.22   The Wrong Way to Eliminate a Schedule Variance

DILBERT: © Scott Adams/Dist. by United Feature Syndicate, Inc

EXHIBIT 9.23
Monitoring Multiple Projects with a Graphical View of Cost Performance Index (CPI) and Schedule Performance Index (SPI)

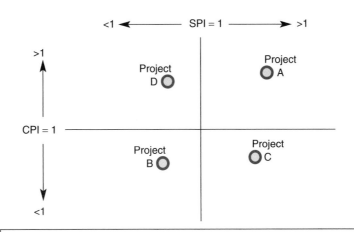

Earned Value Interpretation:
CPI and SPI values greater than 1 are indicators of favorable performance. Values less than 1 are indicators of unfavorable performance.

Exhibit 9.23 reveals that Project A is performing well, with CPI and SPI values both greater than 1. It is under budget and ahead of schedule. Project B is at the opposite end of the spectrum, with poor performance (< 1) on both indices. Project C is ahead of schedule but over budget, and Project D is under budget but behind schedule. If high-level decision makers review these figures with project managers, sponsors, and functional managers, they can collaborate to re-allocate resources to poor-performing projects. For example, if Project B has the highest strategic priority, decision makers could elect to temporarily borrow resources from another project to get it back on track.

Earned Value in Action: Challenges and Solutions

Although earned value systems have grown in popularity in recent years, many organizations have faced challenges when attempting to implement them. Consequently, earned value often fails before the organization has an opportunity to demonstrate or realize its advantages. The following paragraphs highlight specific challenges we have observed in our work with several organizations, and offer ideas for avoiding or resolving them.

Earned Value Game-Playing

Many new earned value users find it tempting to revise planned value (PV) figures once the project is underway and actual cost (AC) and earned value (EV) data become available. This can eliminate gaps among the three measures, and team members hope this will make them look good. Unfortunately, it eradicates historical estimating data and excuses team members from diagnosing or correcting the causes of performance gaps. The Dilbert cartoon shown in Exhibit 9.24 offers a humorous but reality-based perspective on this kind of game-playing, which generally occurs in environments where people believe the monitoring system will be used to cast blame or punish team members. A key principle for implementing any measurement system is to demonstrate that it will be used to solve problems. One way to gain trust is to use earned value in small pilot projects to work out details and gain inputs and insights before implementing the system more broadly.

EXHIBIT 9.24   Dilbert's Perspective on Earned Value Game-Playing

DILBERT: © Scott Adams/Dist. by United Feature Syndicate, Inc

The 90 Percent Complete Syndrome

Many people who manage or contribute to projects would like to avoid the scrutiny that comes with a progress variance that indicates a failure to meet performance thresholds. Consequently, they overreport their achievements, promising week after week they are 90 percent complete and hoping they can catch up.[23] The downside is that if the project manager (and others on the team) are unaware of a problem, they have no opportunity to provide support that could get the activity back on track. In a well-managed earned value system, team members eventually see the benefits of providing accurate progress reports. Some organizations partially avoid the 90% complete syndrome by allowing only three activity progress percentage figures: 0 (task has not started), 50 (task in progress), and 100 (task complete).

"I Have No Idea What My Percent Complete Is!"

Ask stressed and busy project contributors for percent complete estimates, and you might wind up with a team mutiny. Experienced project managers often discover it is better to ask a project team member, "How much more time do you need to finish this task?" versus "What is your percent complete?" People are generally more comfortable reporting in this way, and the project manager can make an estimate of percent complete based on time-to-completion data. For example, if someone performing a programming task estimated at five days says she needs six more days at the end of the second day, the project manager can roughly estimate that the task is about 25 percent complete (two days of what is now forecast to be an eight-day task). A focus on time-to-complete also opens the door for more effective problem solving. When people estimate they will need more time than the schedule allows, the project manager can ask, "What can we do to help you get back on schedule?"

---

[23] D.N. Ford and J.D. Sterman, "Overcoming the 90% Syndrome: Iteration Management in Concurrent Development Projects," *Concurrent Engineering: Research and Applications,* 11, no. 3 (2003), pp. 177–86; and D.N. Ford and J.D. Sterman, "The Liar's Club: Concealing Rework in Concurrent Development," *Concurrent Engineering: Research and Applications* 11, no. 3 (2003), pp. 211–20.

Grappling with Multifactor Costs

Estimating actual cost (AC) can be a challenge because a comprehensive budget includes many components, as we illustrated in Chapter 5. When monitoring performance on a multifactor cost basis, the team must track human resource time, wage rates, travel expenses, material expenses, and other costs for each task. These factors certainly are important to overall project performance, but for the sake of EV reporting, it can be simpler just to include labor costs. (Other costs can be tracked through the organization's accounting system.) An even simpler approach involves using person hours, without wage rates or other costs, as the unit of measure.

Overly Narrow Focus on the Numbers

A team would be naive to assume earned value indices tell the entire story about a project's time and cost performance. For example, estimate at completion (EAC) figures are not unalterable facts. By keeping performance logs and engaging in open discussion about project work and challenges, a team can generally make better time and cost predictions than those portrayed solely by earned value parameters. Moreover, a negative cost variance for an activity, in itself, might not signal a problem. Perhaps the activity is ahead of schedule, potentially justifying the added expense. Team members must dig into underlying causal factors before jumping to conclusions based on the numbers alone. Earned value data inform decisions and assessments. They do not make them.

Distraction from Project Performance Goals

An over-emphasis on earned value monitoring can divert team members' attention away from a project's strategic goals. The exclamation "We finished on time and under budget" does not offer a reason to celebrate if the new product fails market tests because no one sought (or listened to) customer feedback during the development process. Time and cost should not be the only metrics on a project's dashboard. Thus, we warn against allowing earned value to consume team attention to the exclusion of other important project dimensions.

Box 9.1 offers an example of an earned value system implementation story at a Fortune 500 company. It shows the value of involving team members, establishing trust, and starting with a pilot project.

PROJECT CHANGE CONTROL

All project teams need a mechanism to control changes that affect scope or quality of deliverables. In major projects, the project manager should initiate a **change control process** and form a **change control board.** A change control process is a set of formal procedures for introducing changes to a project plan. A change control board is a group of people that includes important stakeholders such as the project manager, sponsor, customers, key suppliers, and leaders of important project subteams. When anyone proposes a change, the change control board follows an established protocol to evaluate its effects on the triple constraint (time, cost, performance) and other important KPIs. Based on an integrated analysis, the change control board decides whether to adopt the proposed change. Many projects flounder out of control because they lack a systematic process for screening changes.

Brianna Clay was an industrial engineering manager for a Fortune 500 manufacturing company. She had studied earned value methods and was intrigued by their potential for her organization. She decided to implement them in her product design group and began with an introductory training session for the 10-person team. She was unprepared for the resistance she encountered. People seemed uncomfortable with the idea of such a tracking system. Their stated reasons were: "This won't work. We don't have reliable time estimates." "You'll be measuring me on things I can't control." As she dug deeper, Brianna discovered the real reasons for their resistance. First, people didn't like the idea of being measured. Second, team members were unsure how the information would be used. They did not want the system to become the basis for punitive actions against them. Third, they were actually correct in their assertions about the weaknesses in the current estimating system. Understanding these concerns early, Brianna was able to convince her team that the system would be used for constructive problem solving and not to punish individuals for their performance. They began by using the system on an experimental basis to uncover and correct weaknesses in the estimating system; this helped to build trust. Still, it took her more than a year to fully implement earned value methods. Once the system was fully operational, Brianna's team members began to tell others in the organization about the performance improvements earned value had helped them to achieve. This initiated a positive "viral buzz" that led other managers to request assistance from Brianna and her team so they could implement similar systems.

Consider additional information about the previous example of a project to transfer production of a product from a facility in China to a new facility in Malaysia. At the end of month 7, the team responsible for Deliverable E, involving the transport and repair of old equipment, expresses doubts about the long-term viability of the equipment it has moved to the new site. While repairing the equipment, team members discovered several machine design issues that rendered the equipment prone to breakdowns. They recommend that the company purchase new equipment and scrap the old equipment. And they have found a vendor who can deliver state-of-the-art equipment in three weeks. This will add $100,000 to the project budget. The team members should report their concerns to the change control board, citing what they think is causing the breakdowns; how the overall project, as well as other project deliverables, will be affected; and how their suggested change will support the project's outcome goals. The change control board should ask team members if they have thought of other ways, besides the new equipment purchase, to solve the problem in the short run as well as in the long run. Before taking action to change the project, the change control board must ensure that other involved stakeholders have bought in to the change. Assuming approval is forthcoming, the project manager then leads a team session in revising the WBS and schedule to accommodate the changes. These changes are communicated to all key stakeholders.

Exhibit 9.25 outlines a change management process involving a change control board. Although it is presented as a formal process, a team or individual considering a change could run through this logic in a less formal way when the change is minor or in the event of a crisis.

EXHIBIT 9.25
Change Management
Process

1. Change proponents clearly communicate the problem or opportunity underlying the need for change to members of the change control board. (This reflects our earlier emphasis on Why Before What or YB4What.)
2. Change proponents demonstrate they have considered several options for addressing the issues motivating change and recommend one or more to the change control board.
3. Members of the change control board discuss the question, "If we don't do anything, what will be the effect on our ability to meet project goals?"
4. The change control board can reject the proposal or continue the process.
5. If the process continues, the change control board engages in a series of what-if questions related to options for solving the problem or seizing the new opportunity. Questions they ask might include:
   - What changes to the WBS will this require?
   - How would this option affect budget and schedule?
   - What other project activities would be affected if we did this?
   - How would this change option affect stakeholders within and outside the project?
6. The change control board might communicate the problem or opportunity and possible strategies to key stakeholders to gain additional insight.
7. The change control board, with input from other stakeholders as needed, decides whether to make the change and, if the answer is yes, which option to choose.
8. The project team revisits the WBS, budget, and schedule and changes them accordingly. If the change involves a supplier, the contract is formally modified in cooperation with the supplier.
9. The project team revises baseline data for the monitoring system if the change is significant.
10. The project team communicates the change to all stakeholders.
11. The project team monitors the effects of the change and communicates results with the change control board and other stakeholders.
12. The project manager and team document lessons learned from the change that would be useful for future projects of a similar type.

Chapter Summary and Onward

This chapter has taken us into the project delivery stage where plans are put to the test. During delivery, the project team needs a monitoring system that fits the project—it must be of the appropriate level of detail and sophistication, must measure the right things, and must provide timely, useful data. An effective monitoring system is used for problem discovery and provides insights that enable a team to take appropriate corrective actions. It is more than just a device for reporting to others. If a monitoring system is misused as a vehicle for punishing people, it likely will be subject to sabotage and, therefore, will not fulfill its intended purpose.

A balanced set of metrics includes many indicators that are project-specific. We emphasize the importance of measuring KPIs that track performance with respect to a project's specific outcome goals (e.g., market share, customer satisfaction). All projects involve generic indicators associated with time, cost, and task completion. Earned value is a widely recognized tool for measuring these generic indicators. Its popularity stems from the way it allows a team to examine a project's variances, interpret indices, and compare these across projects. When project performance differs from the plan, a team must decide on the kinds of actions needed to get things back on course. These include adding resources, re-evaluating the WBS, revising the schedule for remaining activities, revising contracts, and other strategies.

In any project, there will be times when internal or external factors introduce the potential need for change in the plan. The team should have agreed on a change control process at the beginning of the project and should follow it when this occurs. The change control process should focus on whether or not the proposed change supports the project's outcome goals.

Throughout project delivery, major project components will be closed out when complete. At the end of the project, the team will engage in major **closure activities,** as discussed in Chapter 10.

Team Activities

1. Work with a team of three to five classmates. Identify a company that manages major projects such as new product development, market launches, commercial construction, major IT initiatives, and so on. Contact the company and request a 45-minute interview with an experienced project manager. Explain that you are studying project monitoring and control systems and would like to learn about the manager's experience in this area. You are more likely to gain agreement from a busy executive if you limit your request to 45 minutes. However, after you arrive you might be allowed more time if your questions are interesting to the interviewee. Be prepared! Your assignment:

   a. After you introduce the objectives of your assignment, ask the project manager to recall a recently completed, successful project to use as the basis for interview questions. When reviewing your objectives, inform your interviewee that you would like to learn about the way performance was monitored and offer assurance that you recognize every organization uses its own blend of formal and informal, objective and subjective monitoring methods. Enter this exercise with an open mind, recognizing that some of the most effective project managers use intuitive methods that might not exactly mirror those described in this chapter.

   b. Ask the project manager to recall a recently completed, successful project as the basis of his or her answers to the following questions:

      • What was the purpose of the project, what was involved in executing it, and how big was it in terms of budget and planned duration? What kind of monitoring system did he or she, or the organization, use for this project?

      • What performance indicators did the project manager track during project delivery? (See if you can gain insights about measures that go beyond cost and schedule to include indicators of project goal achievement, but be prepared to discuss in your report the presence or absence of a balanced set of metrics.)

      • How often were metrics updated?

      • How did the project manager, the team, and the organization use the data?

      • What challenges did the project manager face in using the monitoring system?

      • What is the project manager's general advice for developing and using project monitoring tools?

   c. Meet as soon as you can after the interview to collect team thoughts while the interview is still fresh on team members' minds.

   d. Write a two-page team report summarizing your findings. In your report, provide an overview of the company and the project that was the focus of the interview. Highlight the interviewee's responses to your questions and include a section with your team's reflections and conclusions. Also include a photo of your team with your interviewee (assuming he or she grants permission, with your promise that it will be used only for this assignment). Send a professional looking thank you note to your interviewee and include a copy with your report.

2. This team-based activity gives you an opportunity to tackle planning, executing, and monitoring a real project. Gather a team of five to 10 energetic classmates who enjoy working together. Poll the group to determine which member has a real but small project for which he or she would appreciate assistance. It should be a project the team could actually execute within three to six hours. Possibilities include planting flowers, organizing a garage or storage shed, painting a room, detailing a car, preparing food in advance of a social event, installing holiday lighting, or a community volunteer project. (This is just a list of potential ideas to get you started. Be creative!) Select the one that seems most realistic and captures the interest of the team. Obtain the instructor's approval for your selection. The remainder of your assignment is as follows:

a. Prepare a plan for the project you have chosen, including:
   - Identification of underlying purpose—why are you doing this?
   - Project goals—what are you trying to achieve?
   - WBS (Note: Try to specify between 15 and 30 individual work packages for monitoring. You will monitor this project as it unfolds and if there is too much detail, the monitoring effort will be a nightmare for this very short project.)
   - KPIs you will measure during and after the project, in addition to time and cost.
   - Time estimates for person hours and calendar hours required for each task.
   - Budget estimates for all work packages based on a cost allocation of $20 per hour. Thus, if a task is estimated to require two people for two hours, the budget will be $2 \times 2 \times \$20 = \$80$. (If you believe your team members are worth more or less than this amount, feel free to use another number, but to keep it simple, pay everyone the same.)
   - A project schedule in network and Gantt formats. Consider using an Excel-based Gantt chart that allows you to calculate planned and actual costs and display them on a time scale.
   - Assign responsibility for tasks. Who will be doing what, when? Keep assignments clean by having each individual work on one work package at a time. One or two people must be assigned to project monitoring and data gathering. Do not assume someone can gather data while also working. Monitoring will be very time consuming. Find a way to randomly select the person who assumes the monitoring role. Do not rotate this role. If there are more than 10 work packages and if the data-gathering interval is 15 minutes or less, you should have more than one person monitoring performance.
   - Based on your Gantt chart and work package budgets, prepare a table and graph that plots planned value (PV) for your project. In calculating planned value, consider not only the cost of the people performing WBS tasks, but also level-of-effort work associated with the one or more individuals who are monitoring the project. These overhead costs are incurred at $20 per hour, per monitor, as long as the project is underway. If one person is responsible for monitoring, this would produce an ongoing cost of $20 per hour, in addition to variable costs associated with project work packages.
   - As a team, agree on reporting frequency with a goal of having at least 10 data points during the life of your small project. So, for a project predicted to

require three hours of calendar (clock) time, 15-minute intervals would be appropriate. For a project predicted to require six hours of calendar (clock) time, 30-minute intervals would be appropriate. The team member who is the monitor will gather data about percent complete and actual cost. Refer to monitoring tips offered in this chapter.

b. Once everyone is clear about his or her responsibility, what is involved in each task, how the schedule is laid out, and how performance will be reported, begin the project. You will have chaos on your hands and data-gathering will be a mess if team members do not understand the schedule, performance reporting, and task responsibilities. So be sure your team has a solid grasp of these elements before actually starting project work. During the project, the monitor will do the following:

- Remind people before work starts that this is a learning process and not a contest to see how fast people can work. Remind them, also, that the work should be of high quality.

- Observe how many people are working on each task and track actual cost per time interval. Note that although task assignments have been made, people might move around to help on tasks for which they were not assigned. Also, some people might be idle during certain periods of time, so their time will not be charged to any tasks. Make careful note of the actual number of team members working on any task at any given time. This will determine actual cost.

- At agreed time intervals, ask for percent complete information. (Remember that if the project involves more than 10 activities and a short frequency interval for gathering data, you will probably need two people as monitors.) Recall a recommendation from this chapter: if a team member cannot come up with a reasonable estimate of percent complete, ask how long it will take him or her to finish. You can then work backward from the original time estimate to approximate percent complete.

- Keep careful records for each task at each time interval. It can be difficult! You may do this manually in tabular form or in a spreadsheet.

- If time and space allow, track performance on a large graph visible to the team.

- Track KPIs beyond cost and schedule, as agreed before the project began.

c. At the end of the project, prepare a complete project report, including the following:

- A description of the project and its purpose.
- WBS, network schedule, and Gantt schedule.
- List of KPIs you chose during the planning process.
- Initial graph of planned value (PV).
- Description of your approach to monitoring (planned frequency, who was assigned to do it, and other decisions). Include comments about challenges you faced or discoveries you made in developing your approach.
- Photos of your team working on the project.
- A spreadsheet-based table and graph incorporating all of your earned value data, including AC, PV, and EV.

- Calculations, for each data-gathering interval, of the following:
  - Schedule variance (SV)
  - Schedule variance percent (SV%)
  - Cost variance (CV)
  - Cost variance percent (CV%)
  - SPI
  - CPI
  - EAC_{cost}
  - Revised duration (also known as EAC_{time})
  - TCPI
- Records of KPI performance, beyond earned value data.
- A two- to three-page post-project assessment, including a discussion of project performance based on earned value and other KPIs, reflections about the monitoring system and process, and what you learned from this project experience.

Discussion Questions and Exercises

1. Based on your own experience with personal or work-related projects, describe examples of two of the phenomena discussed early in this chapter under the heading "Why Project Monitoring and Control Are Necessary."

2. Based on your answer to Question 1, describe what you did, or could have done, to manage the project better in light of the two factors you described in your example.

3. Imagine you have been designated as the project manager for an enterprisewide IT system that includes modules for sales, manufacturing, supply chain, after-sales service, inventory, and accounting. Additional modules will be implemented in the next project. The project has a budget of $15,000,000 and a deadline 12 months from today. For each of the modules, write a short paragraph summarizing your assumptions about the work that will be involved. Then, for each module, identify at least four KPIs you could use to measure its performance. In developing your list of KPIs, consider a balanced set of factors to monitor. This is a creative assignment, so use your imagination.

4. Design a dashboard to display the balanced set of metrics you described in your answer to Question 3. This is also a creative assignment.

5. Imagine you and your family plan to plant a vegetable garden in your backyard. The purpose of the project is to reduce your family's food costs and ensure that your foods are grown organically. The space where you will plant the garden is currently occupied by a gravel-covered parking area. Develop a list of at least six deliverables for this project. For each deliverable, list at least two KPIs, beyond time and cost. Explain why you chose them.

6. Locate the following article: K. McLaughlin, "What's Not Cooking: As Some Luxury Restaurants Close, Others Cut Prices," *The Wall Street Journal*, January 23, 2009, p. W1. Imagine you have been hired by Stephen Hanson of B.R. Guest Restaurants, who has decided to close several of his upscale eateries in New York and Chicago, including Level V in Manhattan, Fiamma in the Soho District, Ruby Foo's Uptown on the Upper West Side, and Blue Water Grill in Chicago. He wants to be certain these restaurants are closed in the most effective manner and is conscious of how the closures might affect his other very popular restaurants. He has asked you to develop a comprehensive set of KPIs you would measure

during the project and after the project is complete. Prepare a report for him in which you:

    a. Explain the importance of performance measurement during project execution.

    b. List at least 10 KPIs and explain your rationale for choosing each one. Also for each KPI, describe how, when, and the frequency with which you would monitor it.

    c. Write a paragraph offering advice to Mr. Hanson about at least three principles he should keep in mind when developing the monitoring system for this set of closure projects. Apply your advice directly to this situation.

7. In this chapter, we described several tools for monitoring projects, including checklists, spreadsheets, percent complete, tracking Gantts, and earned value. Create a three-column table with each of these in the left-hand column. In the middle column, describe a specific type of project for which this method would be appropriate. In the right-hand column, write one or two sentences about why you think each tool would be appropriate for the project you identified in the middle column.

8. Recall three projects in which you have been involved. These may be work-related or personal projects (e.g., a vacation, a job search, a wedding, a fishing trip, a car engine overhaul, a dinner party). For each project, identify which of the project monitoring approaches described in the book would have been the most appropriate to use in monitoring project performance and describe why. What type of monitoring system was *actually* used in each of the three projects you identified? How well did it work? Explain your answer.

9. You have just accepted an overseas position with your current employer. Because you expect to be in the new position for several years, you and your spouse have elected to sell your current home. Your real estate agent strongly advises that you undertake several upgrades including (1) adding landscaping to the front yard to improve curb appeal (e.g., replace old shrubs, add several flower beds, create a walkway), (2) replacing the worn and weathered back deck, and (3) updating the wall colors and replacing the flooring throughout the house (e.g., installing hardwood in several rooms and new carpeting in the others). You have limited funds for the upgrades and the renovations must be complete in two months so the house can go on the market at the best time. You plan to physically move overseas in four months and want the house sold before your departure.

    a. Describe the project monitoring approach you would use for this project and why you would adopt the chosen approach.

    b. When you tell your spouse (who does not have a background in project management) about your planned approach to monitoring the project, your spouse says, "What a waste to spend time and effort monitoring! Let's just do the work." Prepare several arguments in favor of project monitoring that you could use to convince your spouse of the value of project monitoring and the suitability of your chosen monitoring approach.

10. You plan to have a yard sale at the end of the month. Develop a checklist you could use to monitor this project. Describe how you would actually use the checklist while the project is under way.

11. The figure below depicts the schedule for a small project. The budgeted cost is shown within the schedule bar for each activity. For the sake of simplicity, assume costs are distributed evenly throughout an activity's duration. For example, Activity A will take four weeks and has a total budgeted cost of $4,000. Consequently,

expected expenditures for A will be $1,000 per week. In contrast, Activity B will cost $2,000 per week. Precedence relationships are as follows: A must precede B and C, B and C must precede D.

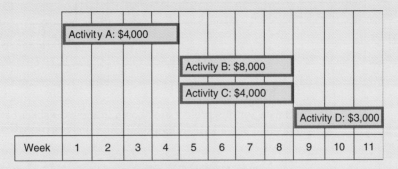

| Week | 1 | 2 | 3 | 4 | 5 | 6 | 7 | 8 | 9 | 10 | 11 |

Activity A: $4,000
Activity B: $8,000
Activity C: $4,000
Activity D: $3,000

a. Plot planned value (PV) over time.
b. Assume six weeks of project work have passed. Team members have reported progress and expenditures as follows:
   - Activity A started on time, but took five weeks and is 100 percent complete at a cost of $5,000.
   - Start dates for B and C were delayed by one week because A took an extra week, so both started on week 6.
   - At the end of week 6, Activity B is 50 percent complete and has cost $5,000.
   - At the end of week 6, Activity C is 20 percent complete and has cost $3,000.

   Assume costs and earned value are incurred in a linear fashion. For example, if A took five weeks and cost $5,000, the incremental cost would be $1,000 per week. Earned value accumulates linearly as follows: A is valued at $4,000 and took five weeks, so EV for A accumulated at a rate of 20 percent per week or $800 per week.

   For week 1 through week 6, use a spreadsheet to calculate:

   Actual cost (AC)
   Earned value (EV)
   Schedule variance (SV) and schedule variance % (SV%)
   Cost variance (CV) and cost variance % (CV%)
   Cost performance index (CPI)
   Schedule performance index (SPI)
   Estimate at completion (EAC$_{cost}$)
   Revised duration (also known as EAC$_{time}$)
   To-complete performance index (TCPI)

c. Provide a progress report for the project sponsor. Discuss your findings from part b and comment on possible reasons for variances.

12. A project schedule is depicted below, followed by a spreadsheet showing percent complete and expense data for each activity. The project is complete and the sponsor has hired you as an outside consultant to conduct a post-project review. Assume planned expenditures (i.e., PV) accrue in a linear fashion throughout the life of an activity. For example, Activity A has a total budget of $120,000, with an expenditure of $20,000 anticipated for each of the six weeks of its planned duration. Precedence relationships are not shown, but assume the schedule involves some fast tracking, with some activities running concurrently in start-to-start relationships.

Month		1	2	3	4	5	6	7	8	9	10	11	12	13	14
Activity	**Budget**														
A	$120,000	A	A	A	A	A	A								
B	$5,000					B	B	B	B	B					
C	$30,000						C	C	C	C					
D	$3,000									D	D	D	D	D	
E	$90,000								E	E	E				

Progress data for this project are shown in the worksheet below. All expenditures are cumulative and all are in thousands of dollars ($1000s):

Progress Month		**Cumulative Monthly Expenditures in $1,000s and Percent Complete**													
		1	**2**	**3**	**4**	**5**	**6**	**7**	**8**	**9**	**10**	**11**	**12**	**13**	**14**
A. % Complete		10%	20%	30%	50%	80%	100%	100%	100%	100%	100%	100%	100%	100%	100%
A. Cumulative expenditure		$20	$30	$50	$70	$90	$110	$110	$110	$110	$110	$110	$110	$110	$110
B. % Complete						20%	40%	80%	100%	100%	100%	100%	100%	100%	100%
B. Cumulative expenditure						$1	$5	$10	$12	$12	$12	$12	$12	$12	$12
C. % Complete					20%	40%	60%	80%	100%	100%	100%	100%	100%	100%	100%
C. Cumulative expenditure					$5	$10	$15	$20	$25	$25	$25	$25	$25	$25	$25
D. % Complete											25%	50%	75%	90%	100%
D. Cumulative expenditure											$1	$2	$4	$5	$6
E. % Complete								10%	50%	100%	100%	100%	100%	100%	100%
E. Cumulative expenditure								$30	$70	$80	$80	$80	$80	$80	$80

a. Calculate cumulative earned value (EV) for each activity in each month.

b. On a single graph, plot cumulative planned value (PV), actual cost (AC), and earned value (EV) for the entire project. At the bottom of the graph, display a table with these values for all months.

c. Calculate cost variances (CV and CV%) and schedule variances (SV and SV%) for each month.

d. Interpret overall trends and specific results.

e. Write a paragraph discussing how the project manager could have used the information in your report early in the project to make modifications or adjustments.

13. You are the manager of an IT project to develop and install a customer relationship management (CRM) module within your company's enterprise IT system. You and your planning team have decided to use earned value for the project. So far, you have planned only the first phase of the project, which does not include the soft

launch (to test the system live), user input, corrections, or final launch. A network diagram showing the first phase of project schedule appears below:

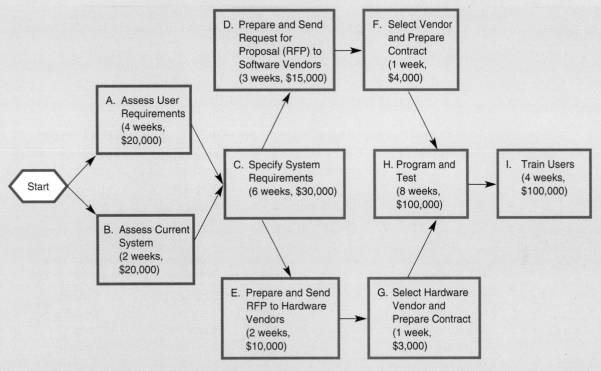

The following information is available about activity progress and actual costs for the first seven weeks of the project:

Activity	Week 1	Week 2	Week 3	Week 4	Week 5	Week 6	Week 7
A. % Complete	20%	40%	60%	100%			
A. Cumulative cost	$10,000	$20,000	$30,000	$55,000			
B. % Complete	75%	100%					
B. Cumulative cost	$15,000	$25,000					
C. % Complete					75%	100%	
C. Cumulative cost					$40,000	$50,000	
D. % Complete							10%
D. Cumulative cost							$ 5,000
E. % Complete							100%
E. Cumulative cost							$15,000
F.							
G.							
H.							
I.							
J.							

Based on the information provided about the project schedule, budget, actual costs, and percent complete through week 7 of the project, complete the following assignment:

a. Create a spreadsheet-based Gantt chart similar to those illustrated in this chapter, with cumulative planned value (PV) tabulated in the bottom row.

b. Plot PV, AC, and EV on a graph with weeks on the horizontal axis and cost on the vertical axis.

c. For weeks 1 through 7, calculate the following: SV, SV%, CV, CV%, SPI, CPI, TCPI, EAC_{cost}, and revised duration (also known as EAC_{time}.)

d. Discuss the managerial implications of the performance results from part c.

14. A project has a CPI of 1.2 and an SPI of 0.8. Interpret what this means and offer a plausible explanation for how this situation might have occurred. Include hypothetical figures for PV, AC, and EV in your explanation.

15. Consider the following information about seven consulting projects that share resources within an organization:

Project	SPI	CPI	Estimated Duration	Calendar Time Consumed (So Far)
Skillingstad project	.4	.6	12 months	11 months
Anderson project	1.4	.8	24 months	5 months
Rietveld project	.5	1.5	36 months	30 months
Clark project	.7	1.4	28 months	10 months
Shaffer project	.9	.7	6 months	1 month
Young project	1.6	1.5	5 months	2 months
Fairchild project	2.1	1.2	8 months	7 months

a. Describe each project's performance based on time and cost (i.e., over or under budget, behind or ahead of schedule).

b. For each project, offer a plausible explanation about how this level of performance could have occurred.

c. Identify the projects for which immediate action is necessary. What could you do to get each one back on track?

d. What are your recommendations to the general manager?

16. Advanced Problem: Review earned value performance data for the plant relocation project example presented in this chapter. Note the somewhat lumpy EV data for Deliverables A and F. In particular, observe that it took an entire month for the team to finish the last 5 percent of Deliverable A. And, for Deliverable F, the team made only 5 percent progress between months 3 and 4. In both cases, the teams made much more significant progress during other months. Offer at least three possible explanations for why progress data are uneven and suggest possible actions the project manager could consider as a result of your reflections.

References

Anbari, F.T. "Earned Value Project Management Method and Extensions." *Project Management Journal* 34, no. 4 (December 2003), pp. 12–23.

Block, A. *Murphy's Law and Other Reasons Why Things Go Wrong.* New York: Price/Stern/Sloan, 1981.

Christensen, D., and C. Templine. "EAC Evaluation Methods: Do They Still Work?" *Acquisition Review Quarterly* 9 (2002), pp. 105–16.

Fleming, Q.W., and J.M. Koppelman. *Earned Value Project Management.* Newtown Square, PA: Project Management Institute, 2005.

Ford, D.N., and J.D. Sterman. "Overcoming the 90% Syndrome: Iteration Management in Concurrent Development Projects." *Concurrent Engineering: Research and Applications* 1, no. 3 (2003), pp. 177–86.

Ford, D.N., and J.D. Sterman. "The Liar's Club: Concealing Rework in Concurrent Development." *Concurrent Engineering: Research and Applications* 11, no. 3 (2003), pp. 211–20.

Goldratt, E. *Critical Chain.* Great Barrington, MA: The North River Press, 1997.

Keil, M.; B.C.Y. Tan; K.K.Wei; T. Saarinen; F. Tuunainen; and A. Wassenaar. "A Cross-Cultural Study on Escalation of Commitment Behavior in Software Projects." *MIS Quarterly* 24, no. 2 (2000), pp. 299–325.

Kerzner, H. *Strategic Planning for Project Management Using a Project Management Maturity Model.* New York: Wiley and Sons, 2001.

Kim, E.H.; W.G. Wells; and M.R. Duffey. "A Model for Effective Implementation of Earned Value Management Methodology." *International Journal of Project Management* 21, no. 5 (2003), pp. 375–82.

Matta, N.F., and R.N. Ashkenas. "Why Good Projects Fail Anyway." *Harvard Business Review* 81, no. 9 (2003), pp. 109–14.

McNamara, G.; H. Moon; and P. Bromiley. "Banking on Commitment: Intended and Unintended Consequences of an Organization's Attempt to Attenuate Escalation of Commitment." *Academy of Management Journal* 43, no. 2 (2002), pp. 443–52.

Pareto, V. *The Rise and Fall of Elites: An Application of Theoretical Sociology.* New Brunswick, NJ: Transaction Publishers, 1991.

Parkinson, C.N. *The Law, Complete.* New York: Ballantine Books, 1979.

Project Management Institute. *A Guide to the Project Management Body of Knowledge.* Newtown Square, PA: Project Management Institute, 2008.

Project Management Institute. *Practice Standard for Earned Value Management.* Newtown Square, PA: Project Management Institute, 2005.

Royer, I. "Why Bad Projects Are so Hard to Kill." *Harvard Business Review* 81, no. 2 (2003), pp. 48–56.

Staw, B., and J. Ross. "Knowing When to Pull the Plug." *Harvard Business Review* 65, no. 2 (1987), pp. 68–74.

Chapter Ten

Finishing Well: Project Closure and Learning

"It ain't over 'til it's over."
Yogi Berra[1]

Chapter Learning Objectives

When you have mastered the material in this chapter, you should be able to:

- Explain the importance of project closure for the customer, the organization, and the project team.
- Recognize the value of planning for project closure at the outset of the project.
- Develop and execute a comprehensive closure plan.
- Lead a team in learning throughout a project.
- Apply effective strategies to promote project learning across the organization.

This chapter discusses project closure, the last phase in managing a project. In this phase, the team completes all project deliverables, affirms customer satisfaction, gains formal acceptance of deliverables, and undertakes administrative tasks required to bring the project to an end. Project closure activities also include assimilating and communicating lessons learned. Box 10.1 describes two contrasting scenarios that set the stage for the remainder of this chapter. (Be sure to read these scenarios before proceeding!)

The two scenarios described in Box 10.1 represent opposite ends of the spectrum in project closure. In the first case, the project drew to a close with the same careful deliberation that should characterize the preceding project phases of selection, initiation, planning, and delivery. Stakeholder satisfaction motivated the project team's decisions and actions to the end. Notably, an effort was made to use the project experience as the basis for ongoing improvement in how the organization engages in project work. In the second scenario, project closure appears to have been an afterthought that took the unprepared project manager and her team by surprise.

---

[1] Yogi Berra, *The Yogi Berra Book* (New York: Workman Publishing, 1998).

PROJECT ONE: ALL'S WELL THAT ENDS WELL

James was pleased as he read an e-mail the plant manager had sent to him, praising the recently completed lean manufacturing project and James's work as project manager. "Your attention to customer satisfaction has been exemplary and did not wane in the closing days of the project, as so often happens," the manager's e-mail noted. "I appreciated that you and your team met with me and our supervisors to identify remaining issues near the end of the project, and I was impressed by the speed with which you addressed them. Moreover, at the handover meeting, you provided us with all the documentation we needed to support the new 5-S* system implemented in our area. I am also pleased that the assembly and test team members who represented us on the project learned a great deal from their involvement and are now serving as excellent in house resources for us as we continue to implement other aspects of lean production."

James was glad the lessons-learned document he and his team put together would be the subject of discussion at the next project managers' roundtable, the monthly meeting of those in the company who routinely lead project teams. The group had been a big help to James several months ago when this project started, and he was glad to have the chance to contribute something this time.

PROJECT TWO: TROUBLE IN HOSPITAL CITY

A passing comment in the cafeteria line brought Sally up short. "You aren't still working on the ventilator-associated pneumonia (VAP) improvement project, are you?" With a weak smile, Sally responded, "Almost done." In reality, the project had lingered in an "almost done" state for six months!

Sally reflected on what had led to this situation. First, there hadn't been a clear picture of what signified the "end" of the project. Though the general focus of the project was clear—identify steps the hospital could take to reduce rates of VAP—Sally had believed the project would end when the team submitted its recommendations to the top-level managers who sponsored the project. However, some key stakeholders believed the project would not be complete until top-level managers *approved* the recommended changes. And some hospital senior executives expected Sally's team to *implement* the changes as well.

After the project sponsors finally approved a small set of recommendations, Sally was disheartened when she and her team learned that their next step would be to develop an education plan to inform staff of new VAP policies and procedures. By this time, several members had left the team, either officially or unofficially. Team size had diminished to the point where the skeletal group that remained was too small and lacked the breadth of skill to do all that was now required. Sally also learned late in the project that she was expected to submit a project file that included documents her team had either never created, or had created but not saved (e.g., several of the early project presentations). Sally wondered what she and her team could or should have done differently and when, if ever, the project would mercifully come to a close.

* 5-S refers to five Japanese words for shop-floor practices associated with cleanliness, organization, and discipline.

Project participants, unrecognized and demoralized, operated in escape mode, pausing neither to reflect on what they had learned nor on what they would do differently in the future.

WHY PROJECT CLOSURE MATTERS[2]

Project closure refers to all those activities that, once completed, permit the project manager and team to say, "We're done!" (Or, if open items remain, the team knows what needs to happen before closure and celebration may commence.) Efforts invested in planning and preparing to close out the project and hand over deliverables to the final users (whether internal or external) directly affect project success.[3] Further, effective project closure yields benefits to the customer, the enterprise undertaking the project, and the project team.

Project closure provides a final opportunity for clients to offer input (perhaps accolades) about deliverables, and to identify loose ends to be addressed before they will formally accept the project as complete. Thus, a well-defined, organized, and executed project closure has the potential to enhance customer satisfaction and confidence in the project's deliverables.

For an enterprise undertaking a project as part of a contractual agreement with an outside customer, final payment will be contingent on project closure. This payment might be the full amount of the contract, a final progress payment, or a smaller amount known as a **retainage** that the customer holds out until all final details are complete. When closure is delayed, payment may be delayed, sometimes for years.[4]

For example, reconsider the EDS case in Chapter 4. In 2000, Electronic Data Systems (EDS) secured a contract with the U.S. Navy to design, install, manage, and support "a single, hacker-proof network" connecting 345,000 computers at 4,000 Navy and Marine Corps locations. However, by 2004, the company had lost $1.6 billion on the project, in large part because of delays in closing out. The Navy contract required that the computers be installed before EDS could bill for the work. However, assembled computers often sat waiting for installation—in certain instances as long as nine months—because users were busy or on assignment, sometimes overseas.[5] This case underscores the importance of gaining agreement during project initiation about what will be paid, when, and how.

In addition to getting paid, an enterprise also benefits from project closure because it offers an opportunity for learning and improvement. One of the biggest wastes in project work is making the same mistake over again, both within a single project and from project to project. By taking project learning seriously, an organization can make great strides in effectiveness and efficiency of project delivery.[6]

Finally, project closure can benefit the project team itself. A carefully planned project closure can ensure the orderly and timely exit of team members, who will move on to other responsibilities. In addition, it can contribute to team members' sense of

[2] This section draws on our experience as observers, consultants, researchers, and participants in project-driven organizations, as well as the literature on organizational learning. Additionally, we found CH2M Hill, *Project Delivery System* (Denver, CO: CH2M Hill, 2001) to offer a very useful framework.

[3] D. Dvir, "Transferring Projects to Their Final Users: The Effect of Planning and Preparations for Commissioning on Project Success," *International Journal of Project Management* 22, no. 1 (2004), p. 262.

[4] P.K. De, "Project Termination Practices in Indian Industry: A Statistical Review," *International Journal of Project Management* 19, no. 2 (2001), p. 119.

[5] G. McWilliams, "Sink or Swim: After Landing Huge Navy Pact, EDS Finds It's in over Its Head," *The Wall Street Journal*, April 6, 2004, p. A1; and R. Richmond, "EDS Chief Sees Brighter Skies," *The Wall Street Journal*, December 15, 2005, p. B5.

[6] D. Leonard and W. Swap, "Deep Smarts," *Harvard Business Review* 82, no. 9 (2004), pp. 88–97.

accomplishment by formally acknowledging their project achievements, recognizing and rewarding their contributions, and providing them with opportunities to build portfolios that showcase their project contributions.

Despite the benefits for the customer, enterprise, and team, project managers tend to give closure less attention than preceding project phases.[7] (If your instructor assigned this chapter for class reading, you should send him or her a note of commendation. In project management courses, this chapter is often skipped, offering a metaphor for what happens in real project settings!) By the time the end of the project rolls around, project team members may have mentally (and sometimes physically) moved on to their next assignments or back to their functional home bases. The time and attention team members are willing to devote to the last 1 to 5 percent of the project, just when handoff to the customer occurs, can be far less than what is required. As we will discuss below, this is one reason that planning project closure at the outset of the project, when energy and commitment are likely to be high, is so important.

WHY AND WHEN PROJECTS CLOSE

If asked to describe what closeout activities were involved in a prior project, project managers are likely to recall a project that went full term. However, projects can close prematurely as well. A project may be completed early but with an abbreviated scope. Or it may end when decision makers, for any number of reasons, decide to terminate it. For example, a project might be terminated when it becomes clear that the desired outcome cannot be achieved (e.g., the development of a new drug for treatment of lung cancer is scrapped when clinical trials fail to show improved patient outcomes), or when a change in the firm's strategic direction (e.g., due to a merger, acquisition, a new business opportunity, or changing economic conditions) reduces the desirability of continuing to expend resources to pursue a particular project objective. For example, a large law firm launched a project to reconcile potential client conflicts that might arise as a consequence of a planned merger (i.e., the merged firm could not represent both sides in a civil conflict). Six months after the project began, the law firm abandoned the merger plans for strategic reasons, and the project to reconcile client lists for conflicts was scrapped because it was no longer necessary.

Sometimes, as in the above examples, project cancellations are unambiguous; the resources required for the project to continue are simply eliminated or redeployed. In other cases, typically when the project sponsor or key stakeholders wish to avoid admitting the project is no longer viable, resources will simply be reduced, providing only a fraction of the funds required.[8] This starvation type of project termination places the project team in a difficult state of limbo.[9]

Regardless of the circumstances under which a project ends, the project team should be systematic in the way it closes a project. The discussion here considers the case of the full-term project, although many of the activities described are valid for projects that end early or before all of their objectives are achieved.

---

[7] De, "Project Termination Practices in Indian Industry."

[8] Dvir, "Transferring Projects to Their Final Users," p. 257.

[9] K. Schwalbe, *Information Technology Project Management* (Cambridge, MA: Course Technology, 2000), p. 394.

PLAN FROM THE BEGINNING FOR PROJECT CLOSURE

During the project initiation and planning phases, the team should develop a formal written closure plan. End-of-project closure activities should appear in the work breakdown structure, complete with work packages representing individual activities, their owners, and time estimates. Further, each major milestone included in the project plan should have associated closeout activities that will signal its completion. Closure activities require resources and consume time and, thus, should appear on the project schedule and in the budget.[10]

A major aspect of closing the project is handing off the finished work product. A clear delineation of the customer's requirements will help define the activities that need to be part of project closure. At the outset of the project, the project team should secure consensus about the completion criteria. What, from the customer's (and other key stakeholders') perspective, will signal that the project or a major deliverable is finished? For example, an in house IT group undertook a project to implement an upgraded customer relationship management system. Discussions with senior managers clarified that the project would not be complete until the 18 employees in the customer service group had been adequately trained to use the system and complete documentation had been delivered. This information prompted the team to dig deeper to discover what was considered "complete" documentation and "adequate" training. The team developed specific checklists related to these, which they asked senior managers to review. After the team obtained agreement on the content, these checklists became an important part of the written closure plan for the project.

Successful completion of any project element typically goes beyond "Did we do it on time?" "Did we do it within budget?" to include other important metrics aimed at results ("Did we get the right information?" "Did market tests indicate the product has potential?" "Did yield rates improve during the pilot test?"). Chapter 5 offers guidelines for linking key performance indicators to major tasks and deliverables. If the project team waits until the end of the project, or even later, to ask these questions, it may be too late and important goals may have been overlooked.[11]

ONGOING CLOSURE ACTIVITIES DURING THE PROJECT

Once the project is underway, project closure is also underway. Informally, one can think of each completed project work package or deliverable as having been closed. In addition to this, more formal closeout activities will occur as the project proceeds. For example, if project tasks have specific billing numbers associated with them, the team will need to close these billing numbers incrementally as work is completed. Below we describe several other ways in which project closure happens during the project.

Project Review Meetings

A good closure plan includes a project review meeting at the end of each project phase, milestone, or deliverable completion. This is an opportunity for stakeholders to review progress, provide feedback, and formally acknowledge that one phase or deliverable is

---

[10] Dvir, "Transferring Projects to Their Final Users," p. 257.

[11] N. Matta and R. Ashkenas, "Why Good Projects Fail Anyway," *Harvard Business Review* 81, no. 9 (2003), pp. 109–14.

A few months after the completion of a process-improvement project, the project manager was asked to reflect on what made it a success. Final assembly time for the volumetric infusion pump line had been cut in half, which had been the target. As he thought back, it seemed to him the reason it went well was because he didn't have many team meetings and just asked people to work it out themselves. From his perspective, this meant that having infrequent team meetings was a best practice he would apply in the future. He had always thought meetings were a waste of time, and this proved it. What he did not realize, or perhaps forgot, was that the highly experienced members of this team were able to handle the problem very effectively without his help once they knew the goal. It was not that they didn't have meetings; they just met on an as-needed basis without him. Perhaps best practices he *should* have taken away from the experience included the importance of having team members with the specific skills needed for the project, and the value of setting clear, specific goals.

put to rest. In many organizations, project sponsors use these project review meetings to formally authorize a project to continue. For example, organizations with robust Six Sigma programs typically require project teams to present their achievements to key department heads as they complete each phase (i.e., define, measure, analyze, improve, control, or DMAIC) of the Six Sigma project methodology. At each of these so-called **toll-gate meetings,** managers decide whether to continue to invest resources in the project.

Ongoing Project Documentation

As part of a team's closure plan, specific tasks (and resources) should be devoted to documenting project work *throughout the project*. Waiting until the end of the project to create required documentation almost guarantees the project files will be incomplete and inaccurate. Time erases details. Also, research on hindsight bias suggests that individuals looking at past events may let the project's end result color their recollections of what happened during the project.[12] Thus, because a particular technical solution turned out to be the best in the end, team members might recollect that they always knew this, forgetting the many struggles and failed solutions they pursued. They also may tend to attribute success to their own skill when, in fact, it may have been the result of a remarkable and unrepeatable stroke of good luck. Box 10.2 offers an example.

DIMENSIONS OF PROJECT CLOSURE

Team activities at the end of the project depend on the nature of the specific project and the expectations of the organization and key stakeholders. However, as described below and summarized in Exhibit 10.1, some general dimensions of closure activities will apply to most projects, even though they might differ in their formality.

Customer Dimensions of Project Closure

One important aspect of project closure is verifying and documenting that project deliverables have been accomplished in the eyes of the customer. This can involve

[12] R. Hogarth, *Judgement and Choice* (New York: Wiley and Sons, 1980); and J.S. Hammond, R.L. Kenney, and H. Raiffa, *Smart Choices* (New York: Broadway Books, 1999).

EXHIBIT 10.1
Dimensions of End-of-Project Closure Activities

Customer Dimensions
- Obtain final customer sign-off
- Assess customer satisfaction

Human Resource Dimensions
- Conduct team member performance evaluations
- Reward and recognize project contributors
- Support project team members as they transition to their next assignments

Administrative Dimensions
- Close out project financial documentation
- Finalize project files

Organizational Dimensions
- Identify and capture lessons learned
- Assess project outcomes and communicate them to the organization
- Celebrate with the team

meeting with the customer to identify remaining items required for closure, completing these activities, and then conducting a formal acceptance meeting with the customer. For example, one of the preclosing activities associated with purchasing a new house is the creation of a **punch list**[13] of activities the builder must undertake before the close. The same process applies in nonconstruction projects.[14]

Ideally, the formal acceptance meeting with the customer will celebrate the successful completion of the project or major milestone. Although the project manager and team should be positive, upbeat, and professional during the meeting, they also should be gracious about customer concerns and demonstrate a willingness to address unresolved problems. Research and practice have demonstrated that a customer is more likely to accept a sincere apology and commitment to correct errors than feeble attempts to cover up problems.[15]

The closure meeting with the client should have a structured agenda, and afterward the project manager should follow up with a letter to the client summarizing the meeting and acknowledging that all the project deliverables and requirements have been met.

Sometimes project closure activities also include formal assessments of the customers' satisfaction with the outcome and process using surveys (online or paper-based), interviews, or other mechanisms for gathering feedback.

Human Resource Dimensions of Project Closure

The project manager should be prepared to address several human resource issues at the end of a project. Doing them well benefits the project manager, the organization that undertook the project, and individual team members. These human resource dimensions of project closure include performance evaluation, reward and recognition, and redeployment.

---

[13] *Punch list* is a term used in the construction industry to describe a list of work items to be completed. Typically, the customer does not make the final payment until all punch list items, including incomplete work or work that does not meet quality specifications, have been finished. Historically, the term is drawn from the pre-digital age practice of punching a hole next to each item on a list when it is completed. www.wikipedia.org, 2009.

[14] G. Heerkens, *Project Management* (New York: McGraw-Hill, 2002), p. 236.

[15] J. Brockner, "Why It's so Hard to Be Fair," *Harvard Business Review* 84, no. 3 (2006), pp. 122–29; and P. Dvorak, "How Understanding the 'Why' of Decisions Matters," *The Wall Street Journal*, March 19, 2007, p. B3.

Performance Evaluations

At the close of the project, the project manager should prepare performance evaluations for team members. This means thoughtfully considering the team members' contributions as well as developmental opportunities (areas for individual technical or managerial growth that arose in the context of the project). These should be documented and communicated both to the individuals and to their direct supervisors (if this is someone other than the project manager). Well-run organizations have formal processes through which functional managers solicit performance evaluation input from project managers. In organizations with less structured approaches, project managers who take the initiative to document and communicate performance information are making an important contribution to the development of individuals and the organization as a whole.

Reward and Recognition

Acknowledging and rewarding the contributions of team members is an important aspect of project closure. While this can take many forms, team celebrations in which individual and team contributions are publicly recognized are essential. Celebrations should take place at the end of the project, but also may be appropriate at the end of major milestones. Though celebrations are often overlooked in the crush of moving on to today's urgent matters, we strongly encourage project managers to honor project contributors by taking time to celebrate. Exhibit 10.2 lists several additional means for recognizing team contributions.

Redeployment of People

At the conclusion of a project to which team members have dedicated all or most of their time, some individuals may simply return to their functional areas. Others may take on roles associated with the project just completed (e.g., to provide day-to-day support for a newly implemented information system upgrade), and some will move on to new project assignments. Regardless of their post-project destinations, the project manager can play an important role in assisting team members with their transitions. For example, the project manager might identify upcoming project opportunities, discussing them with the team member, and where appropriate, advocating on the team member's behalf for a specific assignment. Similarly, the project manager might discuss with the team

EXHIBIT 10.2
Options for Team and Team Member Recognition and Rewards

- Prepare and publish an article in the company newsletter or on the company Web site that describes project outcomes and applauds team member contributions.
- Arrange to have the organization leader express his or her appreciation of the team and individual contributions at an organizationwide event (e.g., company meeting) and follow up with an e-mail. Consider providing the organization leader with a draft that could serve as the basis of his or her comments.
- Send personal letters of appreciation to individual team members thanking them for their specific contributions. Send a copy to each team member's direct supervisor or manager.
- Memorialize the project via a small memento for each team member (e.g., a clock, a paperweight) that has been engraved with the project and team member name. A framed certificate noting the team member and project is another appropriate memento.
- If budgets permit, the project manager may be able to provide cash awards, gift certificates, or stock options. (However, this should be negotiated with the project sponsor early in the project.) Experience has shown that people attach more meaning to a gift than they do to cash. Cash goes into the wallet or bank account and its source is soon forgotten. In contrast, the recipient of a gift certificate for a dinner for two is likely to remember the evening and how it was funded.

member returning to a functional area the ways to best leverage, in his or her ongoing work, the skills and insights gained from project involvement. Providing requested letters in support of team members applying for new responsibilities is another way the project manager can assist in the redeployment of people as the project winds down.

A project manager who develops a reputation for careful attention to the human resource issues associated with project closure likely will have little trouble attracting good people to work with him or her on future project endeavors.

Administrative Dimensions of Project Closure

Administrative closure refers to closing down aspects of the project related to the organization's business systems and procedures. The specific list of tasks will depend on the nature of the project and the administrative requirements of the organization, but we describe a few examples below.

Financial Closure

For most projects, a big part of administrative closure is closing the project financially. This involves closing out billing codes associated with the project (i.e., charge numbers against which individuals billed their time in completing project work). When project billing codes are not closed, individuals may continue to charge work to these accounts, resulting in cost overruns. In contractual projects, financial closure also involves submitting the final bill to the customer, along with all required supporting documentation. This underscores the importance of being very clear at the outset regarding what documentation is required for payment. Discovering at the end of the project that the customer will not reimburse expenses without complete documentation can be an unpleasant surprise, particularly if the project manager has not retained needed records throughout the project.[16]

Finalizing the Project Files

Completing project documentation and submitting required project files is another common task in administrative closure. Most organizations have specific requirements for the final project file. Exhibit 10.3 provides a set of sample contents. The task of assembling the final project file will be less onerous if the team undertakes it in small increments throughout the project, instead of leaving it until the end.

Other Administrative Closure Activities

Other tasks that might be part of administrative closure include closing temporary facilities associated with the project (e.g., a project office at the customer's site), closing out contracts associated with the project (e.g., contracts for mobile office space, Internet access at a job site, or duplication services), disposing of leftover project material (e.g., project binders not required for a training project), and shutting down project-related IT functions such as Web sites, discussion boards, and system access for subcontractors.

Again, the list of specific administrative activities is project- and organization-dependent. The formality of the closure will depend on the size and complexity of the project. A prudent project manager is well advised to query knowledgeable parties at the start of the project regarding what will be required to close the project from an administrative perspective.

Organizational Dimensions of Project Closure

Organizational dimensions of project closure focus on assessing the contribution of the project to the development and success of the organization as a whole. Thus, a major component of organizational closure is summarizing lessons learned from a project

---

[16] CH2M Hill, *Project Delivery System*, p. 197.

EXHIBIT 10.3
**Typical Contents of
the Project File**

1. Project initiation document (describes the project purpose, team composition, project objective, project success and business success measures, final deliverables, etc.)
2. Project planning documents (includes originals and revisions of the work breakdown structure, schedules, etc.)
3. Status reports
4. Design documents (written specifications associated with the deliverables)
5. Meeting minutes (includes minutes from project team meetings, subteam meetings, meetings with customers, and meetings with high-level sponsors)
6. Issues log (describes timing, nature, and resolution of problems that emerged during the project)
7. Uncertainty log (a chronicle of the risks and opportunities identified at various points in the project and the team's response)
8. Change requests (documents the timing and nature of changes requested and details how they were addressed)
9. Presentations made in the course of the project, their timing, and the audience
10. Time and expense reports (lists the resources expended on the project)
11. Contracts, contractual revisions based on change orders, and invoices
12. Final project report
13. Other written and electronic communications
14. Project retrospective report, lessons-learned report, summaries of end-of-phase review and improvement sessions (described later in this chapter)

and communicating them to the organization. In addition to this activity, which is discussed more fully in the upcoming section on project learning, organizational closure also may include evaluating the performance of the project and preparing a final project report. Although the format of the final report will vary from organization to organization, this document normally summarizes project performance with respect to the key project process and outcome objectives. How well did the project meet its objectives? Was the project completed on time and within budget? What has been the effect of the project outcomes on organizational performance? In addition, as part of organizational closure, the project team typically conducts a formal project review with the sponsor and other top-level managers, and communicates the project's results to the entire organization.

An additional element of organizational closure is celebration. As mentioned earlier, at the close of the project, the team should assemble to cheer one another and the completion of the project. A celebration can be anything from a pizza lunch to a full-scale party or daylong outing. What matters most is doing something to honor, collectively, the contributions people have made to the project, and to do so in a fun and positive manner. The celebration is a way to close out any project, even the most difficult and challenging one, in an upbeat way. Last impressions matter.

Individuals vary in what they view as fun, so it can be worthwhile to have the team plan the celebration. One manager with whom we worked created a very negative dynamic by insisting that the end-of-project celebration be a weekend rock-climbing outing. While fun for some, others resented the incursion on their private time and disliked the idea of an outdoor adventure. Another project manager decided, without consultation, that his team would rather have T-shirts than a party. He was mistaken in his view, and his team's last impressions of the project were not favorable.

PROJECT LEARNING

Many organizations regularly apply continuous-improvement thinking to enhance the way they execute the routine work that delivers value to customers on a daily basis. Few organizations, however, apply this type of thinking to project work. Although projects, by definition, represent unique endeavors, there are many opportunities to learn from project to project, or even within the same project.

The widely known and documented *learning curve phenomenon* holds that as organizations gain experience with production, productivity and quality improve.[17] (We discussed the technical and mathematical aspects associated with learning curves in Chapter 5.) Research has shown that *learning rates*—how much improvement happens with each repetition—vary widely from task to task, worker to worker, and within and across industries and organizations. Recently, in an effort to explain this variation, scholars have begun to explore which factors, in addition to cumulative volume, can accelerate or impede the rate of learning.[18]

Exhibit 10.4 offers a perspective on the factors that create learning effects. Industry experience has demonstrated that people, teams, and organizations learn to perform repetitive tasks better and more quickly simply as a function of cumulative experience. Additionally, individuals and teams learn through deliberate activities such as task-specific training and formal improvement projects.[19] When the knowledge of individuals in an organization increases, the result is greater organizational knowledge. However, for that knowledge to have an effect on overall performance, people must change their behaviors to reflect collected discoveries about better ways of working.[20] When this happens, there will be a positive effect on performance.

Applied to project work, the model shown in Exhibit 10.4 suggests that as individuals and organizations engage in more projects, they accumulate useful knowledge about how to run projects effectively. This knowledge will be partly a function

[17] F.J. Andress, "The Learning Curve as a Production Tool," *Harvard Business Review* 54, no. 1 (1954), pp. 87–97; W.B. Hirschmann, "Profit from the Learning Curve," *Harvard Business Review* 42, no. 1 (1964), pp. 125–39; and M. Lapré and L.N. Van Wassenhove, "Managing Learning Curves in Factories by Creating and Transferring Knowledge," *California Management Review* 46, no. 1 (2003), pp. 53–71.

[18] Lapré and Van Wassenhove, "Managing Learning Curves in Factories by Creating and Transferring Knowledge."

[19] Ibid.

[20] Otherwise, as one Fortune 500 executive we know remarked, "Without transfer of knowledge and behavioral change, we have 'lessons observed' but not 'lessons learned'!"

EXHIBIT 10.4
Inside the Learning Curve

Source: Adapted from M. Lapré and L.N. Van Wassenhove, "Managing Learning Curves in Factories by Creating and Transferring Knowledge," *California Management Review* 46, no. 1 (2003), pp. 53–71.

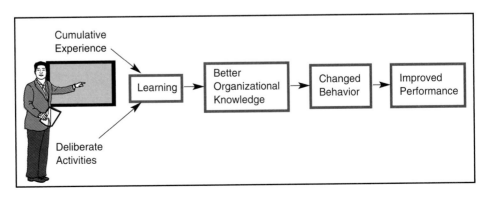

of accumulated project experience and partly a function of deliberate activities. If the organization is effective in capturing and applying this accumulated knowledge, project performance will continue to improve. Organizations with relatively mature project management systems often have in place practices aimed at capturing what has been learned on one project so it may be applied to future projects.[21] Examples of deliberate learning practices include assigning a project management mentor to assist a new project manager in leading a first project, creating project management checklists to mistake-proof the way projects are done, or requiring that all projects follow certain regimens regarding learning and improvement throughout the project.

Projects are, by their very nature, less repetitive than the routine activities that characterize an organization's daily work. Without the repetition that naturally leads to learning, project teams who want to move down the learning curve must focus more on deliberate activities to enhance the performance outcomes of their work and accelerate project learning.

Deliberate Learning during the Project

Organizations often have **lessons-learned** activities where project managers and their teams are required to take time after a project has concluded to identify what was done well or poorly and what was learned. While these sessions can be useful, they are of little benefit to the project being reviewed: after a project is completed it is too late for any lessons learned to be of benefit to that project. An improved scenario is one in which the project team is also learning to do the project better as the project is underway. Most of us are more motivated to seek out and implement ways to improve if those improvements likely will benefit us, and not just some unknown future team. The U.S. Army, as part of its after-action review process, explicitly recognizes this, noting, "Lessons must first and foremost benefit the team that extracts them."[22] Enterprises that aspire to be learning organizations view every event as an opportunity for learning. Applied to projects, this means making learning and improvement a throughout-the-project activity, not a onetime, end-of-project task. Below, we describe several specific mechanisms for making learning a routine part of project work.

Make Learning a Project Goal Embedded in the Organization's Project Management Approach

While every project has specific technical and business goals, organizations serious about improving the way they deliver projects will expect each project to contribute also to the organization's project management knowledge base. As Bowen et al. note, "Every project should have two distinct goals—to successfully develop the product and to advance the learning of the organization."[23] Thus, the list of end-of-project deliverables, created at the outset of the project, should include a lessons-learned summary. Attentiveness to project learning is further encouraged if there are learning or knowledge targets associated with each major milestone and built into the templates governing the organization's approach to project execution. So, just as the team might report at each milestone how it is doing with respect to meeting time, cost, and outcome goals, members would also report how they are contributing to the organization's

---

[21] J. Raelin, *Work-Based Learning* (New York: Addison-Wesley, 2000).

[22] M. Darling, C. Parry, and J. Moore, "Learning in the Thick of It," *Harvard Business Review* 83, no. 7/8 (2005), p. 92.

[23] H. Bowen, K. Clark, C. Holloway, and S. Wheelwright, *The Procedural Enterprise Machine—Seven Keys to Corporate Renewal through Successful Product and Process Development* (New York: Oxford University Press, 1994).

project management knowledge base. Specific targets at each milestone could include identifying and documenting relevant insights, documenting things that have gone wrong and why, and passing experiences on to others who may benefit.[24]

Start with Learning

At a large electronics company, each project launch meeting includes a segment that focuses on lessons learned from past project experiences. After identifying the current project's intended results and measures, and the challenges likely to arise, team members are asked to think about what they, personally, or others, have learned in similar situations. In particular, team members identify the three most significant lessons learned from past projects that might have relevance for the current initiative and share these with the rest of the team. The group, as a whole, then discusses the implications these insights have for the project about to begin. This organization also has a routine practice of having a project manager from a past project that was successful (or unsuccessful) speak to the new project team about lessons learned and their potential relevance for the current project. Project managers, in their follow-on remarks, are encouraged to focus on those lessons learned that are likely to be generalizable to the new team.

Other organizations have a formal step in their project management process that requires new project teams to review electronically stored documentation pertaining to past projects' lessons learned. Such a requirement is based on the assumption that truly useful information is stored, and that it is easily searchable. Learning is not facilitated if the data capture or review is pro forma, where teams and their managers are motivated to simply "check off the box" indicating they have archived or reviewed lessons learned. One computer manufacturer guards against perfunctory review of past lessons learned by requiring that new teams describe, in their project initiation document, the key insights gained from their review of past projects' lessons learned. Managers of past projects are likely to find some satisfaction in the acknowledgment that comes from being publicly cited for their contributions to these future projects, increasing the likelihood they will record and disseminate what they have learned. The team also includes a brief summary of insights extracted from past projects in its presentation to management at the tollgate meeting that concludes the project initiation phase.

Whatever the specific approach, beginning each project with a review and analysis of relevant past project experiences can sensitize a team to issues, challenges, and possible responses. Moreover, project initiation practices such as the ones described above help establish an expectation early that project learning is an important part of the upcoming project effort.

Make Learning Visible

In a project with a designated project room, the team can devote a wall to project learning. The wall might display records of the team's discussions of lessons learned from past projects, summaries of meeting critiques, the most current team ground rules, key insights from review and improvement sessions (described in an upcoming section), and so on. Facility space or geographical separation of team members may limit the feasibility of having a project room. In that case, a project Web site with a component dedicated to learning and a chat room for sharing lessons will be very useful. Such a Web site can also be a useful supplement and long-term repository for learning, even when the team is co-located and there is a project room.

---

[24] M. Schindler and M. Eppler, "Harvesting Project Knowledge: A Review of Project Learning Methods and Success Factors," *International Journal of Project Management* 21, no. 3 (2003), p. 236.

Set a Positive, Open Tone

The project manager must set an expectation that the objective of any project learning activity is to improve project delivery, not blame individuals. If people believe they are likely to be blamed, and fear repercussions, they will hesitate to reveal problems that others might blame on them.[25] In fact, they may even object to attending a learning meeting. Two phenomena of human behavior—negativity bias and the fundamental attribution error—can make it difficult for the project manager to maintain a positive atmosphere during learning sessions.

- **Negativity bias** refers to the fact that people think others will view them as more intelligent if they criticize a situation rather than remarking on its positive attributes.[26] Thus, people involved in a learning session might spend too much time on negative lessons to impress their colleagues, and thus limit opportunities for examining the things that are going well.

- The **fundamental attribution error** (or FAE) refers to the human tendency to find fault in individuals, rather than in the organizational context.[27] The outcome of FAE in a learning situation is that the project manager and team members might not attend to contextual factors in the work environment that could be the true causes of the problem.[28] As a consequence, the team may fail to address system-related causes and may alienate people they have inappropriately blamed. As the Dilbert cartoon in Exhibit 10.5 shows, it is not uncommon for people to begin preparing to cast blame before a project begins. Teams enmeshed in this sort of culture often

[25] D.N. Ford and J.D. Sterman, "The Liar's Club: Concealing Rework in Concurrent Development," *Concurrent Engineering Research and Applications* 11, no. 3 (2003), pp. 211–20.

[26] T.M. Amabile, "How to Kill Creativity," *Harvard Business Review* 76, no. 5 (1998), pp. 77–87.

[27] K.A. Brown, "Explaining Group Poor Performance: An Attributional Analysis," *Academy of Management Review* 9, no. 1 (1984), pp. 54–63.

[28] N.P. Repenning and J.D. Sterman, "Capability Traps and Self-Confirming Attribution Errors in the Dynamics of Process Improvement," *Administrative Science Quarterly* 47, no. 2 (2002), pp. 265–95.

EXHIBIT 10.5 **Dilbert's Perspective on the Fundamental Attributional Error (FAE) in Project Environments**

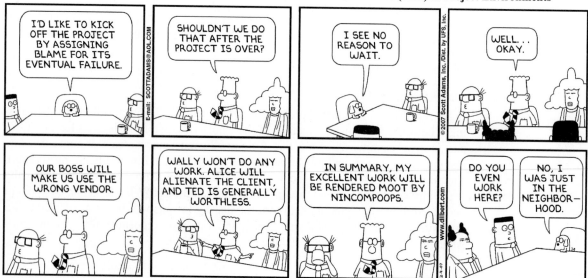

DILBERT: © Scott Adams/Dist. By United Feature Syndicate, Inc

spend more time looking for scapegoats than engaging in productive project work. We must reinforce a cultural caveat here: The FAE operates at full-strength in North American and Western European cultures, but is less likely to occur among members of Asian cultures where people are more inclined to consider the context or environment when attempting to explain poor performance.[29]

To keep things positive and avoid attributional errors, the project manager must continuously remind people of the developmental purpose of learning sessions, begin each learning session with positive observations rather than negative ones, focus on measurable performance rather than individual behaviors, and build trust over time by demonstrating there will be no repercussions for individuals when the team identifies problem areas to be corrected.

Maintain Up-to-Date and Accurate Records

Time erases details. Accurate documentation is essential to identifying what has gone well in the project that should be remembered and what has not gone well that should be corrected. Without accurate data on what has happened, team members will make judgments about effectiveness based on their own limited perspectives, anecdotal evidence, rumors, and predisposed opinions.[30] Further, if the team does not collect knowledge on an ongoing basis throughout the project, members can be influenced by hindsight bias. As mentioned earlier in the chapter, hindsight bias is the human tendency to build faulty memories of what actually happened. These memories are based primarily on final outcomes and often ignore the underlying events and actions that led up to them.

Involve the Team

The careful reader will have observed that we recommend team involvement at every stage of a project. Project learning is no exception. Gathering all those who played a role in the project provides a more complete picture of the project and helps assure that varied perspectives are represented in identifying what went well or poorly and what to do differently next time. Not only does the team gain valuable perspective, but the process of shared learning also helps individuals to absorb best practices from each other and redirect their behaviors in ways that will better support the team.

Methods for Continuous Learning during the Project

Building on the principles described above, we offer three approaches for continuous learning during the project. The first one, the **traffic light process,** is somewhat informal and might be appropriate for a small project. The second one, an **after-action review** or **AAR,** has military origins but can work in certain types of organizations. The third is a more formal and systematic process that we have labeled **end-of-phase review and improvement** (**EPR** for short).

The Traffic Light Process

One quick and effective technique useful at regular intervals throughout the project is the *traffic light process.* The project manager or a facilitator asks each team member to work silently to record one idea about what is happening in the project that should *continue.* Each idea should be recorded on a sticky note. The facilitator places each note on the

[29] R.E. Nisbett, *The Geography of Thought* (Yarmouth, ME: Nicholas Brealey Publishing, 2003).

[30] Repenning and Sterman, "Capability Traps and Self-Confirming Attributional Errors in the Dynamics of Process Improvement."

board, closely locating items that appear to be related. Practices to continue might include "People pitching in to help others when they are behind schedule or need technical assistance" or "The ice cream deliveries on Friday afternoons." The group then follows the same process in identifying things happening in the project that should *stop*. Examples might include "Late handoffs" or "Long team meetings." Next, the facilitator instructs the team to follow the same process in identifying what actions they believe should *start*. Examples might include "Gather feedback from customers before key milestones are complete" or "Send notes to team members' functional bosses letting them know about the individual's contributions to the project." Again, as comments are offered, the facilitator posts them, closely locating items that appear to be related. The team next reviews the clusters of related ideas in each category (i.e., *continue, stop* and *start*) and discusses what they can do to ensure these lessons become part of the project as it moves forward. Keep in mind that each person contributes only one idea in each category. This keeps the process brief and forces people to focus on what is most salient to them.

Where conflicts and tensions have created an environment of low trust, the project manager may wish to make the traffic light process more anonymous. This approach also works if there is not enough time to run the fully-facilitated process during a team meeting. In this case, each individual can write one activity to continue, stop, and start on separate pieces of paper and submit them anonymously (or not, depending on the circumstances) to the project manager. The project manager can then group them after the meeting and prepare and distribute a summary for discussion at the next team meeting.

After-Action Reviews

The U.S. Army's *after-action review,* or AAR methodology, provides a particularly effective process for making ongoing learning a routine part of the project experience. While not everything in this approach is relevant to project teams in other settings, the focus on reviews at each milestone or phase is directly applicable.[31] These sessions are designed to identify what to do differently and better in the next phase. Continuous feedback processes such as these can "help a project team maximize performance and develop a learning culture over time."[32]

At the conclusion of each significant phase of an action, the leader and his or her direct reports meet in an AAR session. They begin by collectively reviewing the ground rules (participate; no thin skins; leave your stripes at the door; take notes; focus on our issues, and not the issues of those above us),[33] and the leader or facilitator summarizes the mission, intent, expected end state, actual end state, and any "events and metrics relevant to the objective."[34] The meeting then focuses on four key questions:

1. What were the intended results?
2. What were the actual results?
3. If there was a difference, what caused it?
4. What will we sustain or improve?

The forward-looking nature of the session is important to underscore: at the close of an AAR meeting the leader identifies two or three lessons of greatest relevance to the next phase.

[31] T. Ricks, "Lesson Learned: U.S. Army Finds Way to See What Does and Doesn't Work," *The Wall Street Journal,* May 23, 1997, p. 1.

[32] Darling et al., "Learning in the Thick of It," p. 92.

[33] No thin skins is a metaphor to suggest that people should avoid being acutely sensitive to criticism and blame. Leave your stripes at the door is a metaphor to suggest that people should not be concerned with organizational hierarchy and that all participants should feel comfortable saying what they think.

[34] Darling et al., "Learning in the Thick of It," p. 88.

Some civilian organizations have begun benchmarking the Army's AAR process, attempting to emulate the military-style approach. Many of these have found the immediacy, structure, and guidelines to be very useful.

Formal End-of-Phase Review and Improvement Sessions

A more formal approach for continuous learning, which incorporates elements of the AAR approach, is to engage the team in a project-to-date team-based review and improvement session at the conclusion of each major phase of the project (initiation, planning, and delivery). This end-of-phase review or EPR asks the team to identify what has gone well, not well, and lessons learned thus far in the project. It can be helpful to probe specific dimensions of the project such as risks, communication, and assumptions (e.g., Are there risks we have failed to identify? How are we doing in communicating among ourselves or with our key stakeholders? What assumptions did we make that proved not to be true?). Importantly, review and improvement sessions also should include action plans—what should be done differently going forward to take best advantage of the lessons learned? If specific tasks are identified (e.g., increase to once a week the frequency of status communication with the client), these should have assigned owners and deadlines as well. Notably, the next review and improvement session should check in on how effectively the lessons learned were actually practiced in the follow-on phase. Exhibit 10.6 provides a structure for a review and improvement session.

The Project Retrospective: Capturing Knowledge at the End of the Project

The principles and processes for learning that occur on a continuous basis during project delivery apply equally well at the end of a project when the activity becomes more formal. This is sometimes called a project postmortem, but we prefer the term **project retrospective** because of its more positive connotation. These sessions offer organizations a formal mechanism for capturing the important lessons learned from project successes and failures. The intent is to capture collective insights so they do not escape into the ether when the team breaks up. Retrospectives should be both a review of what happened well or poorly in the project and an opportunity to plan how projects should be approached differently and better going forward.

In terms of agendas and duration, each retrospective is unique. Some are multiple-day events; others take just a few hours. At the core, however, should be a desire to discover answers to these questions:[35]

- What worked well that we do not want to forget? (What is important to remember, but is at risk to be forgotten if we do not capture it?)
- What did we learn?
- What should we do differently next time?
- What still puzzles us? (What do we still *not* know how to do well?)
- What recommendations would we make to upper-level managers and future teams based on the above?

Some retrospectives begin with the joint creation of a visual timeline using large paper and sticky notes that document, from the participants' varying perspectives, the significant events in the project. This timeline serves as a reference point for identifying and discussing when and where things went well or poorly. A team may wish to return to the high-level sticky note schedule developed during the project planning stage.

---

[35] N. Kerth, *Project Retrospectives: A Handbook for Team Reviews* (New York: Dorset House Publishing, 2001), p. 125.

EXHIBIT 10.6

Sample Plan for an End-of-Phase Team-Based Review and Learning Session

- State session objectives:
  - To identify what has gone well, not well, and lessons learned thus far in the project.
  - To develop an action plan for upcoming phases of the project.
- Review project objectives, accomplishments to date, and results of past traffic light feedback.
- Assess what has gone well so far. (We recommend beginning with positives rather than negatives.)
  - Each team member identifies three to five things that have gone well in the project and records each on a separate, large sticky note.
  - Team members may then offer these in round robin format. Specifically, each person, in turn, offers one idea about what has gone well, placing the corresponding note on the whiteboard or flip chart. Team members pass if all their responses have been noted by other team members. The process continues until all ideas have been posted. If an anonymous process seems more appropriate, team members can hand notes face down to the project manager. The project manager reads each one aloud and places each on a whiteboard or flip chart.
  - The team collaborates to group similar items.
  - The team then reviews the grouped notes and agrees on a title or summary phrase that captures the essence of each of the groupings. These represent the aspects of the project process that are going well and that should continue as the project moves forward.
- Assess what has *not* gone well so far.
  - Each team member identifies three to five things that have detracted from performance so far in the project and records each on a separate, large sticky note.
  - Team members then offer these in round robin format, using the process described above. Again, if an anonymous process seems more appropriate, team members can hand notes face down to the project manager. The project manager reads each one aloud and places each on a whiteboard or flip chart. The team collaborates to group similar items.
  - The group then reviews each cluster of notes. The team may agree on a title or summary phrase that captures the essence of each grouping. These represent the potential improvement areas.
  - The team then assesses the relevance of each improvement area to the next phase of the project. The goal is to identify the three to five improvement areas most relevant to the next phase of the project. If a discussion does not result in a consensus, then the group can vote to narrow the list.
- For three to five of the factors or practices the team views as having contributed to success so far, the group should agree on ways to sustain them as the project proceeds.
- For the three to five most relevant improvement areas, the group develops an action plan for addressing each improvement area. The group discusses what to do differently going forward in the project. For each item, the group identifies an owner and, if appropriate, sets a deadline for implementation.
- The project manager documents the outcomes of the review and improvement session. These are distributed to team members and posted in the team meeting area or on the project Web site. Ultimately, these will accumulate to become part of a project learning document.

Members can revise the original schedule to reflect what actually happened by adding or subtracting tasks or by changing sequential linkages. Once they have established the timeline of actual events, they have a useful visual to aid them in a discussion of what happened along the way. This visual approach can jog people's memories and make it easier to bring their recollections and insights to the surface. Exhibit 10.7 shows a project team engaged in this type of retrospective activity.

EXHIBIT 10.7
Project Team Engaged in an Exercise to Recreate a Project Event Timeline

The results of the retrospective should be summarized in a report distributed to participants and other stakeholders who might benefit from the information. In an organization with a project learning database, these lessons would also be submitted there. Exhibit 10.8 summarizes typical contents of a project retrospective report.

Keep in mind that a project retrospective that emphasizes a collective and relatively open assessment of the project process and outcomes may be unproductive in cultures that lack a tradition of public self-examination. In such cultures, where saving face is all-important, other approaches to project reflection may be more acceptable and therefore more effective. For example, a neutral third party might interview participants individually and create a carefully constructed summary highlighting lessons learned and key takeaways for future project endeavors. Where culturally acceptable, however, team-based retrospectives can provide valuable insights for organizational learning.

EXHIBIT 10.8
Sample Retrospective Report Contents

Source: Adapted from N. Kerth, *Project Retrospectives: A Handbook for Team Reviews* (New York: Dorset House Publishing, 2001), pp. 254–55.

1. Title page (name of project, date and location of retrospective, report authors, company confidentiality statement)
2. Executive overview of the retrospective report
3. Project overview
4. Effort data (project duration, resources used, cost and schedule-plan versus actual)
5. Performance data (extent to which the project achieved performance targets)
6. What worked well
7. Lessons learned
8. What to do differently next time
9. What still puzzles us
10. Recommendations for management
11. Summary of retrospective timeline developed by team
12. Names of participants

Facilitating Learning from Project to Project

Although many organizations engage in post-project assessments, research shows that rarely do teams actually put to work lessons learned by prior teams.[36] Although companies may expect the lessons learned to flow naturally from one project to the next, experienced observers have noted this rarely happens.[37] Sometimes, in the interest of expediency (e.g., who has the time?), post-project assessments are not done at all[38] or are done in only the most cursory way. Teams may view the post-project debriefing as a formality—something that must be done to meet organizational requirements—but not an activity believed to serve as an engine for improvement. For these and other reasons described below, new project teams tend to reinvent the wheel instead of learning from previous project efforts.[39]

Organizations serious about improving the process of project delivery have adopted a number of strategies for promoting learning from project to project. Used in combination, these practices can contribute to creating a **learning organization,** an organization focused on continually finding ways to do work better, faster, and at lower cost.

Focus on Process and Procedural Lessons Learned

Although the output of each project is unique, the processes and procedures of initiation, planning, and delivery of project work are similar from project to project. This means that lessons learned about decision making and assumptions, collaboration methods, risk identification, team structure, communication, meeting processes, stakeholder management, conflict management, and so forth, may be of great value to future teams. Teams should be encouraged to capture and share what they have learned about these dimensions of the project. In most industries, the audience for these *managerial* lessons learned is far larger than it is for technical lessons learned that may apply to a very narrow class of highly similar future projects. New project teams should be encouraged to think about the types of process issues and problems they might encounter (e.g., What is the best way to communicate with one another? How often should we inform top-level managers of our progress? What types of problems should we escalate upward?) and to recognize that other teams have probably dealt with similar issues and may have good ideas about how to overcome them.[40]

Maintain and Encourage the Use of an Organizational Database of Project Lessons Learned

Many organizations maintain project management databases in which lessons learned from each project or phase of a project are logged and can be accessed, along with other project documentation, on an as-needed basis. "The idea is that other project teams can then search these documents by project title, staff, or keywords; assimilate the knowledge they contain; and so learn from them."[41] These databases are typically

---

[36] Darling et al., "Learning in the Thick of It"; S. Newell, "Enhancing Cross-Project Learning," *Engineering Management Journal* 16, no. 1 (2004), pp. 12–20. and Schindler and Eppler, "Harvesting Project Knowledge."

[37] Darling et al., "Learning in the Thick of It"; and Leonard and Swap, "Deep Smarts."

[38] R. Glass, "Project Retrospectives, and Why They Never Happen," *IEEE Software* 19, no. 5 (2002), p. 112; A. Keegan and R. Turner, "Quantity versus Quality in Project Based Learning Practices," *Management Learning* 32, no. 1 (2001), pp. 77–98; and Schindler and Eppler, "Harvesting Project Knowledge," p. 221.

[39] L. Prusak, *Knowledge in Organizations* (Oxford: Butterworth-Heinemann, 1997); and Newell, "Enhancing Cross-Project Learning."

[40] Newell, "Enhancing Cross-Project Learning," p. 19.

[41] S. Newell, M. Bresnen, L. Edelman, H. Scarbrough, and J. Swan, "Sharing Knowledge across Projects: Limits to ICT-Led Project Review Practices," *Management Learning* 37, no. 2 (2006), p. 168.

available via a company's intranet. These information and communications technology-aided approaches to cross-project learning also often include a "corporate 'yellow pages' directory" of project knowledge.[42] These directories, also called **knowledge maps,** indicate what individuals or groups in the organization have specific types of knowledge or experiences.

Although information technology-based knowledge-management systems can provide rapid and easy access to past project experiences, they contribute to organizational learning only if they are routinely used, and research suggests they are not. In one study of 18 project-based organizations, researchers determined that none of the project teams studied used stored knowledge from past projects, even though project documents were electronically stored and easily searched and retrieved.[43] Another investigation of 13 teams in six companies found that teams were either unaware that relevant data existed or they deemed the data captured as not relevant to their projects.[44] Similarly, Schindler and Eppler observe that the "not invented here" syndrome may limit new teams' willingness to learn from the experience of past teams, even when those lessons are well documented and easily accessible via company databases.[45]

Despite these limitations, searchable databases of lessons learned have potential value. To be effective, however, project lessons must be captured in ways that make them relevant to future projects. The documentation of what was learned should include enough context to convey the essence of the insight. A long, unorganized list of bullet points, rich with project-specific jargon but without sufficient explanation, is unlikely to be useful to future project managers. An alternative way of capturing project lessons learned is the **micro article,** a half-page magazine article-style document that records the project experiences and insights in easy-to-read prose and engaging visuals (e.g., embedded video clips, mind maps, photographs).[46] In addition, as noted above, descriptions that capture what was learned about the process of working through the project (e.g., how and why the team did things, solved problems, worked together) may be more useful than insights regarding how specific objectives were achieved.[47] As described earlier, organizations can also encourage, reward, and even require that teams consult the database for relevant lessons when embarking on new projects.

Strengthen Social Networking among Project Managers

When assigned an unfamiliar task or confronting a problem at work, you might seek the advice of a colleague who has dealt with a similar issue. Your personal network is acting as the mechanism for transferring knowledge. Project learning can take the same approach. In a recent study of cross-project learning in four organizations, researchers found that effective transfer of learning was more dependent on social networks than information and communications technology-based lessons-learned systems.[48] Also, the most effective organization members are those whose social networks span **structural holes** and who interact frequently with people outside of their work groups or functions.[49]

---

[42] Ibid., p. 169.

[43] Keegan and Turner, "Quantity versus Quality in Project-Based Learning Practices," p. 90.

[44] Newell, et al., "Sharing Knowledge across Projects: Limits to ICT-Led Project Review Practices," p. 167.

[45] Schindler and Eppler, "Harvesting Project Knowledge," p. 221.

[46] Ibid., p. 223.

[47] Newell, et al., "Sharing Knowledge across Projects: Limits to ICT-Led Project Review Practices," p.182.

[48] Newell, "Enhancing Cross-Project Learning," p. 16.

[49] R.S. Burt, "Structural Holes and Good Ideas," *American Journal of Sociology* 110, no. 2 (2004), pp. 349–99. Structural holes are the white spaces between functions.

Promote Project-to-Project Learning through Team Member Selection

Given the importance of learning from other people, organizations can encourage the transfer of learning from one project to another by forming teams that reflect staffing continuity. For example, if the organization has just completed a new product development project, it will be valuable from a learning standpoint to assign some members of that team to the new project. "The veterans will bring lessons from the first project with them and will be sources of experience and know-how for first-time project members."[50]

Provide Resources for Just-in-Time Learning

One recent study of cross-project team learning observed that project contributors tended to rely primarily on the experience of others within their team when solving problems. They sought the help of outsiders only when internal team knowledge was insufficient.[51] Organizations can facilitate project learning by providing project teams with the ability to pull relevant knowledge from past project experiences just in time. Searchable databases of past project experiences, yellow pages or knowledge maps indicating where information about specific problems might reside in the organization, and personal networks are all sources of just-in-time information.

Create a Project Improvement Advocate Role

Some organizations assign an individual or group the responsibility for collecting, packaging, and internally marketing the organization's accumulated wisdom about project management.[52] A project improvement advocate archives and reviews the retrospective reports and other lessons-learned documentation, synthesizes these into meaningful summaries, and publishes them in places where they are likely to be seen (e.g., project team meeting rooms, prominent bulletin boards). The advocate may also serve as a resource for project managers and their teams. The advocate might, for example, meet with new project teams to explore how the organization's accumulated project management wisdom may be of use to team members as they move forward with the project. Having an individual (or group) responsible for internally marketing the knowledge base helps ensure that valuable lessons remain visible.[53]

Chapter Summary and Onward

Project closure is an important, though often undermanaged and underleveraged, phase in the life of a project. Carefully planning and effectively executing the closeout of project phases and the completed project are hugely important. This is the project team's last opportunity to influence, in a positive way, stakeholder satisfaction. When project closure is not properly handled, costs can escalate, team morale may suffer, stakeholders may be dissatisfied, payment for work can be delayed, future business may be at risk, the opportunity for learning is forgone, and mistakes made may be repeated. Importantly, poor project closure can tarnish the project manager's reputation: last impressions matter, so he or she must close out the project with the same attention to detail that characterized the prior phases.

---

[50] R. Austin, *Managing Projects Large and Small* (Boston, MA: Harvard Business School Press, 2004), p. 152.

[51] Newell, "Enhancing Cross-Project Learning," p. 16.

[52] Kerth, *Project Retrospectives: A Handbook for Team Reviews,* p. 256.

[53] Ibid.

**Team
Activities**

1. Using a scenario introduced in Chapter 4, assume you and three classmates work for the same small electronics organization. The four of you have just been asked by your division manager, Noah Tolk, to organize a two-day, off-site year-in-review and "what's next" management retreat. The division manager has explained that he hopes the retreat will (a) provide an opportunity to celebrate recent accomplishments, (b) enhance community and interdepartmental cooperation within the organization, (c) provide time and space, without distraction, to focus on big-picture issues facing the organization, and (d) increase managers' ideas about, understanding of, and buy-in to, a set of strategic initiatives for the coming year. Noah is concerned that a lack of interdepartmental cooperation and understanding is causing delays in customer service, compromising the organization's ability to get new products to market, and, in general, limiting the organization's performance. Approximately 25 managers will attend the retreat, which is to be held off-site but within driving distance of the company offices.

   Noah has asked that the program be organized so there are sessions/activities devoted to: (1) highlighting key accomplishments of each area, (2) gathering input to shape next year's divisional strategic initiatives, and (3) informal team building and energizing the team for the year ahead. The retreat should occur sometime in the next three months. Resources allocated to the retreat include $15,000 to pay for facilities, materials and services; two hours per week per project team member; and 20 total hours of administrative time. Noah would like to see a draft plan for the retreat in four weeks and would like a written report two weeks after the retreat. That report should briefly describe the retreat itself and the project that created it.

   a. As a team, identify the project's intended results (expressed in several sentences), measures (a bullet list of five to seven key measures), and the challenges likely to arise (a bullet list of five to seven likely challenges). You may go beyond the situation described above when identifying performance metrics.

   b. Individually, identify the three most significant lessons learned from your past project experiences that you feel might be relevant to the retreat project. Record each on a large sticky note and share these in round robin format. Place the notes on a whiteboard, grouping those that seem related. Discuss, as a large group, the implications these insights have for the project about to begin. Take a photo of your group gathered around the whiteboard and embed it in the document you submit to your instructor.

   c. As a team, put together a closure plan for this project. Your closure plan should include closure activities during the project as well as those at the end of the project.

2. This is an extension of Team Activity 2 described at the end of Chapter 9. The assignment involves planning, executing, and monitoring a small project with a team of classmates. In addition to other actions assigned for the project, do the following:

   a. Add a closure plan to the plan you have developed for the project, incorporating all of the dimensions identified in this chapter.

   b. Midway through the project, stop all work and have a short team meeting of 15 to 20 minutes. During the meeting, use the traffic light process described in this chapter to quickly identify things the team should continue doing, stop doing, and start doing. Agree on specific actions your team will take during the remainder of the project. Record the results of your analysis and include them as part of your final report for the project.

c. Conduct a formal learning session at the end of the project, following guidelines from this chapter.

d. Incorporate results of your learning activities into your final project report.

Discussion Questions and Exercises

1. In your own words, describe the benefits of effective project closure. Use examples, real or otherwise, to support your answer.

2. Why is it important to plan project closure at the outset of the project? What is likely to happen if the team does not do this?

3. Describe the major categories of project closure activities and give an example of each (not the examples offered in the chapter).

4. For the "Trouble in Hospital City" vignette presented at the beginning of this chapter, identify at least four closure-related problems the project manager and her team have encountered. For each problem, describe at least one action the project manager and team could have taken to avoid or correct it.

5. Think of a recent project in which you were involved. It can be based on your experience in work settings, school-related efforts, family events, or community service. Prepare a bullet list of the activities that actually happened to close the project. Now, based on what you learned from the chapter, prepare a bullet list of the activities that *should* have been part of closing the project. Identify the activities that were overlooked. Why were these activities omitted?

6. Find the following article: G. McWilliams, "Sink or Swim: After Landing Huge Navy Pact, EDS Finds It's in over Its Head," *The Wall Street Journal,* April 6, 2004, p. A1. EDS began a project worth nearly $2 billion, but did not seem to attend to some important details. Consequently, the project was over budget, behind schedule, and a blight on the reputation of EDS.

   a. Imagine the CEO of EDS has asked you to identify and briefly describe six key lessons EDS should learn from this experience and apply in future projects. What are they?

   b. Imagine the Secretary of the U.S. Navy has asked you to identify and briefly describe six key lessons the Navy should learn from this experience and apply in future projects. What are they?

7. You are the project manager for your parents' wedding anniversary celebration, which will be a dinner for 50 friends and family at your parents' favorite restaurant. Develop a closeout plan for the project. Be sure to consider the administrative, organizational, and personnel dimensions of project closure.

8. A 150-person event planning company serving the corporate market is creating a formal project management process. Company officials have requested your assistance in developing a template they can use to guide project closure.

   a. Conduct an Internet search of "project closure template."

   b. Select and download two templates and compare them. Prepare several bullet points summarizing the differences between the two.

   c. Which template would be more useful to you as a starting point for developing a closure plan for the event planning company and why?

   d. Using the template you selected as a starting point, amend it to create a draft project closure template for the event planning company.

9. This exercise will involve venturing into your local community to interview an individual who has experience with project learning. This can be an individual or team activity, depending on your instructor's assignment guidelines. Identify an individual who has been a team member in a recently completed project. This

could be an employee in a local corporation, a small business, or a non-profit enterprise. Contact the individual and request a 30-minute interview. During the interview, seek answers to the following questions:

a. What was the project objective?

b. What worked well in the planning and delivery of this project that you do not want to forget?

c. What did you learn from the project experience?

d. What should you and the project team do differently next time?

e. What, if anything, still puzzles you about the project and its delivery? In other words, what do you believe the project team still does not know how to do well?

f. Based on your experience with this project and the answers you gave to the questions above, what recommendations would you make to upper-level managers to improve project delivery in your organization?

Prepare a report summarizing the interviewee's answers to your questions. Write a concluding paragraph identifying three insights you can draw from what the interviewee said (or perhaps what he or she did not say). Describe how you could apply ideas you gained from this exercise when you participate in future projects.

10. For a recent project in which you were involved, answer items (a) through (d) in Question 9. From among the items you listed in your response to (c), what did you learn from the project experience?, identify those lessons learned that you anticipate will be of greatest use to you in future projects and explain your rationale.

11. You have been hired as a consultant for Russell Robotics, a firm specializing in the design of innovative scientific instrumentation using robotic technologies. Top-level managers have decided they would like to enhance cross-project learning in the company. Specifically, they would like to implement initiatives that would help project teams and project managers learn from one another so the company will be able to deliver projects faster and with better results. Prepare a one-page document describing five actions you recommend the company take and why.

12. You are the project manager of a yearlong project that created standardized project management training for your organization. You plan to use a portion of your upcoming team meeting to encourage team members to participate in a daylong project retrospective retreat. A capable facilitator, external to the organization but knowledgeable about the general area of your project, will lead the retreat. Prepare a five-slide presentation to use at your final team meeting that will persuade the project team to participate. Your presentation should emphasize how the team and organization will benefit from the retrospective retreat.

References

Amabile, T.M. "How to Kill Creativity." *Harvard Business Review* 76, no. 5 (1998), pp. 77–87.

Andress, F.J. "The Learning Curve as a Production Tool." *Harvard Business Review* 54, no. 1 (1954), pp. 87–97.

Austin, R. *Managing Projects Large and Small.* Boston, MA: Harvard Business School Press, 2004.

Bowen, H.; K. Clark; C. Holloway; and S. Wheelwright. *The Procedural Enterprise Machine—Seven Keys to Corporate Renewal through Successful Product and Process Development.* New York: Oxford University Press, 1994.

Brockner, J. "Why It's so Hard to Be Fair." *Harvard Business Review* 84, no. 3 (2006), pp. 122–29.

Brown, K.A. "Explaining Group Poor Performance: An Attributional Analysis." *Academy of Management Review* 9, no. 1 (1984), pp. 54–63.

Burt, R.S. "Structural Holes and Good Ideas." *American Journal of Sociology* 110, no. 2 (2004), pp. 349–99.

CH2M Hill. *Project Delivery System.* Denver, CO: CH2M Hill, 2001.

Cook, C. *Just Enough Project Management.* New York: McGraw-Hill, 2005.

Darling, M.; C. Parry; and J. Moore. "Learning in the Thick of It." *Harvard Business Review* 83, no. 7/8 (2005), pp. 84–92.

De, P.K. "Project Termination Practices in Indian Industry: A Statistical Review." *International Journal of Project Management* 19, no. 2 (2001), pp. 119–26.

Dobson, M. *Streetwise Project Management.* Avon, MA: Adams Media Corp., 2003.

Dvir, D. "Transferring Projects to Their Final Users: The Effect of Planning and Preparations for Commissioning on Project Success." *International Journal of Project Management* 22, no. 1 (2004), pp. 257–65.

Dvorak, P. "How Understanding the 'Why' of Decisions Matters." *The Wall Street Journal,* March 19, 2007, p. B3.

Ford, D.N., and J.D. Sterman. "The Liar's Club: Concealing Rework in Concurrent Development." *Concurrent Engineering Research and Applications* 11, no. 3 (2003), pp. 211–20.

Glass, R. "Project Retrospectives and Why They Never Happen." *IEEE Software* 19, no. 5 (2002), pp. 111–12.

Hammone, J.S.; R.L. Kenney; and H. Raiffa. *Smart Choices.* New York: Broadway Books, 1999.

Heerkens, G. *Project Management.* New York: McGraw-Hill, 2002.

Hirschmann, W. B. "Profit from the Learning Curve." *Harvard Business Review* 42, no. 1 (1964), pp. 125–39.

Hogarth, R. *Judgement and Choice.* New York: Wiley and Sons, 1980.

Keegan, A., and R. Turner. "Quantity versus Quality in Project-Based Learning Practices." *Management Learning* 32, no. 1 (2001), pp. 77–98.

Kerth, N. *Project Retrospectives: A Handbook for Team Reviews.* New York: Dorset House Publishing, 2001.

Kirby, J., and T. Stewart. "The Search for the Path to Peak Performance." *Financial Times,* August 23, 2005, p. 14.

Kotnour, T. "A Learning Framework for Project Management." *Project Management Journal* 30, no. 2 (1999), pp. 32–38.

Lapré, M., and L.N. Van Wassenhove, "Managing Learning Curves in Factories by Creating and Transferring Knowledge." *California Management Review* 46, no. 1 (2003), pp. 53–71.

Leonard, D., and W. Swap. "Deep Smarts." *Harvard Business Review* 82, no. 9 (2004), pp. 88–97.

Matta, N., and R. Ashkenas. "Why Good Projects Fail Anyway." *Harvard Business Review* 81, no. 9 (2003), pp. 109–14.

Newell, S.; M. Bresnen; L. Edelman; H. Scarbrough; and J. Swan. "Sharing Knowledge across Projects: Limits to ICT-Led Project Review Practices." *Management Learning* 37, no. 2 (2006), pp. 167–85.

Newell, S. "Enhancing Cross-Project Learning." *Engineering Management Journal* 16, no. 1 (2004), pp. 12–20.

Nisbett, R.E. *The Geography of Thought.* Yarmouth, ME: Nicholas Brealey Publishing, 2003.

Prusak, L. *Knowledge in Organizations.* Oxford: Butterworth-Heinemann, 1997.

Raelin, J. *Work-Based Learning.* New York: Addison-Wesley, 2000.

Repenning, N.P., and J.D. Sterman. "Capability Traps and Self-Confirming Attribution Errors in the Dynamics of Process Improvement." *Administrative Science Quarterly* 47, no. 2 (2002), pp. 265–95.

Richmond, R. "EDS Chief Sees Brighter Skies." *The Wall Street Journal,* December 15, 2005, p. B5.

Ricks, T. "Lesson Learned: U.S. Army Finds Way to See What Does and Doesn't Work." *The Wall Street Journal,* May 23, 1997, p. A1.

Schindler, M., and M. Eppler. "Harvesting Project Knowledge: A Review of Project Learning Methods and Success Factors." *International Journal of Project Management* 21, no. 3 (2003), pp. 219–28.

Schwalbe, K. *Information Technology Project Management.* Cambridge, MA: Course Technology, 2000.

Sharp, D. "Knowledge Management Today: Challenges and Opportunities." *Information Systems Management* 20, no. 2 (2003), pp. 32–37.

Swan, J.S.; S. Newell; H. Scarbrough; and D. Hislop. "Knowledge Management and Innovation: Networks and Networking." *Journal of Knowledge Management* 3, no. 4 (1999), pp. 262–75.

Von Zedtwitz, M. "Organizational Learning through Post-Project Reviews in R&D." *R&D Management* 32, no. 3 (2002), pp. 255–68.

Appendix A

Quick Guide to Using Microsoft Project

This appendix is a beginner's guide for using Microsoft Project (MSP).[1] It also offers guidance to somewhat experienced users who would like a fresh start. Before you launch into MSP, or any other scheduling software package, you must have an idea about the purpose for which you will use it. Will it be for team decision making or problem solving? Will it be for dissemination to project stakeholders? The purpose will determine the type of display, the level of detail, the time scale, and other attributes of the electronic records and printouts you create.

All readers must understand that the software does not manage a project; it is merely a tool that fits into a larger process. Before entering data into MSP, the members of the project team must have completed several important steps, including:

- Agreement on project purpose. This is based on a clear understanding of an underlying problem, opportunity, or mandate. (See Chapters 3 and 4.)
- Work breakdown structure (WBS). A project team must develop a comprehensive list of project activities before it can competently create a schedule. For most projects, we recommend the mind-mapping approach involving key team members. (See Chapter 5.)
- Network schedule. The team should develop a precedence-based schedule using a collaborative approach that allows members to see the big picture. Developing the initial schedule should not be a solo activity. (See Chapter 7.)
- Preliminary estimates of time and resource requirements for project tasks. (See Chapter 5.)
- Uncertainty assessment. The team should have performed a thorough assessment of potential project uncertainties and adjusted the WBS accordingly. (See Chapter 6.)

This appendix is not intended to be a full tutorial on all features and functions of MSP, but it should offer sufficient guidance for most people. We have used a trial version of Microsoft Project Professional 2007, demonstrating that you can practice using it before purchasing it. However, MSP is available to students at very reasonable prices.

---

[1] Tamara Reid played a significant role in the development of this guide, developing screen shots, reviewing instructions, and testing it with her students. We are deeply indebted to her for her contributions.

STEP-BY-STEP PROCESS FOR BUILDING AND USING A MICROSOFT PROJECT SCHEDULE

In this appendix we walk through a set of procedures for setting up defaults and project parameters, creating network and Gantt chart schedules, adjusting schedules to accommodate resource conflicts, and monitoring progress. These procedures are built around a small information technology (IT) project. As you proceed with the steps shown here, be sure to save your work along the way.

1. **Set Default View to Network Diagram.** Move the cursor to TOOLS in the pull-down menu at the top of the screen. Select *Options*. Change the "Default view" (Gantt Chart) to **Network Diagram.** (From now on when you open MSP, you will see the Network Diagram view instead of the Gantt Chart view.) See Exhibit A.1.

Each individual has his or her own preferences, but we recommend starting with the Network Diagram view because it highlights task relationships more graphically

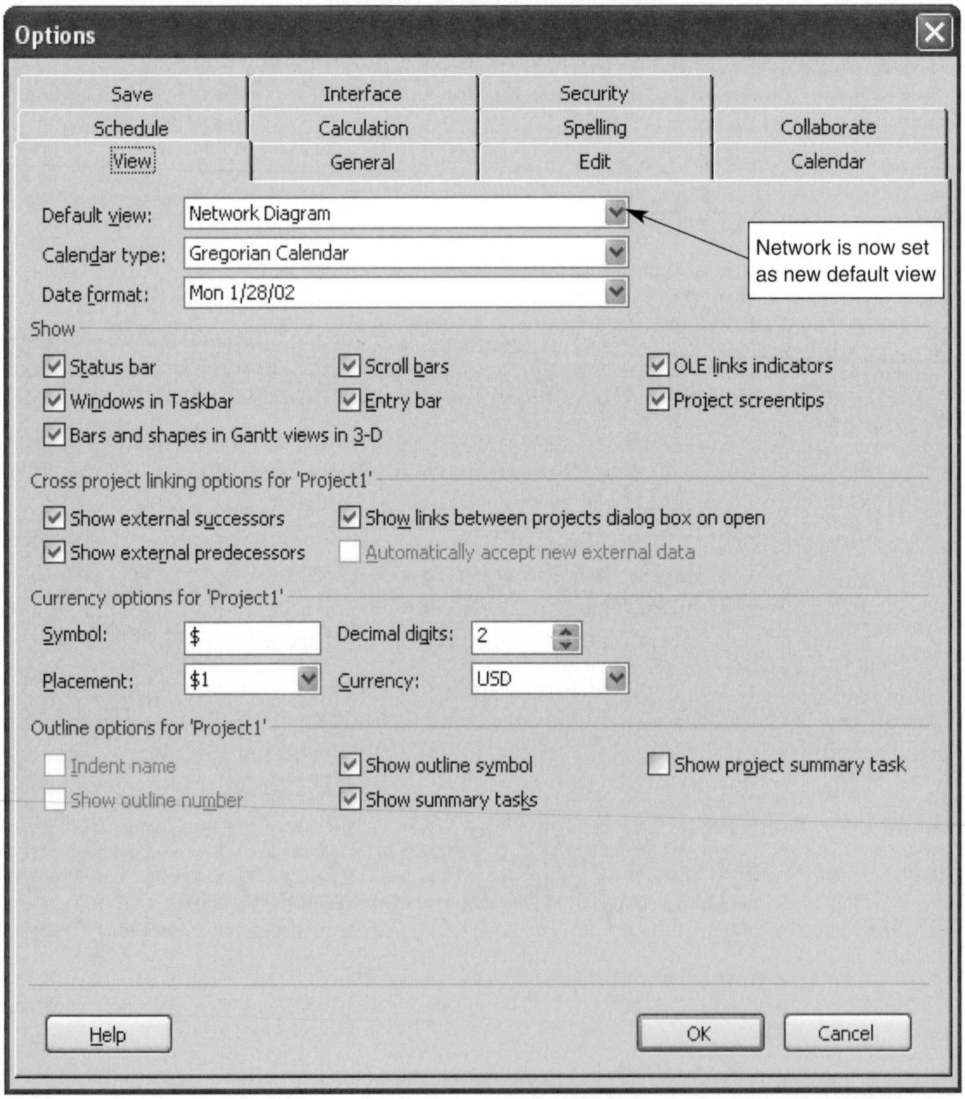

EXHIBIT A.1 Step 1: Setting Network Diagram as the Default View

than the Gantt view does. Also, it represents a natural outgrowth of the team scheduling effort that should have preceded use of the software. People tend to think in a more linear manner when they start in Gantt view, and they do not necessarily look for connections among subelements.

2. **Changing Defaults for Assignment Units and Task Type.** In the *Options* dialog box (TOOLS, *Options*), select the Schedule tab. First, change the "Show assignment units" to **Decimal.** The default is percentages, a setting appropriate for use with specialized resources such as individual team members. The realities of your project will determine which approach is appropriate, but we use the decimal approach to depict generic team members for this example. In addition, change the "Default task type" to **Fixed Duration**. Finally, deselect "Split in-progress tasks." These changes will give you more control over activities; without them, you are likely to find MSP to be quite mischievous. Click "Set as Default" at the bottom of the screen, then click "OK." MSP now will apply these settings to every new project you create. See Exhibit A.2.

EXHIBIT A.2   Step 2: Changing Defaults for Assignment Units and Task Type

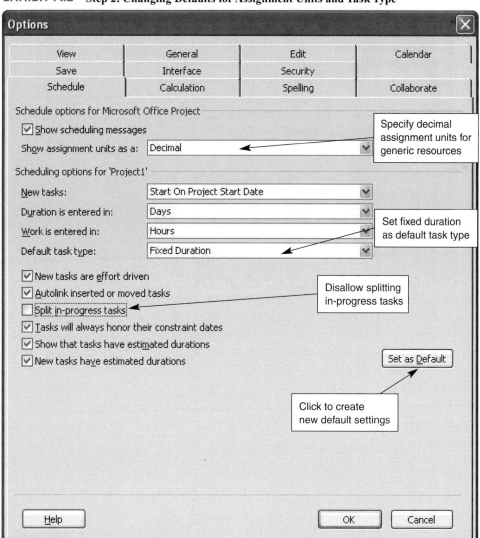

Note that the screen in Exhibit A.2 is also the place where you can specify the level of detail for the schedule by showing duration time units (hours, days, weeks, months, years). The default units, days, are appropriate for our example, so leave this as is.

3. **Setting Resource Leveling to Manual.** Go to TOOLS again and select *Level Resources*. Confirm that **Manual** leveling has been selected. This gives you control over rearranging tasks if you have too much work scheduled in relation to the number of people available for a particular time period. You may regret it if leveling is set to automatic. Click "OK" to close the pop-up box. MSP will apply this setting to every project you create until you change the default. See Exhibit A.3.

EXHIBIT A.3
Step 3: Setting Resource Leveling to Manual

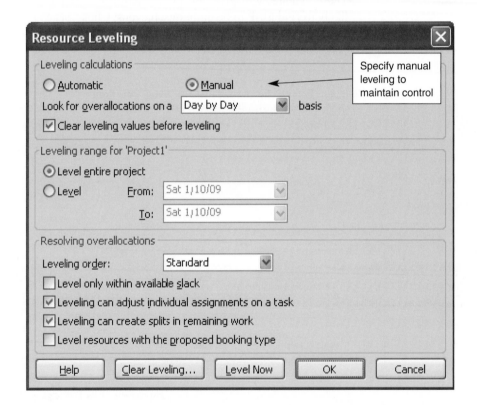

4. **Adding a View Bar on the Left of the Screen.** Place the cursor on the VIEW pull-down menu and select *View Bar*. This adds a bar on the left-hand side of the screen with icons for each of the views MSP offers. If you have completed Step 1, your project is already in the Network Diagram view. If not, select the Network Diagram icon from the view bar on the left-hand side of your screen. MSP now displays the view bar and the Network Diagram view until you change these settings. See Exhibit A.4.

Unlike Steps 1 through 4, the adjustments made in Steps 5 through 8 must be made for each project. These settings do not carry forward to new projects automatically.

EXHIBIT A.4   **Step 4: Adding a View Bar on the Left of the Screen**

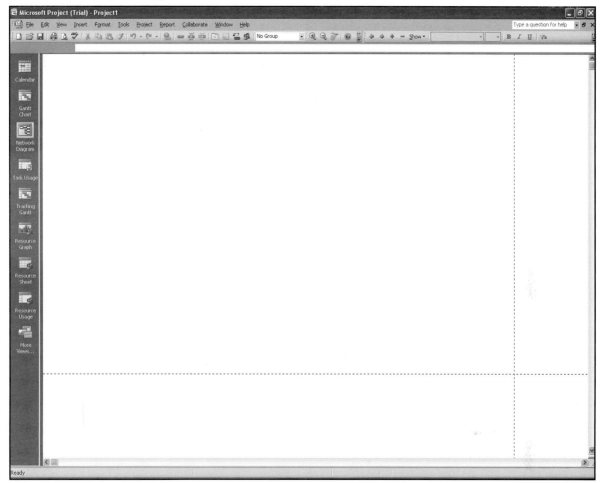

5. **Setting Up Layout, Link Style, and Link Labels.** Make certain you are still in the Network Diagram view for this step. Go to FORMAT in the pull-down menu at the top of the screen. Click on *Layout.* At the top of the pop-up frame that appears, change automatic box positioning to **Allow manual box positioning.** This allows you to control where your activity boxes are placed in the Network Diagram view. After you make this change, you will be able to more easily visualize, as well as print, your network. In automatic box positioning mode, MSP spreads even a small, 10-activity network in a messy array across multiple pages.

In this same pop-up box under "Link style" select **Straight.** This is a matter of personal preference, but we believe it creates a more understandable network. Try it with this example and decide for yourself.

Also, in this same pop-up box under "Link style" select **Show link labels.** This will allow you to see the type of relationship (e.g., Finish-to-Start, Start-to-Start, etc.) between each pair of sequentially related tasks (see Chapter 7 for details). And it permits you to see lags (e.g., B can start five days after A finishes) and overlaps (e.g., B can start three days after A starts). The link labels, in combination with lag and overlap information, are handy when you are moving tasks around to accommodate resource constraints. Without them, MSP provides no clear indicator of lag or over-lap decisions you may have made, and the rationale behind the resulting schedule can seem mysterious. Click "OK" to close the pop-up box. See Exhibit A.5.

EXHIBIT A.5   Step 5: Setting Up Layout, Link Style, and Link Labels

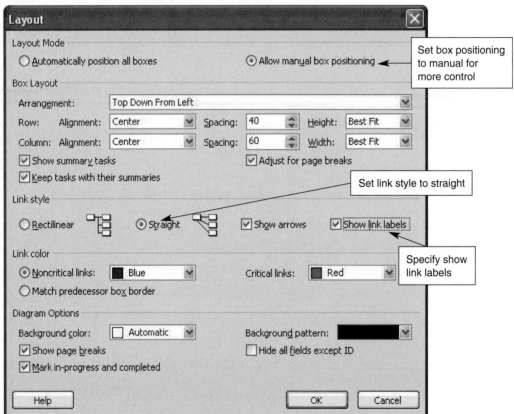

6. **Selecting Task-Box Styles.** Return to FORMAT on the top pull-down menu and select *Box Styles*. The word "Critical" will be highlighted in the list of task types at the top left of the box. To specify the look of all critical activities in the Network Diagram, under "Border" find the "Shape" attribute. Select the smallest rectangular box shape (first selection in most Microsoft Project versions). Go back to the top left of the box and highlight **Noncritical**. Under "Border" find the "Shape" attribute and, again, select the smallest rectangular box shape. Choosing this smaller box size permits you to fit more project activities on a single page. (If we had any clout with Microsoft, we would persuade key decision makers to resurrect the slightly smaller boxes available in earlier versions of the software.) You can also change the color of your critical and noncritical network boxes and specify shape and color for other Network Diagram elements in this screen. For now, leave these other options as they are. Click "OK." See Exhibit A.6.

EXHIBIT A.6
Step 6: Selecting
Task-Box Styles

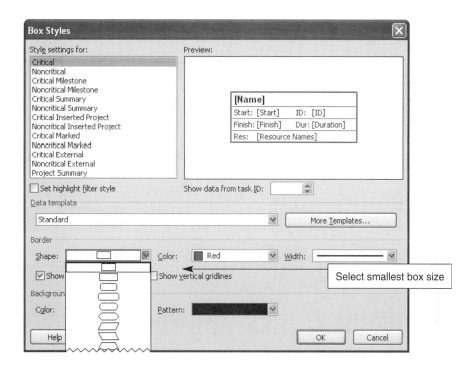

7. **Setting the Project Start Date.** Go to the PROJECT pull-down menu and select *Project Information.* Specify a project start date of your choosing under "Start date." The software will now schedule activities forward from that date. (You also could specify a completion deadline and have MSP schedule backward to give you a start date, but that approach can be a little messy, and if you have done your group scheduling work before entering the information into MSP, you should know what start date meets your requirements.) Click "OK." See Exhibit A.7.

EXHIBIT A.7
Step 7: Setting the
Project Start Date

Project Information for 'Project1'

Specify project start date

Start date:	Mon 8/16/10	Current date:	Sat 1/10/09
Finish date:	Sat 1/10/09	Status date:	NA
Schedule from:	Project Start Date	Calendar:	Standard
	All tasks begin as soon as possible.	Priority:	500

Enterprise Custom Fields

Custom Field Name	Value

Help   Statistics...   OK   Cancel

8. **Changing Calendar Working Days.** Go to TOOLS in the pull-down menu at the top of the screen and select *Change Working Time.* Here we are going to add a holiday. Do this by highlighting the day on which you will not be working (select the first Friday of the project) and then clicking on the "Name" column under the Exceptions tab that appears beneath the calendar. Then hit Enter or tab over to the start column and this date will be marked as nonworking time. This is just to give you a feel for the flexibility you have with the calendar. If you wanted to select all Fridays, you would highlight the "F" column to give your team members four-day workweeks. The working time default is 8:00–5:00 Monday through Friday with an hour for lunch from 12:00–1:00. Leave working time as-is for now. Close this menu by clicking "OK." See Exhibit A.8.

EXHIBIT A.8   Step 8: Changing Calendar Working Days

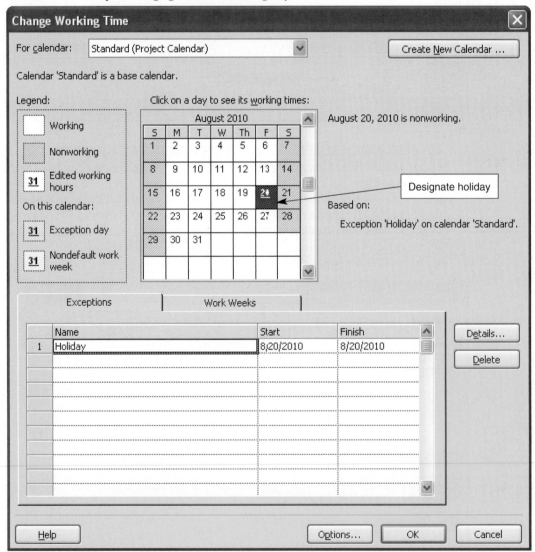

9. **Entering Project Activities.** You are now ready to enter project activities. For the sake of this exercise, we will plan a small IT project. When you close the previous dialog box, MSP should return you to the Network Diagram view. In this view, click and drag the cursor to form a box. A network task box should appear. Click on the top line of the box and type in the name of the activity. Name this activity "Define system requirements." On the "Res:" (resource) line at the bottom of the box, type "Project Team." This line is simply asking for the type of resource needed for this task. For this example, assume all team members possess interchangeable skills. Now place the cursor on the "Dur:" (duration) line in the box and type in the duration, "2d" (MSP knows you mean two days). To specify two weeks, you would enter "2w." See Exhibit A.9A.

EXHIBIT A.9A   Step 9: Entering Project Activities

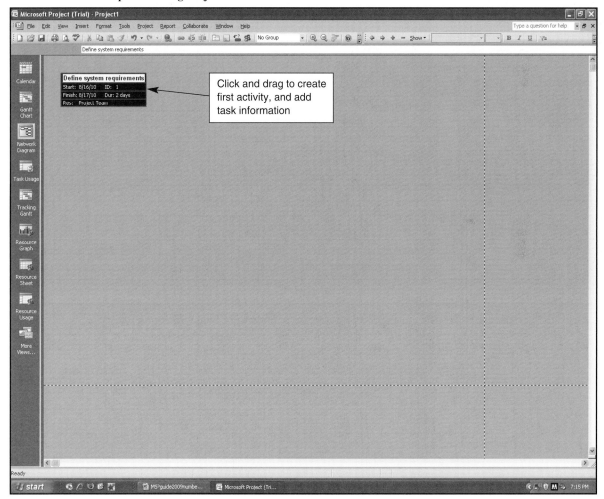

There is another way to add information about a task. Direct the cursor to the INSERT pull-down menu and select *New Task*. When a new task box appears on the screen, double-click on it. A dialog box labeled *Task Information* will appear, and you are in the General (for general information) frame. In the space for "Name," type "Develop application." Under "Duration" type "6d." Then click on the Resources tab at the top of the pop-up box. The pop-up box then displays the Resources box for this task. Type in "Project Team" under "Resource Name." Click "OK" to close this box. It is also possible to enter all of the necessary information using the Resources box. The "Name" and "Duration" fields are at the top of the box. See Exhibit A.9B.

EXHIBIT A.9B   Step 9: Entering Activity Information in "New Task" Box

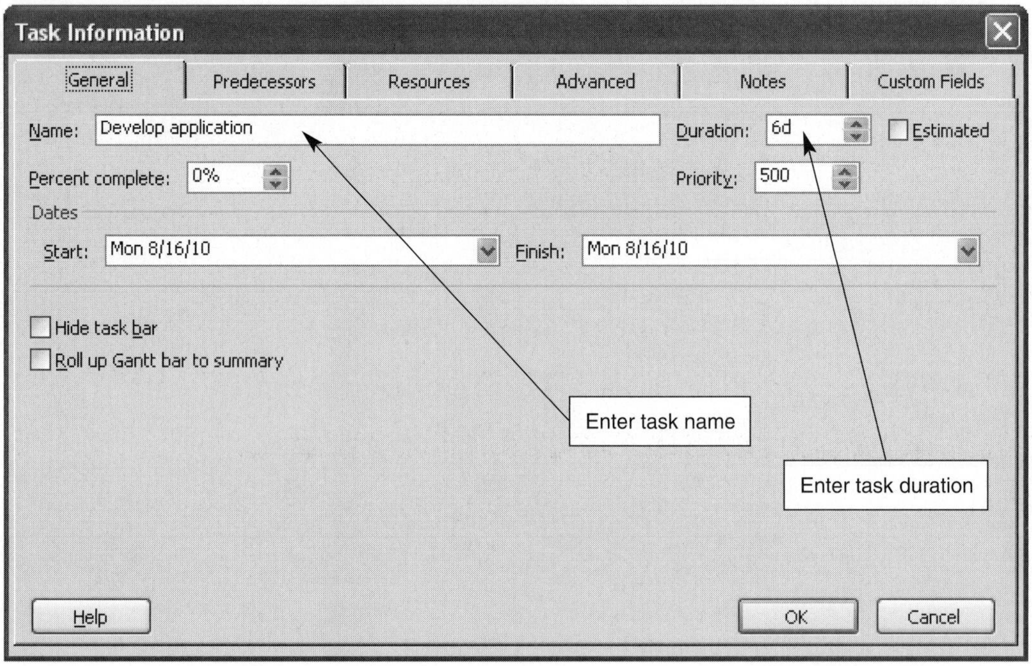

Task Information

| General | Predecessors | Resources | Advanced | Notes | Custom Fields |

Name: Develop application   Duration: 6d   ☐ Estimated

Percent complete: 0%   Priority: 500

Dates

Start: Mon 8/16/10   Finish: Mon 8/16/10

☐ Hide task bar
☐ Roll up Gantt bar to summary

Enter task name

Enter task duration

Help   OK   Cancel

As depicted in Exhibit A.9C, the screen now shows both of the tasks you have created, even though you used two different methods to create them.

EXHIBIT A.9C   **Result of Data Entry for First Two Activities**

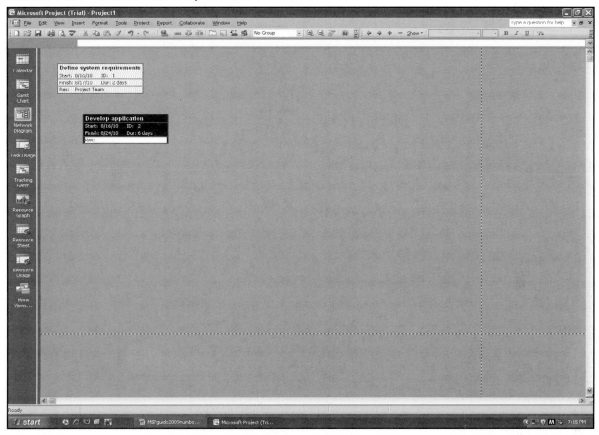

Using the information in the table below, create activity boxes for Tasks 3–7, using either the click-and-drag method or the task information box method.

	Task	Duration	Resource
1	Define system requirements	2d	Project Team
2	Develop application	6d	Project Team
3	Integrate and test application	4d	Project Team
4	Install application	1d	Project Team
5	Develop training	3d	Project Team
6	Train users	2d	Project Team
7	Deploy application	.5d	Project Team

The screen shot in Exhibit A.9D shows how the plan should look after all tasks are entered. They will be arranged in whatever positions you have placed them, but at this point they are not yet connected by precedence arrows. That is the next step.

EXHIBIT A.9D **All Activities Created but Dependency Relationships Not yet Specified**

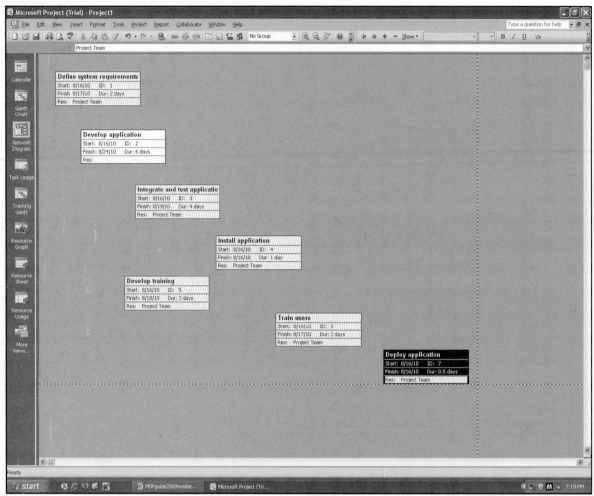

10. **Specifying Dependency Relationships.** To specify dependency relationships among project activities, place the cursor in the center of the Define system requirements box. A small cross should appear (⊹). Hold the mouse down and a link symbol should appear as you move the cursor toward the left side or top of the Develop application box. When you let go of the mouse button with the link symbol on the Develop application box, an arrow between the two boxes appears. Using the predecessor relationships identified in the table below, create the appropriate links in the network diagram. See Exhibit A.10.

	Task	Immediate Predecessor
1	Define system requirements	-
2	Develop application	1
3	Integrate and test application	2
4	Install application	3
5	Develop training	3
6	Train users	4, 5
7	Deploy application	6

EXHIBIT A.10   **Step 10: Specifying Dependency Relationships**

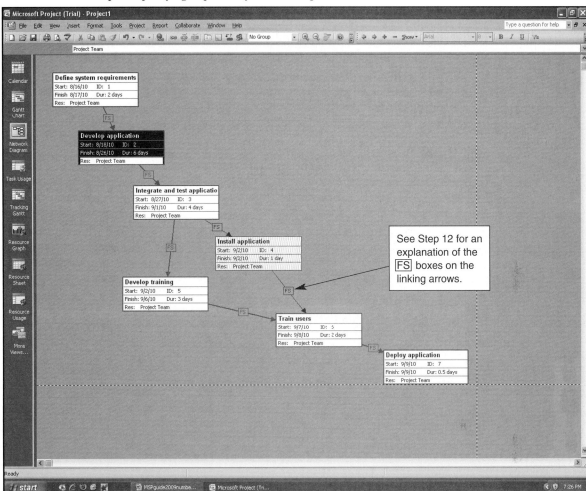

At this point, the network might be somewhat messy, with lines crossing or boxes in odd positions. Reposition the boxes by putting the cursor at the edge of a box (you should get the classic crossed arrows symbol (✛) that you get in PowerPoint) and dragging it to a new spot. You would not be able to move the boxes if you had not selected manual box positioning during the setup process.

You will see that critical path activities are a different color from noncritical activities. They should be red, unless you changed the colors when setting box styles earlier.

If you have successfully created connections among all of the activities in your network, you are far ahead of most beginning users of MSP. Many people attempt to use the software before they know anything about network schedules, critical path, float, and so on. Consequently, they naively omit the connections and simply specify a start and finish date for each task. This misses the point of using the software and exposes the person's lack of knowledge about project scheduling. Remember, every task should be tied into the network. That way, when you make a schedule change, the software can show you the effect of your change on every other task in the project.

11. **The Gantt Chart View.** Select the Gantt Chart icon on the left-hand side of the screen. (You can also go to VIEW and select *Gantt Chart* from the pull-down menu.) The Gantt chart for the IT project should appear. The software places the view on today's date, so if the project is set to start in the future, scroll forward until you reach the horizontal Gantt bars on the project start date. Shaded areas are nonworking days (including the holiday specified earlier). MSP automatically interrupts activities for nonworking days, even though the activity bars appear to suggest that the work continues through the weekend. (This is another one of those areas where we believe Microsoft could make schedule displays easier to use; simply shade the bar differently on the weekend.) In this view of the Gantt chart, the critical path is not apparent. If you want to see the critical path highlighted in the Gantt chart view, select Tracking Gantt on the left-hand side of the screen. This view will differentiate critical activities from other activities. See Exhibit A.11.

Any changes you make in one view (e.g., task name, duration, resource name) automatically update themselves in other views.

EXHIBIT A.11   Step 11: The Gantt Chart View

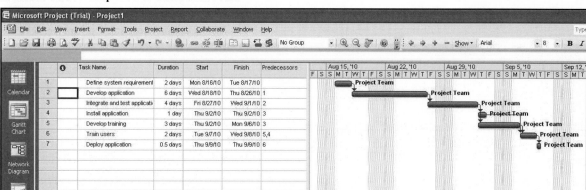

12. **Changing a Task Dependency.** Imagine the team has decided it needs to have the application installed three days before the training begins.[2] This is to ensure everything is running properly before they use the software in the training sessions. Select the Network Diagram icon on the left-hand side of the screen. Double-click on the connecting precedence arrow between Install application and Train users. A small box labeled *Task Dependency* should appear with an entry for "Lag" time. In this box type "3d." It also asks for "Type". The default is Finish-to-Start. Leave this as it is. This simply means installation must finish before training may start. (There are other types of dependencies, as described in Chapter 7 and Chapter 8.) See Exhibit A.12A.

[2] Assume it will be running in parallel to a existing system during this time.

EXHIBIT A.12A
Step 12: Changing
Task Dependency

Close the dialog box and in the network view you should see a small box with
$\boxed{FS + 3d}$ inside it on the line between the Install Application task and the Train
Users task. And, compared to the network diagram before insertion of the lag,
there is a slight change in the critical path. See Exhibit A.12B.

EXHIBIT A.12B   **Step 12: Network View with Lag Displayed in Task Link**

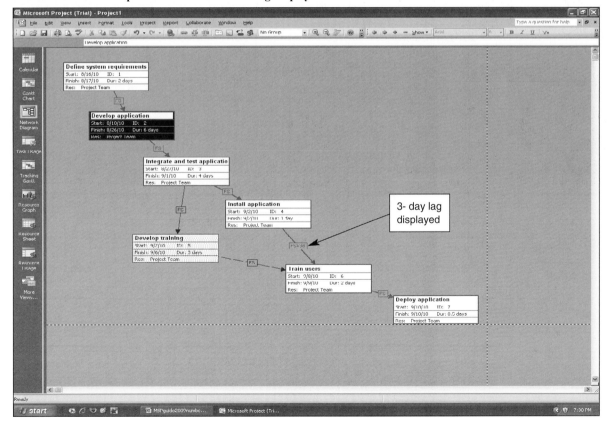

Select the Tracking Gantt icon on the left-hand side of the screen. With the insertion of the three-day lag, the task **Develop Training** is no longer on the critical path. See Exhibit A.12C.

EXHIBIT A.12C   **Step 12: Tracking Gantt View with New Critical Path Highlighted**

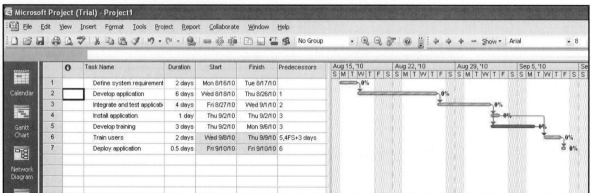

13. **Establishing Resource Parameters.** Select the Resource Sheet icon on the left-hand side of the page. (You can also go to the VIEW menu and select *Resource Sheet.*) The only line in the sheet should say "Project Team." Under "Max Units" in this view, type in "**10.**" This tells MSP there are 10 team members (our resource) available to perform all project tasks. See Exhibit A.13.

EXHIBIT A.13   **Step 13: Establishing Resource Parameters**

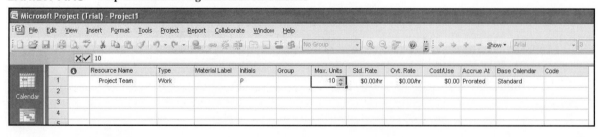

14. **Specifying Resource Usage for Project Activities.** All 10 project team members will be required to complete each task, so we must add this information to the project file. Go to VIEW and select *Network Diagram.* In turn, double-click on each box in the network to get the *Task Information* dialog box. Select the Resources tab and in the space for "Units," enter the number "**10**." When you have finished, the "Res:" line of every task should read Project Team[10]. *Note: Do this for EVERY task!* Although we could add costs in the Resource tab, it is not necessary to do so in this example. See Exhibit A.14.

EXHIBIT A.14
Step 14: Specifying Resource Usage for Project Activities

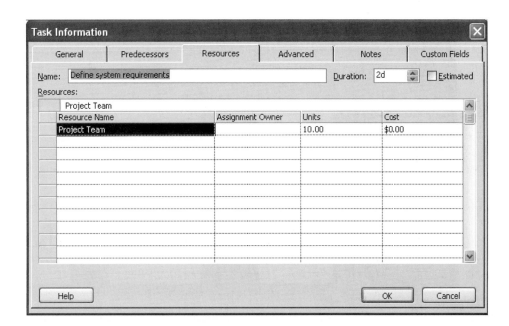

15. **Interpreting the Resource Graph.** Direct the cursor to VIEW and select *Resource Graph* or select the Resource Graph in the view bar. You should see a histogram that shows the days of the project along the horizontal axis and the people used on each day on the vertical axis. (Once again, if you chose to start your project on a future date, scroll forward in time to see horizontal Gantt bars displayed.) The red-hashed bars show where the current schedule requires more than 10 people on a given day. You should see a red-hashed "overutilization" segment in the upper part of the vertical bar on the day when Install application and Develop training are concurrently scheduled. See Exhibit A.15.

EXHIBIT A.15 Step 15: Interpreting the Resource Graph

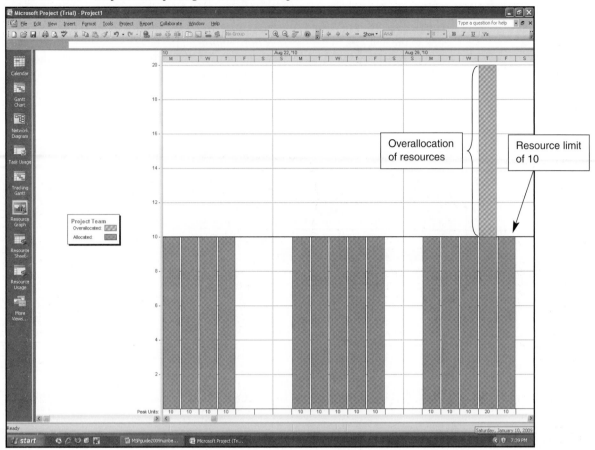

16. **Viewing Resource Allocation in Split-Screen Mode.** To adjust the screen to create a more comprehensive view of what is happening, move the cursor to WINDOW on the pull-down menu bar at the top of the screen and select *Split*. The screen is now split horizontally. On the top is the Resource Graph view. Move the cursor to the bottom half of the screen and click on the Gantt Chart icon on the left-hand side. A Gantt chart view should appear on the bottom half of the screen. The double display shows the relationship between the schedule and resource usage. Install application and Develop training overlap by one day, and each one requires 10 project team members. One obvious solution is to delay development of the training until the application is installed. Develop training is not on the critical path and it has one day of float (both total float and free float, in this case). It is possible to delay it a day without changing the anticipated completion date of the project, and without affecting any other task in the schedule. See Exhibit A.16.

EXHIBIT A.16   **Step 16: Viewing Resource Allocation in Split-Screen Mode (Partial View of Schedule)**

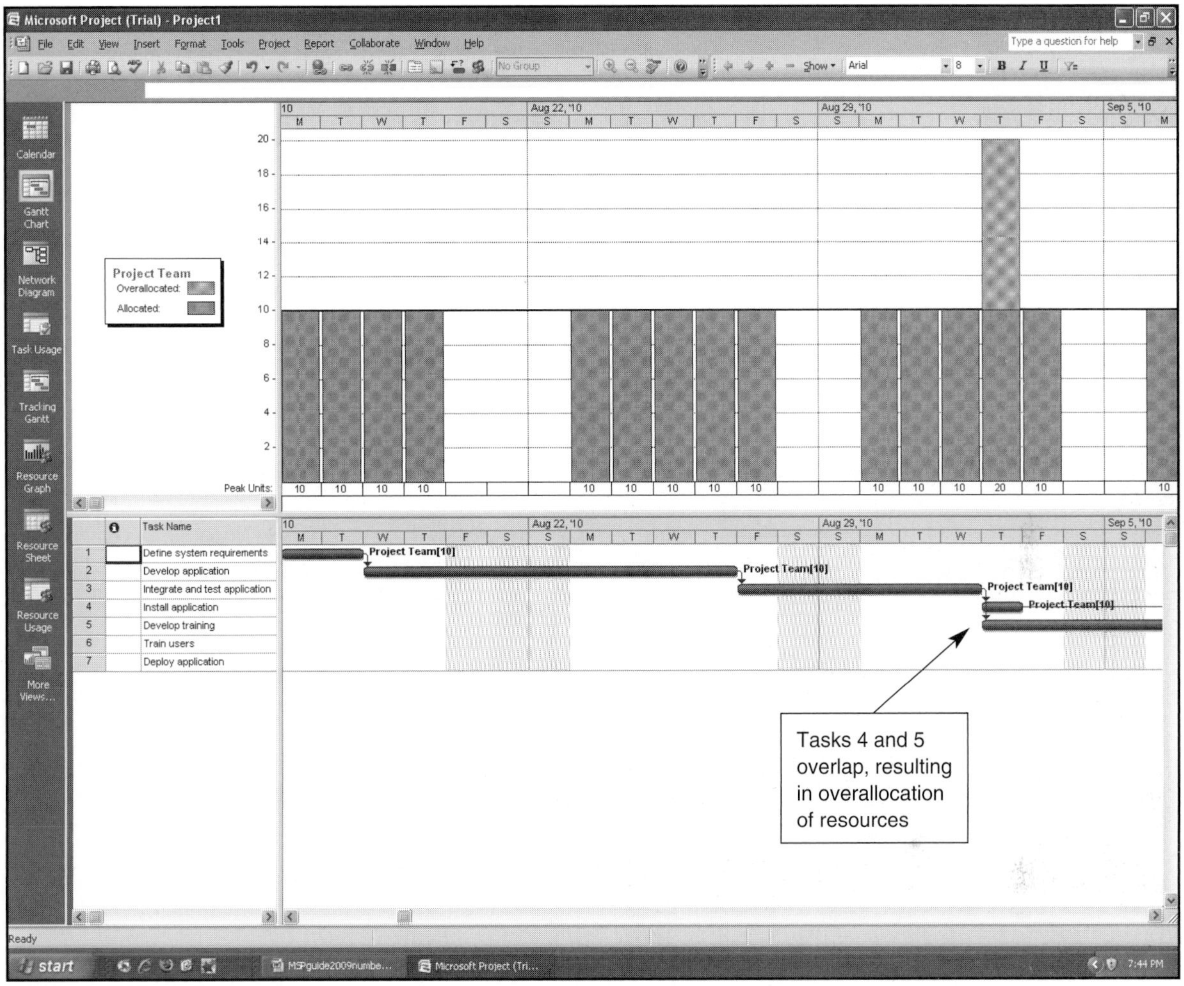

Tasks 4 and 5 overlap, resulting in overallocation of resources

17. **Resolving the Resource Conflict.** There are two ways to resolve the resource conflict that appears on September 2: (1) make the needed adjustments yourself by moving tasks where resource conflicts present themselves or (2) employ the MSP resource-leveling tool.

First we demonstrate the intuitive do-it-yourself method. As noted earlier, **Develop training** can be delayed by one day, allowing **Install application** to be completed by all 10 team members. On the bottom half of the screen, shift from the Gantt Chart view to the Network Diagram view by selecting Network Diagram on the view bar. Double click on the FS box located on the arrow that connects **Integrate and test** with **Develop training**. Add a lag of one day (1d) in the *Task Dependency* box that appears, and hit "OK" to return to the network. If you have succeeded in making the change, an $\boxed{\text{FS} + 1}$ appears in the dependency box on the arrow and the overallocation on the histogram disappears. See Exhibit A.17.

EXHIBIT A.17 **Step 17: Resolving the Resource Conflict**

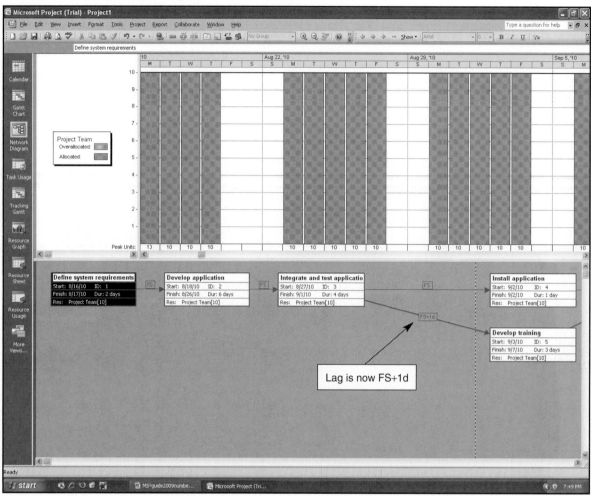

Notice that none of the precedence relationships has been violated to accommodate the resource conflict. We have simply used available float. Some people are tempted when they see resource constraints to change precedence relationships—for example, by making Install application the predecessor of Develop training. However, if this is not a hard logic dependency, you will have specified an unnecessary constraint that might limit flexibility as the project proceeds.

This is one approach. Now, undo the preceding changes (i.e., reset the lag between Integrate and test application and Develop training to 0d) to prepare for the automated approach.

18. **Automated Leveling.** This time, we direct MSP to do the leveling work based on its own algorithms. Make sure you have returned to the original situation with a resource overload on day 13 of the project (here, September 2). Go to TOOLS, *Level Resources.* "Manual" leveling should be selected. Click on **Level Now** at the bottom of the box. You should see your resource graph level out with no more red hashes shown. What the program has done is what you did intuitively—delayed development of the training until installation of the application is complete. Notice

that MSP does not indicate the lag on the link between **Integrate and test application** and **Develop training**. This makes it very difficult to determine what has happened and how the float has been used. (Another area where we wish we had more clout with Microsoft!) See Exhibit A.18A.

EXHIBIT A.18A   Step 18: Results of Automated Leveling with Network View

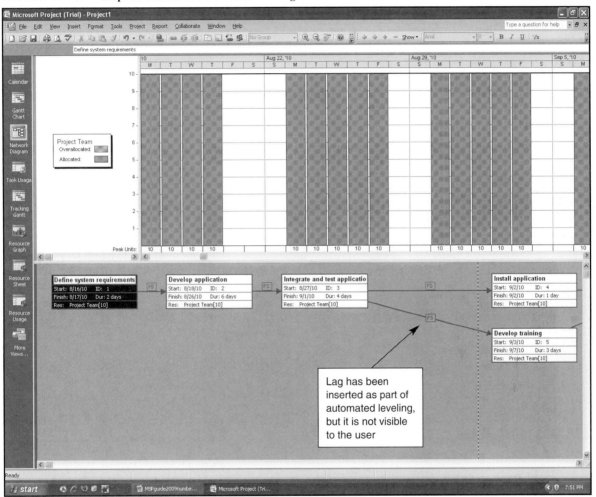

Warning: In this case, MSP came up with a logical solution to the resource constraint—one you made yourself. In more complex networks, the software will not behave as intelligently. Although the leveling tool has been improved over the years as computer speed and the software's analytical sophistication have evolved, it is still not as reliable or intuitive as the human brain. Consequently, it can produce less-than-optimal solutions, and, in many cases, create quite a rat's nest. Be very cautious about using this feature. As one of our former students who was an experienced project manager once remarked, "Don't touch that leveling button!" See Chapter 8 for more information about intuitive solutions supported by decision rules and team input.

To see what happens to the Gantt chart after leveling, place the cursor in the Network Diagram and select Gantt Chart from the view bar. Notice that Task 5, **Develop training**, has been slid to the right until **Install application** is complete. However, its position as an immediate successor of Install Application is intact. See Exhibit A.18B.

EXHIBIT A.18B   Step 18: Results of Automated Leveling with Gantt View

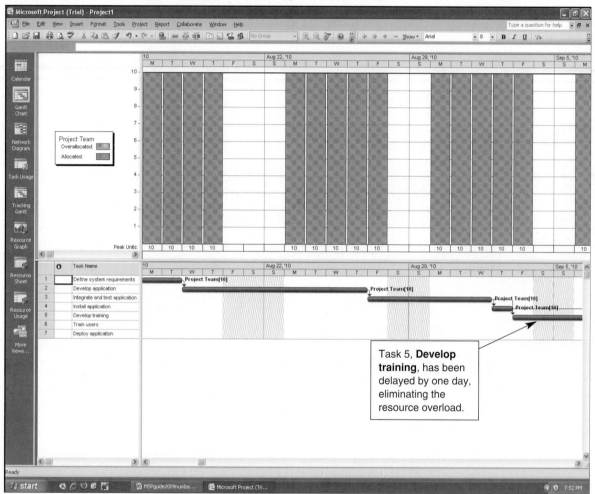

Task 5, **Develop training**, has been delayed by one day, eliminating the resource overload.

19. **Reporting Progress.** Shift the view in the lower half of the split screen back to the Network Diagram view. In the network diagram, double-click on the **Define system requirements** box. The *Task Information* box should appear. Go to the General tab and find the line for "Percent complete." Type in "**100%**" complete. Then double-click on **Develop application** and make it "**40%**" complete. See Exhibit A.19.

EXHIBIT A.19 **Step 19: Entering Percent Complete Information**

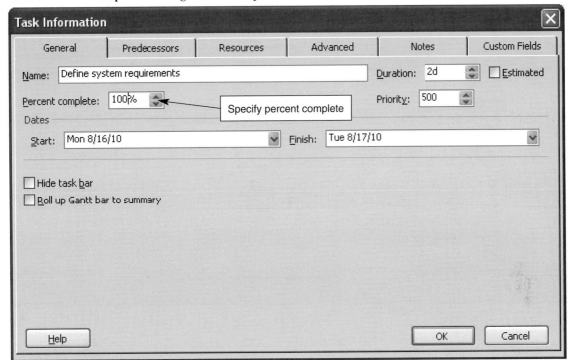

It is also possible to specify percent complete for a task in the Gantt and Tracking Gantt views. Click and drag on the center of the task bar until the percent complete indicator reflects the progress you wish to depict.

20. **Displaying Progress Information.** In the upper half of the split screen, select the Gantt Chart icon on the left-hand side. You should see the Gantt chart appear. Notice that there is a horizontal black line through the center of **Define system requirements** and another black line about 40 percent of the way through **Develop application**. These dark lines represent activity completion. When MSP shifts to the Gantt chart view it initially shows only the highlighted tasks in your network view. Don't panic. Just highlight the "Task Name" column by clicking the top of that column near the title "Task Name." Then you will see the complete network, as shown in Exhibit A.20A.

EXHIBIT A.20A Step 20: Displaying Progress Information for a Selected Activity

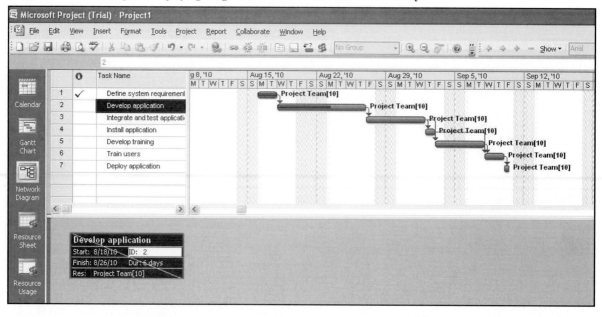

After the "Task Name" column is highlighted, the entire network appears in the lower half of the split screen. Looking at the Network Diagram view, you should see that the completed activity (Define system requirements) has two diagonal crossbars through it indicating that it is complete. Develop application has one diagonal crossbar through it indicating it has begun but is not yet complete. See Exhibit A.20B.

EXHIBIT A.20B   **Step 20: Displaying Progress Information for All Activities**

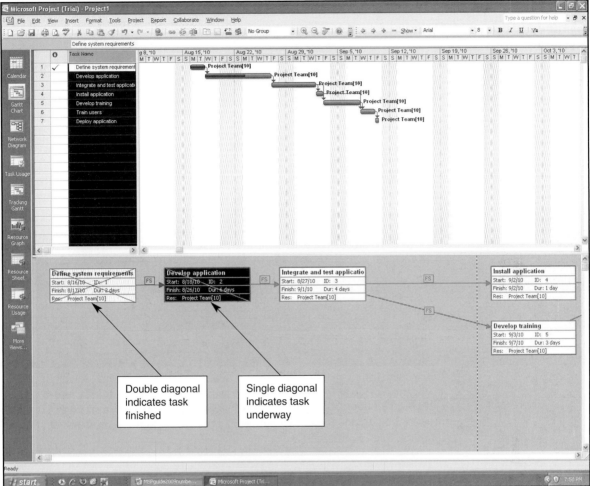

21. **Displaying Revised Schedules as the Project Unfolds.** Imagine the team is 11 days into the project. Develop application took nine days instead of the six days originally planned. To reflect this status in the schedule, first set a project baseline. A baseline records the original plan and then allows us to reflect deviations between actual progress and planned progress. To save a baseline for this project, select TOOLS from the top pull-down menu. Select *Tracking* and then *Set Baseline.* Click "OK" at the bottom of the *Set Baseline* dialog box.

Now update the status of the project to reflect the delay in Develop application. Click on the "Dur:" box in the Develop application task and change the duration to 9d. Notice the Develop application bar on the Gantt chart has extended to the end of the day on August 31 and the project end date has been pushed out to the end of the day on September 15. See Exhibit A.21A.

EXHIBIT A.21A Step 21: Displaying the Revised Schedule for Develop Application (Partial View of Schedule)

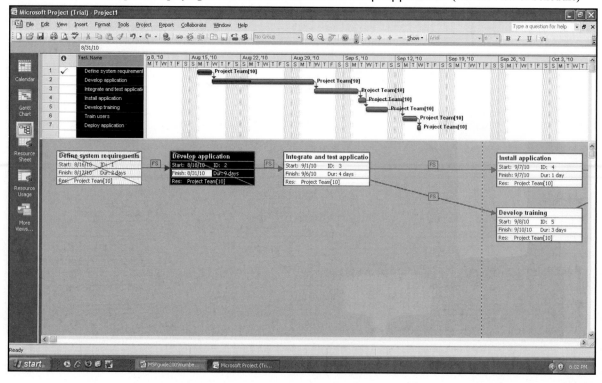

Now double-click on the Develop application box. Notice that MSP has revised the percent complete from 40 percent to 27 percent to reflect the longer duration. See Exhibit A.21B.

EXHIBIT A.21B
Revised Status Based on New Duration
for Develop Application

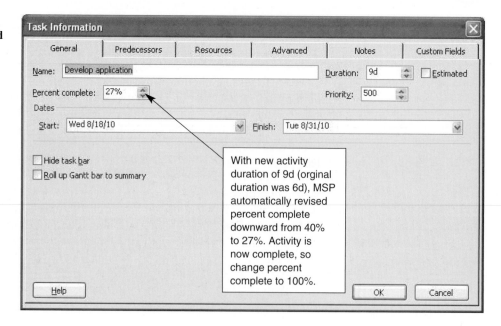

However, **Develop application** is now complete, so revise 27% to 100%. The result of the revision is shown in Exhibit A.21C.

To see the effect of **Develop application's** delay on the project, select the Tracking Gantt icon on the view bar. This chart compares the original plan (baseline) with the current performance. This is displayed in the lower half of Exhibit A.21C.

EXHIBIT A.21C   **Full Update on Status**

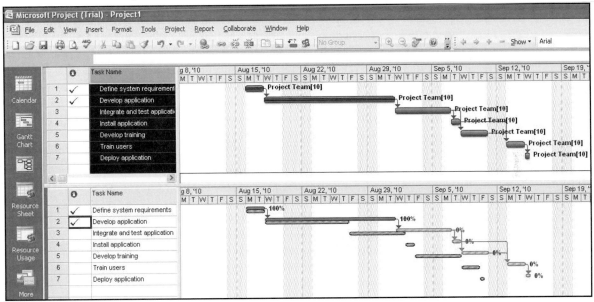

USING MICROSOFT PROJECT EFFECTIVELY

MSP (or any scheduling software) can be used for one or more purposes, and it is important that you know why you are using it at any given time. The following are potential reasons for which you may need scheduling software:

1. To electronically document the scheduling efforts of a project team. This can create a baseline for further deliberations, or an archival record. A team might continue to use a manually prepared schedule displayed on large paper on a conference room wall, but keep a computer-generated schedule as a record.

2. To create a printed project display for hands-on use during project meetings. In this case, the schedule should be printed on plotter paper and be large enough to allow several people to gather around it. Do not hesitate to write on it—you can use it for posting notes and updating progress. Messy is OK. For a short-duration endeavor, a team could use the pencil-marked version of the schedule as its only scheduling document, perhaps creating an "as it actually happened" version at the end for archival purposes. For longer projects, a team could update the pencil-marked schedule and reprint it weekly or monthly.

3. Another important use of a computer-generated schedule is for communication with project stakeholders such as customers, sponsors, subcontractors, and support

personnel. Most stakeholders outside the core team probably do not want to see an intricate level of detail. Additionally, they are unlikely to appreciate or understand the complexities of a network schedule. You could create a separate version of the schedule that shows only the major deliverables in Gantt form. Think of your stakeholders as customers, and consider how you can make the information accessible to them. If the Gantt chart spreads across several pages, be sure to cut and paste the pages into an accordion form that folds out for a full view. Do not simply clip all of the pages together and expect an outsider to understand the flow of the project. Do *not* print schedules in double-sided mode.

A high-level (i.e., showing major deliverables only) Gantt chart also can be posted on a company intranet site for projects that affect people across the organization (e.g., an ERP installation, a new product launch, a plant closure). Sites such as these also should include explanatory information geared toward audience members with a wide range of training and education. The schedule should not appear as a hocus-pocus mystery.

> You are now ready to do battle with Microsoft Project! Although there is much more to it than what we've presented here, you should now be able to create schedules for most common types of projects.

Appendix B

Decision Analysis: Using Payoff Matrices, Decision Trees, and Implications Wheels in Project Management

"If you see a fork in the road, take it."

Yogi Berra

Decision making is a core activity essential for managing all aspects of project work. We have addressed this topic in virtually every chapter, beginning with a discussion of decisions about project selection and continuing in other chapters with material on project options, scope, stakeholders, uncertainty preparation, scheduling, schedule modification, and project change orders. One set of tools, having to do with decision analysis, offers valuable structure for decisions in virtually all stages of a project. We have mentioned these tools briefly elsewhere in the book, but because of their universality, we have reserved details about their structure and use for presentation in this appendix.

WHY USE DECISION ANALYSIS TOOLS?

Individuals and teams can fall prey to several biases and limitations that reduce their ability to make effective decisions.[1] One of these is a bias toward status quo,[2] which appears to block people from considering options that could lead to better outcomes. Exhibit B.1 pokes fun at those who are paralyzed by their inability to make decisions.

[1] A. Campbell, J. Whitehead, and S. Finkelstein, "Why Good Leaders Make Bad Decisions," *Harvard Business Review*, February 2009, pp. 60–66.

[2] J.S. Hammond, R.L. Keeney, and H. Raiffa, "The Hidden Traps in Decision Making," *Harvard Business Review*, January 2006, pp. 118–126.

EXHIBIT B.1
**The Perils of
Indecision**

© Jerry Van Amerongen 2009.

According to Howard, et al., people tend to pay too much attention to **sunk costs,** which can reinforce **status quo bias** because it helps them to justify past decisions.[3] They also note that people are prone to looking for information that confirms their own opinions rather than seeking contrary opinions and evidence. This **confirming-evidence** trap can lead to dangerously narrow thinking in high-stakes project situations. The ill-fated NASA decision to launch the space shuttle Challenger in 1986 is an often-cited example.[4] And Howard, et al., also remind us that we are probably overconfident in our estimates of likelihood or outcome magnitude.[5]

The first step for any decision maker is to recognize that the limitations described above are real, and they do not apply just to *other people*. The decision maker's second step is to circumvent the potential ill effects of biases by using structured methods that assist him or her in clarifying objectives, considering a range of possibilities, improving ability to envision outcomes, gathering objective data, and creating a constructive team environment. The tools we present here are designed to help leaders and teams engage effectively in these processes.

DECISION ANALYSIS TOOLS

A team can use one or more of the tools we present here, **payoff matrices, decision trees,** and **implications wheels,**[6] to structure its discussion of options, future scenarios, assumptions, and possible outcomes. Teams can use these tools in a subjective fashion, or they can take a more quantitative approach through the use of financial data and

[3] Ibid.

[4] For example, see D. Vaughan, *The Challenger Launch Decision: Risky Technology, Culture, and Deviance at NASA* (Chicago: University of Chicago Press, 1996).

[5] Hammond, Keeney, and Raiffa, "The Hidden Traps in Decision Making."

[6] J. Barker, Implications Wheels Training Video, 1994; http://strategicexploration.com/implications-wheel/ and http://implicationswheel.com/ (accessed August 22, 2009).

statistical forecasts.[7] *Payoff matrices* and *decision trees,* in their purest forms, allow teams to consider only a single category of outcome (e.g., cost or financial gain). In contrast, *implications wheels*[8] offer a team the opportunity to envision multiple types of outcomes (e.g, market share, customer response, support from stakeholders, technical failures). All three have potential value, and the choice of which one to use depends on project circumstances and team preferences. We describe these three tools from simplest to more complex, beginning with payoff matrices.

Payoff Matrices

A payoff matrix allows decision makers to consider two or more options in relation to a single-criterion outcome, and to place these considerations into the context of likelihood estimates. By combining information about quantifiable outcomes with estimated likelihoods, a project team can calculate the expected value of each option and make a decision accordingly. An important rule in payoff matrices is that the decision options must be exhaustive and mutually exclusive. An example helps to illustrate how a payoff matrix works.

Hope Mountain, a country singer, is scheduled to tour 19 cities in North America (Canada, the United States, and Mexico). Her concert tour team is planning the details for each venue in the cities where she will play. During past tours, some Hope Mountain concerts have been booked into facilities that proved too small to meet demand, resulting in lost sales and unhappy fans. Also, ticket resellers have made large sums of money as market scarcity has inflated the value of concert seats sold in the secondary market. In other cases, tour planners overestimated ticket demand and wound up with minimal profits (and sometimes losses) because of the high numbers of unsold seats.

Based on historical records from the previous 10 Hope Mountain tours in North America, members of the planning team have a fairly good perspective on her popularity in each location. They have decided to use a payoff matrix to assist them in laying out the options and assumptions for the first city on the tour, Montreal, Quebec, Canada. They will use this analysis as a test case to guide concert venue decisions for the other 18 cities. Three possible venues, which are equally appealing in terms of facilities, location, access, and acoustics, are available in Montreal. The respective seating capacities of these venues, which we will call A, B, and C are 4,000, 6,000, and 8,000. Using reliable records from past tours, as well as insights from other sources, team members estimate a 50 percent probability they can sell at least 4,000 seats, a 25 percent probability they can sell as many as 6,000 seats, and a 25 percent probability they can sell as many as 8,000 seats.[9] The team also has used historical records and current information to forecast the profit associated with the combinations of choices and demand outcomes. These profits incorporate financial data about the cost of renting each facility and the revenues that would accrue under each condition. They have simplified the profit analysis as follows: Unit cost is the same for all three facilities at $5 per seat. Every sold seat will produce $25 in gross profit, before rental costs are deducted. Fixed costs are not included here because they will be roughly the same for each venue. A matrix of outcomes and options is shown in Exhibit B.2.

---

[7] R. Greenwood and L. White, *Decision Trees* (Boston: Harvard Business School Press, 2004).

[8] Barker, Implications wheels Training Video; and J.W. Schreier, "Thinking about Thinking: A Meta Analysis of Joel Barker and Edward de Bono Thinking Skill Programs," 2002. Available through the Institute for Strategic Exploration, www.implicationswheel.com (accessed August 22, 2009).

[9] In reality, the cutoff points would not be this clear cut, but the demand figures and likelihood estimates represent reasonable forecasts in this case.

EXHIBIT B.2
Decision Options
and Outcomes for
Hope Mountain Tour
Venues in Montreal

Decision Options

Demand Outcomes, Probabilities, and Profit Estimates			
	Low Demand (50% likelihood) 4,000 Tickets Demanded	**Medium Demand (25% likelihood) 6,000 Tickets Demanded**	**High Demand (25% likelihood) 8,000 Tickets Demanded**
Book Facility A, 4,000 Seats	(4,000 × $25) − (4,000 × $5) = $80,000	(4,000 × $25) − (4,000 × $5) = $80,000	(4,000 × $25) − (4,000 × $5) = $80,000
Book Facility B, 6,000 Seats	(4,000 × $25) − (6,000 × $5) = $70,000	(6,000 × $25) − (6,000 × $5) = $120,000	(6,000 × $25) − (6,000 × $5) = $120,000
Book Facility C, 8,000 Seats	(4,000 × $25) − (8,000 × $5) = $60,000	(6,000 × $25) − (8,000 × $5) = $110,000	(8,000 × $25) − (8,000 × $5) = $160,000

Exhibit B.2 shows the calculations of net profit outcomes for the six possible combinations of decision options and ticket-demand outcomes. The cost of lost sales in each cell is implied in the model. The process of setting up the matrix can be very helpful to a team in developing a shared understanding of possible scenarios.

Given that the team also has likelihood information based on historical data, members can take the analysis further by calculating the **expected value** or **EV**[10] for each option. They do this by summing weighted profits across rows. These calculations are as follows:

$$\text{EV for Option A} = (.5 \times \$80,000) + (.25 \times \$80,000) + (.25 \times \$80,000) = \boxed{\$80,000}$$

$$\text{EV for Option B} = (.5 \times \$70,000) + (.25 \times \$120,000) + (.25 \times \$120,000) = \boxed{\$95,000}$$

$$\text{EV for Option C} = (.5 \times \$60,000) + (.25 \times \$110,000) + (.25 \times \$160,000) = \boxed{\$97,500}$$

For each decision option, the team multiplied the decimal value of the corresponding demand probability by the profit outcome value, then summed across the row. In each row, decimal values associated with the three possible outcomes must sum to 1.

If the team chooses to take the result of the payoff matrix at face value, it will choose to book the Montreal concert in the 8,000-seat venue because this produces the highest **EV** for profit ($97,500). However, the team might also decide that the expected value of choosing the medium-sized facility is close enough to this value at $95,000. After all, these are forecasts and not certainties. Thus, a team that is somewhat **averse to risk**[11] might play it safe and go with Option B. Team members might also consider the **least-worst** or **maxi-min** payoff option. To do so, they would ask: "Which choice has the highest minimum profit?" In this preferential model, the solution would be to go with Option A, which appears to guarantee $80,000 in profit,

---

[10] Although we used EV to denote earned value in Chapter 9, this is a different use for this acronym.

[11] Some people are more prone toward risk aversion than others. For more on this, see J. Spencer and C. Crossen, "Fear Factors: Why Do Americans Feel That Danger Lurks Everywhere?" *The Wall Street Journal,* April 24, 2007, p. A1.

EXHIBIT B.3
General Structure of
a Decision Tree

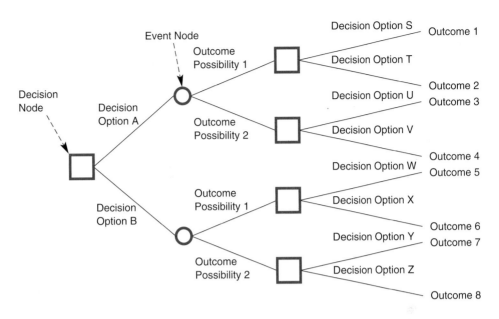

regardless of the demand outcome. The other two options offer lower profits in their worst-case scenarios ($70,000 and $60,000). The team could also use the payoff matrix as a jumping-off point for discussing other decision criteria such as the marketing image each facility might convey, potential secondary sales of CDs and other memorabilia, and so forth.

A payoff matrix offers a useful mechanism for laying out decision options and can be a great aid to a team. However, it has a static perspective that does not allow for changes in a course of action over time. In reality, the team planning the concert tour might want to add flexibility to its decision model by delaying the final venue choice until preliminary demand information is available. In this case, they could add a layer of sophistication to the discussion by employing a decision tree.

Decision Trees

Decision trees are based on the same logic as payoff matrices; they can aid a team in structuring decision options in relation to outcome and probability estimates. A tree differs from a matrix in that it allows a team to consider secondary decisions, and beyond, that might evolve after more outcome information becomes available. Exhibit B.3 shows the general structure of a decision tree.

As depicted in Exhibit B.3, the general format of a decision tree involves the use of multiple branches emanating from each initial square decision node, followed by circular event nodes, and repeating decision and event nodes as necessary to carry out a scenario. Events refer to uncertain states of nature, the occurrence of which are, at least theoretically, independent of the decisions that precede them.[12] In complex scenario planning, decisions and outcomes could continue alternating several times. As with a payoff matrix, a team might find value in laying out the options and outcomes, then discussing them and reaching a conclusion. However, to make full use of a tree, a team can add numerical data and likelihood estimates to the event nodes and outcomes.

---

[12] For example, if you were trying to decide whether to carry your umbrella to work in anticipation of possible rain, the weather condition (rain or no rain) would be the event, the occurrence of which would not be influenced by your choice (umbrella or no umbrella).

EXHIBIT B.4 **Initial Decision Tree for Hope Mountain Concert in Montreal**

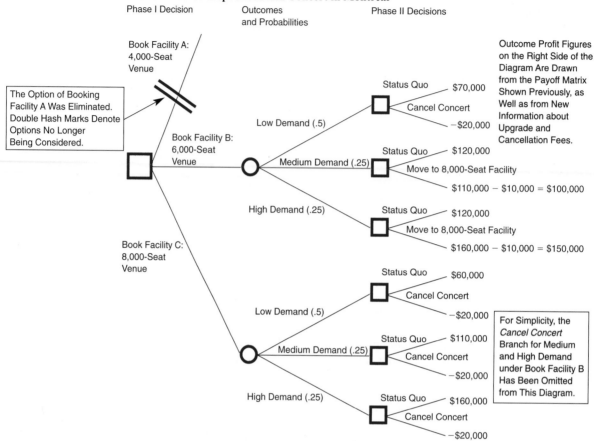

Continuing with the Hope Mountain concert tour example, we demonstrate how a decision tree could be applied to examine a series of decisions. Members of the planning team have decided to offer concert tickets for sale six months in advance of the concert. After the first month of sales limited to VIP fans,[13] they will have more information about demand for tickets and can then make a decision about whether to cancel the event, accept the status quo, or move the event to a different facility. Given that renting the small facility produced the lowest EV in the payoff matrix, and given their confidence in Ms. Mountain's popularity, they have decided to limit their next stage of analysis to the medium and large facility options.

Team members have arranged a flexible contract with the company that owns and operates both venues. If they initially rent the 6,000-seat facility and early ticket sales suggest demand will be high, the contract allows them to move to the 8,000-seat facility. However, they cannot move to a smaller facility if demand is lower than expected. The facility owner will charge a fee of $10,000 if the concert planning team decides to shift from the 6,000-seat facility to the 8,000-seat facility after early ticket sales figures are available. The team can, for any reason, decide to cancel the concert, but the Hope Mountain Company will be required to pay a $20,000 cancellation fee to the facility owner. A **multistage decision tree** for this analysis is displayed in Exhibit B.4.

[13] Registered fan club members and those who have purchased tickets for at least five Hope Mountain concerts in the past three years.

EXHIBIT B.5   **Completed Decision Tree for Hope Mountain Concert in Montreal**

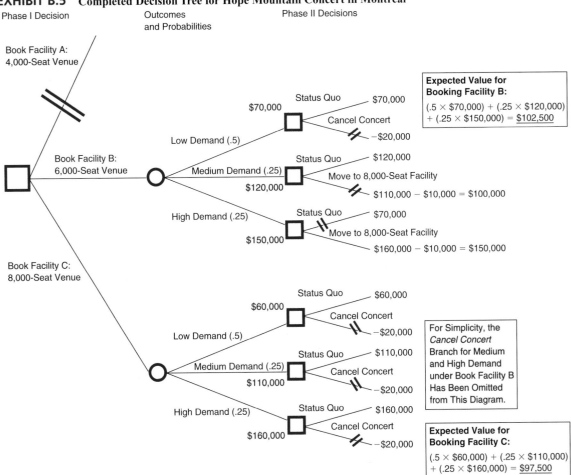

The procedure for analyzing a decision tree involves moving from right to left, first eliminating unattractive options, then calculating EV for each of the most attractive decision options. Exhibit B.5 presents a completed version of the decision tree for the Hope Mountain concert.

The steps for analyzing the Hope Mountain Tour decision tree depicted in Exhibit B.4 are as follows:

1. Assess the value of Phase II decisions to select the most attractive option under each scenario. Eliminate and mark unattractive options. We have used double hash marks for options the team has determined it would eliminate should a particular set of conditions arise. For example, under the Facility B option, if demand is low, the team could either accept the status quo with $70,000 in profit, or cancel the concert at a cost of $20,000. The status quo would be more attractive financially, so a double hash mark is placed on the decision branch for canceling the concert.

2. Move the EV of each secondary decision that has *not* been eliminated to the box node to its immediate left. This is the EV for that node. For example, if the team chooses the Facility B option (6,000-seat venue) and demand is high, it is more profitable to move to the larger facility even with the $10,000 upgrade fee. The gross profit for

the larger facility, minus the upgrade fee, results in a net profit of $150,000, which is higher than the status quo profit of $70,000, so $150,000 is the value noted over the square decision node to the immediate left.

3. Multiply the decimal values associated with each outcome possibility by the EV selected in Step 2, and sum the EVs to determine the EV for each Phase I decision. The weighted EV calculations for booking Facilities B and C are shown in the text boxes on the right side of Exhibit B.5.

The result of the decision tree analysis suggests the team should choose Option B, the 6,000-seat venue. But if early ticket sales to VIP fans indicate demand will reach 8,000, the team should be prepared to move up to the larger facility. The decision tree enables team members to agree, in advance, how they will respond under different circumstances. It is much better to handle these sorts of questions during the planning stage, rather than waiting for a crisis to suddenly demand a decision team members might not be prepared to make.

The decision tree's orientation toward multiple-stage decision making opens the door for the team to discuss additional implications for the scenarios they are examining. For example, members of the group could envision the possibility of increasing advertising if initial demand is lower than expected. This could be built into the decision tree as part of the secondary decision phase, or possibly as a tertiary decision option following another month or two of demand data availability.

Decision trees and payoff matrices are powerful tools for teams to use when considering future project scenarios under conditions of uncertainty. As we have emphasized, they are most fully used when the team has valid data about likelihood and outcome values. However, a team can benefit tremendously from the structure of these two tools for scenario planning, even when using qualitative data.

Implications Wheels

One major limitation of payoff matrices and decision trees is that they restrict a team to considering only a single, quantifiable outcome criterion (e.g., profit, revenue, cost, sales volume, etc.). Implications wheels, developed by Joel Barker, are built on concepts from decision trees.[14] However, they offer a more creative approach to decision analysis by encouraging a team to consider outcome sequences and loosening some of the constraints and assumptions of their conceptual predecessors.

Barker developed implications wheels (IWs) to help teams envision future scenarios and assess potential negative and positive implications. For example, if you were trying to decide whether to accept a job offer in Mumbai, India, you might go through the following thought process: "If I take the job, I'll have an opportunity to learn new skills. On the down side, the pay is lower than what I would make if I accept the other job I've been offered. But, if I learn new skills and have the experience of working in India, my career prospects and lifetime income might be greater in the longer term. My spouse's parents might object to our move, creating some tensions in the family. But, we might appreciate the autonomy for our family."

In the job offer example above, the individual is considering chains of events and decisions in a much more freewheeling way than he or she could do with a decision tree. Moreover, outcomes do not have to be mutually exclusive, may be of different types, and do not necessarily have to be measurable. According to materials available through the Institute for Strategic Exploration (http://strategicexploration.com), implications wheels

[14] J. Barker, Implications Wheels Training Video,1994; and http://implicationswheel.com/ (accessed August 22, 2009).

EXHIBIT B.6
**General Format
for an Implications
Wheel**

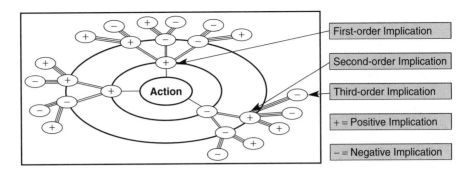

can push people past innate biases that tend to limit their vision to first-order implications when they are considering possible outcomes of a decision. Numerous organizations have used implications wheels to improve their ability to envision the future.[15]

The general approach for developing an implications wheel involves placing a future decision or action in the center of a page, then brainstorming first, second, and third (maybe more) levels of implications. A **first-order implication** is anything that can happen as a direct result of the decision or action in the center of the wheel. **Second-order implications** result from first-order implications, and so forth. A general guideline is that for every implication, the team should try to think of at least two higher-order implications. At least one of these implications should be positive (beneficial) and at least one should be negative (detrimental). To determine what is positive and what is negative, the team must have a particular stakeholder in mind (e.g., customers, the company, employees). Exhibit B.6 displays the general format for an implications wheel.[16]

As shown in Exhibit B.6, the implications wheel is set up to include three (or more) levels of implications. The first question a team would ask is, "What outcomes might occur as a *direct* result of the project or project option in the center of the wheel?" These are added to the wheel in the first ring emanating from the central action node. They are linked to the node with a single connecting line. Next, the team asks what might happen as a direct result of each first-order implication, linking those with double lines. The process continues to **third-order implications,** and sometimes continues beyond those.

According to Barker, implications wheels promote more open-minded and balanced discussion if participants attempt to look for at least one positive and one negative implication emanating from each lower-level implication.[17] Thus, something that might be bad can actually lead to something good. (We depict this guideline with the "+" and "−" signs in Exhibit B.6.) The process incorporates a scoring element that mirrors the approach used with decision trees. For every implication, team participants attempt to reach consensus on its likelihood and the magnitude of its positive or negative effects on the project.

[15] M.A. Potter, H.K. Burns, G. Barron, A. Grofebert, and G.D. Bednarz, "Cross-Sector Leadership Development for Preparedness," *Public Health Reports,* 120 (2005), pp. 109–15.

[16] We acknowledge that an IW, on first glance, might look quite a bit like the mind maps we have introduced in this book. However, the content is quite different. A WBS mind map captures categories and subcategories of work activity. It represents a hierarchical structure that can be converted to an outline. An IW is a type of causal map showing chains of events. An IW shows what we *believe* will result from something else, and what, in turn, *could* result from that.

[17] Barker, Implications Wheels Training Video.

Members of the planning team have decided to apply IW concepts to the Hope Mountain concert tour, building on insights they gained from the payoff matrix and decision tree they developed previously. They have narrowed their focus to an issue that has been troubling them. If they do need to upgrade to a larger facility after a month of strong VIP ticket sales, what outcomes might they expect? Those who purchased tickets early are likely to be the most enthusiastic Hope Mountain fans, and the shift to a different facility could create some problems. On the other hand, it might open the door for some opportunities. The team's first attempt at an implications wheel to brainstorm possible outcomes associated with moving to a larger venue is shown in Exhibit B.7.

As the implications wheel in Exhibit B.7 shows, the team brainstormed first-, second-, and third-order implications associated with moving the concert to a larger venue after a preliminary VIP sales period. They identified the potential for both negative and positive outcomes at each level. This might be sufficient background for a discussion of whether it is appropriate to move the concert to a larger venue, and what to do to prepare if this does become necessary. However, the team could apply Barker's scoring methods to further analyze the wheel.

To score the wheel, the team attaches a likelihood number of 1, 3, 5, or 9 to each implication. The higher the number (e.g., 9), the higher the team's consensus estimation of likelihood. The limitation to odd numbers conveys the general subjectivity of these estimates. The team can then assess the magnitude of the outcome associated with each implication by attaching a score of -5 to $+5$, where negative numbers represent undesirable outcomes and positive numbers indicate desirable outcomes. Barker also offers the possibility of a -50 or a $+50$ for outcomes that are absolutely disastrous or

EXHIBIT B.7   **Partial Implications Wheel for Moving Hope Mountain Concert to a Larger Venue**

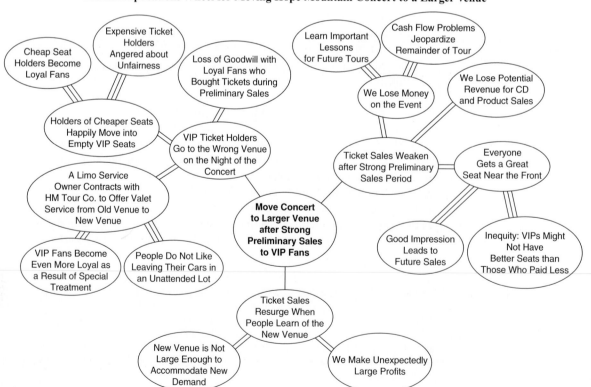

so incredibly positive that they would change the organization's fortunes profoundly. As the team reviews the IW with the scoring information, members look for chains of implications with high likelihoods and major negative outcomes, working to come up with solutions or ways to prevent them from happening. They also look for major positive outcomes that currently have low likelihoods and seek ideas for increasing their likelihood.

Although it is possible to become mathematical with these scores and multiply them in a way similar to the one we described for decision trees, we recommend stopping at this point and using the wheel in a more qualitative way to develop plans and contingencies. In the case of this IW, team members decided the move to a larger facility would be a good idea if high demand prevails. However, as a result of their IW-based discussion, they decided to restrict VIP seating in the larger facility to those who purchased tickets for the medium-size facility during the early ticket-sales period. This would reduce potential feelings of unfairness among loyal fans. They also decided to offer free valet parking for those who mistakenly arrived at the wrong venue. They would be dropped off at the correct facility and their cars delivered to them at the end of the concert. The team is also considering offering free Hope Mountain CDs to VIP ticketholders as a way of further appeasing them.

Summary

This appendix has introduced structured and semistructured approaches for teams to use in analyzing decisions. These tools include payoff matrices, decision trees, and implications wheels. All three offer frameworks for teams to use in structuring decisions, understanding potential outcomes, and overcoming human decision biases. They can be applied at several stages in the life of a project—wherever a decision must be made and there are multiple options and outcomes.

References

Campbell, A.; J. Whitehead; and S. Finkelstein. "Why Good Leaders Make Bad Decisions." *Harvard Business Review,* February 2009, pp. 60–66.

Barker, J. Implications Wheels Training Video, 1994. **www.joelbarker.com/ downloads.php**; and **http://implicationswheel.com/case-studies/**.

Greenwood, R., and L. White. *Decision Trees.* Boston: Harvard Business School Press, 2004.

Hammond, J.S.; R.L. Keeney; and H. Raiffa. "The Hidden Traps in Decision Making." *Harvard Business Review,* January 2006, pp. 118–126.

Potter, M.A.; H.K. Burns; G. Barron; A. Grofebert; and G.D. Bednarz. "Cross-Sector Leadership Development for Preparedness." *Public Health Reports* 120, Supplement 1, (2005), pp. 109–15.

Schreier, J.W. "Thinking about Thinking: A Meta Analysis of Joel Barker and Edward de Bono Thinking Skill Programs," 2002. Available through the Institute for Strategic Exploration, **www.implicationswheels.com**.

Spencer, J., and C. Crossen. "Fear Factors: Why Do Americans Feel That Danger Lurks Everywhere?" *The Wall Street Journal,* April 24, 2007, p. A.1.

Vaughan, D. *The Challenger Launch Decision: Risky Technology, Culture, and Deviance at NASA.* Chicago: University of Chicago Press, 1996.

Name Index

Subject Index